Dancing across Borders

Dancing across Borders

Danzas y Bailes Mexicanos

Edited by
OLGA NÁJERA-RAMÍREZ,
NORMA E. CANTÚ,
AND
BRENDA M. ROMERO

UNIVERSITY OF ILLINOIS PRESS
Urbana and Chicago

∞ This book is printed on acid-free paper.

Library of Congress Cataloging-in-Publication Data
Dancing across borders : danzas y bailes mexicanos /
edited by Olga Nájera-Ramírez, Norma E. Cantú,
and Brenda M. Romero.
p. cm.
Includes bibliographical references (p.) and index.
ISBN 978-0-252-03409-1 (cloth : alk. paper)
ISBN 978-0-252-07609-1 (pbk. : alk. paper)
1. Dance—Mexico.
2. Dance—Mexican-American Border Region.
3. Folk dancing, Mexican.
4. Folk dancing, Mexican—Mexican-American Border Region.
5. Religious dance—Mexico.
6. Religious dance—Mexican-American Border Region.
I. Nájera-Ramírez, Olga, 1955– II. Cantú, Norma Elia, 1947–
III. Romero, Brenda M., 1949–
GV1627.D355 2009
793.3'2—dc22 2008036540

To the dedicated teachers, musicians,
dancers, and scholars whose love
of Mexican *danzas y bailes* have
made this work possible

Contents

Part II: Dimensions of Space and Place

Part III: Trajectories of Tradition

Part IV: Politics of Tradition and Innovation

Acknowledgments

I am grateful to everyone who supported me on this project, particularly to all the contributors for their good will and cooperation and to my coeditors Norma and Brenda for their friendship and hard work. A special thanks to my research assistants Claudia Andrade, MaryHelen Guadiana, Jorge Rodolfo de Hoyos, and Marisa Fernández for helping me with the bibliography; the Chicano/Latino Research Center for funding my research assistants; and to Kathryn Caruso for her invaluable assistance. *Muchas gracias de todo corazón a mi mamá* for instilling the joy of dance in me, to my friends and my entire family for all the happy times we have spent dancing together, and to Ronaldo and Elisa for their love, patience, and good humor throughout.

Olga Nájera-Ramírez
Santa Cruz, California

I acknowledge the support of various family members and friends throughout the process of getting this book together. I thank my coeditors Brenda and Olga for their tenacity and critical eye, *y no se diga*, for their hard work. My gratitude to my academic home for the past seven years, the University of Texas at San Antonio, for its support of my work through research assistance and a faculty development research grant in the spring of 2005. At various points I was assisted by graduate assistants in our program: June Pedraza, Marco Cervantes, and Megan Sibbett, ¡*gracias!* My deepest gratitude to Elvia Niebla for her patience and understanding. Finally, *gracias* to all the contributors and our collaborators, as well as my coeditors for their love of dance.

Norma E. Cantú
San Antonio, Tejas

I wish to thank my colleagues Norma and Olga for their friendship and for all I have learned from them in the process of working on this anthology. Special thanks to Sara Holman for her work with the photographs and other figures, to Ernesto Maestas for his helpful information, and to José Luis Sagredo del Castillo, Gonzalo Camacho Díaz, and Guillermo Contreras Arias for their willingness to share their immense knowledge of Mexican music and dance with me. I am grateful also to all the contributors and many others who made this work possible, including Elisa Facio, Lorna Dee Cervantes, and Lisa Peñaloza for their unflinching encouragement, the dean of music, Daniel Sher, and the musicology/ethnomusicology faculty at the University of Colorado at Boulder for their support on the local scene. My deepest gratitude to my mother Eufelia for her love, guidance, and prayers, to my brothers and sisters for their constant encouragement, and to my children, Sonya, Bethrah, Juanita, and Nathaniel, who gave up many comforts so Mom could go to school.

Brenda M. Romero
Boulder, Colorado

Introduction

Dance is a dynamic cultural expression widely practiced throughout Greater Mexico.[1] According to early Spanish writers, dance was an important and integral part of indigenous peoples' lives (Sahagún 1829; de las Casas 1875–76). Many dances were associated with specific rituals, but others were more secular in nature.[2] Although European sacred liturgical dancing, conceptually more similar to indigenous ritual dancing, was no longer practiced at the time of the conquest, the Spanish highly valued both profane, carnivalesque *danza* in the celebrations associated with Catholic feast days[3] and secular group and couple dancing for entertainment and as markers of social refinement.[4] The subsequent European colonization led to the devaluation of indigenous dance practices throughout the Americas, but it did not fully erase them. Although the missionaries and colonizers initially prohibited indigenous *danzas* because they wanted to eradicate native religious practices, they ultimately incorporated some of the *danzas* into their own Christian celebrations for didactic purposes and to make the new imposed religion more attractive to the native peoples. The superimposition of European dances upon existing traditional dances in the Americas further resulted in a fusion of indigenous and Euro-Christian beliefs and practices.

Dance was similarly at the center of religious observances for the African slaves who arrived in the Americas with the Spanish as early as 1519.[5] To this day, elements of African religious dance and music survive in much contemporary popular dance music throughout the Americas.[6] Moreover, throughout the colonial period (1500–1800s) and into the postcolonial epoch[7] of the nineteenth century, new dance forms developed due to increased interaction among the people of Greater Mexico as well as to increased contact with the outside world. For example, popular pan-European ballroom dances, such as the *vals* (waltz), *polca* (polka), and *chotís* (schottische) were brought to Mexico via Spain and France. These dances underwent transformations consistent with the socioaesthetic preferences of the local populations. Dances that developed in other parts of Latin America, such as the *danzón,* also became popular in Mexico (Flores y Escalante 1993), as elucidated in chapter 14 of this anthology. In the Americas, *danza* and its accompanying narratives, but also social dance, often served as important media for documenting and transmitting history, and they subsequently became a significant means of expressing the complicated tensions of the colonial and postcolonial periods.[8] As a result, the changing dance traditions testify to the political and historical trajectories of the people.

At present, dancing continues to be one of the most popular and diverse forms of cultural expression in Greater Mexico. Widely practiced as a form of entertainment, dance also constitutes an important component in religious ceremonies. In Spanish, the term dance is translated as "*danza*" and "*baile.*" In standard Spanish, the words are interchangeable but in vernacular speech, *danza* primarily (although not exclusively) refers to ritual or ceremonial dance. Some of the best-known *danzas* still practiced today include *la danza de moros y cristianos, la danza de los matachines,* and *danza azteca.* Despite the broad variation in names and in hybrid characterizations, *danza* is almost always associated with or reflects "*lo indio*" or "indigeneity," with notable exceptions such as the case of some groups in New Mexico and Texas.[9] This is true even though many poor Mexican villagers identify only as mestizos.[10]

Baile, on the other hand, refers to secular social dance typically enjoyed by people at parties, commercial dance halls, and nightclubs. During the late eighteenth century, waves of European immigrants brought popular ballroom dances, such as the *contradanza,* that served as contributing sources for the development of mestizo regional dances. African-based traditions also sparked the development of new song and dance styles. The *cumbia,* for example, emerged out of both indigenous and African-based traditions of coastal Colombia and has become a popular pan-American (if not global) dance and musical style. Played by various regional ensembles such as the *conjunto* from the Texas-Mexico border and the *mariachi* from Jalisco as *música tropical,* the *cumbia* has acquired new identities. *Bailes folklóricos* represent another type of popular dance. These are regional dances that are stylized and choreographed for stage presentations and often serve to express national pride and promote tourism.

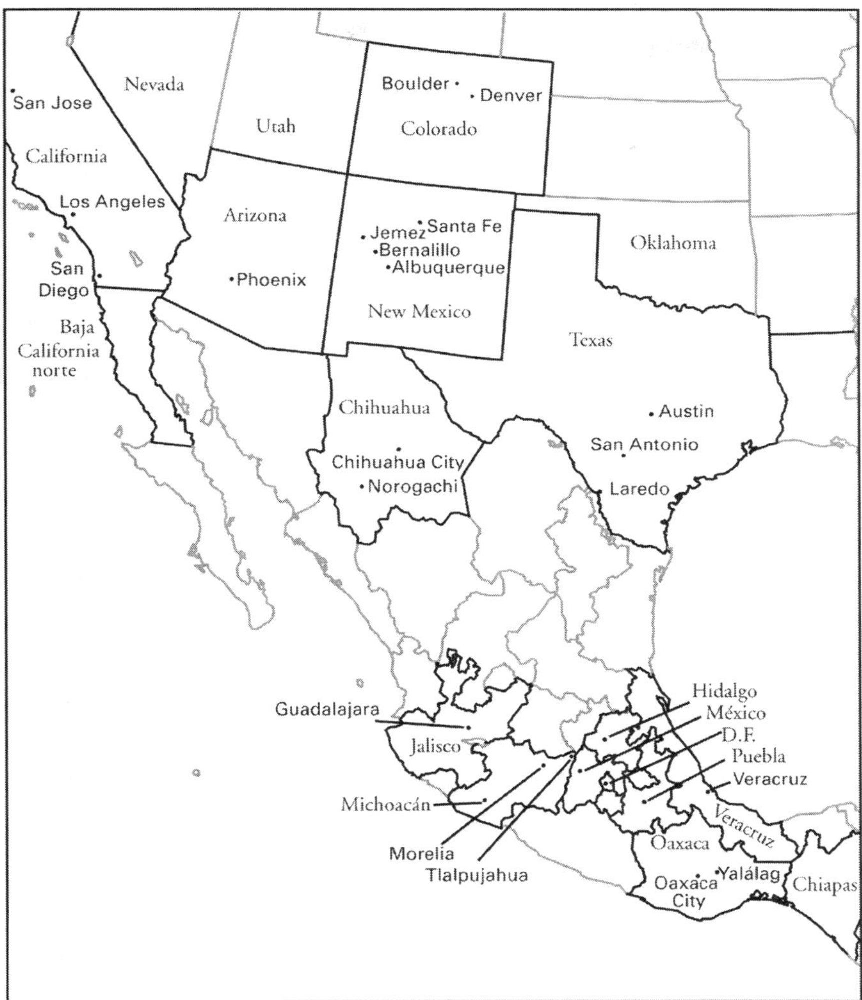

Map of Greater Mexico. Produced by Helen Cole.

Today, the economic demands of globalization have increased the mobility of peoples and their dance expressions within and across national borders. As a result of migration in conjunction with readily available audiovisual technologies, regional dances increasingly circulate beyond their places of origin. Adapting to new places and circumstances, the dances continually change in function, form, or style and are among the most important and widespread expressive forms that continually cross the U.S.-Mexico border in both directions, as evidenced by the essays presented in this collection.

Despite the rich diversity of dance forms in Greater Mexico and the abiding popularity of dance as an artistic cultural expression, Mexican dance forms have not received adequate scholarly attention to date. This is surprising given that dance scholarship in general has grown significantly over the past several decades. According to Reed, "since the mid-1980s, there has been an explosion of dance studies as scholars from a variety of disciplines have turned their attention to dance" (1998, 503). Brenda Farnell's *Human Action Signs in Cultural Context: The Visible and the Invisible in Movement and Dance,* Susan Foster's *Choreographing History,* Jane Desmond's *Meaning in Motion: New Cultural Studies of Dance,* Sondra Fraleigh and Penelope Hanstein's *Researching Dance: Evolving Modes of Inquiry,* and Ann Dils and Ann Cooper Albright's *Moving History/Dancing Cultures: a Dance History Reader* represent important anthologies on dance scholarship that advance the theorizing of dance from an interdisciplinary perspective and promote critical thinking on issues of politics, representation, and identity. Although these anthologies offer important methodological and theoretical insights for anyone interested in dance studies and are obviously not intended to be comprehensive in their treatment of dance, it is surprising that none of the chapters in the aforementioned anthologies deal with Mexican dance.

Dancing across Borders: Danzas y Bailes Mexicanos is a collection of previously unpublished essays that focus specifically on Mexican popular and ceremonial dances practiced within the transnational context of Greater Mexico. Written by noted scholars in various disciplines as well as several dance practitioners and students of performance and expressive culture, this anthology constitutes a path-breaking endeavor to promote and expand intellectual exchange. As a whole, *Dancing across Borders: Danzas y Bailes Mexicanos* highlights the centrality of dance as a cultural expression in Greater Mexico and showcases the vibrant nature of these dance traditions. Contributions by dance practitioners who offer their *testimonios* (personal testaments) of how dance affects their lives are essential to the volume. As these dance practitioners reflect on their engagement with dance, they contribute to scholarly understandings of kinesthetic and other bodily experiences confirming the distinct ways of knowing that dancing produces. As dance scholar Sklar notes, "[m]ovement, in other words, combines felt bodily experience and the culturally based organization of that experience into cognitive patterns. Ways of moving are ways of thinking" (2001, 4). Although not the first or only anthology to focus on Latino[11] or borderlands[12] dance forms, it represents a significant contribution toward a fundamental understanding of theoretical and methodological issues related to a variety of Greater Mexico dance practices and social processes, including, among others, those related to the construction of identity, to culture contact, and to cultural resistance through dance. An ethnographic approach, central to all the contributions,[13] captures dance as a living expression and highlights the importance of the cultural and social contexts in which dances are practiced.

The collection includes essays on innovative dance genres such as Butoh Mexicano and Zapateado Chicano, as well as several chapters on readily recognizable Mexican dance genres such as *baile folklórico, danza azteca,* and *matachines.* The intellectual framework of the anthology emerged organically from the submissions, resulting in four sections: Contested Identities, Dimensions of Space and Place, Trajectories of Tradition, and Politics of Traditions and Innovation. We must underscore that these categories are not mutually exclusive and most essays could easily fit in more than one section. Below, we briefly outline the four thematic categories and give an overview of the individual chapters.

Contested Identities

Dancing is a powerful means to express personal and cultural identities. The essays in this section map indigenous, transnational, and gendered identities. In her essay, Elisa Huerta identifies the sociopolitical goals of the Chicano movement inherent in the "celebration and recuperation of indigenous ancestries," and moves the discussion to the body's ability to know and articulate "oppositional consciousness" through the *danza azteca.* Her essay reveals the extent to which the performer engages in implicit and explicit processes of identity formation.

Similarly, Renée de la Torre's essay analyzes the dance traditions celebrated around *Día de la Raza* (literally the Day of the Race) festivities in Guadalajara, Jalisco.[14] She discusses the ways contemporary *danza* in homage to the *Virgen de Zapopan* is revitalizing ancient dance practices. She posits that a proliferation of youthful groups and *danzantes,* in conjunction with a move away from Catholicism, produces multiple identities characterized by a new consciousness of an empowered mestizo located between an imagined indigenous and colonial past and contemporary urban realities.

While de la Torre looks at dance as the site for the production of new identities, Xóchitl Chávez provides a gendered reading of the performance of the *parachico danza.* Chávez argues that cross-dressing in the festival re-enactment contributes to the redefining and expansion of community gender norms. Women are empowered by performing roles in the festival that were previously restricted to men.

Exploring another perspective on gender and focusing specifically on Mexican American youth, Marie "Keta" Miranda also illuminates the creation of a new identity through dance. Her semiotic reading of a 1960s dance phenomenon in Los Angeles offers a discussion of how the youth explored the potential of creating new identities in their dance and dance hall contexts. She claims, "Communicating the incommunicable, dance symbolizes the ability to articulate one's identity in a society that racializes bodies." Miranda focuses on the dancing bodies of teenage Chicanas as they create their own choreographies to a song iconic of their urban experience, "Whittier Boulevard."

María Teresa Ceseña explores the social activism associated with *danza azteca* in San Diego, California. Ceseña's essay complements Huerta's opening essay to this section by providing an historical overview of *danza azteca* in the United States within the context of the Chicano movement. In particular, she addresses the dynamics of spiritual and political approaches to reclaiming indigenous identity with two different groups, describing the various ways the groups use the danza "to gain agency through affirming their cultural identities" and, in one case, to create "interracial political alliances."

Dimensions of Space and Place

The location of the dance event and the site where the dancing itself occurs impacts the theorizing and complicates the analysis of performance and ritual. While several essays grouped elsewhere could easily fit into a category that explores the space and place of the dancing, the essays in this section exemplify a particular concern with location. Several of the essays in this section take the idea that place is "space with meaning" and find that performing a dance on a particular site lends meaning to that place.[15] We use the term "placiality" in the essays found in this section to talk about how such meaning manifests. Place and space are concepts inherent in a discussion of movement, which dance is, as the geographical space shapes the ritual and the ritual creates a spiritual space. Authors look at how regional traditions are uniquely and distinctly situated in time and space.

In her essay, Norma E. Cantú argues that the action of the *matachines danza* transforms the space from secular to sacred. The spaces where the dancing occurs, along the streets during the procession, in front of the church, and in the neighborhood site, *el terreno,* are at the center of her analysis, but she also discusses the object of veneration, a cross, and how it spatially anchors the celebration and the dancing. Her essay complements those of Peter García and Brenda Romero, who also focus on the *matachines.*

In contrast to Cantú, who examines a group that has been firmly rooted in the community for more than a hundred years, Adriana Cruz-Manjarrez investigates the practices of deterritorialized Zapotec groups in Los Angeles. She describes various elements of Zapotec dance events and compares the Los Angeles dance practices with dance events in the fiestas of Yalalág, Oaxaca. She reveals ways in which dance events become social spaces that complement and reinforce group identity.

The gender concerns of groups in Mexico studied by Alberto Zárate Rosales introduces the role of place in identity construction. Zárate Rosales searches for a "*patriarcado dansístico tradicional,*" a patriarchy embedded in various traditional dances found in the eastern Mexican state of Puebla. He also explores a cultural hybridity that has developed in these communities as a result of emigration and return, with new cultural norms that change the worldview of the community. Transcultural movement of these social dance traditions has led to changes in the social dances themselves.

In contrast to Zárate Rosales's study of dance traditions influenced by emigration to the United States, Shakina Nayfack's essay focuses on a dance form imported to the small town of Tlalpujahua de Rayón, Michoacán. He explores the ways in which Butoh, a dance with origins in postwar Japan, is taught in a local Mexican dance school. A complex and multifaceted signifier of self, Butoh has become a hybridized form in the hands of local teacher Diego Piñón. Nayfack dwells upon the interactions between the townspeople and the students in response to this new dance form, and on elements of their traditional dances.

In his essay, José Sánchez Jiménez demonstrates the loss of meaning and ritual efficacy in a *comunitas* eroded by migration and generational change. He notes that when approached from the perspective of tradition, both the ethnographer and members of the community inscribe the dance in a "folkloric" image and situate its meaning in the past. The ancient conceptualization of "place" is shown to be in conflict with the "social temporality of the young people."

Trajectories of Tradition

Historical processes have imbued the dance traditions of this large geographical area of Greater Mexico with complex layers of meaning that are imparted and renegotiated depending on time and place, and cultural imperatives where the traditions are enacted. The essays in this section reveal the persistence of genre, as well as the vitality and efficacy of dance movement, gesture, and visual imagery in communicating the deepest emotions.

Brenda M. Romero's essay provides a historiography of the *matachines* and calls attention to different perceptions of *matachines* on both sides of the U.S.-Mexico border. She summarizes the significant scholarly studies of this *danza* and discusses the varying motivations of authors. Romero's essay compares the defining elements of this quintessential mestizo genre, arguing that the name refers to a wide number of variants and cultural manifestations that maintain local formats and meanings.

In contrast to Romero's focus on localized variants and meanings, Sydney Hutchinson's essay addresses the power of dance to communicate nationalist ideologies through concepts such as *mestizaje* (racial mixing) and *indigenismo* (indigeneity) in discourses of race and authenticity. Through the specific example of the far-reaching influence of the Ballet Folklórico de México, Hutchinson focuses on how the staging of folk dance has been used to construct the Mexican nation as well as Mexican identity in the United States.

Rudy García continues the discussion of folkloric dancing, relating a practitioner's intimate understanding and experience through an essay that traces his personal trajectory as *folklórico* dancer and teacher. He situates himself as a dancer in the United States who travels to Mexico to learn from local *maestros* and then brings this experience to reinvigorate dance traditions in his U.S. community. In their essays on this important and ubiquitous dance genre, Olga Nájera-Ramírez and Russell Rodríguez provide further insight.

Susan Cashion, the director of a Mexican dance company in California, traces the history of the social *danzón*, from its origins in nineteenth-century Cuba to its popularity in early twentieth-century Mexico, its subsequent decline in the late 1950s, and its recent rebirth among young and old alike. Cashion teaches us to dance (literally), gracefully bringing various social issues such as racial difference and moral character into the discussion. Through her essay, we begin to understand why *danzón* became such a vital artistic inspiration in Mexico City and why it remains a favorite dance genre.

Nancy Ruyter provides a brief historical overview of modern dance in Mexico, addressing the female-centeredness of Mexican modern dance through a focus on Barro Rojo (Red Clay), a social activist dance troupe. Ruyter's analyses of the troupe's works reveal how their nuanced presentations of "situations and experiences" of women's personal lives go beyond a purely feminist agenda.

The Politics of Tradition and Innovation

The scholarship on traditions convincingly demonstrates that efforts toward preservation have been met with equally forceful efforts to eliminate or in some way transform them.[16] The authors of the essays in this section interrogate factors that produce or prevent change in both long-standing and newly emergent dance traditions. They explore the politics underlying certain expressive forms and ask how and under what conditions particular changes occur.

For example, Olga Nájera-Ramírez notes that *folklórico* dance undergoes change as choreographers adapt regional Mexican community dance forms for stage performances. Despite these changes, *folklórico* dance performances are often advertised as "authentic." Nájera-Ramirez questions how authenticity is constructed in *folklórico* dance, and to what end.

Chris Goertzen's chapter also explores authenticity. He traces the history of this regional event and provides ethnographic data to highlight what is at stake for various social actors—the state, the dancers, the musicians, the local communities, the tourists—in promoting and supporting the Guelaguetza. Despite numerous changes over the years in size, participation, and sponsorship, the Guelaguetza continues to be touted as an "authentic" regional celebration. He ends with a brief commentary on the 2006 cancellation of the event and what occurred in 2007.

Similarly, Peter J. Garcia's essay explores the performance of various types of music and dance featured in an annual religious festival in Bernalillo, New Mexico. Garcia provides the reader with insight into the larger sociohistorical and political climate of this long-standing regional tradition. He shows how certain changes have evolved over the years and how particular expressive forms, such as regional New Mexican dances, have acquired new meaning over time.

Presented as personal testimonials, the chapters by Russell Rodríguez and Martha González offer introspective analyses. Rodríguez's essay presents a provocative perspective on *folklórico* dance and asks: Why is it that this dance form rarely includes representations of the Chicano experience? He also presents other expressive forms (e.g., *teatro*, mariachi, and *jarocho* music) as models of how to integrate Chicanos' lived realities into artistic forms.

As if in response to Rodríguez, Martha González, Chicana lead singer for the Los Angeles–based group Quetzal, reminisces about her life as a child performer in East Los Angeles and explains how she developed her own unique dance form inspired by the fandangos (community music and dance performances)[17] that she witnessed in Veracruz, Mexico. Trained as a *folklórico* dancer and later as a percussionist rooted in Afro-Cuban musical traditions, González was impressed by the improvisational aspects of the fandango dances, sometimes "represented" but virtually lost in the *folklórico* presentations. She describes in detail how she integrates *zapateado* in composing and performing her original works.

* * *

Drawing on extensive research in culturally specific dance forms, these scholars address questions of authenticity, aesthetics, identity, interpretation, political activism, and research methodologies in dance performance. Through their essays, the authors offer us a glimpse into the rich panorama of dance traditions in Greater Mexico. Not only are the motivations for dance and the forms changing, but the processes of transculturation, appropriation, and relocation expand the matrix of possibilities. Dance may function as a cultural refuge or a site for cultural reaffirmation. At the same time, the mainstream appropriates the traditions and they become objects of consumption. This situation brings into relief the necessity of further fostering and fomenting a dialogue among those invested in the traditions as emblems of culture and identity.

Because of the paucity of resources for dance scholars interested in the area of Mexican dance traditions, Olga Nájera-Ramírez has prepared a selected bibliography of published works on folk, ritual, and social Mexican dance traditions. In doing the preliminary work and research for this project, we found that dance scholarship in Greater Mexico is dispersed in different disciplines, and we attempted to gather in the bibliography the key resources from a widely cast net. Ultimately, through the essays and the bibliography we seek to facilitate further engaged scholarship and communication among dance scholars in Greater Mexico and beyond.

Notes

1. Folkorist Américo Paredes coined the term "Greater Mexico" to refer to "all the areas inhabited by people of Mexican culture—not only within the present limits of the Republic of Mexico but in the United States as well—in a cultural rather than a political sense" (Paredes 1976, xiv).

2. Kurath and Martí 1964 provide an excellent discussion of the historical sources on pre-Hispanic dances of Mexico.

3. For more discussion on dance and religion in the Americas, see Ricard 1994 and Coleman 1995.

4. Both types have a long history in Western European artistic expression. See Romero 1993; see also McKinnon 1991.

5. In his classic study, *La población negra de México, 1519–1810: Estudio etnohistórico* (1946), Gonzalo Aguirre Beltrán notes that the first African slaves in Mexico arrived with the Spanish conquerors in 1519.

6. See Sheehy's article "Music of African Diaspora in the Americas" (2005).

7. Arguably, indigenous people have never reached a "postcolonial" era.

8. Particularly relevant to our discussion are the "*danzas de conquista*" (conquest dances). See, for example, Jáuregui and Bonfiglioli 1996a and Harris 2000.

9. For details on Texas and New Mexico, see essays by Cantú, P. García, and Romero in this volume.

10. The term "mestizo" refers to a person of mixed racial ancestry, especially a mix of indigenous and European peoples in the Americas. In Mexico, the term is also used to refer to expressive forms rooted in indigenous, European, and African cultures (as in "Afro-mestizo").

11. For a collection on Latino/a dance, see Delgado and Muñoz 1977.

12. See Polkinghorn, Muños, and Reyes 1994.

13. Although not all contributors to this volume are anthropologists, we consider their work ethnographic because they have conducted extended fieldwork as part of their dance research.

14. In Latin America, October 12 is referred to as the Day of the Race to commemorate the arrival of Columbus to the Americas as the creation of the mestizo race.

15. The literature on place and space is quite extensive. For a concise discussion of "place" and "space," see Brown 2001. Extended on the subject include Feld and Basso 1996 and Low and Lawrence-Zuaniga 2003. For a discussion of "place" in dance studies, see Drid Williams's "Space, Intersubjectivity, and the Conceptual Imperative: Three Ethnographic Cases" and Farnell's article "Where Mind Is a Verb: Spatial Orientation and Deixis in Plains Indian Sign Talk and Assininboine (Nakota) Culture" in Farnell 1995.

16. For a discussion on "invented traditions," see Hobsbawm and Ranger 1983.

17. For more discussion on fandangos, see Sheehy 1979 and Ochoa 2000.

PART I

Contested Identities

1

Embodied Recuperations

Performance, Indigeneity, and Danza Azteca

ELISA DIANA HUERTA

> Cultural resistance is not a totalizing affair, but one based on particular struggles and negotiations waged on turf that, in the grander scheme of things, may appear to be of little consequence. But this negotiation cannot be ignored. Producing a place in which one's collective identity is forged to a principle of solidarity affects, quite significantly, the social construction of reality. The purpose of such activity is to control one's world and oppose those who may have other plans.
>
> —Richard Flores, *Los Pastores*

Hurriedly pulling into the crowded parking lot of the Mexican American Cultural Arts Center an hour later than scheduled, I am relieved to see a number of *danzantes* huddled around the backs of trucks and minivans talking and getting dressed, a good sign that the day's ceremony has not yet begun. Most are already wearing their *huipiles* (traditional embroidered dresses), *tilmas* (cape-like garments used primarily by men), loincloths, and ornately beaded and sown shoulder and chest pieces. I pause briefly to watch a young *danzante* struggle to secure her *chachayotes*[1] (seeded ankle-wraps) around her ankles, sending the seeds into a frantic percussive rhythm. Next to her, another *danzante* methodically decorates her *copilli* (head piece) with parrot, eagle, and white-tipped pheasant feathers. Mothers, fathers, friends, and teachers paint designs on the faces, arms, and legs of younger *danzantes* in rich hues of red, green, white, blue, and black, modeling their designs after traditional Mesoamerican symbols and etchings. The sweet, smoky smell of sage and copal[2] calls to all of us, telling us it is time to gather and dance.

Following a group of *danzantes* through the back gates of the Mexican American Cultural Arts Center, I pass various vendors as I walk into a large, open-air cobblestone plaza where the *danza* will take place. Approaching the ceremonial site, the smells of copal and sage grow heavier and heavier in the air, compelling me to seek out the source. After only a moment, I focus my eyes on a steady trail of white smoke rising from a *sahumador*[3] (a clay vessel in which incense is burned) that sits near the central altar. The smoke dances in the wind, moving over the bodies of all those present, burrowing into our hair and clothing. The smoke rising from the *sahumadores* is one of the most sacred elements of a *danza* ceremony as it serves as a conduit, a bridge between the heavens and the earth, carrying the *danzantes'* prayers from this world and the other. In each group there is at least one person whose responsibility is to keep the *sahumadora,* the sacred fire, burning during the ceremony. This person is almost always a woman and she is often called the "*malinche,*" "*malintzin,*" or "*sahumadora.*"[4]

There is a thin circle of orange reflective tape, at least thirty feet in diameter, in the middle of the plaza that marks the area within which the *danza* will take place. This thin marker separates the ceremonial area from where the audience sits. The one break in the circle is marked by a wide arch of fresh flowers, bamboo, and palm leaves, through which all *danzantes,* drummers, and other ceremonial participants enter and leave the space. Sitting around the circle are community and family members, *danzantes,* and non-*danzantes.* The moments just before the ceremony are a time for last-minute preparations, rushed conversations, and quick reunions. The sounds of voices, hellos and good-byes, rise and fall against the chaotic sounds of *chachayotes* and hand rattles, the tuning of drums, large and small, and the shuffling of bags and chairs. Spanish and English, and all the variations in between, being spoken amongst the hundred or so people mingling in the plaza generates a feeling of familiarity. People are friendly with each other and with me, but as a relative newcomer it is difficult to know where everyone is from and what their relations are to one another. I pick up clues here and there, catch references to hometowns, references to distances traveled and to delays along the way. It seems as though most people are from San Jose, California, and the surrounding areas, including San Francisco, Oakland, Santa Cruz, and Watsonville. A close friend who is from the area and has been a *danzante* for many years soon joins me, and he is able to confirm this for me. He explains that since this ceremony is a *veintena,* a smaller gathering that marks one of eighteen twenty-day periods of Aztec and other Mesoamerican calendars, and not one of the larger ceremonies, most of the participants are "locals."[5] While not the case for this particular gathering, families and groups often travel long distances to dance in ceremonies, especially when there is a strong relationship between the hosting *danza* circle and those who are traveling, or when there is a tradition of participation. The economic restrictions of travel are significant, and most *danza* groups must pay their expenses out of pocket. Regardless, it is common for groups to travel from out of state or even from México (and vice versa) to participate in larger ceremonial gatherings.

Before I am able to ask my friend more questions, the unmistakable deep, solid sound of the conch shell rings out over the crowd, signaling the beginning of the *danza.* An anticipation-filled calm washes over everyone. *Danzantes,* ranging in age from around five to fifty years old, the majority of whom seem to be in their twenties and thirties, make their final preparations and begin to line up at the opening in the circle. I notice that an equal number of women and men will be dancing today, an ideal situation that is not always achieved. As each person enters the ceremonial space, he or she is blessed with smoke by one of two women, each with her own *sahumador,* and then directed to his or her position in the circle by a *capitán* (captain), whose responsibility is to help maintain the balance of energy in the ceremonial space and to "hand out" the dances as the *danza* progresses. The arrangement of the ceremonial space depends greatly on the physical layout of the area within which the dance is occurring and the number of *danzantes* who are participating. Today, the *danzantes* are placed in two concentric circles, as opposed to one large circle, because of space constrictions and the number of participants.

Drumming rings out over the crowd. What begins as a dissonant combination of layered rhythms and beats produced by the two *huehuetls* (large, traditional, three-footed drums of ancient lineage), hand rattles, *chachayotes,* and voices quickly coalesces into a strong, steady, rhythmic cadence of the *danza del permiso* (dance of permission). This particular *danza,* which is relatively short, is danced frequently throughout the ceremony as it is a means for *danzantes* to ask permission to begin their dance offering and of giving thanks once they have completed it. *Danza azteca* is, after all, *un rezo encarnado* (embodied prayer). While there are variations of this dance, as is the case for most dances, the rhythmic pattern of the dance is fairly consistent and deviations occur most often in the speed with which *danzantes* execute *pasos* (steps) and the addition of unique flourishes that may include more complicated steps or other physical movements that demonstrate athleticism and agility. As the ceremony begins I wonder how far into the surrounding neighborhoods the smell of the copal and the heartbeat rhythms of the *huehuetls* will carry.

Danza azteca exists as a significant mode of expressive cultural production throughout México and the United States. This chapter seeks to critically interrogate Chicana and Chicano participation in *danza azteca* in order to illuminate processes of representation, identification, and historical and cultural recuperation in relation to theories of cultural performance and embodiment. It is my contention that the multilayered practices involved in the performance of *danza azteca* offer particularly rich sites for the articulation, negotiation, and contestation of Chicana and Chicano notions of indigeneity.[6] Central to this project is the conceptualization of Chicana and Chicano constructions and performances of indigeneity as complex configurations of cultural-national sentiments, oppositional consciousness toward racist objectification, and a means of meeting community needs, especially in terms of youth outreach through cultural knowledge and healing practices. My own experiences as a cultural activist, as well as my discovery of the dearth of academic resources directly engaged with my central areas of inquiry, have been a driving force behind this project. While there are various videos that address my topic, there have been few articles, and fewer books,[7] dedicated to the subject of *danza azteca* and Chicana/o indigeneity.

Since the Chicano movement of the late 1960s and 1970s, the celebration and recuperation of indigenous ancestries has been central to the formulation of counterhegemonic sociopolitical projects. In most cases, Chicano ancestries have been traced back to the civilizations occupying the central valley of México at the time of European invasion, namely the Azteca-Mexica (Roberto Rodriguez 1997). While this particular genealogical construction has been vigorously questioned, particularly in terms of cultural essentialism and pervasive patriarchal ideologies,[8] it remains a dominant narrative within many communities, as it was foundational to classic Chicano nationalist philosophies.

Taken up as a critical space for the development of oppositional consciousness and a sense of belonging for many communities throughout México and the United States, *danza azteca* is emphasized by *danza* groups as important for *danzantes* to recuperate their indigenous heritage and identity. For this reason, the dance tradition of *danza azteca* is a critical medium through which Chicanas and Chicanos[9] are able to claim and embody an indigenous (Azteca-Mexica) ancestry. *Danza azteca* participants sensually embody (see Stoller), through their physical movements, *trajes* (regalia), music, and the ceremonial burning of copal and sage, understandings of indigeneity. Key

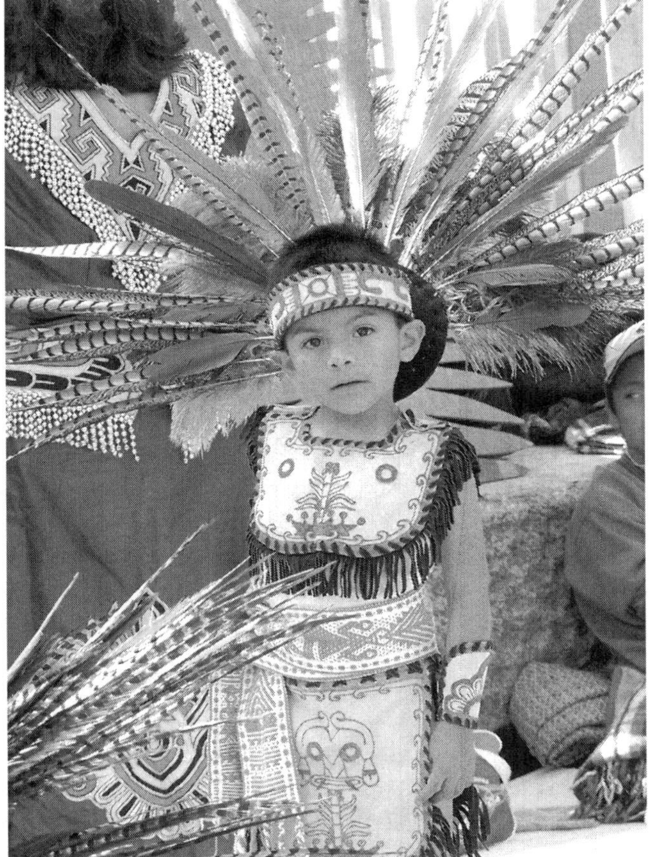

A young *danzante* in his full *traje* at a ceremony in Mexico City. Photograph by author.

to *danza azteca* epistemologies is the idea of knowing through the body, a concept I will further examine in subsequent sections.

Historical Overview

Danza azteca is but one of many dance forms drawing upon pre-Columbian choreographies and pedagogies that can be found in contemporary México and, to a lesser extent, in the United States. In their text, *Dances of Anáhuac* (1964), Gertrude Kurath and Samuel Martí give a detailed genealogy of many of these dance forms in México, most notably *los voladores* (flying pole), *danza de la pluma* (dance of the feather), and el *comelagotoazte* (small ferris wheel) (9). Often categorized as "folk dances" or "*danzas*" (versus "*bailes*"), these dance traditions are often a complex assembly of pre-Columbian practices and Catholicism (Pugh 1944, 11). Generically, the term "*danza*" is used throughout México to identify dances whose choreography draws heavily from autochthonous, indigenous dance traditions. Within the *folklórico* tradition, *danzas* are distinguished from *bailes.* While there are a number of differences between *danzas* and *bailes,* the central distinctions that are made are (1) *danzas* tend to utilize group formations, whereas *bailes* prioritize couples, and (2) *danzas* most often have spiritual or religious foundations whereas *bailes* are primarily for performance, entertainment, or social purposes.[10] It is within this rich history that contemporary forms of *danza azteca* find their philosophical, spiritual, and choreographic foundations.

Danza azteca, a physically rigorous dance tradition consisting of rhythmic steps, deep squats, rapid turns, and other intensive acrobatic movements, is often said to have been introduced to the United States during the Chicana/o movement of the late 1960s and early 1970s (Maestas 1999; Hernández-Ávila 2005; Valencia 1994). It was during that time period that Chicana and Chicano social activists, scholars, artists, and musicians collectively made concerted efforts to reclaim the indigenous histories and cultural traditions and practices that they felt had been denied them through processes of conquest and imperialism. Although it is true that contemporary manifestations of *danza azteca* in the United States can be placed in this time period, it is important to acknowledge that *danza azteca* and other indigenous dance and cultural traditions were practiced in the United States long before the 1960s. In her 1994 interview with Harry Polkinhorn, Marylou Valencia speaks to this issue. She says, "The last time when I went to Querétaro and Zapopan I met a lot of people who were my elders, in their 60s and 70s, who spoke about being invited and coming to the U.S. to do *danza azteca* with the powwows" (1994, 13).

The sociocultural and material battles that were waged during the Chicana/o movement created a moment, or perhaps a series of moments, that fostered a reincarnation of *danza* as a possibility for continued relationships between indigenous peoples of the north and those of the south, between Chicanas/os and Mexicanas/os. It was within this context that the teachings of maestros of *danza azteca* from México, in particular Maestro Andrés Segura and Maestro Florencio Yescas, began weaving their way into the spiritual, cultural, and political consciousness of many Chicanas and Chicanos. Segura and Yescas are widely considered to be the first two Mexican practitioners of *danza azteca* to introduce the tradition to Chicanas and Chicanos in the United States.[11] In spite of many variations of the *danza* tradition, as well as names for dance traditions (*danza de los concheros, danza chichimeca, danza guerrera, danza mexica, danza de conquista, and danza azteca*), there are two branches that were more widely adopted by Chicanos. Decisions as to which tradition to follow, *la danza de los concheros* or *Mexica danza azteca,* marked significant political and spiritual differences. These two traditions overlap in ceremonial and ritual practices and diverge from each other along political, spiritual, and religious affiliations. *Conchero* dancers in both the United States and México maintain a *synergetic* (Hérnandez-Ávila 2005) relationship between indigenous (specifically Mesoamerican) spiritual and philosophical belief systems and Catholicism. *Conchero* groups are named after saints who are simultaneously evocations of particular Catholic icons and referents to *azteca* divine essences or deities. In her 1978 article "*La danza de concheros: una tradición sagrada,*" María Angela González writes: "In my opinion, the survival of this religious manifestation is a very special phenomenon that has been given to us under the vision of our ancestors, who formally reinterpreted it into the Catholic tradition. They took common religious elements, changed the names of the ancient divinities and translated the songs; always struggling to maintain the ritual cycles and their objectives" (1978, 21).

It is precisely this issue of syncretism between indigenous belief systems and Catholicism that proves to be a primary division between *conchero danza* and Mexica *danza.* While the Mexica tradition of *danza azteca* can be considered derivative of the *conchero* tradition, Mexica *danzantes* have widely disavowed affiliations and references to Catholicism that are highly visible in the *conchero* tradition, including the use of religious banners, ceremonies connected to Catholic feast/saint days, as well as the use of stringed instruments, including *conchas* and *mandolinas,* that are considered European impositions. Many Mexica *danzantes* also make a point of using all-natural fibers and materials for all aspects of their ritual practices, including *trajes,* as commonly seen in Chicana/o communities.

I have had the privilege of interviewing a series of *danzantes* in Northern California, México, and Central Texas. These interviews have offered a rich and complex panoramic view of transnational *danza azteca* traditions. Of particular interest to me was a series of interviews I conducted in January of 2005 in Santa Cruz, California, with a mother and her two sons, all of whom were, at the time of the interviews, active participants in a *danza azteca* group in San Jose, California. Luz, a child psychologist, and her two sons, Cuitláhuac and Tomás,[12] had been dancing for close to twelve years with various groups in San Jose and Santa Cruz County. As we began our conversation, she told me she took her oldest son to *danza azteca* for very personal reasons that stemmed from a comment he made when he was four years old about being ugly and not liking his hair, which was long and dark at the time and is now a style that he proudly wears. Luz was eager to find a way to help her son have a positive self-image and a connection to tradition. Continuing with the story, she shared the following:

> I had no idea what *danza* was about, but I always liked it when I saw them dance and I was hoping that my son, my older son Cuitláhuac, would join. We would follow these dance groups all over San Jose, or whenever we'd see them advertised; we'd go to expose him to it because I had heard that's how you get somebody interested, especially little kids. But we had no idea until he actually joined . . . we found this group, [in San Jose] and Cuitláhuac was like four and a half, and the maestro said to bring him to practice. . . . It was free and we thought it was great, so he started at four and a half. Two years later I started to dance. It took me a long time to lose my embarrassment. Now I have no embarrassment, no shame, *nada de nada,* nothing of anything.[13]

Highly interested in the issues that Luz and other *danzantes* might have experienced as they first began to dance, especially in terms of the physicality of the movements, I wanted to hear more about her process of entering the *danza* group. And so she continued with her story:

> Well I think, for two years I sat on the sidelines. One thing is that I had my little one, a challenging two year old. So I always had to be in back of him, so of course I used that also as an excuse, as a front. I'd say, "Oh I can't dance because I got to take care of him." . . . We have an older woman, *una señora* who would dance and I would watch her dance and think "*Ay, esa señora,* how can she dance," you know, and I always thought she was kind of like my role model. If she can dance, I can, and I was in my thirties, even then I felt really embarrassed. But, eventually the beat got so good and once I got out there, though, it was hard to sit down ever again.[14]

Luz's narrative of joining a *danza* group is important for a number of reasons. First, it demonstrates how her identification and discussion of the difficulties she experienced in raising her son in a predominantly Anglo neighborhood motivated her to find a way to connect him and herself to a community that would provide a space of identification for her young son. Second, she reveals her hesitation to actually begin dancing because of the physicality of the movements. This latter issue has surfaced as a common thread throughout a number of my interviews. But, as I will discuss in the following section of this chapter, these same movements provide a kind of embodied knowledge for *danzantes* that is based in philosophical, spiritual, and scientific Mesoamerican traditions.

Notably, Luz identifies as Mexicana and Apache, but she also identifies politically as Chicana. When asked about her Mexicana-Apache identities, she responded:

> We were always brought up in my family *que somos indios, pero, 'shhh, no le digas a nadien,*[15] because we knew that other Mexicanos look down at "*indios.*" They would say, "eres indio?"[16] and we'd say "no, no!" We'd get all scared because my mom and dad always taught us to say no. Whereas, of course, my kids don't say that now. We're like, "yeah we are." They're raised in a certain way because we're both, we can't separate it. We acknowledge both sides. We do know that we don't know enough about the Apache side because we've been living so far away, but they're starting to get to know more things.[17]

The silencing that Luz experienced growing up, and that she worked against in raising her sons, is an unfortunately common narrative within Mexicana/o and Chicana/o communities. In our conversation, Luz speaks to the imbricated relationship of Azteca and Apache traditions within her life. In our conversations, it has become clear that *danza azteca* has offered a kind of bridge to enter into conversations with her sons about an "indianness" that was silenced for her, that is, her Apache heritage. Through their participation in *danza* she and her sons have also entered into activist relationships with other indigenous peoples in California. As *danzantes,* they have participated in powwows, which in turn has exposed Cuitláhuac and Tómas to other forms of indigenous dance, which they are currently beginning to learn.

Corporeal Recuperation and Embodied Knowledge

The initial draw to *danza azteca,* as discussed by Luz in the previous section, and her subsequent desire to continue in the tradition can be understood in a number of ways. I propose that the embodied knowledge of *danza azteca* provides important spaces for community building and personal identification, two aspects Luz signaled as important for her and her sons as they entered into their *danza* group. As each dance corresponds to a particular philosophical-scientific principle within Aztec/Mexica thought, I have chosen to highlight a few examples within *danza azteca* practices to help clarify the ways in which I am employing the concepts of embodied knowledge and corporeal epistemologies.

The power and energy of *danza azteca* is highly sensuous. As with other expressive forms such as theater, poetry, and music, *danza azteca* allows Chicanas/os to articulate cultural knowledge and indigenous legacies. Additionally, it allows for an *embodimen*t of indigeneity. This is important as it speaks directly to the notion of "knowing through the body," an alternative epistemological possibility for knowledge production and perpetuation. The senses (sight, touch, hearing, taste, smell) are important in the various ways people can understand themselves as "being-in-the-world" (Geurts 2002, 3).

Through *danza* practices, Chicanas and Chicanos embody their indigeneity and learn through movement in a variety of ways and in multiple physical and philosophical registers. In the first instance, *danzantes,* through the preparation and donning of their *trajes,* embody a complicated and at times fraught aesthetic of indigeneity. *Danza trajes* most often include a *copilli,* a *manta* (material that covers the body; it can come in a variety of styles, usually decided upon by the leader of the group; varies along gender lines), *chachayotes,* and a *sonaja* (a seed-filled rattle). Colors, symbols, and overall design are chosen in ways that express an individual dancer's energy or disposition, as well as his or her position in the group. Often, *danzantes* are responsible for designing, sewing, and arranging each part of their *traje,* down to the smallest detail, which proves to be a great commitment of time and energy. The visibility, the aesthetic markings of indigeneity employed in *danza,* create powerful possibilities for sensuous identification.

According to Marylou Valencia, *danza azteca* "had a big impact in the Chicano movement in that it gave Chicanos something that was very visible, something that was very beautiful to identify with insofar as the cultural past was concerned" (1994, 50). *Danza azteca* is not only visually striking, but it is an overall deep sensory experience that evokes all of the senses. While much attention is often paid to what *danza azteca* looks like, it is also important to consider the importance of the other senses in the creation of ceremonial space (Stoller 1997). Indeed the sounds and smells of *danza azteca* are as distinct as its visual nature. For example, the distinctive sounds of *danza azteca* consist of multilayered percussive rhythms that at any given moment include the deep, resonating sound of the *huehuetl;* the staccato sound of hollowed-out seeds of *chachayotes* hitting against each other as *danzantes* walk, step, jump, turn, and spin; sonajas, hand drums; *teponaztli,* and so on. In addition to the sights and smells of *danza* is the ubiquitous smell of copal and sage. During interviews and informal conversations, *danzantes* and people associated with *danza* often referred to the ways the sounds and smells of ceremonies would draw them into ceremonial spaces. Specifically, they would reference how the sound of the drums and the smell of the smoke travels across distances and that they were often able to hear and smell the *danza* before they were able to see it.

Danza azteca is an expressive cultural form based on the movements of the sun, moon, and planets. An important shift within Azteca-Mexica social organization and scientific knowledge production came with their shift from a lunar to a solar calendar (León-Portilla 1963, 21–22). While lunar cycles remain an important aspect of everyday practices, especially in terms of ritual and agricultural cycles, the solar calendar took on an added importance during the height of the Aztec civilization. The majority of dances within the *danza azteca* tradition take place in a circle, or a series of concentric circles, with one *danzante* (or representatives from a participating group) leading the dance in the center near the main altar. This formation is directly linked to the sun and the movement of the planets, with the "lead" *danzante* representing the centrality of the sun and the other *danzantes* representing the moving planets around the sun. In most circles, each *danzante* has the opportunity to lead a dance, but the *danzantes* have the option of passing their turn if they feel they are not yet ready to lead a dance or for any other reason. This physical embodiment of the sun and planets is recognition of the advanced astronomical understandings that Mesoamerican societies had as well as a means of enacting cosmic or universal movement. In this way, the *danzantes* themselves not only recognize a heliocentric model of the solar system, but also embody the cosmos itself. Additionally, an active acknowledgment of each person's participation as a *danzante* in ceremony occurs as each *danzante* takes her or his turn to dance in the center of the circle; this rotation speaks to the centrality of respect and balance found in *danza azteca* philosophy.

In a similar vein, several of the dances themselves are metaphors for everyday activities. For example, a number of the dances include *pasos*, or a series of steps that represent the planting, growing, harvesting, and preparation of corn for consumption. For many Chicanas/os, the planting of corn is not a part of everyday life. The inclusion of such movements allows *danzantes* to physically embody a process that is central to understandings about the environment and nutrition. María Sten elaborates this connection in her discussion of *danza* as a vehicle for social understanding (1990, 20). Corn holds an important place in Native cultures throughout the Americas. For many Mesoamerican groups, corn was the foundation of nutritional intake in addition to playing a key role in creation mythologies. During these movements, *danzantes* are creating and performing themselves as workers of the land, as generators of energy, and as storytellers.

I will touch on a final example of corporeal recuperation of indigenous beliefs for *danzantes:* the concept of death and rebirth as a constant throughout Azteca-Mexica philosophical thought and culture. Death was thought of as another part of life, one that a person would prepare for with all of her or his heart. For *danzantes* the idea of death and rebirth is constant in their ways of knowing through the body. One example of this is their understanding of self-sacrifice and discipline. The shedding of skin, from calluses for example, and pain from dancing for hours, if not days, is literally a physical understanding of the concept and processes of regeneration. Bodies regenerate themselves, as life regenerates itself through death. It is important to note that this kind of embodiment and knowing through the body is highly individualized, but it also has strong reverberations through the collective. Self-sacrifice and discipline are central principles for *danzantes.*

Importantly, each of these forms of knowing through the body is meaningful on both the individual and collective levels. *Danzantes* simultaneously explore teachings through their own body movements, their unique processes of learning the *pasos* of each dance and their correlated philosophical teachings, and through their relation with other *danzantes* and the social, cultural, and political contexts in which they dance.

Politics of Belonging and Cultural Performance

Benedict Anderson's notion of imagined communities (1991) is useful in thinking about how Chicanas/os and Mexicanas/os in the United States imagine themselves as indigenous and how they imagine their relationship with other communities. He suggests that the nation is "an imagined political community" and "communities are to be distinguished, not by their falsity/genuineness, but by the style in which they are imagined" (6). The implication of such a model is that it breaks with conventional notions that communities are easily identifiable and recognizable to everyone, and highlights that even in the smallest communities, especially those that number in the thousands of people, it is unlikely that an individual will know everyone else in the community. So then, in any community there is at least some aspect of imagining. While Anderson's primary focus is on print media, the styling and mechanisms of community imaginaries, the ways in which individuals, groups, and communities identify and know themselves, is directly related to cultural performances where "members of a society put their culture on display for themselves and others" (Bauman 1986, 133). In the case of *danza,* the connection between imaginaries and cultural performance is at the heart of the political and social implications of *danza azteca* practices and the narratives created and embodied by *danzantes.* Specifically, transnational imaginings are central to many *danzantes'* understanding of belonging, as many have family and community in both the United States and México. Moreover, many of the social, cultural, and ritual practices followed and performed are based in autochthonous, pre-Columbian traditions of México, which includes much of the U.S. Southwest. Thus, for some groups, like Mexica dancers, a different type of imagining takes place. Not only are they in conversation with contemporary *danzantes* transnationally, they also imagine and understand themselves as the carriers of the legacy of Azteca-Mexica cultural, political, and social practices. At times, this particular mode of imagining can be controversial both in practice and philosophy, particularly in the instances in which static representations of indigeneity are formulated and continually re-inscribed."[18]

Everyday practices and rituals are central to the ways in which communities are imagined. These practices are often centered on the self, the individual *danzante* (but not necessarily the *danzante* as individual). In *Breathing Spaces,* Chen interrogates "the ways in which practices of self cultivation in certain times and places enabled the transformations of existing spaces and even transcendence of spatial and institutional boundaries" (2003, 18). The practice of *qigong,* which is centered in breathing practices and self-cultivation, is both a healing practice and a response to shifting political and social realities marked by the economic shift to a market economy. The imbrications of self-healing and political readjustment speak directly to how the *danza* practices of self-discipline and self-sacrifice (elaborated in the previous section) create a sense of collective belonging, a space for the development of cultural and political consciousness and identity. It is necessary to contextualize how work on the "self" can and does have political ramifications (Chen 2003, xi) and how body practices can be important in the (self-)positioning of individuals within community contexts.

As stated earlier, the visual power and energy of *danza azteca* is deeply emotive. Enrique Maestas writes in the January/February 1997 issue of *Raza-Teca Magazine:* "Chicano's *danza* is how many of us come to know ourselves as indigenous people of these American continents . . . when we make our ceremony, we are indigenous people making indigenous ceremony in honor of all those who serviced to give birth to us and have taught us to stand our ground as indigenous people" (1997, 45). Here, *danza* is constructed as a place of indigenous "knowing" through the body and through dance. Thinking about *danza* as a space in which identity and knowing are constructed opens up a range of possibilities for Chicanas/os who participate. The performative aspects of *danza,* then and now, allow for corporeal articulations of oppositional consciousness and potentially, although not necessarily, for progressive politics.

* * *

It is an hour into the *danza.* The drummers have found their stride and are pounding out the ancient heartbeat rhythms of dance after dance. My eyes finally begin to discern intricate patterns of movement and design. The *danzantes' trajes* range from the simple to the boldly ornate. In some cases there is a consistency of colors and/or execution of design within a group. It is easy to pick out the few *danzantes* who are dressed in clean, simple *trajes:* beige cotton dresses or cloaks and small headpieces, if at all. These *danzantes* carry either a single feather or a *sonaja.* The majority of *danzantes* are dressed in elaborate *trajes* created from a combination of natural and synthetic materials: lamé, leather, beads, sequence, and feathers. Two men are dressed in full, head-to-toe, leopard print body suits and carry large shields. *Copillis* come in all shapes and sizes. Some are fashioned in the shape of animal heads and others are so large that their feathers extended well past the fingertips of outstretched arms. Almost all the *danzantes* use *chachayotes,* adding the rhythm of their own dance to that of the drum. Even though they dance on a cobblestone plaza, the majority of *danzantes* do not wear shoes, and those that do wear thin-soled *huaraches,* leather sandals.

Each *danza* is a complex combination of intricate footwork, deep squats, high jumps, and fast-paced turns. *Danzantes* dance relatively close to one another and I marvel that, although there are a few close misses, no major collision of bodies occurs, even as *danzantes* begin to tire. This is quite a feat as the *danza* circle is a conglomeration of various groups who may only dance with each other once or twice in a year. Two hours into the *danza* the *jefes* invite three other groups to join the circle: three Zuni dancers, four Apache dancers, and two young female fancy dancers. Each group takes its turn in the middle of the circle as the *danzantes* move gently with them to the rhythm of the new drum in the circle, adding their own quiet rhythms with their rattles and *chachayotes.* The fancy dancers complete the offering of their dance; the *danza azteca* begins again and continues for another two hours.

As the morning turns into afternoon, the sun bears down on the *danzantes* and the clouds become fewer and farther between. The wind rises up now and again, carrying feathers from hands and headpieces, and coaxes more thick, white smoke from the *sahumador.* The sun remains hot and bright until the last half hour of the *danza,* when clouds reappear, this time heavy with rain. Intermittent sprinkles soon become a heavy downpour, and the *danza* continues through it all.

At the end of the *danza* the emotionally charged, physically exhausted, and rain-soaked *danzantes* gather in the center of the plaza for a talking circle. Each *danzante* is given the opportunity to speak, even as the rain pounds harder against them. As the talking circle ends, the *danzantes* quickly file out of the circle, change, put away their rattles and feathers, and join their group members, friends and families for *pozole,* hominy stew, at a nearby building.

Notes

1. Also referred to as "*ayayotes.*"

2. Copal is a resin from the copal tree of Oaxaca. It was considered sacred in pre-Columbian times and is thus still burnt in ritual ceremonies and cleansings.

3. In Spanish, the *sahumador* is also referred to as an *incensario,* or by the Náhuatl name, *popochcaxitl.*

4. Terms used to describe the person(s) responsible for taking care of the fire during ceremonies varies from group to group. The use of the term *malinche* is interesting as it is the same name used to reference the young, indigenous woman identified as Hernán Cortes's "companion" and translator. There is much debate as to who La Malinche was, how she came to accompany Cortes, and her relationship (forced or willing) to him. Contrary to popular portrayals of Malinche as the ultimate traitor to her people that are tethered to sexist mythologies, Hernández-Ávila argues that la Malinche's role was that of a translator and path opener, and within *danza,* the responsibilities of those who carry her name are the same. The second term, "*Malintzin,*" is closely related to the first, as it is the Náhuatl name from which the Spanish derived the name "Malinche." The name Malintzin itself may derive from, or refer to, "*malinalli,*" the day sign in the Aztec calendar meaning "winding plant, or grass" under which Malintzin/Malinche would have been born. The third term, *sahumadora,* is a Spanish term that is a direct reference to the vessel in which incense is burned (*sahumador*).

5. Groups present included Danza Tezkatlipoka (San Jose), Danza Tonatiuh (San Jose), Ixtatutli/White Hawk Indian Council (Watsonville), Xiuhcoatl Traditional Danza Azteca (San Francisco), Danza Xitlalli (Berkeley).

6. Throughout this chapter, I use the term "indigeneity" to refer to representations, actions, and performances rooted in and expressing "indigenous" identities.

7. Sten 1990; Gonzalez Torres 2005.

8. Important to this project is a fleshing out of pedagogical discourses and praxis that essentialize Chicana and Chicano indigeneity, especially as they affect gender relations, representations of sexuality, and articulations of cultural pluralism. The writings of Anna Nieto-Gómez, Marta Cotera, and Alma M. Garcia's in the anthology *Chicana Feminist Thought: The Basic Historical Writings* (1997) have made important interventions and critiques of sexist and heterosexist discourses with Chicano nationalisms that inform my formulation of this project.

9. Both during and since the Movimiento, the term "Chicana/o" has been contested and redefined. Originally deployed in the battle to claim the right to self-determination and as a means to call attention to the oppressive and racist practices openly occurring in the United States (Zavella 1997, 45), the term also took on problematic sentiments of paternalism, homophobia, sexism, and nationalism. Much work has been done to both problematize and refigure the term Chicana/o. Drawing on the work of Norma Alarcón (1990), Gloria Anzaldúa (1987), Cherríe Moraga (1993), Patricia Zavella (1997), and José Limón (1981), I will further problematize the legacy and possible futures for the term Chicana/o as an identity category. During preliminary fieldwork, all the *danzantes* I spoke with self-identified as Chicana and Chicano. Through future interviews I hope to gain a stronger understanding as to why *danzantes* use the terms Chicana or Chicano and why others may not. I am also interested in exploring other identity terms (e.g., Mexican, *Mexicana/o, indígena,* and so on) that they may use.

10. It's interesting to note that *folklórico* groups often incorporate *danzas* in their repertoire, highlighting the performative, not religious or spiritual, aspects of the traditions. In this context, the meanings and symbolic movements of the *danzas* take on different cultural, social, and spiritual significance.

11. For a further discussion of the contributions of these two particular *maestros,* please see my forthcoming dissertation, and for a discussion of Maestro Segura's influence on Teatro Campesino, see Broyles-González 1994.

12. Pseudonyms.

13. Luz (pseudonym), interview by Elisa Huerta, Santa Cruz, California, January 30, 2005.

14. Ibid.

15. "that we are Indians, but, shhh, don't tell anyone"

16. "Are you an Indian?"

17. Luz (pseudonym), interview.

18. A major controversy circulating around *danza azteca* is whether or not *danzantes* (and more broadly Chicanas/os) are "truly" indigenous peoples. Enrique Lamadrid (2003) discusses a similar challenge of who is indigenous among those who enact "Comanche" commemorative ceremonials in New Mexico. For more on this topic, please see my dissertation (forthcoming).

2

The Zapopan Dancers

Reinventing an Indigenous Line of Descent

RENÉE DE LA TORRE CASTELLANOS

Translated by Nicholas Barret

En pocos lugares del mundo se puede vivir un espectáculo parecido al de las grandes fiestas religiosas de México . . . El tiempo deja de ser sucesión y vuelve a ser lo que fue, y es, originalmente: un presente en donde pasado y futuro al fin se reconcilian.[1]

—Octavio Paz

In Mexico the dance is an expression of popular religion, originating in pre-Hispanic and colonial times, that has managed to stay alive till present times as a form of devotion associated with the central images of Catholicism. Up until a few decades ago, the religious traditions of the dance seemed to be dying out or losing strength (see Medrano de Luna 2001), but today there is a revival in this way of paying homage to the Virgin by dancing, much as the indigenous peoples of Mexico used to dance in honor of their deities. This can be seen in the proliferation of groups and companies of dancers, the increasing number of young people and children taking part, and in the renewal and diversification of dance styles. It is also important to note that in the past few decades some of the *conchero* or Aztec dancers have ceased to identify their religion as Catholicism and have started to search for what it means to be Mexican in cultural terms, by tracing the pre-Hispanic origins of the nation's culture.

I am interested in seeing how current dance practices are able to re-create the memory of being identified with a tradition and a sense of being Mexican[2] in a way that links Catholic believers to an imaginary indigenous line of descent, reinventing the founding myth of the nation and allowing the historical continuity of the cultural mix between an indigenous past and colonial Catholicism to be renewed.[3]

The Context: A Creole Culture Waking Up to the Indigenous

Somos el borrador de un texto
Que nunca será pasado en limpio
Con borrones y con tachaduras
Y párrafos enteros cancelados
Nuestro ser es un texto
Que busca redondearse
Con el paso insensato de los días[4]

—Julian Palley

This study of dance companies honoring the Virgin of Zapopan was conducted in the city of Guadalajara, which is the second largest urban concentration in Mexico (accommodating some four million inhabitants) and also second largest in commercial exchanges, though it is only the third most industrialized (Ramírez Sáiz 1998, 40). In spite of its being a modern city in cultural terms, it is above all else the capital of a region where the predominant, essentially Creole, culture[5] has systematically denied the city's indigenous past (Ávila Palafox and Calvo Buezas 1993; De la Torre 1998; Aceves, De la Torre, and Safa 2004), and where a culture that discriminates against its indigenous people continues to this day (Martínez Casas 2001).

A number of local products from Guadalajara have been adopted as Creole symbols of national identity and folklore, such as the *charros*, the *mariachi*, *tequila*,[6] and the "Jarabe tapatío," a typical Mexican folk dance also known as the Mexican hat dance, which lends its name to the people of Guadalajara, or "*tapatíos*." One characteristic of Creole identity that became the pride of the region was extolling the white features of the population, creating a stereotype of superiority of such features over the features of the indigenous people of Mexico. These emblems also take no notice of the value of the continuous indigenous presence in the city from its foundation to our own days, and they seek to erase any appreciation of their culture.[7]

The Virgin of Zapopan Pilgrimage is a procession that takes place on October 12th to accompany the "traveling" Virgin on her return to her sanctuary. The journeying effigy leaves her altar in Zapopan during the rainy season (from May to October) and visits the 172 parishes of the diocese to offer the local inhabitants her protection against rain, lightning, and storms. On her return, the length of the procession, from the Cathedral of Guadalajara to the Basilica of Zapopan, is 11 kilometers (6.8 miles). Despite the hegemony of the Creole construction mentioned earlier, what defines the atmosphere of the principal feast of the city, the Virgin of Zapopan's procession,[8] currently celebrated on the twelfth of October and attended by more than two million pilgrims, is the indigenous Catholic character of the thousands of dancers who accompany the Virgin.

Although the dancers are mestizos living in a modern city in the twenty-first century, they have decided to "indigenize" their bodies and conquer the streets of Guadalajara through their dancing, their rhythms, their music, and their costumes.[9] But why should an indigenous identity emerge at the principal religious festival of a city that prides itself on being Creole? My hypothesis is that the experience of the dance companies allows new arrivals to construct ways of thinking and feelings that they belong to the city of Guadalajara and lets them reinvent the ethnic past and popular tradition in innovative ways.[10]

Types of Dance: Identities and Otherness

> *Los géneros dancísticos no son otra cosa que lenguajes dancísticos asentados históricamente. Cada lenguaje dancístico posee objetivos definidos dentro de las comunidades o culturas que le dan vida.*[11]
>
> —Alberto Dallal

In previous studies I have shown that the city of Guadalajara has been growing at an ever-faster pace and without regard to planning, provoking urban problems that have reduced the area of social spaces in the city. Just two of many circumstances that limit the spaces to socialize are a growing segmentation and polarization of the population by social class, and insecurity and violence that have become a fact of urban life. Along with these two circumstances, there are two factors that dramatically affect the ways of getting along with each other in the city. First, at present more than 20 percent of the inhabitants of Guadalajara live in irregular settlements, where precarious living conditions and the distance from the center of the city make it difficult for people to participate in the life of the metropolis. The popular barrio or neighborhood is no longer the stage for harmonious relations based on mutual solidarity, trust, and self-help; it has become a territory fragmented by violence and daily insecurity. Second, the better-off social classes (middle and upper) have opted for exclusive privatization.[12] *Cotos* (private estates or gated communities) have been creating a kind of society separate from the rest of the city, which "produces a fragmentation of the consciousness of citizenship, annihilates the distinctions between those who live close to each other, solidarity with those in need and responsibility to the city as a whole" (Aceves, De la Torre, and Safa 2004, 291).

Despite this situation, every barrio, every *colonia,* and every popular settlement in Guadalajara has its own dance company. These organizations and their activities play an important role in the construction of neighborhood identities, but especially in integrating distinct ways of living the urban experience into a single ritual into which the traditional inhabitants of the city (who have taken part in this ritual for centuries) converge. Also converging are more recent arrivals who live in popular *colonias* and residential areas, those who live in new irregular settlements, and people from townships with an indigenous past close to the city that have been incorporated into the urban zone.

At present there are three hundred dance companies on record, the largest of which have as many as five hundred members, and the smallest around forty.[13] This incorporation of the city's inhabitants into the dance creates one of the main spaces of cross-class and cross-neighborhood conviviality in the urban area, as rehearsals take place in public places nearly everywhere from July to October.

Around thirty thousand multicolored dancers turn up at the pilgrimage and use their bodies to make an offering that will please the Virgin, whom they recognize as "the Great Mother." The companies of dancers are organized by wards. The Franciscan friars are in charge of each ward, and the time and the place where the dancers are to perform is decided by competition. There are three wards in the city: Guadalajara with eighty companies registered, Zapopan with ninety, and Tonalá and Tlaquepaque with forty each; these are in addition to the groups that visit the city on the day of the pilgrimage from other towns in the state of Jalisco and from elsewhere in the country. The wards are in charge of making sure the norms are respected, which means the dancers must be "evangelized," which means they have to attend meetings the first Sunday of each month.

The people who make up the dance groups are not members of particular ethnic groups in the city, but mestizos who on this special day are proud to wear a whole array of garments to re-create their indigenous origins. The dancers are all from the popular class, though in recent years the dance tradition has begun to include artists, professional men and women, and students as well.

Among the various companies of dancers harking back to an indigenous tradition—whether their own or an appropriated or an invented one—a number of different types may be distinguished: (1) dances of the Conquest, (2) the *conchero* and Aztec dances, (3) autochthonous Indian dances of the region (Tuxpanese and *matachín* dances),[14] (4) the *lanceros* (lancers) and the *sonajeros* (rattlers) who re-create the aesthetic of the North American Indian, and (5) the pre-Hispanic dances of the *mexicanidad* movements. Groups who wish to restore the values and the spirituality of pre-Hispanic times through the dances lead these movements, which are composed of an urban mestizo population that desires to revitalize and belong to a native identity. One type of movement is the *mexicanidad*. It stems from the Movimiento Confederado Restaurador de la Cultura Anáhuac (Confederate Movement to Restore Anáhuac Culture), which seeks to vindicate indigenous traditions and does not accept subsequent varieties mixed with Catholicism. Another is the *neomexicanidad*, which has a more esoteric and spiritual character, accepts the mixture with Catholicism, and forges links with New Age networks. Both these movements have approached the ancient *conchero* dances,

Staging of the Conquest, dance group from the Retiro Barrio. Photograph by author.

believing that the ancestral knowledge has been kept alive in such sites (see González Torres 2005 and De la Peña 2003).

DANCES OF THE CONQUEST

The dances of the Conquest are the product of assimilated, autochthonous, pre-Hispanic dances that were taken over by the Spanish missionaries in order to portray the great battles between the *conquistadores* and the native Indians. The dance was a cultural instrument the conquerors used to impose the new faith by assimilation with the festive religious character of the indigenous peoples, and especially with the processions and the pre-Hispanic dances. The Christian dances were laid over these to provide a language that could transmit miraculous stories, extend the culture of the conquerors over the conquered, and reinforce the position of "the Lord's chosen people" (Warman 1972, 80). Originally, missionaries used dances in the colonial period as instruments of acculturation and evangelization that would replace the pagan cults of the indigenous people:

> *Pero, mediante su reproducción a lo largo de varios siglos, la danza de Conquista ha sufrido sucesivas reelaboraciones que han desembocado en diferentes versiones contemporáneas y, por supuesto, en otras que se han perdido por haber llegado a ser disfuncionales a sus portadores* (Jáuregui 1990, 68).[15]

The dance traditions of the Conquest, though possessed of a colonial past, have been reinvented in the course of history. In fact, among current companies of Conquest dancers, which have been maintained by family inheritance, the most ancient were founded halfway through the nineteenth century. This is because, as mentioned in the note, the traditions of popular culture were interrupted on several occasions in the nineteenth century and in the early part of the twentieth century. Conquest dance companies enact, in the form of dialogues and skits, the confrontations between the autochthonous Indian culture and Spanish culture, between Christianity and the gods of the Aztec pantheon, and between nature and nurture (see González 1996). Narrators accompany the Conquest dances and portray the history of events, allowing the history to be remembered by means of oral transmission:

> *Se darán cuenta qué pocas danzas hay de Conquista; antes en este barrio ("El Refugio") había 18, y ahora podríamos decir que somos la única ya en la actualidad, y eso es lo que nos llena más de orgullo, poderles mostrar a los niños lo que pasó en la historia de México. Aunque no sea exacta, porque en algunos párrafos sabemos que nosotros los seres humanos somos capaces de cambiarla,*

por ejemplo, yo o algún danzante puede decir diez mil soldados y eran dos mil, o puedo decir un párrafo que no entra. Para volver a contarla como de veras fue, necesitaríamos hablar con nuestros ancestros que ya murieron y eso es imposible, estamos tratando de sacar lo más fiel que se pueda esta tradición.[16]

Most of the Conquest dance companies of Guadalajara have included a presentation of the confrontation of the Indians (with characters like la Malinche, Cuauhtémoc, and eagle warriors) and the Spaniards (represented by Hernán Cortés), but they no longer show the battle of Mixtón, which is the founding myth of the evangelization of Jalisco. The dances are, however, a way of teaching history to the populace:

En la danza de Conquista se relata todo lo que supuestamente pasó en los años cuando los aztecas y los españoles de la conquista se enfrentaron, entonces cuando vinieron a conquistar los españoles para vencer a Cuauhtémoc y por medio de embajadas, como las que hicimos hace rato, que veníamos y se mandaban a avisar que cedieran y se rindieran y Cuauhtémoc a no rendirse mandando sus tropas y nosotros como reyes a decirle que no se rendían y escenificamos cuando empezaba la guerra de españoles contra aztecas.[17]

In the traditional barrios, most of the Conquest dances have been recycled as Aztec dances. Some of them retain the name and keep the tradition of the ambassadors and the flags so as not to lose their identity, but they no longer present the dialogues. Others, such as the tastoanes (in honor of Saint James), survive in the ancient indigenous pueblos (Indian villages) that used to be some distance from the city but now are part of Guadalajara.[18]

THE AZTEC DANCES

> *La danza de los concheros y los valores culturales*
> *que en ella se expresan poseen características sincréticas*
> *y reculturalizadas, entendiendo con este último término*
> *un movimiento de reconciliación con las antiguas raíces*
> *de la "mexicanidad"*
>
> —Anáhuac González Torres 1996, 224.[19]

The Aztec dances, also known as *concheros,*[20] portray the indigenous past by re-creating the Aztec culture of the high plateau of Mexico.[21] Their rituals are a syncretic manifestation of the Mexican national sense and religious spirit, in which pre-Hispanic rites combine with symbols of Catholic devotion. The key to autochthonous knowledge is kept alive in religious syncretism, by which the religious culture of the ancient Mexicans lives on beneath the signifiers of Catholic culture.

Sonajeros Apaches, el Moreno (the Dark One) represents the temptation of the Table Dance. Photograph by author.

Don Mario Gutiérrez, currently captain of the group called Primera Danza Azteca (First Aztec Dance), founded by the Gutiérrez family in 1927, is one of the few dancers who remembers when the dancers first performed at the pilgrimage. He inherited the dance tradition from his maternal grandfather, who was nicknamed *el gran jefe*, the "Big Chief." Don Mario recalls that he started dancing in the 1930s to fulfill a sacred vow and that in those days things were different. Because the Callista government did not allow pilgrimages, there were only fifteen dance groups. He continues:

> *Era el tiempo en que hubo gobernantes que no dejaban que los católicos saliéramos a peregrinar, ni siquiera nos dejaban ir a misa. Fue hasta los años '40, cuando cesó la persecución religiosa de Calles, la primera vez que la imagen fue recibida en Zapopan y trasladada entre una gran manifestación de gentes.*[22]

Although people speak of the tradition of dancing to the Virgin of Zapopan and of accompanying her on the pilgrimage as dating from the earliest years of the colonial period, it is clearly a tradition that in its present form is no more than a century old.

Aztec dance companies have proliferated, and with their coming many of the Conquest dances have disappeared; in fact, it is said with some pride that Guadalajara is "the city of the dancers." The popularity of this fashion of pleasing the Virgin with dancing has meant that some of the companies are temporary and do not last longer than the time it takes to get ready to dance at the pilgrimage. It also means, as can be seen in the interviews, that many of the dancers today have no knowledge of the significance of the tradition, the symbolism of the dances, or of the roots that feed them. Though there are fewer of them than before, dance companies that have held fast to a family dance lineage have survived, and in these groups a consciousness of the historical roots of Mexicanism and the culture of the dance has developed, transcending the ritual around the Virgin.

> *La mayoría de los grupos se mantienen por familias. Las familias son las que se encargan de seguir viva esta tradición que no se acabe, que no se pierda. Manejamos nosotros lo que es tradición, para nosotros nuestros antepasados, mi padre y mi abuelo nos dejaron tradiciones. Esto se viene manejando como un ejército. Hay celadores, hay capitanes, hay las malinches, que son celadoras también. Están también los soldados.*[23]

The elders know the sacred meaning and the ritual function of the choreographies, of the ceremonial objects (such as copal resin), of each instrument—the *huehuetl,* vertical tree trunk, footed drum; the *teponaztli,* a horizontal wooden slit drum; and the conch trumpet—and of each step, each sound, each movement, in relation to a ritual cosmogony. For example, the elder Francisco Ayala comments:

> *La danza además de ser una esencia, un movimiento, es una preparación física, espiritual, mental y emocional. Es una medicina, una plataforma que te impulsa a conocer muchos aspectos del mundo. Nosotros con las danzas sostenemos nuestras raíces autóctonas y exploramos la infinitud de estas experiencias.*[24]

The Aztec companies (the *concheros,* the *Mexicas,* and the *Chichimecas*) perform pre-Hispanic rituals to venerate the Virgin, re-creating the indigenous according to the current image people have of the Aztecs: wearing large plumes made of exotic feathers, breastplates, loincloths, bracelets, knee pads, and a *tilma* (blanket used as a cloak). Although they are inspired by the Aztec apparel of pre-Hispanic times, they acknowledge contemporary tendencies and introduce brightly colored plastic fabrics, velvet, sequins, (semi-)precious stones, and so on. The Aztec dances include sets with very complicated steps (leaps, flying turns, and fast spins), so their *guaraches,* sandals, tend to be made by hand of leather, though some of the dancers dance barefoot, offering their pain as a prayer. The dancers say they are keeping an ancient tradition alive, one that goes back to the pre-Hispanic period and that used to be performed to placate their own gods and the dead in their own pantheon but is now related to the main Catholic observances.

> *Sí todo tiene su significado, las plumas representan lo que es la fuerza que recibimos aquí de nuestro padre Tonathiu. Todo esto es el sonido [hace sonar los cascabeles]. Los movimientos que hacemos con los sones, significan el movimiento de la serpiente, que es pues la vida. Hay que llevar todo a cabo como debe ser. Nosotros llevamos a cabo lo que es la cultura y el movimiento, los sones, las danzas se llevan a cabo de lo que es los ayoyotles, esto es parte de la danza—¿por qué?—porque es el movimiento de todo tu cuerpo, sonido, movimiento, hay que darle ritmo a la vida.*[25]

The Aztec dance ritual starts with a salute to the four cardinal points, "the four winds," and then the dance is offered to the deity. The dances produce a

Aztec dance group. Photograph by author.

syncretism between the Christian cross and the *cruz-olín* of the four winds, which in turn represents the four elements (water, fire, air, and earth). The choreography is performed in a circle, around the cross and the copal incense.

It is important to observe that while the Chichimeca variant still exists among the dance companies, differing from the Aztec dances in apparel, footwear and the steps, in recent years most of the dance companies of Guadalajara have incorporated the ritual aesthetic of the *conchero* groups from Mexico City into their repertoire. These reproduce the national ethnocentrism that elevates the Aztec past and imposes it as a symbol of "national ethnicity," and reduces the diversity of indigenous cultures in Mexican territory.

Unlike the dance groups of Mexico City and the center of the country, the groups from Guadalajara claim to be autochthonous. They call themselves Aztecs, rejecting the name of *concheros*, because, as they say:

> *Aquí hay más grupos danzantes que en el D.F. Pero aquí no somos concheros, sino aztecas, porque aquí somos danza autóctona. Nosotros no le decimos cascabeles a las tobilleras, sino que son "hueseras," porque están hechas con huesos de frutos conocidos como "hueso de fraile." Nosotros los cortamos de los árboles, vamos al campo y los recolectamos, les sacamos la pulpa y les metemos municiones para que suenen.*[26]

In the 1950s the *conchero* dance in Mexico City and other places in the center of the country began to be secularized by the Mexicanism movements, especially due to the influence of the Movimiento Confederado Restaurador de la Cultura de Anáhuac (Confederated Movement to Restore Anáhuac Culture), which aims to restore society by rescuing the purity of pre-Hispanic culture. It disdains any admixture with the European world, above all else the use of stringed instruments, and it proscribes the dance around Catholic images. However, in Guadalajara the Mexicanism movement has been much more marginal than in Mexico City, and it has no relation with the established traditional dance groups.

Nonetheless, late in the 1980s members of a neo-Mexicanism movement known as the Reginos made contact with the chiefs (captains) of the principal Aztec dance companies (the most ancient and the most extended), referring to them as their guides and regarding them as authentic guardians of the tradition. This encounter has brought important transformations to the interpretations of the dancers, who no longer consider the dance to be only a religious practice, but also an instrument for awakening the *chakras*[27] of the earth, or else as a form of therapy or a way of doing "meditation in movement."

THE AUTHENTIC IS FROM TUXPAN

Some dances are intimately associated with the historical memory of the colonization and evangelization of the region. This memory of local ethnicity is kept alive through religious dances linked to the festivals of some of the indigenous pueblos (villages or towns) of the region, but a few years ago some of the dance companies of the city began to take them up as models of ethnicity.

The Compañía Sonajeros de Lourdes (Company of Lourdes' Rattle Dancers), founded in 1935, provides one example. It used to be called the Sonajeros de Lourdes de Tepopote (Rattle Dancers of Lourdes of Tepopote), when Lourdes de Tepopote was an Indian village close to Guadalajara, but by the 1970s the village had been invaded by the city, and it was there that the land was parceled out and the *colonia* of El Fresno was established. This group stands out from the rest as one of the most colorful. The costumes and the dances correspond to the tradition of the pueblo of Tuxpan, in the south of Jalisco. This town "came into the twentieth century as an indigenous exception in a region of creoles and mestizos" (Lameiras 1999, 254). Institutions, practices, and customs of Nahua Indians still survive today in Tuxpan, but if the ethnic identity itself survives in Tuxpan, it is because ethnicity has found a refuge in the festive tradition. As José Lameiras explains,

> *El mantenimiento de las diversas cuartillas de danzantes, la atención por reclutarlos, desde la socialización primaria, por disciplinarlos y estimularlos parece sostener a nivel organizativo, de sistemas simbólicos y de emotividad cultural, buena parte de la identidad étnica.* (Ibid. 228)[28]

Although none of the Tuxpan group of dancers is originally from there, nor have they gone there to dance, the director of the company still believes that Tuxpan is the most authentic of the indigenous dance traditions, and he explains it as follows: "*Tuxpan es para los danzantes, lo que las chivas es para el fútbol: lo más autóctono, lo más mexicano. Es el original.*"[29] In order to keep the Tuxpan dance tradition "autochthonous," they design the costumes, the tunes, and the steps of the dance using video recordings of the original dances of Tuxpan.

Among the Tuxpan-style *sonajeros* (rattle dancers), there is a conflict between the desire for authenticity and the need to renew the tradition. For example, the *sonajeros* of Lourdes call the *sonajeros* of St. James the Apostle of Tonalá "*danceros*" (dancers) because the latter have started to use laminated sandals or suede boots and renovate the tunes with the music of contemporary bands. This is how don Rubén, director of the Sonajeros de Lourdes, explains the difference:

> *Ellos renuevan las costumbres, no lo hacen como los auténticos. Nosotros sí. Ellos le ponen metal en los guaraches, y aunque hacen mucho ruido y llaman la atención, cada vez se parecen más a los sonajeros apaches y menos a los de Tuxpan. Lo más grave es que ya no pueden bailar bien porque con las láminas se resbalan. Por ejemplo, nosotros danzamos con guaraches de cuero, y sólo con ellos podemos dar vueltas y pasos que serían muy arriesgados con las suelas de metal. Además, ellos sacan música de banda y la adoptan a sus danzas (como "la cucaracha"), la nuestra sí es autóctona, no como las de ellos.*[30]

The banner of the San Martin *lancero* dancers.
Photograph by author.

The Tuxpan-style dancers form group figures with their bodies and movements.[31]

The costume of the Tuxpan *sonajeros* is both original and showy. It is made of unbleached coarse cotton cloth, as was the indigenous apparel known as *calzón de manta* (cotton trousers) that came to be identified for a long time with the dress of the Mexican peasant. A vest is worn on top, adorned with silk ribbons of different (lively) colors that hang down to form a border like a rainbow. Beneath the waistcoat is coarse cotton clothing: "*Si me quito el chaleco quedo vestido como un campesino de antes, en calzón de manta y con ceñidor rojo.*"[32] The dress also includes a *calzonera,* a pair of black trousers buttoned on both sides of the legs, with laces that make shapes alluding to the Virgin, and tied to the waist by a band of red thread. The colors of the trousers and the fringe of the pants cannot change; the only thing that can vary between one group and another is the color of the waistcoat ribbons.

Don Rubén is the captain of Sonajeros de Lourdes. He is thirty-seven years old and explains that he is keeping alive a tradition that was passed down through his family and which he is passing on to his children. Don Rubén was born in the city of Guadalajara. He does not know Tuxpan and has not lived as a peasant, but as a construction worker. At the age of ten he started to dance in the company he is now captain of, and he explains that he learned to dance the family's traditional dance not because his parents were originally from Tuxpan, but because they also danced in the barrio, and now his children will keep it alive because they too like the dance. Although don Rubén does not consider himself to be indigenous, he says:

> *Para mí es un orgullo traer este traje, que yo mismo con ayuda de mi esposa confeccioné . . . en realidad, si no se danzara por amor y fervor a la Virgen, yo no lo haría. No me vestiría de indio, ni de ranchero, si no le tuviera tanto amor a la Virgencita.*[33]

APACHE TRADITIONS IN CHICHIMECA LANDS

> *Muchas danzas están echadas a perder.*
> *¿Cómo van a tener respeto a la Virgen,*
> *a los estandartes, al traje, a los demás grupos,*
> *si no toman en cuenta las raíces de la danza?*
> *¿Cómo vamos a alabar a Dios con nuestros*
> *orígenes indígenas si estamos vestidos,*
> *como algunos, de piel roja?*
>
> —Juan Plascencia, founder of the Plascencia Brothers Aztec Ritual dance[34]

But just as the tradition is kept alive, so it is also renewed and reinvented. Many of the dance companies are of recent creation and are formed by young people, even children, from the new urban settlements. These groups can be distinguished from the traditional groups by their apparel, which is supposedly inspired by the indigenous "redskin" and Apache of the United States: shirts with large sleeves and pants made with brightly colored sequins, decked with long barbs, and wearing "*cíndulos,*" headbands attached to their foreheads. Those in charge of the companies dress as tribal chieftains, with tufts of feathers that fall to the ground, and they carry axes.

These groups are disliked and criticized by the other dance groups, who believe they are deviating from the tradition and have nothing to do with the indigenous traditions or the history of Mexico. Some say that the proliferation of this "northern band" aesthetic is due to the recent massive success of northern music bands and especially the group Cuisillos, whose choreography includes extravagant designs based on the garments of the Indians of the north. Although these indigenous tribes never lived in Jalisco except on movie screens, on television, and in the *cómics* (generally little booklets of romantic adventures in the form of strip cartoons, often set in "the Wild West"), in the new aesthetic of the bands the members create their own idea

Compañía de Lanceros: Pieles Rojas de Zapopan (The Lancero Dance Troupe: Redskins of Zapopan). Photograph by author.

of the tradition, their own conception of indigenous roots, and their own way of continuing the lineage. They belong to the nation by means of the *mestizaje,* a new admixture that fuses mass media images with traditional religious meanings.

For example, Mr. Ramos founded la Compañía de Lanceros del Colli (the Colli Lancers Company) in 1991, and he says he designs the Indian dress and gets his inspiration from the Libro Vaquero (Cowboy Book), the comic with the largest circulation in Mexico. Another dancer, Arturo Salas, who founded the Sonajeros del Tepeyac in 1988, says that one of his brothers designs the costumes in the style worn by the Apaches and that he copies them from cowboy-and-Indian movies. He acknowledges that his apparel is more modern than that of the Indians, as *"ellos usaban pieles y nosotros usamos tela de peluche que parece pie."* Some members of these companies go so far as to assert "the Apaches are our ancestors." *"Los apaches don nuestros antepasados." "Aquí en Jalisco hay mucho género revuelto porque aquí vivió una diversidad de etnias: los azteca, los huicholes y los apaches Mexicanos."* They are also criticized for using *tehuas* (suede boots) and because *"Ya no bailan, nomás hacen puro ruido."* The *tehuas* are a kind of ankle boot made of suede leather with wooden soles, padded with *balines* (pellets) and *rondanas* (thin round pieces of leather or metal with a hole in the middle), and laminated with strips of metal underneath. They can weigh nearly nine pounds. As Martín, dancer with the Sonajeros del Tepeyac puts it, *"bailar con estos zapatos es un sacrificio para recompensar lo pecador que es uno."*[35]

These groups do not re-create traditional dances—they do not even know the original tradition. Characteristically they show simple scenery, and they are the noisiest (with strips of metal on the soles of their footwear); still, the elements of their dance (the steps, the apparel, the footwear, the tiredness) constitute a sense of the sacred and a way of practicing the tradition just by being in the dance.

To understand how one group assumes the value of what is traditional and its relation to the sacred, I shall describe the case of the La Compañía de Danza del Sagrado Corazón de Jesús (Sacred Heart of Jesus Dance Company), named after the temple of Ixtacán. This company classifies itself as lancers because the dancers have spears, but as Julián, the director of the group, explains, his group is traditional because it is an "Indian" type of group. Don Julián started to dance when he was just thirteen years old, and he explains in his own words how he created his very own dance tradition by dancing: *"Cuando yo era niño yo no sabía qué era eso de danzar, me nació de corazón danzar y después yo sólo quería danzar. Y danzando me di cuenta de que salí danzante."*[36]

Don Julián explains that to have the dancer's dress is an honor, and the dancers have to respect the dress and the honor they wear with it. He compares his group with others that to me look the same, but he says they are not the same because the others look like northern music bands. I ask Julián whether the dress worn by his company is not made with the colors of the Mexican flag (green, white, and red), and he replies that the meaning of the dress is that these colors represent Mexico and should therefore be worn with pride and respect. He says it is not just any dress, it is the symbol of our nation; "*representamos a México.*"[37] He also thinks the dress is sacred because it has been blessed by the priest.

I ask him what the indigenous origins of the dances may be, and he answers:

> "*Las danzas vienen de los indios. Ellos tenían sus dioses y sus reyes, nosotros bailamos para la patrona,*[38] *la Virgencita de Zapopan. Los antiguos indígenas se vestían con penachos para agradarlos con danzas. En la biblia, no estoy seguro quién fue, pero creo que fue David el que la danzó a Dios. Nosotros tenemos que arrimarnos a lo bueno. Nosotros hacemos lo mismo pero con la Virgen. Somos indios.*"[39]

Julián knows that the ancient indigenous groups used to dance (though he could not say which groups), and he also knows that they did not dance as his group does. He reflects:

> "*Quizá ellos podían bailar mejor. Nosotros traemos nuevos pasos, por ejemplo yo adapté el corrido de Juan Colorado dentro de las danzas. También los indígenas vestían de manta, pero ahora usamos terlenka y telas más nuevas, para que los trajes sean más vistosos. Ya nadie quiere vestirse de manta.*"[40]

I ask him if he knows about his own indigenous origins, and he thinks for a moment and then says, "*Claro que sí, fíjese el nombre de mi abuelo: Bulmaro, y claro que somos indígenas si yo nací en la cultura del sembradío, fíjese cómo hablo y mire mi color. Ahí donde yo vivo hay comunidades agrarias, ejidos de indígenas.*" When I ask him if they have some ethnic name to distinguish them from other indigenous people, he says, "*No, somos indígenas, pero no Tarascos, por eso representamos la bandera como nuestro símbolo nacional.*"[41]

The *Chakras* and the Rescue of the New Mexicanism

Another type of new group is made up of young middle-class dancers (some of them professionals and university people) who identify themselves with cultural movements, from the rescue of Mexicanism to ecological move-

Lanceros apaches guadalupanos. Photograph by author.

ments, and New Age religious groups.[42] These groups re-create indigenous dances as part of a search for transcendental, mystical experiences. They dress in coarse white cotton, without adornment, and during their dances they perform purification rituals. This search for religious mysticism is undertaken by cultural movements such as the Reginos y Mancomunidad de la América Iniciática Solar (the Commonwealth of the Solar Initiation of America, hence the acronym "MAIS," i.e. "*maize,*" corn), who interpret the sanctuary of the Virgin of Zapopan as being on one of Mexico's most important *nadis* (channels connecting the energy between *chakras*) and believe their participation in the rituals helps to liberate the flow of energy of the planet.

Local groups such as the Movimiento Cultural de la Mexicanidad en Jalisco (Cultural Movement of Mexicanism, known in Jalisco as "Xalíxca Mexikay-oólin") and the Unidad de Apoyo a Comunidades Indígenas (Support Unit for Indigenous Communities), who have assumed the task of awakening the spiritual consciousness of the city. Their first task was to search for the "line of hidden energy" left for posterity by the pre-Hispanic civilizations of the area. Since then they have gone on pilgrimages along the sacred routes to cleanse them from the contamination and obstruction caused by lack of respect for and appreciation of the value of indigenous cultures.

These groups have assumed the task of finding the surviving indigenous old people who are the custodians of the millenary culture of the people of Mexico.[43] In 1989 the Reginos group went on ceremonial marches with the aim of discovering the sacred route that balances the energy of the city. After long ceremonial marches they discovered that the route connecting the Cathedral of Guadalajara to the Basilica of Zapopan is the masculine route, and the route from the Basilica to the Cathedral is the feminine route. For seven years after that day, on every Saturday closest to the equinoxes and solstices, the group of mestizos, directed by Luciano Pérez (Chief Lakota),[44] undertook a pilgrimage of purification to awaken the consciousness of the city's inhabitants:

> *Así como todos los días una barredora limpia avenidas para levantar la basura, nosotros debemos levantar la conciencia y sembrar semillas de paz; es muy sencillo. Los indígenas lo habían hecho por mucho tiempo.*[45]

To date there have been twenty-five peace walks, on every solstice and every equinox, as a form of active prayer for peace. The route they use and consider to be sacred is the one thought of as feminine, from the Basilica of Zapopan to the Cathedral, because, as the coordinator of the Reginos group of Guayabos explains, "it is necessary for women to start playing the part that will be theirs to play for the next two thousand years."[46]

Some members of the Guayabos ecological community have joined one of the most traditional Aztec dance groups, los Hermanos Plascencia (the Plascencia Brothers), which started in 1936. Both Tata Juan ("Father" Juan, who died recently) and his brother Jefe Chendo (Chief Chendo), directors of the dance group, were named "guardians of the tradition" by the Guayabos community. In contrast with members of other dance groups, the Plascencia Brothers' rituals are not only intended to make the Virgin happy but to awaken a cosmic consciousness. In other words, the sense of the dance does not coincide with traditional popular religion, but has an esoteric meaning.

On the basis of this meaning, they interpret the route taken by the Virgin's pilgrimage to be a sacred route that is reactivated by energetic marches, which not only allows the indigenous consciousness of the city of Guadalajara to be awakened, but also helps to maintain world harmony thanks to the rituals which connect the *chakras* and allow cosmic energy to flow through.

These movements combining elements from different cultural and religious traditions re-create a syncretism that incorporates the knowledge, symbols, and rituals of various traditions: Asian (Indian and Tibetan), indigenous (Lakota, Aztec), and popular devotions linked to Catholicism. But they acquire coherence in the light of the holistic framework of the New Age discourse that is present in the New Mexicanism movement. The synthesis or juxtaposition of different frames of knowledge constitutes a new syncretism in which the Catholic sanctuaries and the ceremonial centers of the pre-Hispanic cultures—for example, ancient regional centers for ceremonial activities performed on the solstices and equinoxes, and purification rituals such as *Temaxcales* (collective steam baths)—are interpreted as *nadis,* channels connecting one point with another and allowing the *chakras* to work; it is a holistic conception of the universe (planetary consciousness and cosmic consciousness) and a spiral view of history.[47] This discourse, strongly influenced by the New Age view, is intertwined with the search for the millenary wisdom of the Mexicas, which has been stored and can be found alive in the knowledge of the old indigenous people. They grant traditional legitimacy through their knowledge and their rituals and reconstitute an ancestral historical memory, but one that is deciphered and reinterpreted in the light of the concepts that belong to the New Age discourse.

It is important to highlight the writer Antonio Velasco Piña, who became famous with his novel *Regina,* which is not considered by his followers to be a work of fiction so much as "a living testimony of the events that it was their fate to have lived through." Velasco Piña himself witnessed the Mexicanism movement started by *Regina.* After her death, the author dedicates himself to spreading the movement. As one person informed me:

> *Yo he estado en el Zócalo, y he participado en los rituales en Teotihuacán, y somos testigos de lo que muchos no ven, pero que en realidad está pasando, en el plano espiritual. Muchos creen que el '68 fue un evento político y que las marchas del 2 de octubre sólo tuvieron una dimensión política, pero no saben, o no quieren admitir, que detrás de lo político, nosotros hemos estado haciendo un trabajo espiritual. Aunque para los ojos de los demás los libros de Velasco Piña son una novela, para nuestros ojos son experiencia y testimonio de eventos históricos importantes.*[48]

Some adherents of Mexicanism consider Velasco Piña as well as the old surviving indigenous people to be authentic guardians of Mexica culture. The interpretations that can hold together a coherent discourse and that give these movements a sense of New Age religion with Mexican soul are to be found in Velasco Piña's novels (especially *Regina* and *El retorno de lo Sagrado*).

The dances are not only important because they keep the memory alive, but in this case because the novelty of the New Age discourse requires the legitimization that the pre-Hispanic tradition gives, since this allows the newly emerging identities to be perpetuated backward and forward. These identities are renewing the most ancient traditions in their search for the "imaginary constitution of a lineage of believers and their social realization in a community" (Hervieu-Léger 1996, 39).

Final Reflections

Based on the study of dance companies that take part in the pilgrimage of the Virgin of Zapopan, I have highlighted the way in which the experience of the dance companies allows urban dwellers to create ways of feeling and thinking that they are part of the city (through the appropriation of public spaces) and at the same time allows them to reformulate their identity as Mexicans. They identify themselves with two anterior traditions, the indigenous and Catholicism, which are incorporated into rituals of popular faith where the traditions and the lineage of Mexican identity are reinvented.

In the course of this work, four modalities for practicing the dance tradition around the Virgin of Zapopan were distinguished. The Aztec and Conquest groups seek to renew the founding sense of the Mexican *mestizaje* (cultural mix), whether it be in the dramatic portrayal of the cultural confrontation between *conquistadores* and Indians, or through the Aztec choreography that shapes a synthesis in which the religious significance of the ancient Aztecs is kept alive under the mantle of Catholic images. Then there are the groups of autochthonous dances that are most linked to the regional traditions, and these perpetuate the indigenous tradition by keeping up the "originality" of typical costumes and choreographies, though there is no sense of appropriating the cultural significance of such practices. Another type is that of the Apache companies, who appropriate to themselves the mass media images of American-style "natives" and give them a new significance in a discourse where the mutual presence of Indian, Mexican, and Catholic generic ingredients gains some weight in the tradition simply by being piled on top of each other. In this case the legitimization of the tradition is mostly in the consecration rituals linked to popular Catholicism. Although they know that their dances are of recent invention, they are still aware that through repetition their dances will generate the idea of being traditional. The last type is represented by the dance groups of the New Mexicanism, dissociating themselves from the Catholic meaning of the dance tradition and recuperating the "occult" meaning of the indigenous past, which is reinterpreted in the light of a new discourse in which neo-Mexicanism is part of the planet-wide New Age movement. This group is conscious of participating through their dances in a spirituality that connects the local movement to a national network, participating from Mexico in planet-wide networks with the objective of liberating the energy of the Earth.

It is true, as we have seen in every case, that the experiences of identity generated by the dances reinvent the sense of origins, tradition, and ethnicity, but I consider, as Guillermo de la Peña put it, that "[t]o ignore the ethnic dimension of these groups is to deny them the possibility of constructing their own history, distinct from that which has been written from the viewpoint of those in power" (de la Peña 2001, 62). The four modalities of the dance are lived experiences that are signified as sacred, that is, they are sustained in a religious dimension that looks to the past so as to face the future and that justifies, authorizes, and brings up to date the needs people have to construct a sense of their new social identities.

It is important to note that the Indianized identity is constructed not as an identity of belonging to one particular ethnic group or another, but as an identity referring to symbols, aesthetic markers, and a past seen as "our roots." In fact, in various interviews with dancers conducted during the 2004 pilgrimage, we were able to establish that most of the dancers assume themselves to be a hybridized and contemporary representation of an autochthonous past, which is based on "the Indian." But there is an awareness of the distinction between themselves and "real" or "true" indigenous people, that is, those who form a part of the ethnic communities today. These people generally live in conditions of extreme marginalization and differ from the urban mestizo population in that they keep up their own languages and rural ways. The notion of the dancers having an indigenous identity is a vague idea, since being indigenous is taken to mean forming part of the glorious past of the nation. Hence it is seen as something separate from everyday reality and not simply as a condition of normal life in today's complex Mexico. To illustrate the point, there is no interaction or solidarity with the Otomí, the Purépecha, or the Huichol, who do participate in the pilgrimage, but not as dancers, only as part of the informal commerce.[49]

This work has emphasized that through the experience of taking part in the neo-indigenous dances, the tradition is being renewed, but more importantly, an ethnic lineage is being reinvented for the mestizo urban populations. Through the dances, not only are cultural traditions kept up as folklore, but above all the sense of being mestizo is negotiated, the *mestizaje* that has been described as "one of the most contradictory axes of the Mexican nation today . . . and the marrow of its present cultural identity" (Jáuregui and Bonfiglioli 1996, 7). *Mestizaje* is the cultural feature that marks the encounter (sometimes conflictive, sometimes conciliatory) between indigenous and Spanish cultures. But the dances also show the dynamic presence of contemporary culture, because while keeping the mythical past of our indigenous roots alive, they depend for their vitality on the resignifying of our current multiculturalism, one that is based on a *mestizaje,* and regenerate the bonds of identity between the indigenous-colonial past and the traditional-modern present. This is clearly demonstrated in the processes of adaptation and the aesthetic and symbolic reworking and innovation that allow this tradition to be represented as an element for facing the present and prefiguring the future.

Notes

1. "There are not many places in the world where you can witness a spectacle to compare with the great religious festivals of Mexico . . . / Time ceases to be a succession of events and reverts to what it was, / —and is originally: a present where past and future are reconciled at last."

2. *Tradition* is used here in the sense proposed by Hobsbawm and Ranger (1983), who referred to it as a dynamic cultural construction that is reinvented in order to make it contemporaneous, rather than as a static narrative reproducing a memory of what the tradition was.

3. This work forms part of a more extensive project with the title "Cultural transformations and popular Catholic religion in Guadalajara." The information used in this chapter derives from an ethnographic study (participative observation and interviews with dancers) conducted during rehearsals and during the religious Feast of the Procession of the Virgin of Zapopan in the months of August through October 2001, 2002, and 2003. I have chosen to withhold the names of the interviewees cited in this chapter.

4. "We are the draft of a text / That will never be copied out clean / With smudges and bits crossed out / And whole paragraphs cancelled / Our being is a text / That is trying to round itself off / With the senseless passing of days."

5. Creole in the sense of a culture with Spanish antecedents in Mexican territory, which is distinct from Iberian culture by having developed in Mexico and is also

different from the indigenous culture of the country and from the mestizo expression of indigenous culture. As part of the Bajío region, Guadalajara stands out as the capital of this regional culture. Creole culture is, in a sense, a mestizo culture, but it differs from the indigenous version of mestizo because, although it incorporates native elements that create a new synthesis when brought into contact with the Iberian, it is the Spanish part that is exalted, and in particular the primacy of Catholicism, Hispanicity, and racial features that enhance the whiteness of the skin. Jaime Tamayo and Alejandra Vizcarra describe the city's Creole culture as follows: "In Guadalajara itself and to a lesser extent in the rest of the state of Jalisco, a 'creole' culture has been established that does not, as in the rest of the country, assimilate the autochthonous heritage; which is reflected . . . in the indisputable presence of morality in the social and political life of the person who lives in Jalisco, one that is determined by the weight of the Catholic religion" (2000, 19).

6. "skilled horsemen, West Mexican music ensemble and symbol of Mexican culture, a prized Mexican alcoholic beverage made from the agave plant"

7. The foundation of Guadalajara is taken to refer to what we think of today as the center of the city or historical center, which was established by the Spanish in 1542 in the Valley of Atemajac near two indigenous villages: Mezquitán (inhabited by Tecuexe Indians) and Mexicaltzingo (inhabited by Mexican Indians and some Tarasco). At nearly the same time as the foundation of Guadalajara, another indigenous town, called Analco, was founded on the other, eastern, side of the river to be inhabited by Indians from Tetlán (Chávez Hayhoe 1944–48, 59).

8. From the end of the nineteenth century until the early part of the twentieth century, the public procession of the Virgin was not allowed to proceed every year, first because of the application of the Reform Laws and then because of laws enacted by President Plutarco Elías Calles in 1926. These laws suspended religious cults and privileges and led to an armed Catholic rebellion known as the *guerra cristera* (Christian war), which lasted three years. As recently as 1948 dancers were not allowed to take part in the pilgrimage. It was not until 1950 that the return of the Virgin of Zapopan to the Basilica was reinstated. Notwithstanding such interruptions, popular fervor and the Feast of the Pilgrimage have kept up, even to present times (González Escoto 1998). Since 1953 the pilgrimage has been celebrated on the 12th of October to coincide with a civil holiday to honor Hispanicity (the day Columbus is supposed to have discovered America); previously the pilgrimage took place on the 5th of October (the eve of the Feast of St. Francis).

9. See de la Torre 2001, 2002, and 2005 on the representation of the Creole and the indigenous during the pilgrimage of the Virgin of Zapopan.

10. The dances are both cultural and religious practice; see de la Torre 2005.

11. "The different types of dance are merely / dance languages established at different times in the course of history. / Every dance language has definite objectives / within the communities or cultures that give it life."

12. By the year 2000, the number of private estates built had reached 150, a trend which is not confined to the most privileged classes; houses in closed-off estates are now being offered for "social housing" (Ickx 2002, 126).

13. Although rehearsals take place in the streets and the squares of the neighborhoods, those who join the dance companies come from all over the city and are not necessarily neighbors living in the same barrio or *colonia*.

14. Other scholars group *matachines* as dances of the Conquest (see Jáuregui and Bonfiglioli 1996). See also Romero's and Cantú's essays in this volume for questions on the status of *matachines* dances and their presence among autochthonous peoples of the Americas, as well as their prominence among mestizo communities.

15. "But in the course of its reproduction over the centuries, the dance of Conquest has undergone successive transformations that have led to a number of contemporary versions as well as producing others, that were, naturally, lost whenever they became dysfunctional to their bearers."

16. L. A. R. "Hernán Cortés," interview with Renée de la Torre, November 11, 2003. "You will notice how few Conquest dances there are; there used to be eighteen in this *barrio* ("El Refugio"), and now we might say we are the only one left, and what we are most proud of is being able to show the children what happened in the history of Mexico. It's not necessarily accurate, as in some places we know that as humans we might change it, for example, I myself or one of the dancers might say ten thousand soldiers when there were two thousand, or might add a passage that wasn't there. In order to tell the story the way it really was we would need to talk to our ancestors, which is impossible as they are dead; we are trying to be as faithful to the tradition as possible."

17. H. G. R. "el Rey Tizoc," interview with Renée de la Torre, November 10, 2003. "The Conquest dance tells what is supposed to have happened in the years when the Aztecs and the Spaniards of the Conquest confronted each other, then when the Spaniards came to defeat Cuauhtémoc, and they also used ambassadors, as we just showed when we came and advised them to stop fighting and surrender, and we showed how Cuauhtémoc refused to surrender and sent his troops and ourselves as kings to tell him we would not surrender, and we showed how the war of the Spaniards against the Aztecs started."

18. Although the dances of the *tastoanes* and *santiaguitos* are also dances of the Conquest, they have an ancient tradition in the region studied and are not considered in the current work, as they do not participate in the pilgrimage of the Virgin of Zapopan. Their patron saint is the Apostle James (Santiago), and their representations take place in the plazas of the ancient pueblos, now conurbated with the city (see Rodríguez Aceves 1988).

19. "The dance of the *concheros* and the cultural values / expressed in it have syncretic and recultured features, / using this last term to mean a movement of reconciliation / with the ancient roots of 'Mexicanism.'"

20. The term *conchero* referred originally to the shell of an armadillo used to make a guitarlike instrument, and not, as one might suppose, to the conch carried by a dancer.

21. The *conchero* tradition started in Querétaro and Guanajuato and commemorates the myth of origin in which the Chichimeca Indians convert to Christianity in the course of a battle. In the nineteenth century it was imported to the center of Mexico. The *conchero* dance is known indifferently as the Chichimeca, Aztec, or Chichimeca-Aztec Dance (de la Peña 2003, 100).

22. Mario Gutierrez, interview with J. C. Chavira Cárdenas, published in *Vida en Cristiano* 137 (October 19, 1999): 2–6. "It was when there were governors who would not let Catholics like us go out on a Pilgrimage; we weren't even allowed to go to Mass. It was only in the '40s that the religious Calles persecution stopped, the first time the image was received in Zapopan and transferred through the midst of an immense turnout of people." See also note 8 for more details on President Calles and the prohibition of religious pilgrimages.

23. G. S., member of Danza Azteca Xalixtli, interview with Renée de la Torre, December 11, 2003. "Most of the groups are maintained by families. These families assume the task of making sure that the tradition stays alive, that it doesn't get lost. We deal with what we call the tradition; our ancestors, my father and my grandfather left us traditions. This is managed like an army. There are wardens, there are captains, there are the *malinches* [the only woman in a dance, to whom certain reverences and ceremonies are proffered], who are also wardens, and then there are the soldiers."

24. Francisco Ayala, interview with Ricardo Ibarra. *Gaceta Universitaria*, November 12, 2001. "As well as being an essence, a movement, the dance is a physical, spiritual, mental and emotional training. It is a medicine, a platform that pushes you into learning many things about the world. With the dances we manage to maintain our native roots and explore the infinity of these experiences."

25. G. S., member of Danza Azteca Xalixtli, interview with Renée de la Torre, December 11, 2003. "Everything does have a meaning: the feathers stand for the strength that we get from our father Tonatiuh. All this is sound [shakes ankle rattles]. The movements we make to the tunes, they represent the movement of the serpent, which is, in effect, life. Everything has to be done the right way. What we undertake is culture and movement, while the tunes and the dances are accompanied by the *ayoyotles* [the stones of the fruit of the *yoyote*], and that is part of the dance: why?—because it is the movement of your whole body, sound as well as movement, you have to give life a rhythm."

26. F. A., Danza Azteca Quetzalcóatl, interview with Renée de la Torre, November 12, 2002. "There are more dance groups here than in the Federal District (Mexico City). But here we are not *concheros*, we are Aztecs, because here we are the autochthonous dance. We don't call the ankle rattles 'jingle bells' [*cascabeles*], but 'ossuaries' [*hueseras*] because they are made with the stones [*huesos* or 'bones'] of the fruit known as friar's bones [*Thevetia thevetioides*, said to be an apocynaceous narcotic

plant; could be St. Ignatius' bean]. We cut them from the trees, we go out into the country to get them, we take out the pulp and add pellets to make them sound."

27. *Chakras:* ancient Indian Sanskrit yogic term for "wheels" as metaphors for focal points of energy.

28. "Maintaining several wards of dancers, attending to their recruitment, starting with primary socialization, then by disciplining and stimulating them, appears to have been able to sustain at the organizational level of symbolic systems and cultural emotion, a good part of the ethnic identity."

29. R. R., interview with Renée de la Torre, October 12, 2002. "Tuxpan is to the dancers what the Chivas team is for soccer: the most traditional, the most Mexican. It's the original." Chivas is Guadalajara's soccer (called *fútbol* in Mexico) team and the best-known in the republic.

30. R. R., interview with Renée de la Torre, October 12, 2002. "They renovate the customs; they don't do it like the authentic groups do. As we do. They put metal on their sandals, and even though they make a lot of noise and get people's attention, they look more and more like Apache rattle dancers and less and less like those of Tuxpan. The worst of it is, that they can't dance well any more because with the metal strips they slide. For example, we dance with leather sandals, and it is only using them that we can do turns and steps that it would be very risky to do with metal soles. Also, they get *banda,* popular band music, and adapt it to their dances (like "the Cockroach"), where ours really is autochthonous, not like theirs."

31. They have more than sixty steps rehearsed, and each one has a name to indicate the figure being re-created. For example, *las morismas,* the Moorish, is a step where the tambourine is passed between the legs; the windmill, representing a flower with the tambourines in the center; the carousel, a gyrating wheel formed by the bodies of the dancers; or *el caballito,* the merry-go-round dance.

32. R. R., interview with Renée de la Torre, October 12, 2002. "If I take my vest off I am dressed like a peasant from before, in cotton trousers with a red waistband."

33. R. R., interview with Renée de la Torre, October 12, 2002. "For me it is a source of pride to wear this outfit, which I myself made with the help of my wife . . . in reality, if there were no dancing out of love and devotion to the Virgin, I wouldn't do it. I wouldn't dress like an Indian, or a cowboy, if I didn't have so much love for the little Virgin.

34. "Many of the dances have gone to rack and ruin. / How can they respect the Virgin, the standards, the regalia, the other groups, / if they don't take the roots of the dance into account? / How can we of indigenous origin / praise God if we are dressed, / the way some dancers are, as 'redskins'?"

35. Z. M., interview with Renée de la Torre, October 11, 2002. "they used fur and we used velvet that looks like fur" / "The Apaches are our ancestors." / "Here in Jalisco there's a lot of racial mix-up because a variety of people lived here: the Aztecs, the Huicholes and the Mexican Apache." / "They don't dance anymore, they just make a lot of noise." / "dancing with these shoes is a sacrifice to pay for the awful sinner one is"

36. J. J., interview with Renée de la Torre, October 11, 2002. "When I was a child I did not know what all this dancing was; dancing got into my heart and then all I wanted to do was to dance. And it was dancing I discovered that I had become a dancer."

37. J. J., interview with Renée de la Torre, October 11, 2002. "We represent Mexico."

38. Although "*la patrona*" means the patron saint, when the word is used as a term of endearment to refer to the Virgin of Zapopan, the principal meaning is "chief" or "chieftain." She is also known as "La Generala" (The General) and receives an annual pension; the use of the diminutive "little virgin" may require further explanation, but insofar as it refers to the effigy itself, the Virgin of Zapopan is indeed very small.

39. "The dances come from the Indians. They had their gods and their kings, and we dance for the *patrona,* the little Virgin of Zapopan. The ancient indigenous people dressed with feathers in order to please them with their dances. In the Bible I'm not sure who it was, but I think it was David who danced before the Lord. We have to hold fast to the good. We do the same but to the Virgin. We are Indians." J. J., interview with Renée de la Torre, October 11, 2002.

40. "Maybe they could dance better. We have introduced new steps; for example, I adapted the *corrido,* folk ballad of Juan Colorado to include it among our dances. The indigenous people also dressed in *manta,* coarse cotton, but now we use *terlenka,* polyester, and newer materials, to make the outfits look flashier. Nobody wants to wear coarse cotton now." J. J., interview with Renée de la Torre, October 11, 2002.

41. "Yes, of course; think of my grandfather's name, Bulmaro, and of course we're indigenous if I was born in the culture of sowing crops. See the way I talk and the color of my skin. Where I live there are agrarian communities, *ejidos* of indigenous people." "No; we are indigenous, but we are not Tarascos. That's why we show the flag as our national symbol." J. J., interview with Renée de la Torre, October 11, 2002.

42. The interpretations that have articulated a more or less coherent discourse and that make sense of the symbolic practices of New Age religion with a Mexican soul can be found in Velasco Piña 1997.

43. These movements, which Yólotl González identifies as "*Nueva mexicanidad,*" "New Mexicanism" (i.e., a new sense of what it is to be Mexican), get their inspiration from Antonio Velasco Piña, who was not only the person who started this movement in Mexico but through his novels was able to establish an interpretive link that allowed the rescue of what-it-is-to-be-Mexican to connect with a New Age vision of the cosmos (González 2000, 29). In Velasco Piña's novel *Regina,* a young Mexican woman comes back from Tibet in 1968—just at the time of the student movements—where she had acquired certain esoteric knowledge, and she starts a movement to awaken the nation. She undertakes a search for the guardians of the traditions of Mexico, and these reveal the sacred routes that will allow the energy paths of Mexico City to be unblocked.

44. Luciano Pérez died on September 16, 2003. He was of Purépecha origin and had emigrated as a child to the United States. When he came back from the Vietnam War he got in touch with the chieftains and medicine men of the Lakota (Sioux) nation and became their disciple. He was later recognized as Chief Lakota. In the 1980s he made contact with the Guayabos ecological community in Guadalajara, where he went to conduct a ceremony called "*Búsqueda de la Visión*" (Vision Quest) and organized walks for peace, whose aim was the cleansing, the unity, and the peace of the Earth.

45. R. P., coordinator of the Reginos ecological community group of Guayabos, Zapopan, interview with Ricardo Ibarra. "Entre el cielo y la tierra, la danza tradicional mexicana." *Gaceta Universitaria* 12 (2002): 14–15. "Just as a street-sweeping machine cleans the avenues every day picking up the rubbish, so we ought to raise consciousness and sow seeds of peace; it's very simple. The indigenous people did the same thing for years."

46. Patricia Ríos, interview with Ricardo Ibarra.

47. For Velasco Piña (1997), the *chakras* are "nervous fluid" centers that have a close relationship to the internal secretion glands. The Earth as well as the individual is thought of as a living organism, with seven *chakras* that have been located in those places where cultures flourished that allowed humanity to progress. One of the most important is in Mexico, and the rituals performed by these groups contribute to reactivating the *chakras*.

48. S. R. M., interview with Renée de la Torre, March 4, 2005. "I have been in the Zócalo and have participated in the rituals in Teotihuacan, and we are witnesses of what many do not see, but is really happening, on the spiritual plane. Many people believe that what happened in '68 was a political event and that the demonstration marches [prior to] the 2nd of October only had a political dimension, but they do not know, or would rather not admit, that behind the political, we have been doing spiritual work. Although in the eyes of others the books of Velasco Piña are a novel, in our eyes they are the experience and the testimony of important historical events."

49. An ethnographic essay by masters students in anthropology at CIESAS Occidente (the western branch of Centro de Investigaciones y Estudios Superiores en Antropología Social, or Center for Research and Advanced Studies in Social Anthropology) records the different discourses constructed by the mestizo dancers about the "real" indigenous people that belong to ethnic groups in the city (Ajú, González, and Talavera 2004).

3

La Feria de Enero

Rethinking Gender in a Ritual Festival

XÓCHITL C. CHÁVEZ

During the month of January each year, the community of Chiapa de Corzo in Chiapas, Mexico, parades and dances in honor of its local patron saint, Saint Sebastian the Martyr, and celebrates the colonial legend of the city's benefactor, Doña María de Angulo. La Feria de Enero or the January Festival, which officially began in 1599, is the principal festival of Chiapa de Corzo and is celebrated January 8–23. In this re-enactment, men dress and participate as *chunta*, the benefactor's servants, a role that was in the past filled by women. Similarly, some women now dress and participate as *parachico* dancers, a role traditionally reserved for men. In this chapter, I explore how women and men have redefined gender norms in this ritual festival. Although this festival is not an everyday event, its ritual performance deeply affects the everyday lives of Chiapacorzeños, the inhabitants of Chiapa de Corzo. It is during this festival period that Chiapacorzeños may occupy a liminal space rather than adhere to the boundaries of mundane social structure. In an analysis that speaks to the challenges, major concerns, and new spaces that have been created by participants who cross-dress during the January Festival, I argue that at the same time that the festival participation reaffirms the community's sense of history and allegiance to tradition, the festival is also a present-day site for gender negotiation and, by extension, identity formation.

Literature on Chiapas and Festival

The anthropological literature on Chiapas has for many decades predominantly focused on the highland area. In the late 1950s dozens of ethnographies were produced under the direction of the Harvard Chiapas Project led by Evon Vogt. Until recently, most analyses of Chiapas have focused on indigenous communities and how rites and rituals sustain a community structure that is understood to be separate from the larger society (Gossen 1974). According to Aguirre Beltrán, analyses during the same time period also left out any serious mention of the state of Chiapas. In 1983 Robert Wasserstrom broke from this tendency with his book *Class and Society in Central Chiapas*, as did Jan Rus a decade later with his analysis of the state and how it involved itself in cargo systems in the Tzotzil *municipio* (municipality) of Chamula.

During the 1960s and 1970s, the literature on Chiapas by a number of women anthropologists reflected a more general trend toward correcting the prevailing male bias in social science by focusing on women's experiences. Here, too, the focus was on indigenous communities that were seen as distinct and self-sustaining. According to Eber and Kovic (2003, 9), "empirical research in Chiapas about women's experiences during this time took place primarily in indigenous communities where researchers expected to find alternative gender and household relations to those of Western cultures."

Early ethnographic studies of social structure and relations in native communities described the gender specialization that characterized life in the highlands of Chiapas. These studies noted that involvement in tradition was a daily aspect of life for women, complementing the more formal roles that men adopted in ritual events (see Collier 1968, 1973; Linn 1976; Nash 1964, 1970; Cancian 1964; Greenfield 1972; Laughlin 1963; Modiano 1973; Price 1966; Siskel 1974; and Wali 1974).

Since the late 1970s anthropologists began integrating data on women and gender into whole fields of study, including economics (Nash 1977; Rus 1994), health and reproduction (Freyermuth Enciso 2001), sexuality and religion (Barrios and Pons 1995), tradition and myth (Rosenbaum 1993), and alcohol studies (Eber 1995). Early in this period scholarship about women and gender took its place in a larger body of literature about Latin America and the global economy that analyzed the contribution of women in domestic production and the new international division of labor into which women were increasingly drawn (Nash and Fernandez-Kelly 1983; Nash and Safa 1980).

Since the 1994 uprisings of Ejercito Zapatista de Liberación Nacional (EZLN), a new wave of literature on Chiapas by journalists, activists, and scholars in Spain, Mexico, and the United States has emerged. This literature continues to focus on indigenous communities, but they are now seen through a lens that looks at social conflict rather than community stability (see Rojas 1994, 1995; Rovira 1996; Hernández Castillo 2001; Collier 1999

[1994]). As the focus is generally on political conflict, none of these works makes any mention of how the communities are culturally surviving or if any of these communities have ceased to practice their traditional rituals.[1]

Unlike other studies that have focused primarily on remote indigenous communities in the highland region of Chiapas, I focus on Chiapa de Corzo, in the lowland region. The town of Chiapa de Corzo is historically significant as it was the first township in the region, established in 1528 (Cifuentes-González 1964, 22). Existing literature on Chiapa de Corzo and La Feria is sparse. Works such as Pineda del Valle's *Las Fiestas de Enero en Chiapa de Corzo, Chiapas* (1999) and Corzo's *Chiapas: Voces desde la danza* (1999) include only schematic overviews that offer minimal analysis. Cifuentes-González's *La Fiesta de Enero y la danza de parachicos* (1964), which highlights the choreography of the dances in the festival, is concerned primarily with demonstrating how the intricacies in choreography and dance style correlate with how highly a *danzante* is regarded within the community.

Regardless of political climate, fiestas remain one of the constant and most visible features of urban and rural community life in Mexico. Festivals typically include feasting, drinking, and dancing; in addition, fireworks, candles, flowers, and traditional attire are common features. Not surprisingly, festivals require a considerable amount of time, money, and other resources. As Nájera-Ramírez writes, "the complex nature of these events demands a comprehensive examination of specific festivals as they are practiced in specific communities, in order to appreciate the many ways in which a given festival may intersect with other areas of social and cultural life" (1997a, 9).

Nájera-Ramírez's book *La Fiesta de Los Tastoanes* (1997) is one of the few comprehensive studies of a single festival in Mexico. Nájera-Ramírez explores what the festival means to Jocoteño culture and identity and shows how it helps in adapting to and resisting the dominant social order that Christianity symbolizes. Because most festivals involve elements of life such as religion, identity, tradition, belief, and cultural change, they are often mentioned in anthropological studies of Mexico but are not seriously examined. Even though religious festivals have been studied extensively in Mexican ethnography for several decades, they are typically viewed as only one part of larger ethnographic projects. Giving specific attention to a cultural performance, as Nájera-Ramírez does, allows us to see how social and cultural life intersect and become re-imagined by festival participants. Major trends that emerged from this school of thought have concentrated for the most part on rural communities in which class, ethnicity, and rural/urban distinctions may appear obvious. Where anthropologists tended to develop oppositional models to explain community dynamics, those oppositional models (new/old, Indigenous/European, and rural/urban) have tended to be identified as static. In contrast, Nájera-Ramírez's analysis focuses on the mutability of those categories and the ways in which "traditional" festivals provide a forum for the expression of cultural change.

Whether explicitly or implicitly, anthropologists have also customarily analyzed indigenous communities on the basis of language, dress, and economic status.[2] These approaches tend to provide "ideal types" that do not reflect the actual lived experiences found within the communities they describe. In particular, such analyses fail to acknowledge the complex blurring that has resulted from the constant negotiation of two or more distinct cultural systems operating in a single community for hundreds of years. I agree with Friedlander's (1981) call upon the anthropological community to further examine and document the identity of indigenous people. In particular, I believe there is a need for analyses documenting the expression and definition of cultural identity through these cultural practices.

Mendoza's *Shaping Society through Dance: Mestizo Ritual Performance in the Peruvian Andes* (2000), which concentrates primarily on Cuzco, Peru, asserts that identity is not only enacted and expressed through *danzas*, but that the performance contexts of the *danzas* during the fiesta are in themselves key public vehicles through which identity is defined. By providing historical evidence dating back to the Andean colonial period of the sixteenth century, Mendoza illustrates that *danza* performance has long been a site for the confrontation and negotiation of identities.

Festival sponsorship and the civil-religious cargo system have customarily been a focal point of study for anthropologists. The civil-religious cargo system, also referred to as simply the "cargo system," represents a distinct formal characteristic of Indian communities in colonial Mexico; its presence today is understood to reflect a community's indigenous roots (Greenberg 1981; Smith 1999). Traditional fiestas are typically sponsored by and for the community, and resources for the production of fiestas must therefore be found within the community (Nájera-Ramírez 1997a). Although a cargo system continues to operate in the example of La Feria de Enero, over the past forty years commercial sponsorships have assisted in financing the festival. In some communities the cargo system has disappeared completely, whereas in others it has been recently revitalized (DeWalt 1975; Rus and Wasserstrom 1980). Differences in the functioning of civil-religious hierarchies over time demonstrate the profound variation in the ways communities adapt to the macro changes affecting their lives and express this in traditions (Nash 2001).

The concern over resources has been a point of debate with regards to the economic and political implications of the festival. Indeed, some scholars have concluded that festivals serve the hegemonic order as a means of socially controlling subordinate indigenous communities because fiestas consume local resources, which keeps participants from working in other activities to effect political or social change (Nájera-Ramírez 1997a, 10). However, literature that focuses too narrowly on the function of festival sponsorship can obscure dynamics such as reciprocity and networking, which have economic implications. By solely addressing the function of cargo systems, these studies negate the possibility that participants may utilize festivals as a forum for the articulation and advancement of competing political agendas.

My research adds to the existing body of literature in addressing how men and women express versions of their cultural and gender identity through participation in a ritual performance. This work illustrates how some of the participants choose to display their cultural identity by cross-dressing and fulfilling the role of the opposite sex.

La Feria de Enero: From Colonial Legend to Present-Day Festival

According to oral tradition, La Feria de Enero and the term "*parachico*" have their origin in a mid-sixteenth-century colonial legend in which Doña María de Angulo, a wealthy Spanish woman, is said to have traveled to Mexico in search of a cure for her nine-year-old son's paralysis. According to the legend, Doña María sought the help of *curanderos*, or healers, from Soctón Nandalumí, the capital city of the Los Chiapas nation.[3] Immediately after the boy was healed, a horrible drought struck the town. The community then told Doña María that for the drought to cease, she needed to offer a gift to the gods. She placed her son on a post for an entire day, without food or drink, as an offering. As dusk fell, so did the first raindrops, signifying that the gods were satisfied with her offering. The child was then taken down and returned to his mother. Legend also has it that while in Chiapas Doña María de Angulo observed the state of poverty in which the indigenous people lived, and in order to demonstrate her gratitude, she employed her male and female servants (*chunta*) to distribute meat, vegetables, grains, and gold coins to the people of the city.[4] The community returned the favor by inviting Doña María and her son to an indigenous ceremony displaying adoration for the gods and gratitude for their benevolence toward the people. The dance that had been traditionally performed in honor of Saint Sebastian was thus expanded to include a dedication to Doña María's child as well. While praying and dancing, the participants called out "*para el chico*."[5] Thus the term and dance "*parachico*" was created and gave way to the formation of the annual La Feria de Enero.

The Festival and Its Participants

Historically, both men and women participated in a variety of festival roles, such as *parachico* dancer, musician, *artesano/a* (artisan), *prioste* (the cargo holder or spiritual leader), chunta, *comidera* (cook), and *chiapaneca* (representing the traditional woman from Chiapas who is the partner of the *parachico danzante*). Traditionally, men took the role of the *parachico* dancers in daytime processions honoring the festival saints, particularly Saint Sebastian, while women acted the roles of *chunta*, Doña María's servants, by dancing and distributing food to the community during evening processions. Through the adoption of a role formerly held only by men, the formation of women's identity is influenced in four dimensions. These dimensions are the challenging of traditional roles, the formation and perpetuation of self-assurance, the blurring of gender roles, and the creation and continuity of cultural identity.

The women that dance as *parachico danzantes* are able to publicly exhibit the same desire and physical endurance as men, thus creating a sense of equality. This sense of empowerment is frequently transferred into their homes, liberating them from their socially prescribed roles as domestic workers during the festival period. In addition, as festival participants they become more confident about their abilities and prouder of their roles in upholding their community's history and culture, as Faustina remarks:

> I know how to dance and very well. I learned to dance like the men dance. When I would participate, men would lift my mask and would say, 'Oh, you are a little girl!' They were surprised, and it would cause them a sense of pride to see that I was female. I know how the dance is supposed to be done, not like now, how these [men] dance like monkeys, they look like marionettes. You just laugh to see them dance. My father is a traditional *parachico* dancer and by watching him dance is where I learned.[6]

Faustina's comment is an indication of her knowledge regarding the dance of the *parachico* and also makes the point that she is a woman that is knowledgeable about her tradition. She is also critical of the men that neglect to perform the *parachico* dance properly. The verbal affirmation from the community—especially that of women—that accompanies festival involvement has also influenced the voices of female participants. When I asked the female interviewees what responses they had received as *parachico danzantes*, Yrene, who has participated as a *parachico* for several years, replied: "[Other women] flatter you. They tell me, 'you enjoy everything and you know the dance very well.' I tell them that they need to partake in the festival so they too can enjoy it. They need to live the same experience that I speak of."[7] This "experience" can be understood as a mark of personal and cultural fulfillment, as the *parachico* role is one of the most revered in the festival.

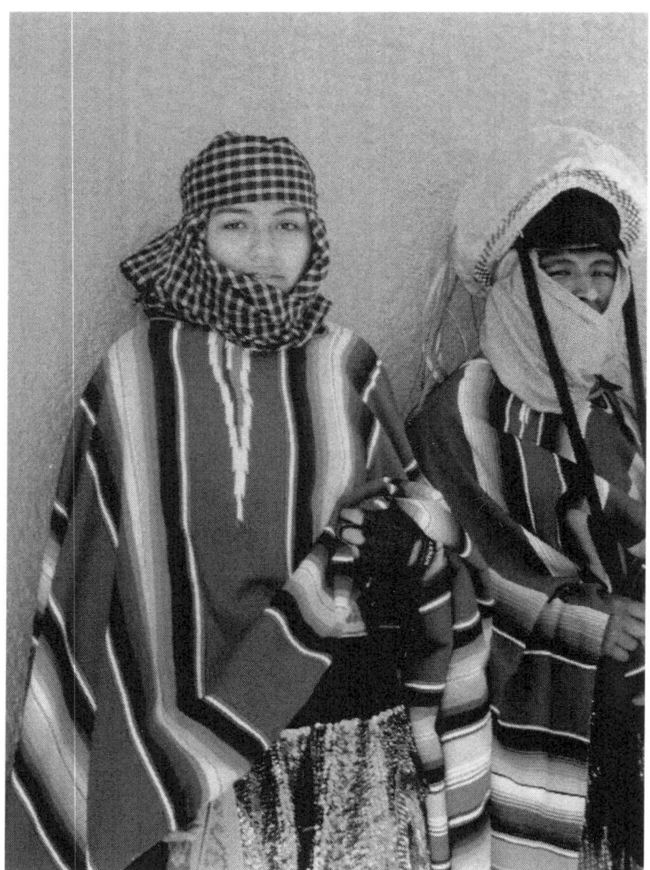

Young female *parachico danzante* with her male family member. Photograph by author.

The *parachico* is also a physically demanding dance. The dancer executes a continuous *doble zapateado*, moving from one foot to another in a circular motion while also moving counterclockwise in double time. At the same time both arms are held out, and the left hand is held open while the right hand energetically shakes a rattle. Given the layers of clothing, mask, and headpiece, the costume may weigh more than twenty pounds, adding to the physical strength required of the dancer. Participation has influenced many women's sense of self-worth and confidence on a physical level; it is a step toward a sense of agency. Yrene conveyed this idea of self-assurance best: "You really take pleasure in participating in La Feria de Enero; we're delighted that we can dance in the manner that men do."[8]

Although there may be affirmation for women's involvement, some men have expressed opposition to women's participation. In interviews, women disclosed the kinds of sentiments their male counterparts have expressed. Elena, one of the most well-respected female *parachico* dancers, said, "Yes, originally the men used to say that women shouldn't go out as *parachicos*, but we women are also Chiapacorzeñas and we also feel the same as they [the men]. We are also part of this community, so yes, we can dance."[9]

When women dance as *parachicos* they are stepping out of their traditional festival roles, (e.g. cooks, *madrinas*, *chuntas*, *chiapanecas*, etc.) and hence challenging gender norms. Women who participate in these traditional roles are vital to the production of the festival, but they do not allow them to gain the same recognition as a *parachico* dancer. For instance, the cooks assist in the preparation of the principal traditional meals such as *pepito con tasajo*, a ground pumpkin seed paste with strips of dried beef, and *chanfina*, a pork dish. All food preparation is done at the home of the *prioste*, or cargo holder, out of the public eye. *Madrinas* are the women who donate items, such as handkerchiefs, candles, flowers, or food products for processions or novenas and rosaries. The *chunta* carries a basket filled with fruits, vegetables, tamales, and chocolate gold coins, which are distributed during the *chunta* procession. Lastly, the *chiapaneca* represents the beauty of Chiapas and plays a supportive role to the *parachico* by bringing water or food to the dancer.

Women who choose not to fulfill these traditional roles threaten societal expectation and in turn usurp male prerogative (Senelick 2000). By entering and partaking of a male-dominated public role, women have demonstrated that they possess not only the physical strength but the cultural authority to play that role. With such demonstrations, women continue the process of asserting their cultural identity beyond their prescribed gender roles.

Liminality

In Van Gennep's formulation of *rite of passage*, liminality refers to "a structural place that is situated outside the realm of everyday social interaction, and in some cases, between two distinct structural planes" (cited in Bohannan and Glazer 1973, 123). A rite of passage takes place in three phases: (1) separation, the separation of the individual from previous status, (2) limen (liminality), the threshold or a condition of not having full membership within any social status, and (3) reincorporation, the reincorporation of the individual into a new status (Ibid.). Victor Turner (1995) follows this model by arguing that *communitas* develops within the liminal phase. During *communitas* one may feel an intense or shared emotion of togetherness or an ideal view of society. In *Los Pastores* (1995), Flores states that a "special license is accorded to the members who occupy this space. Such license is connected to behavior that, under ordinary circumstance, would be unacceptable in the public domain and that in some cases is the inversion of everyday practice" (57).[10] Similarly, La Feria de Enero provides a liminal space during which set notions of gender, class, and social roles become blurred. I contend that ritual *separation* from previous status takes place as *parachico* and *chunta danzantes* assemble and don their elaborate *trajes*, or regalia. The *parachico* costume entails multiple layers of clothing, a *montera* or head piece made of *ixtle*, maguey fibers, a wooden-carved mask resembling the face of Saint Sebastian, a wool serape, and *chalinas*, similar to western chaps, made of black cloth and adorned with colorful sequined images. As the costume completely covers the body, it conceals the identity of the individual. This separation is further marked, as only the *danzantes* are permitted to "dance" in the processional route.[11]

Those participating as *danzantes* move into liminality when dancing in the procession. Interviewees described feeling during this procession what seemed to be a sense of *communitas*, or as Turner puts it, an "Edenic" view of society. Social markers—such as economic status, gender, age, and marital status—become insignificant during the Feria de Enero setting. Alicia, a *parachico* dancer, states that Mexico is a classist society, but that during the January Festival this idea of classism seems to disappear.[12] Likewise, Soraya, a *chunta*, mentions that education is not a factor in participation: "In the group of *chunta*, they are from all types of professions. They are from all levels, laborers, students and professionals."[13] David, a homosexual male who participates as a *chunta*, also brings up an interesting point concerning gender. He states, "If you see people in a procession you cannot tell whether one is a man or a woman, because they are all dressed the same . . . their faces are covered with masks."[14] Finally, Elena tells us that age is evidently also blurred during participation in the festival. "When we dance, for example as *chunta*, an older woman can dance just the same as a young girl, their participation is the same. There is nothing that says, 'Well you can't dance because you're old.'"[15] These testimonies speak of *communitas*, a state where all participants are equal and this equality is achieved through participation in the festival dances.

As *parachico danzantes* complete this rite of passage, for many the main purpose of dancing was to ask for spiritual assistance from Saint Sebastian before reintegrating into society. Petitions that are made to Saint Sebastian are most commonly asked by the *danzante* on his or her behalf or on behalf of someone else with dilemmas of health or livelihood.

As petitions to these dilemmas are answered and remedied, *danzantes* return to pay homage to Saint Sebastian. For many faithful *danzantes*, this festival serves as a crucial step for reintegration into society as sober or healthy individuals returning to their community.

Intricate Processes of Challenging Gender Boundaries

The navigation of gendered performance at the individual and community levels in the January Festival is an intricate process. While transcending traditional gendered roles, festival participants deal with major concerns and constraints such as the maintenance of one gender identity while performing another, a request for balance among gendered participation in the role of *chunta*, and a respect for gender boundaries in the roles of Doña María de Angulo and the leader of the *parachico danzantes*.

By taking on the traditional male role of the *parachico danzante*, women are not only able to exhibit their physical capability but are also able to subvert traditional patriarchal values and norms. Although today most of the community of Chiapa de Corzo tolerates women *parachico danzantes*, historically, young women fulfilling this role were not accepted. In the past, most young women participating as *parachico danzantes* did so by defying their parents' traditional beliefs that women should not participate in a role customarily reserved for males. Claudia, a modern female *parachico* dancer, states that "there were those who would participate without their parents knowing it, it looked bad when a woman went out as a *parachico* . . . they didn't see it as proper for a woman to go out as a *parachico*."[16] Claudia clearly speaks to the struggle of the older generation of women who resisted traditional gender roles. The following quote by her mother, Daniela, illustrates that Chiapanecan mothers were indeed instrumental in charting a new course for their daughters' participation in the *parachico* role. "The education my parents gave me was very limiting, and out of spite I participated as a *parachico*. I did so on only a few occasions mostly because my parents didn't like it."[17] As a result of the claims of women like Daniela, female *parachico danzantes* are increasingly accepted within the household and greater community.

In addition, these women are proving that they can move in and out of spaces that have been traditionally reserved for men. Elena brought it to the attention of the men that they have forgotten the purpose of dancing as a *parachico*. "I tell men, I dance better than them, because all they do is go to the bars. I dance for the saints! I tell men not to tell me how to do something that they don't know how to do."[18] Elena's comments point out that a woman's presence in the *parachico danzante* role may draw attention to the meaning of the festival. Her statement serves as a reminder to the community of the festival's original intention of dancing to honor their saints. Women of both generations have proven that they can move in and out of festival roles traditionally reserved for men. A woman's participation in the male-dominated role of *parachico* enables her to fulfill two objectives: to obtain respect from her family and community for her ability as a *danzante* and to acquire a certain degree of male privilege by posing as a male.

In addressing the construction of gender, Butler asserts that gender is constituted through performative acts, and it is real only to the extent that it is performed by the individual (1990a, 278–79). Participants that engage in the act of gender performativity are empowered, for they transcend set gender ideals established by society. My interviewees stated that while participating in the opposite gender role they continue to maintain a sense of their biological sex. For example, Soraya maintains that "although we go out as *parachico* dancers we are still women."[19] As female *parachico* dancers assert "they are still women," their presence in this male role has expanded their social mobility within a festival context. As for homosexual men, the effect of their performance as *chunta* dancers is that they are now moving from the periphery and into the public sphere.

Although homosexual men do participate in the January Festival, for most participants the act of cross-dressing is not tied to sexual orientation. David, a homosexual man who participates as *chunta*, makes a similar comment with Soraya: "Just because men dress as women they don't stop being men."[20]

Women in particular have voiced their concern that a balance of participation based on gender should be maintained in the *chunta* role of the festival.

This need for gender balance is especially important in light of the fact that men have started to outnumber women in the traditional women's role of *chunta* in the festival. During an informal conversation with my host family I asked the eighty-year-old uncle, who also participated as a *chunta*, when men began to participate in this role. To his knowledge, men had participated in this particular role even before he began to do so in the mid-1930s.

During the interview process, I was told several versions surrounding the introduction of the male *chunta*. One version harks back to the colonial period. Rather than submitting to Spanish power, hundreds of the indigenous people of Chiapa de Corzo took to the Sumidero Canyon along the Grijalva River. It is said that some leapt off into the canyon, ending their lives, while others hid in the caves of the canyon. Those that hid in the caves would return to Chiapa de Corzo at night wrapped in *rebozos*, or shawls. While walking through the town they were thought to be women, since only their eyes were visible.

Another version holds that men took on women's roles to provide safety for the women who participated in the evening processions. Several women had reportedly been attacked or assaulted during the *chunta* procession, which takes place during the evening. Fewer and fewer women were participating in the evening processions because of a fear of attacks, so, rather than allow the *chunta* procession to disappear, men began to dress in this role. Ironically, the number of men participating in this role slowly began to outnumber the women. One of the reasons this is seen as significant is that the *chunta* role is one of the only public roles in which a critical mass of women may participate. The only other public role where a large number of women may participate is the *chiapaneca*, the partner to the *parachico danzante*. While *chiapaneca*'s participation is only seen during the *parachico* procession, following along the outsides or tail end of the procession, the *chunta* traditionally stands on her own, unaccompanied. During the interview process some of my interlocutors who participate as female *chunta* called for equal representation in this festival role dedicated to ensuring a female presence, a place to reaffirm their gender identity while contributing to this significant event in the community's culture. As mentioned earlier, the *chunta* role is the only role where women stand alone in public.

Boundaries

There are a few roles in the January Festival where traditional gender boundaries must be adhered to: the role of Doña María de Angulo and the leader of the *parachico danzantes*. Luis, who participates as a *chunta*, explains: "Men have infiltrated the roles of women, clearly it has happened. But if a man were to infiltrate into one of the women's roles such as Doña María de Angulo, well no! The community will hang him, they would burn him alive! Surely, you see there are certain margins that we have to respect just like in any society."[21]

Notwithstanding the fixity of the remaining boundaries, it is important to note that the blurring of gender boundaries with respect to the *chunta* role occurred as a response to the perceived needs of the community. Men entered the role of *chunta* to protect the women from harassment while participating. Men also maintained the almost extinct *chunta* role during the period when a number of women, fearing for their safety, quit participating.

Participation of Homosexual Males

The last finding of this study focuses on the participation of self-identified homosexual males in the festival. Here I focus solely on homosexual males because none of my interviewees made any mention of "out" lesbian participation in the festival. As fiestas offer an opportunity for certain daily restrictions to be lifted, this occasion offers an opportunity for individuals to become aware of and "express their role playing power" (Garcia Canclini 1993, 103). The participation of men in the role of *chunta* has provided a venue for some homosexual males to express a different kind of gender identity in a way that is not accepted in everyday life.

Most of the inhabitants of Chiapa de Corzo tolerate the participation of homosexual males who assist in maintaining the role of *chunta*, but they do not expect acts of homosexual expression. According to those interviewed, the first mass appearance of openly homosexual males in the festival began when an unidentified woman brought a busload of homosexual males to Chiapa de Corzo from Tuxtla Gutiérrez in the early 1990s. She provided them with the traditional attire of *chunta* and introduced them to the festival. This event helped to spur open male homosexual participation in the January Festival. There is some concern among the community of Chiapa de Corzo that the openly homosexual males are making a mockery of the festival's traditions. However, it is clear that the men I spoke to have great respect for their community traditions. Luis, also an openly homosexual male who participates as a *chunta*, states that "the origin of *chunta* has not been lost yet."[22] David, another homosexual participant, says, "The truth is we're trying to rescue the tradition, we're not trying to deform it. . . . I'm not very sure I remember the date of the introduction [of these openly homosexual males]; however, what is more important is the festival. I love my traditions, our traditions that our ancestors did not allow to disappear."[23] Since these men have chosen to participate within the *chunta* role, they are partaking in the maintenance of the tradition and making it part of their cultural identity.

It is common knowledge that the majority of the male *chunta* participants are heterosexuals but that a few are homosexuals. During the festival, homosexual males who participate in the role of *chunta* are easily differentiated because of their stylized attire. Luis assisted in familiarizing me with the adaptations used by openly homosexual men. For example, he points out "they no longer wear braids, there are times we go out in wigs or hair pieces." Whereas the heterosexual men tend to wear medium to long-haired wigs so they make two braids. The present-day dresses used for the procession of *chunta* are designed by the participant and have few similarities to the traditional *chunta* attire.

Needless to say, some community members see the participation of homosexual males as tolerable only if they refrain from expressing their sexuality

Elderly heterosexual male dressed in a traditional *chunta* attire, January 22, 2001. He is an active participant who has danced as a *chunta* for decades, as well as taking up the cargo of hosting the statue of Saint Sebastian in his home. Photograph by author.

during the festival setting. To this effect Xiomara claims, "You can look for them [homosexual males] right now and you'll find them dressed as men. They only dress as women during the festival."[24] Celestina also confirms this idea by stating "these men can't dress as women during their everyday life, normally."[25] Therefore, it follows that the community has not tolerated the crossing of genders on an everyday basis. To further supplement this statement, I turn to Cherríe Moraga, author of *Loving in the Wars Years: Lo que nunca pasó por sus labios*,[26] who discusses the notion that "homosexuality does not, in and of itself, pose a great threat to society. Male homosexuality has always been a 'tolerated' aspect of Mexican/Chicano society, as long as it remains 'fringe'" (2000, 102).[27] Although most of the residents of Chiapa de Corzo have not embraced homosexuality, generally they tolerate the individual as long as actions remain on the fringes of the festivities.

Elena, a member of a *chunta* group called Los Gerries, conveys this sentiment of "tolerance" in the following words: "The only thing that we ask of them is to respect the tradition, that they don't go doing silly acts, relating themselves sexually with another person while we are dancing, because that would be breaking our traditions."[28] Not all *chunta* groups are as adamant as Los Gerries. Indeed, Los Gerries is known for its discriminatory and homophobic nature, as Soraya explains. "Los Gerries don't permit homosexuals to go out [with them], they don't like it. They [Los Gerries] go out because they enjoy the tradition, and those who are [gay] can go out, just somewhere else, they don't permit it. There is a certain amount of discrimination, but not because they won't let them go out, the street is public, but that group, Los Gerries, don't accept that."[29]

The role of *chunta* has proven to be a space where gender identification becomes fluid. From my interviews, it was apparent that there are conflicting opinions regarding the participation of homosexual males. One participant felt that the presence of homosexual males in the procession would turn it into "gay parade." However, Angelina expresses the prevailing opinion of my interviewees on homosexual male participation in the festival: " [I]t's nice to see the [homosexual] men dance, they are conserving the tradition, we are happy for them; that's good that they continue to do this."[30] This comment is accepting of their participation as long as that participation is respectful.

As my research has shown thus far, the January Festival is an important site for challenging and reconstructing gender identity. Both women and men are recapturing the idea of public space and are now re-creating new spaces for themselves within their community and culture. The blurring of social and cultural indicators has given women the space to redefine gender

Queer *chunta* dressed in a stylized gown for the procession. Photograph by author.

boundaries and allowed them to reconstruct their gender identity and privilege. Women are actively reclaiming their space within the role of *chunta* as well as engaging in acts of social resistance by entering the role of *parachico danzante*. Their participation resonates beyond the festival setting as they are publicly recognized for their knowledge of tradition and physical strength as *parachico* dancers. Further, this blurring has created an environment of limited tolerance that has provided a space for homosexual males to express a part of their gender identity within the context of a ritual performance in a traditional female role.

By means of festival participation, both women and men create and reaffirm their individual cultural identities as well as maintain the cultural traditions of their community. The role of *parachico* liberates women by providing them a culturally sanctioned site to challenge traditional gender roles. In particular, participation in the role of *parachico* and *chunta* liberates them from their domestic duties in the home. This liberation is evident through the support of fathers, brothers, and husbands who are more willing take up household responsibilities so their women may participate as a *parachico danzante*. Admittedly, these actions have been met with some criticism from a small percentage of men, but women continue to participate in the role of *parachicos* nonetheless. Traditionally, these types of behaviors (cross-dressing and crossing of gender roles) would not normally be accepted. Both women and homosexual males have recaptured the idea of public space, however, and are now re-creating new spaces for themselves within their culture as well as in their community. As this creation of new space exceeds the festival period and leads into daily life, my interlocutors and others like them are acknowledged for their efforts as contributors to La Feria de Enero and in making it viable for current and future festival participants.

Notes

1. What has been most useful to my study on cargo systems in Chiapas is Rus and Wasserstrom's work (1980), as well as Smith 1977 and Greenberg 1981 on cargo systems in general. I have also consulted Guss 2000, Mendoza 2000, and Nájera-Ramírez 1997a to address cultural performance and ethnic identity.

2. See, for example, Cancian 1964, DeWalt 1975, Friedlander 1981, and Vogt 1969, 1994.

3. Soctón Nandalumí is the pre-Hispanic, Mayan name for the city of Chiapa de Corzo.

4. *Tradicional: Fiesta de Enero en Chiapa de Corzo, Chiapas.* Chiapa de Corzo: Artesanías Díaz Zamora. 2001.

5. The actual chant of the *parachico* is "*Parachico me pediste, parachico te daré con tu máscara de palo y tu chin-chin te sonaré.*" "*Parachico* (For the child) you have asked of me—*parachico*—this dance I will give, with my wooden mask and my *chin-chin* (rattle) I will play" (my translation).

6. Faustina (pseudonym), interview with Xóchitl Chávez, Chiapa de Corzo, May 14, 2001.

7. Yrene (pseudonym), interview with Xóchitl Chávez, Chiapa de Corzo, May 16, 2001.

8. Ibid.

9. Elena (pseudonym), interview with Xóchitl Chávez, Chiapa de Corzo, May 14, 2001.

10. For further discussion see Turner 1995, 19.

11. Those dressed in street clothes are allowed to follow but must remain along the sidewalks or at the end of the procession.

12. Alicia (pseudonym), interview with Xóchitl Chávez, Chiapa de Corzo, May 18, 2001.

13. Soraya (pseudonym), interview with Xóchitl Chávez, Chiapa de Corzo, May 16, 2001.

14. David (pseudonym), interview with Xóchitl Chávez, Chiapa de Corzo, May 17, 2001.

15. Elena (pseudonym), interview.

16. Claudia (pseudonym), interview with Xóchitl Chávez, Chiapa de Corzo, May 21, 2001.

17. Daniela (pseudonym), interview with Xóchitl Chávez, Chiapa de Corzo, May 15, 2001.

18. Elena (pseudonym), interview.

19. Soraya (pseudonym), interview.

20. David (pseudonym), interview.

21. Luis (pseudonym), interview with Xóchitl Chávez, Chiapa de Corzo, May 21, 2001.

22. Ibid.

23. David (pseudonym), interview.

24. Xiomara (pseudonym), interview with Xóchitl Chávez, Chiapa de Corzo, May 19, 2001.

25. Celestina (pseudonym), interview with Xóchitl Chávez, Chiapa de Corzo, May 25, 2001.

26. "What never passed through your lips"

27. At the beginning of the colonial period, Bernal Díaz proposed that homosexuality stems from indigenous Aztec roots (86–87). Such a proposal was based on ignorance and was self-serving for the Spanish, who condemned homosexuality.

28. Elena (pseudonym), interview.

29. Soraya (pseudonym), interview.

30. Angelina (pseudonym), interview with Xóchitl Chávez, Chiapa de Corzo, May 23, 2001.

4

Dancing to "Whittier Boulevard"

Choreographing Social Identity

MARIE "KETA" MIRANDA

Let's take a trip down Whittier Boulevard!
¡Arriba! ¡Arriba!
¡Aaaaaaaaaah Haa Haa Haa Haaaa a!
—Thee Midniters' "Whittier Boulevard"

No movement from the human body is possible without definite relation to life experience, even if it is random or inadvertent.
—John Martin, *Introduction to Dance*

In the dominant imaginary of 1960s youth, little attention is given to the subcultures of youth of color that preceded the development of the identity politics movements. Yet the early 1960s East Los Angeles youth scene boasted of garage bands, rock 'n' roll shows, car club–sponsored dances, cruising down Whittier Boulevard, and a mod style that revealed public space as a synergetic site of cultural production.[1] While the years between 1963 and 1968 are customarily assigned and ascribed as a transitional period—between being Mexican hyphenated American and becoming Chicano[2]—this chapter opens up the site as "history happening."[3] The teenage girls and their dancing bodies who participated in the East Los Angeles scene are the primary focus as they created a local/regional mod dance to Thee Midniters' rock 'n' roll hit "Whittier Boulevard." While the marketing system of rock 'n' roll privileges the male fantasy of fame and fortune through stardom, this chapter examines the choreography of a local dance to a regional scene. Conceiving the body as the articulation of identity formation, I argue that the girls' strategic location as dancers and fans to the band on stage offers a way to reconstruct the history and interpretation of the local, regional subculture among Mexican American youth in 1960s Los Angeles. The body becomes a critical factor in understanding the "structures of feeling" (Williams 1977, 129) operating in the barrios of Los Angeles. Communicating the incommunicable, dance symbolizes the ability to articulate one's identity in a society that racializes bodies.

Centering the body in motion, particularly the relationship between the band and the fans that danced to Thee Midniters' instrumental song "Whittier Boulevard," follows Celeste Fraser Delgado and José Esteban Muñoz's contention about the "dance of identity," where the "endless repositioning of the dancer . . . traces patterns of difference that can be taken up and recognized as new modes of identification . . . suggest(ing) neither being nor even becoming, but a body in motion that breaks into meaning to the polyrhythmic beat of history" (1997, 14). When the body dances as an object of history it produces meaning against and within and to the discourses that form identity. The dancing body speaks a language irreducible to words, and the dancing body acts in relation to interpellating categories of race, ethnicity, class, gender, and sexual identity.[4] The act of stylization and restylization of dance by the dancer as well as the self-instruction—learning to dance by watching and practicing rather than through formal knowledge—are techniques of cultural production by Chicano/a youth during the early and mid-1960s. Additionally, the acts of watching and participating, a relation between spectators and participants, provide a structure for producing community identity. If examination of subcultural style requires looking at culture not as the "study of relationships between elements in a whole way of life" but thinking about culture as "the study of relationships in a whole way of conflict,"[5] then the dance provides a way of exploring identity in a local context.

Dance Elements

The 1960s dancing body is remembered in the uplifting Temptations' walk, the Four Tops' dynamic duck walk, the Miracles' monkey, and the smooth slide of James Brown. Highly stylized performances, these movements of the stars were imitated on the dance floors of union halls, recreation centers, churches, and high school auditoriums throughout the nation, especially in Los Angeles. The mimesis is a corporeal "call and response" between artist and audience, thus a process of hailing or interpellation establishes identity between them.[6] However, there were moves that were uniquely Chicana/Chicano—steps fashioned to particular songs of East L.A. bands. One of the most notable is the dance to "Whittier Boulevard" by Thee Midniters. Chicana/o youth produced a dance with two main elements that are separate and identifiable as bodily *acts* of the dance. The elements I am addressing, or rather notating, assist my evaluation of the dance as a way in which identity is bodily enunciated prior to the articulation of a Chicano identity. The two elements consist of the following:

1. The first element consists of tilting the upper body back and forth. Bending from the waist, chest and shoulders slightly sway toward the floor or to the side then tilt back up to stand straight.
2. At the same time, the foot movement sets a regular pattern of beats and emphasis. Here, the toe marks the first muted beat, where the dancer elegantly balances the bent body. Striking the second beat, the heel pounds. Then the dancer shifts weight from one foot to the other foot marking the third beat, and the heel hammers the fourth. This repeating element suggests the overall mood or effect that characterizes the dance. Unlike Afro-Caribbean dance that is on the balls of the foot, the toe-to-heel movement rapidly beats to the drums of "Whittier Boulevard."

Throughout the driving rock 'n' roll tempo, the dancer maintains a balanced and controlled position throughout the movements.

While boys and girls queued up in rows (boys on one side and girls on the other), the girls would take over the dance nonetheless, disrupting the boy-girl parallelism. By turning to each other to exhibit their rhythm or the proficiency of their dance steps, the girls made the boys secondary to spectatorial pleasure. Because the girls took over the dance, and because of the dance's elements—the body bending at the waist and the type of vigorous heel-toe stampings—many of the Mexican American boys pejoratively called it "The War Dance" or "The Aztec Stomp."[7]

The dance elements were imitative of the band members' movements. The singer of the band had greater mobility and an enhanced choreography. Conversely, the brass—saxophonist and trumpeters—and organist had limited spatial mobility because they had to hold their instruments or because of the immobility of the instrument. In addition, the spatial restriction of the stage restricted the bodies of the brass section to a limited set of movements. More importantly, the musicians were generally secondary to the singer/crooner who pronounced the lyrics of a song, producing the primary meaning. Since "Whittier Boulevard" is a blasting, rocking instrumental, the dance gives the impression of imitating the brass musicians' bodily gestures and footwork.

On the dance floor the gestures and footwork of the brass instead become highly stylized swaying and stampings of the feet by the youth who attended the dance hall events held throughout East Los Angeles.[8] It was an ironic symbolization of the lived experience of the Chicano youth in Los Angeles prior to the nationalist identity politics of the late 1960s and early 1970s: the bending, swaying body gestures as if attempting to break from confinement; the foot stomps as if signaling protest. It is the mimesis of restricted space that is key to my analogy. While there is limited mobility through economic class, the gesturing body marks the overriding problem of racialized bodies restricted from full participation in society.

Choreographing the Dance

Considering the dance as a whole composition, the dance catalogues five segments that follow the arrangement of the music.[9] The first occurs with the shouting appeal by Thee Midniters to "take a trip down Whittier Boulevard." During this segment, the dancer leisurely finds the beat by tapping to the side and forward and concludes with a sweeping foot movement across the line of the body.

First segment:

- Feet are parallel in a closed position.
- Right foot taps out the beat, first to the side, then in front of the other foot. Then back to the side, parallel, and tapping to the front and returning to parallel in an open position.
- Followed by a sweeping motion where the leg crosses the line of the body and sweeps back, landing with the ball of the foot parallel, in an open position.

The second segment combines the main elements of the dance where the position of the torso bends and rocks back from the waist up with the heel-toe step. Characterized by its toe-to-heel work, the body shifts weight from one foot to the other, creating a cross rhythm. Balance is achieved by keeping one foot flat to the floor while the other foot marks the beat from toe to heel.

The third segment is an interlude when the organ predominates. As a short rest from the rhythmic heel-and-toe element, the body is straight and relaxed, the legs crossing the line of the body as in a stroll. The stroll, like the vigorous portions of the cakewalk, is characterized by a "series of walking steps on the toes that is executed with a type of swagger" (Barendrect 1996–2002):

Third segment:

- Straighten the right knee and raise the left foot in small kick in front of the right foot.
- Step onto left foot, and lower it in front of the right foot.
- Transfer weight onto right foot, then onto left foot in a rocking action.
- Straighten left knee, raising right foot in sharp, small kick in front of the left foot.
- Transfer weight onto left foot, then onto right foot in a rocking action.
- Then as the drums pick up the tempo, the feet rapidly shuffle back and forth, so that the footwork emphasizes the three blasts of the brass.

The fourth segment repeats the second segment of bending torso and footwork elements. The fifth and final segment is a boxed movement called "cruising," where the body is upright, with hands swaying in a cool stroll, repeating the third segment.

While the descriptive notation may imply pedantic uniformity, at this point it is important to reassert that it is a vernacular dance created to a rock 'n' roll song, producing a hybrid dance. The variations and improvisations reflect two components of syncretism. On the one hand, the dance borrows from the various strolls and cakewalk styles of African American popular dance.[10] On the other hand, the toe-to-heel beats register adaptation and change. The toe-heel element as an essential character of the dance registers how Mexican American youth—without formal training in folkloric dance—varied and improvised elements of Mexican dance.[11] The toe-heel element registers a syncretism, attempting to combine two different dance systems and practices, in effect bringing Mexican dance to rock. The dance as the body in pleasure articulates identity.

As Pablo Vila argues in "Tango to Folk," the body is crossed by discourses, thus the body performs in and through ideologies. The body competes with ideological interpellations that constitute one's subject position (1991, 107). While subject position can be many (woman, mother, worker, and so on), the dance to "Whittier Boulevard" clashes with those ideologies "that say who we are" (107). In the world in which Mexican American youth lived in the 1960s, outside the dance hall the "mediational power of the dance" conveys not only the personal (leisure) but a dialectics with the political and social (Henry, Magowan, and Murray 2000, 253). The dance to "Whittier Boulevard" is a discursive flowing with the networks that work through and upon the bodies of Mexican American youth.[12]

During the period between 1963 and 1968, when the first wave of East Los Angeles rock 'n' roll revues were occurring, dominant discourse of social injustice was framed in racial terms of black and white. Social issues framed between these two terms devalue the experience of the Mexican American community. As the postwar economy provided social mobility through assimilation for most Euro-American ethnic groups (such as Irish and Italian Americans), Keynesian economics considered poverty as a fundamentally economic issue. In this framework, ethnicity is considered a category that will "disappear" as assimilation occurs. "Race," however, is veiled by that logic.

As the contradictions of the economy—the boom of finance and manufacturing with mass consumerism and extensive poverty—became conspicuous, the welfare state recognized its role in the public sphere and intervened in the free market to protect the general interests of society. This yielded the antipoverty programs for "other" whites—Appalachians and Mexican Americans—which would aid in achieving the American Dream. While the 1954 *Hernandez v. State of Texas* decision considered whether or not Mexicans were white (Handbook of Texas), their reality was the experience of Jim Crow segregation. Disenfranchisement and second-class citizenship, as well as the treatment as a surplus labor force in a dual wage structure, produced the "racial fault lines" of social and racial inequality for the Chicano/a communities of the Southwest.[13]

The dancing body registers the space, an interstice, within the state-regulated discourse about ethnicity and race that constrains the ways individuals and groups articulate identity. At the time, census forms did not include the term Mexican American as a way to claim ethnic-national identity. Thus, many Chicanos marked the box for Caucasian or Spanish-speaking. Yet their everyday lives were anything but the experience of whiteness. The dancing body configured the paradoxical experience about the American Dream and articulated the complexity of identity during a period when there was a War on Poverty, a war in Vietnam, and warring sides in the burgeoning civil rights movements and the emergent youth and student movements.

Quite possibly the dance was not articulating opposition to economic mobility but to the American nationalist project of assimilation where ethnicity/race are erased for Mexican Americans. The dance to "Whittier Boulevard" made visible the Mexican American racialized body. The dance simultaneously revealed the multiple identificatory positions, and the kinesthesis asserted the sense of knowing what it means to be a debased brown body in

America. Positioned as "other" whites, the Mexican American population becomes absent from the social discourse on racial equality. The disconnect between the law and their social reality then leads to an interpretation of the Chicano/a dance to "Whittier Boulevard" as an enactment of their indigenized racialization.[14] Despised as "bandits," "dirty," and only good for working the fields, as well as derogated as a mixed race where the Indian becomes the factor for racialization, the disidentified community constructs an identity through a dance that mimics indigenous dance.

Pablo Vila's discussion on ideological interpellations assists in the project of further evaluating music and dance: " [D]iscourses exist both in written and oral forms and in the social practices of everyday life, and music, as a discourse, has different ways to interpellate: via its lyrics, its music and its performance; each offers ways of being and behaving and modes of psychic and emotional satisfaction" (1991, 107). Recognizing the obvious direct address of lyrics, Vila goes on to examine the music's capability to interpellate subjects. Noting the "imperative rhythms which set bodies moving in specific ways," Middleton (1989, 242) asserts that music calls (hails) particular subjects through "mechanisms of identification whereby listeners' self-image is built into the music."[15] As a process in which subjects recognize and perform identity, I imagine dance as a way of breaking away from the restraint of the dominant social body. Before analyzing the opening stanza of "Whittier Boulevard" as the hailing of particular subjects, I will contextualize the recording's history and reception.

The East Side Sound

Released in late 1965, the instrumental was (and still is) Thee Midniters' most famous recording.[16] In their tour de force on Chicano rock 'n' roll in Southern California, David Reyes and Tom Waldman provide important information on the history and context of its style and ultimately its labeling. While Thee Midniters (and many of the local garage bands) wanted to look like the Beatles, they wanted the funkier rhythm and blues sound of the Rolling Stones. "Whittier Boulevard" was modeled after the Rolling Stones' "2120 South Michigan Avenue." The song's raucous party mood and the famous shouted opening *¡Arriba! ¡Arriba!*, followed by the sounds of cars honking, and ending with the wild, extensive, and delirious yodeling cry has made it a cult classic for CD compilations of frat and garage rock. Defining frat rock as music "designed with keggers in mind," Richard Henderson's liner notes designates place as key to understanding the East Side bands. For Thee

Midniters, place is instructive. "In 1964, Thee Midniters blasted out of the barrio to become (for a moment) East L.A.'s answer to the Beatles, as well as providing a charge of garage energy that inspired many other young Latino bands. 'Whittier Boulevard' is evidence of the latter, complete with the simulated sounds of a street full of low riders" (Henderson 1991).

Yet "Whittier Boulevard" never made the Billboard Hot 100 list nor was its popularity made evident in record sales (Reyes and Waldman 1998, 91). Registering place as the connection between the song and its primarily Mexican American audience, Reyes and Waldman describe how the band members, producers, other Chicano musicians, teens who cruised, partied, met friends, and took their dates down Whittier Boulevard created a weekend scene. It "was a two-mile long party . . . a happening place" (55–56). Reyes and Waldman offer their analysis of the problems with marketing the recording as well as the record companies' classification of the band, which marginalized them in the dominant recording industry. The authors note that due to the song's title, a local gathering spot for Mexican American youth, Thee Midniters were "pegged" as a Chicano band. Since Southern California was segregated, Reyes and Waldman argue, there would be no reason for a white band to celebrate the area and the subcultural scene. The authors maintain that "[w]hile Thee Midniters did not deliberately evoke Mexican-American life," it was the mixture of rhythm and blues, rock 'n' roll, pop, and Latin jazz that illustrate how Thee Midniters refused to restrict categorizing their sound (92–93). Performing on local rock 'n' roll television shows like *Shebang* and *Ninth Street West,* and even on the nationally broadcast *American Bandstand,* Thee Midniters garnered a sizable Anglo following. As their song got greater radio play, they performed in many Southern California suburbs. Yet Thee Midniters were identified as a "Chicano band" by producers and disc jockeys who needed to categorize the "sound." Certainly, the "imperative rhythms," that is, making bodies move, interpellated new subjects among white suburban youth who heard the song.

Felt Meanings and Interpellation

Yet another form of interpellation occurs for the band's Chicano/a fans. As the band members shout "Let's take a trip down Whittier Boulevard," the band hails the dancer/fan who recognizes the geosocial place. The band acknowledges the very street Mexican American youth have appropriated to make a subcultural landmark. Immediately following, a single strident voice shrieks out "*¡Arriba! ¡Arriba!*" Additionally, the singular voice, separating itself and standing out from the boisterous, collective voices in the song's beginning, registers the code switching of the Chicano/a language community. While it may be assumed that the code switching to Spanish is one way the audience recognizes itself, the terms *¡Arriba! ¡Arriba!* have become stereotyped representation. The cartoon mouse Speedy Gonzalez is characterized by his constant shouting of the words *¡Arriba ¡Arriba!* The mouse's ethnically coded expression stereotypes things Mexican, bringing two different reactions. The first is a counteridentification with the stereotype. Yet in the call by Thee Midniters there is another formation occurring, that of disidentification.

José Esteban Muñoz explains that disidentification is the work at a site between identification and counteridentification. Noting that identification is never seamless, Muñoz considers the subject *inside* ideology. While identification registers a subject identifying with the dominant culture, counteridentification finds a subject imagining that he or she is outside ideology or in opposition to the dominant culture. These have been the two poles for examining identity formation (like resistance/capitulation or assimilation/opposition). Disidentification, Muñoz posits, is not simply the identification against, but a process of crafting and performing the self for subjects outside the dominant public spheres. As a process that enables politics, it is a third mode of dealing with dominant ideology. "One that neither opts to assimilate within such a structure nor strictly opposes it; rather, disidentification is a strategy that works on and against dominant ideology" (1999, 12). Instead of buckling under the pressures of dominant ideology (identification, assimilation) or attempting to break free of its inescapable sphere (counteridentification, utopianism), this "working on and against" is a strategy that tries to transform a cultural logic from within. Muñoz argues that counteridentification always labors to enact permanent structural change, thus he values local and everyday struggles of resistance. As a survival strategy, disidentification transforms the raw material of identification (in this instance the stereotyped *¡Arriba! ¡Arriba!*) and simultaneously positions the subject within ideology, who "works on and against" the stereotype. While counteridentification would attempt to dissolve or abolish the racialized coding, *¡Arriba! ¡Arriba!* reworks the shameful component. Neither eliding the harmful nor directly confronting the stereotype, disidentification allows the recognition of the contradictory facet. Since disidentification negotiates strategies of resistance within the flux of discourse and power, Muñoz allows for the variety and diversity in the processes of production and modes of performance.

The final line of the opening stanza, the wild, delirious, and extended cry *¡Aaaaaaaaah Haa Haa Haa Haaaa a!*, is a *grito*, commonly found in *ranchera* or *conjunto* songs. Like the first line of the stanza, "Let's take a trip down Whittier Boulevard," it directly addresses particular subjects. The *grito*, a loud, inarticulate expression of rage, pain, and anger in many Mexican songs, is also an expression of overwhelming joy, or feelings of great happiness or pleasure, especially of an elevated or spiritual kind. Joy is derived from something that is given, a spiritual denotation that connects and creates affinity. The *grito* may be shouted by the performer or the audience. This dialectical vocalization, a sometimes continuous response from the audience to performer, brings a shared emotional world into being. It also marks the relation of the individual to the broader society, a movement between political and cosmological realms (Henry, Magowan, and Murray 2000, 254). Thus, the *grito* becomes an interlocking of emotions. Rage, pain, and anger as well as thrill and frenzy merge so that not one emotion is discernible. Thee Midniters' *grito* calls and interpellates particular subjects to form community.

In the dialectical relation of call and response, the dancers return the hailing *gritos* by producing the first dance segment—tapping out the beat to the side and front, and ending with a sweeping foot movement across the line of the body. While other audiences hear the opening and may begin to assemble for to the dance, fans of Thee Midniters produced this customary opening; thus interpellation is not coerced, and identification is agreed upon.[17] Starting any dance, the dancer takes time to find the correct musical beat to begin on—tapping the foot on the floor, counting the meter. This foot movement is a basic tapping of the ball of the foot to each of the beats. "Let's take a trip" consists of four movements (feet together, one foot steps out in front, returns to feet together, then returns out in front). This is followed by "down Whittier Boulevard," where the foot crosses the body in a sweeping motion across the line of the body and returning to feet together. Then as the blare of a car horn sounds, the foot taps out the beats. As the shout *¡Arriba! ¡Arriba!* is yelled, both feet tap out four beats. When the *grito* rings, a cruising stroll transpires. With the first beat of the drum, the rapid heel-toe element commences. While the opening interpellates—hailing any and all audiences—the customary steps by the fans stress how this particular audience of Mexican American youth interact with the performers. The multiple interaction—the lyrics, the code switching, the disidentification process—registers the formation of a popular identity. The dance demonstrates the productive, creative, and discursive flows and networks through and around bodies. The dance reveals itself as a cultural engine, dynamically producing new meanings as well as reinforcing established ones, simultaneously empowering and constraining the bodies. Ultimately the dance is about power for being and meaning for Mexican American youth in 1960s Los Angeles.

The "turbulent sixties," a period of mass protest and political struggle against class exploitation, unpopular wars, and racial and gender inequality, has been marked as unique because it was the first time youth as youth played a central role in shaping oppositional politics (Muñoz 1989). Early Chicano historians have tended to highlight the Chicano movement of the late 1960s, however. This has had a twofold effect. Dismissing the productive moment of culture and identity making has marginalized the young women who made the youth scene in East Los Angeles during the early 1960s. The other effect has been to write off the mod scene as assimilative. Examining the body as a site of cultural production reveals that the body in motion articulates the social and the political. My project to consider dance as *history happening* attempts to bring the margins and marginalized to the center in order to reconsider the girls as the fulcrum of the events of the later 1960s Chicano movement and today's "Hispanic" generation in Los Angeles. While many of the mod girls bleached their hair blonde, used concealer creams on their lips before applying pink lipstick, and spent a lot of time purchasing the accoutrements of the mod fashion, the young women were not "acting white" or attempting to "pass." Neither can their participation in consumerism be argued as a desire to assimilate. In the world in which Mexican American youth lived outside the dance hall, the realities of police brutality, poverty, and racism were part and parcel of their everyday lives. The dance hall did not release them from nor did it banish the world of class, race, gender, and sexual oppression. Dance as bodily expression operates within temporal and spatial zones as well as within local and national political and economic tensions.

Examining the subcultural mod scene among Los Angeles Mexican American youth and focusing on the bodies of young women in dance offers an understanding of the range of signification symptomatic of broader structural discourses that shape social relations. My semiotic reading of their kinesthetic action to Thee Midniters' song "Whittier Boulevard" has argued that dance, as bodily text, signals the multifaceted production of social identities. Dance is productive and creative and demonstrates the body in the flows of discursive power. A reconstruction of the early 1960s is not just a matter of what people were doing, but of how they invested meaning in the process of constructing and realizing self and society. The girls' bodies in motion offer a potential alternative interpretation to the pre–Chicano movement history. Looking at the fan as dancer for social history, to find new ways of being and the potential of new identities, draws a sociohistorical picture of the early civil rights period through its subculture.

Notes

1. Mod as a subcultural style developed with the "baby boomer" generation. Among the many youth subcultures in Britain (teddy boys, rockers, and beats), mod is associated with the Mersey sound (1962–63). Although there were many variations, the media featured the collarless two-tone suits with narrow ties or small collar shirts and elasticized "Chelsea" boots. (The style was so popular among British youth that the Beatles, primarily a rocker band, changed their outfits and style to mod. In the United States, it became known as the "Beatle look.") While the young men are primarily discussed and celebrated (Hebdige 1972 and McRobbie 1991), mod girls took the Mary Quant style of Chelsea, the pop-art and op-art dresses of bold primary colors or black and white checks or stripes, and, of course, the famous mini skirts. The mod hairdo marked a significant change from the hair-sprayed "beehive" style to the "mop top" (a la Beatles) style or the straight, chin-length hair cut with a deep part down the center of the head. The style was symmetrical simplicity.

2. Providing an insider's view of the Chicano student and youth movement, Carlos Muñoz's (1989) project details the relationship between community and campus activism. Muñoz and other Chicano historians, however, have through a linear and progressive model considered the period before the Chicano movement as a time when the youth of Mexican descent were either on the way to assimilating to the dominant Euro-American majority, or opposing assimilation. In either case, the accommodation/resistance model sets up two opposing poles that obscure the production of culture and identity during the early 1960s. In this chapter, I consider Emma Pérez's (1991) concept of interstitial space, or third space, to understand cultural production as a project of decolonization.

3. Examining dance in relation to the state, ideology, and social structure, Celeste Fraser Delgado and José Esteban Muñoz (1997) consider the performative body as it speaks to the politics of society. Their concept of "history as choreography" registers both diachronic and synchronic aspects of dance, informing my concept of "history happening" of this local/regional dance.

4. The concept of interpellation is derived from Louis Althusser, who explains "hailing" as a process where one becomes subject to ideology. His most descriptive example provides a great insight into power and subjectivity. A police officer yells, "Hey you, stop!" As one turns to the call or hail, one is therefore subject to authority (1971,170–78).

5. Dick Hebdige compares and contrasts the concepts of culture by Raymond Williams and E. P Thompson. In Thompson's project, ideology and ideological state apparatuses produce conflict, opposition, and resistance between dominant and subordinated groups (1972, 6).

6. Jacqui Malone (1996) defines the African American vernacular as those rhythms that originate primarily outside the mainstream: on southern farms and plantations, in northern urban streets and dance halls, and in theaters and cabarets patronized by ordinary folk. She registers African American vernacular dance as a rhythmically

propulsive, call-and-response process that improvises upon the most refined styles of the past in response to contemporary pressures to articulate subjectivity.

7. In my mind's eye the dance elements approximate (1) the indigenous deer dance of the Yaqui and the northwest Mexican highlands where the body bends at the waist and then the upper torso is brought back up, and (2) much like the stampings of a *zapateado* or the vigorous heel-toe of a country *jarabe tapatio,* the foot beat calls to mind the national folk dances of Spain and Mexico. The first time I saw two teenage girls perform this choreographed dance was at a church bazaar. While I previously listened to the song, trying to figure out what kind of dance steps to take up to Thee Midniters' instrumental, the two young women finally nailed it. Memory has made the moment and their dance mystical.

8. While the horn section's swaying—bending from the waist, swinging their horns up and down—are the movements that are imitated on the dance floor, it is unclear whether the band members originated the foot-heel movement or if they imitated the dancers.

9. I use the term "segment" in order to consider the body movement as language, thus a segment is any one of the individual speech sounds that make up a longer string of sounds.

10. The dancers may include other segments such from African American dance, i.e., the Temptations' walk, the stroll, or cakewalk.

11. Like most Chicano/a youth, I had no formal training in Mexican dance or folkloric dance. Thus, I believe the variation and improvisation arises from familial and neighborhood knowledge, where Chicano/a youth see family members dance the *jarabes, jaranas,* and *bambas* and create this type of toe-heel movement—*zapateado*—for the fun of it.

12. Rosita Henry, Fiona Magowan, and David Murray describe the "mediational power of dance" as a term that conveys the same processes as dialectics, negotiations, and becoming. Discussing the power of dance, they engage Foucault's concept of power as "the productive, creative, and discursive flows and networks through and around bodies which simultaneously privilege and marginalize discourses of being, relating and meaning" (2000, 253–60).

13. In their works, both Montejano (1987) and Almaguer (1994) explicate the social construction of race and class for the Mexican communities in the Southwest.

14. In considering the term "indigenization" for the Mexican American community, invaluable discussions with my *colega* Dr. Josephine Mendez-Negrete offered a way for me to characterize the dance as a third space outside the resistance/capitulation binary to examine social practices. While Mendez-Negrete offered a broader conceptual framework for considering the Chicano/a experience whereby the mestizo is considered unassimilable, I present my apology for reducing her eloquent argument.

15. Middleton argues that the "connotative function [of music] operates most obviously in certain sorts of direct-address lyrics (for example, 'save the last dance for me,' 'come on everybody, let's rock'). . . . It may also be associated, however, with

'imperative' rhythms, which set bodies moving in specific ways, and, in a general sense. On this general level, it can be regarded as the function of 'interpellation,' through which listening subjects are located in particular positions as addressees" (1989, 242).

16. Los Lobos rerecorded the song for the film *Mi Vida Loca,* directed by Allison Anders, but their version was not released in the CD motion picture soundtrack.

17. Not every interpellation is coercive (Crease 2002, 112–13). As Thee Midniters hail or call their fans to join in dance, the dancer gives herself to dance in the company of others. Thus felt meanings are summoned up in the hailing, and a collective self emerges in the act of dance.

5

Creating Agency and Identity in *Danza Azteca*

MARÍA TERESA CESEÑA

About a hundred *danzantes* (dancers) stood in formation, making up two single-file lines at the corner of Broadway and Spring Street in East Los Angeles, California, on a Saturday in February 2003 to pay tribute to Cuauhtémoc, the last of the Aztec *tlatoanis.*[1] *Danzantes* from all over California, Arizona, and even Mexico swayed in place as they waited for the traffic signal to change; then they crossed the street. The *danzantes* were women, men, and children. Many were college-educated, bilingual, Mexicanos, first-, second-, third-, and fourth-generation Chicanos.[2] Each moved in unison to the forceful beats being pounded out by the drummer who led them. As they proceeded down Broadway toward the Parque de México, they marched from left to right, in a style resembling an army marching off to battle. Men carried banners displaying images of the Virgen de Guadalupe, and all donned elaborate *trajes* (ceremonial dress or regalia) and *penachos* (feathered headdresses). Upon arrival at the park, the *danzantes* were greeted by a crowd of onlookers awaiting their entrance, among them reporters from the local Spanish-language newscast, people from the East L.A. community, and family and friends of the *danzantes*. Vendors sold snow cones, *paletas* (frozen fruit and cream popsicles), jewelry, and knick-knacks. You could find necklaces and hair clips with natural images such as birds and shells, and various Catholic symbols.

This was only one of the several colorful displays I encountered as I conducted my research comparing two *danza azteca* groups in San Diego, California: Danza Mexicayotl, based in Chula Vista, and a student-run *danza* group based in the University of California, San Diego campus, which I will refer to as *Danza Azteca* at UCSD.[3] Each of the two groups I worked with were strongly invested in claiming an indigenous identity, but how and why they claimed this identity varied between each group, and often among members within the same group. The indigeneity they claimed was tied to political and spiritual beliefs. For example, the student group was quite vocal about their politics. During an interview with their leader, Rafael Navar, he stated, "We'll support the Zapatistas. We'll support all sorts of movements. If anything, that's what we see as our principal job number 1. We'll go to a community protest before we go to anything else."[4]

In contrast to the student group, Danza Mexicayotl maintains that *danza* should be used solely for cultural and spiritual fulfillment. Its leader Mario Aguilar noted, "It isn't about being politically free or empowered through *danza*, cuz it's not that at all. It's spiritual. Now, [if] that gives you the spiritual power and gives you the spiritual peace in terms of peace to go on a political quest, [or an] economic quest, academic quest . . . those are the spiritual bases of *danza* and everything else piles on like icing."[5] Regardless of their differences, both groups found within *danza* a sense of community and pride and a way to assert their identities as culturally and racially indigenous. This chapter aims to reveal a glimpse of the agency created by claiming indigeneity through *danza*.

The indigenous identities manifested through *danza azteca* are linked to the larger move by Chicanos to reconnect with their indigenous cultures, which began in the 1960s and 1970s. Stuart Hall discusses the process involved when oppressed groups attempt to reclaim what colonialism has destroyed. He asks whether this process of reclaiming involves "unearthing that which the colonial experience buried or overlaid, bringing to light the hidden continuities it suppressed? [or] . . . a quite different practice—not rediscovery but the *production* of identity? Not an identity grounded in archeology, but in *re-telling* of the past?" (Hall 1989, 69) To apply the concept of "unearthing" or "rediscovery" to *danza* would presume that *danza* was out of existence until the 1970s. To the contrary, various forms of *danza* have existed in Mexico for centuries. *Danza* was not something that needed discovering in the sense of being unearthed.

However, for some Chicanos, their introduction to *danza azteca* was like an archaeological discovery because *danza* was a practice unfamiliar to them before the 1970s. Just as material culture uncovered by archaeology must then be interpreted and analyzed, Chicano *danzantes* took what they were given by *danza* as clues about how their ancestors might have been, and more importantly, who they as Chicanos wanted to be. The "identity . . . grounded in [a] re-telling of the past" that Hall speaks of applies to the struggle of Chicanos, who, through *danza*, reclaimed their indigenous roots and began telling the story of Chicano *danza*; for many Chicano *danzantes*, *danza* became a tool they used and continue to use to fight for the power to represent themselves, rather than be represented. It is not my intention to either prove or disprove the "authenticity" of one form of *danza azteca* over another. My investigations examine the formation of the form of *danza azteca* so visible in California and how each of the two groups I worked with has used it to gain agency through affirming their cultural identities.

For this research I used several ethnographic methods, including participant observation, formal taped interviews, and informal interviews conducted during *danza* practices. Prior to my research I was not a *danzante* nor was I affiliated with any *danza* group. Most of my information was gathered through my participation at weekly practices and occasional ceremonies and performances hosted or attended by each group.

The first group I participated with was Danza Mexicayotl, based in San Diego, California. Much like the scene I opened with, my first practice with Danza Mexicayotl was in a public setting and generated an impromptu audience. Practice took place at the San Ysidro Recreation Center, just one mile from the United States–Mexico border. On the night I attended my first practice, the center was locked due to its being September 16th, Mexico's Independence Day. All of the *danzantes* had forgotten about the holiday, but rather than cancel practice they danced on the lawn at the adjacent park. As the drummer began to play, people from the neighborhood came out to watch. It was then that I became familiar with how a typical practice is run.

After about an hour of dancing, the *danzantes* stood in a circle for *palabra*, or the word. During *palabra* each person in the circle had a chance to speak and could only do so when he or she was holding the *sahumador* (incense burner). Beginning with the *capitán* or *capitana*, or male or female leader of the circle, each *danzante* took a turn holding the *sahumador* of copal resin[6] as it was passed in a clockwise direction until it made its way full circle, back to the *capitán* or *capitana*. While some passed the *sahumador* to the next person, usually holding it just long enough to allow the smoke from the burning copal to rise into their faces as a way of purifying themselves, others passed it quickly to the next person without pausing at all. Only some took the opportunity to speak; when they did, statements typically consisted of giving thanks, making announcements, sharing personal dilemmas, or asking the group to pray for a friend or family member. *Palabra* really demonstrated the sense of community that *danza* facilitates, and it marked the completion of practice.

The practices in San Ysidro seemed mainly for experienced dancers. During the rest of my observations I opted to attend a beginner's practice. I first attended practice at St. John of the Cross Catholic Church in Lemon Grove, but practices were canceled after a few months due to low attendance. I then began attending practices at Sherman Heights Community Center near downtown San Diego. At Sherman Heights the dances were broken down step by step. Aguilar led all practices since it was one of his obligations as a *capitán* to share *danza* with the community. As a participant at these practices, I received instruction in the Nahuatl language, and I learned about the history of the group and its role in the community.

Danza Mexicayotl was formed in 1981 by *capitán* Mario Aguilar, one of the first Chicanos to participate in *danza azteca* when Florencio Yescas brought it to California during the early 1970s. Yescas brought his group Esplendor Azteca from Mexico City to the Centro Cultural de la Raza in San Diego as part of a commitment to teach indigenous dances and spirituality to Chicanos/as throughout the United States. According to Enrique Maestas, a scholar and *danzante*, Yescas was adhering to the code UNIÓN, CONFORMIDAD, Y CONQUISTA, which was dedicated to reconquering "Mexican people back to their indigenous roots." He also explains that "Nahuatl and Otomí Indians living in central and northern Mexico maintained *danza conchero* and *danza azteca,* and instituted *La Conquista* in order to proliferate the culture throughout Mexico" (1997, 44). *Danzantes* such as Yescas were on a mission to spread the word and practice of *danza* to Mexican Americans north of the border. As Maestas explains, La Conquista was initially a movement in Mexico. It was not until the late 1960s and 1970s that *danzantes* Yescas and Andrés Segura extended the mission of La Conquista across the border into the United States, pioneering the teaching of *danza* to Chicanos, who, for the first time, were aggressively pursuing the indigenous side of their Mexican ancestry. As many Chicanos were taught the dances, they were transformed from spectators of *danza* into *danzantes* themselves.

Maestas also points out the influence of the Mexican Revolution of 1910 on the movements to reclaim indigenous aspects of Mexican culture, of which the mission of La Conquista was a part. "After the revolution there were many never-before-experienced freedoms of religion and culture throughout Mexico. So, during the 1910s and 1920s many of *los concheros* rebelled against their traditional forms and turned to their indigenous roots. Many turned underground to the *huehuenches*, *sonajeros*, and *bastoneros* for knowledge. The result was the birth of what has come to be known as *la danza azteca*. As part of this transformation, some *danzantes* began to reclaim their languages, cut their abrasive robes into dress seen in the ancient Mexican writings, and reclaim their bright plumage and drums" (1997, 34).

The decision to reclaim their heritage marked a split between *danza conchero* and the form of *danza azteca* that Aguilar's group practices. While attending practices with Danza Mexicayotl there were times when Aguilar would point out whether a particular step was from *danza conchero* or *danza azteca*. According to Maestas, *danzantes* who follow *danza conchero* are obligated to support Catholic events, while *danzantes* who follow *danza azteca* must support cultural events (40). *Danza azteca* derived from *danza conchero* and in my experience there is much overlap in terms of beliefs and practices. This emphasis on maintaining distinguishable forms of *danza* relates to Stuart Hall's discussion of the effects of diasporic conditions on the creation of black popular cultures. Speaking to the issue of inevitable cultural fusions that occur when groups are spread out transnationally, especially as the result of colonizing influences, Hall notes:

> there are no pure forms at all . . . forms [of cultural productions] . . . are always the product of partial synchronization, of engagement across cultural boundaries, of the confluence of more than one cultural tradition, of the negotiations of dominant and subordinate positions, of the subterranean strategies of recoding and transcoding, of critical signification, of signifying. Always these forms are impure, to some degree hybridized from a vernacular base. Thus, they must be heard, not simply as the recovery of a lost dialogue bearing clues for the production of new musics (because there is never any going back to the old in a simple way), but as what they are—adaptations, moulded to the mixed, contradictory, hybrid spaces of popular culture (Hall 1996a, 471).

This argument contextualizes *danza* as not simply a newly uncovered, pre-Hispanic antiquity, but as a cultural production that reveals the historical process of *mestizaje*, or mixing. The historical process of *mestizaje* is a reflection of *danzas* as "adaptations, moulded to the mixed, contradictory, hybrid spaces of popular culture" (Ibid.). This is how *danza* teaches us about the way culture evolves as a historical process.

The 1960s and 1970s mark a pivotal moment in the creation and adoption of new Chicano identities, which involved an embracing of the racial and ethnic *mestizaje*. It was Maestro Andrés Segura who introduced *danza conchero* to Chicanos during the 1960s as part of a movement to encourage indigenous peoples to "rediscover their heritage" (Broyles-Gonzalez 1994, 64).[7] Also following La Conquista, Florencio Yescas began teaching *danza azteca* and indigenous spirituality to Chicanos in various U.S. cities starting in the 1970s. Yescas especially inspired many artists at the Centro Cultural de la Raza, including Chicano poet Alurista. Maestas notes that Yescas prompted Alurista to form an "artists commune" they called Toltecas en Aztlán (Toltecs in Aztlán), after the Toltecs (1997, 47). Marylou Valencia, one of the original *danzantes* who learned and practiced at the Centro under Yescas, describes how he was received by the Chicanos at the Centro. "Out of the focus on *danza azteca,* there were a lot of artists, muralists, song-writers, this explosion. We shot all over like sparks out of a fire. Out of that, *danza azteca* has spread throughout California and into Arizona and New Mexico" (Polkinhorn, Muños, and Reyes 1994, 156). Valencia also mentions that *danza azteca* groups have made their ways as far as Missouri, Wisconsin, New York, and Florida (Ibid.). Valencia's words connote the sense of excitement surrounding this vibrant dance that for some Chicanos was a very powerful way to reconnect with Mexico, a place that many had either never known firsthand or had only visited. For Mario Aguilar this connection became a literal one when he was encouraged by Yescas to actually travel to Mexico and be recognized as a *capitán de la danza*. Aguilar admits he was not quite prepared for this major step, but accepted it willingly: "I don't consciously remember saying, 'I'm going to be a *danzante* for life.' You know? 'I'm going to follow this path, my spiritual path.' It was like 'Oh, this is so cool, this is awesome, I love doing this and I love dancing.' . . . I just got into it and there was never a second thought. I was like, I never thought, 'I'm going to be a *danzante* for life, I want to be a *capitán*.' That's the last thing I ever thought I would be, cuz I just thought I'd dance. When Florencio told me I had to go to Mexico to get recognized, I was like 'Oh my God, okay.'"[8]

To be recognized, he had to attend a ceremony in Mexico and receive permission from a veteran *capitán* to begin his own circle. This recognition is difficult to receive and many groups, especially Chicano groups in the United States, do not follow this tradition of traveling to Mexico to be formally recognized. Danza Azteca at UCSD was not officially recognized. When I asked him about formal recognition, Rafael Navar was not concerned with it, stating, "I didn't get permission directly, but in essence, we don't really need that permission, you know? If you're gonna do a circle, then you're gonna do a circle and you're gonna be committed to it serious[ly]."[9] While the *danza* practiced by the student group was much more overtly political, by contrast Danza Mexicayotl stayed very much connected to what they viewed as more traditional Mexican forms of *danza* focused on cultural and spiritual obligations.

Part of this disjuncture can be explained by the generational differences between the groups. Danza Mexicayotl formed just following *danza's* introduction to Chicanos. This, along with the fact that Mario learned *danza* from Florencio Yescas, influenced his group's commitment to maintaining Mexican *danza*, including its connection to Catholic events. When I asked Mario and his son Andrés under which category their group fit, Mario responded, "I think that our group is more Mexican in its traditions than some of the other groups, in the sense that we don't hide or fear our connection to Christianity and the Catholic Church. We participate in the *doce de diciembre*,[10] we have our *velaciones*, which some groups don't because it's Catholic; it's Christian. We play *mandolinas* and guitars, which some groups reject because they're non-indigenous Hispanic. We really don't go out of our way to re-create or rescue pre-Colombian ceremonies like some groups do."[11] Mario's statement that his group does not "go out of [its] way to re-create or rescue pre-Columbian ceremonies" demonstrates that they negotiate between what the past has to offer and their contemporary contexts as Chicanos, actively producing the group's identity, rather than simply rediscovering "that which the colonial experience buried" (Hall 1989, 69). Though he may not have started out wanting to be a "*danzante* for life," Aguilar eventually accepted the obligations of a *capitán* and began learning *danza* with the intention of spreading its traditions through La Conquista, which closely paralleled the Chicano notion of "Aztlán."

Aztlán refers to the mythical place of origin for the Chichimecs, the ancestors of the Aztecs. According to Mexican history, it was from Aztlán that the Chichimecs began their journey south into the valley of Mexico where the Aztec empire of Tenochtitlán was eventually established. Aztlán was an important part of Chicano nationalism, made most popular among Chicanos by Alurista when he presented his epic El Plan Espiritual de Aztlán at the first Chicano National Conference held in Denver in 1969 (Alurista 1995). Alurista's poem became the preamble to El Plan de Aztlán, which listed key points such as unity, economy, education, institutions, self-defense, and cultural and political liberation necessary for reclaiming Chicano cultural identity and, in essence, taking back the land of the Chichimecs.[12] Michael Pina characterizes Aztlán as functioning on two intertwining mythic frameworks. On one level it involved "[a] call for the re-creation of an Aztec spiritual homeland . . . on another . . . the desire to politically reconquer the northern territories wrested from Mexico in an imperialist war inspired by American 'Manifest Destiny'" (1989, 36). Menchaca, in *Recovering History, Constructing Race: The Indian, Black and White Roots of Mexican Americans,* explains that because the area encompassing Aztlán could not be specifically delineated, Chicanos took this place north of the valley of Mexico to mean the Southwestern United States (2001, 19–26).

The points of Alurista's El Plan bore a resemblance to the *danza* code of La Conquista. The call for a "re-creation of an Aztec spiritual homeland" strongly correlated with *danza azteca*, which Nájera-Ramírez states "seemed an ideal way to make tangible their [Chicano's] connection to their indigenous roots" (2002, 3). The quest for a new cultural identity and the construction of Chicano nationalism was in part a response to the more assimilationist attitudes of Mexican Americans in the 1950s. Many Chicanos saw that their parent's attempts to assimilate as Americans had been in vain, and, worse yet, this was done at the expense of their own Mexican cultural identities. The idea of Aztlán was a more radical response involving the quest for a renewed sense of identity—Chicano identity. Richard Griswold del Castillo adds that beyond "educating people to be proud of their Mexican heritage . . . Chicanos linked the corporate exploitation of Chicanos in the fields and the barrios to the multinationals' domination of Mexico's economy" (1996, 44–45). Chicanos saw a connection between their own struggles in the United States and struggles going on in Mexico and the rest of Latin America.[13]

Danza azteca provided an extremely interactive and visible way to connect with Mexico, and it was connected to a much larger *danza* movement that had already been going on in Mexico for centuries. What we think of as *danza azteca* is a mix of different influences, not a preserved, unchanged tradition. Still, many of the dances have been passed down through generations of *danzantes* in Mexico. Aguilar explained his understanding of how *danza* has survived and evolved over the centuries:

> [I]n 1521 when Cortés finally captured Cuauhtémoc, the city was destroyed, there was pestilence, there was smallpox . . . the few people who were left hid in the villages in the surrounding valley and the mountains where they had friends and contacts in other pueblos, and [others] stayed because the Spanish offered . . . some kind of order. When there was enough time passed and the pestilence and the dead bodies had disappeared . . . they could start making the colonial Mexico city. . . . In 1623 there were more black slaves in Mexico City and more Spanish people in Mexico City than there were Native Americans. There was a little barrio that's called San Jose de los Naturales. All the Aztecas, the true Aztecas, the Mexicans who had lived there before the conquest, were forced to live [in that] . . . barrio. They had one of the open chapel churches which was very important in the evolution of *danza azteca* . . . the rest of the city was [the] Spanish and their slaves, and then over the

> generations the mestizos started appearing, and so there were barrios where mestizos lived, but the barrios de los naturales kept getting smaller and smaller and smaller [as the people] passed away or mixed with the mestizos and the Spanish and blacks. So by 1590 there was no identifiable Mexica essence in Mexico City. It was a colonial town starting up fresh, and the Indians, the indigenous people that went to the villa to dance, were from all the other little towns. And even to the 1910s it was pretty much the people from outside Mexico City.[14]

Danza survived in Mexico by adapting and evolving, which meant that in some cases the indigenous dances became hybridized, sometimes by influences from the Spanish. One such influence is reflected in the incorporation by many *danza* groups of the sign of the Christian cross to go along with the honoring of the four directions, north, east, south, and west, as part of asking permission to take part in the dance. Another example is the inclusion of the *mandolina* to accompany the indigenous *huehuetl*, or sacred drum. While there exist sects of *danzantes* in Mexico and the United States who advocate for the practice of what they see as a purer form of *danza* more closely based on the pre-Hispanic, indigenous dances, many groups like Danza Mexicayotl practice a form of *danza* that acknowledges the European traditions that have influenced the fusions of new *danza* traditions—they openly embrace, rather than reject, the hybridity of *danza azteca* because they see it as part of their history that cannot and should not be separated from them. This hybridity within *danza* reflects the hybridity existing within many Chicano families and communities that have mixed racial and ethnic identities and that have adopted, or at least been influenced by, Catholicism. However, not everyone agreed that the group should rely solely on Mexican *danza* traditions. A *danzante* who danced with Danza Mexicayotl for thirteen years shared with me how she distinguished herself and Chicano *danza* from *Mexicano danzantes* and *danza* in Mexico:

> It's [Chicano *danza*] going to be very different from the *danza* tradition in Mexico, which I highly respect. They are not Chicanos and they don't understand the politics that we have to deal with here. They don't understand the issues of culture and identity that we have to deal with here and how this waste we feel from our spirits, because of the institutions that we have to survive through. We're so disconnected from ourselves, you know? We don't know how to be.[15]

Though she still has great respect for Mexican *danza*, she sees herself as part of the new and changing generation of Chicano *danzantes*. Her reasons for moving away from the more Mexican traditions paralleled the very reasons many *danzantes* follow the Mexican traditions: she saw that new influences were beginning to shape a new form of *danza*.

As a group, Danza Mexicayotl maintains ties with *danzantes* in Mexico. When I began attending their practices in 2002–2003, Mario, the *capitán*, was planning a group trip to Querétaro, Mexico, which is considered the birthplace of *danza conchero*.[16] Those who could afford the trip traveled to Mexico and participated in *danza* festivals there. In addition to Mario's group going to Mexico, *danzantes* from Mexico travel across the border to dance in the Chicano Park ceremony hosted by Danza Mexicayotl every July. I personally purchased the *huaraches* (leather sandals) I dance in from a *danzante* who travels from Mexico every year to participate in ceremonies north of the border.

Danza Azteca at UCSD also maintains connections with Mexico through their political activism. For example, they danced as part of a demonstration at the U.S.-Mexico border in protest of Operation Gatekeeper. Their strongest connections with Mexico came through their expressed solidarity with the Zapatistas. As a group, Danza Azteca at UCSD hosted lectures by people involved with the Zapatistas and held showings of documentaries telling the story of the Zapatista uprising in Chiapas. With Danza Azteca at UCSD I got a sense of their politics from the very first meeting. The first practice was announced by flyers posted around school. When I arrived at the Cross Cultural Center on campus, there were white, black, Asian, and Latino students present. This was just the first practice and many students eventually stopped attending, but several of the non-Chicano members attended for several weeks and the group welcomed their membership rather than limiting the group to Chicanos and/or Latinos only. As the dancing ended that first night, several of the *danzantes* yelled out in excitement. I heard one person yell, "*¡Viva Zapata!*" and others joined in, repeating the cry. They also had a form of *palabra* where each person had a chance to share announcements and concerns, but theirs was much more informal in comparison to Danza Mexicayotl's. They did not pass around the *sahumador* of copal; rather they placed it in the center of their circle to create a sacred space while they danced.[17]

This group also encouraged its members to learn Nahuatl, but did so from a very different approach. Instead of students gathering around a teacher, Danza Azteca at UCSD practiced Nahuatl during their opening exercises as they used the Nahuatl names for numbers to count off jumping jacks and push-ups. Much like army recruits yelling responses to a drill sergeant, the

UCSD *danzantes* yelled in unison while assembled in a circle. The counting would vary from group counts to individual counts as each person in the circle was responsible for calling off the next number in the sequence; this was done to the very quick pace set by the drummer. If an incorrect name for a number was given, the *danzante* responsible, along with the rest of the circle, would then have to repeat the exercise and the number until they got it right. This forced every participant to be interactive at a certain level. Responses were forced rather than volunteered. Their practices reflected much more of a militant attitude and a pressure to take action.

The section of *palabra* was used to inform members of political struggles going on in the world and to announce upcoming protests in the area. *Danzantes* often brought in printouts of literature about the Zapatista movement, or statements from political prisoners, that they all took turns reading aloud in the circle. They did this to empower themselves with knowledge and to feel connected to larger struggles. They viewed being political as their primary obligation. I witnessed an example of the way they spread their politics at a "Justice for Janitors" rally held outside of the main library on the UCSD campus during lunchtime. Danza Azteca at UCSD danced about three dances, then addressed the crowd with a microphone, explaining why they were dancing and the cause they were supporting. This was very different from the performance I had observed with Danza Mexicayotl. After the protest, I interviewed the group's leader, Rafael Navar. I asked how he related to other *danza* groups, specifically with groups connected to the Catholic Church. He responded:

> The way we see any group is the way we see any organization. . . . Just because we don't share the exact same politics as you doesn't mean we can't work with you. . . . If anything you're what we would consider with us, or on our side because you're teaching danza. . . . You're still teaching people our history. . . . But we do feel ourselves different from them in many ways, the fact that we came to this protest today when many groups feel that it's [*danza*] just cultural, it's just spiritual, ceremonial. . . . We see it differently. Just by dancing you're being political, you're saying that we're from this land, hey we have a history. We didn't originally speak Spanish, we spoke another language. We have traditions; we have different ways of looking at the world. So [in] that way [it's] political . . . you're going at the roots of colonization when you're dancing. We apply that to our current struggles today. The fact that we still can't get just wages or live dignified with a job is very much connected to why we couldn't dance in the first place. . . . If our community is there, of course we're gonna be there.[18]

Though Navar's group refused to incorporate overtly European elements, such as the *mandolina* or the acknowledgment of Christianity, into their practice of *danza*, his group still reflects the *mestizaje* that Hall alludes to. By emphasizing the need to form cross-cultural political alliances through welcoming non-Mexicans and non-Latinos into the group, Danza Azteca at UCSD participated in what Hall describes as "the process of *diaspora-ization*," which involves "the process of unsettling, recombination, hybridization, and cut-and-mix"(Hall 1996b, 447). Essentially, they embraced their *mestizaje* by encouraging racial and ethnic diversity within the group (including white participants at times), yet selectively choosing to reject any of *danza's* European influences.

As the interview continued, I learned that Navar was introduced to *danza* while he was a student at Garfield High in East Los Angeles. He learned *danza* from Marcos Aguilar, a teacher at Garfield who began offering *danza* to whoever wanted to participate. Along with being a teacher, Marcos was also active in the hunger strikes that took place at UCLA during the early 1990s to get a Chicano Studies department on campus. As the student of an activist, Navar's background definitely influenced Danza Azteca at UCSD's deep investment in reaching the community through political activism.

One major difference between Danza Mexicayotl and Danza Azteca at UCSD lay in whom they saw as their community. Mexicayotl focused on spreading the teachings of *danza* to the Chicano/Mexicano community. For example, the Cuauhtémoc ceremony that I opened this chapter with is a well-known ceremony within the *danza* community organized each year by Xipe Totec, also a veteran group, based in Los Angeles and led by a female *capitana*.[19] The scene I described in my introduction paints a picture of a cohesive Chicano community in Los Angeles. *Danzantes* did not hold signs of protest or chant for a specific cause, but they were highly organized as they took command of the street, marching in perfect unison. Their presence could not be ignored as they crossed through busy intersections, forcing honking SUVs to miss their green lights. Once we reached the park we had an audience waiting for us. We danced at least four hours with only one fifteen-minute break. Visibility was important, but the primary objective was to build community within the *danza* circle.

Danza Azteca at UCSD saw their community as much wider, including people outside the Chicano/Mexicano communities. This expansion of their community was motivated by their goal of forging political alliances with other organizations. Though these *danzantes* did assert their indigenous identities through *danza*, they viewed their group as an organization rather than an ethnically specific cultural activity. By identifying as indigenous, they could stand in solidarity with other indigenous groups who struggle for justice across the globe.

How *danza* should be used to create empowerment is one of the major discrepancies between groups. The student *danzantes* I spoke with wanted to see their dances influence change in the larger community through protests and rallies. As one student *danzante* shared with me, "[i]f you just do it as a ceremony, many people won't find out about it."[20] Also very invested in the community, Danza Mexicayotl limited their dancing to educational performances at schools and cultural events, and within the context of ceremonies. Who each group saw as their community varied, but at the base of each was an adherence to claiming indigeneity and using that indigeneity to empower themselves, either politically, culturally, or spiritually.

In my observations, both Danza Mexicayotl and Danza Azteca at UCSD were political and spiritual; the differences were in where each group focused its energies. Danza Azteca at UCSD held the ideology that *danza* should stay true to its indigenous roots and should not include elements of Christianity or European-style instruments, which they saw as symbols of oppression. As a group they were invested more so in *unearthing* a purer form of *danza* as they believed it existed before its co-optation by Europeans. On another level, Danza Azteca at UCSD was also active in the *production* of new *danzante* identities through their inclusion of all races and their aim of creating interracial political alliances. In a sense, they strove to keep their dances indigenous, but not necessarily the *danzantes* who danced them. Danza Mexicayotl, however, was not interested in *unearthing*, but rather following traditions that had been passed down to them by veteran *danzantes* in Mexico, most of whom are connected in some way to the Catholic Church. As a cohesive unit influential in the community of *danzantes*, especially in California but not only there, Danza Mexicayotl was responsible for *(re)telling* the history and culture of Chicanos through their participation in educational and ceremonial settings. They continue to actively *produce* new traditions, such as the Chicano Park ceremony, which they host every year in July.

By focusing my study on two groups in San Diego, California, it was impossible to demonstrate the diversity of *danza azteca* within the United States, or Southern California for that matter. However, it was clear from my observations with Danza Mexicayotl and Danza Azteca at UCSD, along with other groups I encountered at larger ceremonies, that *danza* teaches *danzantes* the importance of leading a life in balance with the rest of the universe. Regardless of each group's ideological differences, both achieved balance through sacrifice and the fulfillment of obligations, whether those obligations were to one's own family, the group, school, the wider community, or to the Creator. What all *danzantes* seem to share is a pride in their indigenous heritage and a strong desire to express, rather than suppress, this heritage.

Notes

1. "emperor or exalted one." Cuauhtémoc was the nephew and successor of Monteczuma II, the Aztec ruler who initially greeted Hernán Cortés in 1519.

2. I use the term *Mexicano* to describe the *danzantes* who had traveled from Mexico to participate in the ceremony, and also to describe *danzantes* who originally come from Mexico but who are now living in the United States. My use of *Chicano* is referring to *danzantes* who were born in the United States and who are of Mexican ancestry. As I conducted this research I encountered several identifications used by *danzantes*, including Native, Native American, Mexica, indigenous, and names of specific groups, such as the Yaqui.

3. When I participated with the student group at a community celebration, and when I observed their performances at political rallies, they were introduced as "Danza Azteca." At the start of the 2003 school year, this group announced their first practice by posting flyers around campus telling students to come and check out "Danza Azteca." I interpreted the group's identification as *danza azteca*, rather than a more specific group name, as a reflection of both their unrecognized status among more traditional groups often connected with the Catholic Church and their desire to be known for what they do rather than who they are.

4. Rafael Navar, interview with María Teresa Ceseña, La Jolla, California, February 26, 2003.

5. Mario Aguilar, interview with María Teresa Ceseña, Chula Vista, California, January 20, 2003.

6. Copal, the resin from the copal tree of Oaxaca, is considered sacred incense.

7. Broyles-Gonzalez also discusses the vital role Segura played in introducing the Chicano theater troupe El Teatro Campesino's to indigenous worldviews and philosophies (1994, 64).

8. Aguilar, interview.

9. Navar, interview.

10. Literally translates to the 12th of December. This date is significant because according to Mexican Catholic tradition, on December 9, 1531, the Virgin Mary appeared to an indigenous man named Juan Diego at Tepeyac, northwest of Mexico City. The Virgin told Juan Diego to have the bishop of Mexico City build a church at the site of the apparition. Three days later, on the 12th, she then told Juan Diego to pick some flowers for the bishop. When Juan Diego presented the bishop with the flowers, roses fell out of his mantle; upon his mantle appeared a painted image of the Virgin. See Jeanette Rodríguez 1994.

11. Aguilar, interview.

12. Maestas argues that Alurista's involvement with the Centro Cultural de la Raza and his many influential writings, published by the artistic group Toltecas en Aztlán, helped set the stage for the reception that *danza* received by Chicanos in San Diego and other cities in the Southwest. Though not a *danzante* himself, Alurista supported Florencio Yescas by giving him a place to stay.

13. In *Youth, Identity, and Power,* Carlos Muñoz Jr. argues the shift from integrationist efforts to an embrace of third-world radical politics was greatly influenced by the visit to Cuba by Luis Valdez and Roberto Ruvalcaba in 1964. Valdez, one of the founders of El Teatro Campesino, was especially influential to the Chicano movement's focus on a renewed identity. During their visit they observed the Second Declaration of Havana, in which Fidel Castro stated, "Mexico is the country robbed of half of its territory by the United States; Mexico is the country that has suffered in its flesh and its blood from the claws of imperialism." Valdez was also able to witness firsthand that Cuba was the first Latin American country to provide free education, food, and jobs for its people. As a result of the visit Valdez came to identify Castro as the true leader of Latin America, one capable of enacting change and resistance against imperialism. Valdez and Ruvalcaba published their experiences in a manifesto titled "*Venceremos!* Mexican-American Statement on Travel to Cuba."

14. Aguilar, interview.

15. *Danzante* (name withheld by mutual agreement), interview with María Teresa Ceseña, La Jolla, California, May 14, 2003.

16. *Concheros* trace the beginning of their dance tradition to the Battle of San Gremal, which took place in 1531. According to their history, it was during this battle between converted Indians and non-Christian Indians that the sky turned dark and a cross appeared in the sky, causing both sides to stop fighting. The *concheros* dance in veneration of the cross (Stone 1975, 197).

17. Danza Mexicayotl also followed the tradition of placing a *sahumador* (incense holder) filled with burning copal at the center of their circle. This is the job of the *malinche de copal*, which is traditionally the role of a female.

18. Navar, interview.

19. Traditional *danza* groups are led by either a *capitán* or a *capitana*, meaning captain. Female *capitanas* are not as common as *capitanes*. Marylou Valencia, a student of Florencio Yescas, was the first Chicana *capitana*. She was recognized as a "Capitana de la danza," by Mario Aguilar during the fiesta for Chicano Park in 1992.

20. Patricia Segura, interview with María Teresa Ceseña, La Jolla, California, May 30, 2003.

PART II

Dimensions of Space and Place

6

The Semiotics of Land and Place

Matachines Dancing in Laredo, Texas

NORMA E. CANTÚ

> Our dance is . . . a prayer *a la santa cruz*.
>
> —Florencio Ortiz Jr.

Introduction

For centuries, the *matachines*, a religious folk dance tradition practiced in Mexico and Greater Mexico, has offered testimony to the faith, belief, and devotion of the mestizo population. It is among the many cultural practices that are part of daily life for the inhabitants of the South Texas region, along with foodways and musical traditions such as *conjunto* music,[1] that give the region an identifiable identity. The existence of several *matachines* groups in Laredo, Texas, and across the border in Nuevo Laredo provides one more example of how inherently transnational cultural practices exist in the United States and Mexico despite the geopolitical divide. Anthropologist Sylvia Rodríguez defines the *matachines* as such: "A ritual drama performed by a variety of Indian and Hispanic communities throughout parts of Mexico and the Southwestern United States. It exhibits common characteristics of choreography, music, costume, and personae, as well as locally idiosyncratic forms and meanings" (1991, 235). Indeed, the dancing in Laredo and Nuevo Laredo is recognizable as *danza de matachines*, exhibiting the elements found in all, and yet because it is informed by local and historical factors, it invariably incorporates variant forms of dress, choreography, and music.

In this chapter I focus on one particular group from Laredo, Los Matachines de la Santa Cruz, to explore the meanings and messages that the location of the dance itself presents, including the meanings that the object that is venerated through dance, the Holy Cross, may connote for the dancers and the barrio and *colonia*[2] communities at large. I argue that the central icon of the fiesta, the Holy Cross, the location itself, and the space where the fiesta occurs have meaning for the dancers and for the community. Because the dance itself is often seen as a mixture of indigenous and European traditions, such signification exemplifies the *mestizaje* of the community. I also argue that the dance is sacralizing, transforming the space where it is practiced into a sacred place.[3]

While *matachines* traditions inhabit and take place in special spaces reserved for the fiestas—whether in Mexico or in the United States—the tradition also transforms the space where it occurs. In most fiestas, the dance occurs in an area set apart and designated "sacred" by the dance itself, but "profane" when put to secular use, such as as a street. In similar fashion to dancers in other Mexican dance traditions, such as the *conchero* dance, the *matachines* also dance in front of a church as part of the fiesta, whether in front of the Basílica of the Virgen de Guadalupe in Mexico City, in front of the reservation church in San Juan Pueblo, in the courtyard in front of the church in Guadalupe, Arizona, or in front of the San Judas Tadeo church in a northwest subdivision in Laredo, Texas. When the fiesta occurs outside and inside of the church, we can say that where the dance takes place is considered sacred space to begin with, but in other locations, such as when the dancers are invited to private homes or in the processions, the space is made sacred by the dance.

What makes the space sacred is not only the dance itself but also the presence of the icon that is the object of veneration; in the Laredo tradition that is the focus of this chapter, it is the Holy Cross, while in other traditions it is the sacred image that goes on procession from the church through the streets of the barrio or town. Whether the space is viewed as sacred or profane depends on factors that date back to pre-European contact, particularly religious factors intimately informed by the contact of two worldviews, two belief systems. For example, the worship of mother earth and the adherence to seasonal feasts in indigenous traditions sometimes fit well into the liturgical calendar of Christian feast days. Such is the case with spring rituals and Easter, as processions of Holy Week and other Christian spring *romerías*[4] have merged with indigenous spring celebrations. Another factor is the faith-based worship of the Holy Cross with origins in medieval European tradition. The folk religious celebrations it gave rise to are still practiced in Spanish towns, such as Almagro, where the town plaza becomes sacred space as the cross is prominently displayed and celebrated for its feast day, May 3. So indigenous peoples' spring celebrations honored mother earth and her gifts. But, as Linda T. Smith has noted, the indigenous way of looking at time and space shifts when the imperialist power establishes colonizing notions of the Western tradition and imposes its own schemata over the indigenous (1999). Thus, what was sacred space to an indigenous community can remain so under the new European "god," but the sense of the sacred may not remain the same and the resulting celebrations acquire a new meaning. The feasts become hybrid folk religious celebrations that wed the colonizers' traditions to those in the area before European contact. The *matachines* dance tradition exemplifies the confluence of traditions: the earlier Spanish and indigenous, and more recently what can be called Mexican and Tejano aesthetics of space and the concurrent meanings for sacred space. The land becomes a site of multiple spatial meanings and locations, a layering of texts from various spiritual traditions.

Limiting my discussion to the Día de la Santa Cruz and the Virgen de Guadalupe celebrations in Laredo, Texas, I situate the traditional *matachines* fiesta in the space within the community of Laredo and the whole barrio of La Ladrillera. In order to further explore the way the space is configured for the celebration, I then briefly look at the actual *terreno*, the physical location where the dancing occurs that is the size of a regular lot in the neighborhood, for it is in this specific place where the icon, the object of veneration, resides. Finally, I look at this icon, the Holy Cross, for the icon sacralizes the space and provides an anchor to the faith belief at the center of the fiesta. In semiotic terms, it is the cross that as a signifier renders the fiesta and the dancing meaningful; the belief in the cross functions as the signified.

The Matachines de la Santa Cruz dance in spring and winter, for the fiesta honoring the Holy Cross in May and for the day honoring the Virgen de Guadalupe in December. Situated geographically in significant spaces, the community of the Matachines de la Santa Cruz exists in a very real space only about one hundred feet from the Rio Grande, in the barrio traditionally known as La Ladrillera, after a brick factory that was located in the barrio until it ceased production in the mid 1980s.[5] In the past ten years, the barrio name has shifted to "La Santa Cruz," further emphasizing the iconic presence of the Holy Cross in the people's sense of their community. The route that the dancers have traditionally taken in the processions and the *terreno*, as well as the barrio itself, can be seen as spaces of defined parameters. The center of the fiesta is a ten-foot-tall wooden cross that looks even larger mounted on a homemade frame, or *andamia*, for the fiesta. But the cross isn't just a physical artifact; rather this manifestation represents that what really holds the community together is its devotion to La Santa Cruz.

The Barrio

In their study of the built environment of the border towns, Arreola and Curtis claim, "In both material and organizational ways, the Mexican border towns reflect, symbolize and affirm the culture from which they sprang" (1993, 43). I would venture to add that the barrios in these communities follow similar patterns and reflect the cultural expressions that occur there. That is to say, the specific barrios also reflect the "culture from which they sprang"; La Ladrillera reflects the transplanted culture that includes the *matachines danza*. While plazas functioned as the main public spaces in the early settlements and well into the twentieth century, many of the barrios outside of the initial settlement area didn't include a public space in front of the church. Often, the barrio *tiendita* (neighborhood store) or the church itself became the public space where the neighborhood children congregated to play and the adults found entertainment.[6] When in the nineteenth century Laredo was growing outwardly from the original eighteenth-century settlement, the streets were renamed and the residential areas platted. The area west of the railroad tracks was settled in the 1930s by a group of miners who had been deterritorialized from the coal mining communities upriver. The dance tradition of the Matachines de la Santa Cruz came with this group of working-class families.

In a survey conducted in the mid 1970s, I found a total of twenty-five names for the residential areas of Laredo, commonly called "barrios."[7] By the end of the millennium in 1999, the proliferation of new subdivisions, like River Oaks (about eight miles from the *matachines terreno*) and impoverished *colonias* like San Carlos (about ten miles east of the city limits), had increased that number to more than fifty. Some of the barrios had *matachines* dance traditions that have not survived, while some, like the River Oaks subdivision's San Judas Tadeo Church, host dance groups from elsewhere in the city for the annual church festival or *jamaica*.[8] Cultural geographers Arreola and Curtis point out that the border communities, "the barrios (e.g., the *colonias* and *fraccionamientos*) have remained distinct residential entities characterized by a sense of community" (1993, 49). La Ladrillera is one such barrio. Arreola and Curtis also note that "most residents identify with and have a certain allegiance to their respective neighborhood" (49). Although they were specifically looking at the border towns on the Mexican side, some of the traditional elements that they claim persist apply to the towns on the U.S. side as well; at least in some respects it is true for Laredo, as residents of the various barrios, even after moving away, cling to their barrio membership.[9]

The land, the location where the people live then, becomes a source of identity, and along with other self-referents, residents usually say they belong to a certain barrio. While there may even be smaller sections identified by the inhabitants, everyone in town is familiar with the general parameters for the older barrios. According to Arreola, in the 1980s Laredo officially identified nineteen barrios (2002, 88). Many radio stations will play *dedicatorias*, dedications that identify the barrio or *colonia* the person is calling from and where the intended recipient resides (see Cantú 1991). I remember listening to such programs since the mid-1950s, especially one of the first Spanish-language programs broadcast in Laredo, "Serenata Nocturna," a program that has recently re-emerged on the local radio waves.[10] Since the late 1980s, a proliferation of radio shows, both night and daytime, continue the practice, as the majority of those calling from either Nuevo Laredo or Laredo identify their *colonia* or barrio. The radio programs are only one very clear sign that the town is divided into neighborhoods and that the residents of those neighborhoods identify with that space. The Santa Cruz barrio and the *matachines* are no exception.

Los Matachines de la Santa Cruz de la Ladrillera, 1942. Personal collection of the Florencio Ortíz Jr. family.

Yet with the onset of subdivisions and urban sprawl, there may be some shifting as the traditional markers—churches, buildings, or other characteristics—give way to commercially imposed names. Older barrios retain their identity, but they may not always retain their traditional celebrations. For example Corpus Christi processions have ceased at Christ the King Church (in what was at one time the outskirts of the eastern part of town and is now centrally located) and in all the Catholic churches in town. While there are still some of us who recall the processions and the sense of community they elicited in the participants, the community is changing. While these changes are more evident in the more acculturated areas of town, especially as the older residents die and their children move to the suburbs, some of the barrios, including La Ladrillera, maintain traditions such as the *matachines* fiesta and procession. The sense of unity the barrios have held historically for almost two centuries may be drawing to a close due to another recent phenomenon. According to the 2000 census, in this city that was the second fastest growing in the country, newcomers who do not have the same sense of allegiance to the barrio, either via family or social ties, may bring with them other traditions, and the old folk religious practices fall by the wayside. That is why barrios like La Ladrillera and their adherence to traditions like the *matachines* merit study. Historian Andrés Tijerina has identified the unity forged by Tejanos in communities like Laredo during the nineteenth century. He attributes the close-knit nature of barrio communities to the fact that "the early Spaniards had brought with them the strong neighborhood concept of the barrio" and that "when superimposed over the Mexican Indian's traditional concept, the *calpulli*, the result was a reinforced sense of social unity" (1994, 46). He is referring to the mostly mestizo, Tlaxcalan, and Aztec immigrants who came to Tejas in the seventeenth and eighteenth centuries; Tejas in the early nineteenth century was a borderlands with communities divided into barrios with clear group identity (28). He further points out that in addition to an *alcalde* who served as leader of the town, the *comisario* of each barrio served as "judge of the barrio," in charge of the social welfare of the inhabitants of the barrios (46). Dance traditions such as the *matachines* cement these relationships in specific barrios.

The border towns' particular development and the particular urban cultural space their inhabitants have constructed would indicate a move away from the earlier social identity of the people living in the barrio. But even after families have moved away and new immigrants from Central America and recent immigrants from Mexico have moved into the area, the integrity of the group remains. Some would hold that it is a rarity for a barrio like La

Ladrillera to persist; its survival, along with that of its cultural expressions like the *matachines danza*, is attributable to elements and forces that at once depend on the shared historical memory and on the faith and deep commitment of the families that first came to the area from Las Minas in the 1930s, bringing their sense of community and loyalty. The strong communal bonds made it easier to recruit new dancers. Nevertheless, it is the recognition of the dance tradition and of its place in a community that played a major factor in this process.

Most of the dancers are the offspring of the people who came from the mining communities; it is the same families, the Liendo, Martínez, Ortiz, and Castillo families, among others, that dance today. But there are some who have joined after witnessing the faith and dedication of the dancers. One family whose daughter recovered from a terminal illness, for example, has vowed to honor the Holy Cross although no one in the family had ever danced or participated in the procession. So the tradition persists in the barrio as a signifier of the faith belief and as a place where individuals can perform their act of thanksgiving and of celebration, the *danza de matachines*.

El Terreno/The Land

The *terreno*, the lot on Camp Avenue, but a couple of blocks away from the riverbank, is the site where the holy images reside and where the most significant dancing occurs, including the last *son* (dance tune), "*La Despedida*," or the farewell. While there are various designated spaces where the *matachines* dance within the confines of La Ladrillera, such as the street and the church, the *terreno* is the most identified with the tradition, for it is where the *capillita*, a small chapel that houses the Holy Cross, the three-by-five-foot painted image of the Virgen de Guadalupe, and a smaller cross, la Cruz Chiquita, reside during the year. The *terreno* is directly behind the Ortiz family home; the area in front of the home on West Anna Street also becomes the site of the dance during the fiesta. A third site of worship is a few blocks away on Lee Avenue, La Capilla de la Santa Cruz, an official, church-sanctioned chapel under the jurisdiction of the nearby parish, Holy Redeemer Church. It is in the *capilla* that Masses are said and that the Virgen de Guadalupe is honored on her day. And finally, the most dispersed location, the street, includes the twenty blocks or so that make up the procession's path from the *terreno* to the Holy Redeemer Church grounds, where the *matachines* dance before and after the procession. The street in front of the church is also a site of dancing, but in spite of the *capilla* and Holy Redeemer Church being the church-sanctioned places of worship, it is the *terreno* that holds a special place in the hearts and minds of the community, for it is here that the fiesta begins and ends every year. Because the church grounds and the *capilla* are sacred space by definition and de facto since the dance also occurs there, I will focus on the *terreno*, the folk religious space where the *danza* is deployed. It is in the *terreno's capillita*, not *la capilla* on Lee Avenue, where the image of the Virgen de Guadalupe and the Holy Cross "rest" during the year.

The *terreno*, communally owned by the not-for-profit corporation the Santa Cruz Association, became the focus of a bitter dispute in the community in the 1960s. It is unclear whether the dispute was ever resolved to everyone's satisfaction. The *terreno*, approximately sixty by forty feet, faces

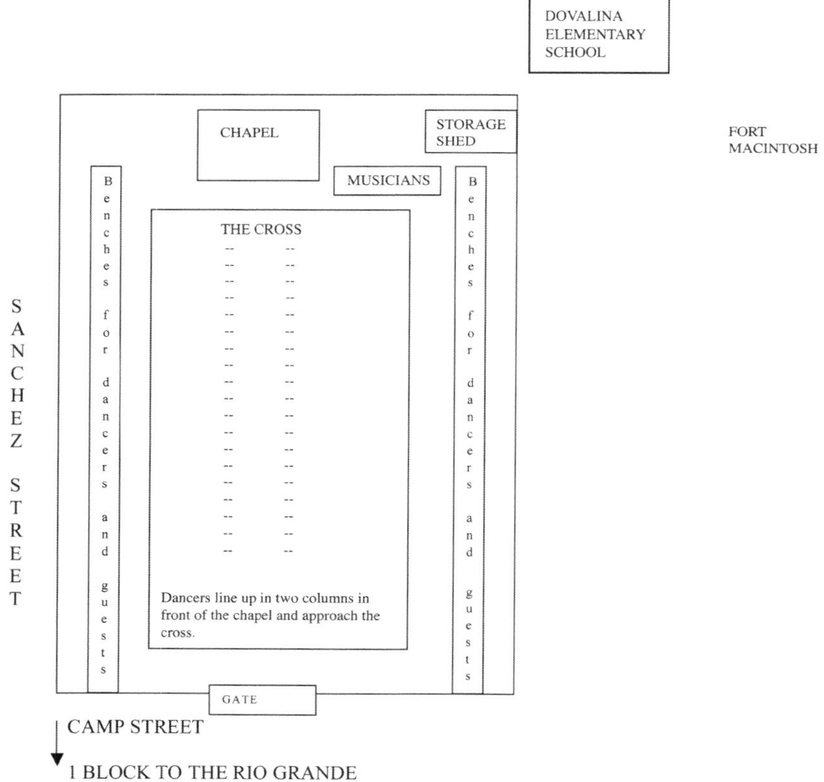

The *terreno* where the Holy Cross resides year-round and where the *matachines* dance during the May celebration.

Camp Avenue one block east from the banks of the river that flows southward in this area. To the south there is an old stone wall that survives from the original Fort McIntosh walls. The wall continues up and marks the boundary of the Ortiz lot. On this spot along the wall, Dovalina Elementary School was built in the 1980s; Roberto Ortiz, one of the leaders of the fiesta, teaches there. On the east, the *terreno* is adjacent to the Ortiz backyard. On the north side is a private home, and a chain link fence marks the boundary there as well. The *capillita*, a small chapel made of cinder block, sits facing the west a few feet from the chain link fence that separates the *terreno* from the Ortiz lot. The location of *la capillita* is significant because it determines how the dancers move, from west to east, as they dance.

Approximately eight by ten feet, *la capillita* was built in the 1980s to house the Holy Cross. The outside is painted a pale seashell pink with lavender trim and the inside is pastel blue. Inside, the Holy Cross sits on a raised concrete platform in the center of the chapel; it is held in place by the *andamia*. Wrought iron candleholders stand on each side of the cross. For the dancing the cross is taken out, "dressed," that is, decorated with fabric and flowers, and placed in front of the structure. The addition of an electric

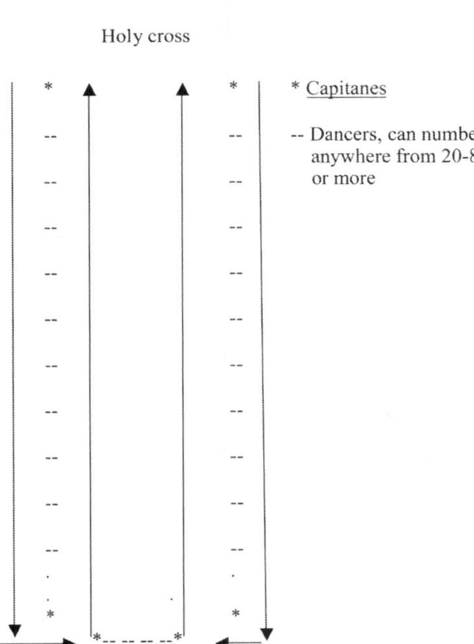

Basic dance greeting for all *sones* (dance tunes). The dancers are lined up in front of the cross. For each *son* they execute different steps, but before beginning the *son,* they "greet" the cross. The basic matachin dance step is used to approach the cross and while on procession. For the greeting, the *capitanes* dance on the outside, to the rear and bring forth, between the columns, four dancers who kneel and pray in front of the cross while the *capitanes* dance back to bring the next group of four until all the dancers have greeted the cross. Then dancing of the specific steps for the *son* begins.

floodlight allows the dancing to continue into the night without having to string up regular light bulbs the way they do when dancing occurs on Anna Street, in front of the Ortiz home. The *terreno* is considered holy ground, as the *matachines* dance and the cross resides there; as Javier Castillo says, it is where the Holy Cross "*descansa durante el año,*" where it rests during the year, between the fiestas.[11] The image of the Virgin "rests" there, coming out each year on the 12th of December for its procession and fiesta. Few Masses have been said in the *terreno*, but at least twice in the more than thirty years I have been attending the fiesta, the priest from Holy Redeemer has come by to say Mass and bless the *terreno*. But that was an unusual case where the priest was from Mexico and knew the tradition well. This case bears mentioning because the priest was not just accepting of the tradition, he was intimately involved in the celebration, a highly unusual occurrence. It provides further proof that it isn't the church's approval that will render the site sacred, it is the dancing. In the past, when the priest has not been of Mexican descent and has had little knowledge of the tradition, there have been conflicts as to the place of the very much identified "folk" celebration within the liturgical celebration in church. At times, the parish priest has not only not supported the *matachines*, but has only barely tolerated the *matachines* bringing the Holy Cross for the Saturday night stay in the church, a clear case of conflict between the "folk" and "formal" Catholicism, to use Redfield's terms. In his discussion on folk religion, Don Yoder cites Redfield's work in Yucatán and in Tepoztlán to distinguish between the two sites of Catholic religious worship (1974, 261, 267). The issue of church-sanctioned celebrations has come up, especially with the Virgen de Guadalupe celebration, since that fiesta is more clearly aligned with official liturgical practices. The Mass that concludes the procession on the evening of December 11 takes place in the Capilla de la Santa Cruz on Lee Avenue. In spite of community efforts to make the *capilla* a full-fledged parish, the diocese has not granted them permission, claiming that there are not enough people to sustain an independent parish, and so it remains under the auspices of Holy Redeemer Church. Our discussion of the politics of negotiating folk religious practices within the official Catholic bureaucracy is beyond the purview of this chapter, however.

As we return to the discussion of the *terreno* and the *capillita*, we need to discuss la Cruz Chiquita, a smaller cross—about eight feet tall—specially built for the American Folklife Festival in Washington, D.C., in 1987. The group believed that their prayer dance could only happen before a properly dressed and blessed cross, and transporting theirs was out of the question; the community would not have approved removing the Holy Cross from its place. So the Cruz Chiquita was constructed by a Laredo furniture maker and blessed by a priest in Washington D.C., ensuring that the dancing on the Mall between the Capitol and the Washington Monument was also sacred. The cross came back with the group and it remains as part of the celebration.

In preparation for the May 3rd fiesta, both crosses are dressed, but only the "real" (read "original") one is placed on the *andamia* to go in procession to Holy Redeemer Church, where it spends the night of the Saturday closest to the third of May. That night the *matachines* dance before the cross that has stayed behind, the Cruz Chiquita, but not in the *terreno* itself; instead the dancing occurs in an area that has been prepared for the fiesta in front of the Ortiz family home on the 1400 block of Anna Street. On Sunday, led by the *andamia* and the cross, the procession of dancers and other worshipers makes its way back to the barrio after a morning Mass, and the dancing resumes at this location. The area "prepared" by the Ortiz sons and some of the others was actually the runway for the old Fort McIntosh military installation, according to Alfonso Peña, "until the fort was closed down in the 1930s" (1972, 9). The dances have been occurring here since the 1920s, when it was Benito Castro, a musician and dancer, who led the group (Ibid., 4). Da Camara (1949) and Peña each mention the location where the dancing occurs, at the corner of Sanchez Avenue and Anna Street. This strip of land, one block long, was an unpaved empty lot for many years. After the Dovalina Elementary School was built, the space was partially paved to become the street leading into the parking lot of the school. Whereas before, the dancing occurred on dirt, where muddy puddles formed during the spring rains that usually happen during the fiesta, now there is a mix of the same plus a small area of paved road. The fact that the city had not paved the road underscores the fact that it has neglected the area in a number of ways. It was not until the elementary school was built that children didn't have to cross dangerous railroad tracks as they walked to the nearest school, McDonnell Elementary on Main Avenue. More in line with our discussion of the fiesta and its symbolic elements is the fact that this strip of land lies in a north to south direction. Symbolically, during the entire fiesta the dancers dance in a cross—north to south on Anna Street and west to east in the *terreno*. It may be pure coincidence, but given that so many of the dances also incorporate movements to and from the four directions, I am inclined to believe that the spatial location of the dance signifies one more way of honoring the cross and by extension the earth.

The *terreno* on Camp Street, along with the block-long space on Anna Street, constitute areas where the dance takes on symbolic meaning. Whether the current dancers acknowledge it or not, their dancing retains vestiges of Amerindian traditions that honored the earth through music and dance. Such elements as the red and yellow color of the *nagüilla* (skirt) and the use of *carrizo*, or reed cane, to decorate their *nagüillas* and vests attest to the indigenous roots in Coahuiltecan native tradition. At least one scholar has collated the various documents that attest to the regional Indian groups' use of dance and music in celebrations, and according to him, one such document tells how the Comecrudo danced every day in March (Salinas 1990, 133). Scholars have documented the development of a hybrid culture, a hybridity that includes the local Coahuiltecan tribal peoples, the Tlaxcaltecans, brought by the Spanish and others, including Sephardic Spanish, Arab Spanish, and Anglo-American settlers. The traditions of the region have survived and offer palpable proof of the indigenous roots of the cultural practices. Thus, I hold that this South Texas *matachines* tradition has roots in indigenous culture, albeit a *mestizaje* of indigenous cultures that incorporates the practices of the local Coahuiltecan and the immigrant Tlaxcaltecan groups that lived in the area in the eighteenth and nineteenth centuries, traditions that survive in the present inhabitants of the area. But how does a traditional indigenous origin celebration come to honor the epitome of Christian symbol that is the cross?

The Holy Cross

In other publications I talk about the medieval origin of the holy day that celebrates the finding of the true cross on which Jesus was crucified and the root legend that made it a faith celebration in medieval Europe. In the elders' comments I often found references to the Holy Cross and to the legend of Santa Elena.[12] The young dancers may have a commitment to the cross, but often it does not include a belief in or even knowledge of this legend that accounts for the conversion of the Roman Empire. Nonetheless, they too claim that their dance is a form of prayer and they remain firmly devoted to the Holy Cross. The story that the cross was brought from Dolores, a town about thirty miles upriver from Laredo, however, is well-known even among the younger dancers, and most, even those who did not come from Dolores, acknowledge Las Minas as the root of the tradition. Some of the elders remember the fiesta in Dolores and their pilgrimage or procession up the hill to where the Holy Cross permanently stood. According to Crawford, a lamp was lit at the foot of the cross (1925, 33). Crawford also tells how "*un cierto Don Fermín estaba encargado de la cruz, y cuando se cerraron las minas hace poco, don Fermín se trajo la cruz consigo y le hizo una pequeña capilla cerca de su casa*" (69).[13] When I asked what were the requirements for a new *matachín*, invariably the answer was "to be a devotee of the Holy Cross."

All who dance and those who perform the various tasks during the fiesta say they do it "to honor *la Santa Cruz*." One such task involves dressing the cross. When I interviewed Sarita Liendo in 1976, she was in charge of "dressing the cross." "*Todos bailan, todos ayudan*,"[14] she said of the group, but when I asked who helped her decorate the cross she replied, "*No, nadie me ayuda en nada, yo nomás la visto; le rezan, la llevamos a la iglesia*."[15] While this may sound like a contradiction, it is not. She did dress the cross on her own, while everyone helped with the celebration. She also noted that, "*Muchos no van [a misa], nomas llegan a bailar*"[16] and commented on what a sacrifice the most recent fiesta in 1975 had been, for "*yo fuí y estaba llovido; sobre el soquete nos fuimos*."[17] It is still so thirty years later, as many of the dancers will dance to and fro in procession but will not stay to hear Mass nor participate in the church services. Their devotion is for the Holy Cross and that is why they dance; the formal Catholic rituals are not necessarily their way of worshipping. Nevertheless, many of the *matachines*, especially the women, are active parishioners and combine their folk and formal Catholicism in very efficient ways. For example, on the day of the fiesta, they will participate in the *jamaica* at the church, then participate in the procession, and come back to the *terreno* to dance.

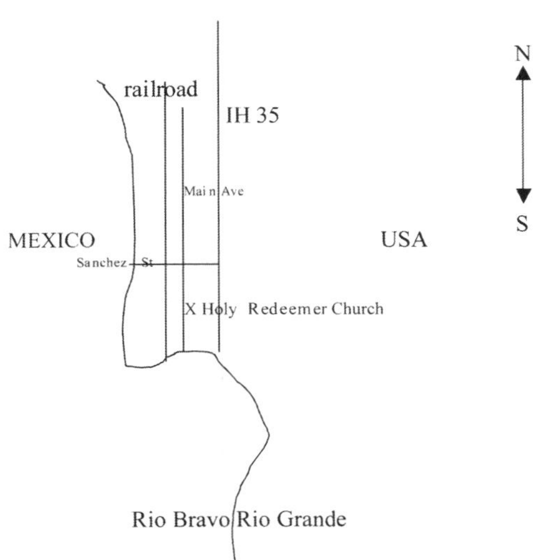

Procession route from *la capillita* to Holy Redeemer Church.

In 1987, in an interview conducted on the grounds of the American Folklife Festival, Florencio Ortiz Jr. explained: "*Hay una persona que la viste. La viejita tiene más de 50 años de vestir la cruz. [Ahora] su nuera se encarga [de vestirla]; ella ya está muy viejita.*"[18] I asked if it was because it was her turn, and he replied, "*no le toca exactamente.*"[19] He goes on to describe how the work is self-selected: "*es una cosa seria y va a invertir unos $100 y la gente gana poco y no puede.*[20] I then asked if the flowers lasted, and he replied, "*Sí, y el siguiente año se le quitan, son de trapo. Cuando lo hace con fe y la gente sabe y dicen que bonita quedó, y la gente queda conforme. Es que ella lleva 50 años.*"[21] Alfonso Peña tells how Doña Sarita was in charge of dressing the cross and someone who lived in Minnesota had sent the money to pay for the flowers "to ask for a quick recuperation for her mother-in-law who had recently been operated on" (1972, 15). He goes on to relate how Claudina Liendo had to dress the cross one year because Doña Sarita was just getting too old to manage the task anymore.

In 2006 Claudina Liendo was still in charge of dressing the cross, but due to her cancer treatments she was not able to do it alone, so she sought the help of her daughters. She proudly points out that she does not get any help from the other families. She has inherited the responsibility and talks about how it is her way of worship. In 1976, when I asked Sarita if there had been any changes, she smiled and in her raspy voice said, "*Sí, como no*"[22] and proceeded to tell me how it was when the cross was dressed with real flowers and greenery, how later paper flowers were used and then it was plastic. By 1987, they—Sarita and Claudina—were using silk. In 2006, Claudina used silk flowers again. The "dressing" of the cross entails wrapping the wooden structure in cloth and, as Ortiz explained, "stapling it so it's all covered, and you can pin the flowers on." Doña Sarita used safety and straight pins. The person wraps the cross in sheets, and she can either cut the sheets in strips or keep them whole, but the strips are more economical. Sometimes some greenery or large bows of netting are also added for effect. They pin the flowers onto the cloth, beginning at the top. And, finally, they drape a new white sheet over the crossbar to symbolize the resurrection.

Each year the flowers are different, as a color scheme is selected ahead of time. Doña Sarita told me she would either save money all year and buy the flowers at once, or she would slowly buy flowers all year long as she could afford it; she would buy the sheet that is draped over the crossbar when there was a sale.[23] So she knew far in advance what the color scheme would be, and for months she planned for the dressing of the cross. Because she had been doing it for more than fifty years, she could pretty well figure out how much it would take to cover the cross. For several years before Doña Sarita died in 1988, Claudina helped, first by doing the stretching and reaching, which were too much for the octogenarian, but later she was entrusted with buying the flowers. In 1988 she assumed the duties of dressing the cross as the nearly 100–year old Sarita watched and approved, still intimately involved and still "dressing" the cross. "One commits to the cross for life or not at all," Doña Sarita told me once. She had told Alfonso Peña that she had vowed to decorate the cross every year that she was alive, and she did (1972, 15).

Every year, Claudina Liendo waits, usually saving money to go and buy all the flowers at once. She knows the color she wants and what kind she's looking for even before she embarks on the shopping expedition. And how does she decide on the color scheme or the kind of flowers? She responds, "It just comes to me, what I think will look nice." During Desert Storm, yellow ribbons and white flowers bedecked the cross. The year after Florencio Ortiz died, it was Easter lilies and a purple banner with the words "In memory of Florencio Ortiz Jr." She, like Doña Sarita, prefers silk flowers, but the cost is sometimes prohibitive and plastic will have to do. In 2003 it was red, white, and blue felt roses with some yellow ribbons. Claudina explained that the colors were for the U.S. Marines and the other armed services, and the yellow ribbons were a symbol of our hopes for peace and the return of all soldiers alive and well. Thus the cross also carries the community's collective wishes and desires, as well as nationalist or patriotic sentiments.

While other materials are sometimes used, everyone agrees that the silk flowers last longer and keep their color most of the year. Claudina often rushes to dress the cross, since she might also be finishing the embroidery on a vest or a *nagüilla*, or skirt, for one of her children or for a grandchild. But the job of dressing the cross is not without risks. As Ortiz said, if the group sees it is nice they tell you, if not they criticize you. One year, the cross sported Christmas lights that blinked on and off, which was too much for the purists who found it totally out of place. But those who didn't like it had to bear it, and the minor crises erupted and were gone before the fiesta was over. The next year, though, the only innovation was yards and yards of pastel-colored ribbons that fell from the top and from the crossbar almost to the ground.

Teresita has taken on the task of dressing the Cruz Chiquita every year, although not as elaborately as the larger cross that goes in procession to the church. Teresita covers it with cloth—usually red or yellow—and pins the flowers and bows, but in a much more sparse fashion; she drapes a twin size sheet over the crossbar.

Now what is the meaning of the cross for this community? How can we assign it a semiotic meaning? Primarily, it is a function of Christian belief and tradition, as William Christian has noted for Spain. But how and why

Dancing in the *terreno* in front of La Santa Cruz and La Cruz Chiquita in front of *la capillita*. Photograph by author.

does a community on the border between Texas and Mexico retain this celebration and continue its annual devotional practice? The communicative power of the image to elicit faith and devotion, and the dancing itself, can provide answers to these questions. When speaking of the Holy Cross, many *matachines* express reverence and give it human qualities and claim to speak to it in their prayers. Indeed, it is the holy icon that is the center of the fiesta and that unites the community of dancers and believers. The chapel may be the physical space where it resides, but it is in the hearts and minds of the faithful that the tradition survives. The meaning of the cross cannot be overemphasized; it is the iconic representation of the community and of its faith. Even a former resident, Mr. Bustamante, who moved out of town and whose group only performs for the Virgen de Guadalupe feast in Stockwell, Texas, says that he started the troupe in honor of the Holy Cross. The sacred space that is created unifies the group and provides a textual plane where the community can find solace and perform its celebratory pleas, either in thanksgiving or in fulfillment of a vow.

It is obvious that the celebration would not exist without the icon, the Holy Cross. Elsewhere I discuss the root origins of the tradition of venerating the

Holy Cross and the trajectory this particular celebration has undertaken in the area of northern Mexico and South Texas (see Cantú forthcoming). The persistence of the cultural celebration could be attributed to the social function it serves in the community of La Ladrillera, but I would submit that the celebration fulfills first of all a faith-based belief and as such functions in true folk religious ways as both secular and religious, and even spiritual, ways to fulfill needs beyond the merely social, to establish a bond between the community, the individual, and the supreme power the cross represents. Just as in the many Holy Week celebrations in southern Spain, especially in Andalusia and in a number of Latin American, Mexican, and U.S. Latino communities, the location of the dramatic enactment of the *matachines* story is crucial to its meaning. The processions along narrow streets in Toledo or the procession around the block where the church sits in Omaha, Nebraska, mark the space as sacred, and in the participant's everyday life, it is a time and space set aside for worship.

Notes

I would like to dedicate this chapter to all the members of the Matachines de la Santa Cruz, first and foremost the Ortiz family, especially Reynaldo, Javier, Roberto, and Doña Panchita, and to Teresita González, Alicia Martínez, Carolina Liendo, and Claudina Liendo. I am grateful to the many comments and suggestions of many readers, but especially my *comadres* and coeditors Brenda M. Romero and Olga Nájera-Ramírez.

1. In this context the *matachines* musicians are often proficient in *conjunto* music that features the accordion.

2. When I was growing up in the 1950s and 1960s, the term *colonia* in Laredo referred to government-subsidized housing projects; since the 1980s, the term has come to refer to impoverished peripheral settlements outside of the city limits. The term *barrio* is a general inclusive term that refers to the established neighborhoods of the city such as "Sal si puedes" ("Leave if you can"), "El Puente Blanco" ("The White Bridge"), and "Canta ranas" ("Singing frogs").

3. Various scholars have dealt with the origins of the tradition as a syncretic or hybrid form of European and indigenous dance (see Romero 1993, 2003; Harris 2000; and Treviño and Gilles 1994, 1997). I use Brown's term "placiality" to look at space that has meaning, that is, place.

4. *Romerías* are often pilgrimages to hermitages out in the countryside, but can also refer to religious processions.

5. The barrio was also at one time known as "La Mina" because many of its residents had migrated there from a mining area upriver.

6. Tijerina notes, "To the nineteenth-century Tejano the barrio was home, and the *vecindario*, or neighboring populace, was family" (1977, 46).

7. Cantú 1974. The term *colonia* in 1974 was rarely used on the U.S. side to designate anything other than the federally subsidized housing projects, while in Nuevo Laredo the term was used to designate any specific area, the way that the term *barrio* was used in Laredo. So in Nuevo Laredo one would identify as being de la Colonia Viveros or la Colonia Victoria while in Laredo one identified as being from el barrio de La Ladrillera or el barrio de Guadalupe. Nowadays, the term *colonia* is used in the United States to designate the numerous settlements outside the city limits that, unlike the more affluent subdivisions, lack many of the basic services like running water and sewage.

8. A *jamaica* is a church festival akin to a fair. It is secular and features games such as bingo and cakewalks and is held on the Sunday closest to the patron saint's feast day. So the Holy Redeemer Parish *jamaica* is held on the Sunday when the Matachines de la Santa Cruz dance, but it is held on the grounds of the church, and the *matachines* dance is simultaneously held in the community and not in the church grounds.

9. Arreola in his cultural geography of South Texas claims that it is not just individual communities or barrios within the communities, but that the whole area of South Texas is a cultural region; he uses the existence of fiestas like the *matachines* and of particular language and foodways and other cultural expressions to support his thesis (2002).

10. Serenata Nocturna's radio host, Luciano Duarte, was the first Spanish *locutor* (radio announcer) on the radio in Laredo in the 1940s when he returned from military service in World War II and began broadcasting on KVOZ. Prior to the war, he had worked in Nuevo Laredo, broadcasting with Ramoncita Esparza's program, an amateur hour (Cantú 1991).

11. Javier Castillo, interviews with Norma E. Cantú, Laredo, Texas, 1975–2006.

12. In my discussions on the origins of the local tradition I rely heavily on the personal communication and formal interviews with members of the *matachines* group, especially Josefina Negrete and Florencio and Pete Ortiz.

13. "A certain don Fermín was in charge of the cross, and when the mines closed . . . don Fermín brought the cross with him and made it a small chapel close to his house." There are actually two concurrent fiestas in two adjacent barrios—the Mother Cabrini *matachines*, named after the church they go on procession to on May 3rd, also dance for the Holy Cross and came from Las Minas, and the Matachines de la Santa Cruz de La Ladrillera, the group that is the subject of this chapter.

14. "Everyone dances, everyone helps."

15. "No one helps in anything, only I dress it; they pray and we take it to church."

16. "Many don't go [to Mass], they just come to dance."

17. "I went and it had rained so we went in the mud."

18. Florencio Ortiz Jr., interview with Norma E. Cantú, Washington, D.C., 1987. "There is a person who dresses her. The old woman has been dressing [the cross] for over fifty years. [Now] it is her daughter-in-law who is in charge [of dressing the cross]; she [Doña Sarita] is already too elderly."

19. Florencia Ortiz Jr., interview with Olivia Cadaval, Washington, D.C., 1987. "No, it isn't exactly her turn." This interview is housed at the Smithsonian Institution Office of Folk and Cultural Studies.

20. "It's a serious thing. One will invest $100 and the people earn little and they can't."

21. "Yes, and the next year they remove them; they're made of fabric. When it is done with faith and the people know it, and they say how pretty it turned out, and people are content. She's been doing it for fifty years."

22. "Yes, of course."

23. Sarita Liendo, interviews with Norma E. Cantú, Laredo, Texas, 1975.

7

Dancing to the Heights

Performing Zapotec Identity, Aesthetics, and Religiosity

ADRIANA CRUZ-MANJARREZ

The impact of migration on individual and collective identities is complex. The migration process affects the perceptions of identity and shapes the construction and reproduction of ethnic identity among immigrant groups. Also, it restructures the social relations and the culture that immigrants bring with them. Anthropologists and sociologists have shown that many immigrant communities reconfigure their culture to assert their ethnic identity and reinforce their group solidarity in the country of immigration. In addition, they point out that immigrants tend to remain socially, economically, and culturally connected to their home communities to strengthen their sense of identity and belonging because of the exclusion or marginalization that immigrants experience within the host society. The maintenance of economic, social, and cultural connections to the home community and the development of multiple identities within the receiving societies have been characterized as transnational identity (Appadurai 1996; Glick Schiller, Basch, and Blanc-Szanton 1995; Gupta 1992; Hall 1998; Kearney 1991; Levitt 2001; Rouse 1991; Waters 1990), and this chapter contributes to current discussions in anthropology and sociology that look at how transnational social, economic, and cultural processes inform the culture and identity of immigrant groups (Adler 2004; Brettell 2003; Glick Schiller, Basch, and Blanc-Szanton 1995; Gross, McMurray, and Swedenburg 1996; Levitt 2001; Manuel 1989; Smith 1998; Vertovec 2001).

In this chapter, I present a case study of the relationship between expressive cultural forms and the shaping of ethnic identity of Zapotec immigrants[1] who live in Los Angeles, California. Also, I focus on the multiple connections that

Zapotec immigrants of the village of Yalálag sustain with their home community in Oaxaca, Mexico. Drawing upon ethnographic data, I analyze the crucial role of Zapotec dance and music, the celebration of religious festivals to honor patron saints of Yalálag,[2] and the continuation of three native forms of social organization that are at the core of group cohesion and maintenance of ethnic identity among Zapotec immigrants. I argue that the *bailes,* which are community dance gatherings for the celebration of patron saints of Yalálag, create a context where forms of social organization, religious beliefs, intergroup relations, cosmology, and aesthetic practices are perpetuated, re-actualized, and performed within the context of Los Angeles. I conclude that a new interpretation of Zapotec dance and music and religious celebrations locates them as a symbolic vehicle for maintaining Zapotec culture, for bringing together immigrants, and for reinforcing their sense of identity in the United States.

Zapotec Migration to Southern California

Mexican migration to the United States is a complex historical process that began at the end of the nineteenth century, when economic and political conditions in Mexico generated a significant expulsion of impoverished peasants, who became a source of cheap labor within the United States after the annexation of the northern states of Mexico into the U.S. economy (Canales 2003, Martínez 1996). During the first decade of the twentieth century, the first groups emigrating to the United States came from rural areas, mainly from Jalisco, Michoacán, and a few northwestern states in Mexico, whose population consisted of non-Indian, peasant, single men. In the 1940s, major transformations in the patterns of Mexican migration to the United States began to take place. The points of origin in Mexico and the destinations in the United States diversified. Also, the number of immigrants and their ethnicity, race, gender, and class changed. In the 1960s, the Zapotec people from the state of Oaxaca were drawn into this international migration process. Recruited in Mexico City and Oaxaca City to work in the Bracero (farmhand) Program, the Zapotecs[3] from La Sierra began to migrate to California.[4] In that program, male Zapotecs were admitted as farm workers on short-term contracts[5] to work in agricultural fields. In the 1970s, changes in the selection of labor market opportunities from the agricultural sector to the service and domestic areas in the city of Los Angeles transformed the destiny of this group. Circular and permanent migratory patterns and new migratory routes developed among Zapotec immigrants to California (Hirabayashi 1993,

Hulshof 1991, Klaver 1997). As a result, migrations of almost entire communities of young single people, and of families attempting to consolidate, began to increase. In 1986, many Zapotecs began to legalize their migratory status when Congress finally passed the Immigration Reform and Control Act (IRCA). Consequently, Zapotecs already settled in the United States began to invest in private property and acquire legal residency.

Currently, approximately three thousand Zapotecs from Villa Hidalgo, Yalálag, live in the United States. Since the 1970s, they have begun to settle permanently in the states of California, North Carolina, and Chicago (Cruz-Manjarrez 2001). However, the major concentration of Zapotecs of Yalálag, henceforth Yalaltecos, is in Los Angeles. For them, the experience of migration has implied a process of adaptation to new social and economic conditions and a continuity of their cultural practices. Also, cultural and social connections between Zapotec immigrants and their communities of origin have reinforced the persistence of the Zapotec culture in the receiving society and the permanent participation of Zapotec immigrants in the social, economic, and cultural life of their home village. As a result, Zapotecs who live in Los Angeles have developed a transnational consciousness (Clifford 1997; Glick Schiller, Basch, and Blanc-Szanton 1995; Gross, McMurray, and Swedenburg 1996; Vertovec 2001) that marks dual and multiple identifications and attachments between "here"—Los Angeles—and "there"—Yalálag. Namely, Zapotec immigrants embrace a double relationship or dual loyalty to their place of origin in Oaxaca, Mexico, and also to their new home in the United States. According to Lavie and Swedenburg's ideas of transnational identities, the Zapotec people of Yalálag occupy "no singular space, but are enmeshed in complex circuits of social, economic, and cultural ties encompassing both the mother [land] and the country of settlement" (1996, 14).

Since the 1980s, Yalaltecos living in Los Angeles have been engaged in the process of building and reorganizing their community through a series of communal gatherings, known as the *bailes* (Cruz-Manjarrez 2001). Unlike other immigrant groups, which have reorganized locally and transnationally through the development of community projects for the restoration and prosperity of the home village (Smith 1998; Levitt 2001) or have joined or established transnational political and social organizations (Hamilton and Stoltz 2001), the Yalaltec immigrants have reconstituted their community through the celebrations of the patron saints of Yalálag in Los Angeles and by the maintenance of transnational connections with the home community on the basis of religious activities and cultural networks.

In Los Angeles, Zapotec immigrants continue to celebrate their main religious festivities and perform Zapotec religious and social dances during the *bailes*. As in Yalálag, the immigrant community in Los Angeles reproduces three native forms of social organization that allow them to organize the celebrations of the Yalálag patron saints—the *bailes*—as if they were in the home village. They are the *gwzon* or the *guelaguetza*,[6] the barrio organization, and the committees, called *comisiones*. The *gwzon* or *guelaguetza* is a Zapotec system of mutual aid expressed through the exchange of economic or symbolic goods (de la Fuente 1949, 1994). It allows Zapotec immigrants to secure communal participation for the realization of the *bailes* according to the norm of reciprocity. The barrios are political and geographical units as well as religious and cultural institutions that constitute the village of Yalálag. These barrios are Barrio San Juan, Barrio Santa Catarina, Barrio Santa Rosa de Lima, and Barrio Santiago. In Los Angeles, the barrios continue to serve as religious and cultural entities and no longer designate physically demarcated spaces. As in Yalálag, in Los Angeles, each barrio is composed of several committees that are in charge of organizing *bailes* for the celebration of the Catholic patron saints. Although in Yalálag the committees plan and collect money for the patron saint fiestas, in Los Angeles, the barrio committee organizes the *bailes* to collect money for more than just the celebration of the religious fiestas. They also fund the restoration of the *casas de los barrios* and the churches of the barrios back in the home village. The barrio committees in Los Angeles work for a period of one year in the same way as the barrios in the community of origin. But more importantly, central to the maintenance of long-distance transnational relations between the barrios in Yalálag and Los Angeles is the improvement of communication technology and modern transportation (Rouse 1991). For instance, the barrios in Los Angeles receive their *nombramientos* (appointments) by fax, mail, or telephone from the barrio committees and the municipal authorities in Yalálag. But sometimes, when the barrio committee members return to Yalálag to visit their families or to participate in the patron saint fiestas, they pick their appointments up in person. The *nombramiento* is an official document issued, sealed, and signed by the municipal and barrio authorities in Yalálag that describes the tasks, meaning the community service, that the barrio committee members are expected to do in Los Angeles. The *nombramiento* also gives the name of the person who is supposed to carry out the service or task and when the appointment starts and ends. In addition, in the main office of the municipal building of Yalálag, a list of all committee barrio members of Los Angeles is displayed throughout the year. Consequently, through the reconstitution of the barrios and the work accomplished for the barrio committees in Los Angeles, the immigrant community has become inextricably bound to their community of origin. According to Rouse's ideas of "transnational migrant circuit," the Yalálag community and what I call its satellite communities have come to constitute "a single community spread across a variety of sites" (1991, 14) and have consolidated on the basis of their social institutions—the barrio system—and native forms of social organization—the *gwzon*.

The *bailes* have been oriented toward maintaining cultural, social, and economic relations with the home village. Also, they have warranted immigrants' continuing membership to both their home community and the immigrant community in Los Angeles. However, over the years, these community events have evolved in such ways that they have become attached to the native calendar of the patron saints of Yalálag. In Los Angeles, the *bailes* do not take place in random manner; they are regulated by the Yalálag fiesta system of Catholic patron saints that acts as the axis on which the social life of the Yalaltec immigrant community turns. To be precise, in Yalálag, the fiesta system is regulated by the Zapotec ritual calendar consisting of six Catholic festivities: two communal fiestas and four barrio celebrations (de la Fuente 1949). The two communal fiestas, which are planned by representatives of the whole community, are the fiesta of San Juan Yalálag in February (a week before Carnival) and the fiesta of San Antonio de Padua on June 13th. The four barrio fiestas, which are exclusively planned by the barrio committees, are (1) San Juan Bautista on June 13, (2) Santiago Apóstol on July 25, (3) Santa Rosa de Lima on August 30, and (4) Santa Catarina on November 30th. In Los Angeles, the immigrant community has reconfigured the Yalálag fiesta system of the Catholic patron saints, though, unlike Yalálag, it is composed of one communal fiesta, San Antonio de Padua, and the four barrio celebrations. Originally, the celebrations of the Yalálag patron saints in Los Angeles were carried out months before the communal and barrio fiestas in Yalálag. But today they take place during the same month the patron saints' fiestas take place in the home village, and if possible on the same day. In his study of Mexican migration to the United States, Robert C. Smith found that mestizo Ticuanis, who live in Brooklyn, New York, and Ticuani, Puebla, enhance their sense of commonality and imagine themselves as members of a transnational community by means of simultaneity. This finding is in line with my research because the synchronization of the religious celebrations of the Yalálag fiesta system across national territories makes Zapotec immigrants and non-immigrants move forward in time as Zapotecs. To be exact, knowing that the home village and the immigrant community will be celebrating and performing for the Yalálag patron saints around the very same days creates a sense of community and reinforces a sense of ethnic distinctiveness.

For the Zapotec immigrant community of Yalálag, following the social and cultural patterns of the home village has to do with the social processes that inform the symbolic construction of the Yalálag community in Los Angeles. But more precisely, celebrating the religious festivities in a traditional fashion reflects a collective need to retain distinctive ways of doing things. During the *bailes*, Zapotec immigrants celebrate their patron saints with the performance of Zapotec religious and social dances, the participation of Zapotec brass bands, at times Catholic processions and masses, and the preparation of traditional foods. The performance of religious dances that revere the celebrated patron saints are the same ones performed by Zapotecs in Yalálag. Dances such as Los Cuerudos, San José, Los Huenches, and Los Negritos[7] are considered among the most important performances. Each dance is representative of each barrio and corresponds to the patron saints of Yalálag: the dance of Los Cuerudos to the barrio of Santiago; the dance of San José the barrio of Santa Catarina; the dance of Los Huenches the barrio of San Juan; and the dance of Los Negritos the barrio of Santa Rosa.

A number of secular events occur in the religious fiestas in Yalálag, such as horse racing, bullfights, fireworks, and basketball games, and some semi-religious and religious events, such as el Convite, la Calenda, and los Maitínes,[8] do not take place in the *bailes*, outside the community of origin. Yet, as I said before, there is a conscious effort in the immigrant community to follow the Zapotec ways of celebrating their Catholic patron saints. But how do Zapotec immigrants organize these community events? What does a *baile* in Los Angeles look like? What does it mean for Zapotec immigrants and their communities to participate in these *bailes* in the United States? These questions frame my discussion of the *bailes*.

The *Bailes:* Dance and Music Performances in Los Angeles

The *bailes* are complex events where forms of social organization, religious beliefs, intergroup relations, cosmology, and aesthetic conceptions are perpetuated, reproduced, and performed. In particular, the Zapotec dance and music performances are a context for understanding the symbolic dimensions of cultural performances and the social processes informing the sense of ethnic identity of Zapotec immigrants. By *baile* I refer to a "dance-event" (Kealiinohomoku 1979; Cowan 1990; Kaeppler 1992; Rönstrom 1999), meaning the community gatherings for occasions such as the celebration of the patron saints of Yalálag and regional holidays.

EL CONVITE L.A. STYLE

Yalaltecos conceive of working for and participating in the *bailes* as a moral and religious obligation to the patron saints and also to the community. One of the most notable aspects I have observed in the *bailes* is the enthusiastic participation by the members of the barrio and the barrio committees. As in Yalálag, each of the four barrios organizes its own *baile* through voluntary cooperation and makes *gwzon* or *guelaguetza* between them. As one committee member explained to me, "[e]ach barrio plans its own fiesta, but the other barrios always offer us their support by attending or helping to organize our *baile*." Four months before a *baile* takes place, the barrio committee members[9] begin meeting to organize it. Personal word-of-mouth invitations start circulating among Yalaltecos. The president of the barrio rents a ballroom, and the secretary and the treasurer of the committee invite one or two Zapotec brass bands and hire a DJ or a *grupo tropical* (a tropical music ensemble) to liven up the *baile*. While the *grupo tropical* might be there primarily for entertainment, the brass bands aren't there merely to liven things up. They are an essential part of the ritual aspects that take place in the *baile*. The *vocales* (barrio committee assistants) usually ask the local newspaper *El Oaxaqueño*[10] to print the announcement of the *baile* within the Zapotec immigrant community. Also, they make phone calls to their *paisanos* (compatriots) urging them to buy tickets for the *baile*. Sometimes, however, the *vocales* go door to door among their *paisanos* requesting donations for the preparations and selling tickets for the *baile*.

In the *baile*, a religious dance is usually performed to commemorate the patron saint of the fiesta. Every weekend for three months prior to the *baile*, eight male *danzantes* along with the *maestro de la danza* (dance teacher) meet in a *paisano*'s house to rehearse the religious dance that will be performed. Usually, the *danzantes* are immigrant volunteers who have previous knowledge of the dance to be performed. When U.S.-born male Zapotecs join the dance for the first time, the dance teacher is in charge of teaching them the steps and choreographies. When the dance includes a female character, she is chosen from a waiting list that is managed by the barrio committee members. For instance, the dance of San José and the dance of Los Huenches include female characters: the Vírgen María in the dance of San José (barrio Santa Catarina) and Santa Rosa de Lima (barrio Santa Rosa), or the Yalaltec woman in the dance of Los Huenches (barrio San Juan). In Los Angeles, these female characters are usually U.S.-born Zapotecs whose ages range from ten to seventeen years old. However, at times, men can play these characters.

A week before the *baile*, in the late afternoon on a Saturday, the Zapotec brass band and the *danzantes* come together to rehearse the dance. Each barrio committee invites its community to attend the dance rehearsal. While the *danzantes* and the musicians rehearse the dance and music performances, a group of women offers *atole*, *tamales*, and traditional bread from Yalálag to the guests. At the end of the rehearsal, the guests thank the committee members in person for the invitation. Some of them may buy tickets for the *baile*. Before the *danzantes* and musicians go home, the committee members invite them for dinner and organize rides for those without transportation.

The success of the *bailes* reflects good coordination among committee members, but perhaps more importantly it is a testament of how the people of their barrio and the rest of the immigrant community cooperate and participate. The work carried out for the commemoration of the patron saints is considered a sacred duty. For example, some Yalaltec women volunteer to manufacture the attire worn by the *danzantes*. Others prepare food to be sold in the *baile*. Some Yalaltec men are in charge of selling drinks and buying supplies for the *bailes*. They also give rides to the dancers or musicians and at times transport the instruments of the brass bands. To be precise, for the Yalaltecos, working for the celebrations of the patron saints is conceived of as a blessing itself (Sklar 2001, 75) and a religious obligation to the patron saints. As Irma Canseco, one of the volunteers, stated, "I am participating in the planning of the celebration of Señor Santiago, because this is the *fiesta del santito* (the patron saint festivity). I am from the barrio of Saint Santiago. Therefore, I have to participate and serve the *santito*."

Thus, the issue of religiosity is more complex for indigenous immigrant Yalaltecos than it seems on the surface. The *bailes* appear to be no more than community events organized by idle Yalaltecos. However, for many Yalaltec immigrants, participating in the *bailes* is tied to their need to assert their cultural identity as Yalaltecos through acts of religiosity. Within the context of the *bailes* in Los Angeles, the Yalaltecos serve their patron saints. The *bailes* are also significant for them because they represent "a reflection and extension of their traditions"[11] through which they resist homogenization in the American mainstream while at the same time carving out a place for themselves in the United States.

Llalní: The Day of the *Baile*

Although Zapotecs have left behind their homeland, they have been able to adapt to their new social environment and transform temporarily the spaces where they gather to socialize. Since the early 1990s, Juarez's Dancing Club[12] has become the common site where the *bailes* are held in Los Angeles. Indeed Juarez's, as everyone refers to it, is a site of "re-encounter" for the Zapotec community. At least three hundred individuals attend these *bailes* each weekend of the fiesta, where musicians, dancers, and complete family groups get together to celebrate. Most of the participants in the *bailes* come from Yalálag and some from neighboring Zapotec villages of La Sierra of Oaxaca. But not all are from La Sierra region. The clothing they wear, and their way of dancing, their racial characteristics, and general behavior give them away. Some are from the states of Jalisco, Guanajuato, or Michoacán. At 7:00 P.M. Juarez's Dancing Club opens its doors. In the main entrance, three of the committee members of the *baile*, who remain sitting on folding chairs behind a small wooden table, sell tickets for twelve dollars each. On the table, there are flyers advertising upcoming events in the Zapotec communities of La Sierra and El Valle. The security and safety of the group is assured as everyone entering the ballroom must pass through a security inspection where all bags and jackets are inspected carefully.

Juárez's Dancing Club accommodates at least 150 couples. The floor is made of wood. Orange, green, red, yellow, and white bulbs illuminate the room. The walls are painted pink and reddish-purple. On each side of the room there is a row of small square and round tables with metal folding chairs. At the end of the room, in the central area, there is a platform for *tropical* music groups that habitually play Mexican mainstream popular music. For fourteen years, Zapotecs have organized their *bailes* at Juárez's Dancing Club. Location and cost make it the most logical place, for it is one of the closest ballrooms to the place where most Zapotecs live and it is one of the least expensive spaces in East L.A. Located in a lower-class area of Korea Town about one block off the 10 Freeway, surrounded by Korean grocery stores, car dealers, a few Salvadorean and Mexican restaurants, and Hispanic bodegas, it is a gloomy-looking place and resembles a storage space. It fulfills the minimum requirements of a nightclub, however dilapidated and dismal its condition. Attached to the walls are many lights that do not always work, but they provide what little light there is, as there are no windows. Pieces of shiny cloth, made of print fabric, hang from the roof. The room is usually hot since the building has a tin roof and lacks air conditioning. All the chairs and tables are uncomfortable, too small, and not very clean. There are two small restrooms at the end of the right side of the room, one for women and the other one for men. The women's has two toilets and one washbowl. Unlike middle-class ballrooms or nightclubs, there is no checkroom for protecting personal belongings. On the right side of the room is a bar that is usually attended by two men, one African American and one Mexican. There, one can buy cold water, soft drinks, and beer, but no food. In spite of its dismal condition, the ways the physical space is used is central to the social and symbolic dynamics that develop during the *baile*. For example, usually, one or two Zapotec brass bands provide entertainment for the *bailes*, and sometimes a *grupo tropical* also joins them for the evening. The Zapotec brass bands are accustomed to playing separately in two circles, either to the right side of the room or the left side. There is a strong tradition among Zapotec musicians that they learn to read music at a very early age; therefore, each musician has his or her own musical score that rests on a music stand (see Figure 7.1). Once I asked Donato, one of the musicians, why they sit in a circular fashion. "This is the traditional way of playing," he responded, "but also, this arrangement eases the communication and coordination between the director of the brass band and the musicians, and among the musicians." During the music performance, all musicians are accustomed to following the director of the brass band, who also sits in the circle. The musicians follow the melody that is marked by the instrument of the director and his bodily movements.

There is a tacit agreement that dictates that the brass band that initiates the *baile* has the privilege of establishing the musical set to be played by the second brass band. The first brass band can play a march, or a waltz, or a bolero, and then a set of social dances, known as the *sones y jarabes Yalalte-*

Zapotec brass band distribution. Photograph by author.

cos. Consequently, the second band will have to respond in the same order but will try to improve on the complexity of the pieces as well as the performance. "It is like a competition," one of my consultants explained to me. "Usually the second brass band does not know what we are going to play, so that they must be ready to improve upon our performance."[13] During the *baile,* it is common to hear comments among Zapotecs about the quality of the performance of each brass band. Generally, the comments refer to the way each brass band plays and to the quality of the performance; one of my informants expressed, "To tell the truth, the brass band of Yalálag deserves my approval. It is obvious that they are getting better."[14] During the music performance, the brass band's members are expected to understand the audience's responses to their music and to improve upon their performance based on audience response.

During the *baile,* each brass band enjoys its own group of aficionados who usually place themselves behind the musicians and lend their support by clapping, yelling, and sometimes whistling. In fact, one can see that some fans like to record the music, others like to video, but most of them just prefer to listen. These competitive performances seem to give a special atmosphere to the *bailes,* as Donato, one of the musicians, explains it: "It is the euphoria and the enjoyment of our *paisanos* that make the brass bands play better." Furthermore, "when we feel that the *baile* is in its best moment, we start playing better. For instance, I like to add notes when I feel that the *baile* is becoming really good."[15] What Donato means by "adding notes" is that he embellishes his performance when the collective euphoria of his *paisanos* is at its peak.

After witnessing and participating in several *bailes,* I realized that the *sones y jarabes yalaltecos* and the music for the religious dances are always played by ear. Once I asked one of the musicians why they did not use musical scores when they play these genres. He responded, "The *sones y jarabes yalaltecos* and the *danzas* are solely learned by ear. In La Sierra, we learn to play this music in the fiestas. One joins the brass band's rehearsals and begins to study music with our *paisanos.*"[16] Zapotec musicians learn to play social and religious dances and any kind of Zapotec music through the oral tradition. However, when they play other music genres during the *bailes* such as Western or popular music, they read musical scores. In contrast to the immigrant musicians' training, the U.S.-born Zapotec musicians play the *sones y jarabes yalaltecos* by reading musical scores. As Juan Montellano, one of the most renowned Zapotec musicians and director of the Banda Filarmónica de Yalálag in Los Angeles, said, "I had to transcribe the *sones y jarabes* and some of the *danzas* to let our children participate in our brass band."[17] In other words, during the rehearsals, the director of the brass band teaches Yalaltec teens to read music and play music for the religious and social dances to be performed in the *bailes.*

One of many significant changes in the music performances is the incorporation of female single teens born in the United States. Playing music has been a male-oriented practice, but today, female youth are joining the brass bands in Los Angeles. To some extent, the impact of transnational migration in gender roles and ideology has not only transformed gender relations within the immigrant community, but also within the brass band gender relations and hierarchy. For example, the U.S.-born Yalaltec female teens who participate in the brass bands have become part of the music ensemble and established a new type of relation with male musicians. Also, Yalaltec immigrants have allowed their daughters to do things that are still restricted for female teenagers in Yalálag, like participating in the brass bands or performing in religious dances. As a result, changing gender relations in the immigrant generation has taken place even though community gender norms are still at work.

Once the Zapotec brass band starts playing the *sones y jarabes Yalaltecos,* the dancers go onto the dance floor. Men hold the women's hands to begin dancing. They keep their arms in front of their chests, and start to dance at will counterclockwise and clockwise on their spot. Donato explains that "it is the tune of one *jarabe yalalteco* that announces the beginning of the dancing." As a general rule, step motifs are simple; however, the harmonious synchronization between the dancers takes practice. "A good dancer keeps and knows all the rhythms." A well-known connoisseur of the *sones y jarabes yalaltecos* stated, "And of course he or she never sits down or asks his or her partner to have a break until the music is over."[18] One of the most surprising aspects of the social dances is their duration. Music for the *sones y jarabes yalaltecos* lasts between forty and sixty minutes without a pause, as different *sones* and *jarabes* are combined into a musical *popurrí* (suite). Juan Montellano explained: "The majority of the *sones* and *jarabes* have their own name and we can play a great variety of them because there are more than two hundred different musical pieces."

Beyond the freedom to change direction at will, improvisation is not allowed in the social dances because everyone is accustomed to following the same step motif. Steps are combined into several rhythmic patterns that indicate if you are dancing a *son* in 2/4 or 4/4 rhythms, or a *jarabe* in a quick 6/8 meter. In descriptive terms, the basic step patterns of the *sones* are based on the combination of step-hop/step-hop, and the *jarabes* are step-step-step/

step-hop step-hop. Particularly, "all female dance movements," I was told, "depend on male leadership."[19] As in other dances, the male dancer leads and the female follows.

Yalaltec dancers told me there is not a specific order in the performance of the *sones y jarabes Yalaltecos.* Only at the beginning and in the very last part of the dance performance the Zapotec brass band plays the *jarabes* called "La hermanita" (the little sister) or "Agua de horchata."[20] The brass band signals that its performance is beginning or coming to an end when it plays either of these *jarabes.* "La hermanita" indicates to the other Zapotec brass band that it should begin to gather and prepare to reply musically. One of the musicians of the second brass band takes note of the order of the pieces that the brass band should play in reply and begins to arrange the musical scores.

Indeed, dancing and playing music are two of the most significant actions that transform Juárez's Dancing Club into something meaningful and pleasant. But most importantly, dancing and playing music serve as a means "for bringing . . . [Zapotecs] together, for articulating who they are . . . and for making their lives meaningful" (Turino 2003, 5). During the performance of the social dances, one can hear and see expressions of excitement, euphoria, and contentment among dancers and members of the audience. When the brass band plays the *jarabe* named "El torito" for instance, Yalaltec men are accustomed to whistling and yelling. Many times, the social dances last longer because Zapotecs do not want to take a seat. I consider that these euphoric expressions reflect the aesthetic experience at the time of the performance, but also that the smooth synchronized movement among all dancers, the close emotional relationship between dancers and musicians, and the characteristic Yalaltec way of dancing all provoke the euphoric expressions and reinforce and enhance a sense of group cohesion in the migratory setting. Likewise, the composition created by the bodies on the dance floor, the music, and the characteristic spontaneity of the people of Yalálag create a common sense of identity.

The *bailes* have become a site where aspects of social identity are continuously negotiated and reframed. As a result of the migratory experience and contact with other peoples, Yalaltecos have already incorporated new cultural practices that reflect social changes in the ways of doing things. When the barrio committee cannot hire two brass bands for the *baile,* then a *grupo tropical* or a DJ is hired by the organizers as a complement. In principle, this allows Zapotec musicians to take a break. However, it also reflects a process of hybridization in which new cultural practices are incorporated into the *baile.* Usually, the tropical musical ensembles play *cumbias, salsas, corridos, polkas,*

Performance of the social dances *sones y jarabes Yalalatecos* during the *baile* dedicated to Santiago *Apóstol,* July 2001. Photograph by author.

and *rancheras.* The DJ may play rock *en español* (in Spanish), merengue, or Mexican pop music. It is important to note that the Yalaltec immigrants scarcely participate in these social dances because they do not know how to perform them, although they are learning. By contrast, the younger generations, mainly Zapotecs born in the United States, like to perform them.

For Yalaltec teens born or raised in the United States, participating in the social dynamics of the immigrant community has become extremely important for gaining an understanding of one aspect of their social identity. Namely, one of the most significant happenings in the *bailes* is that the second and 1.5 generations—still quite young—have the opportunity to socialize with the older generations and learn about their culture. Teenagers and children are introduced to all kinds of conduct and behaviors, such as how to properly dance, sit, walk, court, and look at, listen to, and talk to one another. For them the *bailes* are the place to learn about their traditional dance and music, to become involved in the social organization, to manifest their support for the celebration of the patron saint back in Yalálag, to meet new *paisanos,* to consume special food prepared solely for communal gatherings, and to participate in the performance of the Yalaltec religious and social dances and music. For the Zapotecs born in the United States, the *baile* is therefore the primary place where they experience and learn their own Zapotecness. One of the most important meanings of these *bailes* is to inculcate respect and reinforce the continuity of these expressive cultural forms among Yalaltecos born in the United States. There are at least two reasons that descendants of Zapotecs in Los Angeles are integrated positively within the entire Zapotec orbit. First, they are conscious of belonging to and being Zapotec as opposed to the mainstream American culture and other Mexican mestizo communities. Second, the Zapotec immigrant community promotes and preserves their culture by passing their traditions on to future generations.

The Sacred Dimension of the *Baile*

Throughout my attendance at several *bailes,* I became conscious that Zapotec immigrants not only organize the *bailes* to collect money for the celebration of their patron saints back home, but Zapotec immigrants also honor their patron saints throughout the *baile.* As I said above, in Los Angeles the *bailes* are framed by the sacred calendar of community fiestas of Yalálag back in Mexico and they tend to take place during the same month the religious festivals are carried out in Yalálag. Also, the majority of *bailes* are impregnated with religious observances. Namely, there is a series of religious enactments such as the performance of religious dances, spoken prayers, temporary altars, and processions that mark the temporary transition from an "ordinary time" into "religious time" and back again (Leach 1979, Eliade 1981). When I arrived at one of these *bailes,* I noticed a tiny altar placed to the side of the room. On a small table covered with a white tablecloth rested a picture of Santiago Apóstol. Natural flowers, *veladoras,*[21] a plate with *tamales,* and a glass of *atole* ornamented the altar. Santiago Apóstol, dressed in a white gown riding his horse, was there, at the center of the fiesta, to remind us of the reason for the celebration. This little altar made me realize the religious dimension of the *bailes.* That is, these religious enactments were something more than simple social gatherings.

On another occasion, at the very beginning of a *baile,* one of the Zapotec brass bands led a procession outside of the ballroom. On the sidewalk, on all sides of the ballroom, elderly people, men, women, and children followed the musicians. Girls were dressed in the traditional attire of Yalaltecas—Yalaltec *huipil, enredo, rodete,*[22] the necklace of three crosses, and Yalaltec *huaraches* (leather sandals). Boys wore *calzón y camisa de manta,*[23] a black hat called the hat of the donkey's stomach, and traditional sandals. Some of them carried the picture of Santa Cecilia (the patron saint of musicians). Others had white gladiolas and *cirios* (candles). In the dark, while we walked, women intoned religious chants and the brass band responded with sacred music. Turning at the corner of Vermont Avenue and Venice Boulevard, the procession entered into the ballroom by the rear door. The setting of the altar included the pictures of Santa Cecilia with white and red gladiolas, candles, and food, arranged by a group of women. A *rezadora,* a woman in charge of saying the spoken prayers, knelt down along with other women in front of the saint. Many of them held rosaries in their hands. Meanwhile, the other people of Yalálag remained seated around the room following the rosary. The spoken prayers to the saint lasted approximately an hour and a half. As in the procession, the rosary was accompanied by religious music played by the brass band. During the entire rosary, Zapotec women remained kneeling before the impromptu altar. The brass band kept close to the Yalaltec women right behind them. Those who were not close to the altar remained quiet and seated until the rosary was over.[24]

The presence of these religious enactments and objects, the altar, the procession, the religious music, and the spoken prayers revealed to me the symbolic dimension of these *bailes.* "Each *baile* of our community," I was told, "honors the patron saints of Yalálag."[25] In particular, each religious dance of these *bailes* was performed to revere the barrio patron saint being commemorated, since the religious dances are considered the dances of the patron saints. To me, these religious performances were the doorway and scenario to understand the sacred dimension of the *bailes.*

Dancing as *Promesa:* Religious Performances and the Sacred Dimension of the *Bailes* in L.A.

During the *bailes,* Zapotec immigrants not only come together to amuse themselves and to socialize, but they also come to revere their patron saints. Like all Zapotec religious obligations, dancing is a fulfillment of a *promesa,* a sacred vow for the patron saints (Cruz-Manjarrez 2001; Mendoza 2000; Sylvia Rodríguez 1996; Sklar 2001). In other words, a *promesa* is a personal sacrifice that includes the commitment and devotion of dancing for the patron saints on the day of their fiesta. As the *maestro de la danza* of San José said, "the dancers are accustomed to dancing for a *promesa.* When we dance for the patron saints, we pray either for help or thankfulness. Our dancing is a promise to the patron saints."

On the evening of November 25, 2001, the barrio of Santa Catarina celebrated its annual barrio fiesta at Juárez's Dancing Club. It was around 9:00 P.M. when one of the barrio committee members announced the presentation of the religious dance of San José, also known as Danza de San José. While the presenter asked everyone to remain in their places, the *danzantes* appeared at the main entrance of the ballroom. Everyone, children seated with their families, young single men piled up in the two doorways, and even the security personnel, directed their attention to the *danzantes.* A journalist from the *El Oaxaqueño* began to take some pictures among the participants and I prepared to record the dance performance on video. The *Banda Zempoaltepetl* waited to receive the signal of the *capitán de la danza* to begin playing the first dance, titled *son de la entrada.*[26]

When everyone was seated, the *danzantes* lined up in two rows and walked silently into the center of the ballroom. The *danzantes* wore long-sleeved white shirts, vests, and short pants of bright colors in black, blue, red, and yellow. Their costumes were embroidered with flowers and ornamental designs of silver-colored thread and spangles. All the *danzantes* had handkerchiefs made of silk hanging on the left side of their waist. The *danzantes* wore the Yalaltec male sandals and held sticks about a meter long (39 inches) wrapped with two colored ribbons. Each *danzante* also wore a conical hat with yellow fringe on its edges and a small adornment made of rooster feathers on its peak. The *danzantes'* faces were completely covered with wooden masks painted pink with big eyes, black moustaches, and red lips. At that moment, no one could recognize the identity of the *danzantes.* The Vírgen María character, represented by a fourteen-year-old girl, wore a pink dress made of satin and fine lace scarves on her head. She wore a delicate pink hat ornamented with two bows of pink ribbon and small flowers on it. She had a white belt wrapped around her waist and two long handkerchiefs hanging at her sides. The girl had the female Yalaltec sandals and earrings and the Yalaltec necklace that consists of three crosses representing the three regions where Zapotecs live in Oaxaca, Mexico: La Sierra, the Isthmus, and the Central Valleys. When the *capitán de la danza* signaled the director of the brass band with a bow, the music began. During the musical introduction the *danzantes* put their left hands on their waists and lifted their sticks with the right hands in front of their bodies. Surrounded by the music, the dancers began to dance. After many turns and crossings among the *danzantes* they formed an X formation that resembled the Christian cross. The step motifs were based on combinations of *puntillas,* hop-steps, and turns. Each dance had its own choreographic patterns, such as crossing between lines, circling counterclockwise, simple chains, and turns. During the dancing, all dancers, including the young girl, followed the same choreographic patterns and step motifs.

In the middle of one dance, a woman gave the *capitán de la danza* a baby dressed the same as the *danzantes*. According to Yalaltecos, the baby represents the Niño Dios, or Christ Child. First, San José (the captain of the dance) performed a solo dance with the baby. Then he began to move back and forth along the lines where the *danzantes* were standing. San José, who represented the father of the Niño Dios, allowed each of the *danzantes* to perform a short part of the dance with the infant. In his spot, each dancer, looking up and cooing to the baby, performed a subtle dance with the Niño Dios. At that moment, the grandparents of the Niño Dios appeared, dancing around the room. The grandmother character, a man dressed as Yalaltec woman, wore the traditional dress of the Yalaltecas—*huipil, enredo,* female Yalaltec sandals, and a brown mask made of wood. The grandfather character dressed in *camisa y pantalón de manta,*[27] a brown hat, wooden mask, and the male Yalaltec sandals. On his back he carried gifts, a small chair for the Vírgen María, and a woven palm mat for the Niño Dios (see Figure 7.3).

As the dance evolved, the grandfather offered the chair to the Vírgen María and put the mat on the floor for the baby. Seated on the small chair and carrying the baby on her arms, the Vírgen María started to sing a lullaby. While San José and the Vírgen María performed, the grandparents conversed in Zapotec. I was told they usually say funny things in Zapotec about their *paisanos* to amuse the people that stand close to them. Then the Vírgen María gave the Niño Dios to San José. Surrounded by music, the *danzantes* and the Vírgen María rendered the last dance for the baby. In the very last part of the dance, the grandfather took the baby on his back and, accompanied by the grandmother, left the room. Thereafter, the *danzantes* along with the Vírgen María finished dancing and left the room.

As a general rule, once the religious dance is over, the brass band starts to play the *sones y jarabes yalaltecos,*[28] but most times, the musicians start to combine music for social dances and music for religious dances. Not recognizing the *sones* and *jarabes* that the Zapotec brass band was playing at one dance, I asked Donato, one of the musicians, the names of the dances they were playing. "Oh, this music was part of the Danza de Los Negritos,"[29] he said. But his answer went further than what I was expecting to hear: "Here in Los Angeles, we are accustomed to mixing the *sones y jarabes yalaltecos* and the *sones,* tunes, of religious dances. I think we do this because we cannot dance all the religious dances that are performed in Yalálag during the fiesta of our patron saints. Here, the brass band tries to play most of them.

Dance of San José. Photograph by author.

You know playing and dancing them make us recall the day of the fiesta. It is like if you were there, in Yalálag. Yet, if we forget to play some *sones,* our *paisanos* come to the brass band and ask us to play them."

Namely, although Zapotec immigrants cannot see and perform their religious dances as in the fiestas of Yalálag, they play a "*popurrí*" (potpourri) of them and they still dance and celebrate. Moreover, the performance of religious dances as social dances seems to be another vehicle for continuing, experiencing, and preserving the religious observance of their *bailes.* While Zapotec immigrants recognize that the setting in which the *bailes* are held in Los Angeles is quite different from that in Yalálag, they still experience their religiosity through these performances of religious music and dance.

Conclusions

In this chapter I have argued that the *bailes* are a context for understanding both the continuity of cultural practices and some of the social changes that are taking place in the culture and identity of Zapotec immigrants who live in Los Angeles. Studies of migration, culture, and identity (Turino 2003; Nahachewsy 1995; Gross, McMurray, and Swedenburg 1996; Brettell 2003; Adler 2004) show that religious and secular events are arenas in which immigrants create livable spaces for themselves in their new social environments. It is in this sense that I have proposed that the *bailes*—as dance-events—retain deep symbolic value for the immigrant people of Yalálag. On the one hand, Zapotec native forms of social organization—the barrio organization, the *gwzon,* and the *comisiones*—have been fundamental in the realization of the *bailes.* On the other hand, they have been at the core of the formation process of the immigrant community of Yalálag in Los Angeles.

My main argument here has been that the *bailes* have become a site where Zapotec immigrants negotiate their multiple senses of belonging and reinforce their senses of ethnic identity. In other words, Zapotec immigrants work hard to remain linked to their home community. They do that through their continuous economic, social, and symbolic support for the religious fiestas of the patron saints. But Zapotec immigrants have also struggled to remain Zapotec and stay together as a differentiated community in the migration context. That is, Zapotecs work hard to make a living in the United States, and they are involved in various processes of adaptation in response to the political dynamics and social and economic demands that U.S. society imposes. But their need to participate in the *bailes* and their need to express their religiosity through acts of dancing or playing Zapotec music is what makes them redefine their senses of identity as Zapotec in the United States. Moreover, although Zapotecs remain to a great extent Zapotecs, it cannot be denied that there are a series of new cultural elements and ideas that are combining and informing their cultural practices and senses of ethnic identity, such as those dealing with changes in gender roles and ideology and the incorporation of new dance and music genres in the *bailes*—salsa, merengue, and rock in Spanish.

Zapotecs are aware that they are an invisible community to the U.S. mainstream. However, they seem to challenge the pressures to become part of this mainstream by doing things as if they were in their village. In addition, although second-generation Zapotecs are being raised in the United States and their social identity is shaped by the host hegemonic culture, Zapotec immigrants are educating their children according to the Zapotec values and ideas they grew up with and are passing their traditions on to them.

Notes

I want to dedicate this work to the immigrant community of Yalálag and to express my gratitude for sharing their enormous heart and cultural knowledge with me. Thanks to Dr. Olga Nájera-Ramírez, Dr. Norma E. Cantú, and Dr. Brenda M. Romero for their critical readings of earlier versions. Thanks to Dr. Colin Quigley, Dr. Peter Nabokov, and Dr. Christopher Waterman for their support and earlier comments on this work. Thanks to José Bollo, Cindy García, Paulina Sahagún, and Heriberto Avelino for their unconditional support throughout this work. This chapter draws upon my master thesis written between 2000 and 2001 while I was a graduate student in the Department of World Arts and Cultures at UCLA. Some of the new ideas contained in the paper developed as a result of my ongoing doctoral research. This paper is also based on fieldwork carried out between 2003 and 2004 under a dissertation research grant from the UC-Mexus, the Research Grant Scholarship from the Latin American Studies Center, UCLA; and the Summer Research Scholarship 2003 from the World Arts and Cultures Department, UCLA.

1. Throughout this chapter, I use fictitious names for the sites in Los Angeles where I am conducting research.

2. Villa Hidalgo Yalálag is a Zapotec village located in La Sierra of Oaxaca, Mexico.

3. Zapotec or *ben'zaa,* which means "people from the clouds," are one of the largest indigenous groups in Mexico. Zapotecs are settled in three geographical areas of the state of Oaxaca: (1) Central Valleys, (2) Northern and Southern Highlands, and (3) Isthmus of Tehuantepec. Although Zapotecs from these areas receive the same ethnic label, they are different in various ways (Nader 1969, de la Fuente 1994 [1960]). Each Zapotec village differentiates by a dialect of Zapotec, attire, dance, music, food patterns, and forms of social organization.

4. Specifically, after World War II, the U.S. and Mexican governments established the guest-worker program known as the Bracero Program, in which Mexicans worked in agriculture and transportation and helped to maintain the American railways.

5. Information provided by Zapotecs who migrated in the 1960s. The research of this study is primarily ethnographic. It consisted of interviews and participant observation.

6. According to the current norms of the International Phonetic Association the corresponding transcriptions are: *Gwzon* /wzon/ and *Guelaguetza* /gelaˈgetsa/. See also Goertzen's essay (chapter 17) in this volume.

7. "The Ones in Skins," referring to the *cueras* (jackets); San José is "[the Dance of] Saint Joseph"; Los Huenches is "[the Dance of the] ancient Zapotecs"; and "Los Negritos" is "[Dance of] Black Folks" [as diminutive].

8. El Convite, la Calenda, and los Maitínes are important events of all Yalálag religious fiestas and follow a strict order. In Yalálag, el Convíte is a late afternoon ceremonial procession that announces the beginning of the fiesta. Along with the Zapotec brass band, the barrio committee and the barrio people walk through the village and invite all Yalaltecos, including municipal and religious authorities, to attend the fiesta of the barrio. In Los Angeles, the *convite* takes a new form, but it is still carried out to invite Zapotec immigrants to support the upcoming *baile.* La

Calenda is a late evening walk that takes place two days before all patron saint fiestas in Yalálag. It starts around 10:00 P.M. and ends after 2:00 A.M. Along with the Zapotec brass bands, the residents and the visitors dance through the village as an invitation to the principal day of fiesta of the celebrated patron saint. Los Maítines comprise a Catholic Mass that takes place a day before the main day of the patron saint fiesta. It is usually scheduled around 7:00 P.M. and is accompanied by one of the local brass bands and the church choir, which provide band music and religious chants.

9. The barrio committee is composed of a president, a secretary, a treasurer, and two *vocales* (committee members).

10. This free newspaper is distributed in Los Angeles and Oaxaca. It is printed every two weeks in Oaxaca, Mexico.

11. José Bollo, interview with Adriana Cruz-Manjarrez, Los Angeles, April 2001.

12. This is a pseudonym for the nightclub where Zapotecs gather.

13. Sergio Aquino, interview with Adriana Cruz-Manjarrez, 2000.

14. José Bollo, interview with Adriana Cruz-Manjarrez, Los Angeles, November 2000.

15. Donato (pseudonym), interview with Adriana Cruz-Manjarrez, Los Angeles, October 2001.

16. Yalalteco musician, personal communications with Adriana Cruz-Manjarrez, Los Angeles, February 2002.

17. Juan Montellano, personal communications with Adriana Cruz-Manjarrez, Los Angeles, February 2002.

18. Bollo, interview, November 2000.

19. Santiago García, interview with Adriana Cruz-Manjarrez, September 2000.

20. *Horchata* is a drink made of rice or melon seeds.

21. "votive candles in glass containers"

22. "Yalaltec woven top, skirt, Zapotec headdress"

23. "white pants and long-sleeve shirt made of coarse cotton muslin"

24. It is important to mention that all the religious enactments occurring in the *bailes* take place outside the institutional context of the Catholic Church in Los Angeles. Also, there is not a direct involvement or interest on the part of local churches even though the barrio committee members have invited them to participate. On two different occasions, two priests offered a religious Mass before the *bailes* started. After receiving their payment, they left.

25. Bollo, interview, April 2001.

26. "entrance song or tune"

27. "Cotton shirt and trousers"

28. "Yalalteco song and dance forms"

29. "Dance of the [diminutive] Black People"

8

Traditional Dances of the Sierra Norte of Puebla

Identity and Gender Relations

ALBERTO ZÁRATE ROSALES

Translated by Norma E. Cantú

There is a strong correlation between traditionalism, poverty, and exploitation and the persistence of dances, especially ritualistic ones.

—Mercedes Olivera

Introduction

In this chapter I show the importance of traditional dance and its ties with different cultural practices in poor and marginalized rural indigenous communities in the Sierra Norte in the Mexican state of Puebla. Under the auspices of the traditional culture of the Indian towns, different activities are developed that implicitly involve other actions, such as alcoholism, overspending, and the development of patriarchal relations, that alter the everyday life of the towns. Due to their quotidian nature, these other actions are considered natural for those who practice and perpetuate them.

Puebla has a population of more than five million people who reside in 217 townships. The indigenous population is registered in 201 of these townships with a total population of more than half a million people over the age of five who speak indigenous languages.[1] These townships, which have an extremely highly marginalized status in the northern sierra, contain the greatest number of dances in the indigenous barrios and towns, with almost 60 percent of the 832 being traditional dances.[2] In sixty-two indigenous towns, the most prominent dances include Negritos, Toreadores, Santiagos, Voladores, Quetzales, and Moros y Cristianos.[3] "In some of these, we note the masculine presence interpreting female roles of la Malinche or la "Maringuilla" (Murguía 1975, 65). In contrast, in the urban centers and in the large municipalities, we note the existence of mestizo dances featuring girls and themes associated with religion and fertility. The principal dances of this latter type include Pastoras, Xochipitzahua, Jícaras, Monarcas, and Tocotines (Zárate 2003, 78–85). The worldview of the community is reproduced and reinterpreted constantly; these ideological tenets are rooted in a people's ontological and epistemological systems. The questions that impel the writing of this article are: What is the bond between the traditional dances and the processes of identity formation? What are the characteristics that these dances present and what is their connection to gender relations? Can one refer to a patriarchal dance tradition? I use the term "patriarchal dance tradition" to refer to pre-established social structures that validate and recognize masculine participation while excluding the feminine as part of an ideological reproduction of patriarchy. Moreover, even in dances with women, the participation of women does not imply their empowerment, but a reaffirmation of patriarchy itself, as I will demonstrate shortly.

Processes of Change and Continuity in Traditional Dances

According to Olivera Bustamente, dance "can be considered as a social product, a collective expression generated and practiced by different social groups, with a specific social function determined by the historical moment in which it exists." He adds, "It is a language that manifests itself through the human body and where motivations and messages are expressed in a succession of rhythmic and dynamic movements that possess an observable determined form in space" (1974, 9). He also notes that traditional dance is situated in a "ceremonial context, with meaning, function, and a magico-religious nature, with apparently rigid patterns established by tradition and undergoing gradual changes" (Ibid.).

Dance is tied to the festive system, as it integrates a local social organization, the economy, and the sociocultural life of the region, through which reciprocal relations of a different type are strengthened. Dance in its religious sense functions as a vehicle for communication, a petition from and honoring of gods, but it also serves as a rite of passage. Dance, consequently, remains framed in theatrical processes even as it constitutes a framing to register the various elements of identity and gender in any given culture.

The processes of contact have always been present in this region, as has the imposition of the hegemonic culture onto the subaltern ones—as is the case in contemporary times with the incorporation of the process of "globalization." These aspects have been tied to the economic crises as well as to various events that accelerate the erasure of sociocultural practices in these places. Traditional dances die out due to various factors, such as the presence of new religious cults, change in local economic practices or the increase in the migratory processes, and a lack of interest in continuing these dances among the new generation, who search instead for new cultural expressions to practice such as the ones spread through the media.

Traditional Dance and Identity

According to Barth, dance is tied to diverse subjective aspects including feelings of belonging to a place of origin, values shared by the collective, customs, rituals, and religious, linguistic, and ideological practices (1976, 9). Identity is understood as a way of life, of thinking, of feeling, of belonging, and of organizing. Belonging is related to the appropriation of space and time and with the relationships enjoyed by its members (Portal 1990, 67). Regarding the concept of identity, Giménez explains how it is a variously determined process constructed permanently at the outset of an individual's interaction with others who occupy the same position in a shared space (1978, 127–28). Similarly, Serret indicates that it is important also to consider exclusion, difference, and opposition regarding other collectives in reference to the interpellation of subjectivities derived from other referents, such as culture, ethnicity, race, religion, and gender (2001, 25).

Identity foregrounds the differences between the hegemonic group and others that are subordinated to it in terms of ethnicity, class, gender, or generational relations, subordinating material and ideological reproduction of the rest of the groups and social classes. For Aguado and Portal, subordination does not imply the disappearance of the subaltern classes, but rather their location in diverse places with a constant classist specificity, modifying various cultural values that allow a community to exist with its own characteristics within the greater society (1991, 67).

Within this sociocultural dynamic, we can observe that traditional dances travel a trajectory between the traditional and the modern, the rooted and the faddish, the ancient and the new, the sacred and the profane, the economy of prestige within the context of the financial crises, and between the local and the global. In our countries we face recurring economic crises at the macro-economic level whose effects are felt at the microeconomic level. The generational confrontation can be seen in participants who seek to maintain specific aspects of traditional life as opposed to the new generations who hold different views of the world and of life (Gramsci 1981, 288). In the northern sierra, several factors altered the organizational scheme of the traditional dances. The economic crises, the high cost of the ceremonial regalia, temporary and permanent migration, flexibility in recruitment of new dancers, the presence of other religions, the disinterest and disregard of the young in continuing their traditions are some of the factors that continue to affect the dances. Thus the dances cease to be valued by the new generations, especially when faced with new cultural expectations that come from the larger society.

Traditional Dance and Gender Relations

All known societies distinguish individuals by gender in terms that serve as a basis for constructions of masculinity and femininity. "Gender" refers to a constitutive element of social relations based on differences that distinguish sex and gender and is therefore a primary form of significant power relations. The gender perspective seeks to contribute to a subjective and social construction of new configurations, arising from the resignification of history, society, culture, and politics (Lagarde 1993, 60). In folklore studies in Mexico, the category of gender has not been treated in depth, and even less so in research on traditional dances. At the outset of this chapter, I underscored that female participation in the dances of the region is limited to only five dances (recently created), all with a religious background and performed by mestizo communities (Murguía 1975, 19).

Female participation is limited in official Catholicism and in folk Catholicism. The rituals in the dances systematically exclude women's participation simply because the rituals are based on the patriarchal organizational system. This exclusion of female participation from the rituals and dances allows us to situate the masculine as a neutral thread that strengthens the historically expressed sexism that exists in the majority of exclusively male performance roles. In addition, historically, dance is considered a bond between "men" and gods, such as in the documented references of some chronicles by scholars such as Fray Diego Durán and Fray Bernardino de Sahagún.

All associations with sexual abstention are related to "purification": sexual abstinence, fasting, contact with society, particularly with women because their minds are focused on emotional states that are different from those of men, that is, the rest of humanity. Practicing abstinence allows the men to be in contact with the divine. What is relevant, however, is that women are considered essential, as they must support the men in their practice of sexual abstinence so that the rituals will end well. Pedro Diego, the Totonaca musician, says "*los dioses norman, ellos hicieron las danzas para los hombres, no para las mujeres, ellas no son para esto.*"[4]

If a *volador* dancer suffers an accident, it signifies that he or one of the other dancers engaged in sexual relations,[5] thus bringing bad luck and "contaminating" the dance. The normative is determinant: "in the religious code, the Gods set the norms, they are the ones from whom all rules and existential principles that are the root of sacred expressions come" (Báez-Felix 1988, 13). This is so in dance as well, as Mircea Eliade notes (1981).

Celibacy, a synonym of chastity, functions within folk Catholicism as a means of maintaining the purity of the principal actors, the dancers. Fertile women represent all that can alter the states of purification and all that is susceptible to sin, sexual tension, and they are associated with that which is "dirty," such as menstruation. Women are avoided during periods when they "can contaminate" (Douglas 1996), because of the fear that they may affect the crops, hunting, and fishing, and that they may violate sacred space and time (Bonfil Sánchez 1999).

The majority of the dances found in the northern sierras of Puebla are masculine. One exception has been recorded in Chiconcuautla, however, where adult women participate. There, at the request of the teachers, two women, related to the town's mayor, participate representing two *maringuillas*. Although they dance, they do not participate in the various rituals. The answer as to why they participate was that they "made the dance more showy."[6]

Some young girls do participate in dances in the indigenous communities, which allows us to suppose that they have not had their first menses. Other women allowed to participate are women elders. We must note that both groups of women—young girls and elders—are at the margins of female fertility. Socially it is not conceivable that a potentially fertile female interact with men in closed spaces isolated from the rest of the community. Culturally, women have clearly defined spaces, such as domestic spaces; in contrast men can navigate public spaces at will.

In almost the entire region of the northern sierra, a man plays the role of *la maringuilla*. His movements emphasize sexual thrusts, exaggerated poses, and parodying what they consider "feminine." These characters are easily identified in the dances through their dress or through relevant expressions that signal and represent the feminine (Godelier 1986, 140). Therefore, playing *la maringuilla* remains a task for a man who represents "woman" symbolically.

Their interpretation of women remains within a masculine thought structure in a masculine space and in "masculine" time (Cazés Menache 2001, 1–24).

These dances are used to petition to the gods, virgins, and Catholic saints. The requests are not exclusive to men (who may ask for good harvest, control of rain, freezes, and hailstorms, for example); they are also the domain of women (who may ask for good health and the family's well-being). If culturally, women are excluded from active participation in offerings and rituals, the absence of women is resolved by having the "other" assume the role of the female "other" (Colaizzi 1990, 14).

The man who dons the *maringuilla* costume to represent a woman is rendered a "non-man" while the fiesta lasts; during this process it is assumed that he is "protected" in the various processes of the dance. All the dancer may do to exaggerate his feminine role, his eccentric behavior, will be forgotten or omitted at the event's conclusion. It would appear that there is a contract of understanding whereby his behavior remains silenced in a "gentleman's agreement."

Is There a Traditional Dance Patriarchy?

In the northern sierra region, men primarily perform traditional dances. This is normatively sustained within pre-established systems, as Van Gennep claims for rites of passage, and in the rules of participation that exclude women. Male participation is allowed, but female participation is not. Rehearsals and isolation prior to the event last about eight weeks, day and night, and constitute a form of brotherhood, or "cofradía" (Moreno Navarro 1985). The ideological construction of what "should be" has a different weight according to each gender. In these locations it is not prudent nor is it considered proper for a woman to go out alone and leave her domestic duties to perform public activities such as the dance or the rituals. Cultural gender stratification applies to the whole community, and life conditions are rigidly established for both genders. A man must comply with what is expected of him. He must rise within the internal social structure of the community from the *topil,* or police, to the *mayordomo,* or festival sponsor, to participation as a dancer. Female presence in a public space may weaken a man's performance (Mummert and Carrillo 1998, 17).

The dance is masculine and not feminine. Thus, if women participate, they do so under very special conditions. Their participation occurs within the domestic sphere and is very limited in the public stages. The traditional dance patriarchy refers to a system of social relations sustained within the patriarchal order that centers the figure of authority and of knowledge in the masculine. This system assumes the functions and known social practices. The concentration of male power and authority in the dances reflects the centralized nature of the practices and the dance knowledge on the popular religious sphere; therefore, the patriarchal structure refers to the male power exercised over others, men and women, as in the constructions of discourses that sustain the value and validity of the *cofradías* and groups that exclude women and some men. This power is strongly identified with Catholicism in the indigenous communities of the region.

Although some dances feature women, female participation does not signify "empowerment" of women within the organization nor their dispensation from culturally assigned tasks or the marginalization resulting from the patriarchal mentality. Within this scenario, one can explore the possibility of the development of a sexism understood as a way of thinking or of acting within the patriarchy that is expressed on a daily basis as machismo, misogyny, and homophobia. That is, it refers to behaviors and attitudes that discriminate against, violate, dominate, subordinate, or exclude others simply because they belong to a particular gender. These dances are integrated within the domain of masculine activities; feminine participation is relegated to the domestic sphere and consequently to the education of new generations reproducing the pre-established cultural model, strengthening what I am calling the "dance patriarchy" (Green 2001).

At the same time, new contexts are emerging. The globalization expressed in the contact between the rural communities and the mainstream is becoming increasingly evident, as is reflected in the technology, the means of communication, and education, among other factors, that impinge upon the changes of everyday life and in the ways of perceiving the world. The *danzas* that have gone from being a central activity to a marginal one have been replaced by other more recognizable ones with which new generations identify, such as social dances and sports tournaments. This is combined with influences brought by those who emigrate and return with new cultural norms. Señora Guadalupe, a Nahua informant, described the cultural clash as follows: "*Nunca había visto bailar aquí hombres con mujeres tomados de la mano, me dío mucha risa, me puse nerviosa. Se veían bien chistosos bailando la música nueva (de un grupo musical) aquí no bailamos las mujeres.*"[7]

Also, new conflicts contribute to family and community divisions, as is the case with new religions in the region. Catholicism is nurtured by traditional structures based on the support and participation of the community, while other religions appeal to individualism and the benefit of the individual family, thus generating conflicts between the communal participation and individual benefit.

There are other stratified, gender-based activities, for didactically, dance is an exclusively masculine activity. José, one of the informants, commented ironically: "*ninguna mujer toca el pito (la flauta).*"[8] The discourse refers to ability but also implies the metaphor where "*pito*" the instrument connotes "penis." For Mateo, a Totonac dancer, musical instruments are "not women's things." In the dances of Moros y Cristianos, Tejoneros, Quetzales, Voladores, and Acatlaxquis, the use of instruments is considered an exclusively male activity; women's participation is not conceivable. Dances are accompanied by musical instruments made with local materials; the musicians themselves gather the reed cane since it is only found in relatively inaccessible areas and therefore instruments are restricted for women. In the case of string instruments, it's training to play them that is an exclusively male domain.

In the Carnival dances, it is common for dancers to disguise themselves by donning the costume of the characters most representative of the community or those likely to be mocked or criticized. The costume may refer to different characters from daily life: doctor, priest, or some thief or lowlife. During our research, there were no cases of dancers who were openly homosexual, although certain characters frequently highlighted certain mannerisms they associated with homosexuality.

Men have the knowledge about the dances and the rituals. They know the dances and how to play the instruments that provide the music for the dances. It is widely known that when the musician dies "the dance dies with him." Some men are specialists, but it is not always these men who reproduce the know-how for the rituals, the music, and the dance. But the teachings are restricted exclusively to time and spaces where men interact, as Margarita Pizano claims in other contexts (2001).

With the dance, certain values and socially accepted stereotypes are exalted, which when combined with other aspects of popular culture, contribute to form the beliefs, customs, and norms of a society (Buxó 1991). Such patriarchal ideology is managed through signs and symbols, according to Leach (1979), that legitimize the virile as "natural," that is, make the masculine the normative. In accepting dances as cultural heritage, it implicitly accepts the strengthening of the sexist ideology (a complex composed of machismo, misogyny, and homophobia) that justifies and legitimizes the oppression of women (Bourdieu 2003; Cazés Menache 2001; Gutmann 2000).

The different aspects regarding dance that are here noted reveal an ideological discourse based on cultural heritage that strengthens the construction of masculinity supported by historical cultural and ideological referents meant to monitor and sanction through a patriarchal ideology (see Foucault 1977). In a rural indigenous arena this ideology is related to a universal vision presented as unique and indomitable (Amoros 1985; Lagarde 1993; Valcarcel 2002).

Conclusions

The theoretical referents that Mercedes Olivera proposed more than thirty years ago are still valid. Persistent poverty and marginalization continue in communities that adhere to traditional cultural expressions. Traditional rituals nourish the conservative patriarchal ideologies that reflect the development of hierarchical relations between men and women. These relations are not exclusively endogenous; on the contrary, the exogenous or external agents, the media, education, and religion, express the national culture in the images that show what is masculine and what masculine duty is.

The changes and possible improvement of the economy and other sociocultural aspects do not necessarily imply the modification of the patriarchal ideology of the region. Furthermore, it is easier and more likely that the traditional dances will disappear than that women will be integrated in any substantive fashion into the various existing processes. If they were to integrate, surely it would signify a relaxing of the existing rules.

The body we have referenced throughout this chapter, through which messages are sent, is a masculine one. All cultural referents are related with the masculine from a humanist philosophy and nourished by Greek philosophy and the dogmas of Catholicism. This latter aspect is fundamental for folk Catholicism. These lines of thought signal "man" as the universal referent of humankind, made in the image and likeness of God.

If the dances noted and researched in this chapter show that rituals are substantively masculine activities in space and time, it is salient that the content of petitions focuses on the needs of men in their roles as providers. This shows that the rural and patriarchal model seeks to exalt male characteristics and abilities, thus underscoring the limits of the feminine, which minimizes or erases women's contributions in the domestic units.

On the other hand, Mexican folklore is often viewed as a part of a living museum, as part of a bucolic past that must be conserved in its totality at all costs. Nevertheless, in this work we have observed that cultural expressions incorporate aspects of a positive and valued folklore without questioning those pernicious factors that strengthen gender hierarchies.

Finally, we must ask which parts of the cultural elements require questioning, especially since they favor a violence fed by gender relations that are disguised as an element of the Mexican folkloric cultural heritage. Such is the case with alcoholism, which is commonly tied to ritual fiestas, elopements, and *el derecho de pernada* (male sexual privilege over women), and so on. The other point is that culture, and therefore dance and traditions, are social constructions, which can be documented and modified.

Notes

1. For comprehensive figures, see Instituto Nacional de Estadística, Geografía e Informática (INEGI) 2000a.

2. This figure does not include those of pre-Hispanic origin or the relatively recent ones such as those of the Carnival cycle.

3. "Black Folks [diminutive form]," "Bullfighters," "St. James Hobby Horse," "Flying Pole," "Quetzal Birds," and "Moors and Christians."

4. "The gods set the rules; they created the dances for men not for women; they (women) are not for these things."

5. With this concern, what is relevant is to know whether homosexual relations imply a transgression as would heterosexual ones.

6. Seidler (2000) underscores the importance of subjectivity as something preestablished. With women as *maringuillas,* for example, in spite of having a bond of trust with the rest of the informants, they claimed to be participants "because they liked it," and positing the mayor's tolerance that allowed them to dance.

7. María Guadalupe Hernández, personal communications with Alberto Zárate Rosales, San Marcos Eloxochitlán, Puebla, September 2003. "I had never seen men dancing with women, holding hands; it made me laugh. I got nervous; they looked funny dancing to the new music (of musical groups). Here, women do not dance."

8. "No woman plays 'the flute.'"

9

¿Por Qué Estás Aquí?

Dancing through History, Identity, and the Politics of Place in Butoh Ritual Mexicano

SHAKINA NAYFACK

The following analysis concerns my field stay in the *municipio* of Tlalpujahua (tlahl-poo-HAH-wah) de Rayón, in the state of Michoacan, Mexico, during the month of August 2004. Supported by a Humanities Graduate Student Research Grant from the University of California, Riverside, I was striving to uncover the actual and theoretical connections between the history of Tlalpujahua, the ways in which the local townspeople construct their identities around their environment, and the role of place in the emergence of Butoh Ritual Mexicano dance. I was questioning how, if at all, these placial[1] perspectives might be in dialogue with one another and in what ways that dialectic might be shaping a new social, historical, and economic conception of the community itself. In the third week of my stay I received word that a close friend of mine back in California had taken her own life. Suddenly, writing about this colonial pueblo more than a thousand miles away from my own community seemed less than important. I struggled to separate my anger and sadness from my work, and yet when called to dance for her I fell back into the soil, finding that the same *tierra* was there to support me. As a foreigner who has come to Tlalpujahua seeking healing through a locally rooted ritual dance, I feel a need to return to the land and the people something of what they have offered me. In some way, I hope this chapter can be a part of that much larger and longer process.

El Sítio—The Site

She sits in the same place every day, on a little wooden chair with a little blue cushion, in front of a little blue door, and watches silently as people pass by on the narrow cobblestone road. During the rainy season, she brings the chair just inside, her feet resting on the concrete floor slightly below street level, peeking out through the threshold. Occasionally you can see her climbing the stairs carved into the hillside along her house, one hand holding a bar of laundry soap or a weathered broom, one hand gently tracing the outside wall with aged, arthritic fingertips.

Every morning, passing by her home on the way to the workshop, I would offer a friendly "*buenos días,*" to which I always received the same reply. Her hands folded neatly in her lap, she would lean forward, smile widely with squinted eyes, and simply echo my salutation. Again, during the evening, after hiking back to the hotel sore and exhausted, we would share a similar exchange, and then her eyes would return to the road, watching and waiting.

Tlalpujahua de Rayón, as of this writing, is a forgotten town. During the last days of the international mining industry in Mexico, the 1910s and 1920s, Mina Dos Estrellas had made Tlalpujahua the richest town in the state of Michoacan and arguably one of the wealthiest *municipios* in all of Mexico. For at least one year, most locals will assure any passing traveler, their mines produced more gold than any other worldwide. The economy was booming and the population was diverse, as more than five thousand workers were needed to keep the mines in business. Even the New York Yankees paid a visit to the humble recreational park, playing a game of *beísbol* against the miners' own local team.

All that changed on May 27, 1939, when unpredictably heavy rains caused a disastrous landslide, sending forty years of displaced earth rumbling through the town, burying everything in its path and leaving only a church bell tower and the image of the town's *patrona,* Nuestra Señora del Carmen, standing in its wake. Some call this *la catástrofe* (the catastrophe), others *el milagro* (the miracle), and for everyone it is near impossible to separate the two. For some forty years after Tlalpujahua was a ghost town, with most families having fled to nearby Morelia or Mexico City and many more sending fathers and sons north to find work in the United States–sponsored Bracero Program. It wasn't until the 1980s that the locals began to return, and the community could embark on its search for a newfound identity, one that would embrace its particular history of exploitation and suffering, uphold its proven faith in divine grace, redefine its relationship to the landscape, and help earn Tlalpujahua its rightful place on the map.

Like many postcolonial communities, the terrain of Tlalpujahua is scattered with sites of contestation. Natural and architectural landmarks trace a historical narrative that finds alternate retellings in all forms of cultural life. In a town such as this, notions of the old and the new, the local and the foreign, face symbolic convergence on a daily basis. Arguably the freshest controversy in this regard belongs to Diego Piñón and the Butoh Ritual Mexicano Dance Center, a small school founded in 2001, where students from across the globe come to train in his sacred energetic movement practice.

El Síntoma—The Symptom

The dance of Butoh was formed in postwar Japan under the creative leadership of Tatsumi Hijikata and Kazuo Ohno. In 1959, Hijikata set out to reclaim the darkness of his personal and national history through a dance that would reject the increasing Westernization experienced in Japan during the years of military occupation. "Ankoku butoh," the Dance of Darkness, was a performed attempt at fracturing identity through an often violent submission of the body to its inherent state of crisis, a struggle for life from the place of a symbolic death. Although Hijikata avoided proclaiming his work as outrightly political, the form is inherently tied to the sociopolitical moment from whence it came. The year 1959, when Hijikata first presented "Kinjiki" (Forbidden Colors), was the same year that student protests filled the streets of Tokyo in opposition to the Japan American Mutual Defense Treaty, a heavily contested agreement which allowed the military occupation of Japan to continue in hopes of securing economic stability for the war-torn nation. This moment of crisis was one in which a trauma of immeasurable scale (Hiroshima and Nagasaki) had created a fissure in the fabric of state and social ideology, a rupture that not only destabilized the economy but exposed the arbitrary and fallible nature of previously unquestioned notions surrounding Japanese history, culture, and identity. That such an abrupt laceration of subject formation would be sutured by the thread of U.S. imperialism was the inevitable reality Hijikata was resisting in his most radical performance, "Tatsumi Hijikata and the Japanese: Revolt of the Flesh" (1969). In preparing for this piece, Hijikata fasted for months on a diet of nothing but water and miso. The performance itself culminated with the sacrifice of a live chicken and the nearly naked, malnourished body of Hijikata hoisted by ropes, Christ-like, over the audience.

In its fantasy of resistance, the grotesque and avant-garde nature of Hijikata's Butoh can be seen as a symptom (Žižek 1989) of the ideological conflicts present in postwar Japan.[2] Fighting against modernization while rejecting the possibility of nostalgia, Ankoku Butoh carved out a bodily presence characterized by hedonistic masochism and a performance practice, which, rather than mend the quilt of ideology, sought to tear it to shreds. In "Revolt of the Flesh," it is the conflict between body and nation, history and future, self and other, that symbolically destroys Hijikata, even as it becomes his only reliable measure of consistency as a Japanese citizen. Beyond simply expressing the fragility of the human form, it must be recognized that Butoh has its origins within this ideological crisis and emerges as an embodied resistance and alternative envisioning of the conflicted social order in which it knows it cannot believe, but likewise cannot escape.

During the past four years that I have been coming to Tlalpujahua to train in Butoh Ritual Mexicano, I have been seeking to understand the translation of this ideological crisis as it surfaces through Diego Piñón's own form of the dance. While the town continues on its quest to reinvent itself, Piñón has been building on his own creative vision, cultivating a place and a practice of radical awakening. These two processes, destined to confront eventually, reveal multiple understandings of Tlalpujahua's sociopolitical present. As a symptom of a new, unspoken ideological crisis, Butoh Mexicano reveals what's at work and what's at risk in the reimagining of a globalized community.

La Escuela—The School

Diego Piñón, born and raised in Tlalpujahua, Michoacan, had no exposure to Butoh when he began training in Mexican indigenous dance as a restless teenager in 1975. Similarly, when he began his university studies in psychology and bioenergetics, he was equally unfamiliar with the practice. When his own creative investigations led him to explore the ritual traditions of the Huichol shamans, as well as a wide variety of modern dance techniques, Butoh still had yet to appear on his horizon. It was not until 1993, when the Japanese company Byakko-Sha was presenting "Hibari to Nejaka" in Mexico City, that Piñón stepped into what would become the final ingredient for his signature form, Butoh Ritual Mexicano. Following a guest performance with Byakko-Sha, which he auditioned for not knowing the profound impact it would have on his work, Piñón traveled to Japan to study Butoh first with Hijikata's disciple Min Tanaka, and later on several occasions with the cofounder of the dance form, Kazuo Ohno. What began as a natural integration of his trainings at home and abroad slowly took shape until a new approach to the practice was formed, one that combines both the sacred and avant-garde sensibilities of this postmodern Japanese dance with the ritual structure and energetic consciousness of indigenous traditions from the western regions of Mexico.

His approach to the form begins with exercises meant to open the dancers' energetic centers, targeting every joint as a conduit for moving and transforming the forces within and external to the body. Emotions are awakened through movement-based exchanges and confrontations, structured activities, or improvisations that enlist simple props to represent complex desires, fears, or obsessions. From this heightened sense of physical and emotional permeability, the practitioners then work to experience an alternative understanding of their environment through explorations that create a sensory challenge to everyday notions of space and time. This may include a meditative walking of a labyrinth, or a full day's journey in the mountains, moving step-by-step to the sound of a gentle bell with your eyes covered and a long train of knotted fabric binding you to the other students in the group. The "dancing" happens last, when the body and mind have been pushed beyond their preconceived limits and the expression of all things experienced leads to a new source of energy, bringing with it a new, personal form of movement.

Diego Piñón's mission statement, which informs his work at the Butoh Ritual Mexicano Dance Center as well as his international training sessions and performances, reflects his intentions behind this symbiotic fusion:

> Butoh challenges us to empty our ordinary judgments, expectations, habitual actions and needs, to allow the emergence of a deeper self, propelling us to awaken and explore all human qualities, both subtle and outrageous, beautiful and ugly, to touch, if only for a moment, our inexplicable matter—the human soul. Through this process we can transform our dance and our daily life, to offer more creative energy to our community.[3]

The philosophies and methodologies of Butoh Mexicano could be simultaneously described as both basic, in the sense of cultivating elemental human properties, and incredibly profound, as these elements transform in what Piñón describes as "the alchemy of the Butoh process."[4] What separates Butoh Mexicano from other forms of meditative or introspective practice is that its focus moves beyond the initial accumulation of these complex human energies and insists upon a conscious offering in both staged performance as well as manner of living. Concomitant with the individual awareness such a deep investigation will arouse, the work of Butoh Mexicano is ultimately a ritual performed on behalf of the community.

As stated before, training for this energetic exchange begins at the level of the body, with long days of physical exploration at the Butoh Ritual Mexicano Dance Center. The school itself is made up of three separate buildings. The first is a large dance studio, which also houses a small dressing area and a library completed in the spring of 2004. The building is made of brick and concrete, with wooden support beams buttressing the walls, and corrugated plastic sheeting serving as the roof. Over the door sits a ceramic plaque with the face of Kazuo Ohno dancing with a lily flower in front of the mountains of Michoacan; the name "Butoh Ritual Mexicano" is inscribed in both Spanish and Japanese above and alongside the image.

Behind the studio is an enclosed sand pit, also used for physical training, and in front, a few stairs above the open patio, sits a large communal kitchen where students meet during the workshops to discuss their progress over green tea, seaweed, mango, and blue corn tortillas. Apart from these two units is a separate structure, a small stone house that serves as Piñón's place of residence during times of instruction and/or construction. The landscape of the center is continuously evolving, as students and community members bring gifts to contribute to the environment. Perhaps the most remarkable of these offerings is a six-foot-tall Buddha carved from a solid trunk of wood, with the posture and shape of the traditional standing image, but physical and ornamental additions characteristic of the nearby Purépucha community from whom the gift was presented. The land upon which the school is built has been in Piñón's family for three generations, and he often recounts stories of childhood moments spent beneath the giant eucalyptus tree that marks the property line, just above the small river that winds behind the town.

While his work has been sponsored by both the Japan Foundation and arts and culture grants from the Mexican government, the Butoh Ritual Mexicano Dance Center was built almost entirely with capital accrued through Piñón's workshops and performances in the United States. His U.S.-sponsored Culturally Unique Artists Visa, which must be reapplied for annually, is arguably the most important document in ensuring the school's existence and upkeep. As any close family member or friend would testify, every dollar Piñón earns abroad he puts into the school, for either new additions or necessary repairs.

When the school first opened, workshops were offered for two different groups of students, usually somewhere between eight to sixteen people at a time: Mexican students (mostly from Mexico City and Morelia) and foreign students (mostly from the United States) who have worked with Piñón on multiple occasions during his travels in Europe and North America. The workshops for Mexican students, presented as an ongoing training program in Butoh Ritual Mexicano, have traditionally met over the course of a weekend, usually once a month. International "intensive" workshops, which last seven to eight days and are taught in English, are offered only three times a year. The division, which was made for both linguistic and economic reasons, is often suspended on the last day of the intensive workshops, when Mexican students are invited to attend a joint class and view the final offering of the foreigners, a performance of the work-in-process undertaken throughout the week. These shared workshops always prove to be the most invigorating, as up to forty students, from ages eighteen to sixty, come together and dance, exchanging powerful physical and emotional energy in spite of the language differences. With relationships forming between the two student groups and members from both parties beginning to demonstrate some sense of proficiency in both English and Spanish, there are hopes that intensive workshops may one day be open for both Mexican and international students to train together.

Students who arrive for the intensive workshops stay together in a hotel owned and operated by Davíd, a community organizer and activist who works for the leftist Partido Revolución Democrática (PRD) at the local and state level. The hotel, El Último Refugio (The Last Refuge) consists of six modest rooms and a detached communal kitchen overlooking the canyon that curves east to meet the river by the ruins of the old Iglesia del Carmen. Between themselves, the students form a strong, temporary kinship, but within the predominantly conservative (though ideologically shifting) community of Tlalpujahua, relations have not always been so smooth nor so simple.

In the spring of 2002, Diego Piñón accepted the first group of foreign students at the Butoh Ritual Mexicano Dance Center. While most of the training occurred inside the studio, there was also a great deal of work outdoors. Students, myself included, were led blindfolded and barefoot through the mountainous outskirts of Tlalpujahua, one of the exercises meant to awaken the bodies' sensory connection to the environment. We walked the trail of the river and again without sight, passed through the trenches of the *iglesia*'s halted excavation, and climbed the spiral staircase inside the broken bell tower. We scoured the landscape, collecting twigs, stones, and trash, tying them to our bodies, assigning an object to each joint, and to each object a memory and a meaning. We created active meditations, clearing pathways through overgrown weeds while reflecting on our personal histories, leaving a trail that we would ascend once more in our final danced offering.

With each intensive workshop, the outdoor activities developed, taking us on daylong hikes past the neighboring village of Talapujahuilla, or to the man-made reservoir, Presa Brockman. People in the town began to develop a curiosity as to what this small, quiet man was doing with these strange foreigners who passed through the central garden each morning, often sporting eccentric dance fashion, and returning ten to twelve hours later, sweaty and limping their way up the steep cobblestone streets. Occasionally we would hear the schoolchildren laugh as we passed, and on Friday nights, when men of all ages gather on the sidewalk outside the Farmacia de Jesús near the central plaza, some of the female students would be subject to the ever-expected whistles and catcalls. For the most part, though, the people of Tlalpujahua saved the *chisme* (gossip) for themselves.

Over time, curiosity begets suspicion, and it did not take long for some others in the town to develop their own theories as to what was taking place at the building on the hill. The school itself had become a place of mystery and intrigue, with people disappearing inside for hours at a time, while loud, bizarre music and occasional screams and cries could be heard echoing up from the valley. In the spring of 2003, a group of citizens from Tlalpujahua approached the president of the *municipio* and the priest of Señor del Monte, a nearby church, with concerns that Piñón was engaged in the practice of black magic and satanic worship. The sounding of the conch shell, an indigenous ritual Piñón performs at the beginning of each workshop session, was cited as proof of his occult behavior. Piñón met with both town officials, assuring them of the creative intention behind his work, and while the training at the school continues, the sounding of the conch has given way to less conspicuous directional rituals, and an image of Señora del Carmen has found its way to the studio altar.

La Pregunta—The Question

Every intensive workshop brings a bit more interaction between the visiting students and members of the town; simple conversations with vendors in the marketplace who have begun to recognize the returning faces, teenagers who hang out in the two new Internet cafés and want to try out the English skills they are picking up in school, for example. Piñón has a strategy for contributing to these exchanges, and as part of the opening to each intensive workshop he sets out an individual task to be completed within the community. In the past, such exercises have included finding a special place in the town to meditate on the meaning of redemption, establishing a connection with a special person, or receiving a gift from a stranger. Yet this next assignment, offered at the beginning of our late summer workshop, proved to be the most intimidating.

On the first day of the workshop, Piñón gathered the students in the kitchen to set out the goals and intentions of our week's work. As usual, he spoke of the need to exchange energy with each other and with the land, but then he went on to talk more of the exchanges we have with the members of the community. No doubt this was present in his mind given the history of events over the past year. He told us of the townspeople who thought he was bringing evil into Tlalpujahua, of their efforts to close the school, and of his fears that they were going to come to the land one night while he was away and burn it to the ground. Tears welled up in his eyes, and he stood up from the table as if retreating from the accusations. He told us:

> This is not my intention. I came here to connect with my history, to open this space and maybe offer something to the town. If they want to see, they can come and look, they can dance, I have opened this space for that. But no, they are afraid, and they want to crush anything that scares them. Even they call me a foreigner, a gringo, and this was my grandfather's land. Don't I have the right to be here? I ask myself, "Why? Why are they so afraid?" And I ask to the universe, "Please, help me to save this school." But even so, if they did come and destroy it, I would know that it was part of my destiny. Maybe that would be my lesson. Still, I believe no, there is more.

He spoke of the contradictions he saw between the way people used to live on this land, using their bodies to connect to the earth through work and ritual, and how now even the dirt is seen as something evil, how no care is taken for the trash in the river, and when something is dropped on the ground it is said to have "gone to the devil." And he talked also of their talking, of the things you only hear in whispers, the underhanded conversations that might take place in every small Catholic town in Mexico, but especially here in Tlalpujahua.

And from this point, he gave us the instructions to our opening preparation. We were told to find someone in the town, anyone with whom we felt a special connection, and ask them the simple, informal question, "*¿Por qué estás aquí?*"

> *¿Por qué estás aquí? En éste pueblo, ¿Por qué estás aqui?*
> Why are you here? In this town, why are you here?

We were instructed to give something first—an offering, like a flower—and then to watch carefully their physical response to the question. There were students in the workshop who spoke no Spanish at all, so for them, the bodily response would be their only clue to what the answer might be. Yet the intention behind this question, as Piñón would point out, extended far beyond the answer it beckoned.

"How does the reflection of the other affect you?" he asked us. "How do you reflect this attitude? What kind of things do you represent for the people in this town, and how can you see your own image in front of yourself?"

And then he added what to me seemed like the true intention of this exchange. Thinking aloud in the way that he does, a manner that seems more like manifesting than ruminating, he suggested, "Maybe they will find the courage to ask you the same question."

We were also told that we could invite members of the community whom we had met to come share in the final offering at the end of the workshop. This would be the first time in the history of the school that the closing ritual would be open to public viewing, a step Piñón deemed necessary in cultivating support from the townspeople.

I knew instantly whom I would ask. As I listened to Piñón speak, the image of the little old lady in her little wooden chair would not escape my mind. Why was she there every day, in front of her little blue door, patiently watching the street? The next morning I walked in to town and bought a few beeswax candles from Doña María's small store next to the main church, another one of our tasks to be completed before the following meeting. Impulsively, I purchased an extra one and decided it would be my gift. Trudging back up the hill, my thoughts swirled in anticipation, wondering how she would respond to my question and what token of wisdom I would be able to glean from our exchange.

I saw her as I approached the crest of the hill, sitting there as usual, and offered her the traditional "buenos días," which she returned with a smile. Stopping for a moment, I reached into my bag and told her I had a small gift, presenting the candle wrapped in rough, dark paper. She accepted it freely, though I could sense a definite confusion in her gesture. Then, perhaps redundantly, I asked in my mediocre Spanish if I could ask her a question, to which she agreed.

"*¿Por qué estás aquí?*"

Her response was immediate and required almost no thought. She smiled and pointed to the mountains just west of town, near Campo de Gallo. "*Vivía en un rancho allá, hasta que se murió mi esposo. Después vine aquí para vivir con mi hija y sus niños.*"[5] Seeming very satisfied with her clear and commonsense answer, she stood, ready to begin the long, slow journey down the stairs by the side of the house, fingers poised to trace the cold, stone wall. Before she left, I asked for her name, and during the rest of my stay in Tlalpujahua, while I searched for my own meaning within her simple reply, I could at least greet her as Doña Celia.

La Ofrenda—The Offering

It seemed that all the students found nearly the same response. The most common reply to the question, "Why are you here?" was something in the way of, "Because I have always been here, where else would I be?" For those like Doña Celia, who might not be able to claim "always," the same fixed sense of home still resonated. As the week progressed and we began preparing for the final offering, I began to wonder if Diego's intention would come full circle, and what I would say if asked the same question. I thought first about the school and the deep meanings the Butoh work holds in my life. And then I thought about the town, about the rich history and the energetically vibrant land, about the tower of Carmen, standing solemnly in the mud, and how one day sitting in the musky stairwell I had come to understand the death of innocence. I thought about walking blindfolded through the mines, discovering redemption in a Christmas posada, exploring the infinite on a mountaintop of boulders, and recognizing all these sacred experiences by dancing on the landscape. All the lessons I carried with me, the powerful discoveries I had made in my Butoh process, were inextricably linked to the place and time of Tlalpujahua. For me it had become more than just a town. As a dancer and an ethnographer, I had begun constructing Tlalpujahua as my own sort of utopia.

In *Spaces of Hope*, anthropologist, geographer, and cultural theorist David Harvey (2000) engages a post-Marxist critique of globalization, drawing equal attention to the impact of economic development at the macro level of geographic borders and the micro level of body politics. He chooses the term "uneven geographic development" to address the ways in which people and places are classed along scales that shift over space and time. Though manifesting via capitalism as an omnipotent force, globalization, Harvey argues, can instead be localized through an analysis of uneven geographic development, which exposes the transnational technologies of movement, communication, information, and mass production that manipulate spaces and the bodies that occupy and/or travel between them.

Tlalpujahua is certainly a site of uneven geographic development, with a placial history of exploitation that cycles along with its population. It is precisely this history that allows for Tlalpujahua to become utopianized, though its conception may differ greatly between locals and visitors. According to Harvey, utopian spaces are both produced by history and producing of subjects. These sites offer a "spatial play," a "fertile means to explore and express a vast range of competing ideas about social relationships, moral orderings, political-economic systems, and the like" (Harvey 2000, 161). The citizens of Tlalpujahua and the visiting foreigners—be they dancer, ethnographer, tourist, or multinational corporation—are constantly engaged in this process of spatial play. I have seen this from each of Piñón's students, Mexican and foreigner alike, who come to Tlalpujahua and remark on the town's simple beauty, only later through the dance to discover the profound energy of the mountains, the mines, the town, and its people. I hear it from the locals who in nostalgia remind me how wealthy their community once was, in righteousness condemn the moral corruption that led to its demise, or in often unrealized enthusiasm let me in on their plans for redevelopment and renewal. It's not that the town is by any means perfect, but rather the ideology that it could have been, coupled with the latent potential for it to become, say, as great as the cities of Guanajuato, Zacatecas, or San Miguel de Allende—Meccas of culture and tourism, these other colonial utopias of central Mexico.

Since uneven geographic development is an inevitable accomplice to the construction of utopian space, Harvey calls for a process of dialectics that allows for spatial play while resisting economic and geographic exploitation (Harvey 2000, 182). When the multiple envisionings of Tlalpujahua collide, as they have most acutely within and around the Butoh Ritual Mexicano Dance Center, tensions between the different viewpoints open such a dialectical moment. Both local and foreigner partake in the construction of space while contending with the structures of power already placed within it. Butoh Mexicano responds to the ideological crisis of Tlalpujahua, a crisis of globalization and uneven geographic development, by finding the sacred in the scarred and haunted landscape. Piñón's utopian vision of the town is shared by his students, who in turn project that deep, symbolic value back onto the community with the intention of offering an alternate direction for their own redevelopment.

On the last day of the workshop, at the end of the final offering, Piñón invited the guests from the community to stay in the studio for a brief discussion. A few questions were asked about the emotional intensity of the performance, the meaning behind the movement and the costumes, and the background of the students. As the questions shifted toward the process of

The first workshop offering open to the community. Photograph by Osvaldo Berrios Ocaña.

the workshop, I spoke a bit about my latest profound experience giving and receiving energy to the land.

"A close friend of mine died this week while I was here, and I could not make it home for the funeral. Earlier in the workshop I did a dance to bury her body in the earth, and today, I danced again to set her spirit free."

The guests were silent for a moment. Some women in the front nodded their heads in an understood agreement of what they had just seen and heard, and then an old man in the back asked me, "*¿Pero por qué Tlalpujahua? ¿Por qué estás aquí?*"

La Reunión—The Meeting

The week following the workshop, I was invited by Israel, a local friend and administrative official for Tlalpujahua's Partido Acción Nacional (PAN), to the first ever *reunión de trabajo* (work meeting) of the candidates for president of the *municipio.* The meeting was sponsored by the Asociación

Butoh Ritual Mexicano students Julie Becton Gillum, Nicole LeGette, and Vangeline, dancing as part of the final offering in the August 2004 workshop in Tlalpujahua. Photograph by Osvaldo Berrios Ocaña.

de Prestadores de Servicios Turísticos (Tlalpujahua Association of Tourist Service Lenders) and provided a forum for invited representatives from the community to address the presidential candidates with their concerns for the future of their town. Held in the Zocabón restaurant, the meeting lasted for several hours, with each speaker allotted several minutes to make his or her presentation. The candidates, of whom only three of the five were actually present, were given ten minutes each to speak at the opening, and five more at the end of the evening. The topic was the Movimiento del Cambio (Movement of Change) in Tlalpujahua, and themes raised were concerns for the environment, public health, education, transportation, architecture and urbanism, craft workers and artisans, civil protection, and social activities. The sentiment was the same across the board: *Tlalpujahua needs to be redeveloped, there is no culture, the history is lost, and these changes must be made to restore our community to the status it once had.*

As I left the *reunión* and walked back up the newly repaved sidewalk, laid fresh sometime during my stay, I could not help but wonder at the ideological fantasy that was motivating this movement of change. Tlalpujahua's particular history of uneven geographic development must shape the nostalgia the citizens feel for the buried glory of their small town. This time around, however, the socioeconomic pressures of globalization are less interested in the riches beneath the soil and are leading the community to choose Culture and Tourism as the primary reasons and resources for redevelopment.[6] By constructing a new vision of the town against the ghost of a nostalgic utopia, the citizens of Tlalpujahua are in fact deepening themselves within the matrices of their ideological crisis. Returning again to Žižek's psychoanalytic reading of the symptom, "[t]hey know that, in their activity, they are following an illusion, but still, they are doing it . . . [even if their ideas for restoring Tlalpujahua are] . . . masking a particular form of [self]-exploitation (Žižek 1989, 33)."

Una Teoría—A Theory

Butoh Mexicano can be thought of as a locally rooted (site specific, place-based) ideological intervention operating within a history of uneven geographic development. The cycle of exploitation and underdevelopment in Tlalpujahua has left specters on the landscape, ghosts that both citizens and students are forced to interact with on a daily basis. The history of Tlalpujahua is written in the architecture, the agriculture, the geology. These memories are also inscribed within the social imaginary, as seen in the community's own re-imagining of itself. The trauma of the historic disaster, coupled with the contemporary globalizing of the community, has placed Tlalpujahua in an ideological crisis. The emergence of Butoh Mexicano marks a symptom of these haunting forces of past and future that are conflating upon the space of an ideologically shifting present.

In a town with its own parable of divine judgment, moral dramas are played out on a daily basis. Some see the arrival of foreigners digging in the mud as a warning sign, a return of the same hands that brought destruction to Tlalpujahua in the era of Mina Dos Estrellas. Those who dance with the mud on our faces are forging our own connection with the history of the land, working to preserve and cultivate the contested site of the Butoh Ritual Mexicano Dance Center. And then there are those locals who are trying to forge their own redevelopment of the *municipio,* one that contends with the complex history of the community even as it navigates the ever-increasing pressures of globalization.

My concern, in regards to this research project and the creative work that stems from it, is that the most common argument (and widely agreed upon means) for initiating this redevelopment is to find a place for Tlalpujahua within the globalized industries of Culture and Tourism, two areas where Butoh Mexicano is perhaps unwittingly implicated but as yet unrecognized. The townsfolk struggle for means of external recognition, and Butoh Ritual Mexicano, as of this writing, is the only source of international tourism Tlalpujahua has known, at least since the era of Dos Estrellas. What happens now, now that they've asked us why we've come? How will the reflection of our utopian Tlalpujahua alter or conspire with their Movimiento del Cambio? I'd like to think that Piñón and his students offer Tlalpujahuenses the chance to see their town through our eyes, that for them we might validate something now felt to be lacking in the community identity. A sense of place, perhaps. Gentle, grounded, and forgiving amidst the chaos of social and economic redevelopment.

Of course, it is also interesting to draw a parallel between the work of Piñón and the original intentions of Hijikata. "Revolt of the Flesh" symptomatically asserted Butoh as a sacrificial resistance to the sweeping forces of military-led U.S. imperialism ten years after the Japan American Mutual Defense Treaty. Now, in the age of rampant U.S. economic imperialism, we can see Butoh emerging again as a less violent but equally radical way to counter and contend with the ideology of globalization. Ten years after NAFTA (the North American Free Trade Agreement) opened borders for trade while keeping them closed to bodies, with the economic violence moving from the symbolic to the real,[7] Butoh Mexicano might also be seen as a symptom of a larger ideological crisis, one that extends far beyond the spatiotemporal scale of Tlalpujahua.

The dialectic opened by Butoh Ritual Mexicano is the shadow-space of the globalized subject, hovering between resistance and acceptance, participation and alienation, (sociopolitical) conscious and unconsciousness. It is a symptom calling attention to a universal lack, the terrifying realization that we can no longer believe in the ideology of globalization, nor escape from it. As a performance strategy, Butoh Mexicano offers a defense against this reality while simultaneously forcing submission to it. It emerges as a specter manifest amidst the schizophrenia of global capitalism, a weeping spirit trailing along the riverbed, mourning the loss of her children, La Llorona of post-modernity.[8] From the muddy creek that winds its way behind the ruins in Tlalpujahua, farther north to the Rio Grande, scarred with its pink, wooden crosses, to the quiet suicide of one transgender Latina, Butoh Mexicano signals our catastrophe and patiently makes way for the miracle.

Notes

1. In his essay "How to get from Space to Place in a Fairly Short Stretch of Time: Phenomenological Prolegomena," philosopher Edward S. Casey offers the term "placial" as a frame for rethinking local knowledge "appropriate to the particularities of places . . . their felt properties and cultural specificities" (1996, 45). I follow his theory that we come to understand places through the collision of body, space, and time and suggest here that dialogic experiences of place might in turn affect notions of identity for those who inhabit that place, as well as those just passing through.

2. Žižek's discussion of "the symptom" furthers a psychoanalytic approach to the cultural analysis of late capitalism. For Žižek, the symptom emerges as a means of negotiating displacement while preserving the subjects' ability to enjoy the self-serving participation in the fantasy of ideology (1989, 75). Here and throughout this chapter I use the symptom in a more limited spatiotemporal scope to metaphorically frame conflicting responses to the ideological crisis brought about by globalization and U.S. imperialism.

3. Diego Piñón, interview with Shakina Nayfack, Tlalpujahua, Michoacán, August 2004.

4. Diego Piñón, interview with Shakina Nayfack, Tlalpujahua, Michoacán, April 2004.

5. "I used to live on a ranch over there, until my husband died. Later I came here to live with my daughter and her children."

6. I use capitals here to refer to the globalized industries of Culture and Tourism, reflecting their structures as (contestable) economic relations of power and exploitation (see Kirshenblatt-Gimblett 1998).

7. Ciudad Juárez, for example: A border town in the state of Chihuahua, Mexico, the sister city to El Paso, Texas, where NAFTA *maquiladoras* (factories) have relocated to capitalize on cheap labor, mostly provided by young Mexican women. In the past ten years that these factories have been in operation, more than five hundred of these women have been kidnapped, raped, mutilated, and murdered with, until recently, little or no investigation by either the Mexican or U.S. governments. Large, pink crosses mark the places where their bodies are found (see Livingston 2004).

8. La Llorona, the weeping woman, a ghostly figure of Mexican folklore. While there are many versions of her legend, they always surround the death of children, her own or the ones she steals in the night. She appears as a howling siren and is often seen and heard late at night, crying her way through the street or trailing along the banks of a river.

10

El Baile de los Elotes

The Corn Dance

JOSÉ SÁNCHEZ JIMÉNEZ

In memoriam
Flora Vite (+):
Prophetess who examined the night
To celebrate the birth,
To conjure the dream,
And to reinvent auroras,
Her wheelchair
Was never an impediment
For her to fly far away,
For her to walk forever.
On one of those trips,
She never returned.

Ethnographic Context

As part of their patron saint celebrations every October 4th, the inhabitants of the Nahua town of Coshuaca in northern Hidalgo state in central Mexico perform the Corn Dance as part of what they call the *tlamanes* ritual. The word *tlamanes* derives from the Náhuatl term *tlamanalli,* which means offering, present, or gift (Rémy 1999, 609). In this context, the Corn Dance itself thus constitutes a preamble to an offering of corn that certain officials of the church, *los fiscales,*[1] carry out in honor of Saint Francis, the town's patron saint, who up until 1950 was better known as Tata Huehuetzin (elderly father) in Náhuatl.

This performance offers an opportunity to socialize people in the dance's "frame of meaning" and to learn about the way in which the elderly, the younger generation, and children honor the first fruits from their cornfields.

The dance is thus nothing less than the corollary of a very special meaning that is re-created generation after generation by fostering respect for this people's staple food (corn), even though—as residents themselves recognize—those peasant farmers who continue to cultivate corn today do so only because "it's their wont." The central figure in the staging of the Corn Dance is Saint Francis (the elderly father), although Saint Michael—whom Catholic iconography represents as a warrior who guards the boundary between heaven and hell—is also recognized as a patron saint of this town. According to native interpretations (Sánchez 2000), offered by "Joel" and "Miguel" (two informants in Coshuaca), Saint Michael is considered by the townsfolk as a warrior who protects their town from attacks or misfortune.

The festival itself revolves around the vicissitudes of a figure in a local tale that concerns the origins of corn. This personage is called Centeuctli, which means "little blessed corn,"[2] and it is through this protagonist that the people come toward a mirror in which they re-create the traits that should characterize the coming generation of *campesinos,* peasants (men and women). This event, then, begins to teach children the "ways of being and doing" characteristic of the people of this particular town. The town of Coshuaca has approximately eight hundred inhabitants, who devote most of the year to cultivating corn, rotating it with chili peppers that they grow in small seedbeds, and squash and beans of the creeper variety. Their agricultural cycle is divided into three stages: (1) hot season planting, called *tonalmilli,* that takes place in the months of March, April, and May; (2) dry land farming that takes advantage of the rains that come in July; and (3) an "off-season" stage, so called because people may or may not succeed in obtaining a harvest. This latter stage is also known as *cehualmilli,* or "cold cornfield," because the corn is planted during the coldest months of the year, November, December, and January.

In the context of the changing nature of the relationship of belonging to towns in the sierra of Hidalgo, this ritual offering of corn promotes, among other meanings, one which is ludic, nostalgic, pedagogical, ethical, normative, and situational. Corn has been representative of the local pathos since time immemorial, but as the symbolic efficacy of the rituals associated with it has crumbled, so too has its emblematic force. Yet its representation is a burden upon the collective memory that reflects the current condition of the sierra *campesinos,* who still have good reasons to revere corn.

The cargo systems in Coshuaca, as in several other towns in Hidalgo's high sierra, reached their limits when Juárez's liberal government undertook its ideological reconversion of the manifestations of Catholic liturgy in the second half of the nineteenth century. Later, during Plutarco Elías Calles's government in the early 1930s, orders were given to cancel all manifestations of Catholicism in public spaces. Up to that time, the representatives of the Catholic Church had appropriated the control and administration of those ludic-religious manifestations that local inhabitants had once practiced as they organized their agricultural cycles in accordance with their patron saints' festivals.

In addition to these political assaults on such native ludic-religious manifestations, the deities of Mexico's indigenous peoples were transmuted into patron saints from the Catholic Church's ritual calendar. It was Aguirre Beltrán (1986) who first realized that changes in Nahua appellations were underlain by fusions of the names of those patron saints with their Nahua equivalents. This was not just some simple act of convergence but, rather, a real conversion that brought two systems of thought or ideologies into confrontation. It is precisely the Corn Dance that allows us to question the centrality of the patron saints and, in contrast, to understand the event as an act of resistance that revolves around the *campesinos* themselves, and not as an act of ideological subjection through which this cult was reduced to an expression of Catholic emblematics.

In this process of conversion, the displacement of native languages toward the private domain, and the ever greater domination of Castilian speech in public spaces, allows us to observe how such dances apparently came to lose their symbolic efficacy in those places where people no longer carry out rituals such as the *tlamanes* and where, moreover, both local speech and the meaning of Nahua toponyms have been lost.

The symbolic efficacy of such phenomena consisted in articulating meaning to the emblems of socioterritorial belonging in two directions: first, the toponyms fulfilled the cognitive and metaphorical functions of affixing meaning to the relationship between man and the natural environment; and second, they were used as cultural and ritual markers in local liturgy, either to transmit petitions for water, seed, or other benefits to the deities represented by the *altépetl* (mountains) or to disseminate an ethics of commitment between man and the environment that was based on respect and responsibility (as exemplified by the Corn Dance). Dances have thus become much more than just a form of recreation or a simple "staging" of symbolic and cognitive mechanisms, as had been the case in Coshuaca up to the 1950s. They have been increasingly transformed into a text that requires a certain interpretive charity on the part of the reader, and a listening based on the complicity of actor and narrator: meaning seems to be lost or relegated to a secondary plane, removed from the model that characterized the generation of those who are now approaching their seventies. It is also possible, however, that the ethnographer's need to interpret is linked to her or his fear of losing the discipline's traditional object of study (see Jacorzynski 2004). The risk one runs in doing interpretation consists in fixing the meaning of rituals in some mythical past, an act that essentializes culture, thus leaving the anthropologist only one possible way out: to situate "current" performances of dance in the museum of memory as folkloric curiosities. Such a tendency would not only characterize those anthropologists who fear losing their object of study, but would also become an issue for "cultural policies" designed to "rescue" "traditions."

My point of view, based on the present, is that the Corn Dance has been used to "stage" territorial limits and the bonds of belonging; that is to say, the people dance from "place," and, in so doing, the plight of the life cycle of corn is ritually transfigured into the perilous life of the *campesino.* Not only is a story narrated or performed, but an act of realization takes place that contributes to prolonging and updating the idea of belonging. It is to the degree in which corn is revered that the linking identity between humans and land makes the residents of the sierra into "peasants." In this space, which is at one and the same time ludic, religious, and public, as well as intimate (because each individual has her or his own distinct attitudes and reasons for giving thanks), the twelve *sones* (traditional songs) of Xochipitzahual (the Festival of the Flowers) that supply the rhythms of the Corn Dance are performed with jubilation and purpose: *to please the corn.* This is a festival *for the people,* one that represents the life of the *campesino.*[3]

The meaning of this celebration, then, lies in its uses, and these are circumscribed by a sociohistorical context that updates the tradition of the festival. In the 1950s, the rituals for giving thanks to the land for providing the benefit of the corn harvest ceased to be practiced as "communitarian" acts and passed into the private domain. The reason for this was that certain transgressions committed by the region's longstanding *cacique,* Don Pancho, had violated the idea that the Corn Dance was celebrated in honor of the patron saints. Later, in the 1960s, the arrival of certain non-Catholic religious cults led to a rupture of the communitarian ideal that had been based largely on that church's liturgy. In addition, the 1970s and 1980s were marked by conflicts over land boundaries that altered the people's conception of the land itself as well as their ideals of belonging. Finally, toward the 1990s, generational change brought about a transformation in the region's social activities, as the peasants lost their intimate relationship with the land based on agriculture and came to devote their time increasingly to wage work and seasonal employment, sometimes planting cornfields during the dry land farming season, at other times working in construction or in the mines.

In the current context of migration to the United States and Mexico City, October 4th in Coshuaca has become a resource of identity: feelings of nostalgia bring people back to their place of origin, a site where the "old folks" no longer insist that the *tlamanes* be performed in accordance with the ethics of their epoch. The social temporality of the young people, together with generational change and increased mobility, are the factors that have transformed the Corn Dance into rather more a "meeting place" than any kind of "re-encounter" with themselves. The explanation of this lies in the fact that the relationship between human beings and land has changed. Today, peasants plant corn only because "it is their wont" and not out of any sense of "profitability" in terms of gaining status, prestige, power, or even food. It must be remembered that the *tlamanes,* the ritual offering made to the land in order to obtain the benefits of cultivation, were organized through the cargo system and, in general, by the large-scale merchants and *arrieros* (muleteers), who had the economic capacity to hire peons to work their fields.

Nowadays, the efficacy of the *tlamanes* no longer depends on mediations. For the first time, this ritual has gained its independence from the cargo system and is free from the condemnation of locals and outsiders. Today it is celebrated voluntarily by peasants who still feel an obligation to give thanks to the land and to obtain the benefits of a ritual that is celebrated to grant them identity, belonging, and a reason to exist: that of being "men of corn."

The celebration of the Corn Dance brings together the elderly, women, and young people. Later that evening, after the Corn Dance is over, the fiesta becomes the "young people's time," as they re-create the possibilities of the marriage market. At this time people participate in the game of jockeying for positions of prestige and status. But this competition, which in times past revolved around the number of hectares of corn that each individual cultivated, is now decided on the basis of one's economic capacity, reflecting the fact that migration has allowed certain returnees to accumulate wealth.

The Corn Dance has been largely displaced by this "young people's time" because it is commonly considered "an old folks' thing." Young people who have brought with them other styles and routines of living have appropriated the evening of October 4th. For them, this period constitutes an opportunity to re-create the city in the countryside. The sound of their Afro-Caribbean and *banda*[4] rhythms allows the younger generation to distinguish themselves from their ancestors, whom they refer to as "the ancient ones." The identity of these two groups is simply and completely blurred. The desire of the elderly to participate in the festivities has largely vanished, as has their interest in teaching their traditions, because almost as soon as young people finish junior high school they abandon their hometown to explore other territories. When they return, October 4th no longer represents a mirror for them, but rather a kind of public theater that allows them to show off their histrionic talents and thus distance themselves from everything they consider old-fashioned and which, in their view, reduces them to *indios,* "natives," an attribution they now consider offensive.

Nonetheless, the Corn Dance does prove the effervescence of memory. A tale is re-created through gesture, and participants are, at one and the same time, actors and spectators. At a certain point, the differences disappear and all those present come to agree on something they do indeed have in common: their respect for corn. Religious creeds and political factions are set aside and it no longer matters whether one is a native or a renegade, a local or a migrant. How else are we to explain the fact that every year on October 4th and 5th in the kitchens of Coshuaca, the corn that is prepared and offered is enveloped in the smoke and aroma of incense?

Approaches to Dance

Popular dances in Mexico have been studied and documented in five stages and thematic approaches (Rodríguez 1988): (1) the antecedents of dance in pre-Hispanic and colonial Mexico, (2) dance during Mexico's independence period, (3) dance in the postrevolutionary setting in which their folkloric aspect was emphasized, (4) the founding of the Sociedad Folclórica de México (Mexican Folklore Society) in the modern era; and (5) the period from 1960 to 1986, which focused on the ideological and theatrical aspects of dance. *Grosso modo,* we can identify the following ethnographic interests in the documentation of dance: (1) reconstructing the hegemonic or dominant forms ascribed to the ideology of emerging political systems, including the Aztec empire, the vice royalty, and the revolutionary governments, which continued right up to the political artifices of "Mexicanness," (2) expounding detailed ethnographic descriptions of the particularities of local dances, and (3) as experiences of collective resistance, memory, and identity.

In the public sphere, dances in the state of Hidalgo have been reduced to artistic expressions whose meaning is administered by the representatives of government. Political functionaries use dances as forms of narrative construction that can be staged at different levels and distinct settings of social interaction, from educational institutions to public events organized by mayors and even as a means of delighting incoming governors. Moreover, the fact that these performances are contextualized in the framework of "tradition" means that the indigenous peoples who present them are subsumed and reduced to a static image of the past. The objective is to please the "honored guests" and, at the same time, to promote an image of local culture that is totally naïve. However, one can catch glimpses of certain features that reveal the intentions of the author (choreographer) of the dance and of its sponsors (the political functionary), elements that allow certain contents and expressions to escape from the author's intentions and thus elude apprehension and challenge the spectators' imaginations.

This is the situation that prevails among dances in the state of Hidalgo. In the case of the sierra region of Molango, Coshuaca is the only town that celebrates the *tlamanes* fiesta. The government does not intervene in this festival, nor do the cargo systems, which ceased to exist some time ago. As the local people say, the Corn Dance is celebrated "voluntarily." The neighboring town of San Miguel (municipality of Tepehuacán) performs this dance only occasionally because, as the townspeople themselves put it, if the cornfields are not cultivated communally, then there is no reason to "give thanks" as a community.

In the municipal administrative center of Tepehuacán, however, people do not think in this way. There, in addition to celebrating the *tlamanes* every year on July 25th (after their own fashion), the town brings folkloric groups from the school zone in the high sierra to entertain the visitors and political functionaries, who are usually friends of the local oligarchy. On most occasions, the members of these groups who are in charge of disseminating their interpretations of such dances as the *matlachines, santiagos,* and *huapangos*[5] are members of well-off families or of the local elite. Thus, the idea, far from any kind of celebration of "social bonds," is clearly to underline and increase the differences between the elite and the common folk. The people dance in order to please their rulers. And the same is true of university events held in the state of Hidalgo, at the end of which the audience is invariably treated to acts (*clausuras* in the local argot, which literally means closing ceremony) that include performances by a fledgling municipal ballet ensemble. The word *clausura,* in fact, derives its meaning from the concept of the "frame" of events that are organized by teachers (i.e., regional educators). After all, Hidalgo's elites have written the golden history of teachers in the region, where *maestros* often become highly influential in politics and every new generation adjudicates pedagogy and the state's educational system as their own personal creations. The term *clausura* has different uses, but the setting in the state of Hidalgo is a recursive one. A *clausura* marks the end of the school year for primary and secondary education, as well as the end of congresses, colloquia, or political assemblies. In this semantic context, dances fulfill a performative function by closing an event or cycle but also, beyond this, by shutting off the discourse itself. I suspect that on a second plane—one that remains tacit—these actuations, which seem to be a rule of courtesy, actually function in ways similar to the strategies of Goffman's cynic (1987, 1993), who in order to silence another person offered her or him a banquet, thus placing her or him in the unassailable position of the supposed "honoree." Such forms of courtesy follow rigid prescriptions, and if anyone were to reject such a generous offering as a banquet they would be displaying disdain for the hosts.

The Corn Dance

Dance is a language, and its purpose and function tend to be not only descriptive but also representative and performative, because it is through dance that a story unfolds, one in which the performances of the characters who participate are foreknown. There are no surprises here; everyone apparently knows just what to do and in what moment to do it. In this sense, the ritual of the *tlamanes* in Coshuaca seems to follow a model in which people recognize movements, gestures, and outcomes.

The standardized movements, the tracing of certain patterns and the participation in a game in which everyone knows what they are playing (Schechner 1994, 617), are all adapted to certain activities that are carried out, in this particular case, in the framework of mediation between human beings and nature. It is through these movements that the art and ritual of the *tlamanes* are created. Those who originate such dances do so with some particular purpose in mind. In the case of Soviet dancers, to cite but one example, the former USSR utilized the expressive arts as instruments of social change; through the use of certain types of gestures and movements they attempted to create the meaningful bases of a new national identity. In other settings, dance has been used consciously by artists as a form of expressing their rebelliousness and unconformity with the status quo (Doi 2001).

In general terms, the following can be affirmed: "The Corn Dance is expressed through gestures, movements, and postures whose meaning is denotative of human actions" (Meier 2002, 167). This idea is common to linguists and psychologists, who have drawn attention to the significant role that gestures play in the production and reception of language. Several studies of gestures exist in the literature, from those that conceive of gestures as ways of anchoring knowledge and spatial descriptions (Levelt 1996; Levinson 1997, 1998; Haviland 2000), through others that link them to the expression of emotions (Bateson 1977; Lakoff and Johnson 1980), to those that inquire into their roles in the forms of socialization and learning of referential languages, as a type of prelinguistic phenomenon (Haviland 1993; Levinson 1996).

Though the dance of the *tlamanes* is not linked *in situ* to oral expressions, but rather to gestures, the older generation is clearly capable of recognizing whether or not a dance has been performed well. Thus, we can affirm that the dance of the *tlamanes* expresses local theatricality by permitting the evocation of a central motif that condenses the meaning of the Corn Dance. Participants follow the movements and rhythm marked by the music of the band that accompanies them as they parade through the streets around the town, starting out from—and finishing up at—the local church, which is dedicated to Saint Francis. Each participant plays a different role as they represent distinct aspects of the maturation cycle of corn. This is a ritual representation, as the Corn Dance combines theater with ritual (Schechner 1994, 620). The dancers are differentiated according to the social division of agricultural labor; men dance as *ayateros*, that is, they represent themselves as they return from their fields, their *ayates*[6] laden with ears of freshly picked corn. Meanwhile, the lines of cornstalks re-created by the children, young people, and women constitute a theater of space by visually reproducing a cornfield in a liminal state. The drama acted out by the central figures of Centeuctli and Xilonen—the ears and kernels of corn, respectively—presents a tale in which tension forms part of a story that will be resolved at some moment.

The harvesters, called *ayateros*, who accompany the procession represent the peasant farmers themselves and proffer a framework of meaning to the theater of space as they are physically accompanied by the cornfield, represented metaphorically by the children and women who carry the cornstalks. It is there that space and time are re-created, as each station that they visit in the cornfield represents a season in time. By the time they triumph—that is, arrive at their destination (the church, where the offerings are made)—they have re-created the twelve months of the year (theater of time) through the performance of the twelve *sones* (traditional songs); the "extra time" they may dance beyond the seasons of the year is carried out as a means of defeating the adversity of "bad weather." Here, then, we are dealing with an act of resistance. Does the drama end when the tension is resolved? (cf. Turner 1995). When the women and children, holding their cornstalks, form a chain around Centeuctli and Xilonen, who are accompanied by the harvesters, it is not to close a cycle. This is not a closing (*clausura*) like in official, state-organized events, but rather a horizon of meaning that opens up to reveal the vicissitudes of corn, between its planting and harvesting, as it passes through its liminal state in the form of fresh corn (*centeuctli,* corn on the cob) up to the time it matures and hardens (*xilonen,* hard, dry corn).

PREPARATIONS

On the day before the *tlamanes* fiesta, the town delegate in Coshuaca orders his five *mandaderos* (assistants) to call at the homes of the members of the community and ask for donations of *centeuctli,* fresh corn, from those peasants who may have some in their fields. It must be fresh, tender corn because if it is partially dried or hardened it no longer fulfills the idea of the ritual, which is to show gratitude to a small child, in this case, "the blessed young corn." Those who decide to donate ears of fresh corn then have to go out to their fields to bring back perhaps thirty cornstalks. On the appointed day, the farmers leave for the hills where their fields are located early in the morning to select the stalks with fresh corn, which they then proceed to pull out by their roots and tie into bundles. They return to the town with these bundles on their backs supported by the fiber bag and the strap that they hook on their foreheads. Upon their arrival, they head straight for the church, where they empty their loads. Once a sufficient quantity of cornstalks has been collected, a *fiscal,* an official of the church, bathes the ears of fresh corn in the smoke and aroma of locally extracted incense. As he covers the stalks with smoke, he recites the Lord's Prayer and makes an offering of the corn to Saint Francis and Saint Michael to thank them for having allowed the farmers to obtain a successful harvest. He then calls the faithful to come together in the church by ringing the church bell slowly three times. As the people arrive, they form two lines, one made up of boys and girls, the other of women of reproductive age. Two antagonistic figures then take their places between the two lines, where they act as the leaders of the procession. They are Xilonen, the grandmother, and her grandson Centeuctli, "the blessed young corn."[7]

Also between the two lines, but behind Xilonen and Centeuctli, comes the procession of the harvesters, men of reproductive age or, as they are commonly called in Coshuaca, "those who now count." The harvesters carry a sack of fresh corn tied to a strap around their foreheads and must dance with this burden during the entire procession that sets out from the church and winds its way through the main streets of the town until finally returning to its starting point in the atrium.

The harvesters continue their march through the "cornfield." Photograph by author.

THE PROCESSION

Xilonen carries in her hands a kind of portable clay grill, filled with burning embers, where the incense is slowly consumed, leaving a trail of aromatic smoke in its wake. She advances a few steps with this censer raised, while Centeuctli dances behind her. Further behind, the harvesters also take a few steps forward, dancing all the while, and then retreat toward the contingent that is bringing up the rear. This cycle is repeated continually as the procession advances. Meanwhile, the two lines also advance, though slowly, forming a wall around the central figures. These rows of boys, girls, and women carry cornstalks in their right hand, raising them straight up in the air and shaking them to the rhythm of the music of the band as it intones the songs of Xochipitzahual.

When the procession reaches the first corner of the town, located east of the church, a large firecracker is launched skywards. The procession waits until it hears the explosion of this *cohete* (literally "rocket") before advancing on to the following station, which is located to the north. There the same ritual is repeated. This sequence is then re-enacted also at the eastern and southern cardinal points, after which the entire throng returns to its starting point in the central square in front of the church, and it is there that the procession transforms itself into what the local people call the Corn Dance.

The vertical cornstalks the children carry are analogous to the tender ears of fresh corn. Just like the cornstalks they hold, these children will also grow upwards. In fact, when you ask someone in Coshuaca to describe a child or other individual, they use their index finger to point upwards, indicating their belief that life develops just like physical growth does. Women of reproductive age are in charge of looking after the children, who are considered similar to fresh corn. The swishing of the cornstalks produces a sound and movement that mirrors the way one cradles and rocks a newborn baby. As the harvesters come and go, carrying their product on their backs, they also represent an allegory of carrying a baby, a synecdoche that substitutes fresh

Centeuctli leads the Corn Dance, accompanied by the harvesters and surrounded by a wall of cornstalks. Photograph by author.

corn for babies. The back-and-forth movements represent the ups and downs of the corn's cycle of cultivation, while the coming and going of the peasant farmers to and from the hills represents the social trajectory of their life, thus representing their fate.

Finally, the circular form of the dance and its return to its starting point leave no doubt that what we are watching is indeed the staging of alliteration. The twelve traditional songs represent the twelve months of the year and their performance emphasizes the fact that the *campesinos* must always tend their fields with great care and attention. Indeed, in order to express their gratitude to the corn, the celebrants may play fourteen songs or more, depending on the stamina of the participants. It is there that this dance acquires its connotation as a demonstrative act: *corn is revered.*

In figure 10.3, the position of the town of Coshuaca is represented in relation to the Claro River, blue linen, and the four cardinal points mark the places where the people launch the *cohetes* (rockets) into the sky as the procession passes by.

The firecrackers are a metaphor for thunder, as their explosions represent the loud claps of thunder that announce the onset of the rainy season, which brings with it the moisture needed to nourish the cornfields and assure their development. In synthesis, then, the Corn Dance re-creates space and time through figurative acts that mirror the life of the peasants; this dance, in effect, brings together their conceptualization of life and its resemblance to the life cycle of the corn they cultivate.

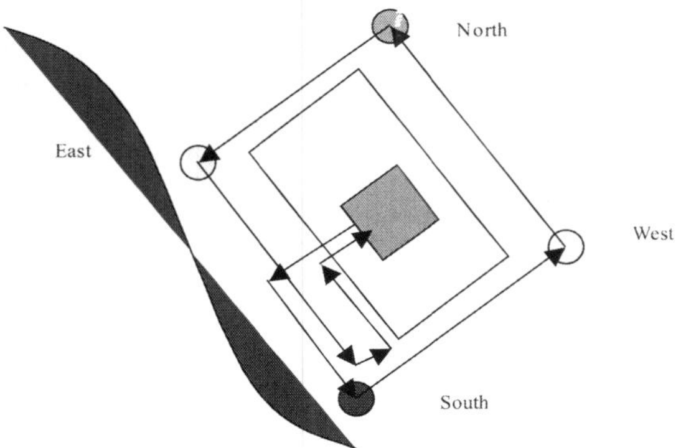

The arrows indicate the route the procession follows from its starting point in the atrium of the church.

Conclusion: Presenting Corn . . . or the People's Concept of Belonging?

There is no single answer to the question of the meaning of the Corn Dance. Rather, its meanings depend upon its uses and its contexts of reference. From the perspective of Don Miguel—who considers himself the heir of local memory—the modern staging of the Corn Dance no longer corresponds to its ancient roots, because its older ritual meaning has been lost. The symbolic efficacy of this dance came to an end with the disappearance of the town's cargo system, that is, when the ritual practice and meaning of the Corn Dance ceased to be a motive that brought people together to solidify their community's boundaries, and when it was freed from the administration of meaning imposed by the so-called "lords of the land": the *caciques,* local oligarchs, and landowners. The various reasons that may influence the decision of the residents of the neighboring town of San Miguel to perform the Corn Dance only when they work their cornfields in a communal fashion offer an ethical reading of the ritual meaning of this dance. As the reasons for social reunions become diluted, there is simply no longer anything to celebrate. Thus, individualism is a signal of the loss of religiosity. Everything that people consider "common" seems to dissipate before their very eyes, and, in stark contrast, a world made up of "differences" opens up before the townspeople. The loss of ritual meaning thus marks not only the termination of the relationship between man and land, but also the limits of the relationships among the people themselves.

By the same token—and as in the case of Coshuaca—the idea of community that might be celebrated by staging the life trajectory of the *campesinos,* who devote so much of their lives to cultivating corn each year, is one that is both precarious and fragile, accosted by other ideological systems. The followers of the evangelical religion fragmented the idea of community at the same time as the imposition and adoption of Castilian Spanish through the efforts of rural schoolteachers and municipal officials penetrated the town and began to displace indigenous systems of thought and belief. Today, the members of the new generations—the children and grandchildren—look upon their forefathers as people who pertain to the past, dismissing them as "the ancient ones," individuals characterized by their old-fashioned way of thinking. Finally, the idea of territorial belonging itself has been assailed and modified by the state's land distribution programs and its systems for adjudicating and registering property.

The ritual meaning of the Corn Dance in Coshuaca and San Miguel—in contrast to its significance in Tepehuacán—is that it is not staged specifically as an offering to the land, because the land does not belong to particular individuals. Rather, it is offered up to the "lords of the land," those who used to grant its gifts but who demanded in return offerings of the kind represented in the Corn Dance. Now, the personages who once mediated the relationship between human beings and the land have been lost, and only memories remain of what those dancers might one day have been: intermediaries between gods and people, vehicles through which people were socialized in the ideas and values that gave corn, and by analogy the peasant farmers, its *raison d'etre.*

The staging of the Corn Dance thus promotes a representation of the theater of memory and identity. It is a moment in which the life of *campesinos* is re-created through theater and the marriage of time and space. In the view of the younger generations, the ludic aspect remains alive and offers sufficient reason to emerge from their tedium and, though perhaps only fleetingly, approach the horizon of "ourselves." In spite of everything, however, the liturgy maintains its touching significance: "corn is revered." Corn is the fundamental motivation of the lives of the *campesinos.* Their children, even though they now live "out of town," do indeed understand the importance of this festival and thus line up with their cameras and handicams. "At least we'll have a reminder," they say. At some point, after all, they too were peasants.

When the Corn Dance is performed, our bodies follow the rhythmic steps of a song. Its effervescence brings us to ecstasy. The culmination comes when the body can bear no more; at that point the dance seems to acquire meaning as an act of resistance, but against who or what? And why, or for what purpose? The answer: Because it is good to push the body to its limits, to immerse oneself in ecstasy, and then to re-emerge having fulfilled a promise. "I succeeded in dancing all twelve songs. I stuck it out longer." But what is the reward? Is it just that one is seen or appreciated? Does one's recompense lie in simple satisfaction and Dionysian enjoyment? Is all that exertion therapeutic? As long as the young people and children continue to attend, this remembrance will enjoy success, and they will be figurations of what they/we are. The situational ethics expands through the unfolding of a story that is recounted, though we cannot determine just where it should be inscribed. At the same time, we are dealing with an ethics that is re-created in a space that has been inhabited since human beings began to plant, cultivate, and praise the fruits of the earth: corn.

Today, Coshuaca has ceased to be a "community" in the agglutinating sense of the term. The monopolization and administration of the meaning of the ritual find their limits in the exhaustion and weariness of the elderly, those who have discovered that their voice no longer echoes there. The migrations of young people to Florida and North Carolina, and to the metropolitan area of Mexico City, inhibit the social reproduction of *comunitas* and fix the meaning of this ritual as a performance of nostalgia.

The incursion of new ideologies in the 1950s, such as the Pentecostal cult introduced by a religious leader named José Cruz (originally from Poza Rica, state of Veracruz), who reinvented the idea of tradition and cult, divided Coshuaca into two groups: Evangelists and Catholics. It is only the latter group that still stages the celebration of the corn. Indeed, when a member of the evangelical church is appointed to the position of community delegate, as was the case on October 4, 2004, it is highly unlikely that there will be a successful celebration. The explanation lies in the fact that the delegate is in charge of organizing the festival and of obtaining the collaboration of the members of the community through collective work parties. However, the religious cult to which he belongs classifies such activities as manifestations of "idolatry" that his peers would never pardon. On this plane, the very same activities that award certain people with prestige and recognition bestow upon others only denigration and place them in a predicament with respect to the groups to which they belong. When we turn our eyes to the domestic sphere, though, it turns out that it does not matter to which cult residents belong, because everyone holds corn dear and reveres it, whether it be by preparing tamales or by relishing a tender ear of corn on the cob.

In summary, the Corn Dance has reached a limit in the public domain, where it is now considered a "performance of nostalgia," though in the domestic sphere people still remember that corn is nothing less than an intermediary between human beings and land that gives meaning to the biography and social trajectory of Coshuaca's *campesinos* and to those in many other places in the high sierra of Hidalgo: men and women who once dreamt of being Centeuctli, the corn itself.

Notes

1. *Fiscales* are individuals in charge of organizing the Catholic cult in these towns, in the absence of priests, but upon the latter's express petition.

2. Centeuctli is a reverential word used by residents of Coshuaca to refer to corn. According to their translation, it means "the owner of the corn," though in other

contexts it means "the blessed little corn." Its roots are *centli,* which means "corn," and *teuctli,* meaning "lord."

3. Nahua celebrations were accompanied by the twelve *sones* of "Xochipitzahual," a song dedicated to the mother in her personification as giver of life and symbol of agricultural fertility.

4. Popular music dance band, typically made up only of wind instruments and percussion.

5. *Matlachines* is a dance performed by peasants who brandish machetes to simulate, among other things, the act of weeding a cornfield (*matlayar*). *Santiagos* are hobby horse dances. *Huapango* is the name given to a musical genre characteristic of the Huasteca areas in Hidalgo, Veracruz, and San Luis Potosí. It is also the name given to the dance that accompanies the music performed by a trio on the violin and two guitar-like instruments known as *jaranas* and *huapangueras.* The music of *huapangos* re-creates epic tales that allude to mermaids, towns, the countryside, and local personages.

6. The *ayate,* or fiber bag, is a kind of carrying bag or net that *campesinos* use to transport corn. It consists of a piece of cloth tied at the ends and attached to a strap that is placed on the forehead to support the weight of the sack of corn that is carried on one's back.

7. According to the local imaginary, Xilonen is the grandmother of the "blessed little corn." When the cornfield has matured, peasants can see a reddish spot on the tip of the corn that they call *jilote,* which indicates that the corn has ripened.

PART III

Trajectories of Tradition

11

The *Matachines Danza* as Intercultural Discourse

BRENDA M. ROMERO

The *Matachines* (Matlachines)

This chapter provides a brief historical and bibliographical overview of *matachines danzas* and describes varying elements in a broad sample, clarifying some of the *danza's* important roles and guises in an extended region that reaches across the U.S.-Mexico border. The variety of *matachines* types and variants is intriguing, and in New Mexico this has generated a layer of scholarly polemics about the origins of *matachines* that this chapter also seeks to resolve (see also Romero 1997, 2003; Stephenson 2001). Similar polemics bring to bear on historical approaches, which many contemporary scholars eschew in favor of ethnographic analyses. Yet it is as incomprehensible to conceive of ethnographic studies that ignore historical events and processes as it is to think that any understanding of historical events could ignore ethnography, and so this work is squarely based on fieldwork in a variety of contexts. Confusions of all kinds surround *matachines* studies, a situation that begs for a comprehensive study, of which this chapter is only a part.

Those new to the tradition sometimes assume that all *danzas* are *matachines,* but this is not the case. In Mexico there is little ambiguity regarding its status as only one kind of *danza de conquista,* conquest dance-drama, appearing in saints' day celebrations, referred to as *fiestas patronales. Matachines* are particularly prominent in north central Mexico, but an important exception is found in Oaxaca (where it is increasingly called *monos*), and if one looks farther south, *matachines* are also to be found in Colombia (see also Stephenson 2001), Brazil, Puerto Rico, and Peru.[1]

Mural on the wall at San José Parish in Huahuapan, Oaxaca, with jesters flanking the boast of "Bienvenidos al Barrio de San José, Cuna de los Auténticos Bullangueros Matachines," "Birthplace of the Authentic and Raucous *Matachines*." Photograph by author.

Distinct *matachines* variants thrive in New Mexico in both Pueblo indigenous and Hispano (Spanish Mexican) contexts, in Arizona among the Yaqui (as among the Yaqui south of the border), and in south Texas among mestizos. The local importance of the tradition is reflected in people's beliefs in some provincial New Mexican locations that theirs is the "original" Spanish music and dance; indeed, many have only seen other versions on television. If Hispanics in New Mexico have maintained the *matachines* as an icon of Spanish tradition, in Mexico *matachines* allow for the expression of indigenous ideals and formats (Romero 2003). Here large, communal groups of *matachines danzantes* participate in local and neighboring fiestas far and wide, as fiestas are large events that recur annually to coincide with many different saints' day celebrations. Mexico did not experience the reservation system of the Southwestern groups, and this led to a greater *mestizaje*, with a strong indigenous character in many isolated locations. The gathering together of different groups at large events may itself have been a preconquest tradition, as it was among northern indigenous groups, around naturally occurring, calendrical events like first fruit or harvest celebrations. Such gatherings were common in Europe—Spain—around the same seasonal events, and this coincidence may partially explain the vitality of the Mexican fiesta today.

Different processes of culture contact in Mexico also resulted in *danzas* different from those among Hispanos and Natives in the Southwest, whose distinct variants survive only in New Mexico and in some parts of Texas, although a Hispano group in southern Colorado reorganized itself after many years for a short time in the mid-1990s. It is important to note that the early Southwestern variants arrived with the Spanish, which accounts in part for the differences from more recent ones that have arrived with Mexican immigrants. The Catholic contexts are the same in the Southwest as in Mexico; however, Southwest *matachines* was the only surviving Hispano *danza* from early colonial times until the Chicano movement provided fertile ground for the reinvention of tradition through *danza azteca* in recent times.[2] On the other hand, Pueblo indigenous dance-drama traditions have survived for millennia in New Mexico, with occasional abrupt modifications, such as when the Spanish colonial government outlawed the use of ceremonial masks. *Matachines* were exempt from this rule.

A "received" tradition, Matachina (its Pueblo name)[3] is one of only two Native Southwest traditions dating back to colonial times that use European-derived instruments. While the guitars and violins are the lone survivors of the Pueblo revolt in New Mexico (1680), in Arizona the Yaqui continue to play guitars and harps in some "Matachini" ceremonials.[4]

Mexican versions of *matachines* have existed for many years in the United States wherever large immigrant populations have settled, as in Dallas, Detroit, and Chicago,[5] and newly arriving immigrants continue to maintain this noncommercial, prayer-like tradition on the north side of the border. There are at least three troupes in the Denver/Boulder area, and there is little doubt that the tradition will be disseminated widely in the north during the twenty-first century, as *ballet folklórico* has been since the 1930s.[6]

The *matachines danza* is characterized by a standard double-file formerly made up exclusively of male dancers, or *danzantes,* who create symbolic, sometimes virtuosic choreographic formations over the course of a performance or enactment. The most widely accepted origins theory is that *los matachines* was, in Europe, a profane dance event displayed as entertainment on Catholic feast days (see Lozano 2007; see also Shipley 1987). In the Americas, however, the Spanish saw its potential for converting the Indians to Catholicism and substituted or superimposed it as something congruent with the seriousness of Aztec and other indigenous dance rituals. A competing theory suggests that the tradition is indigenous to the New World (see Treviño and Gilles 1994; see also Stephenson 2001), but this theory does not explain the established *matachines* traditions as *moriscos*[7] in Europe during the sixteenth century. The decidedly Iberian qualities of the *danza* still dominate among Hispanos in New Mexico and Afro-mestizo elements dominate in Colombia, suggesting that the process of reinterpretation is enough to account for the *matachines*' widespread indigenous character in most Mexican contexts. The case of the Pueblo of Jemez's Matachina, discussed further below, provides a transparent example of the process of reinterpretation. One ceremonial moiety enacts a "Spanish" version accompanied by violin and guitar, and the more conservative ceremonial moiety enacts a reinterpreted version that looks more traditionally Native (see also Romero 1997).[8]

The term *matachin* is most closely related to the Italian *mattaccino*, or buffoon, a role assumed by early *matachines* groups in Spain for theatrical interludes in burlesque comedies of the *comedia del arte*, during the Siglo de Oro, or Golden Age of Spanish theater (Hurtado and Mata Induráin 2002, 164). Remnants of this important satiric genre, in the form of long-nosed masks associated with *el "dottore"* (the "doctor"), survive in *carpa* (tent theater) in Mexico and the Southwest. This same mask is essential in an elaborate Peruvian line dance that resembles *matachines*, called *Huaconada*, "a dance that controls—or, if necessary punishes—the misbehavior of the inhabitants . . . during the first three days of the year in the city of Mito, located on the right margin of the Mantaro River, 16 kilometers from Huancayo" (Silva Meinel and Muñoz Monge 1998, 33). The same half mask with large nose characterizes some regional variants of *danzas de matachines* in Colombia, tying the tradition also to Carnival celebrations. *Matachines* was the name given to a wide variety of troupes that dressed up and danced in sixteenth-century holy day processions, much as they do today. They are often described as having carried animal bladders filled with air or water and pelting each other or the crowd with them, as children do with balloons. Today the *matachines danza* is commonly referred to as *los matachines* or simply *matachines*. In central Mexico the *danza* is also called *matlachines;* this is in accordance with the Nahua linguistic practice of forming a glottal /tl/ where a single unaspirated /t/ would be sounded in Spanish. The Mexican anthropologist José Sánchez Jiménez notes that the term among the Nahua today is associated with the use of machetes, an implement the Spaniards also introduced.[9] There are still Mexican *danzas de conquista* that use machetes, presumably instead of swords, in dangerous dance exchanges, such as one that enacts choreographed battles between Pontius Pilate and Saint James.[10] As previously mentioned, the term *matachina* is preferred among the Pueblo Native groups of New Mexico, and *matachini* among the Yaqui of Arizona and Mexico, a term also used among the Rarámuri of the Sierra Tarahumara and other indigenous groups in northwest Mexico.

Over time, a differentiation of types has evolved, and it is fair to say that the term *matachines* has become a generic appellation (or perhaps always was), and the *matachines* of New Mexico are quite different from the *matachini* of the Sierra Tarahumara, which are yet again quite different from the *matlachines* of Aguascalientes, in central Mexico. A confounding aspect of researching *matachines* is that different appellations are common in different parts of Mexico, as, for instance, a *danza del agua* (water dance) in the Huastec region of Mexico that includes elements similar to those of the Rarámuri and New Mexican Hispano versions. Norma E. Cantú cites three kinds that are in the Coahuiltecan tradition, *matachines* (or *matlachines*) *de la pluma, de la palma,* and *de la flecha.*[11] These terms are used widely in north central Mexico, in addition to which I have heard *danza del indio,* which I believe to be synonymous with *de la flecha.* Field interviews provide evidence that the terms are sometimes used interchangeably by *danzantes.*[12] Dance scholars in Mexico attribute a victorious Spanish narrative to those *danzas* categorized as *de conquista,* dances of conquest, and a victorious indigenous narrative to the Oaxacan *danza de la pluma* (Jáuregui and Bonfiglioli 1996a, 29), which differs markedly from the *matachines de la pluma* types of north central Mexico, although arguably the underlying theme of resistance could be said to apply to reinterpreted versions in the north as well.

Matachines Research in the Southwest

In the United States there were quite a few short articles published in the *New Mexico Magazine* and other local magazines and newspapers in the mid-twentieth century. Typically such articles speculated on the origins of the *matachines,* in keeping with the goals of folklore studies at the time. These included short articles by composer John Donald Robb (1961), folklorist Aurora Lucero-White Lea (1963–64), anthropologist Gertrude Kurath (1957), and many others. Their wide dissemination, proliferation, and variety provoked serious scholarly publication on the *matachines,* starting with Gertrude Kurath and Antonio Garcia's inclusion of *matachines* and its Labanotations in their *Music and Dance of the Tewa Pueblos* (1970). The next publication followed ten years later, with John Donald Robb's *Hispanic Folk Music of New Mexico and the Southwestern United States* (1980), which included transcriptions of a substantive number of *matachines* melodies from Robb's field tapes, collected between the 1930s and 1970s. Then came Flavia Champe's *The Matachines Dance of the Upper Rio Grande* (1983), which focused on the *matachines* music and dance of San Ildefonso Pueblo and is still unique for including transcriptions of the music in addition to detailed dance Labanotations.

Since the 1960s the Chicano movement stimulated many researchers to center on traditions that might reveal something of a previously hidden cultural history in which Hispano indigenous roots or Hispano-Native relations could be foregrounded. This was especially true in New Mexico, where *los matachines* thrive both in the indigenous Pueblos and in Hispano communities. New Mexican researchers in this category included anthropologist Sylvia Rodriguez, amateur ethnomusicologists Adrián Treviño and Barbara Gilles, literary folklorist Enrique Lamadrid, documentary photographer Miguel Gandert, folklorist Claude D. Stephenson, ethnomusicologist Peter J. Garcia, and myself, a composer and ethnomusicologist. In the same spirit, a few scholars grew up with the tradition and began writing about it; of these, literary folklorist Norma E. Cantú, who is from Laredo, Texas, is the best-known.

The first attempt at serious ethnographic analysis of *matachines* appeared in 1991, with Sylvia Rodriguez's article in the *American Ethnologist,* "The Taos Pueblo *Matachines:* Ritual Symbolism and Interethnic Relations." I followed her seminal article with my ethnomusicology dissertation "*The Matachines Music and Dance in San Juan Pueblo and Alcalde, New Mexico: Contexts and Meanings*"(1993), in which I argued that *matachines* have fostered a symbiotic intercultural relationship between Pueblos and Hispanos. While Pueblos have often relied on Hispano musicians and *danzantes* to maintain the tradition, it is unclear whether the tradition would have survived among Hispanos of New Mexico had it not been for the Pueblo and other indigenous ritual dance models. I also tried to determine the role *matachines* had played in Spain prior to the Conquest and the extent to which the tradition is transformed in New Mexican contexts today. I made the case that the contexts and beliefs of *matachines* enactments in Pueblo and Hispano communities are different, and that the meaning of the *danza* thus varies culturally, even while the choreography, music, and other elements are the same or similar. Finally, I transcribed the repertoires of Alcalde (a Hispano community) and San Juan Pueblo, today called Ohkay Owingeh[13] (both very near to my childhood community), which are closely related to each other, and of the

Pueblo of Jemez. I compared these three repertoires to each other and to Robb's eighty-seven transcribed melodies (1980), showing the distribution of related New Mexican *matachines* melodies among the entire sample. The exercise revealed obvious links between musical gestures and choreographies, something I also observed as a violin player for the Pueblo of Jemez. I have continued to explore various dimensions of *matachines* in a number of articles (see 1997, 1999, 2007), and a book-length manuscript is forthcoming.

In 1996, Sylvia Rodriguez published *The Matachines Dance: Ritual Symbolism and Interethnic Relations in the Rio Grande Valley,* in which she focused on finding the "hidden transcript" of interethnic relations in *matachines,* focusing closely on Arroyo Seco and nearby Taos (where she is from), but also examining a number of other New Mexican locations. Her status as "*coyota*"(mixed Hispana and white) gave her a unique position from which to examine dynamics of interethnic relations, and her emphasis on ritual symbolism, although insufficiently developed, inspired many scholars, myself included. Our work paralleled each other's between 1987 and 1993, and we often saw each other in the field.

One of the most significant articles for *matachines* research of the mid-1990s was an article published in the *New Mexico Historical Review* by amateur ethnomusicologist duo Adrian Treviño and Barbara Gilles. Their article, "A History of the *Matachines* Dance" (1994), proposed an indigenous New World origins theory for the *danza.* The article, based on secondary sources, suffered from a lack of ethnographic rigor and largely ignored published evidence that the *matachines* originate in long-standing Western European buffoon traditions. Their article did contribute to an understanding of how some indigenous dances might have transformed or replaced the Spanish *matachines* in some places over time, however.

More recently, in his dissertation "La Onda Nuevo Mexicana: Multi-Sited Ethnography, Ritual Contexts, and Popular Traditional Musics in New Mexico" (2001), ethnomusicologist Peter J. Garcia addressed the blurring of the sacred and secular in the juxtaposition of *matachines* and the secular *baile,* a typically New Mexican practice. He also focused on issues of gender, class, and sexuality in leadership roles in the Bernalillo *matachines.* Claude D. Stephenson's dissertation "A Comparative Analysis of *Matachines* Music and Its History and Dispersion in the American Southwest" (2001) made no attempt to address choreographies but is still the most comprehensive analytical work on the music itself, providing transcriptions of a wide sampling of *matachines* pieces from both sides of the border and noting gesture variation in the music. As I had done in my dissertation, he also studied the distribution of related

New Mexican *matachines* melodies among Robb's sample. Most significantly, he provided several insights about the musicians who play *matachines*, based in part on his own performances for the Bernalillo *matachines*. The biggest weakness in the dissertation was Stephenson's determination to confirm Treviño and Gilles's indigenous American origins theory, thus essentializing the tradition in the opposite direction to Hispanophiles. Finally, Max Harris, who also supports Treviño and Gilles's theory (Stephenson 2001, 41), made problematic references to *matachines* in his *Aztecs, Moors, and Christians: Festivals of Reconquest in Mexico and Spain* (2000).[14] It is clear that these scholars were not wrong in positing that present-day *matachines* are (or have become) indigenous, but to generalize that they always were, or that they are perceived as such by practitioners, undermines our understanding of the intricacies of historical processes and ignores the full extent of the cultural devastation brought by the Conquest.

A number of articles (1989, 1992a, 1992b, 1995a, 1995b, 2003, 2005), a dissertation (1982), and a forthcoming book, *Soldiers of the Cross: Los Matachines de la Santa Cruz*, by Norma E. Cantú document the *matachines* in the border town of Laredo, Texas, and in Nuevo Laredo, across the border in Mexico. These include descriptions of the elements of the *danza* and are good attempts at capturing a sense of the inner processes of *matachines* enactments. Cantú also assisted producer Marlene Richardson in an award-winning television documentary, *Los Matachines de la Santa Cruz* (1996). Finally, documentary photographer Miguel Gandert has published many photographs of *matachines* in many locations (Figure 11.2; see also Gandert 2002, 73–90).

Mexican Sources

As previously mentioned, the debate regarding origins is not occurring in Mexico, where *matachines* is considered a *danza de conquista*, among many others. As such, *matachines* is one of several *danzas* that relate colonial events in one form or another and are often closely linked to theatrical traditions, the informing narratives of which have often transformed over time (see Jáuregui and Bonfiglioli 1996a). Furthermore, in Mexico there have been few attempts thus far to isolate *matachines* from other dances of conquest, so no comprehensive overview of Mexican *matachines* is currently available. Carlo Bonfiglioli published the only book-length study that focuses closely on *matachines* (1995), although he naively applied his conclusions on the *danza*'s role in maintaining cosmic harmony among the Rarámuri (Tarahumara of north Mexico) to the New Mexican versions. Bonfiglioli

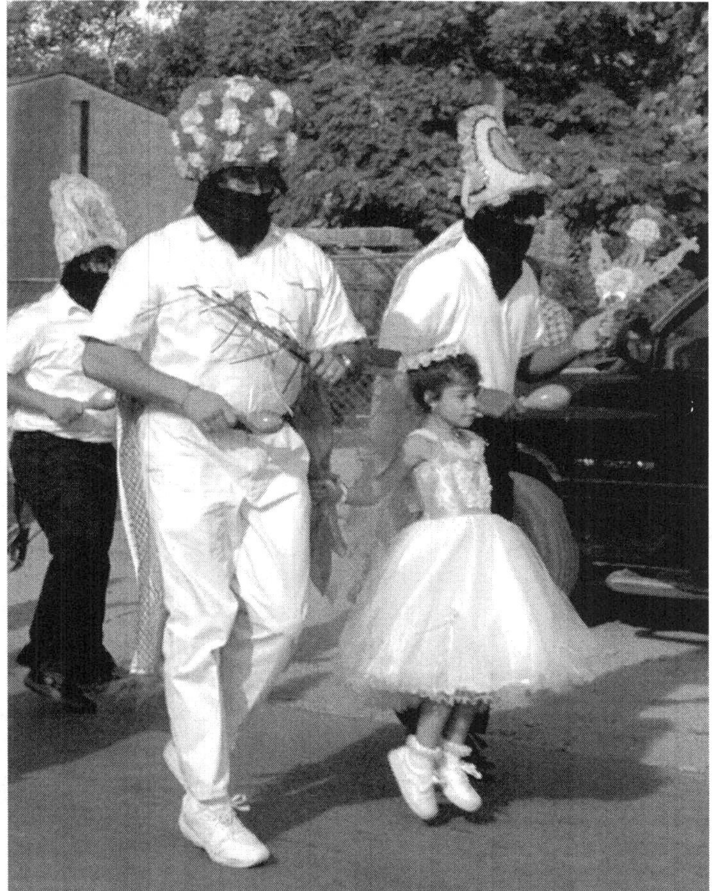

"*La Malinche Salta*" ("La Malinche Jumps"). Photograph by Miguel Gandert.

joins anthropologist Jesús Jáuregui as co-editor of *Las Danzas de conquista, I. México contemporáneo* (1996), where one learns a great deal about *danza* in general but less about *matachines,* per se.

Bonfiglioli's chapter on the Rarámuri, "Fariseos y matachines: el conflicto y la armonía cósmicos,"[15] in *Las danzas de conquista* relies on materials from his book published the year before, but this time includes helpful musical transcriptions and dance notations. Another chapter by Bonfiglioli, "Chichimecas contra Franceses: de los 'Salvajes' y los Conquistadores,"[16] describes the inclusion in this *danza* of various elements I have observed in central Mexican *matlachines*, elements that may have been adapted to this one as described by Bonfiglioli: "*Según el Nahual, la danza de chichimecas se compone de una decena de bailes 'autenticos,' es decir, exclusivos de esta danza, más otros tomados en préstamo de otras danzas y adaptados a ésta*" (1996, 100).[17] In the same anthology, Demetrio Brisset's chapter, "Cortés derrotado: La Visión indígena de la conquista,"[18] focuses on the *danzas de la pluma* from Oaxaca and includes three pages on the inclusion of Malinches as symbolic objects of the struggle between opposing groups (85–87) (discussed further below).

Pedro de Velasco Rivero includes a lengthy chapter on *matachines* in his overview of Rarámuri religion and resistance to domination, *Danzar o morir* (*Dance or Die*) (152–88). Finally, as in the United States, many short articles have been and continue to be published in local Mexican newspapers, mostly in reference to local troupes and enactments.

Prototypes, Spiritual and Social Contexts

Matachines are significant in part because they continue to be a dynamic tradition in spite of factors that threaten their existence. Along the border in Tortugas, New Mexico, and Juárez, Mexico, the *matachines* troupes are large communal groupings, similar to the Pueblo corn dances, which are also danced in Tortugas among descendants of Pueblo ancestry. At Ranchos de Anapra in Juárez I was told that fundamentalist Protestant groups, commonly referred to as "*los aleluyas*," are attracting many participants away from Catholicism and therefore away from *matachines*, as the *danza* is typically tied to the Catholic ritual calendar. While the numbers of participants are fewer than before, troupes along the border are still large (twenty to more than a hundred), although farther south the troupes are much smaller and not as communal. In Trancoso, in the northern part of the state of Zacatecas, a *danzante* told me they dance *matachines* as a prayer for rain. An interesting exception to the religious contexts, in the state of Zacatecas, Mexico, regional, state-supported organizations, called Centros Culturales (Cultural Centers), have begun to preserve the *matachines* as cultural forms through regional competitions, as in the area of Pinos, Noria de Angeles, and Loretto. This trend will likely spread, at least regionally.

Farther south, in Matehuala, in the Mexican state of San Luis Potosí, a woman I interviewed had stepped into the role of *mayordoma* (female steward of the *danza*) and trained a youth group that includes boys and girls through their teens, because the men are mostly working across the border in the United States (or Canada). Women are the *mayordomas* of several groups in Laredo, Texas[19] and I documented a *mayordoma* in Alcalde, New Mexico, in 1992 who fulfilled the obligation when her husband passed away. Most often, while women are considered *mayordomas,* it is in complement to their husbands' roles as *mayordomos.* In 2004, however, the same woman in Alcalde organized a female *matachines* group, called Las Matachines de Alcalde New Mexico Rainbow Dancers.[20]

The *matachines* among Hispanos in New Mexico and mestizos in Juárez evidence some of the oldest Iberian ceremonial dress (although in Juárez the choreographic formats are more indigenous); farther south of the border, in Mexico, the Iberian qualities are obscured. There are some very old Iberian *matachines* versions represented in Ranchos de Anapra, Juárez, in which the *danzantes* wear white tunics, much as men wore for similar enactments throughout Europe until the early part of the twentieth century. Perhaps they were a rendition of Islamic dress, as they strongly resemble today's Sufi tunics. In Ranchos de Anapra, as in the New Mexican versions, the *danzantes* carry a gourd rattle, often covered by a handkerchief and turned inward, in one hand and a trident in the other, similar to what the *matachines de la palma* would carry.[21] The use of the gourd rattle is indigenous, however.

One Iberian element is the character of the *abuelo,* or grandfather, featured in New Mexico, who differs from his Mexican counterpart in playing an integral role cueing the sequences of the *danza.* (In Mexico, and in Mexican versions on the U.S. side of the border, as in Laredo, Texas, the *capitanes,* or leaders of each line, cue changes in choreography.) There is sometimes also an *abuela,* or grandmother, who is a man dressed as an elderly woman, in a comedic role, a Spanish festival tradition that is still visible in Spanish contexts today.[22] This tradition dates back to historical European times when women were not allowed in theatricals, so men played female roles.[23] I have not seen a woman playing this role to date, as it is pejorative, a symbolic reversal that teaches how older women must *not* behave. This character is called *la perihundia* in Taos and a few other places documented by Sylvia Rodriguez (1996) in New Mexico.

In Mexican contexts, the *viejo de la fiesta* is an essential part of the *danza,* ensuring that everything go as it should, but not cueing the sequences. The *viejo* is dressed as a comedic figure, often a hobo-like character; additionally, many *viejos* play lesser roles than the main *viejo.* One sees increasing numbers of the lesser *viejos* wearing ghoulish Halloween masks in *matachines* celebrations in New Mexican Hispano towns, as they do in Mexico. In New Mexico, too, one sees *vaqueros,* or cowboys, who are less important than the *abuelo* and who more closely resemble the Mexican *viejos* in providing entertaining sidelines for the audience. The *vaqueros* control the *toro*, or bull.

In the Pueblos of Jemez and Ohkay Owingeh, New Mexico, the *danza* has been reinterpreted in a completely local fashion and the dress and music have changed over time to conform to Pueblo practices, although the choreographies remain much the same.[24] The Jemez male chorus and drum version requires completely traditional regalia. Although traditional regalia are also required in Ohkay Owingeh, there the music is still played on guitar and violin.

The dramatic enactment of conversion is choreographed in the New Mexican versions. There is always a Monarca (Monarch), sometimes called Moctezuma, who overcomes his spiritual weakness in the course of the *danza*. It is common to feature a young girl as Malinche, in a white communion dress, although in the Pueblos she dresses traditionally and is more of a young woman than a young girl. The Malinche does not have the same connotations in New Mexico as in Mexican folklore, however, where she is much maligned as traitor of Moctezuma, and thus of the Aztecs. This is because the *matachines* arrived in New Mexico long before the Malinche figure acquired the negative character she subsequently developed in Mexico. Along the border it is common to see a Monarca and three or more young girls as Malinches, a tradition that might recall that Moctezuma had more than one wife (see Brisset 1996, 85–86), but they typically wear the same colors as the troupe, and the drama is in the choreography as described below for Mexico. The inclusion of multiple Malinches has been adopted in New Mexico, notably in Bernalillo, where it is desirable to allow as many young girls as possible to dance. The presence of Malinche with a male protagonist of the *danza* symbolizes either Moctezuma's wife or Cortez's mistress (given as a slave to Cortéz) in both Mexico and New Mexico. Brisset provides some perspective on the Iberian origins of a female protagonist in the *danza* and her context in Christian enactments:

> *En otros trabajos he identifacado "el rapto de la doncella" como uno de los motivos básicos de las danzas de conquista en la Península Ibérica, aunque actualmente se encuentra en un nivel arcaico, residual y metafórico. El personaje de la doncella no tiene tanta relevancia en ninguna representación actual como en Oaxaca. Puede ser que en el antiguo culto al dios zapoteco de la fertilidad y de la muerte intervinieran doncellas que representasen divinidades, pero,para interpretar su actual significado, habría que compararlas con las otras Malinches de los rituales mexicanos. Para terminar, solo añadiré que la Malinche cristiana desfila con las tropas españolas cuando éstas aparecen en escena.* (86–7)[25]

In addition, in New Mexico and occasionally in Mexico there is also a *toro* (bull), usually played by a young boy. The *matachines* sequence in which the bull is "killed" is found exclusively in New Mexico,[26] although the bull is occasionally seen in the Huastec region as part of a *danza de agua*. The bull is perhaps the most telling Iberian element of the New Mexican *matachines* versions from Albuquerque north to southern Colorado, as the bull did not exist in the Americas prior to the Conquest. On the other hand, it was a salient symbol for early European civilizations such as the ancient Minoans, but also among the ancient Romans there existed the soldiers' mystery cult of Mithra, in which a bull was killed in celebration of the triumph of good over evil.

Finally, in New Mexico the Río Abajo *matachines* practices (Bernalillo north to the Keres Pueblo of Cochiti, where it is sometimes performed) and those of the Río Arriba *matachines* (north of Santa Fe) are similar enough to constitute a northern version, as opposed to the southern versions that begin to appear in Tortugas, approximately fifty miles from the Mexican border. As previously mentioned, the Pueblos incorporate two versions, Spanish-Mexican and Pueblo.

A marble statue in a grotto at the ruins of Ostia Antica (Old Rome) of the legendary Mithra slaying a bull in celebration of the triumph of good over evil. Photograph by Phillip B. Gallegos.

Danzantes are generally characterized locally by the type of headdress they wear, which can vary by troupe in single towns. In New Mexico *danzantes* wear tall, decorated hats called *coronas,* or (king's) crowns, from which multicolored ribbons fall, with scarves covering the mouth, neck, and back, and with a bead or cloth fringe covering the eyes. The combination looks like North African desert tribal dress, presumably harking back to the time in Europe when *matachines* represented conquered and converted Turks or Arabs. This image is seen in both Hispano and Pueblo contexts, although the Puebloans decorate the crowns lavishly with turquoise and silver jewelry that helps to ensure prosperity through the ritual, as a kind of sympathetic magic, in spite of a general level of poverty (more so prior to gaming, although not all Pueblos have casinos).

Starting at the border south into Mexico there are a variety of headdresses, or *penachos,* from which different groups may choose, depending on the type of *matachines: danza de indio* or *danza de pluma.* Variants of the *corona* described above are still common in the *danza de pluma,* especially north of the Mexican state of Durango, although each *corona* is unique within the style, while a uniform dyed feather war bonnet, the type worn in the past among Plains groups in the United States, is common in the *danza de indio.* The war bonnet further associates the *matachines* with North American currents of Native resistance to European hegemony, even when appropriated from the popular media.[27] Some Mexican groups wear a round *penacho* made of feathers thickly interwoven, as did a group from Aguascalientes that I observed in Mexico City at the feast day of Our Lady of Guadalupe in 2000.

The groups of central Mexico, including the states of Zacatecas, San Luis Potosí, Aguascalientes, Durango, Nuevo León, Tamaulipas, and Chihuahua, typically wear a kind of skirt, called *nagüilla,* that is decorated with *carrizo* (river cane), a material that has historically seen many uses among Mexican peoples.[28] It is common also for these groups to carry a gourd rattle turned inward, but more often they carry a bow and arrow, *la flecha,* used to make a snapping sound; *la flecha* is not used in New Mexico. In Texas, the Laredo *matachines* who dance *de la flecha* or *del indio* carry both the stylized bow and arrow and the gourd, demonstrating the Mexican rather than New Mexican style. In Nahua codices, the bow and arrow is a symbol of light. The dance regalia for these groups features a particular color, which is red among the oldest groups, often called Chichimecas after the last resistant indigenous nation of northern Mexico. The *danzantes* often make their own regalia differing in detail from any other, while conforming to a uniform look overall.

A common feature across borders is the use of Catholic images, including saints on the back of the shawl hanging from the shoulders. Most often it is the image of the Virgin of Guadalupe, whose importance is paramount among Mexicans everywhere, and this is true for New Mexicans as well. In many places her image or that of a particular saint is also displayed on the headdress and embroidered on the *nagüilla*, just below the navel.

Another tradition exists between the New Mexican and Mexican ones, and is represented by the Yaquis, Rarámuris, and other indigenous groups of southern Arizona and Chihuahua and Sonora in north Mexico. The choreography is Mexican (described below), but the dress consists of long, draped robes of colorful cloth worn over everyday clothing. There is a central *abuelo*-like figure (the *chapayeke*), who wears a white-faced mask worn on the back of the head so that he appears to see from both sides. The *danzantes* carry only a gourd rattle turned inward (see also Bonfiglioli 1991).

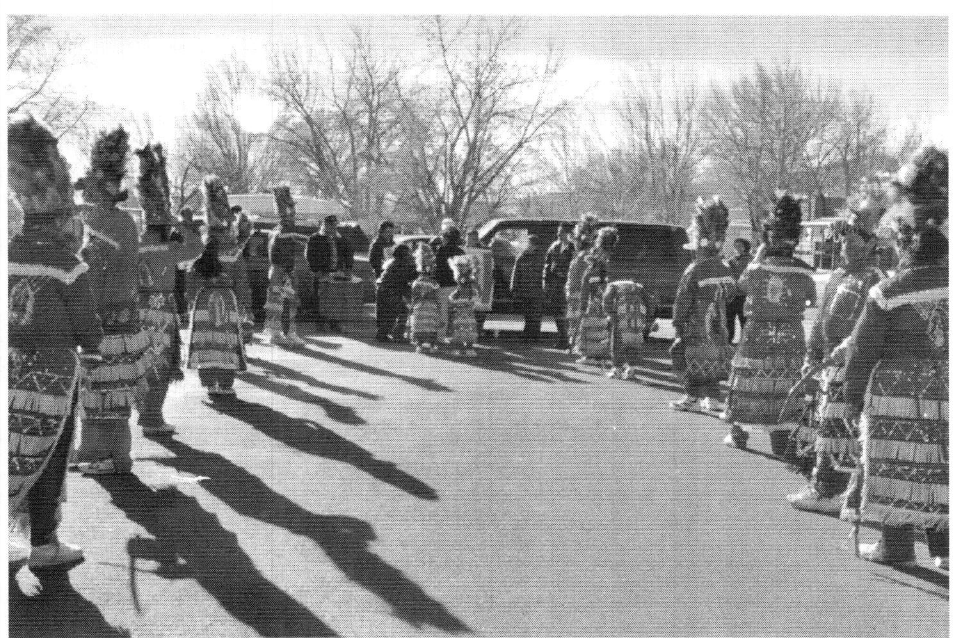

The red Chichimeca group, featuring a *nagüilla* with *carrizo* (cane) fringe, as commonly seen in northern Mexico. This group, in Boulder, Colorado, is transplanted from the state of Durango. Photograph by author.

The Dance and Choreographies

In most places, it is still important that the *matachines* arrive in procession, as in pilgrimage, to the place where they will dance.[29] In the Pueblo of Jemez, New Mexico, for instance, the dancers always arrive from afar, cueing the musicians to begin so the *danzantes* can enter the dance space dancing. In Mexico, *danzantes* typically arrive at their *danza* locations in a procession, called *romería* or *peregrinación,* both terms meaning "pilgrimage." The *danza* typically takes place at the plaza or other designated spaces in, but mostly around, the church. For Mexican fiestas the *matachines* do not always dance other than in the spaces around the church, for which they have been commissioned, while in New Mexico there are always subsequent performances at the houses of important people in the *danza* organization. These troupes can be very family-oriented, although this is not always the case. Groups on both sides of the border rarely accept payment for religious fiestas but may accept donations, which go into maintaining the *danza.* The groups are almost always fed, however. *Matachines* are increasingly invited to dance for important secular occasions in many places, and this may change attitudes toward accepting payment.[30]

Significant action takes place between the two lines of dancers. In New Mexico (and southern Colorado) the dance sequences are tied to a pantomimed story line of Catholic fundamentalist tone, so each dance sequence has its own melody and is repeated, in cyclical fashion, until the choreographic requirements of that sequence formation are met. The pantomimed story line is not usually articulated other than as the performance.[31]

There is a particular order in which the *sones* (tunes) appear in New Mexico, while this is less obvious in Mexico, where the interest is focused on ever more virtuosic dance steps to matching dynamic drum patterns. I was told in Zacatecas that it takes five days to dance the entire *danza* in all its parts, but that this is rarely done now that they are invited to dance at a local fiesta for one or two days and must adapt to performance circumstances.

Where the *abuelo* cues the melodic and choreographic sequences in New Mexico, in Mexico it is the *capitanes,* the lead dancers of each line, who introduce ever more intricate *pasos* (steps) at the culmination of each set of three *vueltas,* or rounds. That is, there are three repetitions of each choreographic *pisada,* or pattern of sequence of steps; in each repetition each pair of *danzantes* dances to the front and then around to the back of the double file while performing that particular *pisada.* After the third *vuelta* the two *capitanes* intensify the dance choreography, typically adding to it and making it longer, say going from twelve to sixteen, or even thirty-two steps to the *pisada*. Such choreographic patterning can depict important Catholic iconography, such as the cross. As one might imagine, this tradition is rapidly becoming a virtuosic art requiring a great deal of stamina, not to mention memory, flexibility, agility, and speed. It is common in Zacatecas to see young *matachines* troupes, including both teenage boys and girls, dancing at incredibly fast tempos, to two precisely synchronized bass drums played (typically) by young men. Dancing from dawn to dusk is an additional autosacrificial act that the older troupes strive for as they fulfill their *promesas* (vows) or *mandamientos* (requirements) in exchange for divine intervention in their particular prayerful petitions. This tradition of spiritual reciprocation is another common element across borders.

In New Mexico, even in the Pueblo reinterpretations, the dance step is a bouncy, jumping step, with the upper torso held rigidly upright, remotely similar to the Irish River Dance troupe of recent popularity. Traditional Pueblo dances are rarely bouncy, but rather the feet stay close to the ground. In contrast to the New Mexican *matachines,* the Mexican *danzantes* often take a more flexible body position, with knees and shoulders bent to resemble, say, a deer or other animal, and the feet staying close to the ground.

In Texas, as in other *norteño matachines,* accordion and drum duos provide the music. In Mexico, the bass drum has taken over everywhere that the violin has declined. Groups still prefer the violin (except in Oaxaca, where a unique version is accompanied by the municipal band), but fewer violin players are available or able to play the rapid repertoires. Where the violin is replaced by drum, the names of the *sones* played by the violin are retained, but the *sones* are rendered rhythmically.

I finish this whirlwind *matachines* tour in the state of Oaxaca, where we begin to hear about who made the *matachines,* or *monos.* This is because they are wooden figures, much like the *gigantes* (giants) one still sees in Spain during feast day celebrations today.[32] Spanish sources say that *matachines* (sometimes called *mojigangas*) were performed as *entremeses* (interludes) in popular comedic plays.[33] Oaxaca is the only location I have found where comedic dramas and *matachines* were performed in close juxtaposition until around 2000 in the town of Tezoatlán for the feast day celebrations of San Sebastián (January 20). I surmise that the Oaxacan *matachines* originate with some of the earliest European-imposed carnival contexts. Finally, the dress and choreographies of the Oaxacan *danza de la pluma* are sensational and often soloistic, but distinctly different from the north-central Mexican *matachines.*

The music is provided on two bass drums and an accordion (performed by the director of the group, Manuel Borrego) for this norteño matachines group in Boulder, Colorado. Photograph by author.

Summary

Everywhere they survive, the *matachines* represent an active expression of faith. Today's *matachines danzas* primarily honor Catholic saints, but *matachines* are also danced ceremonially for important secular occasions in many places. In Zacatecas special attention has focused on the tradition in minifestivals that recognize its importance and encourage its development, especially as a means of incorporating youth in meaningful artistic and spiritual activity. In other parts of Zacatecas, the *matachines* is believed to bring rain. Mexican mestizo *matachines* dance in lavish and colorful fiesta contexts, sometimes in public squares where the drum sets off car alarms!

Hispanos of New Mexico incorporate traditional Spanish theatrical devices as a form of entertainment and social commentary. *Matachines* is the only religious dance ritual allowed in rural New Mexican Hispano Catholicism. Its revival, made possible by the ideals of the Chicano movement of the 1960s, is motivated in part by the desire to regain what has been lost, but obviously there is much more to it than that. The sheer joyfulness of the *danza* and its music may be the main reason it has survived in a culture with little material basis for happiness, equally among the Pueblos as among Hispanos.

As a transnational tradition, the *matachines danza* has original roots on both sides of the United States–Mexico border among Hispanos and indigenous peoples. New traditions are constantly evolving, as they are among recent immigrants in Chicago, Denver, and Detroit (and perhaps even in Canada, where many Mexicans have immigrated). Additionally, the *danza* is beginning to change contexts due to staged performances for special occasions, as in Pinos, Zacatecas, and by professional dance troupes like Amalia Hernandez's Ballet Folklórico de México.

The *matachines danza* crosses many borders, and, much as human nature itself, it has changed in response to a myriad of factors. It has helped people to survive as much as people have aided its own persistence. It has helped people to connect with something deeper than its external elements might suggest, which is the subject of Norma E. Cantú's chapter in this volume.

Notes

I wish to thank my *comadres* Norma E. Cantú and Olga Nájera-Ramírez for their guidance in editing this essay. María Teresa Guillén Becerra facilitated my initial fieldwork in Colombia, for which I am eternally grateful. Fieldwork for this work was funded by a Fulbright García-Robles Scholarship (2000–2001) and by numerous grants from the University of Colorado Graduate School, including the Graduate Council on the Arts and Humanities, the Council on Research and Creative Work, and others. I wish to thank the people of the Pueblo of Jemez, New Mexico, who opened their hearts to me as my heart opened to them in the nine years I played the violin for their *matachina*. I wish to dedicate this work to the late Jemez educator and tradition bearer Randolph Padilla (1951–2004), without whose friendship and support none of this would have been possible.

1. John Galm, personal communication with the author, 2001.

2. Norma E. Cantú notes in personal communications with the author that a group in Laredo was performing *mojigangas* and dances such as "*la del caballito*" (hobby horse type) at other times as well. *Caballito* is rarely seen in New Mexico, appearing in the August 2nd feast day celebration in the Pueblo of Jemez. See also note 23 below.

3. The term "Matachina" is also used in Colombia when referring to the lone female character, suggesting that the Pueblo people of New Mexico identified the single female character as the center of the *danza*. It is unclear what they would have

thought about men dancing the female role, a tradition that continues in some places or has only recently declined.

4. Peter J. García, personal communications with the author, 2006.

5. Norma E. Cantú, personal communications with the author, 2007.

6. See Olga Nájera-Ramírez's essay in this volume.

7. "of or referring to the Moors"

8. See also Romero in "La Danza Matachines as New Mexican Heritage," 2007.

9. According to José Sánchez Jiménez, the term derives from the hispanicized Nahua verb *matlayar,* which is the act of weeding a cornfield (see note 6 in Sánchez Jiménez' essay in this volume).

10. I witnessed one such choreographed exchange where both men and boys used machetes at the *velación,* night vigil, for the Virgin of Guadalupe at the Basilica in Mexico City, December 11–12, 2000.

11. Norma E. Cantú, personal communications with the author, 2005.

12. To add to the confusion, in Jesús María, in the Altos of Jalisco, I saw a group dressed as medieval Europeans, dancing in double file to the music of the violin, but they were not called *matachines.* I speculated that some Mexicans wishing to emphasize their European roots would no longer call themselves *matachines,* which in Mexico appear so thoroughly indigenous today. I base this conjecture on similar attitudes among older New Mexican Hispanos. See also de la Torre's essay in this volume.

13. In November 2005 San Juan Pueblo community members voted to return to their pre-Spanish name, Ohkay Owingeh, meaning "Place of the Strong People."

14. I discuss Harris's work in my article "La Danza Matachines as New Mexican Heritage" (2007).

15. "Pharisees and Matachins: Conflict and Cosmic Harmony"

16. "Chichimecs versus the French: Of the 'Savage' and the Conquistadores"

17. "According to the Nahual [the principal informant], the *danza de chichimecas* is comprised of ten 'authentic' dances, that is, exclusive to this *danza,* in addition to others borrowed from other *danzas* and adapted to this one" (my translation).

18. "Cortéz Defeated: The Indigenous Vision of the Conquest"

19. Norma E. Cantú, personal communications with the author, 2005.

20. See http://www.webspawner.com/users/elainegarcia/

21. Norma E. Cantú, personal communications with the author, 2005.

22. I have photographs documenting this tradition in Andalusía in 1990.

23. More elaborate cross-dressing occurs in *mojigangas,* a genre closely related to *matachines* in fifteenth-century Spain (see Romero 1993) that survives in the southern Mexican states of Guerrero and Oaxaca today.

24. Traditional Tewa costumes, for instance, become dance symbols (see Snyder 1972), which reflect a desire to be in harmony with the natural order. In some rituals, the men wear no shirts; they wear brilliant parrot feathers which symbolize light and life; spruce branches are held to unite the dancer with the undying life of vegetation;

a fox skin on the regalia represents man's dependence on animals; the rain sash, agitated by the dance, represents the falling rain; the gourd rattle is the sound of falling rain on the leaves of the growing corn (Estabrook 1931, 85).

25. "In other publications I have identified the rape of the young maiden as a basic motif of conquest *danzas* in the Iberian Peninsula, although actually this is at an archaic, residual, and metaphoric level. The character of the young maiden does not have such relevance in any present representation as in Oaxaca. It could be that the ancient cult of the Zapotec god of fertility and of death intervened with maidens that represented divine beings, but to interpret their actual significance would require comparing them with the other Malinches of Mexican rituals. Finally, I will only add that the Christian Malinche lines up with the Spanish troops when these appear in a scene" (my translation).

26. Riflemen are only present in the New Mexican Hispano *matachines*. Typically a rifle fires blanks into the air at the point that the young bull is killed and symbolically castrated.

27. See also de la Torre's essay in this volume (chapter 2).

28. Pablo Ortega, Rarámuri musician, personal communications with the author, 2002.

29. A priest in Jesús María, Jalisco, explained to the public that the procession was a commemoration of Christ's arrival into Jerusalem riding on a donkey. See also Cantú 2005.

30. In the Pueblo of Jemez, where I played the violin for nine years, I followed the same practice as the previous fiddler, Adelaido Martinez, who did not accept payment on December 12, the feast day of the Virgin of Guadalupe. But I accepted half of what was collected on January 1, the other half going to the guitarist.

31. One group for a stage presentation I once helped organize narrated the evangelistic religious significance between sequences. It was awkward to explain why this was inappropriate for the venue. In this case, the troupe's efforts to be "authentic" by sharing the fundamentalist text with the audience served to reinforce negative stereotypes of Spanish colonial domination of indigenous people in the Southwest.

32. In his book *Aztecs, Moors, and Christians* (2000), Max Harris includes a photo of the feast of San Sebastián in Catalonia, where the *gigantes* figures closely resemble those called *matachines* in Oaxaca.

33. The term *entremeses* today signifies dramatic religious floats (see Harris 2000), but originally referred to interludes in dramatic plays.

12

The Ballet Folklórico de México and the Construction of the Mexican Nation through Dance

SYDNEY HUTCHINSON

The nation is a slippery, insubstantial concept—an "imagined community," in the words of Benedict Anderson (1991). Yet it is also a powerful symbol that is communicated via an ideological discourse present in a variety of mediums, including the arts. In the past decade, many significant works of scholarship have expanded on this concept, arguing that in most national projects race also plays a significant role (Appelbaum, Macpherson, and Rosemblatt 2003; Omi and Winant 1994). The connection is clearly evident in Latin America, where the concept of *mestizaje*, racial mixing, has played a significant role in nationalist discourse throughout the twentieth century. In the case of Mexico, numerous scholars have examined the roles that film, the visual arts, literature, and music have played in nationalist and racial projects (see, for example, Hershfield 1999; Sommer 1991). A few works have even discussed the connections between dance and cultural nationalism in Mexico and among Chicanos in the United States (Nájera-Ramírez 1989; Tortajada Quiroz 1995, 2000). However, in spite of these authors' contributions, dance continues to play a marginal role in most discussions of Latin American nationalisms.

Nestor García Canclini writes, "Although Mexico has a potent literature, its cultural profile was not primarily erected by writers . . . the conservation and celebration of patrimony, its knowledge and use, is basically a visual operation" (2001, 168). If this is true, surely dance must play a central role in our analysis of the construction of the Mexican nation. Dance also communicates primarily through the sense of vision but it reaches a larger audience than many visual arts because of its spectacular nature; it is also more powerful because so many participate in it and thus "feel" its message. This chapter will therefore focus on how dance has been used to construct the Mexican nation as well as "Mexicanness" in the United States through the specific example of the Ballet Folklórico de México (BFM) and its far-reaching influence.

Dance is an important means of constructing and disseminating images of race and nation. It reaches perhaps a broader audience than any other form of art, particularly in the form of the national folkloric dance companies that have proliferated throughout Latin America since the 1940s.[1] The Ballet Folklórico de México is one of the earliest formed and most influential of these companies. Since its inception in 1952, it has been closely tied to Mexico's political interests and policies, first as an official organ connected to the Department of Tourism and later as an independent interest that nevertheless was officially favored as a representative of Mexican culture at home and abroad. Amalia Hernández, the company's creator, was a member of Mexico City's political elite, the daughter of a revolutionary general and one-time mayor of the city, and was deeply influenced by and involved in postrevolutionary romantic nationalism. She was not the first to take an interest in regional dance, nor was she the first to attempt a theatrical presentation of Mexico folk dance. Yet Hernández was by far the most successful proponent of theatrical folk dance in Mexico, most likely because she so effectively integrated official discourses of *mestizaje* and *indigenismo* (indigenism) into an aesthetically appealing format.

Mestizaje in Motion: Racial Ideologies and National Folk Dance in Latin America

In Latin America, theatrical presentations of traditional, regional dances have proliferated since the 1950s. Writing of nationalist musical projects in Latin America, Thomas Turino explains that "in spite of the differing local conditions that led to populist projects in specific Latin American countries, they occur close together in time and produce very similar musical results—suggesting common underlying models, motivations, and causes" (2003, 170). A central motivation, he further explains, was the need to create large markets and a mass of consumer citizens in order to achieve economic as well as political independence. I argue that nationalist dance projects are subject to similar processes, but I suggest that race and racial ideologies also play a central role. The ideology of *mestizaje* and the proliferation of national folk dance companies were both critical in the nation-building processes of the postcolonial period.

At present, *mestizaje* is a contentious issue among scholars, even as it continues to play an important role in popular conceptions of nation in Latin America as well as among some Latinos in the United States. In Mexico, for instance, it has long been thought that the mix of Spanish and Indian biology and culture gave the country a unique identity. One oft-repeated origin myth traces the beginning of the Mexican people to the birth of Martín Cortés in 1522. As the son of the Spanish conquistador Hernán Cortés and the Aztec princess Malintzín, "La Malinche," Martín was the first mestizo and thus the first Mexican (Krauze 1997, 52). During the twentieth century, *mestizaje* was at the center of nationalist discourse after 1910, when Justo Sierra proclaimed that "we are the children of two nations, of two races . . . this fact dominates our whole history; to it we owe our soul" (cited in Krauze 1997, 50).

However, since the 1950s revisionist scholars have argued that *mestizaje* and related ideologies are "insidious myths" that only mask discrimination and prejudice (Appelbaum, Macpherson, and Rosemblatt 2003, 9). For instance, in her important study of early Latin American national romances, Doris Sommer notes that, while *mestizaje* has been "practically a slogan for many projects of national consolidation," its use as a rhetorical device in novels often serves as a symbolic "pacification of—in other words, a means of placing value judgments and expressing domination over certain groups" (1991, 22). And Robin Sheriff and other students of Brazilian racial politics have criticized that nation's ideology of *democracia racial* (racial democracy) as a "mystifying" discourse that "prevents the development of social movements" that might expose racism and oppression (Sheriff 2001, 30). Indeed, the symbolic inclusion of minority groups in nationalist racial discourse and in arenas such as national folk dance has done little to alter the political and economic circumstances of disenfranchised populations in Latin America. At the same time, as historian Enrique Krauze has noted, *mestizaje* is vastly preferable to the extermination of Indians that occurred throughout much of the New World, and "it is one of Mexico's most original contributions to the social and moral history of the Western world" (1997, 55).

In short, *mestizaje* can be viewed in one of two ways. In the words of anthropologist Peter Wade, it is either a "democratic process leading to a symbolic of racial harmony" or "a rhetorical flourish that hides racist and even ethnocidal practices of whitening" (Wade 2003, 263). Though outside observers tend toward the latter view, many Chicano scholars and writers prefer the first view and offer a more personal take on the subject. Among that community it has inspired works of art from Gloria Anzaldúa's poetry to Amado M. Peña Jr.'s silkscreens. Many Latin American governments have also chosen to promote the positive view of *mestizaje* as a process that can produce national unification. As such, the idea has often played a central role in the selection of "national" dances and music throughout the Americas. From the Dominican *merengue* to the Brazilian *samba*, the Colombian *cumbia* to the Venezuelan *joropo* and *tamunangue*, particular styles are chosen because they are seen as symbolic of the particular race mixture that formed their nation.

In Mexico, mariachi music was chosen in the early postrevolutionary period as the best representation of Mexican national culture (Jáuregui 1990; Sheehy 2006). This music from Mexico's central west region in and around the state of Jalisco is often cited as an example of *mestizaje*, combining European instruments like violin and guitar with Mexican creations like the *guitarrón* and rhythms considered both Mexican and Spanish in origin.[2] Accordingly, a national dance was selected that is associated with this music and this region, specifically, the "Jarabe tapatío" or "Mexican Hat Dance." First performed in Mexico City in 1790, banned in 1802, revived under the rule of Emperor Maximilian (Bruno Ruiz 1956, 47–48), and reappropriated as nationalist symbol in the revolutionary period,[3] the *jarabe*'s format and costuming make the discourse of *mestizaje* further apparent. For example, *jarabes* are those songs that combine bits of many other songs (often European in origin) into a distinctly Mexican whole and are danced with a foot-stomping zapateo or zapateado. The female costume typical of this dance is the *china poblana*, itself said to have originated with a kidnapped Chinese princess who mixed Philippine shawls, Chinese embroidery, and local Mexican styles. The male, originally portrayed as "a man of the pueblo, with no special outfit" (Saldívar 1937, 5), later adopted the *charro* suit described by a 1950s scholar of Mexican dance as "an unmistakable sign of American mestizaje" (Bruno Ruiz 1956, 48). Since the style was initially worn by Spanish gentlemen in Jalisco, however, it seems to more truthfully represent a wealthy European heritage. Later a different type of women's *folklórico* dress was chosen to match the men's upgraded attire: the Adelita costume, named for the revolutionary *soldaderas* who adopted this high-necked colonial dress of Jalisco.[4]

Mestizaje was promoted through other arts besides music and dance, even (and particularly) in the "high" arts with which Amalia Hernández, an educated urbanite, would no doubt be familiar. Beginning in the 1920s, visual artists focused on producing art that would be accessible to large numbers of the general public. The initiation of the Mexican mural movement is credited to José Vasconcelos, who was secretary of education in the early 1920s and commissioned the "Big Three" (Rivera, Orozco, and Siqueiros) and others to paint large works in public buildings, many of which promoted the ideology on a monumental scale. Vasconcelos also established cultural missions throughout the republic where folk dances were collected and disseminated for educational purposes (Nájera-Ramírez 1989, 19). But Vasconcelos is best known as the author of *La raza cósmica*, the 1925 book extolling the virtues of the mestizos, or the "cosmic race." The ideology of *mestizaje* that Vasconcelos preached became the dominant paradigm for Mexicans' understanding of their own racialized nation. During the next two decades, the concept and lived experience of *mestizaje* formed the basis for novels like *Nayar* (1940) by Miguel Angel Menéndez, while films like *Allá en el rancho grande* (1937) and *Ay Jalisco, no te rajes* (1948) disseminated romanticized images of Jalisco and its mariachi music.

Though *mestizaje* was the dominant ideology of the time, during the 1930s a counterpart to it was elaborated. This ideology, known as *indigenismo*, first appeared during the presidency of the populist Lázaro Cárdenas, who championed Indian rights. Subsequent presidents shifted priorities from social to economic progress, and scholars came to believe that the country's large Indian population would need to be studied and incorporated into the mainstream in order for Mexico to move forward. Thus, in the 1940s, government-employed anthropologists like Miguel Gamio stressed the positive in Mexico's Indians, creating a romanticized image that could serve as a basis for a national identity while still encouraging racial mixing. Gamio wrote of their "beautiful and epic tradition" and "high examples of ethics and aesthetics," urging Mexicans to preserve Indian arts and to take inspiration from them (Doremus 2001, 383–84). At the same time, the ultimate goal of Gamio and other anthropologists was not to preserve Indian autonomy but to integrate them into a "solid patriotic union" (Knight 1990, 84).

Indigenismo also found its champions in the arts, as romantic nationalist works were created in a variety of media. Carlos Chávez composed works like the *Sinfonía India* (1935–36), which used indigenous melodies from Sonora and Nayarit, and *Xochipilli* (1940), which used indigenous percussion to create "an imagined Aztec music" (Delpar 2000, 562). Novels like *El indio* (1935) by Gregorio López y Fuentes focused on Indian communities, and paintings by Frida Kahlo such as *Self-portrait as a Tehuana* (1943) celebrated images of Indian women. In film, *Redes* (1934), *Maria Candelaria* (1943), and others told stories of Indians' struggles set to nationalistic music, though they tended toward one-dimensional depictions of the "noble savage." The latter was the work of Emilio "El Indio" Fernández, who depicted his vision of "authentic national identity" by tying together Mexico's past and present through romanticized portrayals of Indian characters—usually played by light-skinned actors (Hershfield 1999, 87).

By rhetorically promoting the dignity and rights of Mexico's Indians, *indigenismo* appeared to contradict the "melting pot" ideology of *mestizaje* that effectively erased indigenous cultures. But in reality the philosophy reproduced racist assumptions by continuing to promote belief in innate, primordial characteristics that differentiated Indians from Europeans (Knight 1990, 87). In addition, *indigenismo* was always a view imposed from without—by white or mestizo intellectuals casting their gaze upon poor, indigenous Mexicans. For example, great thinkers of the time like Agustín Yáñez and Luis Villoro adopted and expanded on the anthropologists' ideas, but by tending to emphasize pre-Hispanic culture they often made contemporary indigenous cultures appear inadequate (Doremus 2001, 287). Some urban mestizos adopted an even more extreme "Indianist" position. These "parlor *Aztecófilos*" romanticized ancient Mexican cultures and wanted to rid Mexico of foreign influences (Knight 1990, 81), yet the result was the same: a veneration of Mexico's pre-Colombian past but continued ignorance about its indigenous present.

Amalia Hernández drew from all these ideologies—*mestizaje*, *indigenismo*, and romantic nationalism—and their corresponding artistic expressions when she created the Ballet Folklórico de México. She was clearly a member of the "generation of Medio Siglo," as Enrique Krauze calls the intellectuals of the 1950s and 1960s who were influenced by the progressive magazine of that name. This generation was committed to revolutionary nationalism and "looked for 'Mexicanness' in colonial and pre-Hispanic history and in the phenomenology of everyday life" (Krauze 1997, 651). Amalia looked and seemed to find it all around, since she believed that music and dance were a "way of life" for the Mexican people, something she expressed in one of the earliest films on the company, *Place of the Plumed Serpent* (1960s).

Indigenismo is apparent in Amalia's many Indian-themed choreographies, which from 1961 to 1983 typically comprised four to six out of the nine or ten items on each program. She choreographed *Sinfonía india* after the Chávez work in 1946, and in return, Chávez watched her development closely and offered advice.[5] The later work "Danza del venado" (Deer Dance), one of the company's signature pieces, is loosely based on a traditional dance of the present-day Yaqui Indians of Sonora (this dance will be further examined below), and "Los tarascos" depicts the indigenous people of the Lake Pátzcuaro region. But many of these pieces are modernist choreographies that Hernández based not on living traditions but on pre-Colombian artwork. In an official publication, such dances are classified as "pre-Hispanic" (Aguirre and Segura 1994) although they are actually Amalia's interpretations of what ancient dances may have looked like based on depictions in codices, architectural ruins, or ceramics.[6] Descriptions of such dances typically emphasized Amalia's meticulous research on pre-Colombian sources, but could differ significantly between English and Spanish-language programs. For example, *Los hijos del sol* was advertised in English as an actual set of "ancient Aztec ritual dances, dating back to the thirteenth and fourteenth centuries,"[7] while in Spanish it was only a "presentation based on how pre-Hispanic celebrations *could have been* in reality"[8] (emphasis mine).

Though poses and costumes vary depending on the civilization depicted (Aztecs, Mayas, and Olmecs have all been subjects for Amalia), certain features are common. Her romanticized visions are set to newly composed music similar to Chávez's indigenist works and played on "Aztec" instruments like *teponaztli* drum, flutes, conch trumpets, and leg rattles. The dancers maintain serious expressions and stiff, regal postures throughout, upholding the stereotypical image of the stoic, melancholy, yet noble Indian. The company thus serves to further the glorification of Mexico's imperial Indian past by focusing on Aztec, Mayan, and Olmec myths and monuments, while continuing to marginalize modern-day indigenous groups by largely excluding them from representation.

In spite of the large number of *indigenista* pieces in the BFM repertoire, the centrality of *mestizaje* to Mexico's image both at home and abroad is also made clear by an analysis of the company's programs and self-presentation. For one, Amalia self-identifies as a mestiza and "claims to celebrate both her Spanish and Indian heritages in her choreography" (Shay 2002, 89). A 1964 magazine article described her as "half Indian, half Spanish, and aristocrat."[9] A French program went so far as to state, "Amalia Hernández is a pure Mexican, her ancestors descended from a tribe from the central part of Mexico."[10]

The discourse of *mestizaje* is further played up in the company's public relations materials and programs. The film *Place of the Plumed Serpent* opens by panning around the Plaza of Three Cultures at the center of Mexico City. The camera moves past the excavation of an Aztec temple with a Catholic cathedral looming behind it and ends with a focus on a plaque noting the site's representation of the "painful birth of mestizo Mexico." More recently, the company's coffee table book tells readers, "As the Mexican people are the product of miscegenation, so is their artistic expression: the formal elegance of its indigenous history with its exquisite Asiatic nature, the spirited impetus of its Spanish past and the syncopated, painful rhythms of Africa transported to its coasts. All are part of the mestizo culture that is Mexico today" (Aguirre and Segura 1994, 126).

BFM programs typically feature four or five items focusing on mestizo dances. These include regional dances of Michoacán, Tamaulipas, Veracruz, Jalisco, Zacatecas, Guerrero, and Yucatán. (Though the Yucatán is usually considered a more Indian region, BFM programs emphasize the combination of Mayan and Spanish influences there.) A typical program note on "Sones antiguos de Michoacán" explains, "It is in the mestizaje of the indigenous and the Spanish where one will find one of the essential traits of the Mexican people: A whole series of expressions are colored by their own, vigorous style."[11]

The discourse of *mestizaje* is also espoused, though less obviously, through the regional division of the company's repertoire. In his ethnography of the El Paso–Ciudad Juárez border area, Pablo Vila argues that for many Mexicans regional discourse is used as a euphemism to replace ethnic or racial discourses (2000, 26). For example, those from central and southern Mexico, who are darker-skinned and more "Indian," are often contrasted with those from the north, an area considered relatively untouched by *mestizaje*, through negative stereotypes of southern laziness and backwardness. I believe that the repertoire of the Ballet Folklórico can also be read in this way. The BFM's own souvenir program confirms the company's acceptance of the stereotypical equation of the South (or the Indian) with nature and the past, and the North (or the Hispanic) with progress and the future: "the South knows how to dream of the beauty of nature, of the beauty of the art that links us to the past; one feels proud of its incredible history, but the North teaches us there is a future to be conquered" (BFM 1968). The BFM thus chooses the middle ground, emphasizing the mestizo center in accordance with official nationalist discourse. Except for the polkas of the "Revolution" suite and the Yaqui deer dance, no dances of the predominantly white northern states like Baja California, Sonora, or Chihuahua are performed, while dances from the extreme south, like those of Chiapas and the Yucatán, are only occasionally included. The audience's focus is instead directed to the central (principally north-central) region where *mestizaje* has been practiced more successfully and longer—to the Huasteca region, to Michoacán, to Veracruz, which always closes the first act, and of course to Jalisco, which provides the piñata-breaking, foot-stomping, hat-waving grand finale.[12] At the same time, the political message of the focus on Jalisco as the center of *mestizaje* must be questioned. For one, the Jaliscan image relies on stereotyped gender roles—those of the "gallant" *charros* and "coquettish" women, as one program described them.[13] In addition, this is probably the "whitest" state of Mexico's central region, and its European roots are emphasized through the choice of the gentlemanly *charro* costume and the eventual selection of the high-necked, European-derived "Adelita" dress for dance performance over the *china poblana*.

Amalia Hernández: Biographical Issues

Because works of art are never produced free of the influence of personal bias and individual experience, it will be useful to briefly examine the biography of the creator of the Ballet Folklórico de México, Amalia Hernández. Her story has been widely disseminated through the company's press materials and reprinted in countless newspaper reviews. These differ only slightly from one another and always emphasize certain key features. The following version is a representative one that I have taken principally from the official "coffee table" book of the Ballet Folklórico (Aguirre and Segura 1994).

Amalia Hernández was born on September 19, 1917, in Mexico City. Her mother was a schoolteacher and her father a "prominent military and political figure of the day" (Aguirre and Segura 1994, 16). He owned land in several states and in later life Amalia fondly recalled her visits to his ranches in far-off areas, particularly the family's sugar plantation in Tamaulipas.[14] Amalia's experiences there formed the basis for an early choreography titled *La zafra en Tamaulipas* (Sugar Harvest in Tamaulipas).

Hernández was a privileged child who received every advantage her well-connected parents had to offer. When she expressed interest in dance, her father built her a dance studio in the house and provided her with ballet lessons from teachers such as Russian exile Hypolite Sybine and Madame Nesly Dambre of the Paris Opera. She also studied indigenous and regional Mexican dance, tap, modern, Spanish, and "Oriental" dance, as well as theater and Mexican art (Aguirre and Segura 1994, 18). Her nearly flawless English was a result of having been sent to the United States to learn it; she also continued her ballet studies in San Antonio and later completed her dance education at Mexico's National School of Dance.

In 1946 Amalia began to work as a professional dancer, teacher, and choreographer with the Mexican Academy of Dance, a part of the government's Instituto de Bellas Artes (INBA). One of her first creations was the *Sinfonía India*, influenced not only by Chávez, the composer of the work by the same name, but also by the "passion" she had shown for indigenous dances since her childhood vacations in the provinces. However, after Chávez created a Department of Dance within INBA in 1950 and appointed Miguel Covarrubias its director, she found she had to leave her post. Covarrubias did not approve of her plans to create performances based on traditional dances, since for him Mexican dance should arise from "the new nationalist, revolutionary, and essentially indigenist ideology" and should be based on a modern dance vocabulary (Tortajada Quiroz 2000, 56). Hernández therefore left the Academy to form her own company and develop her own concept of nationalist dance (Ibid., 57). In 1952, she formed an eight-member troupe called Ballet Moderno de México and created the suite *Sones de Michoacán*, a number still performed by the Ballet to this day. Although her family did not always support her artistic goals in this early period, she persevered, on one occasion pawning her father's limousine to pay the dancers' wages.[15] The group soon began performing weekly on the TV show "Función de Gala." In total, sixty-seven different programs of Mexican dance were produced and transmitted nationally, while the group grew to twenty dancers (Aguirre and Segura 1994, 36).

This was an opportune time for the creation of a nationalistic dance company. The 1950s and 1960s were a time of relative prosperity and stability in Mexico, as well as a time of searching for national identity, and profits could be reaped by a well-placed cultural organization. A look at presidential priorities in 1940s–1960s Mexico shows that Amalia's work was also in line with the Mexican government's goals for the country. For example, in 1940, the Mexican government cosponsored a major art exhibition at New York's Museum of Modern Art titled "Twenty Centuries of Mexican Art," which they saw as a way of increasing understanding of Mexico in the United States (Delpar 2000, 558). The government's interest in promoting Mexican culture abroad only increased in the post–World War II era, a time of optimism and entrepreneurialism. President Miguel Alemán, the "businessman president," made the increase of tourism to Mexico a priority from 1946 to 1952 (Krauze 1997, 545); he continued to work in tourism as an ex-president (Ibid., 605) when the tourism department began its promotion of the BFM. Adolfo Ruiz Cortines (1952–58), Adolfo López Mateos (1958–64), and Gustavo Díaz Ordaz (1964–70) followed in his footsteps. As the time of stability continued, so did the country's economic progress and the government's ties to the BFM.

In 1958, the company became an official representative of Mexico's folklife when the Mexican Department of Tourism asked the group to tour North America, including stops in Cuba, Canada, and Los Angeles. In the following year, the director of the government's International Cultural Promotion Organization asked the group, now fifty members strong, to represent Mexico in Chicago for the Pan-American Games. At this time, the group's name was changed to "Ballet Folklórico de México" and Felipe Segura joined the company for a brief term as artistic director, bringing in ballet dancers to "raise the technical level" (Tortajada Quiroz 1995, 479). In Chicago, their performance included the numbers "Los hijos del sol" (a reconstruction of Aztec dance), "Antiguos sones de Michoacán," "El cupidito," "Fiesta veracruzana," "Los quetzales," "La danza del venado" (of the Sonoran Yaqui people), and "Navidad en Jalisco,"[16] many of which still form part of the company's repertoire today (Aguirre and Segura 1994, 38). The group then accompanied future president Díaz Ordaz to City Hall in Los Angeles (Tortajada Quiroz 1995, 480). Also in 1959, new president Adolfo López Mateos "offered all of his support in order to make it 'the best dance company in the world'" (Aguirre and Segura 1994, 40), which meant that the BFM was then "officially born by presidential decree" (Tortajada Quiroz 1995, 481). INBA, under whose auspices the group functioned, named the BFM its "official" folkloric company and scheduled weekly performances for tourists twice on Sunday and once on Wednesday, the resident company's permanent schedule (Aguirre and Segura 1994, 40). In fact, the director of INBA was such an enthusiastic supporter of folkloric dance that he even attempted to make his organization's classical ballet troupe perform traditional repertoire (Tortajada Quiroz 1995, 482).

The 1960s were a busy time for Amalia and her company. The Ballet Folklórico represented Mexico at the Festival of Nations in Paris in 1961, introducing their dances to an audience then unfamiliar with most Latin American dance and taking first prize. López Mateos continued his close relationship with the group, which was a particular favorite to perform for distinguished foreigners including John F. Kennedy. The American president was so impressed that during the company's first formal North American tour in 1962 he invited them for a private performance at the White House. The 1963 tour saw the Ballet Folklórico performing to full houses in Peru, Argentina, Chile, Uruguay, Brazil, Panama, Costa Rica, and Indonesia; in 1964 they visited London, Paris, Switzerland, and Italy to great acclaim. That same year, Amalia converted the BFM into a civil association "with the purpose of gaining its own legal status," but at the same time she presented a tribute concert to president López Mateos—perhaps to maintain their privileged relationship with the politician even as an independent company (Aguirre and Segura 1994, 46–58).

By 1963, the company had split into two—one resident and one touring company, with a total of 120 members, including seventy dancers, two choruses, musicians, and technicians. In 1965, the BFM touring company visited Eastern Europe and the USSR for the first time, the birthplace of the worldwide folk dance movement. The Soviets approved; the magazine *Tempo* reported, "Our guests demonstrated, with great strength, how magnificent is art created by the people" (in Aguirre and Segura 1994, 62). In 1966 a new president took power in Mexico, but Gustavo Díaz Ordaz continued the government's support of Amalia's efforts, bringing the company with him on a goodwill tour of Central America, including Guatemala, El Salvador, Nicaragua, Costa Rica, and Panama (Ibid.). In 1968, Mexico had the opportunity to showcase its culture to the world at the XIX Olympic Games in Mexico City. Of course, Amalia was chosen to play a key role, and she created the "Cultural Olympics," consisting of two large-scale dance works: *Ballet of the Five Continents* and *Ballet of the Americas*. The first program combined the work of choreographers from around the world and consisted of Greek, Eskimo, Peruvian, Soviet, Aztec, African, Colombian, Turkish, Australian, Indian, and North American dance—the latter choreographed by Alvin Ailey. The *Ballet of the Americas* included Colombian, Panamanian, Guatemalan, Bolivian, Venezuelan, Mexican, Argentine, Costa Rican, and Cuban ballets (Ibid., 68–70).

The 1960s also saw the creation of the Ballet Folklórico school, which began in two dance studios in the INBA buildings. Amalia's brother would later design the school's own avant-garde building, completed in 1968. Education is now one of the company's primary goals, and its programs include a youth program for ages seven through thirteen, a four-year teen/adult program awarding the diploma of "practicing dancer," and a continuation program lasting an additional one to two years. Courses are offered both on school year and summer schedules; they include classical ballet and modern dance technique as well as the expected folkloric dance classes. Of the performing company members, 70 to 75 percent are graduates of this program (Ibid., 92–94).

During the 1970s, the company continued the trajectory began in the previous decade. Tours reached still more countries, from the Dominican Republic to Israel. New works were premiered, including some in honor of politicians: 1970 saw *Tonanzintla* debuted for President Gustavo Díaz Ordaz, while in 1977 two works "inspired by the dances of Veracruz" were presented to former president Miguel Alemán Valdes, a Veracruz native. A significant addition to BFM activities during this decade was a greater focus on outreach. For example, the group performed on open-air stages in poor neighborhoods around the capital city "to expose people of various classes to the Ballet" (Ibid., 110–11). Also, in 1973 the school formed an experimental group to feature regional dances collected by regional researchers. In the 1980s, outreach was expanded to the provinces, and since that time, the company has presented approximately fifty performances yearly in outlying areas, particularly in Guadalajara, Puebla, Toluca, Torreón, Villahermosa, Mérida, Tuxtla Gutiérrez, and Aguascalientes (Ibid., 112–14).

One element of the BFM often emphasized by the press is that the Ballet Folklórico is a family affair. Amalia's sister Delfina Vargas worked on costume design while brother Agustín Hernández contributed to set design and designed the Ballet school building. Amalia's two daughters, Norma López Hernández and Viviana Basanta Hernández, were "born into the ballet," often accompanying their mother on tours. Later Norma became artistic director, Viviana performed as a dancer and became the school's coordinator, and Amalia's grandson Salvador López López is now general administrator, tour coordinator, and a trick roper performing in Tamaulipas and Zacatecas suites. Upon Amalia's death in 2000, Norma continued as director (Ibid., 24–30).

Though the Hernández family certainly plays a central role in the company's management and they are the principal decision makers, it is important to note the less frequently promoted fact that the company was also an international one since its inception. From the beginning, Amalia's principal set designer was the Englishman Robin Bond, and her highly influential costume designer was New Yorker Dasha Topfer. Early reviews and programs often lavishly praise the efforts of these two, while in later years, their role is downplayed or goes unmentioned, perhaps because nationalist sentiments made Mexicans in general and dancers in particular feel more proprietary of the company's productions. Still, the international aesthetics created when Bond, Topfer, and Hernández came together gave the company a broad appeal that contributed to its international success.

Another common element in most biographies is their portrayal of Amalia as a woman who struggled to knock down Mexico's gender barriers, her "triumph" bringing "new freedom and opportunity to women."[17] Certainly her refusal to follow a preplanned role (her family expected her to become a schoolteacher) and her pursuit of leadership positions was atypical and shows great strength of character. No evidence has been offered to support the assertion that her career brought any benefits to Mexican women as a whole, however. In addition, Shay observes that the field of folkloric dance was not exactly inundated by male professionals (2002, 93), so her gender was less of a problem than it might have been in other endeavors.

In conclusion, Amalia's close personal relationships with the ruling elite helped win official favor for her company, as did her ability to advance national goals like the promotion of tourism. But the BFM's success as a national symbol can also be attributed to its adherence to the nationalist ideologies developed and espoused by intellectuals of the time. Amalia's work clearly incorporated the racial-political ideologies and romantic nationalism characteristic of the revolutionary period. Her biography also reveals a number of other important facts. First, Amalia Hernández was a child of privilege whose primary contact with regional and indigenous dances came in a decidedly colonial context—as she visited her father's ranches and plantations on childhood vacations. Second, she had an international education and international contacts, from her Russian and French dance teachers to her North American and British designers. This easily enabled her to see an international role for Mexican culture in general, as reflected in her creation of the Olympic *Ballet of the Americas* and her company in particular. Third, she began the company with a slightly different, possibly more progressive conception of its role, reflected by the name change from Ballet Moderno to Ballet Folklórico; the change may have resulted from politicians' encouragement of her folkloric work. Fourth, even though she privatized the company early in its history, Amalia always maintained a close relationship with Mexico's ruling class, currying the favor of a succession of presidents. Fifth, the company's choreographies were widely disseminated early on, from the national television broadcasts of the 1950s to the world tours of the 1960s and the regional presentations of the 1980s. Finally, the BFM's primary roles since the early 1960s have been twofold: providing Mexicans with a cultural education and promoting tourism among foreigners.

Neocolonialism and the Ballet Folklórico

The promotion of the ideologies of *mestizaje* and *indigenismo* through folkloric dance is certainly an improvement over the European-dominated colonial period. However, as we have already begun to see, these ideologies are not unproblematic, and in many ways colonialism still casts its shadow over these works. Anthony Shay has observed that the BFM's longstanding ties to Mexico's government and continuing role in education and tourism have functioned to constrain its representational options (2002, 94–95). Yet the forms of representation the company employs are conditioned not only by external situations but also by the internal subjectivities of its creator. For example, a 1960s filmstrip shows that the company musicians acted as private entertainers to the Hernández family, performing at their gracious estate in peasant attire each weekend as guests in business suits mingled around them. Thus, her view of the world and the artistic works she created were colored by colonialism and the exotification of the "folk" that is part and parcel of colonial conceptions of the world.

Anderson has described how colonial powers use antiquity to legitimate their power, explaining that "colonial regimes began attaching themself [*sic*] to antiquity as much as conquest. . . . Monumental archeology, increasingly linked to tourism, allowed the state to appear as the guardian of a generalized, but also local, Tradition" (1991, 181). Hernández's treatment of indigenous dances shows a similar ideology at play. Indigenous cultures are valuable only in their ancient forms—as part of a glorious past when the Aztecs built fantastic monuments and the Mayas were great scientists (see the 1989 video *Ballet Folklórico de México*). Modern-day peoples are depicted only when they maintain the "purity" of their "ancient" traditions or when they have submitted to the processes of *mestizaje*. In some cases the colonial gaze is evident only through costuming, since the costumes chosen for the most central items of the repertoire, Jalisco and Veracruz, are those that were typical of the colonial period. However, in some cases the results of her colonialist viewpoint are not so benign. For example, in the company's portrayal of the state of Chiapas, representation and reality have little overlap and they combine to produce a politically problematic message. Although this state is best known at present for the Zapatista rebellion of indigenous people demanding their rights, the dance depicts an idyllic scene of graceful women in black lace dresses while program notes dwell on the region's beautiful beaches, mountains, and flora, an incongruity that disturbs some viewers (Shay 1999, 36).

The most politically problematic of her choreographies is her version of the Yaqui *danza del venado* (deer dance). This dance serves as a symbol of the company and is used in its logo. Programs and press releases typically emphasize the dance's "ancient" history and the "purity" of the tribe and its cultural expressions. For example, a 1962 Seattle World's Fair program states that it is "part of a rite preparatory to the hunt which has existed among the Yaqui Indians since their origin hundreds of years ago. . . . The music is as ancient as the dance itself and is performed on primitive instruments." A program from the Palacio de Bellas Artes in Mexico City adds, "The Yaquis have kept themselves free of all mestizaje and compromise with modern cultures" (June 19, 1963), while an early film describes them as "the oldest existing [tribe] in Mexico," who still live as they did "before the conquest" (*Place of the Plumed Serpent*). Jorge Tyller, the Ballet soloist who became famous for his performance of this dance, is subject to a similar exotifying discourse. He is described as "a Yaqui Indian boy from Sonora, [who] was discovered in an orphanage"[18] and "has been trained since childhood to execute this sacred and exciting ritual dance, seen nowhere else in the world."[19] He is also the "one dancer in her company who is simply himself," presumably because he is a Yaqui performing a Yaqui dance (*Place of the Plumed Serpent*).

All this is not so different from the discourse surrounding other indigenous dances on the BFM's programs: the Mayos are also "pure in custom and ancestral traditions;"[20] the Sonajeros dance also comes from the "most ancient of rituals;"[21] and the Concheros too is an "ancient ritual . . . [that] links modern Mexico with its past."[22] What is different is the unique history of the Yaqui people. Mexico waged a full-scale genocidal war against this tribe for nearly a hundred years, ending in 1927. As a result, most of the tribe was forced to leave Sonora and settle in Tucson, Arizona, where they still live today on two reservations. The BFM's erasure of this history in their performance and program notes and the Mexican government's subsequent appropriation of Yaqui symbols, both in dance form and as an image on Sonoran license plates, is thus particularly problematic. Adding to the complication is that in Yaqui performances of the *danza del venado*, the deer does not die, yet this forms the central theme of the BFM's choreography. Anthropologist David Rojas notes, "I know the maestro in Sonora who taught her the dance. He is still mad" (in Preston 1997). Though Amalia argued that this alteration was necessary to supply the dance with a plot line, a symbolic interpretation of the dead deer might yield a more sinister message.

Amalia often found it necessary to alter traditional dances in ways other than the practical requirements necessitated by the transfer from field to stage, such as a reduction in length. Things that were too "simple" were made more complex and demanding in technique. She explained,

> It is as if the people of Mexico, in expressing their dances and their folklore, would have liked to possess greater technical ability to further develop all of these skills, in terms of their dance and culture and its needs and traditions. So first, I tried to be like them, and later to use the techniques that I had learned and my knowledge of dance to develop each one of these works. . . . Sometimes you find a material that is very rich in dance, but with music that is simple and primitive, that must be worked with. Other times the music is marvelous, but the steps have very few elements of dance to them." (Aguirre and Segura 1994, 134–36)

This statement makes clear that her alterations were not only made for practical reasons, but also as a result of value judgments.

In spite of their problematic nature, these depictions of Mexico's cultures have been legitimized by the discourse of authenticity with which the company surrounds itself. The aura of authenticity is imparted through attention to dancers who have "trained since childhood" like deer dancer Jorge Tyller or the Pueblans who perform Los Quetzales (in *Place of the Plumed Serpent*). Costumes, too, are said to be "authentic copies of the original dress,"[23] "exact" in every detail. Even Amalia's modern dance-based reconstruction of *The Mayans* has an "authentic jeweled wardrobe."[24] It is also achieved by emphasizing Amalia's lengthy and meticulous research on Mexican dance in both archival and field situations. *The Aztec Gods* choreography required two years' research into the "records left by the scribes and priests who accompanied Cortez,"[25] as well as field study in "remote areas in the interior of Mexico such as Oaxaca, Mazatlán, the sites of the tombs of ancient kings" (Anon.). Dasha Topfer, too, "analyzed wall painting, ancient sculpture, pottery and old textiles to secure her ideas" for costumes (Anon.), and her cloth is supplied by traditional weavers using "techniques that have not changed since Aztec times" "whenever possible" (*Place of the Plumed Serpent*). As a result, no irony is intended when one video announces that this is "original and authentic folklore created by the genius of Amalia Hernández" (*Ballet Folklórico de México*, 1989 video).

In conclusion, although the BFM's presentations of Mexican dance are the work of one individual, they have become universalized through their promotion by the Mexican government, tourist industry, and educational programs and legitimized through a discourse of authenticity. The removal of contemporary realities from the Yaqui and Chiapas dances seems to depoliticize them. However, because the company's repertoire underhandedly promotes particular racial ideologies and replicates a colonialist gaze, the Ballet Folklórico's portrayals of regional and indigenous cultures are in fact inherently political.

Conclusions

The research and presentation of regional traditional dances are a direct outgrowth of postrevolutionary romantic nationalism. Yet one cannot forget that in this case a vision of national identity was constructed by one woman and therefore was influenced by her personal history and subjectivity. Some see the *folklórico* repertoire as an accurate representation of Mexican diversity because of its incorporation of a wide variety of regional traditions. In fact, Tortajada Quiroz tells us that in the early postrevolutionary period, nationalist dance did help to create cohesion amongst the diverse Mexican populace, as their connection to the state was symbolized on stage in the connection between individual bodies and the collective (2000, 62). Yet, while Nájera-Ramírez agrees that the *folklórico* repertoire stems from a desire to "acknowledg[e] diversity within the Mexican nation," she also notes that such representation is only superficial and in reality allows distinct ethnic groups to be "incorporated into the dominant Mexican hegemonic order" (1989, 19). Shay adds that groups like the Ballet Folklórico actually "embod[y] essentialism" by attempting to show that all Mexicans are "the same" (1999,

41). Expanding on the work of Nájera-Ramírez and Shay, in this chapter I have shown that the regionalism expressed in *folklórico* dance repertoire can also be read as a discourse of racial hierarchy informed by a colonialist mentality, and that that discourse is highly problematic for modern indigenous peoples.

The Ballet Folklórico de México is to be commended for its artistry, precision, and efforts in cultural education, and Amalia Hernández must be admired for her talent, vision, and hard work, along with the tremendous effort she made in researching and presenting as many of her country's dances as possible. Her work should be understood within the context of its time, a time when *indigenismo* was considered progressive rather than problematic. Yet because these theatrical presentations reach such a large audience and have been so influential, it is imperative to understand them in context and to view them with a critical eye appropriate to our time and our new understandings of cultural politics. García Canclini writes, "The unification under national colors and symbols . . . becomes distorting and depoliticizing when it leaves out the differences and contradictions that it includes in reality. Museums and shows that conceal hardships, history, and conflicts that produced an object or a dance promote disinformation as well as preservation, oblivion as well as remembrance. The identity they extol is denied when its explanation tapers into its exhibition" (1993, 65–66.) The Ballet Folklórico de México is clearly implicated here by depicting a depoliticized Chiapas, a premodern Tarascan region, and a Yaqui deer dance where the deer is killed. García Canclini suggests that in order to produce a counterhegemonic culture, the classes of people who created the decontextualized objects must be able to reappropriate the symbolic meaning of their products, to recapture some control over them. National dance companies should therefore be taking a more politically progressive role. For the BFM, this would mean long-term participation by indigenous peoples in the Ballet's choreographies and publicity materials. A new conception of intellectual property might also be warranted, which would allow for the payment of royalties to indigenous groups whose dances are performed. In the short term, the Ballet might attempt to correct the stereotypes and misconceptions they have either created or not contested by creating more accurate and more critical program notes and press materials.

Notes

A shortened form of this chapter was given at the graduate student conference "Music, Performance, and Racial Imaginations," which took place at New York University on March 4–5, 2005. The author wishes to thank Arlene Dávila, Mercedes Dujunco, and the editors of this volume for their comments on earlier versions. All translations are the author's own.

1. I will list just a few of these dance companies here, together with their dates of inception:

> Danzas Venezuela, 1954; Conjunto Folklórico Nacional de Cuba, 1962; Ballet Folklórico Garifuna (Honduras), 1962; Bafona (Ballet Folclórico Nacional de Chile), 1965; Ballet Folklórico Nicaraguense, 1969; Curime (Costa Rica), 1974; Ballet Folklórico Nacional de Bolivia, 1975; Ballet Folklórico Nacional (Dominican Republic), 1975/1981; Ballet Folklórico Nacional de Argentina, 1986.

Dates obtained from dance company Web sites and online articles, accessed June 29, 2005:

> Venezuela: http://www.fpolar.org.ve/encarte/fasciculo21/fasc2108.html,
>
> Cuba: www.folkcuba.cult.cu/historia.htm,
>
> Honduras: http://www.laprensahn.com/portadas/9708/s13.htm,
>
> Chile: http://www.emol.com/noticias/cultura_espectaculos/detalle/detallenoticias.asp?id noticia=182750
>
> Nicaragua: http://www.primeradama.gob.sv/actividad_septiembre1404_2.htm,
>
> Costa Rica: http://www.costaricaweb.com/curime/,
>
> Bolivia: http://www.cultura.gov.bo/empresas/cultura/Ballet_Folklórico/index.asp,
>
> Dominican Republic: http://rsta.pucmm.edu.do/bellasartes/balletfolklorico.htm,
>
> Argentina: http://www.cultura.gov.ar/organismos/musica/musica_ballet.php

2. For example, one film notes that mariachis "add the bite of chiles to the pervasive music of eighteenth century Spain" (*Place of the Plumed Serpent*).

3. Saldívar reports that *jarabes* were the music of choice for soldiers during the Mexican-American War, the French Intervention, and the Revolution of 1910, giving the genre clear nationalist associations; he also recalls that Vasconcelos caused the dance to be taught in public schools beginning in 1921 and even had it performed by three hundred couples in Chapultepec Park to mark the centennial of Mexican independence (1937, 3, 9).

4. Costume is a fascinating topic that I cannot fully explore here. The choices of national costume in Mexico reveal contradictory class- and race-based concepts at play. The *china poblana* has long been considered the national costume for women and

the most appropriate for "Jarabe tapatío"; however, the Adelita has replaced it in most performances. This is likely due to the popularity of the extra-wide Adelita skirt for the *faldeo*, or skirt-twirling steps; yet the fact that the *china poblana*—originally worn by servants in central Mexico—was replaced by a dress derived from nineteenth-century upper-class European attire and later appropriated by revolutionaries merits further consideration.

5. Program, Oklahoma City Great Artist Series, January 15, 1964, 37.

6. The concept of dance reconstruction deserves further explication since many national dance companies use this process, but it is beyond the scope of this chapter.

7. Program from the Seattle World's Fair, 1962.

8. Program of the Palacio de Bellas Artes, August 19, 1961.

9. *Pulse Beat*, December 1964.

10. Program of the Festival International de Lausanne, June 23, 1964.

11. Program of the Palacio de Bellas Artes, August 19, 1961.

12. Earlier choreographers inspired by traditional dances seemed to display no such regional preference. For example, works composed by Nellie and Gloria Campobello in the 1930s took their inspiration from indigenous dances of the Tarahumara, Yaqui, Otomí, and Huave peoples as well as the *concheros*, southern Mexican dances like the *sandunga*, and the seemingly obligatory *jarabe* (Tortajada Quiroz 2000, 18, 21). During the same time, the company Interpretaciones Aztecas y Mayas drew upon archeology to present dances based on ancient Mesoamerican culture, much as Amalia would later do (Ibid., 22–23).

13. Playbill v.7 n. 11, November 1970.

14. Program, Oklahoma City Great Artist Series, January 15, 1964.

15. Ibid.

16. "Children of the Sun," "Ancient Songs of Michoacán," "The Little Cupid," "Veracruz Fiesta," "The Quetzal Birds," "Deer Dance," "Christmas in Jalisco."

17. Program, Butler University, Indiana, January 2, 1964.

18. "New Ballets Highlight Folklore of Mexico," *Lafayette Daily Advertiser*, October 30, 1966, 34.

19. Playbill v.6 n.38, p.19, September 17, 1962.

20. Program of the Palacio de Bellas Artes, 1960s.

21. Program of the Seattle World's Fair, 1962.

22. Program of the City Center NY, November 1983.

23. Playbill v.6 n.38, p.19, September 17, 1962.

24. Press release by Hurok Concerts, March 22, 1969.

25. Press release by Hurok Attractions, October 16, 1963.

13

Dancing Culture

A Personal Perspective on Folklórico

RUDY F. GARCÍA

Folklórico sits at a juncture between performance theater, traditional cultural arts, and national identity (political theater).[1] It draws from its roots in traditional Mexican culture, and it is shaped to entertain a consumer audience in a theatrical setting. Folklore is a term coined by the British archeologist William John Thoms in 1846 to denote the collective cultural knowledge of a people.[2] This includes oral and written literature, linguistic characteristics, music, dance, crafts, religious beliefs, and social values. These are the things that bind us together as a cohesive social group, with shared values that underlie society and custom without having to be overtly expressed. Dance, an essential element of folklore, celebrates life, mourns death, and offers prayers to the gods. Dance expresses the joy of being alive with movement through time and space. This is especially true in Mexico, where music and dance, as well as traditional crafts, form an integral part of the matrix of life. The term *folklórico* is short for *ballet folklórico* and is used to denote a particular kind of folk dancing from Mexico. *Folklórico* plays a role in shaping a cultural or national identity, both here in the United States and in Mexico. It is important to understand the role each of these three fundamental elements—performance art, traditional cultural art, and political theater—plays in *folklórico* because if one assumes that only one is dominant it can lead to disillusionment with the art form or abuse of it. In this brief essay, I propose to examine these three supporting foundations of *folklórico* within my own experiences and compare and contrast their relationships with each other.

The key to examining these relationships is the cultural perspective, or the outlook, that a dancer brings to *folklórico*. This perspective is completely different if one is an immigrant looking back on a tradition lived as a member of a community, or if one was born in the United States and is seeking to identify with the family cultural traditions. In the first case, the dancer may want to reestablish contact with a cultural matrix that once gave her or him a sense of community. In the second, a dancer may be trying to establish a relationship with the culture of her or his parents, essentially as an outsider looking in from a different culture. A third case is that of transcultural participants in *folklórico*. These are persons of other cultures who immerse themselves in Mexican culture because they enjoy the values it expresses or because they perceive a cultural identity they would like to explore. Each of these participants offers a unique outlook that influences what they bring to *folklórico* and how they dance it.

This perspective also changes with the emotional, physical, and artistic maturity of the dancer/director. As a young dancer, one delights in the exuberance of the dance, and the faster and more energetic the dance, the better. This sometimes leads to a distortion of the perceived culture, especially when young and inexperienced directors create acrobatic works that bear little resemblance to traditional dances. They enhance the entertainment value over the cultural values, trying to make up for a lack of depth with energy and flash. One sad side effect of this is the resulting perception that only young people can dance *folklórico* because only the young can perform the gymnastic movements that are embedded in this style. Immature directors forget that folklore involves a community and draws on all its members, from little children just learning their first steps, to young adults who can dance with virtuosity, to mature adults that express their experience and joy in the dance. One of my favorite *maestras* was Marta Arévalos de Alaminos, from Tuxtla Gutiérrez, Chiapas. My wife and I visited her in her home to review some dances. It was a joy to watch her move through the steps of "El alcaraván" and "El riito." Her whole body expressed the imbued feelings of her life in the community, and her face radiated pleasure with each movement. Once I was invited to dance at a private birthday celebration of a Hawaiian family. After we performed, the grandmother, whose birthday was being celebrated, danced a hula that reflected the same joy in movement I had seen with Maestra Arévalos. When the little kids joined in, the feeling of community was complete.

Another side effect of this artistic immaturity is the dance competition. These are forums where groups compete against each other to see "who is the best." They basically respond to the need of some directors and their groups for recognition. However, the competitions force the groups to "enhance" their performances with more energy, brighter or slinkier costumes, bigger smiles, and more complex choreographies with flamboyant moves. It moves *folklórico* from the realm of a cultural art to a sport. Looking at these through the filter of my experience I find that, like political expression, competitions subvert the true nature of the art and apply it to forums that use it for their own ends.

As one acquires a greater understanding of the dance, it becomes more interesting to present more subtle values of the culture. The proud bearing of a humble fisherman in Mandinga, Veracruz, who can play the *requinto*[3] with incredible virtuosity; the way one asks a partner to dance in a *jarana*[4] in Mérida, Yucatán; the way the Tehuanas sway elegantly in their beautifully embroidered dresses in the dance at a wedding in Juchitán, Oaxaca; the melancholic but wonderful sight of three generations of women, from little girls, mothers, and grandmothers, maintaining an all-night vigil over the graves decorated with beautiful *cempasuchitl*[5] flower altars, candles, and food, awaiting the return of the beloved's deceased spirits to visit during Día de los Muertos in Janitzio, Michoacán, while the men wait outside the cemetery chatting. All these experiences are the "folk" element that one needs to experience, either directly by visiting small towns that still maintain their traditions, or indirectly by talking to persons with these experiences, or by reading about them, before one can really present *folklórico.* Without them, one can only project from one's own cultural perspective, and, in my opinion, give a distortion, a caricature of the culture.

In my own case, my cultural perspective is a convoluted one. I was born in San Diego, California, in 1954. At that time, it was politically correct to assimilate as quickly as possible into mainstream U.S. culture, speaking only English, and even changing one's name to erase all ethnic traces that would mark you as "not a real American" or "FOB" (fresh off the boat) or "wetback," in less elegant language. Speaking Spanish was not allowed in schools, and the only heroes one was allowed to emulate were the mainstream U.S. icons. The United States, we were told, was a "melting pot," and one was expected to lose all ethnic traces in the process. Famous movie stars would change their names so they wouldn't appear too ethnic. Such was the case with Rita Hayworth (Margarita Carmen Consino of Spanish and English parents) and Raquel Welch (Jo Raquel Tejada of Bolivian and Irish parents).

It was in this political climate that my father said, "*No quiero pochos en mi familia!*"[6] and decided to send my two brothers and me to school in Mexico. I was four years old at the time, spoke only English, and fully identified with U.S. cultural values. My name reflected this situation. My legal name is Rudy

Flores García, while my baptismal name, used only for ceremonial purposes, is Raul Rodolfo García Flores Ybarra Romero. It wasn't until much later that I understood how much my name reflected my cultural identity. "Rudy" replaced "Rodolfo" because it is easier to pronounce. "Flores" became my middle name because there is no room for the mother's surname in the U.S. legal system. The rest of the surnames, which reflect my family history, were shed like so much unwanted baggage. This "shedding" was typical of the assimilation process at the time.

My brothers and I went to school in Tepic, Nayarit, a beautiful small city that was thoroughly Mexican in a time before U.S. media reached into Mexico. My father's family was from a small rural town called Tecuala, on the northwest coast of Nayarit. My mother's family was from Guadalajara, the capital of the state of Jalisco. We would get to spend vacations with both, and in this way we experienced the full span of Mexican culture, from urban to rural. I felt just at home "*pajareando la milpa*"[7] or spending Sunday afternoon on the rowboats at the Parque Alcalde after going to Mass in the *catedral*. We spent five years in Tepic, and by the time we returned I spoke little English and pretty much considered myself Mexican. Then I began my second assimilation, back into U.S. culture. The *cholos* and *vatos*[8] that I met at school did not meet my social values and for the most part didn't even speak Spanish, and I rejected them as role models in favor of mainstream ones. Since my interests were in science, this proved particularly easy, and I turned my back on my Mexican childhood.

It wasn't until 1974, my last year at Stanford, when I saw a performance of the Ballet Folklórico de Stanford at the Chicano graduation ceremonies, that I found a longing for a culture that I had once known and that had become a faded memory. I wholeheartedly started the process of reclaiming my Mexican heritage by joining the *folklórico* dance group. *Folklórico* dance was great exercise, gave me a social circle to interact with, and gave me a new cultural focus. I started to relearn Spanish, building up my vocabulary, and I began reading everything I could get my hands on about Mexican history and culture. In this process, I discovered many things about the dance form and its expression that came from my particular background. I relearned things I had already been exposed to in Mexico, but in doing so as an adult with an academic interest, I gained the feeling for the culture that a native has, combined with the depth of knowledge that an outside observer needs to understand the culture.

As I immersed myself in *folklórico*, I explored all of its various manifestations and expressions. One of the first things I was exposed to was the use of *folklórico* as a focal point of political rather than cultural expression. The Chicano movement was in full swing in the 1970s, and there was a hunger for positive role models to shape the image of the new Chicano identity, replacing the negative ones in vogue by mainstream culture. Posters of Aztec warriors, Emiliano Zapata and Pancho Villa, or their modern equivalent, César Chávez, decorated the walls of college dormitories and overlooked the barrios in huge murals painted on any available wall. The *folklórico* groups were always the rallying point for a political demonstration, the entertainment to draw and hold the crowd before the speeches began. I objected to this use of the art form because I was trying to express my culture, my joy of dance, not my political views. I now realize, however, that what I experienced personally when *folklórico* became the focal point of my rediscovery of my Mexican roots was happening on a larger scale in the Chicano community, giving a cultural anchor to people who were trying to define themselves. There were, and are, many labels used to describe the community: Latino, Hispanic, Mexican American, Chicano, La Raza; none of them quite fit, each describing only aspects of the culture. *Folklórico* didn't define these terms, but dissolved them by providing direct connection to the cultural roots.

As I eagerly learned new dances and read more history, I ran into another phenomena common in *folklórico,* that of "artistic license." An artist is a creative individual seeking to express some inner vision in the medium of his choice, be it dance, poetry, painting, or any other art form. In Western culture since the Renaissance, the emphasis has been on the individual vision and creativity of the artist. In a traditional society, on the other hand, the emphasis is working with the traditional forms to develop an individual expression. In Western culture this is termed "crafts" and relegated to second-class status compared to "real art." From my own perspective, I wanted to present real, traditional dances of Mexico, not created works that drew from these traditions but sought to express an individual's creative urges. I didn't consider myself a creative artist; I thought myself a curator of a culture and sought to preserve and express that culture. I discovered the Asociación Nacional de Grupos Folkloricós (ANGF), whose annual dance conference brought *maestros* (teachers) directly from Mexico for the purpose of teaching the dances directly to aspiring directors. In these conferences I met many wonderful *maestros,* and I would usually follow up by visiting them in Mexico. I spent many years traveling to the backwater areas of Mexico, seeking *maestros* in their native settings, to learn directly from the source without the filter of anyone's artistic interpretation. I stayed away from places like the Universidad de Guadalajara and the Ballet Folklórico de México school because they offered prepackaged consumer visions of the culture. There are so many wonderful memories of my travels: a traditional wedding in Juchitán, Oaxaca; *fandangos*[9] in Tlacotalpan, Veracruz; learning the steps for the Danza de los Chichimecas from a *capitán* in Salinas, San Luis Potosí; experiencing Día de los Muertos in Janitzio, Michoacán; witnessing a traditional *jarana* in Mérida, Yucatán; watching Don Esperanza, a ninety-three-year-old man, dance *sones de tarima*[10] in Tixtla, Guerrero; enjoying a traditional *mariachi* in Tepic, Nayarit; watching the *guelaguetza* in Oaxaca, Oaxaca; listening to *huapangos*[11] in a hut in Tamaletón, San Luis Potosí. All these experiences are the breath that gives life to my vision of *folklórico,* what gives flavor to the cultural *pozole* that I cook![12] As I accumulated these experiences, I could draw from them to better interpret with greater depth the dances I had learned from *maestros* in Mexico. This experience was sometimes lacking in other directors, who either preferred to "do their own thing" and make "folkloroid" creations that lacked substance, or simply lacked the opportunity to gather the same type of experiences and so came to the same end. The members of a *folklórico* group express the cultural intent, or lack of it, of the director; it is the responsibility of the director to immerse himself or herself in the culture, to soak in the everyday experiences that make up a folk culture. Without this, the director's work becomes a shallow caricature that mocks the culture rather than emulates it. The way people greet each other, their expressions of joy, grief, anger, their clothing, their food, the way they earn a living; all these are the colors we need to paint a portrait of the culture with subtle intonation and soul. Without these experiences, we merely make comic books that entertain but certainly do not educate the mind and uplift the heart. I considered myself a cultural craftsman, drawing from the threads of the experiences I had gathered to create a tapestry of traditional patterns. The greatest compliments I would get would be from people of the small towns of Mexico, who, after seeing our performances, would come to us and say that they felt close to their home town because our dances reminded them so much of their home.

As I progressed from dancer to director of Los Lupeños de San Jose in 1987, I drew from these experiences to present dances with the best costuming we could afford and with as much cultural detail as we could gather. Compromises were always made in the process because of limited budgets or limited access to traditional costumes, but even when we made our own costumes, we tried hard to stay within the cultural bounds of the region. I always tested myself by imagining myself in a small town of the region in that costume, doing that dance, and asking myself if the people would accept it as belonging to their tradition. If the answer was no, then back to the drawing board! Of course, this process was more complicated with historical dances because you had to imagine the cultural setting (through examining period art pieces and reading novels and history books) rather than actually experience it. These are the normal problems that a director faces, and the best guide to see a director through are his or her experiences, sense of judgment, and sense of cultural community. It was wonderful to see how this process was reflected in the pride our dancers had in themselves, in the work of the group, and in their culture.

Assuming the role of director was not as difficult as I had imagined, mostly because I had taken the role of dancer very seriously since the beginning and had thoroughly studied the culture. All the dances and choreographies that I learned were carefully annotated, although this meant researching methods of notation to do this, and when these methods failed, I created my own. The difficulties lay in organizing the dance group, finding and training new dancers, and establishing ties with the community. The long hours of rehearsals, performances, board meetings, and costume-making sessions

Rudy Garcia dancing a Gusto from Tierra Caliente, Guerrero, with his wife and partner, Maria Luisa Colmenarez. OPSU Campus Communications photo by Micah Donaldson.

were a labor of love. The end product was a fine performing company with a wonderful reputation. When I traveled to Mérida, Yucatán, and mentioned Los Lupeños, I was amazed that the local *maestro* said, "Yes, I've heard a lot about you." Many times it was mentioned by *maestros* in Mexico that they were amazed at how seriously we took our work. We worked hard but enjoyed every minute of it. The group was a tight-knit family, but we always welcomed new dancers as long as they realized how serious we were about our avocation.

Of course, there is a major shift in perspective as you progress from a small, community-based performing group, to a larger performing company that serves a more diverse audience in larger venues, and then to a semiprofessional performing company that entertains a commercial audience that expects a "quality" show. You have a responsibility to the audience to present a great show, and you must use the tools of the medium to create a presentation worthy of the group. The dance, choreographies, and costumes are the basic elements that must now be merged with music, lighting, set design, and stage management, as well as new skills to express the culture. But again, they are spices that should enhance the flavor of the *pozole,* not become the dominant factor. I had progressed from being a member of a group to assuming the role of artistic director. The group itself had progressed to the point where it was a recognized and respected performing company with a diverse dance repertoire. It was a joy to watch it grow and learn, almost like a young child learning new skills, demonstrating new abilities. There came a point in 1992 when we were chosen to perform with Linda Ronstadt in her second show, "Fiesta Mexicana." We became elements in an entertainment world that had very different motivations and responded to different rules than we were accustomed to.

The transition from a self-motivated, culturally oriented environment to a professional entertainment forum was a difficult one. In the group, we were very disciplined about rehearsals and performances. We had strict rules about presenting a positive image to the community when we were wearing our costumes. No alcoholic drinks were allowed while in costume. In short, we were used to being our own strict taskmasters in order to achieve our goals. When we began rehearsals with the "Fiesta Mexicana" show, we were required to be at rehearsals, under penalty of being fired from the show. The rehearsals were set by union rules, so breaks were required every hour, whether we needed them or not. We also had to learn a new repertoire with a new, high-visibility styling that went hand in hand with the commercial aspect of the show. This was the most difficult for me to do, to put aside the traditional styling I had so carefully crafted and assume this new role: cabaret dancer. Of course, the styling was exactly correct for this entertainment forum. The audience expects a high-energy, engaging performance, and one must adapt it if one wishes to be on this stage. The dances themselves were very stylized, designed to keep a high energy level in the show. Skirtwork, of which we were particular, was high and showy. The men's footwork was at a very exaggerated level, using ballet *folklórico* poses. All in all, it grated on us to dance outside our style and to have our avocation become a job, with obligations motivated by money. But that is the world of show business, and we were willing to be part of the show! Don't think I'm trying to denigrate the experience. This was a new discipline necessary to perform in this environment, and if you want to participate, you have to learn the ropes. It's just that the experience was so different from what we were used to that it was a true challenge.

The talent level in the show was extremely high, and it was a pleasure to watch the group respond to the new setting. I had long talks with my very good friend Lalo García regarding the difficulties that would accompany this transition. He had performed with the first of Linda's shows, "Canciones de mi padre" ("Songs of My Father's"), and had plenty of good advice to offer. There was suddenly a lot of interpersonal tension and jealousy because not all the members of the group had been chosen to perform, and I had to smooth over the ruffled feathers of the ones not picked. Some of the best memories of my career are those of listening to Linda sing "Crucifijo de piedra" ("Stone Crucifix)" to the accompaniment of Mariachi Los Camperos de Nati Cano, and dancing "La charreada" ("The Mexican Rodeo") on the stage of the Orpheum Theater in San Francisco.

As I grew older, my responsibilities to my family and "real" career grew, so I stopped performing in favor of the next level of cultural involvement, that of nurturing other members of the *folklórico* community, teaching and sharing my knowledge so that others might benefit from my experiences. This is in many ways the best part of a long career in *folklórico*, passing on the torch to a new generation, ensuring that they have, at least by retelling, some of the same experiences that I gathered. This maintains the continuity of experience that is essential to a traditional culture. Without this, the culture has to reinvent itself with each generation, and it leads to that certain feeling of free-floating identity that drives many of us to seek our roots in our ancestral culture to help us maintain a perspective of the ever-changing present.

A teacher has the responsibility to carry on the cultural torch given by his or her teachers. All the knowledge gathered from other teachers, combined with one's own experiences, is what nurtures that next generation. My teaching has taken three forms: teaching the actual dances, teaching the cultural background of the dances, and building the community necessary to make the *folklórico* experience a cultural art. I am involved with Danzantes Unidos, an organization that hosts a yearly festival bringing more than a thousand dancers from throughout California for a weekend of cultural sharing. We bring *maestros* to teach workshops and make contact with the *folklórico* groups. This gives the groups access to traditional *maestros*. The groups perform for each other, providing a forum for their dances to be appreciated and critiqued by everyone. Sometimes, some dances go "over the edge" of cultural bounds and the feedback given in this setting provides the kind of cultural feedback normally applied by the traditional community. Of course, there is also a big *pachanga* that lets everyone interact in the medium that everyone understands: dance!

In my performing years in the Bay Area, I performed many times in the San Francisco Ethnic Dance Festival. Like Danzantes Unidos, it provides a forum for all ethnic dance groups to present to the community in the auditions and, if selected, in a major venue. The best part is meeting members of other ethnic communities, learning their cultural expressions, and making friendships across these boundaries. Understanding the traditional folk communities in this medium has enhanced my knowledge of our own community by comparing and contrasting their experiences. Also, all the dance styles one can see in the *folklórico* community—such as traditional, classical, cabaret, folkloric ballet, competition—all can be seen and examined with the added flavor of different cultures.

I have examined the role that *folklórico* plays in shaping the cultural landscape of an individual and a community. It can provide a firm foundation for self-understanding in a society that prides itself in stripping such culture from the individual. It also provides a medium for the community to present this cultural identity to the world to build bridges and generate respect. What is necessary for this process to succeed is to involve oneself in the experiences that provide the perspective necessary to generate the cultural reality that will then be presented.

Notes

1. Performance theater draws from the personal values of the performer within his or her own cultural setting to present creative works of theater, either spontaneous as in ad lib theater, or scripted as in conventional staged productions. As you cross the boundaries to other cultural settings, there is a mix of the performer's ingrained

cultural values and the ones she or he is attempting to assume to be the character she or he is representing. For an enlightening discussion of the topic of performance theater and traditional culture, please see Richard Schechner's book *Between Theater and Anthropology* (1985). Political theater is the use of cultural arts to present and try to influence a political ideology. It is a vehicle for indoctrination and change, depending on the usage, and has actively been used to shape national identity in the past two hundred years. It was used in Mexico after the Revolución to shape a new identity for the nascent Mexican nation after the Porfiriato. The new identity drew from the indigenous roots to create a "Raza Cósmica," a new national image based on ethnic cultures that had been suppressed before that. An engrossing discussion of this topic is found in Richard M. Dorson's book *Folklore and Fakelore* (1976). Although outdated, Frances Toor's *A Treasure of Mexican Folkways* (1947), written when many displaced U.S. artists suffering from the consequences of the Depression moved to Mexico, is an important collection from her travels in Mexico.

2. British writer William John Thoms (1803–85) is credited with inventing the word "folklore" to replace the various other terms used at the time, including "popular antiquities" or "popular literature" (see also Dundes 1965).

3. The *requinto* is a small four- or five-string instrument from Veracruz, typically plucked melodically with a long quill or plastic plectrum.

4. A *jarana,* in Yucatán, is a fiesta in which you dance *jaranas* (regional dances) to the music played by an *orchestra jaranera.*

5. "Marigolds," used ritually for Día de los Muertos (Day of the Dead) events.

6. "I don't want [cultural] half-breeds in my family!" *Pocho* is a derogatory term for a person of Mexican descent who doesn't speak the language or speaks it badly, a person assimilated into U.S. culture.

7. "using slingshots to keep birds from eating the freshly sown corn seed"

8. In the U.S. context, *cholos* are street tough, inner-city youth that do not fit into mainstream U.S. culture and take on the subculture as a banner of identity. A *cholo* usually wears regalia, such as flannel shirt, a bandana on his head, sunglasses, tattoos, and perhaps drives a low rider car. *Vato* is a "dude" or "homeboy" from the barrio.

9. *Fandango* is a social gathering in which regional music is performed and danced.

10. Tunes meant to be danced to on a wooden platform (*tarima*).

11. The *huapango* is the *son* genre from the Huastec region of Mexico, which overlaps the states of Hidalgo, Veracruz, San Luis Potosí, Tamaulipas, and Puebla.

12. *Pozole* is a delicious stew with hominy corn and pork but varies from region to region in details and flavor! The name comes from *poztl,* Nahuatl for soup or stew.

14

The Mexican *Danzón*

Restrained Sensuality

SUSAN CASHION

Introduction

The *danzón* has been popular for more than one hundred years in Mexican culture. This chapter traces its origins from Cuba in the nineteenth century, its importation and popularization in Mexico in the twentieth, and its rebirth at the turn of the twenty-first. From its birth, the *danzón* was an enactment of restrained sensuality as black and white cultures of Cuba entwined. In the 1940s and 1950s *danzón* enthusiasts packed Mexico City ballrooms to savor its romance and to escape from the grind of industrial, urban life. In the 1960s and 1970s it was pushed to the sidelines of nightclub entertainment when first rock-and-roll and then disco dancing invaded Mexico from the United States. At the end of the twentieth century *danzón* was revived among the urban dancers of Mexico. It became both a participatory event for middle-aged and senior citizens and a performance medium for younger dancers. It also emerged as a symbol of Mexican defiance against globalization. One cultural promoter from Veracruz remarked, "*Danzón* is a return to sanity, which Mexico so badly needs."[1]

Prelude

I first viewed *danzón* in the *zócalo,* or central plaza, of Veracruz during the 1976 Carnival celebrations. One evening I attended a military band concert that was held in front of the presidential palace. Three rows of folding chairs faced the platform, behind which people meandered. Children ran and played along walkways crowded with vendors selling balloons, cotton candy, and ice cream. Nestled under archways on two sides of the plaza, various musicians (*marimba, norteño, jarocho,* and *mariachi* groups)[2] were playing simultaneously for the restaurant crowd, creating a cacophony of delightful sounds.

The military band opened its program with a selection of marches and symphonic works, but the highlight of the evening was their renderings of the *danzón*. Elderly gentlemen were seated in the first row of chairs, smartly dressed in crisp, white *guayabera* shirts, creased white slacks, and white dress shoes. As each *danzón* began, they invited a partner to the area in front of the stage and laced together traditional steps they remembered from their youth. Their selected partners were their wives, daughters, or even granddaughters. The soft romance of the music floated in the warm, evening breeze over the plaza. Spectators applauded the dancers after each selection and commented on the senior dancers' elegance. Everyone was welcome to participate, but most of the younger audience preferred to listen to the music and give the dance space over to the older dancers.

My next encounter with *danzón* was in 1980 in Mexico City, when I accompanied a friend from Brazil searching for the famed *salones de danzón* (danzón salons). We discovered the Salón California, where the dance floor was quite large and had a stage at either end of the room. As soon as the orchestra on one stage finished its set, the curtain on the opposite stage opened and the second orchestra began to play. But we could not understand why couples would pause for an extended time during each dance.

My fascination with *danzón* then led me in 1983 to Havana, Cuba, where I interviewed music historians, musicians, and members of the national folklore company, *El Conjunto Folclórico*. I returned to Mexico City a decade later to film, interview, and dance the *danzón* during the retro movement revival that was occurring.

In 1999, I attended a *danzón* workshop in Colima, Mexico. On the last day, the famed orchestra Acerina y su Danzonera arrived from Mexico City to play in the gazebo situated in the central plaza. Hundreds of *Colimeños*[3] arrived to listen to the evening concert. Platforms extended from the gazebo to feature exhibition couples, who had been invited from Guadalajara. More than five hundred *colimeños* of all ages crowded the plaza walkways to dance their individual interpretations of the music. On the top stair of the gazebo stood Maestra Carmelita Estévez, a workshop instructor, surveying the crowd and softly swaying to the music. When asked to dance, she graciously descended the stairs and assumed a quiet, lifted body position in her partner's arms.

Mexican Danzón, by Ramon Morónes. Personal collection of the author.

As soon as she began to dance, I observed the styling of the ideal female *danzonera*—relaxed, with a slight undulation from the rib cage to the hips, causing the bottom ruffle of her skirt to sway. Occasionally, she spontaneously accented her footwork with a toe tap or slight lift of her lower leg.

My most recent research included a visit in 2004 to the *danzón* community in Guadalajara, Mexico. Since then, I have continued to correspond with two Mexican *danzón* scholars, Miguel Zamudio Abdala of Veracruz and Carlos Aguilar González of Guadalajara. The detailed writings of Mexican *danzón* historian Jesús Flores y Escalante (1993, 1994) have further deepened my understanding, and I have translated and included *danzón* verses from his book in this chapter to reinforce my arguments and observations.

Cuban Origins

Music historians usually credit Cuban cornet player Miguel Faílde as the composer of "Las alturas de Simpson" (1878), the so-called "first *danzón*." Faílde, born of a Spanish father and a mother of mixed African and European descent, began his musical career playing for *bailes de color*.[4] His music quickly gained popularity with the middle-class Cuban creoles that had fought alongside black Cubans during the War of Independence against Spain. Author John Charles Chasteen cautions, however, that Faílde was "not the only musician infusing the dance repertory of Matanzas with the new rhythmic excitement that defined *danzón* in the 1870s" (2004, 75). The creoles were hungry for subtle statements of rebellion against the Spanish, such as the black-infused Cuban music and dance forms. Anthropologist Yvonne Daniel suggests, "The overwhelming tenacity and popularity of *danzón* demonstrated the integration of Spanish and African elements in the late nineteenth century. *Danzón* symbolized the unique position of Cuba in its confrontation with Spain during the War of Independence between 1895 and 1898. Artistically it marked a separation from colonial domination and the emergence of independent Cuban thought" (Daniel 1995, 39).

Danzón was a vehicle for the intersection of black and white heritage elements within Cuban popular music. Faílde's Afro-Cuban orchestra penetrated white society when it began performing at exclusive clubs for the elite in Matanzas. Even the newspapers of the era claimed that the *danzón* had "infected the most distinguished circles of white society" (Chasteen 2004, 73). Its lineage included the Spanish *contradanza* (contra dance), which consisted of a series of set choreographic patterns danced by interdependent couples who formed in long, facing lines, or in chains following the leader and making floor designs in loops and bridges. Proper modesty was maintained when dancers held a partner's hand during the dance. The Afro-Cuban Carnival dancers, who danced *comparsa* (Carnival parade groups) to the lively accompaniment of Faílde's *danzón* compositions, also adopted the highly structured *contradanzas*, thus blending the forms.

The uplifted body carriage of the European dancer fused with the characteristic movements that made up the heritage of Afro-Cubans (*Kongo-Angola, Arará, Yoruba,* and *Carabali*): flexed knees, use of the whole foot on the floor, relaxation of the spine, isolation of torso, individual movement invention, and flirtation. Thus, the European couple dances began to include pelvic movements, although Cuban society discreetly referred to the hip movements as *doblando o quebrando la rodilla*.[5] Just as with American ragtime that began developing during the same period, young Cuban men from upper-class white society began participating in the *comparsa* social gatherings where the *danzón* was making its transition from a dance for groups to a closed-partner, social dance. White men and black dancers of both sexes took to the floor and the seeds of Cuban social dance were sown.

At the turn of the twentieth century, the *danzón* was a model for organizing and patterning social behavior on the dance floor. All Cuban social classes embraced the *danzón,* but over time the *salas de danza* (dance salons) became segregated according to color: *la gente blanca, negra, y mulata.*[6] Yet all dressed elegantly in the style of the time: men in suits with starched collars and cuffs, and corseted women in long, flowing dresses of filmy material. Handkerchiefs were placed in the man's right hand to protect the back of the woman's dress from his sweaty palm smudges. Women carried fans to refresh themselves during the *descanso,* or rest, interludes. *Salas de danza* were so crowded on Sunday afternoons that dancers had to wait turns outside before they could enter. After entering, the best dancers typically gravitated to the front windows of the *salas* so that the dancers still waiting outside might watch them and envy their styles.[7]

Although social dancers of the Americas were familiar with the closed-partner position of the waltz, polka, and schottische, the *danzón* allowed couples to dance even closer, and it directed the dance movement to fluid and soft sways. The couples' close spatial relationship, swaying hips, and minimal use of floor space created the *danzón*'s characteristic "look": couples were to be no more than four inches apart, dance on a 2.5–foot square *ladrillo,* or floor tile, and slide the entire foot on the floor when taking a two-inch step. The Yucatecan lyricist Carlos (Chalín) Renán Cámara Zavala described it thus in his piece entitled *El Danzón:*

> *Pegadito a mi mulata*
> *Sin salirnos de un ladrillo*
> *Damos dos pasos atrás*
> *Y otro más adelante,*
> *Una vuelta a la derecha*
> *Y otra girando al revés*[8]
> (Flores y Escalante 1994, 51)

The musical structure guided the choreographic design. The five musical themes were arranged in a sequence of AB, AC, AD, and AE, and each 2/4 melodic section was sixteen measures long. Whenever the dancers heard the recurring melodic theme "A," a *descanso* (rest) allowed them to stop dancing to rest, chat, cool off from the sexual "rush," watch and listen to the musicians, fan themselves, or press a handkerchief to flushed faces or damp hands, as described by Félix Martínez González in a ten-line (*décima*) *jarocho* verse titled *Danzonero.*

Y solo el Danzón señores
Tiene un tiempo de remanso
Que toman como descanso
Los alegres bailadores.
Algunos se hablan de amores,
Otros secan su sudor
Ella abanica el calor
Esperando atentamente
Que él la tome nuevamente
Para bailar con fervor.[9]
(Flores y Escalante 1994, 52)

During sections B, C, D, and E the dancers danced a slow and elegant basic step. Cuban dancers added syncopation to the *danzón* by beginning on an anticipatory downbeat; the half beat following count 2 that ended the preceding measure was tied to count 1 (the downbeat) of the next measure, which interlocked the dancer even more with the rhythm of the music. Thus the Cuban basic step was a small sliding step to the side (anticipatory half beat), a pause (count 1), a small closing step (count 2), and a shift of weight in place (count "and").

The *danzón* reigned as the Cuban national dance until 1920, when the *son* (not to be confused with the Mexican *son*)[10] began to take its place in popularity. It had more *afrocubano* elements in it, such as the rhythm of *clave* and a *montuno* section of *ostinatos* (repeating patterns) in call and response. *Son* dancers began to embellish the music with accented steps, which pushed the musicians to "catch up" by adding a final musical section called "*cha.*" To keep *danzón* alive, Cuban musicians adopted the innovation of the *son*'s *montuno* to create the "*danzón en su nuevo ritmo,*"[11] or *danzón-cha,* which would develop later in the 1950s into the *cha-cha-chá.*[12]

Modification of the Structure after the *Danzón* Enters Mexico

The Mexican states of Veracruz and Yucatán along the Gulf of Mexico were the first points of entry for Cuba's export of *danzón-cha,* or what Mexicans simply referred to as "*el danzón.*" It was modified to suit the comfortable social distance of Mexican dancers. The basic step of the Cuban *danzón* was simplified to begin on the downbeat of count 1, pause on count 2, and two quick steps in place on counts 3 and "and," rather than beginning the dance step on the anticipatory count before the downbeat. While Cubans were experienced with polyrhythms and could easily syncopate and interlock the steps with the music, Mexicans adjusted the phrasing to begin squarely at the top of the measure, thus making it a simpler task to "stay on the beat."

While Cuban male dancers began the basic step by shifting weight to their left with a side step, Mexican men opened the dance with a forward step, and a couple's embrace was not as close in Mexico as it was in Cuba, because the stricter Catholic upbringing in Mexico mandated a more closely reserved decorum. As with any dance form that moves the woman closer to the man, the *danzón* had a seductive character; one radio announcer is quoted as saying, "The tension between distance and nearness [in the *danzón*] can be erotic" (Dibble 2003). Newspapers of the time warned their readers that the *danzón* was not suitable for proper women. In general, the Mexican dancers de-emphasized the torso accents, rhythmic complexities, and intimate embraces characteristic of Cuban *danzón*. Nevertheless, Mexican dancers retained the original style's subtle hip motion and a general relaxation in the upper and lower body, which Veracruz dancer Miguel Zamudio calls "*natural*" movement.[13]

> *Danzonero* by Félix Martínez González
> *Con cadencia de palmera*
> *Mecida por viento suave*
> *Sigue el ritmo de la clave*
> *Que bien mueve la cadera*
> *Pero sin exagerar.*[14]
> (Flores y Escalante 1994, 51–52)

The musical structure of Mexican *danzón* begins with an easily recognizable musical introduction (theme A) eight measures long that repeats. This theme, the *estribillo* (refrain), traditionally repeats three more times during each composition. During the opening *estribillo,* the dancers enter the space with a small promenade and begin dancing when the melody repeats. During the next two repeats of the *estribillo,* the dancers rest (*descanso*) during the first eight measures and resume dancing during the repeat. Additional melodic themes occur after each *estribillo*—referred to as *melodía* 1 (B), *melodía* 2 (C), and *montuno* (D). Unlike Cuban *danzón,* which strictly adheres to a musical structure of AB, AC, AD, and AE, the Mexican *danzón* may include

Table 14.1. Corresponding Structure between *Danzón* Music and Dance

Estribillo (A)	
Musical introduction	8 measures of *descanso*
Musical repeat of introduction	8 measures to dance
Melodía 1 (B)	Usually 16 measures of basic step
Estribillo (A)	
Musical repeat of Introduction	8 measures of *descanso*
Musical repeat of Introduction	8 measures to dance
Melodía 2 (C)	Indeterminate number of measures to dance
Estribillo (A)	
Musical repeat of introduction	8 measures of *descanso*
Musical repeat of introduction	8 measures to dance
Montuno (D) (More emphasis on rhythm and torso movement)	Indeterminate number of measures to dance

additional themes (F, etc.) before the *montuno* occurs, but the *montuno* is always the final theme, and it is during the *montuno* when the dance becomes more percussive and the dancers' individual personalities come to life. Also during the *montuno,* dancers embellish the basic step with turns, more pronounced hip movements, and *tornillos,* pivots balanced on one foot.

Mexican Regional Acclaim

At the end of the nineteenth century, when Cuban ships docked at Yucatán's principal seaport, Puerto Progreso, their crews introduced the *danzón* into all the clubs near the docks, and it was Mexico's working class that first embraced the *danzón* and added it to their repertory of tropical music (Zedillo Castillo 1996). Cuban touring shows known as Bufos-Habaneras, a comic theater from Havana, provided additional influences in Mexico when Cuban *danzones* were performed between the Bufo acts and during breaks (Pedelty 2004, 145). As these companies toured Mexico, the music became popularized and was added to the repertoire of salon dancing.

Its popularity soared in the early twentieth century. In 1906 Yucatán politicians introduced the new music and dance in a formal reception for President Porfirio Díaz, thus becoming the ribbon-cutting event when the entire Republic of Mexico began to embrace the Cuban import (Flores y Escalante 1993, 29). Still later, after the radio was introduced to Mexico, stations would broadcast publicity jingles to the rhythm of *danzones* (Ibid., 16). But specifically, Veracruz dancers and musicians adopted the *danzón* as their own and gave it a central place in their regional identity.

Danzonerito by Félix Martínez González
Habrá que felicitar
A quien con tanta paciencia,
Te transmite su experiencia
Enseñandote a bailar,
Porque tú has de continuar
La tradición jarochera,
Que no se vuelva quimera
Esa misión tan loable
Tu serás el responsible
De que el danzón ¡Nunca Muera![15]
(Flores y Escalante 1994, 54–55)

In the 1920s, the center of *danzón* shifted from Veracruz to Mexico City as dance clubs sprang up in various neighborhoods. For the next thirty years these ballrooms and cabarets were hubs for nocturnal seduction. Anthropologist Mark Pedelty, in his work *Musical Ritual in Mexico City,* attaches the rise of these music/dance venues to the postrevolution need for a new popular culture to express modernity. He writes that unlike the Mexican *corrido* and *canción ranchera,* "the *bolero* and its dance complement, *danzón,* (were) bittersweet memories of lost love, and evil enjoined, moral ambivalence and cultural relativism, (and) modern catharsis" (2004, 140). As thousands of rural Mexicans migrated to Mexico City after the revolution, *danzón* palaces became a replacement for lost families and rural communities, as well as an outlet for newfound urban freedoms (Ibid., 144).

The ambiance of these palaces dripped with tropical sensuality, driven by the percussive sounds of the *paila* (*timbal*), *clave,* and *güiro.* A "democracy of clientele" (i.e., politicians and prostitutes and everyone in between) frequented the *danzón* ballrooms (Flores y Escalante 1993, 109). The dance venues became a place to escape from daily life, where fantasies of romantic encounters were awakened.

Many of the patrons concealed their real identities to avoid scandals when they left spouses at home, or so that zealous young men could not trace the whereabouts of their dancing partners. For this reason, it was the custom to only use a first name to protect one's identity. In *Danzón,* Mexican director María Novarro's feature film (1991), the dancers and dance halls of the 1940s era are brought to life. In the film, a single mother goes to a *danzón* ballroom every week to meet her favorite partner. Neither has any contact with each other outside of the ballroom, but their hearts are sweetly entwined within the timeless space of the *salón*. When her partner fails to appear for several weeks, she tries to locate him, a search made difficult because she only knows him by his first name.

Competition played an important role in the dancers' self-esteem. The industrial revolution had left its mark on urban dwellers, whose identity blended into the masses and dehumanizing assembly lines. In the *danzón* palaces one might compete for recognition and notoriety. Similar to *tango* in Argentina and swing in the United States, great *danzón* dancers were applauded and acclaimed "heroes" of Mexican nightlife. Displays of virtuosic dancing attracted future partners and also defined one's dominance over rival dancers. Competition on the dance floor sometimes slipped over the fine line of culturally accepted forms of rivalry to escalate into physical intimidation and fights. The unforgivable trespass of bumping into another dancing couple could be countered by a bristling male dancer dutifully protecting his offended partner's honor.

By 1940, more than two dozen dance halls could be found in Mexico City, including Los Salones Colonia, Esmirna, Los Angeles, and El California. Still displayed in neon lights above the door of the Salón Los Angeles is the saying:

> *¡El que no conoce Los Angeles,*
> *no conoce México!*[16]
> (Flores y Escalante 1994, 78)

One of the most famous *danzón* palaces was El Salón México, which was originally built with three separate dance floors surrounding a central bar. It was so large that orchestras could play for each of the dance floors simultaneously without disturbing the other. Within the palace, the social classes gravitated to separate floors: upper classes wearing elegant attire chose one floor, the working middle class another, and the *gente humilde*[17] dressed in denims or work clothes occupied a third. Some of these patrons arrived shoeless, and on the wall there was a sign that read: *No tirar colillas porque se queman los pies de las damas* (Flores y Escalante 1994, 80)[18]

The *danzón* of the 1930s to 1950s often shared the evening with other dances in vogue during this period: fox-trot, Charleston, and swing from the United States; *son, cha-cha-chá,* and *mambo* from Cuba; and *tango* from Argentina. Musicians, such as Veracruz composer Agustín Lara and the famed guitar/vocal trio of Los Panchos, quickly adopted the romantic *bolero,* originally from Cuba. "Eventually, both the *bolero* and *danzón* became viewed as authentically Mexican musical forms" (Pedelty 2004, 151).

Danzón's Reign Ends

Agustín Zedillo believes that a drop in nightlife, which began after a curfew was imposed in 1957 by Mexico City's mayor Ernesto Uruchurtu, largely caused the decline of the *danzón* (Zedillo 1996). The ordinance forced all ballrooms and cabarets to close at 1:00 A.M., thus limiting the hours of activity. Although the ordinance was later repealed, it abruptly shortened the life of many popular dances of that period. During the same era, a flood of new dance imports soon overshadowed the *danzón*. Specifically, two foreign dances, *cumbia* (Colombia) and rock and roll (United States), moved into the spotlight of Mexican popular culture. Mexican dancers no longer held each other close while dancing, and structured dance steps disappeared. As the pace and energy of the era accelerated, more upbeat music and movement better reflected urban hustle and bustle and the growing rebelliousness of youth.

In the 1970s, disco dancing replaced rock and roll and, by the end of the century, the world beat of hip-hop and *salsa* entered Mexico. These forms brought a new type of aggressive energy to the dance floor that many of the *música tropical* dancers considered distasteful. *Salsa* dancers barely listened to the music as they furiously moved, nonstop, from one "trick" to another. Fast spins, increasing use of more floor space, and leg flicks became physically hazardous to other dancers. As *salsa* and hip-hop became driving forces of youth, a *locura,* or craziness, matched the risks of living in overpopulated urban centers.

Passing On Tradition

Beginning in the late 1990s, Mexican people of all ages began to reclaim the *danzón,* similar to the revival of the Argentine *tango.* In his work *Hybrid Cultures,* Néstor García Canclini examines the inseparable concepts of tradition and modernity in Latin America, which helps to explain the impulse for the *danzón*'s retro movement. *Danzón*'s gentle decorum, coupled with its aesthetic of intimacy, provided a buffer against the modernity's dissident forces. As a counterbalance to public insecurity and isolation created by urban violence and the bombardment of technology, *danzón* gatherings were in safe, public spaces that fostered social interaction.

A recent article on the *danzón* "addiction" in the city of Tijuana places the dancers in a public plaza on Sunday mornings, "dancing the way their parents and grandparents did, in pairs that talk quietly and touch carefully"

(Dibble 2003). The article emphasizes "reaching for the past" as a means of preserving order and aesthetic intimacy within a contemporary world of U.S./Mexican border disputes and unrest. In Oaxaca City, *danzón* classes are given by family service organizations such as the Lion's Club and Mexican Institute of Social Security. A class averages twenty-five students who range in age from fourteen to fifty. When community member Nereida Sánchez was asked why *danzón* was so popular, she explained, "Oaxaqueños are sensual people and they like social dances that allow them to move in that way."[19]

García Canclini's work illuminates a second interplay of modernity and tradition in his discussion of staging cultural ritual. "In order for traditions today to serve to legitimize those who constructed or appropriated them, they must be staged" (1995, 109). The rebirth of *danzón* has clearly been facilitated by *ballet folklórico* companies. After forty years of theatricalizing *bailes regionales,* traditional regional folk forms, the artistic directors of *folklórico* performance groups turned to the genre of Mexican social dance, the *bailes de salón,* to augment their repertories. The *ballet folklóricos* of the Universities of Guadalajara and Veracruz each offer dramatized staged *danzónes* in which females wear ankle-strap, high-heel shoes and 1950s' hairdos, and the men wear white suits and panama hats. The *ballet folklórico*'s treatment of *danzón* has changed its image from a vintage dance for elders to a multigenerational, sensual dance vehicle epitomizing romantic fantasy.

Mexican dance and music remain strong symbols of national and regional identity. For this reason, the *ballet folklóricos* enjoy a popularity that Mexican modern dance and ballet companies do not share. Any traditional Mexican dance, among which the *danzón* is included, fosters a spirit of *mexicanismo.* Perhaps now more than ever, Mexicans feel the need to resurrect these dances as symbols of their heritage and identity. Twenty-first-century issues of globalization create growing tensions in Mexico between modernization and tradition. The *danzón* provides a subtle weapon for those who champion retention of Mexican artistry over the satellite blitz of world beat and MTV.

Veracruz City has retained its central position as a stronghold of *danzón,* with more than sixty *danzón* groups in the area.[20] In addition to the older generation's continuing to dance in the *zócalo* on a weekly basis, the younger *jarocho* generation has also been captivated by the *danzón.* Miguel Zamudio Abada, who at age ten in 1986 discovered *música tropical* at a family party, leads this youth movement. He begged his mother for permission to attend *danzón* lessons, and she found a club of elder citizens called the "*Club de Bailadores de Danzón Hoy y Siempre,*" which still meets weekly to dance and create small routines for exhibition. Within the next decade Zamudio started his own group, "*Tres Generaciones de Danzón Veracruzano.*"[21] The group's three separate units of participants—children, young adults, and seniors—perform weekly in Veracruz and represent their city on tours across Mexico and Europe. Perhaps this is why cultural promoter Adrián González refers to the *danzón* as a "family experience" since both the performers and audience include children and seniors. "Everyone in the *danzón* is part of the family, as demonstrated by the traditional dedicatory introduction: "*Hey, familia, este danzón dedicado a . . .*"[22] (Pedelty 2004, 198).

A by-product of Zamudio's passion for *danzón* was the assembling of new orchestras that could perform the music. The mandate for keeping the folklore traditions of Mexico alive has always emphasized the interplay between musician and dancer. Because *música tropical* musicians are commercially invested in well-paying jobs in *salsa* nightclubs, it was difficult for the fledgling *danzón* performing groups to find affordable orchestras that could play a full evening of *danzones. Danzón* groups were forced to rely on recorded music, which greatly diminished their cultural integrity. Zamudio convinced the Instituto Veracruzano de Cultura to invest in building three orchestras so that the music and dance could once more be a united dialogue.

The City of Veracruz sponsors *danzón* musicians to play six nights a week for the community's enjoyment and to accompany the performance groups. Adrián González gauges that the government and popular support for the *danzón* groups surpasses that for the *ballet folklórico* performers of *sones jarochos.* González, a non-dancer, believes the social phenomenon is fueled by a renewed respect for *gente de edad* (the older generation) and a rekindling of regional pride. He says, "Veracruzanos are a little tired of the bombardment of music and dance from other cultures, and have turned toward their own traditions instead."[23] As the lyrics state in this *décima jarocha:*

> *El Danzón* by Armando Gutiérrez Cruz
> *Corazón con corazón*
> *Así debemos luchar*
> *Para poder conservar*
> *Esta hermosa tradición*
> *Aprovecho la ocasión*
> *Decirles a mi manera:*
> *No permitamos que muera*
> *En nuestra tierra de folclor*
> *Nuestra música es mejor*
> *Que la música extranjera*[24]
> (Flores y Escalante 1994, 56)

Mexico City equals Veracruz in intensity of the *danzón*'s retro movement, although participation rather than performance is the main attraction. Community centers, plazas, private dance studios, and hotels offer *danzón* classes on weeknights and Saturdays. Many middle-aged Mexico City couples dutifully attend *danzón* class every week and go dancing on Saturday or Sunday evenings. One female dancer said, "It is definitely better than aerobics as a workout, and my husband can do it with me. We never miss our Saturday class."[25] The average age of these dancers is fifty, and the hotel ballrooms hire the fourteen-piece *danzonera* orchestras from 6:00 P.M. to 10:00 P.M. to accommodate the daily routine and habits of the not-so-young dancers.

The majority of the dancers come from the middle class, which still maintains an elegant dress code, although some arrive dressed more casually in boots and denim. No longer are the dance floors divided by class; all traverse the same floors. What is missing, however, is the romantic fire of the young dancers. Whereas the city's youth frequent clubs where *salsa* or disco/rock music is played until dawn, *danzón* seems to attract married couples enjoying a night out with the added benefit of cardiovascular exercise. Although seniors' bodies are no longer supple and their hand gestures are arthritic, there is a smile on their lips and joy in their movement.

> *Danzonero*[26] by Félix Martínez González
> *Siendo flaco o barrigón*
> *Y aunque tenga edad añeja*
> *Apaña bien la pareja*
> *Y ¡a darle muy duro al son!*[27]
> (Flores y Escalante 1994, 53)

Most *danzón* dancers agree that every teacher, orchestra, or performance ensemble is characterized by its own distinctive style. For beginning dancers, the step variations are simple spatial designs using the basic step: *cuadro* (box step), *medio giro* (half turn), *un cuarto de giro* (quarter turn), *paseo largo* (long stride), *paseos izquierdo o derecho* (side steps left or right), *tornillo* (one-foot pivot), *apuntado* (point gesture), and *vuelta por fuera y adentro* (outside and inside turns). In Mexico City dancers begin *danzones* with a basic box step during the first melody, travel across the dance floor during the subsequent melody (or melodies), and add turning and specialty steps during the *montuno* (which makes up the finale).

Mexico City's *danzón* performance ensembles have a reputation for being overly creative and inventive, a style labeled "*fantasía*." When they innovate excessively, the traditionalists refer to their work as "*folklorizando el danzón*."[28] As mentioned earlier, Mexico City ballrooms of the 1940s usually included many popular dance forms on the same evening's program. Perhaps the creative mixing of outside material borrowed from *tango* and swing has developed into a Mexico City styling all its own.

Guadalajara followed in the wake of the *danzón* in Veracruz and Mexico City. In this urban center of western Mexico, proper *danzón* footwork, structure, and styling had to be introduced rather than revived. Although *danzón* music was always present (e.g., radio, recordings, and musical performances), the proper dance style was not well-known. One Guadalajara dancer in his sixties said, "In my youth (1950) we danced the same steps to all the tropical music. Rarely did anyone realize that each rhythm had its own, distinct steps, much less different styling."[29]

In 1995, the University of Guadalajara offered a three-month summer *danzón* workshop and imported teaching faculty from Mexico City's Academia Nacional de Danzón. In 1996 a second workshop, much more economically priced, was given in a popular nightclub called Club Veracruz. Several dance venues were formed in the plazas during the workshop so that everyone who wanted to participate could join the evening events at no cost. In 2005, three *danzón* spaces in Guadalajara offered classes and dancing on three separate nights each week, which provided amateur *danzón* enthusiasts the opportunity to participate on a regular basis. During these gatherings community-based performance groups have the opportunity to demonstrate their "routines."

To help the *danzón* community broaden its understanding and appreciation of the dance, Carlos Aguilar Gonzáles created an on-line newsletter called "*Boletín Danzonero de Guadalajara,*" which publishes well-documented histories of Cuban and Mexican music and dance, tips on proper dancing, and reports on *danzón* conferences throughout the republic. Here is a sample of the newsletter's pointers on proper dancing, by Carlos Aguilar: "*En el danzón clásico se toman en cuenta los pasos básicos más el ingenio de cada pareja sin perder la posición de pelvis con pelvis, manteniendo el danzón cerrado en las tres melodías.*"[30] Aguilar is a large man who arrives at *danzón* events wearing a white suit and tropical hat. He is the traditional Guadalajaran gentleman: a traditional Catholic, polite and respectful to others, a careful dresser, and generous with his knowledge. When asked what he considers the most important thing in dancing *danzón,* he answered, "The couples that look at each other and share a joy for dancing are always appreciated the most."[31]

Summary and Analysis

Danzón is a vintage social dance that was born in Cuba and moved to Mexico, where it is now enjoying a retro movement that began in the early 1990s. Different regions of Mexico have revitalized the dance for the unique and specific needs of each community. In Mexico City, the central attraction of the *danzón* is its physical activity, in which married couples over forty can participate. As in the United States, the lengthening of the average life expectancy and pressure to increase fitness programs have opened new channels of "healthy" diversions for seniors, and ballroom dancing specifically geared for middle-aged and older citizens has become a popular activity. Whereas the urban youth pursue weekend dances in loud nightclubs that remain open until dawn, middle-aged married couples attend separate dance venues. *Danzón* ballrooms are usually large and well-lit, and they host live orchestras at one end of the room, amplified low enough so that conversation might occur simultaneously. These functions typically end by 10:00 P.M., and the dancers leave feeling relaxed, refreshed, and without any marks of having been kicked or stepped on by other dancers.

In Veracruz, the *danzón* is considered an integral part of the dance tradition of the city. It surpasses the *son jarocho* folk tradition both as a spectator event and as a tourist attraction, and is second in popularity only to *salsa* as a participatory draw in *centros nocturnos,* or nightclubs. All ages are attracted to the *danzón* performances, and government money is readily available to promote *danzón* in cultural centers and dance academies. The events are considered "*familiar*"; families of as many as four generations may attend the open-air performances. The stresses of modern urban life have exacted their toll on the structure of Mexican families, with many city youths becoming ensnared by violence or drugs or simply "dropping out." Daily programming of *danzón* events has helped to revive the historical dance form and served to bind the community while acting to reclaim family life.

What seems to be a thread of agreement throughout Mexico is that the *danzón* is a charming escape into a past when life was not so frantic, when romance was coveted, and when elders were respected. The global community has flooded Mexico with alien images and values, including an accelerated urban life filled with traffic snarls and drive-up kidnappings. Consciously and subconsciously, the population of urban Mexico is searching for connections to its past. One Mexican father spoke nostalgically about his memories of how men used to impress women by opening doors for them or offering an arm when crossing the street. He expressed sadness that his daughter's boyfriend thinks it is proper to announce his arrival with a blast on the car horn instead of walking to the front door to greet her parents. Mark Pedelty amplifies the notion of postmodern Mexico's response to dynamic cultural changes "by reconstructing and reimagining the past as 'tradition,' stable, unchanging truths and values that persevere despite all evidence to the contrary" (2004, 181). He also observes that the *danzón* may well be thought of as a "utopian mirror through which the past is reflected in a more perfect form."

One of the conclusions at a 2005 conference held at the University of California, Berkeley focused on "a sense of a loss of well-being and happiness in Mexican society, combined with a lack of faith and the absence of a vision for the future" (Reyes-Arias 2005, 13). This same message has become a standard format for the Spanish-speaking media in the United States. Radio programs such as "Puro México" and "México Lindo y Querido"[32] are being produced around the theme of comparing Mexico's past with the present. They feature legendary singing artists and composers of popular music (José Alfredo Jiménez, Jorge Negrete, Trio los Panchos) as the narrator remembers Mexico "*en aquellos tiempos.*"[33] He talks about the way things were on the *rancho* where he grew up. He remembers a time when youth respected their elders and took time to enjoy nature and the beauty of Mexico. He criticizes today's urban environment with its graffiti and aggression.

Danzón offers the perfect symbol of decorum and idealized "acceptable" behavior. It is one statement of *mexicanismo* and cultural pride against an invasion of foreign products and telecommunications. It is not a movement that pits youth against their elders; rather it is an opportunity for youth to experience Mexico's traditional values and for older citizens to maintain an active presence in an evolving, modern culture. It has become one of Mexico's answers to the harshness and brutality of rap, urban violence, and the estrangement of urban families. *Danzón* is a quiet communication between dance partners and neighbors, a retreat from the bombardment of urban noise and speed. In this context, *danzón* offers a link between modernity and tradition, a cultural ritual of sanity.

Notes

1. Adrián González, interview with Susan Cashion, Veracruz, Mexico, 2005.

2. *Marimba* music comes from the south of Mexico; *norteño* is from the north and typically employs bass, accordion, and bajo sexto guitar; *jarocho* music is from the coast of Veracruz and typically employs violin, harp, and a variety of small guitars

called *jaranas* and *requintos;* and *mariachi* is from the central western states of Mexico and employs violins, guitars, *vihuelas,* harp, trumpets, and *guitarrón,* a horizontal bass guitar invented in Mexico.

3. "People from the state of Colima"

4. "Dances for colored people"

5. "bending or flexing the knee"

6. "whites, blacks, and people of mixed color" (Lázaro Ros, interview with Susan Cashion, Havana, Cuba, 1983).

7. Lázaro Ros, interview.

8. "Pressed against my black woman / Without leaving a single tile / We take two steps back / And another forward / A turn to the right / And another in reverse."

9. "And only the *danzón,* gentlemen, / Has a pause / That they take as a rest / The contented dancers. / Some talk of love, / Others dry their sweat / She fans away the heat / Attentively waiting / That he will take her again / To dance with ardor."

10. The Cuban *son* is defined by its instrumentation and *afrolatino* character.

11. "the *danzón* in its new rhythmic form"

12. Michael Spiro, interview with Susan Cashion, San Bruno, California, 2003.

13. Miguel Zamudio Abada, interview with Susan Cashion, Veracruz, Mexico, 2005.

14. "With the rhythm of palm trees / Rocked by a soft breeze / She follows the rhythm of the clave / How nicely she moves the hips / But without exaggeration."

15. "We must congratulate / Whoever has the patience / To transmit to you their experience / Teaching you to dance. / Because you must continue / The *jarocho* tradition, / And must not let such / A praiseworthy mission turn into a quarrel. / You will be the responsible one insuring / That the *danzón* never die!"

16. "Anyone who does not know Los Angeles, / Does not know Mexico City!"

17. Literally, the term translates as "humble people," but it refers to the working class.

18. "Do not throw cigar or cigarette stubs on the floor / because they will burn / the ladies' feet."

19. Nereida Sánchez, interview with Susan Cashion, Santa Cruz, California, 2005.

20. Miguel Zamudio Abada, interview.

21. "Three Generations of Veracruz *Danzón*"

22. "Hey, family, this *danzón* is dedicated to . . ."

23. Adrián González, interview.

24. "Heart to heart / Is how we should fight / In order to conserve / This beautiful tradition. / I take this opportunity / To say in my way: / We must not let it die / In our land of folk traditions / Our music is better / Than the music we import."

25. Olga Castillo, interview with Susan Cashion, Mexico City, 1998.

26. The entire décima reads as follows: *El jarocho bailador, / Rie, gosa, se divierte. / No le interesa la muerte, / Mucho menos el calor, / Y si le aqueja un dolor / Viene y se*

avienta un Danzón. / Siendo flaco o barrigón, / Y aunque tenga edad añeja, / Apaña bien la pareja / Y ¡a darle muy duro al son!

27. "Whether skinny or big-bellied / Or even if you are old / Grab a partner / And dance your heart out."

28. "folklorizing the *danzón*" (Miguel Zamudio Abada, interview).

29. Ramón Morones, interview with Susan Cashion, Palo Alto, California, 2005.

30. "In the classic *danzón* you must be aware of the basic step and in addition the inventiveness of each partner without losing the pelvis-to-pelvis position, and always maintaining the closed partner position in the three melodies" (Carlos G. Aguilar, interview with Susan Cashion, Guadalajara, Mexico, 2004).

31. Ibid.

32. "Pure Mexico" and "Beautiful and Beloved Mexico"

33. "in the good old days"

15

Gender as a Theme in the Modern Dance Choreography of Barro Rojo

NANCY LEE CHALFA RUYTER

Since its founding in 1982, the Mexican modern dance group Barro Rojo has carried forward traditions established by predecessors in all the modern Mexican arts: a commitment to investigate social and political issues; to speak to "the people" as opposed to creating works for a wealthy elite; and to encourage, through their art, political and social awareness and responsible action. The focus in this chapter is on the contrasting images of women and men they presented in two of their 1990 works and how these relate to various issues, including feminism. To provide context, I begin with brief overviews of feminism in Mexico and the development of modern dance.[1] Following is a survey of Barro Rojo's history and its distinguishing characteristics. In the description and analysis of the role of women and men presented in the two works, I consider the theatrical settings, the costumes, the range of characters and images, and the movement vocabularies and qualities used by the choreographers.

Feminism in Mexico

The roots of Euro-American feminist movements can be traced to the late eighteenth century and developed through the nineteenth and twentieth centuries, with emphasis on equal rights in education, employment, property ownership, suffrage, medical care, wages, opportunities in government and business, sexual freedom, and so on. By the second half of the twentieth century, much progress had been made in social and economic areas of concern, and women had gained more visibility and power, although there were and still are goals that have not been achieved. In contrast, feminism in Latin America has had a very different history. According to social anthropologists Marit Melhuus and Kristi Ann Stølen, in the 1960s and 1970s "most feminist perspectives were considered not only inadequate but also politically suspect, as they tended to give gender inequality primacy over other inequalities, such as class and ethnicity. Such a position—which aligns women against men—subverted the basis for class struggle, which was perceived as the prime force for achieving social equality" (1996, 9–10).

Historian Anna Macías notes that as late as the 1970s there was a tendency in Mexico to totally deny the very existence of feminist movements in that country, which led her to research the topic and to write a history of its early developments (xii). In her book *Against All Odds,* she traces Mexican feminism from Sor Juana Inés de la Cruz (1648–95) through the nineteenth century and up to 1940. Despite denials that it even existed, the feminist movement was by the 1970s gaining strength and influence through the establishment of action groups such as Mujeres en Acción Solidaria in 1971, Movimiento Nacional de Mujeres in 1972, Movimiento de Liberación de la Mujer in 1974,[2] and others (Lau Jaiven 1987, 18–19, 75–138). Since the 1970s more awareness of gender issues, research into the relevant histories, and groups and initiatives devoted to women's roles and rights have appeared. While the development of feminism in Mexico has not been specifically connected with the development of modern dance, the two movements share certain characteristics which include the placement of women in positions of agency and the exploration and promotion of women's role in the intellectual, social, and political areas of the culture.[3]

Modern Dance and Its Development in Mexico

It has been a characteristic of modern dance internationally to explore social and political themes. In fact, a fundamental motivation for the early twentieth-century pioneers of this genre was the search for an art that would be relevant to contemporary interests and concerns in contrast to late nineteenth- and early twentieth-century ballet, which they rejected as elitist, escapist, and out of touch with modern life (see, for example, Ruyter 1979).[4]

The radical redefinition of concert dance, which began at the turn of the century, was a movement initiated by women artists working independently of traditional structures to develop new languages of physical expression. The early modern dance was a "repudiation of the tenets of nineteenth-century ballet, including its emphasis on spectacle and virtuoso display. It was an avowedly female-centred [*sic*] movement, both with respect to the manner in which the body was deployed and represented and in the imagery and subject matter employed" (Dempster 1998, 223). This statement by Elizabeth Dempster, Australian specialist in dance and performance studies, emphasizes the roles of women such as Isadora Duncan, Loie Fuller, Maud Allan, and Ruth St. Denis in the initial development of a new dance art that would blossom in the twentieth century. They and the following generation, who established what came to be known as "modern dance," explored movement vocabulary, imagery, and choreographic structures that could express concepts, themes, and values they considered important.[5]

As related by the former Barro Rojo dancer and now dance historian Margarita Tortajada Quiroz, the roots of Mexican modern dance were also "female-centred." As she explains:

> *La danza moderna llegó a México a través de dos coreógrafas norteamericanas: Waldeen, de la escuela alemana, y Anna Sokolow, de la estadunidense. En su danza estaba contenida esa lucha que las mujeres habían dado para constituirse como sujetos creativos y expresarse como tales, enseñanzas que muy bien supieron asimilar las bailarinas y coreógrafas mexicanas.* (1998, 18)[6]

These first appearances in Mexico of what can be termed "modern dance" date from the late 1930s. However, Mexican dance artists such as Nellie and Gloria Campobello had already been investigating and experimenting with approaches to choreography and dance performance that would be relevant to contemporary Mexican life. The quest was simply spurred further by the work of Waldeen (Waldeen Falkenstein, 1913–1993)[7] and Anna Sokolow (1910–2000).[8]

Each of these artists had her devoted adherents among both the public and a growing coterie of women devoting themselves to the art of dance. Their dancers, referred to as "Waldeenas" or "Sokolovas," were to some extent in competition with one another in the beginning, but Mexican modern dance began to develop its own voice in the 1940s and 1950s under the leadership of this first generation. Notable early Mexican choreographers include Guillermina Bravo (1923–), Ana Mérida (1922–1991), and Josefina Lavalle (1926–), among others.

One might question how it happened that the modern dance movement in Mexico came to be initiated by women in a society that has been traditionally male-dominated. In the United States and central Europe, however, locations of the earliest modern dance developments, men also overwhelmingly controlled the societies as a whole and the theatrical arts in particular, although cultural differences, of course, result in different kinds of control. Women may have been the icons of nineteenth-century ballet (throughout Europe and the Western hemisphere), but the choreographers, teachers, and directors were male—women had no say over how they were presented. The original pioneers of alternative approaches to dance as an art in the twentieth century were all women with a strong motivation to create images and statements that they considered important. Men eventually came into the movement—the earliest example is Ted Shawn (1891–1972), who became the first male innovator in the United States. After the seminal influence of Waldeen and Sokolow in Mexico, other American modern dancers, including males such as José Limón, Xavier Francis, and David Wood came and provided further stimulation and various approaches to technique and choreography. Limón was of Mexican heritage but had trained with Doris Humphrey and performed professionally in the United States. Mexican dancers and choreographers have also traveled out of their country to work with Martha Graham and other well-known artists. There has been both an eagerness to study with American and European artists and at times resistance against dependence on foreign models.[9] By now, internationally, there are both male and female artists of modern dance.

With a fierce passion for exploring their own heritage as well as addressing current political and social issues, early Mexican modern dancers turned to images and themes from regional popular and indigenous cultures. Modern dance in Mexico was not to be a slavish copy of aesthetics and styles from a northern colonialist neighbor, but rather an expression of Mexican traditions, concerns, and aspirations. As Tortajada Quiroz notes, Mexican modern dance in its first flowering shared with the other arts a commitment to nationalist issues (1998, 19). The tradition of modern dance in Mexico is very strong to this day, with a wealth of excellent groups and choreographers who explore Mexican as well as other themes in their dance works. Influences still come from outside Mexico, including trends from the postmodernist performance of the United States and from the German *tanztheater* of Pina Bausch and others.

Gender, of course, is an issue that is relevant worldwide; modern Mexican choreographers, like their counterparts elsewhere, have addressed this topic in various contexts and for differing purposes. Sometimes entire works are devoted to one or more aspects of the lives of women in general or of particular types or characters. At other times, women are depicted as part of the world they share with men. And while commitment to focused feminist agendas has gained more support in Mexico and other parts of Latin America since the 1970s, modern dance companies variously represent women in the myriad manifestations of their lives as well as, at times, focusing on particular feminist issues.

Barro Rojo

> With its primal images of proletarian struggle, Barro Rojo works in a modern-dance style that seems as classic as Isadora Duncan's *Marche Slav* and as contemporary as the latest activist performance art. . . . Hands desperately reaching out dominated all [of their six works], as did a sense of oppressive weight and fierce communal pride. These artists know what modern dance was created to do—and, for all their beauty and technical skill, they wasted no time on personal display.
>
> —Lewis Segal, *Los Angeles Times,* July 10, 1989.

In the spectrum of present-day modern dance companies in Mexico, Barro Rojo[10] stands out for a number of reasons: its artistic achievement, its longevity without institutional support, its political commitment, its organization as a collective, and its passionate sense of mission. Of course, there are other Mexican dance companies that share many of these characteristics, but it is difficult for independent groups—those without government or university support—to continue their existence over time and to consistently maintain a high level of production and creativity. As in the United States, independent dancers and choreographers in Mexico have to engage in teaching or other work to support both themselves and their artistic endeavors.

Barro Rojo began as a subsidized group in 1982 when it was founded by the Universidad Autónoma de Guerrero in Chilpancingo (UAG), which imported Ecuadorian choreographer and dancer Arturo Garrido as director. For two years UAG provided it with minimal support as one element in the university's political-social activist program in the community. This involved creating works and performing for meetings and demonstrations, as well as choreography geared for the conventional stage. From its birth, then, Barro Rojo has had an orientation to political causes and action, a characteristic that contributes to its overall profile. The first Barro Rojo work to be presented in a theater received major recognition in the form of the 1982 Premio Nacional de Danza sponsored by the Universidad Autónoma Metropolitana (UAM). This was Garrido's "El camino" (The Road), which addressed the struggling of oppressed people in El Salvador. The next year, Barro Rojo was invited by the Frente Sandinista de Trabajadores de la Cultura[11] to perform in Nicaragua at various sites. The group then traveled to Costa Rica to perform in a play against the United States invasion of Grenada.[12] They have continued to participate in alternative theater and political events both within Mexico and beyond. What they stand for is thus not only represented in the thematic content of their works, but it also involves active participation with those whose causes they support.

After moving to Mexico City and assuming independent status in 1984, Barro Rojo continued to produce works that received both enthusiastic reviews in the press and prizes and honorable mention in various annual competitions. This even though their works have often been dark and disturbing—on themes such as slavery, brutality between people, imprisonment of one sort or another, the struggle against oppression, death. The company has also created dances representing more positive aspects of life, for example *El carnaval* (1991).

From the beginning, Barro Rojo has functioned as a collective whose dancers actively contribute to the creative process and to decision making. Modern dance companies are more frequently headed by a choreographer-director (male or female) whose vision shapes every aspect of the group's work. Examples outside of Mexico would include the companies of figures such as Martha Graham, José Limón, Mary Wigman, and Pina Bausch, and many companies within Mexico follow this pattern. In contrast, a collective does not privilege any one member of the group. Individuals will take leadership roles at times, but they are neither absolute nor permanent. At any given moment there is a designated artistic director or coordinator, and each Barro Rojo work is overseen by one or more persons acknowledged as director, coordinator, or even choreographer. These roles may be held by a woman or a man in the group and may change; there are no "star" choreographers or dancers.

Barro Rojo's technical strengths contribute to its high artistic level. The dancers characteristically have advanced movement skills, but physical virtuosity is employed in the service of a dance's meanings and never as an end in itself. In contrast to the contained and controlled quality of ballet and some modern dance techniques, such as those of Martha Graham, the Barro Rojo vocabulary features kinesthetic risk—a dynamic and unpredictable surrendering of the body to gravity, flow, and sudden changes. The dancers fling themselves into space, suspend before a fall, crash onto the floor, stretch out to infinity, sensually stroke their own or another's body. But all is done with focus and underlying control. There is motivation for every movement.

Barro Rojo's choreography is consistently enhanced by artistic collaboration and technical support in sound and music, costuming and props, and stage decor and lighting. Their aural choices have ranged from original music to spoken texts and have included works by Arthur Honegger, Heitor Villa-Lobos, and other classical composers; traditional musics from Latin America, Africa, and Bulgaria; and popular music forms. All elements are integrated with the choreography and never purely decorative.

By late 1999, the company had mounted close to fifty pieces. In the 1980s these were usually relatively short with perhaps four to six making up a full concert. In the 1990s the directors began to develop full-length works of an hour or more. In 1999, they again turned to shorter pieces, often presented with choreographed transitions between them. The artistic level and production values of the company's work have been notable in themselves, but even more so considering that it has lacked institutional support since its early days in Chilpancingo.

It remains to say something of Barro Rojo's sense of mission. In their 1992 prospectus the following poem is given as a gloss on their name:

tierra
tierra de agua
tierra de años y años
tierra nuestra
vasija con huellas
masa para hacer
para crear . . .
venas
venas de sangre
venas que tiñen caminos
venas que tiñen
que tiñen[13]

They chose the image of the red clay as something "*maleable . . . intenso . . . sólido.*"[14] Barro Rojo's commitment to experimentation has been total. From the beginning, they decided that "*el compromiso y la pasión hacia su trabajo es lo único inamovible. Lo demás es como la vida misma: experimentar, buscar, desdoblar, incendiar*"[15] (Barro Rojo 1992). The passion expressed in their words comes through also in their dance works.

Two of the most important members of Barro Rojo have been Laura Rocha[16] and Francisco Illescas.[17] Besides dancing and choreographing for the company, they also shared in its administration and direction for many years (Illescas is now, in the twenty-first century, working independently). Illescas joined Barro Rojo in 1983 and Rocha in 1986. Both of them had trained under the Instituto Nacional de Bellas Artes (INBA), the government-sponsored agency of cultural policy for the nation, and they became prominent teachers in the official INBA Escuela Nacional de Danza Contemporánea and at times have held administrative positions there.

Images of Women in the Work of Barro Rojo

No, pues es parte de mí eso, ¿no? Parte de mi vida, el hecho de plantearnos los géneros . . . Pero la temática en si de abordar los distintos géneros, pues, no es así como mi prioridad, aunque sí, hace parte de mí, y sí es abordar muchísimas obras que hablan especificamente de la mujer, como de mi embarazo, insisto, conforme lo que yo voy viviendo ¿no? Algún momento me vuelco mucho para la situación de la mujer campesina. Cuando empecé a hacer obras, entonces hablaba sobre eso ¿no? Después de mi embarazo, la relación de pareja, como muchas cosas que son parte di mí, como de los otros, como ser humano.[18]

In this passage, Rocha makes clear that her commitment is to explore and represent aspects of the human experience, and that when she focuses on women, it is within that overall intention rather than apart from it. And in fact, since its beginning and under its succession of artistic directors (Arturo Garrido, Serafín Aponte, Rocha and Illescas, and now Rocha alone), Barro Rojo has demonstrated the same kind of general orientation. Whatever oppression women might suffer is viewed as integral to the situation of the society as a whole rather than something unique to women's experience or condition. Indeed, when asked about any involvement she might have with feminist organizations or initiatives, she answered:

No tengo de manera directa relación con organizaciónes de asociación feminista. Pero creo que la temática que abordo en mis obras tiene que ver con la problemática que las mujeres cargamos históricamente. El trabajo creativo tiene necesariamente que ver con el contexto social en que se vive, de tal suerte que el creador va a reflejar en su trabajo sensiblemente el acontecer social que le atañe y lastima de alguna manera y lo transforma en un suceso estético y artístico. El arte se alimenta de realidades para crear su proprio verdad. Esto quizá sea una manera muy personal de entender el mundo.[19]

Barro Rojo has mounted many works that include female characters or focus on aspects of women's lives. One choreography that illustrates quite contrasting artistic conceptions and representations of women is "Mujeres en luna creciente (Nuestra vida está en otra parte)"[20] (1992), with direction, script, and choreography by Rocha and Illescas.

Mujeres en Luna Creciente

"Mujeres" is one of a trilogy of full-length works by Rocha and Illescas that explore gender. All three are more than an hour in length and were designed for presentation in a traditional theater. "Tierno abril nocturno (de la vida de los hombres infames)"[21] was the first of the trilogy and premiered in 1991. It focuses on the male, and its structure is based on Milán Kundera's *El arte de la novela* (The Art of the Novel) (Delgado Martínez 1995, 7). The second of the series, "Mujeres en luna creciente (Nuestra vida está en otra parte)," illustrates various experiences of women's lives, while the third, "Del amor y otras perversiones"[22] (1996), addresses aspects of relationships between men and women. We will look closely at "Mujeres en luna creciente" and compare its images and representations of women with those of men in "Tierno abril."

"Mujeres," set to an original score by Alina Ramírez, was premiered in Mexico City in 1992 at the Sala Miguel Covarrubias of Universidad Nacional Autónoma de México (UNAM) and remained in the repertoire until 1996. It has been performed at the annual festival of contemporary dance in San Luis Potosí, Mexico; at the Cultural Olympics in Atlanta, Georgia, United States; in Bogotá, Colombia; and at other locations. As is true of many of Barro Rojo's works, it continued to develop as long as it was in the repertoire; there were thus a number of versions.[23]

"Mujeres" is structured as a chain of scenes or episodes of various lengths. Discussing a June 1993 presentation of the second version, Mexican dance critic Carlos Ocampo writes that the work "*documenta, episodio tras episodio, diversos aspectos de la condición femenina. De los juegos infantiles . . . a la dificultad de conciliar el deseo con el rechazo, las imágenes fluyen calmas . . . sobre el escenario se desanudan las cuentas de un rosario atravesado por un solo hilo conductor: el imaginario femenino.*"[24] The work does not focus particularly on women in Mexico, although some Mexican elements are suggested in it. Nor does this work depict women in social or political contexts nor present any one interpretation of what women experience. Rather, it shows contrasting types of experiences in women's personal lives that could touch women in any time or place.

"Mujeres" does not give a comfortable or easy view of women and their lives—except in the beginning. It opens with children's games. The dancers portray young girls as simple, innocent, and happy, cavorting playfully with no apparent worries or tensions. They skip off, and from there the work moves to more complex themes in the lives of adult women as they experience the intensity of desire, joy, and despair, and as they are affected by the physical states of menstruation, pregnancy, birth, and child rearing.

While "Mujeres" portrays women in a variety of states or situations of personal life, as described by critic César Delgado Martínez, "Tierno abril" depicts men "in circumstances of confinement, such as prisons, mental institutions, reformatories, and, why not, seminaries and the army. It speaks not only of pain, indifference, suffering, aggression and despair, but also suggests, more playfully, that man—despite isolation—does not lose love, tenderness, and eroticism" (Delgado Martínez 1991a). The contrast in presentation of the two genders can be seen in the scenic and costume choices for each work as well as in the movement choices for the choreography.

Both dance works take place in unidentified space—a kind of uncontextualized black arena in which the generalized scenic elements and the dancers appear and function. But while the women's space is defined with long flowing white cloth panels, the men's contains large boxes. The white panels are flexible. Some hang vertically from the stage flies to floor, and they move as the dancers move into and around them; another is stretched across the stage horizontally in one scene; others are tossed and flung by dancers in another scene. The boxes, in contrast, are heavy, static elements. The men move them into various configurations as the work progresses. They climb on them, jump from them, cower and caress each other within them, and are finally buried in one of them. The impression in "Mujeres" is that the women exist in an unconfined, flexible space that extends upward and outward to infinity, while the men in "Tierno abril" are limited in their focus and possibilities. They are always seen in relation to these confining elements, while the women's attention can move from one sensation or activity to another.

There is also contrast between the apparel of the men in "Tierno abril" and the women in "Mujeres." While the men appear in work shirts and trousers, the women's clothing ranges from baggy coveralls to underwear, nightgowns, and sexy miniskirts, and there is some nudity. As with the scenic design, the costuming of the women represents greater freedom and flexibility, while the men seem more confined to a limited sphere of consciousness and action.

The movement qualities also differ in the two works. The women's movement ranges from soft, sustained, and flowing to passages where it is tense, staccato, and agitated. The men tend to stay in the range of tension and agitation, with sudden movement breaking out. When they do move in a sustained manner, it is mainly with bound rather than free flow in their bodies. The movement characteristics thus also add to the representation in these two works of women living a flexible existence, one with choices and variety, and men limited to a predetermined fate of confinement and enforcement, an interesting departure from the clichéd conceptions of women's limitations and men's freedom.

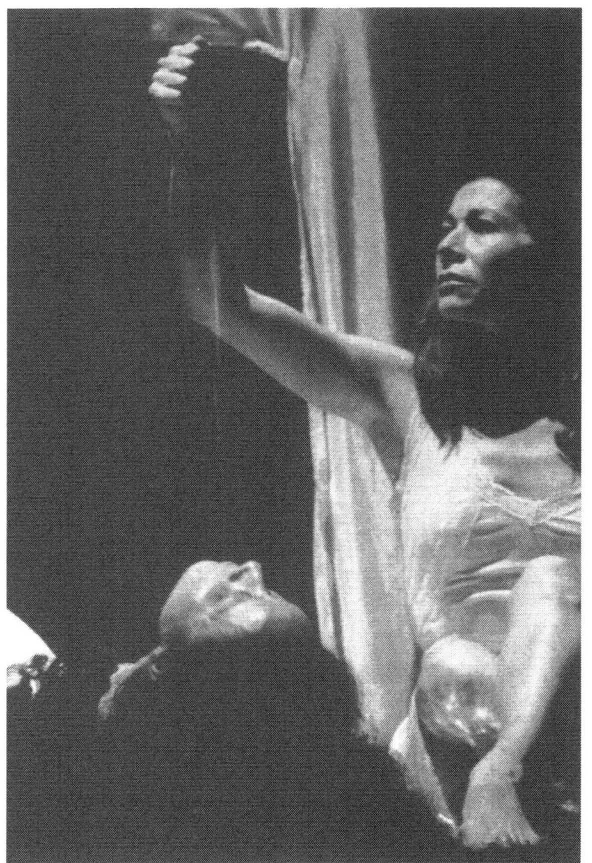

Mujeres en luna creciente at Sala Miguel Covarrubias, UNAM, 1992. Dancers: Soledad Ortíz, Tania Álvarez. Photograph by Ernesto Ramírez.

One of the characteristics of Barro Rojo's work is that they do not shrink from showing images that may offend audience members' sense of propriety. In fact, much of what they create includes elements that are transgressive in Mexico as well as in other cultures, including the United States. One such theme is that of sexual desire. In contrast to theatrical and film works that might feature desire between a man and a woman, and perhaps depict some power struggle within that or impediments to its fulfillment, "Mujeres" shows desire in episodes in which men are not present. In one, men are not even needed as a pair of women dance their intense yearning for one another. Ocampo describes this episode as showing "*las que se aman entre si agobiadas por la sed de orgasmo*" (1993).[25] In his press conference, Illescas was asked about this theme and defended it:

> *[A] la relación de dos mujeres que yo creo que es algo que exista y que tiene que ser público. En algún momento dado tendremos que aceptar esto; creo que va ganando mucho terreno pues en minorías sexuales, las minorías raciales. Cada vez se evidencia más que hay ciertos tabúes en la sociedad que se van derrumbando poco a poco, nuestra última, estos últimos obstáculos serían justamente las minorías sexuales, entonces bueno, es uno de los temas que se tratan en la obra.* (Illescas 1995)[26]

This episode in "Mujeres" can be compared with the section of "Tierno abril" in which two men sensually stroke one another while they are painfully crowded tightly within a box. The men's homoerotic activity seems a result of being forced into physical confinement, while the two women in "Mujeres" are free agents in space, coming into proximity with one another by choice, because of their mutual desire.

Tierno abril nocturno at Festival de Jóvenes Coreógrafos, Caracas, Venezuela, 1992. Dancers: Francisco Illescas, Serafín Aponte. Photograph by Ernesto Ramírez.

Another episode shows a group of women, each with the sweaty shirt of a longed-for absent person (presumably male) whose aroma it embodies. Each woman expresses her intense desire and desolation at being alone through obsessive handling of the shirt. She tosses it away, runs back to it, stuffs it in her mouth, rubs it on her body, pulls it through her legs, tosses it away, runs back to it, unable to abandon it. Does this episode represent obsession with and dependency on the "man"? Or on desire itself? Whichever, it is both shocking—and touching—in its graphic detail.

"Mujeres" also includes episodes on menstruation and pregnancy, female conditions that are usually kept within the private sphere.[27] In one episode, pregnancy is lampooned with two men in drag wearing huge balloons under their garments and cavorting around one another, bouncing their huge bellies against each other and assuming grotesque positions. But pregnancy is exalted in the next episode, danced by an actually pregnant dancer. In her ecstatic sequence, she rapturously caresses her belly, frequently pulling up her garment to expose it. Another episode dealing with pregnancy depicts a woman who has aborted a child and the anguish and guilt associated with that. Illescas notes the concern of one critic who questioned their satiric treatment of pregnancy and also their showing of a pregnant woman making "*movimientos que por tradiciones no debería de hacer porque peligra el producto que trae*" (1995).[28] Although the emphasis is unstated, one can imagine that the emphasis on the pregnant belly—both in slapstick comedic fashion and in actual reality—must have been shocking to its audiences. And while these elements would be extremely transgressive in a Catholic culture that privileges childbearing within the family, they also have other implications. The grotesquely big-bellied men mock any society that might fixate on slimness in women to the extent of finding the pregnant body ugly and unwieldy. The actual pregnant dancer reveals in the loving caresses of her carrying body the sensuality, mystery, and beauty of pregnancy. The aborter touches us with her anguish that ends with a baby's scream and makes us think back to the happy children playing in the first episode.

There are too many episodes to discuss each fully here, but some mention should be made of nudity in the work—potentially transgressive in itself and also in its connection here with the image of the Virgin Mary. Nudity does not seem to present the same difficulties in Mexican dance and theater as it does in the United States, where its incorporation into theatrical works can create scandal and outrage. The Barro Rojo choreographers and dancers are not afraid of nudity; both males and females have appeared without clothes when the theme of a work has called for it. In "Mujeres," an occasional dancer appears nude from the waist up; a group of dancers undresses behind a drape with their bodies seen in silhouette; and, as described above, the pregnant dancer lifts her gown to show her midsection, but not her genitals (covered with a bikini-like panty) or her breasts. The most startling use of nudity is at the end of an episode that features the virgin image moving, swathed in robes resembling those of a Tanagra statue. She finishes her sequence by dropping her robes. Illescas has commented that in the work, "*se tratan las figuras místicas en este caso la virgen que es tan importante para todos los mexicanos y bueno tratamos de desmistificar en ese sentido de decir que la virgen independiente de todo o antes de nada es una mujer a esto nos referimos con los mitos y mistificaciones que se hacen sobre la mujer*" (1995).[29] Actually, this work as a whole demystifies assumptions about women. It raises questions about many aspects of their lives in relation to traditional gender expectations and biological functions. But while some of the episodes involve a group of women, the work is never concerned with women in any kind of revolutionary, social, or political role.

It is interesting to note that *Mujeres* is attributed to both Illescas and Rocha (as are the other two works in the trilogy). In a press conference, the interviewer commented that it was strange to have a male co-choreographer working on a piece about women and asked what gave Illescas the knowledge to do that. Such a query brings up the broader question of whether anyone can or should presume to create on themes not within his or her own experience. Can a man perceive any supposed truths about women? A person of one race about another? Of course, an insider's perceptions are going to be different from those of the outsider, but that does not mean that there is a lack of validity in either. Illescas justified his work on this project as follows: "*Yo me eduqué, bueno me crié, mas bien me crié alrededor de mujeres, tengo tres hermanas más mi mamá, mi suegra, siempre mi vida ha sido rodeada de mujeres, lo cual quiere decir que de alguna manera tengo una sensibilidad femenina o por lo menos mi lado femenino como ser humano lo tengo muy presente.*"[30] This is not the orientation one would expect from a Mexican male, given the stereotype of the macho Latino, but of course, the stereotype is problematic (see Melhuus and Stølen 1996) and individuals develop their own sensibilities.

In 1999, Laura Rocha, Francisco Illescas, and the members of Barro Rojo decided to change their focus. They called this new direction "light" in contrast to the "heaviness" of their prior commitment to social and political themes. The company presented a program of short works in this vein March 4–7 at the Teatro de la Danza in Mexico City and July 29 at the XIX Festival

Internacional de Danza Contemporánea in San Luis Potosí. What the Barro Rojo leaders seemed to mean by "light" was simply dance as a creation of beauty rather than in the service of some commitment outside of itself, but none of these works was light in the sense of being trivial, facile, or non-engaging. And in their explanation of this change of direction, the Barro Rojo members demonstrated their continuing interest in life in general and what it comprises—and in the political and social problems confronting their society. As attributed to unnamed members of the collective:

> *En este momento hay que bailar para repetirnos hasta el cansancio que estamos vivos. Que a pesar de todos los pesares—corrupción, nepotismo, impunidad e ineptitud de los del gobierno de este país—hay una esperanza que nos hace soñar en el cambio que poco a poco se está dando.*
>
> *Bailamos—en el foro de un teatro, en la sala de un departamento o en una disco—para demostrar que tenemos un cuerpo capaz de amar. Hablamos para expresar—no obstante la ruindad y la mezquindad—que todavía existe esa palabra . . ., que se llama solidaridad. Danzamos sin parar para recorrer los rincones de una ciudad amenazada por la inseguridad. . . . Giramos como trompos chilladores porque no queremos ceder los espacios a la desesperanza. Vamos y venimos por el escenario teatral y de la vida como "si la Virgen nos hablara."* (Quoted in Delgado Martínez 1999)[31]

For this concert, Laura Rocha choreographed and performed works that illustrate her courage to expand the boundaries of her choreographic voice. In one, *Luna de mil noches,*[32] she created an exotically beautiful and technically virtuosic duet for two women that evoked images of the "Thousand and One Nights," but without any clichéd use of Middle Eastern motifs. Rather, this work really did demonstrate bodies with the capacity to love—to love life, energy, flow—and the ability to engage in a spectacular kinesthetic daring. In her other work for this concert, *Rojo en son de ausencia,*[33] choreographed with Illescas, they returned to the theme of desire. In this piece, three women in red physically embody the intensity we have all experienced, and find relief finally only in water, a common element in Barro Rojo works. Laura Rocha, now the sole director of Barro Rojo, the other members of the company, and Francisco Illescas, now an independent choreographer, continue to amaze and delight with their explorations of what it is to be human.

Lizbeth Goodman, British specialist on gender, politics, and performance, has written, "'Feminism' and 'theatre' are two distinct subjects: one a form of cultural politics, the other a general category of art or performance. Yet each is political and each is performative. Indeed, most theatre can be analysed in terms of the representation of gender and power" (Goodman 1996, 19). She goes on to distinguish between interpreting theatrical works from a feminist perspective and what she terms "feminist theatre," in which "the politics is not just applied to the 'ready made' art, [but] rather . . . informs the making of the theatre—the choice of working method, topic, form and style" (Ibid.). In considering the work of Barro Rojo, we can see that while they are not creating a dance theater committed specifically to feminism, in their works dealing with gender they are exploring issues that place them squarely in the realm of cultural politics as well as art and performance. Their work can be analyzed in terms of both the message it delivers and the means chosen—what Goodman has listed as choices of "working method, topic, form and style"—and the relation between content and form. Barro Rojo has explored some aspects of women's experiences and men's experiences in the works discussed, but their conclusions don't lead to an impression of women being oppressed and men being in charge. Quite the opposite, the women are shown as psychologically centered and enjoying some measure of control and the men trapped in some inescapable prison—of their own psyches or the culture's impositions. As in much of Barro Rojo's choreography, these works do not answer questions, but raise them and encourage us to seek further.

Notes

Research for this chapter was partially supported by a grant from the University of California, Irvine, Arts Research Committee. I am grateful to Minerva Tapia and the editors for assistance with translations from Spanish.

1. Following general practice, I use "modern dance" and "contemporary dance" interchangeably. In the early years of its development in the United States, "modern dance" was the preferred term. In Mexico and much of Latin America "*la danza contemporánea*" is usually used. For another view on these terms, see Dallal, who distinguishes between an earlier "*danza moderna*" and a subsequent, freer "*danza contemporánea*" (1997b: 10–11). It should be noted that in Mexico, modern dance companies often have titles including the word "ballet," while classical ballet companies will often be called *compañías de danza.*

2. "Women in Joint Action," "National Movement of Women," "Movement for Women's Liberation"

3. For more on feminism in Mexico and Latin America, see also Barbieri 1986 and Tuñón 1997.

4. Ballet as an international art had been developing in Europe since the Renaissance and was transplanted to the Western hemisphere as colonial populations became established, cities developed, and European theaters were constructed. By the

late nineteenth century, the hegemony of ballet as the only approach to dance as an art was being questioned, and the first tentative searching for other kinds of bodily expression began to appear in the United States and Germany.

Ballet's vocabulary and technical training has, with some variation, been a fundamental and defining element in that art. In contrast, innovators of modern dance developed new movement languages and techniques in relation to the content each wished to investigate. Over the years, some of these individual vocabularies have become established, formalized into training systems, and acquired an orthodoxy as rigid as that of ballet. Such established techniques in the United States include those of Martha Graham, Doris Humphrey, José Limón, Hanya Holm (from the German Mary Wigman School), Merce Cunningham, and Alwin Nikolais, among others. The Graham and Limón techniques have been particularly important in the history of Mexican modern dance.

5. For discourses on feminist issues and dance, see, for example, Adair 1992; Campbell 1996; Desmond 1997; Friedler and Glazer 1997; Goodman 1998.

6. Translations from Spanish are by Minerva Tapia and the author. "The modern dance arrived in Mexico through two North American choreographers: Waldeen of the German school and Anna Sokolow of the United States school. In their dance was contained that struggle that the women had made to constitute themselves as creative subjects and to express themselves as such, lessons that the Mexican female dancers and choreographers knew very well how to assimilate."

7. See Delgado Martínez 2000 and Lavalle 1987.

8. For information on premodern dance in Mexico, see Aulestia 1995 and Tortajada Quiroz 1995 and 2001. For Waldeen and Sokolow, see Dallal 1995 and 1997b; Delgado Martínez 2000; Tibol 1982; Tortajada Quiroz 1995 and 2001; Warren 1991; Lynton 1988; Lavalle 1987.

9. Francisco Illescas, "La danza en México es elitista," unpublished interview with César Delgado Martínez, 1985.

10. Since 1996 the company has gone under the name Barro Rojo Arte Escénico. Information on Barro Rojo comes from Laura Rocha (interview with author at the Centro Nacional de las Artes (CNA) in Mexico City in 1999 and revised in 2005) and from clippings, programs, promotional materials, and unpublished transcriptions of interviews provided by César Delgado Martínez.

11. The Sandinista Front of Cultural Workers

12. Illescas, "La danza en México es elitista."

13. "land / land of water / land of years and years / our land / vessel with footprints / dough (clay) to make / to create . . . / veins / veins of blood / veins that dye roads / veins that dye / that dye"

14. "malleable . . . intense . . . solid"

15. "commitment and passion toward their work is the only thing irremovable. The rest is the same as life: to experiment, seek, break down, set on fire"

16. Laura Rocha (b. Mexico City, 1962), dancer, choreographer, and teacher, holds the degree of Licenciada in Artistic Education with specialization in Dance from

INBA and also trained in Mexico at the Centro Superior de Coreografía (CeSuCo). In 1980, she studied contemporary dance in New York City. Her training has included both Graham and Limón techniques. She debuted as a concert dancer in 1979, co-founded the contemporary dance company Contradanza in 1983, and began presenting her own choreography the same year. She has continued choreographing since joining Barro Rojo in 1986 and continues as director of the company.

17. Francisco Illescas (b. Guadalajara, 1959) began dancing in 1980, studying at the Escuela Nacional de Danza Contempóranea of INBA, the Ballet Nacional de México, and the Centro Superior de Coreografía. He has earned from INBA both the Licenciatura in Artistic Education with specialization in Dance and the Maestría in Artistic Education and Research. Illescas' training has included work in the Graham and Limón techniques and work with notable native or immigrant Mexican modern dancers such as Xavier Francis, Luis Fandiño, Lin Duran, and Bodil Genkel. In 1991 he received a grant to study in New York for a month with avant-gardist Alwin Nikolais and the creator of contact improvisation, Steve Paxton. Illescas debuted as a professional dancer in 1982 and joined Barro Rojo in 1983. He is now working as an independent artist.

18. "No, because [the existence of genders], it is part of me, no? Part of my life, the act of questioning gender. . . . But approaching the theme of gender is not my priority, even though it is part of my life, and I have made many works that speak specifically about woman, as I did about my pregnancy, emphasizing what I am living, no? At a certain moment I—get very upset about the situation of the rural woman. When I began to make dance works, then I was talking about this, no? After that, my pregnancy, the relations of man and woman, as many things that are part of me, just as of others, being human" Rocha, interview (see note 10).

19. "I do not have a direct relationship with feminist organizations. However, I believe that the subject matter I address is relevant to the problems that women have historically faced. Creative work should relate to the social context in which it exists and sensitively reflect what happens in the society and how that affects the individual, transforming that into an aesthetic and artistic event. Art is fed from reality to create its own truth. This is perhaps a very personal way of understanding the world." Rocha, interview.

20. "Women in the Waxing Moon (Our Life Is Elsewhere)"

21. "Tender April Night (Of the Life of Loathsome Men)"

22. "Of Love and Other Perversions"

23. Discussion of this work is based on a video of a 1993 performance, attendance at two rehearsals in March 1995, discussion of it by Illescas (Delgado Martínez 1995), and various published reviews.

24. "documents, episode after episode, diverse aspects of the feminine condition. From the games of children . . . to the difficulty of reconciling desire with rejection, the images flow calmly . . . on the stage are revealed the stories like the beads of a rosary carried by a single conducting thread: the feminine imaginary."

25. "those women who love each other, exhausted by their thirst for orgasm"

26. "Regarding the relation of the two women, I think that is something that exists and needs to be public. At a given moment we shall have to accept this; I think that much ground is being gained in relation to sexual minorities and racial minorities. There is increasing evidence that certain taboos in the society are being demolished little by little; one of the last obstacles is justice for sexual minorities. This, then, is one of the themes treated in the work."

27. See Adair 1992, 41–42, 188.

28. "movements that traditionally could not be done because of the danger they were assumed to carry"

29. "are treated the mystical figures, in this case, the virgin who is so important for all the Mexicans, and which we try to demystify in the sense of saying that the virgin before all is a woman to whom we refer with the myths and mystifications that are made about women"

30. "I was educated, well, I was raised around women, I have three sisters besides my mother, my mother-in-law, always my life has been surrounded by women, which is to say that in some manner, I have a feminine sensibility, or at least, my feminine side as a human being is very present" (Francisco Illescas, unpublished press conference, October 2, 1995, in Mexico City. Unpublished transcription by Angélica Del Angel Magro).

31. "At this time, we must dance to repeat to ourselves until exhaustion that we are living. That in spite of all the sorrows—corruption, nepotism, impunity, and ineptitude of those that govern this country—there is a hope to achieve our dream of change that is coming little by little.

We dance—in the venue of a theater, in the hall of a district or in a disco—to demonstrate that we have a body capable of love. We speak in order to express—despite the viciousness and the miserliness—that the word still exists . . . that is called solidarity. We dance without stopping in order to regain the havens of a city threatened by insecurity. . . . We spin like screaming tops because we don't want to hand over the spaces to despair. We go and we come through the theatrical scene and life as 'if the Virgin were speaking to us.'"

32. "Moon of a Thousand Nights"

33. "Red in the Sound of Absence"

PART IV

Politics of Tradition and Innovation

16

Staging Authenticity

Theorizing the Development of Mexican Folklórico *Dance*

OLGA NÁJERA-RAMÍREZ

Introduction

Folklórico dance is a dynamic transnational expressive medium through which Mexican communities on both sides of the United States–Mexico border create and pass on a strong sense of group aesthetics and identity. Although it is an extraordinarily widespread and continually growing cultural expression, Mexican *folklórico* dance has not been adequately studied because it is often associated with the commercialization of folklore for tourist consumption and therefore not considered to be "authentic" folklore (Nájera-Ramírez 1989).[1] I believe, however, that as a cultural phenomenon that continues to attract a large number of participants and spectators, *folklórico* dance merits attention by those interested in issues of cultural representation and interpretation. Furthermore, I argue that in order to fully appreciate the significance of *folklórico* dance, it must be recognized as a genre in its own right with its own unique characteristics.

My goal in this chapter is threefold: Drawing on my ethnographic research and informed by several new publications on the history of dance in Mexico, I develop an overview of *folklórico* dance, providing a discussion of its emergence and development in Mexico and the United States. Second, employing the concept of "cultural performance," I explore the range of goals, intentions, and aesthetic principles among dancers who participate in the "*folklórico* phenomenon" in order to better understand what constitutes *folklórico* dance as a genre. In the process, I also explore the notion of "authenticity." I will show that by understanding *folklórico* dance presentations as "cultural performances" we can better appreciate the diversity among the groups and, more importantly, interpret the performance more effectively.[2]

Danzas Nacionalistas—Nationalist Dances

The interest in collecting and presenting Mexican folk dance dates back at least to the early part of the romantic nationalist period in postrevolutionary Mexico. During the 1920s, the Mexican government sponsored various efforts through the Secretaría de Educación Pública[3] (SEP) to collect folk dances from throughout Mexico and ensure that folk dance was taught in the public schools. In 1921, cultural missions were established with the goal of creating a united national society (Sáenz 1927; Sánchez 1936); by 1928, these missions were specifically assigned the task of studying and collecting folk dance, music, arts, and crafts (Paredes 1970; Jiménez 1932). Writing in a publication for the cultural missionaries, Guillermo Jiménez explains the importance of folk dance:

> *La Dirección de Misiones Culturales al dar a conocer estas danzas, desea que los maestros rurales las utilicen en las fiestas que organizan en sus escuelas: al mismo tiempo les llama la atención (a los maestros rurales), sobre estas expresiones tan bellas del alma popular indígena y les recomienda la representación y exaltación de las danzas locales, así como su estudio, suplicándoles las recopilen, recojan su música, indumentaria, coreografía, etc. y las envíen a esta Dirección de Misiones Culturales, la que, como en el presente caso, hará su divulgación.* (Jiménez 1932, 23)[4]

Since the cultural missionaries lacked even minimal training in folklore theory and methodology, the folklore collection project resulted in a haphazard collection of bits and pieces of folklore varying in quality (Paredes 1970). Despite these limitations, the folklore collections nonetheless fulfilled the larger goal of providing a resource for the creation of a symbolic representation of the diversity of the Mexican nation. Throughout the 1940s, under the auspices of the SEP cultural missions, folk dances continued to be taught in the public schools as a means of instilling national pride in the students and promoting ideals of cooperation and communal solidarity (Booth 1969).

In addition to relying on the work of the cultural missionaries, SEP also sponsored a number of festivals that featured indigenous or regional folk dance. For example, beginning in 1921, the Gran Noche Mexicana, held at El Bosque de Chapultepec[5] in Mexico City, featured a presentation of traditional dances from various parts of Mexico. Similarly, in 1925, the Festival Primavera was established to present "*escenas pintorescas basadas en costumbres, creencias, manifestaciones indígenas*" (Dallal 1995, 54).[6] In 1934, the Festival de Danzas Mexicanas was held at the Teatro Hidalgo with the expressed goal of presenting "ballets" (theatrical dance performances) based on or inspired by Mexican regional and indigenous dance (Dallal 1995, 85). To further institutionalize and systematize the collection, instruction, and dissemination of folk dance, in 1931 SEP established the Escuela Nacional de Danza, a national dance school funded by the government.[7]

During the postrevolutionary period folk dances also earned the attention of several dance companies, whose choreographers began experimenting with the idea of integrating indigenous and folk regional material into their modern dance and classical ballet presentations.[8] One of the first documented experiments occurred in 1919, when Anna Pavlova, a famous Russian ballerina, danced the "Jarabe tapatío"[9] on point in one of her presentations in Mexico. Caught up in the nationalist fever, dance choreographers such as Nellie and Gloria Campobello subsequently developed special suites inspired by the Mexican Revolution. Later, Waldeen[10] and Anna Sokolov produced several folk-inspired choreographies for their respective modern dance companies in Mexico.

Although "*danzas nacionalistas,*" or nationalist dance (Tortajada Quiroz 2000), was the term most commonly used to refer to these early folk-inspired theatrical choreographies, various terms were used to refer to Mexican folk or traditional dance during this period. Such terms include *bailes folklóricos, bailes regionales, danzas tradicionales, bailes típicos,* and *danzas indígenas.*[11] The term "*ballet folklórico,*" while occasionally used, was actually not popularized until the 1950s.

The Emergence of a Dance Genre

The term "*ballet folklórico*" reveals the merging of two types of dance: classical ballet and Mexican regional folk dance. The most well-known dance company of this genre is the Ballet Folklórico de México, founded in 1952 and directed by the late Amalia Hernández. Although other dance companies had created choreographies that incorporated Mexican folk dances and themes into their choreographies, as noted above, it was Hernández who systematically developed and disseminated this new dance form. Using the training techniques of classical ballet and modern dance, Hernández sought to promote Mexican culture by creating *espectáculos* or "staged spectacles" of dance and music, informed by anthropological as well as historical research of the people and customs of ancient and contemporary Mexico. A dance program for one of her shows describes her approach as follows:

> Amalia Hernández goes back to the origins of the culture, folklore or region she intends to develop into a ballet. The art of her ancestors, their sculpture and murals, provides her with information about myths, legends, and especially the aesthetics of the culture. In the museums of Mexico and carved or painted on the walls of towns and ancient pyramids are the sources Amalia shapes into the Ballet's art.
>
> In those cases where the descendants of a culture still exist as a community, Amalia's research becomes anthropological as well as historical. She studies the way the people live, their rituals, ceremonies, and beliefs. From these things she extracts the *essence* of the culture and gives it *drama and meaning for use on stage.*
>
> In the villages where many historic Mexican dances are still performed, the same process occurs. Amalia selects from the costumes, music, and dance steps those elements which will later become *a folkloric ballet.* She retains the artistic expression of the people and creates a *folkloric spectacle* (emphasis mine).[12]

In a 1999 interview, Hernández candidly explained her approach: "I do careful research. . . . It is basically authentic, but we have to make it interesting enough for the public to come. We are, after all, professional performers" (Terry-Azios 1999, 52). Thus, *ballet folklórico,* as popularized by Hernández, was intended as an "interesting" spectacle of "authentic" Mexican dances. From the very beginning, the challenge for *folklórico* dancers was how to preserve Mexican folk dances and customs while creating an entertaining spectacle or show. This raised the question: What degree of creative freedom should the dance instructor or choreographer enjoy? I return to this question later in this chapter, but first I want to trace the development of *folklórico* dance in the United States.

The Rise of *Folklórico* in the United States

Several documents confirm that *folklórico* dance has existed in Mexican-based communities in the United States since at least the turn of the last century (Broyles-González 1994; Huerta 1982; Nájera-Ramírez 1989; Solomon 1941). No doubt people raised in Mexico brought with them the knowledge and practice of their regional folk dances and continued to perform them in the United States. Thus *folklórico* presentations were frequently featured as part of Fiestas Patrias (Mexican national holidays) or other ethnic celebrations in

Dancers (*left to right*) Chandra Frankfort, Ana Fonseca, Celeste Eneriz, and Erica Ocegueda of Grupo Folklórico Los Mejicas from the University of California, Santa Cruz, perform a dance from the state of Guerrero. Photograph by Jon Kersey, 1997.

many Mexican communities in Greater Mexico. During the 1930s, *folklórico* dance was also taught in private academies and dance schools, typically catering to middle-class Mexican Americans. Such schools often included Flamenco classes as part of the repertoire (Zúñiga Benavides 1995).

In addition, during this era, Mexican folk dances were occasionally taught in the U.S. public schools, usually as part of physical education courses. Indeed several books on Mexican folk dance appeared during the 1930s and 1950s in a popular "cookbook" style that provided "recipes" for each dance (see Johnston 1937; Schwendener 1933; Mooney 1957; Sedillo Brewster 1938). Typically, these books included a brief description of the costumes and music (usually to be played by piano) and possibly a few words on the background of the dance. Despite the positive intentions of these authors to promote Mexican dance, the adoption of decontextualized, simplified versions of Mexican folk dance in the public schools in effect appropriated the dance form from the Chicano community and trivialized its significance for that community.

It was in the late 1960s that *folklórico* dance truly flourished in the United States, as part of the Chicano movement. During this period, Chicanos were searching for ways to reaffirm, promote, and preserve their Mexican identity and to express their opposition to cultural assimilation and other discriminatory practices to which they were subjected. Throughout the Southwest, Chicano cultural organizations emerged in an effort to recuperate those aspects of their identity—such as language, history, and expressive forms of culture—that had been denied by the hegemonic forces in the United States. Out of this fervor arose *teatros,* muralists, poets, and *folklórico* dancers, whose cultural productions became important symbols of Mexican identity.

It was no accident that Chicanos used many of the same artistic forms of cultural expression that had been used in the postrevolutionary era in Mexico. In many ways, the Chicano movement drew its inspiration from the Mexican Revolution. Villa and Zapata were proclaimed as heroes of the common people; Chicanas and Chicanos sang *corridos* (narrative folk ballads) from

Carla Preciado and Paul Viazcan, of Grupo Folklórico Los Mejicas from the University of California, Santa Cruz, perform a dance from Oaxaca. Photograph by Jon Kersey, 1997.

the revolutionary period and wore *huaraches* (sandals) and sarapes, indexing a sense of solidarity with the Mexican peasant—in short, the feelings, symbols, and values of the *movimiento* were revolutionary (Paredes 1983).

Young Chicanos recovered control over their own cultural traditions and reinvested them with a new significance. During the height of the *movimiento*, *folklórico* groups in the United States publicly displayed the beauty and diversity of the Mexican heritage, performing in a variety of contexts, including public schools, community events, political rallies, and church gatherings. The unifying principle in these varied performing contexts was the promotion of Chicano issues. *Folklórico* groups affiliated with a university, for example, were often involved in recruitment efforts to attract Chicanos to those institutions. The rationale behind this was that the presence of a *folklórico* group on a university campus indicated to prospective students that higher education was a possibility and that once they enrolled they would receive positive cultural reinforcement. During the 1960s and 1970s, this cultural support was a much-needed element, especially for working-class Chicanos, many of whom, as a result of special scholarships and grants (including the GI Bill), were entering universities for the first time.

For many Chicanos, then, *folklórico* dance offered a means through which Mexican culture could be recuperated and promoted. If folk dance was to be tapped as a historical source of cultural information, however, some measures had to be taken to assure that those dances featured in the performance repertoire were in fact rooted in the traditions of the Mexican people. To that end, Chicanos sponsored dance workshops in the United States that featured *maestros* or dance instructors from Mexico. Eventually, these workshops developed into U.S.-based *folklórico* dance organizations such as Asociación Nacional de Grupos Folklórico (ANGF),[13] founded in 1973, and Danzantes Unidos[14] in 1979.[15] Another option for retrieving information from Mexico was to study with established *folklórico* dance companies in Mexico or even to engage in ethnographic field research. In any case, like their counterparts across the border, *folklórico* dancers in the United States quickly became ensnarled in the question of "authenticity."

(De)Constructing Authenticity

The concept of authenticity arises in many contexts as a way to discriminate between the "real" and the "fake"—a distinction that on the surface appears to be relatively straightforward. Indeed, the problem of "authenticity" is by no means confined to *folklórico* dance but rather is a recurring and critical

Dancers (*left to right*) Maricela Guerrero, Elizabeth Riegos, and Roberto Ruíz, of Grupo Folklórico Los Mejicas from the University of California, Santa Cruz, perform a *jarana Yucateca*. Photograph by Jon Kersey, 1997.

theme implicit in most of the literature on cultural traditions, and it is discussed most explicitly in the "invention of traditions" literature (Hobsbawn 1983; Handler and Linnekin 1984; Nájera-Ramírez 2001). For example, advertisements for a *folklórico* dance performance will often announce that the group will perform "authentic Mexican (folk) dances." But what does it mean to label a *folklórico* dance as "authentic"? And, more specifically, how do *folklórico* groups make claims to "authenticity"? Moreover, new issues have also emerged. Two of the most compelling questions are (1) on what basis can new *folklórico* dances be invented, and (2) can *folklórico* dance be used to present contemporary issues and realities?[16] Such questions plague many *folklórico* groups and have generated heated debates as well as creative responses (Nájera-Ramírez 1989; Wimer 1995).

To begin, I argue that we must take seriously Amalia Hernández's claim that *folklórico* dance is a "spectacle," that is, a theatrical performance or a "display event." These forms fall under the broader rubric of what anthropologist Milton Singer refers to as "cultural performance" (Singer 1972; Abrahams 1983; MacAloon 1984). Folklorist Richard Bauman defines cultural performances as "metacultural presentations in which members of society put their culture on display for themselves and others in performance" (1986, 133).

Understanding *folklórico* dance presentations as cultural performances directs attention to what is being displayed, the content of spectacle, and away from the concern over the authenticity of the dances themselves. That is, instead of comparing the staged dance performance to an assumed original dance form, such an approach focuses attention to how Mexican culture is being represented through the medium of dance and on what is being communicated about Mexicans through the dance performance. In semiotic terms, conceptualizing *folklórico* dance presentations as cultural performances implies seeing dance as the signifier, not the signified.

Using the concept of cultural performance, we can begin to uncover particular strategies employed by *folklórico* dancers to assert their intentions and goals. All cultural performances provide interpretive frames within which the act of communication (in this case, the *folklórico* performance) is to be understood. Therefore, examining the specific labels dance groups employ to identify themselves provides critical information concerning the intentions and ideologies of the particular dance company. As discussed above, the term "*ballet folklórico*" as popularized by Hernández had a very specific meaning in the Mexican republic. It implied the use of classical ballet (and to a lesser extent modern dance) techniques and training, an aesthetic situated within "high art" in Western culture. And indeed, dancers of Hernández's *ballet folklórico* dance troupe train in the technique of classical ballet. Yet precisely because ballet invoked elite or "high" culture, many subsequent *folklórico* dance companies considered it an inappropriate descriptor given their goal to preserve, promote, and display "traditional" or "folk" culture. In an effort to distance themselves from an elitist association, some dance companies thus rejected the term ballet and instead employed such terms as "*grupo folklórico*," "*grupo costumbrista*," or "*danzantes*."[17] Nor was this simply a matter of terminology; some companies also explicitly rejected the notion that training in classical ballet was necessary to perform "*bailes folklóricos*" or "*bailes regionales.*"[18] Despite differences in naming practices and intentions, however, all *folklórico* groups reinterpret and manipulate folklore to create a display of Mexican culture for public consumption. Even dance instructors and choreographers who advocate preservation of the dances acknowledge that mere duplication of the dance is not possible. For example, Marta Heredia, a respected dance teacher from Guadalajara and self-proclaimed traditionalist, observes:

> *Yo procuré siempre respetar lo más posible pero claro yo hacía mi propia versión. Para respetar el material que nos daban en Yucatán, en San Luis Potosí, en Morelia, en cualquier parte que nos daban clases yo trataba de respetar hasta donde era posible. La limpieza, la pureza, lo más tradicional posible.*[19]

Guillermina Galarza, another prominent dance teacher in Guadalajara, explains:

> *Yo siento que el folclór es el alma misma de los pueblos. Y naturalmente que al sacarla de su contexto nosotros la cambiamos. Pero como que hay que tener así como la delicadeza de sacar esa tradición al mundo real pero sin tantos agregados.*[20]

Taking a dance from a community context and performing it onstage always already involves making certain changes such as reducing the time of performance, changing the costumes, developing a choreography, and taking into account a new audience. Therefore, the main difference among *folklórico* groups resides in where they place their emphasis along the continuum of *public spectacle* at one extreme and *preservation* of expressive cultural forms at the other. In Spanish this distinction is often invoked with the terms "*elaborado*" (elaborated) and "*purista*" (purist or traditionalist).[21]

Whether *elaborado* or *purista*, the use of the term "*folklórico*" carries with it the assumption that there must be an explicit or otherwise traceable connection between the staged dance presentations and the folkways of the Mexican people. Without some connection to Mexican folkways, the dance would not be considered "*folklórico.*" However, the nature of the connection varies from case to case. Some dances may have pre-Hispanic roots (such as *los voladores, los huahuas, los quetzales*),[22] while others are of more recent vintage (such as *danzón*).[23] Some ancient dances continue to be practiced in certain communities while others have survived only in chronicles, codices, murals, and sculptures. In some cases, scholars have succeeded in documenting the history and evolution of a particular dance. For example, the "Jarabe tapatío" (popularly known among Anglo-American audiences as the Mexican hat dance) is, as the name implies, a *jarabe* (a specific mestizo song and dance form) from Jalisco (*tapatío* is a term used in reference to the people of Guadalajara). Researchers such as Saldívar (1937) and Lavalle (1988) have uncovered evidence that this particular dance dates from at least the late 1800s. Unfortunately, most of the *folklórico* dance choreographers who actually conduct their own research rarely publish their findings. Instead, they disseminate their findings through their choreographies; hence the written record remains incomplete. While dance historians, anthropologists, and ethnomusicologists have contributed to the literature on Mexican dance, the scholarship is quite limited (see the selected bibliography for a comprehensive listing of notable works on Mexican dance).

With respect to the specific dance steps, some of the movements have actually been named and codified. For instance the step called *lazada,* or roping, from the region of Jalisco, is a movement with the leg that imitates the roping technique of the *vaqueros,*[24] while the *caballito,* or little horse step, is one that imitates the jumping movements of a horse. While the codified steps offer some assurance that the dances are "traditional," choreographers have also expanded the *folklórico* dance vocabulary by naming other dance steps, which in turn can be more easily identified and taught by other choreographers. The codification of dance steps helps establish a particular movement or step as part of a regional repertoire, thus measuring familiarity rather than "authenticity."

In other cases, the idea is to continue the vernacular practice or "folk tradition" of using dance to capture the cultural ambiance of a specific location (temporal or geographic). For instance "El gavilán," "Las alazanas," and "La iguana"[25] are *sones*[26] that are choreographed to imitate the movement and behavior of animals (especially in courtship patterns). Dances imitating specific animals indexically reference particular animals that inhabit the cultural environment being displayed. Using this logic, contemporary choreographers of *folklórico* dance can create new dances designed to represent or imitate animals indigenous to a particular part of Mexico.

Similarly, folk dances have been constructed to emulate other movements found in the landscape. An interesting case in point is the dance called *las olas* (the waves), in which the flowing movement of the skirts imitates the ebb and flow of the waves. However, if one listens to the words carefully, "*las olas*" does not only refer to the waves. Instead, as in many *sones,* the lyrics provide an opportunity for verbal play so that "*las olas*" (the waves) becomes "*las solas*" (the single women) as in the verse "*las solas no las casadas.*"[27] This practice of verbal play allows for double meanings both in the lyrical representations as well as in the choreography. Thus, the women gracefully move their skirts forward and backward to represent "*las olas,*" but also to simultaneously represent "*las solas.*"

Jalisco Contemporáneo represents a more recent trend to choreograph new dances based on recent contemporary regional compositions using the basic principles of traditional Jalisco dances. One choreographer, Gabriela Rodríguez, explains her approach as follows:

> *Todos estos sones se consideran de corte contemporáneo y su servidora, Profesora Gabriela Rodríguez García ha venido conservando y dando nacimiento a nuevos sones, sin perder características propias, pero sí nutriendo al mismo tiempo de formas nuevas; tomando en cuenta el nombre del son, su letra, temas musicales y sobre todo su ritmo. La evolución folklórica nos ha permitido incursionar en la creación de nuevos pasos y coreografías sin olvidar la esencia original de que siempre los sones se caracterizan por el cortejo del hombre hacia la mujer, en estos casos del charro a la china.*[28]

Other dances have no explicit connection to the dance traditions of a region. Rather, the entire *cuadro,* or dance suite, is an imaginative construction of the choreographer informed by anthropology, history, and other archival documents (photographs, paintings, newspapers) to represent a specific time period or regional characteristic. Good examples of this approach include the *Corridos de los Altos de Jalisco* and *El corrido de Rosita Alvírez,*[29] both choreographed by one of the most well-known *maestros* of *folklórico* dance from Mexico, Rafael Zamarripa. A *corrido* is a folk ballad that provides a detailed narrative concerning a particular event or person. When performed by *folklórico* dance groups, the narrative is dramatized and enacted through dance. Once a *cuadro* becomes established, other groups may add it to their company's repertoire and thus it becomes further disseminated. As a result, *cuadros* like Zamarripa's become part of the "*folklórico* tradition," even though they are not the actual dances of the community represented on stage. According to many *folklórico* dance teachers, the *corridos* nonetheless conserve certain recognizable regional characteristics.

This approach to dance, that is, performing a historic event, has enjoyed some popularity among Chicanos as a way to display more localized experiences north of the U.S.-Mexico border. For example, a dance suite based on the Zoot Suit Riots[30] was popularized in a theater performance and later in a film directed by Luis Valdez and choreographed by Patricia Birch. Several performing groups subsequently incorporated zoot suit dances into their repertoire. In a similar vein, Rafael Zamarripa was commissioned by the Ballet Folklórico Rio Bravo from San Antonio, Texas, to choreograph an entire show that would reflect the region's culture and history (Wimer 1995). Through music, dance, and scenery, each of the dance suites reflects a particular period and cultural ambiance. *El Viejo Mercado* (The Old Marketplace) is one of the *cuadros* Zamarripa developed for the company. His process in developing that dance is described as follows:

> In visiting the Market Square, Zamarripa tried to imagine what it might have been like in the past. Then he discovered a painting of the marketplace from the last century that he brought to life for *El Viejo Mercado.* Between the cries of the vendors and a game of *loteria*[31] the company members jump up to dance exuberantly, just as past denizens of the square surely mixed dancing with their daily business. Copying the costumes from the painting, the men wear flared pants and serapes and the women simple dresses. (Wimer 1995, 56)[32]

Calabaceados,[33] created by Mexican choreographer Juan Gil Martínez in 1997, offers a more recent example of newly choreographed *folklórico* dance. Based on the dance practices of the local cowboys in Baja California in the 1950s, Gil Martínez explains:

> *Trece años interrumpidos de investigación de campo y bibliografica no me dejan mentir que el calabaceado es un baile folklórico del Estado de Baja California puesto que es una manifestación que practica el pueblo en sus festivadades sociales, históricas y religiosas.*[34]

These are only some of the principal and innovative approaches that Mexican *folklórico* dance choreographers employ to create dances and ensure a measure of "authenticity." Nonetheless, these few examples are suggestive of the wide range of possibilities available. Clearly, the concern over authenticity, as employed in this realm, means that *folklórico* dances must have some connection to the folk practices of *mexicanos,* but there is a lot of "wiggle room" with respect to what counts as a valid connection. For these reasons, I have concluded that understanding *folklórico* dance as a "cultural performance" allows us to better see the differences among *folklórico* groups and better understand the cultural significance of dance itself.

Conclusion

Mexican *folklórico* dance is a cultural phenomenon that surged during the twentieth century throughout Greater Mexico. Despite its widespread popularity across both sides of the border, *folklórico* dance has not received adequate scholarly attention in large part because questions of authenticity have plagued *folklórico* dance since its inception. However, since *folklórico* dance choreographers and directors must grapple with the issue of authenticity, we must recognize that this is indeed one of the principal distinctive features of this dance genre. Furthermore, the pursuit of authenticity has yielded a variety of creative possibilities. Therefore, we can conclude that as long as *folklórico* groups on both sides of the border remain committed to exploring the power and potential of dance as a creative act of cultural representation, the *folklórico* phenomenon will be a complex and vital cultural expression.

Notes

Acknowledgments: Earlier versions of this chapter were presented at various conferences including the Theatricality of Rituals and Celebrations in Latin America, Luso-Brazilian, Spanish, U.S. Latino Cultures Conference sponsored by the Irvine Hispanic Theater Research Group, University of California, Irvine, February 1–3, 1996; the American Folklore Society Meetings in Albuquerque, 2004; and the European Association of Social Anthropology Biannual Conference in Vienna, 2005. This chapter has been enriched by numerous conversations with *folklórico* dancers and teachers in the United States and in Mexico. Research during 2004 was funded in part by the Committee on Research Faculty Grant at The University of California, Santa Cruz. With the support of a UC MEXUS Grant, I was able to conduct fieldwork in Guadalajara, Colima, Tucson, Los Angeles, and the San Francisco Bay Area. I also wish to thank the 2004 members of the Transnational Popular Cultures Research Cluster at the Chicano/Latino Research Center at University of California, Santa Cruz, Russell Rodriguez, Pat Zavella, Elisa Huerta, Sarita Gaytan, and Steve Nava for their insightful comments, kindness, and support as I have revised this chapter. I am also grateful to Norma E. Cantú and Brenda M. Romero for their many helpful suggestions.

1. Indeed, my 1989 publication remains one of the few academic articles on the subject to date. Since then, however, several new publications on the history of dance in Mexico have been published in Spanish, providing valuable data on *folklórico* dance.

2. Since 1974, I have attended countless lectures, workshops, and conferences, engaged in conversations with choreographers, instructors, and dancers, completed three years of *folklórico* dance education in Mexico, danced with several performing groups, and served as faculty advisor for a campus *folklórico* group. Currently, I am engaged in a research project documenting the contributions of *folklórico* master dance teacher and choreographer Rafael Zamarripa.

3. Department of Public Education.

4. "The Department of Cultural Missions is making these dances known so that the

rural teachers will use them in school festivities; at the same time, we wish to draw (to the) attention (of rural teachers) the beautiful expression of the popular indigenous soul and recommend the representation and exaltation of the local dances, as well as their study, requesting their collection and that of the accompanying music, costume, choreography, etc., which should be sent to this Department of Cultural Missions, for public promotion" (author's translation).

5. "Grand Mexican Night" [held at] "The Forest [Park] of Chapultepec"

6. "picturesque scenes based on indigenous customs, beliefs, and manifestations"

7. Originally the school was named Escuela de Plástica Dinámica (School of Dynamic Plastic Arts). One year later, the name was changed to Escuela de Danza (School of Dance), and ultimately the name was changed to Escuela Nacional de Danza (END) (National School of Dance).

8. See Dallal 1995 for details on these antecedents.

9. For more information on the *jarabe* dance and musical form, see Saldivar 1937; Lavalle 1988; Heredia Casanova 1999; and Chamorro 2000.

10. This choreographer is known simply as Waldeen because she stopped using her family name, Falkenstein, around 1931 (Cohen http://www.uhmc.sunysb.edu/surgery/waldeen.html, from "Waldeen and the Americas: The Dance Has Many Faces" [C]. *American Voice* 16: 58–73.)

11. "folk dances," "regional dances," "traditional dances," "typical dances," [and] "indigenous dances."

12. Ballet Folklórico de Mexico Dance Program (Mexico City, n.d.).

13. "National Association of *Folklórico* Groups"

14. "United Dancers"

15. The formation of the ANGF and Danzantes Unidos coincides with the founding of other national minority-based organizations such as the Society for the Advancement of Chicanos and Native Americans in the Sciences (SACNAS) and the National Association of Chicana/Chicano Studies (NACCS).

16. For a comprehensive discussion on this point, see Rodriguez's essay (chapter 19) in this volume.

17. *Danzantes* also refers to dance groups who devote themselves exclusively to performing pre-Hispanic-based and indigenous dance rituals. See Huerta's and Ceseña's essays (chapters 1 and 5) in this volume.

18. It is important to note that the distinction between the terms "baile" (dance) and "ballet" is not always explicitly acknowledged and, in vernacular speech, the two terms are often used interchangeably, especially in the U.S. context.

19. "I always tried to respect [the traditional] as much as possible but of course, I created my own version. To respect the material that was taught to us in Yucatán, in San Luis Potosí, in Morelia, wherever we were taught, I tried to respect it to the extent that it was possible to do so. Clean, pure, the most traditional possible" (Marta Herédia Casanova, interview with the author, Guadalajara, Jalisco, January 17, 2005).

20. "I feel that folklore is the soul of the people. And naturally when we take it out of context, we change it. But we have to have a certain sensitivity when taking that tradition into the real world (public) but without so many additions (changes)" (Guillermina Galarza, interview with the author, Guadalajara, Jalisco, January 18, 2005).

21. Other terms for *purista* include *danza regional, danza popular,* while the terms that refer to the *elaborado* style include *danza escénica* and *danza teatral* (Marta Heredia Casanova, January 17, 2005, Luis Benjamin Flores, January 18, 2005, and Adrián Lay, January 19, 2005, personal interviews with the author, Guadalajara, Jalisco).

22. " the flying pole, the *huahuas,* the quetzal birds"

23. See Cashion's essay on *danzón* in this volume (chapter 14).

24. Mexican cowboys; *vaquero* is also the origin of the English term "buckaroo."

25. "The Hawk," "the Chestnut-Colored Horses," [and] "the Iguana"

26. For scholarly work on the Mexican *son,* see Mendoza 1956; Saunders 1976; Stanford 1984; and Sheehy 1979.

27. "the single women, not the married women"

28. "These compositions are considered of recent vintage. I have been engaged in conserving and giving birth to new *sones* taking care not to lose their unique characteristics but at the same time nurturing them in new ways—taking into account the name of the song, the lyrics, the musical themes, and above all, the rhythm. The evolution of folklore allows us to engage in developing new steps and choreographies without forgetting the original essence that always characterize the *sones,* the courtship between a man and a woman, in these cases the *charro* and the *china* (author's translation) (Gabriela Rodríguez 1996, 9).

29. *Ballads of the Altos of Jalisco*" [a region] [and] "*The Ballad of Rosita Alvírez.*

30. The zoot suit refers to a high-waisted, wide-legged, ankle-tight pegged trousers and a long coat with wide lapels and wide padded shoulders popular in the 1940s among blacks, Filipinos, and Chicanos. The Zoot Suit Riots refers to a series of riots that took place in Los Angeles during World War II between Mexican American civilian youth and U.S. military youth. For more information see Mazón 1994.

31. *Lotería* is a popular Mexican game similar to bingo.

32. It is worth noting, however, that Zamarripa's dance group has not performed this *cuadro* nor has any other *folklórico* company in Mexico.

33. The term *calabaceado* derives from the word *calabazada,* which means a butt with the head or a blow on the head.

34. "Thirteen years of intermittent field and archival research confirm that the "calabaceado" is a folk dance from the state of Baja California because it is a display that the community performs in their social, historical, and religious festivals" (Gil Martinez, 2002, 43)

17

Dance, Politics, and Cultural Tourism in Oaxaca's Guelaguetza

CHRIS GOERTZEN

Introduction

On two Monday mornings each July, the indigenous populations of the state of Oaxaca, Mexico, collaborate with the state tourist board and various cultural organizations to present southern Mexico's most spectacular festival, the Guelaguetza. A dozen or more dance troupes from all over the state, accompanied by either their own small band or the state brass band—a total of about five hundred dancers and musicians—perform for an audience of more than twelve thousand in an open-air hillside venue built for this purpose, overlooking the state capital, the city of Oaxaca. Thousands more watch on television, and the two mornings of dance combine with dozens of linked events in the city to create a complex and continual fortnight of fiesta. The total event has become quite massive and equally intricate as both aesthetic and political statement.

The city of Oaxaca rests at the intersection of three valleys set high in the mountains. There are a few areas suitable for agriculture, and fishing is adequate along the coast. But the natural resources of the state could not have sustained the modern metropolis of around half a million without the recent growth in trade, industry, and especially tourism. Indeed, the Guelaguetza is inextricably intertwined with Oaxaca's central economic engine of tourism. Without tourist money no festival this large would be possible, and the tourist industry that supports the Oaxaca City of today focuses on two high seasons, the more intense being the weeks surrounding the Guelaguetza, the other being the less tourist-permeated weeks flanking Christmas. In a broader partnership, the Guelaguetza depends on several population groups being happy with the composite event beyond its aesthetic qualities. Tourists satisfy a generalized nostalgia by seeing the Guelaguetza as an "authentic" representation of valuable aspects of a generalized past, the powerful of Oaxaca further their political agendas, and the dancers and musicians welcome both the opportunity to see their indigenous identity celebrated publicly and a trip to the big city. Many among the general populace of Oaxaca enjoy the festivities and the immediate economic benefits as well as any implications for longer-term socioeconomic improvement, though many others harbor serious reservations about the event as a political and economic statement.

The basic facts of Oaxacan history are recorded as reliably in guidebooks as in history texts (see Instituto Nacional de Estadística, Geografía e Informática 1991, Rodrigo Alvarez 1995, Whipperman 2000, and so on). In brief summary, hunter-gatherers arrived in Oaxaca at least twenty thousand years ago. Early pottery and ceramic figures that show cloth skirts, sandals, and jewelry anticipated craft categories of today. Ancestors of Oaxaca's Zapotecs founded Monte Albán high above the junction of the principal valleys. The lack of focused power among the early Zapotecs invited invasion by the nascent Mixtec people. Then, as part of a general expansion of the Aztecs' territory, they subjugated Oaxaca during the 1400s. Cortés and his band of adventurers arrived from Cuba near present-day Veracruz in 1519 and established themselves in the Aztec capital of Tenochtitlán by 1521. By the end of the year, Mass had been celebrated in the region of Oaxaca. As in many parts of the world colonized by Catholics, indigenous religion soon exhibited mixes of Christian and native elements, frequently with European saints and ceremonies taking on both overt and subtle native personalities and qualities.[1] Also, the missionaries learned from and transformed local agriculture and crafts. For instance, working with wool was new in the Zapotec village near Oaxaca now called Teotitlán del Valle—sheep arrived with the Spaniards—but weaving cotton had already been important in that town; tribute to the Aztecs had been paid in cloth. The most prosperous of today's predominantly indigenous villages in the central valleys are those that were able to transform local industries into tourist crafts. For example, the pottery of San Bartolo Coyótepec (a dozen kilometers south of the city of Oaxaca) has given way to plastic and porcelain in local kitchens, but it sells well to tourists. And Teotitlán del Valle (about thirty kilometers [eighteen miles] away) is now a major center for hand-woven rugs (see Stanton 1999). Both villages are affluent enough to send troupes to the Guelaguetza, where they perform their own versions of the *danza de la pluma* for the same tourists that keep their villages in good financial health by purchasing crafts.

The city of Oaxaca grew slowly. The population was less than forty thousand through about 1940, and most of the mushrooming to a total of ten times that number has been during the last four decades. The result is a sprawling metropolitan area with a compact older center. One can walk from the square to the edges of the colonial city in any direction—and thus to most of the locations directly touched by the Guelaguetza—in under a half-hour. The old city streets constitute a north-south and east-west grid, with some curves to the northeast of downtown as one approaches the hill on which the Guelaguetza proper takes place.

The broad outline of the symbiosis between event, government, outsider audience, and local populace is straightforward. It costs plenty to put on the festival, and Oaxaca is not a rich state—it is one of Mexico's poorest, with one of the two highest populations of natives (the neighboring state of Chiapas housing the other). Participants in the Guelaguetza are not paid beyond food, lodging, and transportation, but there are lots of them—I estimate five hundred because there is an average of twenty troupes overall, each filling a bus (twelve or more troupes per Monday, with some overlap between the ensembles dancing the two days). Security involves many more bodies than does the entertainment. Police and temporary security personnel are hired very liberally both because of the sheer size of the event and because it attracts some very high-profile visitors. After all, every socioeconomic level will be liberally represented in the audience, packed more tightly together than in daily life, with the potential for friction. Hundreds of state employees help the city get ready for the onslaught of visitors. The money has to come from somewhere, and the local elite must supplement their own funds—they are affluent per capita, but they are not that numerous—by looking to Mexico City and abroad, to tourists.

I attended my first Guelaguetza in 1995. The event saturated the newspapers, hotel prices were especially high, and taxi drivers charged more than usual. Oaxaca was clearly in high gear. The basic publicity formed a litany that all visitors soon internalize: "Guelaguetza" is a Zapotec word that means sharing generously in a way that inspires reciprocity; some sort of ceremony ancestor to the current one has been going on for a long time. The current Guelaguetza began in 1932, and colorful troupes of "Indians" from the "seven regions" of the state are delighted to dance for an audience now. This information resembles what anthropologists and folklorists call a "memorate," a story told so many times that both its broad outline and intimate details of vocabulary crystallize. But here the memorate belongs not to a storyteller, but rather to the media, flyers given out at the tourist offices, and so on. A modest amount of additional detail appears in scholarly work (see Acevedo

Conde 1997), but this more academic fleshing out of the media's memorate is not readily available to tourists.

Framework of the Fiesta

Each of the two Mondays, audience members arrive by taxi, city bus, tour bus, or on foot. For the pedestrians, the less affluent attendees, it is an easy stroll from downtown for twenty minutes or so, then quite a climb up hundreds of broad steps flanked by dozens of temporary market stands and food stands. Modest lines for the elite paid seats end with the same thorough search by machine-gun-toting teenaged security guards as greets those enduring the infinitely longer lines leading to free seats above.

The stage looks out over the city, with concrete stadium-style arcs of seats reaching quite a ways up the contour of the hill. The audience faces downhill. Thus, as one watches the dancers one also sees the band behind them, with the city distant and far below as a backdrop, with the haze obscuring differences between rich and poor neighborhoods.

The about two thousand seats close to the stage run from about $30 to $50 for guaranteed spots. The free seats—more than ten thousand of them—are first-come, first-served. There is a chain-link fence and armed security between the few well-dressed folks in the inner arcs and the enormous crowds behind. This dichotomy reflects the until recently straightforward division of Mexican citizens into a tiny upper class and enormous much, much lower class, but because the two thousand ticketed seats constitute a much larger fraction of the whole than is justified by the tiny ratio of upper-class to lower-class citizens, tourists *must* enter the picture to fill most of those expensive seats.

Another process of "filling in" the festivities may catch foreign tourists off guard. Many public events in Mexico are free for the majority, including the Guelaguetza itself. Worthwhile free events are packed hours ahead of publicized start times. Over the years, authorities have found that it is considerate—and a simple way to keep crowds peaceful—to supplement the show with warm-up acts starting an hour or more ahead of the advertised event. I arrived at my first Guelaguetza a theoretical hour and forty minutes early. Few of the paid seats were occupied, but I was glad I'd purchased one, because the more than ten thousand free seats behind me were already absolutely full. Ten minutes after I sat down, *chirimías* (shawms, discussed below) played, then the state marimba, and so on through announcements, grandly declaimed romantic poems, and endless patriotic rhetoric right up

Looking toward the stage from the back of the paid seats during the second Monday of the 1995 Guelaguetza. Photograph by author.

to the formal program, which finally arrived precisely when advertised. It starts on time every time, since it is televised.

The Guelaguetza itself opens with a newly crowned "corn goddess" walking around the stage to wild applause. There is a very separate box for a dozen or so special guests at the back of the paying section, and a walkway directly from the stage to that exclusive box, that performers use to visit the rulers of Oaxaca. During the first year I was on the hill, in 1995, the usual high-status guests (the first lady of Mexico, several state governors, sports stars, and other rich individuals) were joined by Lupita Jones, the Mexican 1992 Miss Universe. A multilayered encounter indeed: Miss Universe, heir to ancient pagan harvest rituals, met the eyes of the corn goddess, just crowned in a ceremony structured much like a modern beauty pageant. On another occasion, the state governor was "spontaneously" convinced to come down and waltz with a lissome young dancer (his security guards were moving into a revised formation well ahead of time—they had this "surprise" tightly choreographed on and off the stage).

Now to the main event, a time during which all present are in one or another tourist mode. Twelve or more dance troupes and a total elapsed time of three hours; that *is* long enough, since it's hot. Each troupe owns a slot of just ten to twenty minutes during which they march on, perform a medley of truncated dances, then enthusiastically throw offerings into the crowd. Guelaguetza means sharing, we are reminded as we do our best to catch our share of projectile offerings, ranging from fruit or little loaves of bread to small baskets or other crafts. One of the advantages of the reserved, paid-for seats is that you may get to take some of these offerings home; just a few aerodynamic limes thrown by athletic young men reach the free seats. On my first visit, I caught some rock-hard braided bread and a mango, and was then blind-sided by a pineapple someone else wrestled away. Other years I have trekked very early to the free seats, which are rowdy conflations of locals and budget tourists (a busload of retired electricians from Monterrey sat behind me once). One Monday in 2002, a family group headed by a young *campesina* (countrywoman) adopted me. She performed the miracle of getting her relatives (and me) into contiguous areas in the stands, efficiently delegating responsibilities: "Save those three seats, Cristóbal; Isabel will bring you a drink." We affluent visitors are asked to believe that all of Oaxaca is delighted with the event, and in the auditorium during those three hours there is no evidence to the contrary. Even the poorest folks in the free seats are in fiesta mode, socializing, snacking, and sporadically watching the distant stage.

The mornings of dance are carefully shaped, with the different troupes' contributions ordered systematically and dramatically to yield a strong show. Each ensemble's short appearance is standardized in certain ways. All groups march on as they are announced, then dance, with gender-specific or gender-alternating lines dissolving frequently into twirling couples. Initial short sections of dance done to music sounding like polkas or waltzes eventually yield to quicker ones, with more foot-stomping in prescribed patterns as the music shifts to *sones* and *jarabes* (in a brisk 6/8 or in that combination of 6/8 and 3/4 called sesquialtera). After the dance and music climax, the dancers throw their offerings to the crowds. Beyond that framework for each troupe's time on stage, each group must be special, or there would be no aesthetic point to having lots of troupes. First, each ensemble constitutes a group of models showing off region-specific festive clothes. The men wear relatively standardized white outfits (hats can vary, as can the occasional addition of blankets and other region-specific accessories). The women's dance outfits adventurously explore variations within regional patterns. For instance, if skirts worn by women in a given ensemble are in solid colors with black lateral stripes, there are many different solid colors of parallel intensity for contrast.

Each ensemble offers its own array of dance formations within the basic line dance environment, that is, certain groupings of couples, or a solo couple surrounded by the group, or straight lines or circles, or various kaleidoscopic realignments. Some groups content themselves with those modified line dances, while others incorporate contrasting visual or procedural special features. Attempts to steal kisses are quite common, as are mock bullfights. In other cases, one dancer carries a turkey (usually alive) or a papier-mâché swordfish, or garlands of greens, or a bottle (in one recurring dance in which a man pretends to be drunk). Further contrasts concern musical factors. A troupe may bring its own band, or rely on the Oaxaca state band (in which case there is more room for dancers on the bus the state furnishes to bring them from their homes to the city of Oaxaca). If they employ their own band, this may be a typical village brass band or, less likely, a string-based group. Several troupes always perform a given famous waltz song, and one features salty exchanges of quips between men and women of courting age and bent. And the particular mix of sections of music, metered and paced like marches, polkas, waltzes, and *sones,* will be idiosyncratic. Further, organizers hold to certain patterns in ordering the dances (as illustrated in Table 17.1).

First is an unvarying bold frame. The first ensemble consists of women (only) from the city of Oaxaca. Each of these *chinas,* a nickname for pretty young women, holds on her head a large basket containing a sculpture made of flowers. The women parade in, swaying their skirts to and fro, preceded by a few of the *gigantes* that often participate in religious parades (the people inside these oversized human figures peek out at about the navel level).[2] Balancing this at the end of the day is an all-male *danza de la pluma* ensemble. Here, men wear large flowered headdresses and leap energetically as they express their Zapotec ancestors' happiness at Cortez's triumph over the Aztecs (initially considered a good thing by the Aztecs' vassals). The story can be involved and understandable as historical narrative back in the villages, where the dance takes hours, but it is reduced here. The audiences understand some of what it is about because the story has been told and retold and because these dance outfits are alone in the event in appearing pre-Hispanic.

Next in reliability of placement to those framing ensembles comes the pineapple dance, done by an all-woman ensemble from Tuxtepec, or nearby in a southern tropical area of the state. This dance comes *near* the end (ninth of twelve ensembles in the 1995 event, thirteenth of fourteen in 2002). These dancers' ceremonial dresses vary considerably in color and figuration, but nevertheless are congruent in intensity of visual effect and in that each young woman carries a pineapple on her shoulder. This dance, choreographed specifically for the Guelaguetza, remains a crowd favorite, perhaps due to focus

Table 17.1 Succession of Dance Delegations at the 1995 and 2002 Guelaguetzas

Delegation's Home, 1995	Girls' Dance Outfits	Formations; Features	Delegation's Home, 2002	Girls' Dance Outfits	Formations; Features
1. Oaxaca City	"chinas" with head burdens	mostly a parade	1. Oaxaca City*	"chinas" with head burdens	mostly a parade
2. Huautla de Jiménez*	red and blue skirt stripes	second section involves turkey	2. Huautla de Jiménez	red and blue skirt stripes	line dances; inc. song
3. S. Melchior Betaza	white dresses w/red sashes	line dances	3. San Melchior Betaza	white dresses w/red sashes	line dances
4. Juchitán de Zaragoza	silk/satin w/ embroidery	line dance; song "La Llorona"	4. San Pablo Macuiltianguis	bordado dresses	very tangled bullfights
5. Santiago Juxtlahuaca	all guys, in masks	bullfights; "girl" is matador	5. Tlacolula de Matamoros	red skirts; rebozos; two big balloons	*mayordomía*
6. Huahuapan de León	flowered skirt with ribbons	song "Canción Mixteca" inc.	6. Ciudad Ixtepec	very fancy dresses	inc. hit song "Zandunga"
			7. Juchitán de Zaragoza	inc. elaborate head pieces	girls feign sleep; waltz

Table 17.1 Con't.

Delegation's Home, 1995	Girls' Dance Outfits	Formations; Features	Delegation's Home, 2002	Girls' Dance Outfits	Formations; Features
			8. Santiago Juxtlahuaca	all guys, in masks	bullfights, with horns!
7. S. Miguel Sola de Vega	flowered skirt	line dances; song	9. Tlaxiaco	black skirts; bordado tops	line dance; men = bulls
8. Pinotepa Nacional	single-*solor* skirts; lace!	inc. bullfight	10. Ejutla de Crespo*	pastel skirts; black stripes	partly sung; kiss stealing
9. Tuxtepec	colorful; pineapples	usual pineapple dance	11. Putla de Guerrero	skirts with lots of lace	sectional; girls = bulls
10. Ejutla de Crespo	pastel skirts; black stripes	kissing dance	12. Santa Catarina Juquila	satin; bordado tops	*mayordomía* + sexy quips
11. Tlacolula de Matamoros	red skirts; rebozos; two big balloons	lots of hand kissing; mock wedding	13. San Juan Bautista Tuxtepec*	all women; pine-apple dance	usual fancy pineapple dance dresses
12. Zaachila	usual Pluma outfits	normal Danza de la Pluma	14. Culiapan de Guerrero	unsurprising Pluma outfits	Danza de la Pluma again

*These delegations danced both Mondays during the year in question.

on moves that surprised me the first time I saw them, echoing a can-can or Rockettes maneuvers.

Other patterns of placing ensembles in the sequence of performance also hold over the decades. The most general rule is that simpler medleys of dances alternate with ones featuring flashy novelty. Specific ensembles turn up in customary positions in the roster each time they participate, so that the regular attendee will witness a nice mix of the familiar with a few surprises each year. For instance, the ensemble from Huautla de Jiménez (from a mountainous area in northwest Oaxaca state) does fairly straightforward line dances punctuated by verses of song. The women's dresses are white with embroidered flowers and clusters of lateral light blue and carmine ribbon stripes, as in Figure 17.2.

I have heard that their dance includes a reference to a priest's experience with the hallucinogenic mushrooms characteristic of their part of the mountains, and, more generally, that fertilization of flowers also makes an

The dance troupe from Huautla de Jimenez, in an impromptu performance during a parade through the old city of central Oaxaca the evening before the Guelaguetza. Photograph by author.

appearance, but this information remains in an oral tradition known to few members of the audience. To most in attendance, this performance is simply an attractive array of line dances ornamented with a normal complement of humorous flirting. Nothing in these fragments of dance tells us why it belongs in the second spot on most Monday rosters—the accompanying song, which might be illuminating, is in the local indigenous language, Mazateco—but this dance retains its position in the sequence year after year.

Intensification

Folklore materials moved from detailed cultural contexts to displays intended for new, unevenly-informed audiences inevitably lose some kinds of meanings. But such loss can be balanced through intensification, a family of processes in which *aesthetic* impact is raised through manipulation of the *amount* of traditional materials (see Goertzen 2001). At the Guelaguetza, we witness three kinds of intensification. The most common type, intensification through *addition,* takes place here when lots of natives wearing many different outfits do many contrasting dances within short amounts of time, with each act adding swiftly to the overall density and amount of information. Second, intensification through *selection* occurs when especially striking items are drawn from tradition, even if those items are thin in terms of sheer amount of information. The dances from Huautla de Jiménez furnish an example. In fact, that set of dances has lost information in recent times. Up until the late 1990s, three or four dancers carried some product characteristic of the area, including a turkey. That's no longer done. No one I asked knew why, though I gathered that turkeys had been present simply to show their importance in the local economy, rather than as part of local myth or religion, and perhaps were dispensable for that reason. In any case, deleting the turkey resulted in a visually less crowded performance, one with clean lines and a focus on the embroidered overgarments, or *huipiles,* and provided good contrast with the visually busier flanking acts. Third, we witness throughout the Gueleguetza intensification through *virtuosity:* the practiced, expert precision of dancers' moves strengthens the overall impact.

The Model of the Mexican Fiesta

At the end of the show, we are ready to welcome the familiar *danza de la pluma,* performed by one or another ensemble from the Zapotec central valleys. We then leave, overloaded by the barrage of impressions. This might seem like a good time to rest, but many visitors prefer to continue to celebrate. Indeed, to make the Guelaguetza sufficiently attractive to all involved requires engaging more than the Guelaguetza proper. Three hours on two occasions separated by a week is not enough total festivity for several reasons. Tourists invest substantial time and money to get to Oaxaca, and anticipate days rather than just hours of entertainment. Also, over half of these tourists are Mexican and therefore share, with both the occupants of the free seats and with the performers, a model of how a festival ought to be shaped. That model is the paradigmatic Mexican fiesta based on each town's patron saint's day observances, annual events that typically last a very full weekend. So, doings related to or supplementing the staged dances have gradually accumulated to flank the Mondays on the hill (see Table 17.2).

Yes, dancing is much more central than at a routine village fiesta, but many other customary ingredients have also burgeoned on the coattails of the Guelaguetza's core element of dance. In short, a display designed as a pair of discrete events extracted from village festivals by the state tourist board and intellectuals has effected a return to traditional context in flavor and function, and has thus become an enormous and diverse, but in many ways truly traditional, festival.

Most village festivals begin at the church; the holiday really centers on the local holy day. Much of the Guelaguetza publicity—tourist brochures, newspaper articles, and now websites—asserts that this factor lies behind the choice of dates for the Guelageutza too. The fiesta for the Virgin at the church of Carmen Alto (a half-dozen blocks north of the square) is said to have spawned the modern Guelaguetza. But today this church-centered fiesta simply introduces a busier fortnight (save for parishioners of this neighborhood church). Folks in town for the larger fiesta will notice its prelude, but their "church" part of the Guelaguetza consists of touring the big cathedrals and perhaps staying for Mass. The fiesta of Carmen Alto centers on doings *inside* the church, that is, special Masses plus clusters of baptisms, first communions, and confirmations, all scheduled to be part of the special occasion. In addition, there is a procession headed by men carrying the church religious banners and accompanied by a brass band made up of members of the church, a band that later plays in front of the church. A half-dozen ladies staffing snack stands in front of the church raise funds efficiently. Last, in the church courtyard men affix fireworks to various lathed skeletons. Lighting the largest, a tower several stories high, caps an evening display. Most of the others are set off during a parade to the front of the church. The man bearing the most popular item, the *torito,* a handheld schematic bull, charges toward

Table 17.2. How the Guelaguetza Includes all the Normal Ingredients of Mexican Fiestas

Fiesta Ingredient	This Aspect's Manifestation at the Guelaguetza	Location
Popular Dances	1. Guelaguetza on the hill 2. Evening presentations by individual delegations 3. Other presentations by clubs, by children, in hotels, etc.	1. Hill auditorium 2. Santo Domingo 3. Etc. N. of square
Music	For the above dancing; state marimbas and other year-round performances; at ancillary events; in all parades; by mariachis and others on square (concerts early, for diners later); beggars	At above locations; on square; in markets; on all main streets
Religious Ceremonies	At Carmen Alto and at a smaller church (thus, calendric fiestas partially absorbed into this larger fortnight-long festival)	NW of square 4 and 6 blocks respectively
Processionals	For above ceremonies; by "chirimías" early on the mornings of the Guelaguetza and by dance delegations evenings before	Above locations; on street north of square
Electing a Queen	"Diosa Centeotl" chosen from among representatives of individual delegations the day before the first Guelaguetza	4 blocks N. of square at Santo Domingo Church
Carnival Rides and Games	1. Rides: Ferris wheel plus other rusty turning rides 2. Games: balls-into-holes etc., all easy, with small prizes 3. "Tiro al Blanco": shooting targets to win old-style songs	1. 8 blocks NNE 2. Within markets 3. Within markets
Sport Contests	1. Basic variety sports 2. Half-marathon and bicycle race	1. At university 2. Finish downtown
Food	1. Usual regional snacks in unusual quantities 2. Regional "Festival of Sweets" 3. Regional "Festival of Mescal"	1. Market; stairs to hill 2. Shopping streets N. 3. 8 blocks N. of square
Markets and Other Sales	1. Local crafts: rugs, carvings, black pottery, etc. 2. Crafts from elsewhere in Mexico 3. Anything poor people would customarily buy at markets	1. Crowded (!) square 2. Park 8 blocks north 3. Crowded (!) square
Etc. (here: Pageants)	1. Bani Stui Gulal ("repetition from antiquity"), supposedly the history of the Guelaguetza; college kids showing skin 2. Legend of the Princess Donaji (Romeo and Juliet? Aida?)	1. Formerly near Soledad; auditorium 2. Auditorium

the audience while little firecrackers launch from the lathe frame toward the feet of his target.

Mexican religious festivals always include processions like the one described, and so must the Guelaguetza, though the principle ends up parceled out into fragmentary gestures. First, several villages' *chirimías* assemble outside the cathedral on the square, well before dawn on the two Mondays of Gueleguetza, and start parading (while playing) toward the hill auditorium at about 6:00 A.M.The word "*chirimía*" has an immediate and a general meaning. It's a specific musical instrument, a crude double-reed classified as a shawm, descended from sixteenth-century Spanish versions of Middle

Eastern ones (as are also many Latin American plucked stringed instruments). More broadly, a village *chirimía* is a pipe-and-drum ensemble of a type formerly routinely employed to accompany religious processions, a function now normally assumed by the village brass band.

The few surviving village *chirimías* of Oaxaca each include a handful of drums (often castoff old snare drums from brass bands) and one or two loud wind instruments (bugles, whistles, or, rarely, an actual *chirimía*). While the specific instrument types in Oaxaca's few remaining local *chirimías* trace their roots to the Middle East and Europe, the general idea of pipe-and-drum ensembles that accompany processions is an ancient one in both Europe and the Americas. But these *chirimías,* having largely given up that function, have the climax of their year in the fore-concert to the Guelaguetza. Old men and young boys, playing out of tune and in dubious rhythm, perform a stock medley beginning with the "Mañanitas," the birthday song, and ending with the final phrases of the "Jarabe tapatío," the "Mexican hat dance."

Other links between the Guelaguetza and the procession as a fiesta ingredient include ones already briefly mentioned, the short processions connected with church fiestas during the Guelaguetza fortnight, the slow march onto stage of the Diosa Centeotl (corn goddess) prior to the dances, a five-minute procession with which the Chinas Oaxaqueñas precede their dance (led in by the combined *chirimías*), and the formal entries of each dance ensemble. But the main processions take place Sunday evenings, when dance troupes pass through the city streets of the old town, sometimes marching and sometimes dancing. Several troupes march together, preceded by a few *gigantes.* The streets are so crowded that one can barely see the dancers, but it is fun, and a pleasant advertisement of the next mornings on the hill.

A few other fiesta ingredients have modest but real presences during the eve of the Guelaguetza. In terms of sports, Oaxaca's state university sponsors tournaments during this period in track, field, swimming, volleyball, baseball, karate, soccer, tennis, and chess. These are not visible to most tourists, but a half-marathon includes stints through the city streets, as does a dangerous bicycle race. Rural fiestas often include a rodeo, but as far I could tell this was the single fiesta ingredient absent here. Carnival rides are restricted here to a handful of rusty wheels and the like that generally set up next to the northerly Juarez Park. Games appear within the complex of market stands, many of which are simple and easy to win ball-in-holes types aimed at kids; the prizes are cheaper than the tickets, and the kids have fun. All these standard games and rides are owned and operated by families that tour the state, going from one festival to another in an annual cycle.

Tourists may dine at restaurants that specialize in Oaxacan regional fare all year; all food different from what they consume back home is carnival food to them. Food stands in the extended market feature *tlayudas,* a regional large tortilla—the (rather delicious) fiesta food for the poor. And there are ancillary "festivals" of sweets (local *dulces* are indeed distinctive and tempting), of cheese (Oaxacan pale, highly-textured *quesillo* dominates), and of local mescal. This last is the largest affair subsidiary to the Guelaguetza, and one must actually pay admission to an extended display up north at the Juarez Park. Markets in general are much bigger than usual too. All manner of stands appear incrementally, situated farther into the square and down contiguous streets as the Guelaguetza approaches, until the downtown area is stunningly crowded. Much of what is offered represents normal market fare, ranging from pirated CDs to cheap kitchenware, thus illustrating a simple proportional response to the temporary swelling of the population of the city during this festival season. But there are also special genre-specific markets for the occasion that target tourists or the festivity-loosened purse strings of the local upper class. One such seasonal market, on the square, features Oaxacan crafts, while another, at Juárez Park, features crafts from elsewhere in Mexico, although the entrepreneurs are Oaxacans.

Two supposedly historical pageants are intended to help us understand the cultural backdrop for the Guelaguetza. The Bani Stui Gulal, or "repetition from antiquity," offers four tableaux that symbolize points in the history of Mexico, and include dances. This takes place each Sunday. Then, the evening after each Guelaguetza features the Legend of Princess Donaji, Donaji being the name of a Zapotec Juliet (or Aida?) who fell in love with a Mixtec Romeo (Radames?) of long ago. There is love, disaster, sacrifice. . . . The flavor is of mid-nineteenth-century Italian opera. The pageant is historically dubious and dramatically overdrawn, and it attracts thousands. But the greatest pageant takes place Sunday morning, the day before the first Guelaguetza. Since this entire festival theoretically descends from precontact rites for a corn goddess, a human embodiment called the Diosa Centeotl is chosen each year from among contestants drawn from the visiting dance troupes, one aspirant per troupe. This competition, though run like a one-day beauty pageant, focuses less on physical attributes than on speeches in which the contestants efficiently and humorously present "authentic" knowledge of their home traditions (especially of the elaborate local folk clothing they wear), and glorious history, usually presented first in an indigenous tongue, then in Spanish. Many contestants incorporate gender-based humor into their shouted speeches, and the one with the best combination of spunk and knowledge of tradition wins.

I have saved music for last in this review of how standard fiesta ingredients make their presence known in the Guelaguetza, but this ingredient is as important as the dance events and is of course part of every dance performance. A fairly standard repertory of tunes is employed for extra Guelaguetzas on the city square, often by young dancers-in-training that sat on their parents' laps on the bus to Oaxaca. In addition, an old-folks club puts on their idiosyncratic version of the Guelaguetza twice, and several hotels put on *their* versions as many times as is commercially viable (the same hotels that offer a mini-Guelaguetza with dinner a few times a week throughout the year). When you add all this to the regular Oaxaca city musical fare—weekly evenings from the state marimba, Sunday concerts by the state brass band, evening strolling mariachi bands (plus more marimbas and one *conjunto norteño,* here made up of accordion, nylon string guitar, and bass)—the music and dance calendar for late July is packed. And aside from the calendar of discrete events, there is the music of the *tiro al blanco,* target shooting carnival games (successful marksmen win songs seemingly performed by marionettes), and music played by dozens of itinerant musicians that descend on the city for this fortnight to play selections from the same old-fashioned range of musical genres as the *tiro al blanco* game stocks and the rhythms heard at the Guelaguetza.

Thus, the Guelaguetza is far more than three hours of display twice. It is echoed in shortened performances and supplemented by the usual fiesta ingredients, so that the fortnight of individual events coalesces into a giant unit serving tourists and all populations of locals simultaneously. But the composite fiesta would not be possible without its core, the volunteer efforts of the dancers and musicians who travel from all over the state. Who are they, and what does the Guelaguetza mean to them? How are they chosen? How are the dances they bring from their homes shaped (or reshaped) to fit on the Guelaguetza stage?

The Dancers

Various villages have clubs that cultivate older dances for their own use at their own festivals and also potentially for the Guelaguetza. Many members are single young people who belong to relatively high-status families who can afford for them to take time to learn dances in a social situation and can afford the time and money to obtain a suitable dance outfit. Why do these youths want to dance? For some it is a social activity, pure and simple. Many participants told me they just wanted to get to go to the big city (see Titon

1999) and to have fun, and their banter and sidelong glances at one another made clear that a critical ingredient in that fun was flirting. For others, a factor more old-fashioned enters the picture, the *promesa,* or vow. One common theme is health: a dancer can ask for a return of someone to good health, or give thanks for that having taken place. But the other most common *promesa* theme among dancers I interviewed was to offer up the effort and good will of the dance for the opportunity of finding a good partner in life. That is, dancing for (the) God(s) (or perhaps for tradition's sake) banks a storehouse of virtue, which eventually might be rewarded by the happy circumstance of meeting the right person. Of course, there's no clean line between a *promesa* intended to facilitate courting and the simple fact that being in the dance club places a young person in the company of suitable future mates. Romance is served in either process, or in a mix of the two.

Judging and Innovating Tradition

The shaping of each Guelaguetza on the hill begins when an "authenticity committee" of anthropologists and other upper-class culture mavens visits sizeable native towns. The committee views dances presented by hopeful local culture organizations, and it assesses authenticity (and, more quietly, aesthetics and logistics, that is, both intrinsic attractiveness of a given act to an outsider audience and how that sequence might fit with others a given year). Judging tradition might seem philosophically tricky, but it's simple enough as done here. Checking authenticity just means making sure there is no plastic in the outfits, no rock dancing, nothing that will seem jarringly modern to audiences. *Amounts* of traditional features are not regulated—that is, if one embroidered flower on a woman's shoulder is traditional, a dozen of the same will be perfectly fine. Folkloric intensification of each of the kinds outlined on previous pages is rampant, indeed encouraged, so that all presentations at the Guelaguetza will be vivid and reasonably congruent not just in length but also in generous rations of visual and musical information. The authenticity committee has in the past suggested refinements in choreography to suit the orientation of the stage and the fact that many viewers will be sitting far away. Dancers will retain the traditional steps, but also assemble in lines, or circles, or in other formations that can give a macro shape to the dance. Then the committee places the dances in a certain order to maximize contrast between successive groups and also to frame the series with the two ensembles most visually dramatic due to use of massive headgear, as explained above.

The drastic shortening of village performances for the Guelaguetza is balanced by recommended adjustments, since these tend toward intensification of effect through increased decoration and through choices of especially telling moments in the home dances. Neither process seems to bother the performers much, and perhaps the truncation and intensification balance out for them too. I asked some dancers from Teotitlán del Valle how they felt about their seven-hour *danza de la pluma* being reduced to ten minutes. Was it robbed of its meaning? "That's just a show we put on for the state and the tourists; we know what it really means, and *some* in the audience know, too, " I was told repeatedly.[3] In contrast, the village of Zaachila, which also presents the *danza de la pluma* at the Guelaguetza, doesn't have a long version at home. They acquired (or reacquired) this dance tradition *after* the Guelaguetza was in place and learned a digest of it as their essential form (see Figure 16.5). This sort of contrast between compressed rituals and dances adopted *from* the Guelaguetza (see McKean 1989) is visible to outsiders only through evening performances between the Monday events, when individual delegations offer two-hour presentations of their own in separate concerts. Some delegations present richer and more coherent versions of their region's danced folklore; other groups have the Guelaguetza as their source for dance tradition and therefore know lots of dances from towns other than their own, and present a mini-Guelaguetza as their evening performance. Both approaches seem to work fine for dancers and for audiences. The individuals most likely to be troubled by the wild variations in processes nurturing tradition are in fact the intellectuals who are likely to be on the committee for authenticity. "But this is for the state and the economy: We don't let it get too crazy, but we bend quite a bit, " explained Margarita Dalton Palomo, a prominent anthropologist and frequent member of the authenticity committee. She went on to tell me that a coastal dance celebration cleaves to the letter of tradition more faithfully and that scholars and other intellectuals let the greater authenticity and lesser commercialism of that event balance their personal qualms about the Guelaguetza.

The impact of these endorsed, reshaped, and prominently publicly performed dances is incredible. Yes, there is no shortage of romantic flexibility in rhetoric and interpretation. Traditions said to hark back to pre-Conquest or early colonial times contain plenty of ingredients in apparel, movement, and especially sound reaching back no further than the nineteenth century. The actual youth and the barely acknowledged indigenous/Spanish hybridity of most dances—that they really have changed plenty and recently, contrary

Danza de la pluma troupe of Teotitlán del Valle at home, performing their seven-hour version of the danced playlet, which is condensed to ten or fifteen minutes for the Guelaguetza. Photograph by author.

to rhetoric asserting stasis—may explain the ease with which adjustments made specifically for the Guelaguetza can be accepted back home. The citizens of Zaachila are as happy with their Guelaguetza-shaped pan-Oaxacan tradition as are the citizens of Teotitlán del Valle with their older and more detailed *danza.*

By now, the Guelaguetza's short dances and accompanying tunes constitute a canon worthy of emulation and exploitation. It is not just that the most famous dances are done with abbreviated ensembles in three hotels in Oaxaca City throughout the year and may be taken on tour throughout Mexico and abroad to advertise the allure of Oaxaca. The Guelaguetza has become the signature event of Oaxaca. One each of all kinds of things in Oaxaca are named Guelaguetza: a hotel, a bakery, a brand of chocolate. . . . And representations of dancers are for sale as dolls, as tin Christmas ornaments, in books, in videos of each Guelaguetza. The event certainly includes plenty of ingredients younger than they are claimed to be, but it remains very, very important to the economy and politics of the state of Oaxaca, is enjoyed by most residents of the state, and is enormously popular with tourists of all sorts.

Guelaguetza as Cultural Tourism

In the end, what kinds of pictures of the state of Oaxaca does the Guelaguetza offer, and to whom? All kinds of tourists are well-served. Some approaches to being a tourist feature reduced mental activity and responsibility through emphasizing physical pleasure, thus justifying Huxley's assertion that "we read and travel not that we may broaden our minds, but that we may pleasantly forget they exist" (1925, 12). Such tourists will likely be headed for Oaxaca's beaches. In contrast, MacCannell describes "sightseeing" as "a kind of collective striving for a transcendence of the modern totality, a way of attempting to overcome the discontinuity of modernity, of incorporating its fragments into unified experience" (1975, 13). There is a flavor of a pilgrimage here, which Graburn makes more explicit. He notes that "holiday" formerly meant "holy day," when much of a year's travel would be spent going to religious festivals. Other travels have replaced these over time, but some of the ritual and the hunt for life's deeper meanings remain (1989, 26). Of course, today's tourist-pilgrims vary in how much intelligence and industry they can or care to muster. Also, and of critical importance, the quest that both MacCannell and Graburn describe is often—perhaps usually—mixed in individual tourists with the "switching off" that topped a survey by Krippendorf of German tourists' motives for travel (1987, 23).

Tourists who journey to Oaxaca may concentrate on "switching off" while relaxing in cafés on the square. They can be satisfied with "surgically detached" "ethnographic fragments" (Kirshenblatt-Gimblett 1998, 14). But other tourists really have come on a romantic quest to view an embodiment of an earlier, presumably better—and to them certainly more exotic—way of life. My experience with this population—and I belong to it some days—is that they are intellectually active during their visits, mean well in a general way, and will devote some energy to learning about the culture on which their "holiday" focuses. For these "cultural tourists" (see Van Den Berghe 1994) the Guelaguetza offers a marvelously flexible experience, an efficient visual trip around indigenous Oaxaca for visitors with little time, and an introduction to a more thorough visit for those staying longer. When these tourists see the beautiful *huipiles* worn by women from Huautla de Jiménez, they return *between* the Mondays of the Guelaguetza to the city's museums and read about the meanings woven into that garb, thus contextualizing and enriching their memories of the scant hours of visual pleasure on the hill.

The state government draws on the event as much for political purposes as for economic ones. One hears repeatedly that the visiting delegations represent "the seven regions" of the state (the mantra-like list of regions: "¡Papaloapan, Sierra, Valles Centrales, Cañada, Costa, Istmo, Mixteca!"), a characterization that stipulates diversity even as it asserts that the "seven regions" constitute a viable whole. The Guelaguetza brings native, mestizo, and tourist populations together in a way arguing implicitly that the indigenous populations are happy, healthy, and exotic in a benign way: they decorate the state. The tight control visiting dance troupes endure during the Guelaguetza suggests that the populations they represent, populations that we are intended to accept as standing for all of indigenous Oaxaca, could not possibly be unruly or in any way unhappy.

However, absolutely all who travel to Oaxaca witness evidence of poverty and turmoil. Any visit to the city of Oaxaca entails spending time on its large and charming main square. Shops, nice hotels, and especially high-end restaurants surround most of the square, but the south side fronts on the government palace. The long eaves of this large building have provided shelter for one or another protest encampment for as long as I can remember. In 2002, a new group arrived from rural San Huertas, Teojomulco. In general, there is little government presence in such rural areas. Neither taxes nor services are much in evidence—the traditional social structures of church and family maintain order. But desperate poverty yields long-simmering agrarian disputes, one of which boiled over recently in the massacre of twenty-six men from a village neighboring San Huertas. Citizens of that village claim that men from San Huertas did the killing, while citizens of San Huertas blame local paramilitaries (which certainly exist). The government, in a characteristic response, sent the army in to arrest plenty of men from San Huertas. They did so in the hope that the actual villains would shake out of the mix in time. This typical draconian strategy stripped San Huertas of its leaders and left many families without income. Wives and families moved to Oaxaca, setting up camp in the area on the square that the authorities had only months before coaxed a previous protest group to vacate. The new arrivals set out bedding, built campfires, posted numerous hand-lettered protest signs, and began begging for financial support from passersby, many of them tourists. Therein may lie part of the answer to an obvious question: Why does the government let protesters camp in the city, and in such a public spot? This permission drains off some of the energy of the outrage at the mass arrests, and the location automatically provides a regular and reliable rivulet of outsiders' money to support the bereft families.

During this Guelaguetza, the protest leaders, acting in concert with quite a variety of small antigovernment political groups, directly addressed the discrepancy between their plight and the happy prosperity of rural life as portrayed in the fiesta. The night before the first Monday, when the dance delegations paraded through the streets of the old city, the protesters paraded too. Signs they carried asserted that "*¡La Guelaguetza Oculta Nuestra Miseria y Explotacion!*"; "*¡La Guelaguetza es hoy el exhibicionismo del gobernador!*" "*¡Bajo con los grupos de poder que nos usan como carne de cañon!*"[4] Then, the next day, after the Guelaguetza, protesters blocked intersections near the square, allowing cars through only after donations were solicited from and protest flyers handed to motorists and pedestrians (obvious foreigners received an English-language version). The police quietly dispersed this serial blockade, but a point had been dramatized that the continual presence of dispossessed populations camped on the square continually makes: not all of rural Oaxaca is in good shape. And while reasonably heedless teenagers make up most of the Guelaguetza's dance troupes, not all dancers are willing to be continually complicit in their being caricatured as happy people possessing charming folklore. During the years that families from the government-ravaged village of Loxicha lived on the square, dance delegations (particularly central valley groups presenting the *danza de la pluma*) would occasionally put on a show on their behalf, performing in the street bordering the protest encampment while surrounded by protest banners.

Conclusion

The Guelaguetza offers bridges between socioeconomic classes in Oaxaca, between Mexican and foreign tourists, between tourists and natives via different but compatible feelings of nostalgia, between indigenous peoples and their own complex pasts, and so on. It will doubtless continue into the foreseeable future because it means so many things to so many people. But what about those *indígenas* represented by the women and children residing on Oaxaca's main square? Does the relative prosperity of the natives who dance just rub salt in the protesters' wounds? I will close this essay with a last visit to the Diosa Centeotl pageant. The winner in 2001 was a Triqui, a member of the small and beleaguered population, members of which were the principal protest marchers and square residents before the Zapotecs from Loxicha (thus, two groups of protesters ago as of this writing). Plenty of Triqui still can be seen every day on the square, but as lowest-rung ambulatory merchants serving tourists. They sell gardenias, swiftly woven headbands and wristlets, crudely carved wooden letter openers, and so on. The lives of these particular Triqui cannot be described as prosperous, but they have moved up several steps from their worst times.[5]

To have a Triqui woman become the Diosa Centeotl deliberately made a connection between poor and not-so-poor Indians. Newspaper mention of this young woman, Concepción Martínez Merino, cited her specific ethnic derivation more often than this factor came up in other years. Her ascension as this year's "queen" of Oaxaca offered yet another event both temporally compact and symbolically rich. Like every moment at the Guelaguetza, this succeeded because it conveyed different acceptable messages to the various populations witnessing it. The most general theme was that conflict in the countryside could be resolved, but from that point messages branched out to the different populations at the Guelaguetza. The ruling elite could believe that this moment symbolized their general beneficence and their continuing skill in managing affairs of state large and small. They were keeping Oaxaca stable, a viable political entity, a place safe for themselves and for the economically critical populace of tourists. Those tourists in turn could imagine that ethnic unhappiness in Oaxaca would not effectively nurture a rebel force parallel to the Zapatistas in Chiapas, that populations whose plights gained publicity through delegations' residence on the square could melt back into the general indigenous population in time. It was not simply that these tourists could set aside pinpricks of worry about personal safety, but also that they could mentally return these indigenous groups from an uncomfortable present to the romantic world of the Guelaguetza, a world of aesthetic vibrancy coupled with lively embodiment of nostalgia. And what of the indigenous people and the lower class in general? Having a Triqui sitting by the governor's side in public, however briefly, offered an olive branch to the poor—a message of real hope even for those poor whose frustration periodically boils over into violence, imprisonment, and protest.

Postscript

In late July of 2006, I learned that the Guelaguetza on the hill had not taken place that year. The protest movement of the season—and connected camp on the main square—was by the state teachers' union, which goes on strike for better pay briefly each year. The current law-and-order governor had cracked down on the protest this time, ordering in riot troops who killed several teachers in an unsuccessful attempt to dislodge them from downtown Oaxaca. Nevertheless, the teachers ended their strike roughly on schedule. But the strike had attracted various allied organizations who chose not to disband. These groups first protested the Guelaguetza, much as had been done in 2002, but, inflamed by the paramilitary overreaction to the teachers' protest and especially by the implications of the unresolved national election for president, an angry group marched up the hill the night before the first Guelaguetza was to take place and vandalized and blockaded the auditorium. The Guelaguetza was cancelled. The teachers' union offered alternative entertainments on the university sports fields, and smaller versions of the Guelaguetza took place in many towns nearby, but most tourists left Oaxaca, devastating the local and state economies.

The long-term fate of the Guelaguetza remained unclear in July of 2007. Two occurred. First, a "People's Guelaguetza" was sponsored by the teachers' union and associated dissident political groups. Placards stating that this would take place (for free) the Monday before the "Commercial Guelaguetza," and that it would be staged in the official Guelaguetza auditorium overlooking the city, were replaced as quickly as government workers tore the announcements down. But soldiers with tear gas and clubs dispersed the march of sponsors and dancers to the hill on that Monday. The event reconvened slowly near downtown; it started late and was interrupted by rain, and lasted about seven hours due to the interspersed hoarsely shouted political speeches. It was nevertheless otherwise eerily like the official event. The state-sponsored Guelaguetza did take place the following two Mondays, despite ominous rumblings from the dissidents: "Tourists, we cannot answer for your safety . . ." and such on signs posted at the city square. Many purchased tickets were turned in, the usual visiting dignitaries were absent, and soldiers were everywhere. But the auditorium was full because the governor required state workers to fill the otherwise empty seats. The strangest feature of the official Guelaguetza was that it wasn't the least bit different in form or flavor from previous years, in a sort of bizarre denial of conflict. The rebels and the government are clearly in agreement that the Guelaguetza is critical for Oaxaca's identity and economy, but they continue to disagree concerning ownership of the event, and thus control of the essence of Oaxaca.

Notes

1. See Norma E. Cantú's and Brenda M. Romero's essays in this volume (chapters 6 and 11) for additional examples of this process.

2. These "giants" appear in processions in Spain and in a number of other fiestas and are called *matachines* or *monos* in Oaxaca. See Brenda M. Romero's essay (chapter 11) in this volume.

3. On longer forms of these dances, see Harris 2000, Dallal 1997a, and Peterson 1968.

4. "The Guelaguetza masks our misery and exploitation!" "Today's Guelaguetza is the governor's show!" "Down with the groups in power that use us as cannon fodder!"

5. See Amnesty International 1986 and 1990, and also Mata García 1996.

18

Bailando para San Lorenzo

Nuevo Mexicano *Popular Traditional Musics, Ritual Contexts, and Dancing during Bernalillo Fiesta Time*

PETER J. GARCÍA

The hot summer afternoon is filled with colorful *danzantes* playing their *guajes* (gourd rattles) in strict time to the beat of the repetitive melodies performed by the *músicos*.[1] These ancient-sounding mystical tunes accompany the intricate choreographic patterns by the *matachines* that lead the procession while a prayerful crowd follows reciting the decades of "Ave Marias" in contemplation of *los misterios del rosario*[2] for San Lorenzo. The annual Fiestas de San Lorenzo[3] held in Bernalillo, New Mexico, occurs on August 9th, 10th, and 11th regardless of what days of the week these dates fall. The festival constitutes one of the longest recurring Spanish-Mexican fiestas in the borderlands. Through the performance of the ritual and the various forms of social dancing throughout the events, the annual festival provides insight into the larger sociohistorical context and political climate where it is held. In this chapter I intend to show how during contemporary Chicana/o fiesta time, the dance (both *baile* and *danza*) emerge as loci of community struggle in producing and representing cultural identity through ritual.

Las Fiestas de San Lorenzo are a longstanding regional tradition among Río Abajo descendants based on their own ethnohistorical imaginary and social memory, and as such provide various sites of semiprivate and public ritual. This chapter situates Nuevo Mexicana/o popular traditional music and dancing within these ritualized contexts today. As I've explained elsewhere: "The term *baile* sometimes refers to a certain dance step or, in a different context, to a grand ball. More generally, however, it means a dance party. The *baile*, or local dance party, is one of the most important social traditions among [various groups of] Latinas and Latinos in the United States, a carryover from community-based social festivities dating from New Spain and still popular in contemporary México and the rest of Latin America" (García 2004, 51).

The local residents of Bernalillo would not define their religious fiesta as a dance party, although a grand ball type of social dance brings closure to the final evening. Various forms of *baile,* or social dancing, occur within the confines of a dance hall, or under an outdoor tarp set up in the town square, or in the city park throughout the fiesta. The ethnomusicological analysis of the music, ritual, and dancing offered here attempts to understand this community-based social festivity that bridges the colonial and contemporary time periods, examining what individual performers do musically in relation to the choreography and ritual throughout the fiesta. Other related questions previously asked by Michael Candelaria in his investigation of Penitente Ritual and Santo Art come to mind. Refocusing Candelaria's questions to bear on ritual and dance illustrates the various analytical preoccupations of various New Mexican scholars; hence I raise them here.

What motivates our desire to know the meanings embedded in Nuevo Mexicano culture? Is there some hidden meaning, objectively present, waiting to be uncovered or, rather, some arbitrary and subjective meaning in the process of being constructed? Do the *danzantes, músicos,* and *mayordomos*[4] through ritual and dance preserve, in some way, the spiritual core, the ethos of Nuevo Mexicano culture? What inward essence is being externalized and made objective in religion and dance? What self-knowledge do we hope to discover in the mysterious interplay between inner content and outward form? Dare we find in these cultural expressions a rich resource for an authentic Nuevo Mexicano philosophy? Who has the competency to interpret them truthfully and the right to speak for Nuevo Mexicano culture? (Candelaria 2002, 207). I'm not going to attempt to answer these questions here, but I raise them in hopes of getting the reader to further contemplate and consider the complexity of the San Lorenzo Ritual Time.

The *bailes* taking place throughout the Bernalillo fiesta provide *carnivalesque*[5] contexts for physical activity, choreographic expression, and ethnic solidarity; at times these *bailes* may be sexually charged, offering opportunity for flirtation and courtship. Therefore, the New Mexican *bailes* appeal to people for various reasons across generational, ethnic, class, spiritual, gender, and sexual boundaries. With this level of complexity in mind, we see popular and traditional music and dancing not merely as public spectacle, music/dance party, or even as cultural performance for tourists, but rather as a manifestation of how the musical and dance expression of the "poor reworks the material and concrete conditions of society and history, as well as imagines beyond them" (García Canclini 1993, x). Considering more critically the intensifying context of American domination on New Mexico in general and Bernalillo in particular, anthropologist Sylvia Rodríguez explains:

> Whereas the early context within which Bernalillo defined itself as a bounded community was shaped by the proximity to Sandía Pueblo, today the dominant environmental presence is the spreading city of Albuquerque. . . . The urban expansion of Albuquerque since World War II has created new "bedroom" communities at its peripheries and has revitalized and begun to gentrify some of its older neighbors like Bernalillo. Caught at the near edge of this process, Bernalillo has managed to embark on a slow demographic and economic climb spurred by regional capital development. It is gradually repopulating through natural growth, the return of outmigrated youth, and the influx of mostly Anglo newcomers. Today people in Bernalillo often voice relief that Sandía Pueblo stands between them and the city, creating a buffer against its constant onslaught. Thus the same urban development that enabled Bernalillo to hold its ground also threatens to overwhelm it, a paradoxical situation not unlike that seen in the *Río Hondo* watershed north of Taos. (1996, 117)

However, similar to other parts of the state, the Río Abajo region is subject to intense suburbanization and gentrification but is also experiencing a recent rise in heroin and crystal methamphetamine abuse, addiction, and overdose, especially among the Chicana/o working classes. Journalist Héctor Tobar offers one plausible interpretation of the situation based on his own visits to Cordova, New Mexico, in Rio Arriba County.

> The church that looms over the plaza was built in 1832, sixteen years before the town officially became part of the United States after what's known in American history books as "the Mexican War." As in other conquered places, the locals in Cordova and the rest of New Mexico lost the right to be educated in their own language and in general became second-class citizens. In American New Mexico, a new social construction was born that would dominate the next 150 years of Latino history in all the territories that had once been part of the Republic of Mexico: the barrio. . . . Barrios are insular places, born of de facto and de jure segregation. They have produced proud community leaders, a sense of identity and defiance vis-à-vis the outside world, and also a variety of self-destructive behaviors, from gang banging to paint sniffing. Before heroin arrived in northern New Mexico in the late 1990s . . . self-destruction would have taken a decade or decades to complete, because alcohol would have been their weapon of choice. (Tobar 2005, 170)

Social Imaginary and Barrio Ethnohistory: The Folklore Context

Bernalillo's annual Fiestas de San Lorenzo links the epic Pueblo[6] Revolt of 1680 to the mythic present through the residual elements, the ethnohistorical imaginary, and the superstructure inherent in the overall ritualized performance contexts. According to local ethnohistory, following years of tension, Pueblo Indians under the spiritual and political leadership of a "medicine Man" named Popé[7] from the Tewa pueblo of San Juan successfully avenged the Spanish colonizers in a bloody massacre of Spanish colonists of the northern Río Arriba from Santa Fe to Taos. The survivors, principally from the Río Abajo region (south of current-day Santo Domingo Pueblo to Socorro) were forewarned by Pueblo sympathizers and fled south to the Guadalupe del Paso (El Paso/Cuidad Juárez) area, where, according to tradition bearer Robb Sisneros, "the survivors praised San Lorenzo for their safety, and it was on his feast day that the revolt took place."[8]

While I was conducting fieldwork in 1998, controversy arose following the remodeling of Bernalillo's historical nineteenth-century church building that was rededicated as the Santuario de San Lorenzo. The fear expressed by the fiesta organizers and leaders was that the official institutional church was trying to appropriate the observance and would likely exploit the event by transforming it into a fundraiser for the Our Lady of Sorrows parish and relegating the event to a weekend church bazaar. Community leaders expressed their concerns over the commercial exploitation of the fiesta and their fear that the church would ultimately compromise the spiritual focus or integrity of the observance. In a nutshell, the *mexicano* organizers and supporters did not want the community ritual exploited for commercial gain and directed their efforts to resisting the priest's attempt to gain control. The biggest objection was over the church's departure from the local custom of observing the fiesta on August 10th.

Gentrification and Cultural Tourism: Community Survival and Self-Determination

Today, in many New Mexico tourist centers like Santa Fe and Taos, "the *Fiestas* are the only time during the year when local mexicanos physically reoccupy and thus symbolically reclaim the public spaces of their communities" (Sylvia Rodríguez 1997, 34). In Bernalillo this reclamation has been carried out ritually through the annual fiestas and the elaborate *matachines danza,* which many local residents credit as having prevented or at least partially postponed the gentrification of the town to the same degree as other older Nuevo Mexicana/o communities. According to Rodríguez, in Santa Fe and Taos during fiesta time, "this reclamation signals, ironically, a form of resistance occasioned and defined by the very hegemonic process it seeks to undermine" (Ibid.). In this way the fiestas throughout New Mexico become an effective form of ritual activism used by *mexicanos* as a means of maintaining cultural identity and historical tradition.

The pressure of intensifying capitalist development, which has provoked certain forms of ritual activism throughout much of New Mexico, is like the same gigantic beast with a different face for each locale. Thus Arroyo Seco has been affected by growth in Taos, Alcalde by the growth of Española, El Rancho by Los Alamos, Bernalillo and Carnué or Tijeras Canyon area by Albuquerque, and Tortugas by Las Cruces and El Paso. Whereas the Hispanic *matachines* once celebrated Spanish domination, today it symbolizes Hispano determination to persist against the tide of Anglo assimilation (Rodríguez 1996, 148).

I conducted field research in Bernalillo between 1996 and 1998 and during this time I lived in Albuquerque, the economic epicenter of the state. I have returned regularly to attend the fiestas and other community-sponsored events in Bernalillo and throughout the region and continue doing fieldwork there. Today, as in the past, many mexicana/os who live in Bernalillo find themselves endangered by aggressive economic development and commercial expansion on the part of a thriving cultural tourist market and commercial industry. Such Anglo-driven capitalist ideologies are intended to modernize (read dispossess) Mexican immigrant, regional Chicana/o, and Native American communities through development of natural, historical, and cultural tourist activities, mostly for the benefit of "white" Anglo-American spectators. Enamored with the "enchantment" of the place and the natural beauty and other scenery, many visitors resettle and eventually set out to assume political control of the community and eventually the region.[9] Part of the gentrification process is to maintain a distorted historical continuity among the folkloric social base of mexicana/os (Spanish Mexicans) through the use of a romanticized social memory and local ethnohistorical imaginary. Although the devotion to San Lorenzo is ongoing throughout the year, the actual fiesta is typically a three-day observance. The *mayordomo*'s (fiesta sponsor's) home is open to devotees who wish to pray to the image or meditate with the *santo* (a carved wooden figure—*bulto*—of San Lorenzo), and an official rosary is held on the 10th of every month in the evening. On August 1st an official *novena* begins and the *matachines* rehearse in front of the *mayordomo*'s home following the service. Formal ritualized *danzas* are performed throughout the three days along with Masses, processions, *velorios* (all-night vigils), vespers, and dances, and there is secular entertainment and other food, carnivals, and local vendors, which I will describe in more detail later.

The ritual time and space is not linear but infinite and circular in its conceptual formation. Town mayor and fiesta leader Charles Aguilar pointed this out when we discussed the social and spiritual function of the monthly rosary devotion that occurs on the 10th of every month in the *mayordomo*'s home.[10]

In the overall structure of the festival, August 9th marks the evening service often referred to as "*vísperas,*" or vespers, ending the intense nine-day *novena* where the rosary along with other prayers are recited along with *alabanzas,* or praise singing, as part of the spiritual preparation. A procession follows, carrying the *santo* to the church grounds where the *vísperas* are held in the *santuario* (church sanctuary). The procession is led by the colorful *matachines danzantes* following the *promesa* (vow or promise) dance in front of the *mayordomo*'s home. During the procession the *matachines* dance throughout the main streets of Bernalillo, making intricate choreographic patterns while the crowd follows, reciting the rosary and singing *alabanzas* from behind. Traffic is delayed or detoured, and the crowds line the street as the *danzantes* along with San Lorenzo and the procession pass by.

August 10th is the actual fiesta and it begins with a morning Mass in the *santuario,* followed with another procession accompanying the *santo*'s return to the *mayordomo*'s home. The *matachines* dance again in the afternoon, followed by a *promesa* dance and another procession through the town. The evening continues with an all-night *velorio,* where four *danzantes* armed with rifles at an altar keep a round-the-clock vigil of the *santo,* usually in front of the *mayordomo*'s home, patio, or garage. The ritualized movements of people and the various *santos* depicted on the *danzantes* head pieces, called *cupiles,* throughout the *danza*[11] further become the agents of reclamation of decolonial time and space and assist in the sacralizing of the town. The cast of colonial characters in the colorful *danza*—including a young girl who portrays Malinche, a *monarca* (leader), several *toros* (bulls), twelve *danzantes,* and the *abuelos*[12]—serve as important key symbols and colonial metaphors that help transcend the mythical and historical dimensions of the fiesta. In the past, the *danza* was performed strictly by males; the role of la Malinche was also performed by a male. Since the 1980s more females are participating as *danzantes* and *músicos,* and several gays and lesbians have performed and continue to perform in various roles and are prominent community leaders.

One of the more recent and detailed dance ethnographies devoted to the Bernalillo *matachines* choreography was completed in Spanish by Martha Patricia Espinoza Arreola.[13] The order of the *danzas* within the San Lorenzo ritual is consistent with the narrative of the colonial story and is listed as follows:

1. *La Marcha—Entrada de los danzantes.*[14]
2. *La Cruzada*—Sign of the cross to begin the *danza.*
3. *La Cambiada* (The Change)—Moctezuma directs his people and Malinche sits in front of the musicians while the *monarca* dances with each *danzante* that assumes new positions. The *danzantes* make a cross indicating that Moctezuma's people convert to Christianity.
4. *La Malinche/La Vuelta*—Malinche converts to Christianity while Moctezuma struggles with Christianity and paganism.
5. *La Toreada del Toro* (Controlling of the Bull)—Christianity versus pagan beliefs. The *monarca* begins the bullfight followed by Malinche's *torea,* or teasing with a *pañuelo* (handkerchief). Next, the *danzantes* torment *toro* with their rattles followed by *el abuelo.* Good prevails over evil.
6. *La Cruzada*—The sign of the cross signals the victory of good over evil.
7. *La Tendida/empinadita* (The Laying Out and the Rising Up)—All characters dance in celebration over the conversion of Moctezuma and his people.
8. *La Patadita* (*La Promesa*) (the Little Kick (the Vow))—The promise of the Aztecs to adhere to Christian beliefs. *Danzantes,* finishing their promises, honor San Lorenzo.
9. *La Corrida*—Triumphant procession. This is the *danza* procession that carries the image of San Lorenzo through the streets of Bernalillo (1998 Fiesta Program).

One of the most interesting points in the *matachines* ritual is the final *promesa* dance or "*patadita*" when the community is invited to *bailar para* San Lorenzo[15] for any promises or *ofrendas* (offerings) made throughout the year.

Throughout the final *corrida,* the triumphant procession through the town, and during the *promesa* dance, "individual identity is both created by, and subsumed in, group identity as culturally coded movement that gives valance to each performer's dance, allowing participants to shed their everyday roles determined within white hierarchies of power. In this sense, the dance acts as a shaman exorcising evil" (Gilbert 1995, 343). According to postcolonial critic and ethnochoreologist Helen Gilbert, "[i]t is also an occasion for the exchange of cultural capital between tribes [in Bernalillo's case Mexicana/o, Chicana/o, Genízara/o, and Puebloan], and for the contestation of white dominated space" and time (Ibid.).

Many of Bernalillo's *mexicana/o* residents are descendants of original Spanish Mexican (*Hispana/o* and/or *mestiza/o*) settlers or *genízaros* (detribalized and/or Hispanicized Indians) from neighboring villages (Corrales, Alameda, Placitas, Algodones, and San Isidro). Most of the people I spoke with either lost their ancestral landholdings to Anglo-Americans at some point following the 1848 Treaty of Guadalupe Hidalgo or more recently via the ensuing and ongoing U.S. land grab throughout the twentieth century. They have never forgotten the way the United States's Anglo settlers dispossessed Nuevo Mejicana/os of their family properties by manipulating political control of the region through the legal system. *Mexicana/os* have managed to maintain some local customs such as village spiritual practices, singing, and dancing in Bernalillo. Nevertheless, concerns remain fierce over the increasing Anglo-Americans who continue to relocate to New Mexico determined to purchase the sparse remaining private landholdings, at the same time raising property taxes and thereby forcing older *mexicana/o* residents to sell.

Too often overlooked in the study of ritual or religious ceremony, as Gerholm (1993) points out, are the liminal phases and the transition liberties, which are precisely the point in the ceremony when the lines between *danza* and *baile,* the sacred and the social respectively, are blurred. It is during *la patadita* and *la corrida* where the observers become ritual participants within the *danza* as the masked *danzantes* lead the masses as a social and spiritual offering through dancing. The *corrida* is the point in the ritual where *communitas* most clearly occurs. The repetitive melody or tune played on the violin is especially hypnotic, almost trancelike, rendering a mystical effect on the dancers, participants, and spectators. According to dance ethnologist Gertrude Prokosch Kurath, among Hispano (Spanish Mexican or *mexicana/o) matachines* in New Mexico,

> *La entrada, tanto como la última etapa, lleva un compás de dos tiempos, con pasos semejantes a la polka. Las demás melodías llevan un compás de "jig," 6 a 8, mientras que los Matachines dan brincos y pasos de basques, en figuras complejas."* (Kurath 1967, 263)[16]

The actual choreography consists of alternating foot patterns first danced backwards to the following steps: left-right-left-/right-left-right/left-right-left/right-left-right then repeated forward: left-right-left/right-left-right/left-right-left/right-left-right with two loud group stomps with each foot on the final beat of the melody. The simple folk melodies are performed by the violin accompanied by guitars, although the *danzantes* also play *guajes* (gourd rattles), providing a rhythmic accompaniment to the music and shifting *brincos* (jumps or stomps), which are repeated several times without variations. Typically each sequence within each individual *danza* varies in length but usually consists of about eight sets of choreographed patterns.

The last day of the *fiesta* is the *entrega,* or deliverance, which begins with *mañanitas*[17] sung to the *santo* and another ritual *danza* and *promesa* dance performed in front of the *mayordomo*'s home. Next the *danzantes* lead another procession delivering the *santo* to the home of the new *mayordomo,* who will preside and lead the celebration in the coming year. The *danzantes* return to the former *mayordomo*'s home and a large backyard party ensues, with food, music, and social dancing. A musical *entrega de los danzantes* is composed annually and sung, expressing appreciation to all the dancers, musicians, *mayordomos,* community members, and various participants for their dedication and devotion. The fiesta ends with an evening *entrega* dance that one could classify as a grand ball, with a hired band held at the Sandoval County Sheriff's Posse (a local rodeo grounds with a dance hall) or at one of the ballrooms in the local Santa Ana Indian casino. This secular dance or *baile,* as it is called by the locals, is not part of the official *danza* ritual but does mark the end of the official fiesta and serves as a token of appreciation and gratitude for the *danzantes* who participated throughout the year. That is not to say that other forms of music and dance do not occur throughout the three-day fiesta. In 1997 the fiesta was on a Sunday and various local bands and the local Ballet Folklórico de Bernalillo[18] performed in the town plaza as part of the secular entertainment throughout the entire weekend. Likewise, a carnival with local vendors, food booths, games, and small rides is erected in the local park near *La Calle San Lorenzo* (San Lorenzo Street), where most of the *mayordomo*'s homes are located.

The fiesta, with its processions, prayers, Masses, *santos,* food, carnival, singing, candles, *mayordomos,* crowds, color, and ritual *danza* and secular *bailes,* is not only a mechanism of social or religious prestige and historical commemoration, but also a powerful form of working class Chicana/o ritual activism, resisting the hegemonic domination, gentrification, and commercial exploitation of their community. It is also a creation of an imaginary space in mythological time, in which *mexicano/as* and neighboring Puebloans decolonize themselves from their oppressed social realities under United States rule. The role of the fiesta may be trivialized by critics as an escape from the mundane routines of everyday life or for providing much-needed hope for spiritual, health, or material benefits through the *carnivalesque danza* processions and ritual activities. These kinds of benefits were more personal and were better explained in the *mayordomo*'s public statements printed in the annual fiesta programs handed out to the crowds.

I now wish to shift my focus to more secular dancing taking place during the fiesta and provide some brief comments on New Mexican *conjunto*[19] music. I find the performance of Chicana/o social dancing along with the performance of *conjunto* especially interesting within the same ritual context of *Las Fiestas,* adding another layer of interpretive complexity to this analysis. According to Gilbert, "[a]s well as resisting identities imposed by the dominant culture on individuals or groups and/or abrogating the privilege of their signifying systems, dance can function to recuperate postcolonial subjectivity because movement helps constitute the individual in society" (1995, 342). Without question, *música norteña* or *conjunto* as a style of music and *baile* or dance genre peculiar to the Chicano borderlands is one of the most important cultural expressions that symbolizes the Chicana/o sociohistorical experience of living within and dancing across the borderlands. As such the music expresses the unique aesthetics, composition, and choreography that characterize Mexican American life under United States political control. Intercultural and gender conflict, land dispossession, and the transnational seasonal migration have long shaped the region's diasporic regional Chicana/o cultures.

Since World War II, the push-button accordion itself has become an important musical symbol of the entire region's working-class *raza*[20] that includes migrant farm workers, urban *braceros* who in Albuquerque worked for the Santa Fe railroad, and blue collar Chicana/os who are descendants of original *Hispana/os* (Spanish acculturated *mestiza/os* and *genízaros,* descendants of Native American slaves). Texas-Mexican folklorist Américo Paredes was the first to develop the paradigm of intercultural conflict based on his research along the Texas-Mexico border as symbolically expressed through regional music and dance—specifically, the traditional folk types including Spanish colonial *romances, décimas,* and later nineteenth-century ballads like *corridos* and *inditos* (Texas version of *huapangos*), *canciones rancheras,* and even *danzas mexicanas*[21] (Paredes 1976). Paredes concluded that "since the 1950s what we might call the 'Chicanoized' polka has, in fact, become a hallmark of both the musical and the dance musical styles in the Southwest" (see 1993, 1958).

Regarding the region's instrumental dance music, the leading New Mexican folklorist Arthur Campa noted that by the 1970s,

> the older folk dances of the Hispanic tradition had been elevated to a spectator event performed moreover by those who have had special training. . . . The traditional folk dances once regarded as popular in northern New Mexico were preserved through the efforts of the Folklórico, or Santa Fe Folklore Society. On festive occasions such as the Santa Fe Fiesta, this society presented several (regional) dances such as *la cuna* (the cradle), and a variety of waltz forms such as the *valse despacio* (slow waltz) or the *vals de los paños* (handkerchief waltz). (Campa 1979, 244)

These dances were subsequently known as *folklórico.*[22]

Campa completed fieldwork throughout most of the twentieth century, and his work demonstrates a dual tradition (local/regional and national) in folk dancing that evolved in all of the states of the Southwest borderlands. His efforts helped to preserve the older regional songs and local dances and encouraged the professionalization of these New Mexican *bailes* by performing troupes and academic societies like the Folklórico. Campa spent most of his professional career preserving, reviving, and even at times reinventing[23] New Mexico's past regional Spanish Mexican or Hispano culture and heritage.

At the same time that Campa applauded the salvage and preservation efforts of the Folklórico in their attempt to save what was left of the older Spanish Mexican culture, he was keenly aware of the cultural transformation taking place. Campa wrote that "the Hispanic population of New Mexico tended to follow the current vogues in dancing" (1979, 245). The displacement of the older New Mexican *bailes* and songs and their replacement with newer dance styles and vogues from Mexico, Texas, and the United States was inevitable as the borderlands were integrated into the North American capitalist political economy and commercial media. Historians conclude that it was the social upheaval and displacement of a critical mass of Mexican nationals following 1848 and then again throughout Mexico's revolution of 1910–1917 that introduced the Southwest borderlands to the various regional *bailes folklóricos* of Mexico. However, the 1960s reminded New Mexicans that their connections and ties to the land and place were being seriously eroded under the capitalist development of tourism in the state. The land grant struggles of the 1960s led by Reies López Tijerina, with the support of many local Chicana/o activists, were central to the American civil rights *movimiento Chicano.*

What is clear is that as urbanization intensifies in older *Nuevo Mexicano* towns like Bernalillo, the political dynamics are turned in favor of the foreign Anglos. This likely serves as a catalyst that fuels an aesthetic transformation taking shape within the community and overall region. It is this epic moment in the stylistic development that accompanies the shifts of older Mexicanized dances (appropriated from Europe) toward more recent genres and dances. The former strict association of specific Hispano dances with social groups (*ricos* [landowners]), or elites) and activities considered entirely outside the range of acceptable practice by a vast majority of *Nuevo Mexicanos* was radically transformed during the relatively short period from 1940 to 1970, so that today's *conjuntos* and *orquestas* are believed by older *Nuevo Mexicanos* to hark back to an earlier time.

The accordion[24] was no less popular in New Mexico than it was elsewhere. The accordion arrived with German and Czech settlers in Texas along what is called the German belt of Texas around the turn of the century, and later was diffused throughout the greater borderlands. It seems that the *acordeón* accompanied by the guitar was first introduced to the older New Mexican folk dance music, replacing the violin as the lead instrument in the regional dance music often referred to today as "*la música de los viejitos,*" the elders' music. Old time Hispano fiddlers like Gregorio Ruiz from Pecos continued to play the older social regional dances (*polkas, chotís, varsoviana,* and *redova*), which were being transformed into local forms of *folklórico,* through the late 1970s.

According to Manuel Peña (see 1980; 1982a, 1982b; 1985a, 1985b), the 1950s witnessed a series of changes in *conjunto* music that in a dramatic way climaxed the emergence and maturation of this *tejano* artistic expression in Texas, but in New Mexico the new *conjunto* sound was barely emerging and coming into its own regional aesthetic. The *bajo sexto* has not been used as much in New Mexico, and the four-piece *conjunto* as it developed in Texas did not become standardized further north.

Born in Bernalillo, Nato Chávez was known in New Mexico as "El Monarca[25] del Acordeón," the King of the Accordion. Unfortunately, he died of the alcohol syndrome described earlier by Tobar only a couple of years before I began my field research, so was unable to interview him. Growing up near Bernalillo, I was familiar with his recordings and heard his music played on local Spanish language radio, and I caught his live performances at the annual Fiestas de San Lorenzo. One of his biggest hits was "Polca San

Lorenzo," which debuted on Spanish radio during the early 1970s. It was recorded on the CRISTY label and became immediately popular and was played on KABQ and KAMX radio stations in Albuquerque. Another longtime resident of Bernalillo whom I did interview was disc jockey Alonso Lucero. We discussed Nato Chávez and New Mexican radio in general in his home on November 20, 1997. At the time of this interview, Alonso was sixty-two and recalled that his broadcasting career began in 1970 at KABQ, but he also worked for KAMX (Albuquerque) and KXKS in Belen and he was very familiar with Chávez's style.

Lucero described the Monarca's sound as uniquely "regional with flashy harmonies, lively tempos, and showy melodic fills and interludes." KABQ is the oldest station in Albuquerque and "for years held a monopoly on Spanish radio," and while he worked there, Lucero used "Polca San Lorenzo" as a theme song for his show. The tune expressed Lucero's own pride as a longtime resident of Bernalillo and "the town's long struggle to maintain their *promesa*" in the form of the annual Fiestas de San Lorenzo.[26] The various layers of musical identity may be seen through the appropriation of the accordion as symbolic of Chicana/o political struggle, ritual activism, and community survival. The various references to the *danza,* Bernalillo, and the *fiesta* in *Monarca*'s title and repertoire are complex but no less interesting, especially when examined through various analytic levels of ethnographic interpretation. Although Nato Chávez's "Vamos a Nuevo México" is not an official anthem, at one level it is an important expression of Chicano nationalism expressing pride in the place and the working-class spirit *de la gente* as *música conjunto al estilo Nuevo Mexicano*[27] distinct from Texas and the other Chicano borderlands.

In my research, I also came across several *chotíses, redovas,* and even a *varsoviana* recorded by *Nuevo Mexicano conjunto* artists including Nato Chávez, Max Baca, Felipe Trujillo, and Miguelito Romero, suggesting that the region's working-class popular music and dancing followed a similar pattern as Texas. By 1970 the early wave of New Mexican *conjuntos* had completely asserted themselves and their unique style of performance with important symbolic links to the past, and most of all to Nuevo México as a homeland coming full circle. For example, although the violin had given way to the accordion in the Chicana/o *bailes,* the polka beat remained, and while the *matachines danza* showed influence from the polka in terms of its choreography, it still maintained the violin as its principal melodic instrument. As the quintessential genres of *conjunto* music, the polka along with the older *chotís, redova,* and *varsoviana* were consequently subjected to the most intensive elaboration as the musicians strove both to bring fresh variety to the newly forged style while maintaining what they perceived to be an established socially constructed tradition that they knew extended back at least to the nineteenth century or those earlier days of *la música de los viejitos*.[28]

Polka Royalty

I interviewed Bernalillo accordionist Mike Romero on August 12, 2004, in downtown Albuquerque in the basement of City Hall, where Romero works. Mike Romero's *conjunto* performs regularly at the Fiestas de San Lorenzo and his extended family has been long-standing participants. His mother, Petrita Paiz Romero, was known as "the polka queen" because of her championship dancing skills. She died of cancer in her home in Bernalillo in 1998. Her husband of fifty-five years, Eduardo, was also an accordionist and danced in state and regional competitions from 1976 to 1992. In 1985, they won their age group title in Washington, D.C., at the "Dancing Across the U.S.A. Championships."

The couple received a proclamation, signed by Senators Pete Domenici and Jeff Bingaman, honoring them for representing New Mexico at the championships. Their nickname in Bernalillo was "El Rey y La Reina" ("the King and the Queen"), and they performed at many of the local fiesta dances throughout New Mexico. The Romeros also had a family band, Los Rancheros Alegres, and performed throughout the state from 1970 to 1985. Their musical legacy continues with their son's group Mike Romero y Su Conjunto. Romero recalled his recollections of the San Lorenzo fiestas as follows:

MR: It is a traditional thing because *velan al santo* (they hold a vigil for the saint). And the people really push it. The church has nothing to do with it; it hasn't died because the people keep it going. As I was growing up my mom and I were in the *matachines* in the late 1970s and early 80s. My mom danced for ten years because she made a promise that my brother who was paralyzed would walk. So she danced.

PG: Did the *promesa* work?

MR: Yes, my brother was my drummer until three months ago. I danced for the same reason; my mom was my inspiration. I wrote a *corrido* about her that says always follow your parents' footsteps, what you see and like that's what you have to imitate. And I liked to dance polka because I used to see her dance. Music, the same thing I picked it up from them.[29]

My conclusion is that the first generation of *conjunto* musicians in New Mexico forged their own style and sound by the 1950s, and the fiesta dances provided the local ritual context necessary to develop the style. By the 1970s, a truly regional sound came into its own with artists like Nato Chávez, Max Baca, Felipe Trujillo, and Miguelito Romero, while a second generation of *tejano* musicians was blazing a trail to a newer innovative *conjunto* style in Texas. Finally, in contemporary Chicana/o fiesta time, the dance (both *baile* and *danza*) emerge as loci of community struggle in producing and representing cultural identity. As a ritualized site of competing ideologies, both *danzas* and *bailes* offer unique sites of potential resistance to hegemonic discourses through their representation of the body as a moving subject, whose individual identity is either masked or concealed in the *matachines danza* but reveals a more honest *mexicana/o* and/or Chicana/o face and sound of *Nuevo México* during the *baile.*

Notes

1. Literally "musicians," but in this case, violinists and guitarists.

2. "The mysteries (ten Hail Marys and an Our Father) of the rosary"

3. Las Fiestas is a term commonly used by locals for the entire fiesta complex.

4. Dancers, musicians, and stewards.

5. According to Mikhail Bakhtin, the *carnivalesque* occurs during certain ritualized moments within a festival or social celebration when an inversion of the social order occurs and the lower classes are elevated to a higher status and the powerful elite are demoted to a lower social position. The *carnivalesque* is a ritualized occasion and often involves the body in various popular activities such as dancing, courting, or even praying. However, it may also take place during vulgar, "rowdy," or lewd forms of behavior including drunkenness, fighting, farting, cursing, and obscene gestures.

6. There are twenty Pueblo villages, nineteen in New Mexico and one (Hopi) in Arizona. Anthropologists have grouped Pueblo people geographically (i.e., the six Western Pueblos include Hopi, Zuni, Zia, Jemez, Laguna, and Acoma; and the fourteen Eastern Pueblos include Isleta, Sandia, Santa Ana, San Felipe, Santo Domingo, Cochiti, San Ildefonso, Santa Clara, San Juan (now Ohkay Owingeh; see note 13 in Romero's essay in this volume), Tesuque, Pojoaque, Taos, Nambe, and Picuris. Linguistically, Pueblo people speak several indigenous languages including Tanoan (Tiwa, Towa, and Tewa), Keresan, Hopi, and Zuni.

7. For more detailed information, see Dozier 1970.

8. Robb Sisneros, Annual Bernalillo Fiestas Program, 1998. By the spring of 1693, Spanish *reconquista* leader Don Diego de Vargas organized another expedition, including many of the surviving colonists and their descendents, back up the Rio

Grande to re-establish *La Villa Real de Santa Fe* as the Spanish Mexican capital of *La Nueba Méjico.* During the time of the Pueblo Revolt, all the Spanish-settled areas of New Mexico and some of the Pueblos, including the Tiwa-speaking village of Tuf Shurn Tui (Sandía since colonial times), were abandoned. The area of the earlier Río Abajo settlement was re-established as the Gonzales/Bernal Camp. The Bernalillo area, which was referred to as Real de Bernalillo, was among the first to be resettled after the Reconquest of 1692–93. In thanksgiving for their safe return, and for assistance in creating a new social tolerance among all people of the Rio Grande Valley, San Lorenzo was named patron saint of the settlement and the fiesta in his honor became an annual event. In 1695 Diego de Vargas officially founded the Town of Bernalillo on the site of the Gonzales/Bernal Camp (Ibid.).

9. Tomas Atencio's PhD dissertation, "Social Change and Community Conflict in Old Albuquerque, New Mexico," examines the gentrification and commercialization of la Plaza Vieja, Old Town, Albuquerque. Most of New Mexico's older Mexican communities are currently undergoing a tourist boom and political, economic, and social transformation by outsiders hoping to reap a profit from local culture, history, architecture, and natural beauty.

10. Charles Aguilar, interview with Peter J. García, Bernalillo, New Mexico, December 12, 1997.

11. According to Royball, *danza* is a term that refers specifically to dances that (are) danced for religious purposes and, although often misunderstood, are an integral part of Latina/o, Mexican, and Chicana/o popular culture in the United States. Unlike dances that fall under the more general umbrella of *folklórico, danzas* cannot be altered without jeopardizing the integrity of the *danza.* The alteration of any aspect of a *danza* including costuming, choreography, step arrangement, or musical accompaniment could change or nullify the spiritual devotion of a *danza* in its entirety. Many *danzas* are composed of simple footwork so as to allow for worship without an overwhelming prerequisite of talent and training. There are some *danzas,* however, that are to be danced only by special classes of people and therefore may contain intricate footwork, daring physical exploits, or some other extraordinary display for the purpose of divine worship or sacrifice (Royball 2004, 220). In Bernalillo, only the *matachines danza* is performed for the Fiestas de San Lorenzo although other *danzas* including *los comanches* are performed throughout Advent (see also Lamadrid 2003).

12. Literally "grandfathers" but actually clowns.

13. See also Romero 1993 and 1997 for additional ethnomusicological analysis of New Mexican *matachines* in San Juan Pueblo and Alcalde (Río Arriba) communities.

14. "The March: Entrance of the dancers"

15. "dance in honor of San Lorenzo"

16. "The entrance, similar to the last part, uses a rhythm of two beats [simple duple meter 2/4], with steps similar to the polka. The remaining melodies are set to the

rhythm more like a "jig," 6/8 [compound duple meter], meanwhile the Matachines perform Basque [like] jumps and steps, in complete figures" (translation mine).

17. A morning serenade, traditionally sung for birthdays.

18. See Nájera-Ramírez' and Rodriguéz' essays in this volume (chapters 16 and 19) for comprehensive treatments of *ballet folklórico.*

19. The term *conjunto* refers to dance bands made up generally of an accordion, a *bajo sexto,* twelve-string bass guitar, and a regular six-string guitar and generally found in Northern Mexico (hence "norteño" or *música norteña*) and the U.S. Southwest.

20. Literally "race," but used to refer to a collective of those of Mexican descent.

21. *Huapangos* are from the Huastec region of Mexico; *canciones rancheras* are lyrical country songs.

22. According to Royball, *baile folklórico* refers to Mexican folk dances or dances that bear significant Mexican folk influence and are performed generally by professional, semiprofessional, and amateur troupes throughout México and the United States. Since *folklórico* is a term that describes a developing and dynamic art form, it is important to note that there are within the diaspora of Mexican folk dance many different sects who maintain various views about the true definition, essence, and semantics of *baile folklórico* (Royball 2004, 52).

23. Campa's encouragement of New Mexican local regional culture including *bailes* and *danzas* is well-known and documented. See Mario T. García 1989; see also Arellano and Vigil 1980.

24. It is atypical to use the accordion in New Mexico *matachines;* however, most of the *tejano* (Texas-Mexican) groups use the accordion and not the violin as the principal melodic instrument. See the video documentary "Matachines de La Santa Cruz de la Ladrillera," by Marlene Richardson, 1996 KLRN San Antonio (Alamo Public Telecommunications Council).

25. The fact that la Polca San Lorenzo was used as the theme song for a popular radio show further connects *los matachines* with Bernalillo and Río Abajo community identity. The title of Monarca adapted by Nato Chávez is also another interesting reference to one of the main characters in the *danza.*

26. Alonso Lucero, interview with Peter J. García, Bernalillo, New Mexico, November 20, 1997.

27. "Of the people . . . *conjunto* music New Mexico style."

28. See Loeffler 1999.

29. Mike Romero, interview with Peter J. García, Albuquerque, New Mexico, August 12, 2004.

19

Folklórico in the United States

Cultural Preservation and Disillusion

RUSSELL RODRÍGUEZ

Cada generación tiene el derecho de expresar su interpretación del arte y no más el tiempo y el pueblo dirá si vale.[1]

—Rafael Zamarripa Castañeda, visual artist and director of the Ballet Folklórico de La Universidad de Colima

The early 1970s witnessed an unprecedented blossoming of Latino/Chicano literature, politics, and cultural expressions, due mainly to the efforts of people engaged in the Chicano movement. Thus an interest in *folklórico*, Mexican folkloric dance, emerged.[2] Ethnic Mexicans at community centers, churches, and schools of all levels in large urban centers, small cities and towns throughout the U.S. Southwest began showing interest in this Mexican practice and created new spaces for *folklórico* groups to develop.[3] In the summer of 1975 a new forming organization, the Asociación Nacional de Grupos Folklóricos[4] (ANGF), scheduled a nationwide conference in San José, California, hosted by the dance ensemble Los Lupeños de San José. In addition to generating an annual conference and building a *folklórico* network system, ANGF produced a short-lived journal dedicated to reporting events and developments in traditional Mexican folkloric dance. Today, *folklórico* ensembles are established throughout the United States in major cities, on major university campuses, and in most towns that host a high ethnic Mexican population. Obviously, many people, Mexican and non-Mexican, have at some point participated in or been spectators of this expression.

This chapter is intended to open a serious dialogue concerning the practice and performance of *folklórico* by Chicanos in the United States. I argue that the *folklórico* movement in the United States proliferated from the momentum of the Chicano social and artistic movement. Within this expression, ethnic Mexican dancers focused much attention on collecting, promoting, and preserving dances within a frame of *mexicanidad*. *Folklórico* dancers were rarely concerned with creating dance that would tell the stories of the Chicano experience (a U.S. experience), contextualized in the communities in which many of these dancers lived, which could be received and critiqued by the community, as Zamarripa suggests above. I compare this to other cultural expressions—also inspired by Mexican practices—that came out of the Chicano movement, such as mural painting, *teatro* (theater), film, poetry, and music.

For researchers of Chicano expression and popular culture, artists and cultural products of the aforementioned forms are easily recognized: In theater one thinks immediately of Teatro Campesino, Teatro Esperanza, Teatro de la Gente, Luis Valdez, Socorro Valdez, Olivia Chumacero, Adrián Vargas; in music Danny Valdez, Flor del Pueblo, Los Alacranes Mojados, Los Lobos, Los Peludos; in visual art The Street Scapers, The Chicano Royal Air Force, Judith Baca, ASCO,[5] Juana Alicia, Los Four; in film Jesus Treviño, Sylvia Morales, Moctezuma Esparza; and in poetry Alurista, Lalo Delgado, George Sánchez, Bernice Zamora, Lorna Dee Cervantes, José Antonio Burciaga. Many of these artists crossed into other expressions; for example, José Montoya and José Antonio Burciaga were equally talented writers as they were visual artists, as were Danny Valdez, Ramón Sánchez, Beto Ruíz, Agustín Lira, and Eduardo Robledo comfortable both as *teatristas* (actors) and as musicians. The work of these individuals and collectives has been processed into a collective memory contributing to the formation of a Chicano cultural identity. However, *folklórico,* which emerged concurrently with these expressions, played a different role within the movement and the U.S. community.

Ironically, among the cultural expressions that made up the Chicano artistic movement, *folklórico* was in some ways the most effective in attracting participants and impressing people. Many of the *folklórico* groups had between ten and forty participants in their ranks, compared to most of the *teatros,* which had no more than fifteen members at one time. Actor, musician, and educator Eduardo Robledo has observed that "*folklórico* was very important but it was like an *adorno,*" an adornment.[6]

Robledo clarifies that although *folklórico* had a place in the community and even in the movement, it did not incorporate social issues in its practice, as did many of the other art forms of the time. Issues such as immigration, labor rights, education, access to medicine, representation, the Vietnam war, or racial and class discrimination are not located in *folklórico* as they are in Chicano music, poetry, paintings, and theatrical works of the movement era.[7] He was also correct in noting that *folklórico* was decorating the cultural landscape and soundscape, and it continues to be highly enjoyed in this manner, but it is doubtful that this expression is taken seriously outside of the *folklórico* membership, either by the mainstream or by academics doing work on Chicano cultural expressions. The lack of professional ensembles in which a person can make a living as a *folklórico* dancer provides some evidence of this lack of support. More disturbing is the lack of scholarly interest in this expression, especially given that many U.S. ensembles were developed on university campuses.[8]

What drives my interest in this topic is how *folklórico* affected my life in providing a space to develop talents in performance, but also by causing a real sense of confusion and disillusion around the idea of entitlement of the expression, the contextualization of the practice, and the politics of identity. I was a dancer who lived in a Chicano community and started performing in 1971, experiencing some of the high points of the Chicano arts movement—yet still I firmly identified as Mexican, not Chicano.[9] I came to discover that participating in *folklórico* was an exercise in visualizing the imagined community as one rooted in *mexicanidad*, in this case a cultural and national identity that indexed Mexico. For me, this hindered the process of envisioning cultural performance and practice, which could have been framed within a *chicanidad* representing the community in which I lived.

It is important to ask what the relationship is between *mexicanidad* and *chicanidad*, specifically within cultural expression. Why was it that in *folklórico*, collecting, preserving, and promoting *mexicanidad* was the ultimate aim of the expression? Why wasn't dance seriously developed as an expression that could represent the Chicano community or a U.S. experience? Does the expression of dance have the same possibilities of contributing to a politics of identity as other cultural expressions? Also how does the notion of context fit in the method of preserving and promoting *mexicanidad* in the United States?

In the following pages I hope to initiate dialogue on the question of *folklórico* contributions to Chicano history, identity, and culture by presenting my own narrative as a participant in the *folklórico* realm, by examining the relationship of *chicanidad* and *mexicanidad* within Chicano expressions, and by providing examples of Chicano cultural products, performers, and events maintained through Chicano collective memory and archived/documented history. I conclude by presenting a few examples of how Mexican folk dance is now being cultivated within a cultural frame of *chicanidad* and with a methodology of practice and creativity rather than preservation and promotion.

Reflexive Narrative

Following the examples of ethnographers such as Américo Paredes and Renato Rosaldo, I present a subjective reflexive narrative of my personal experiences as a participant in the *folklórico* scene in San José, California. I do this to offer a specific yet complex view of the dynamics that occurred within the arena of Mexican folk dance between the years 1972 and 1982.

I started dancing *folklórico* when I was eight years old, at El Teatro Indio. It was a small converted house, a grass-roots cultural center that had been established by Sophie Mendoza, one of San José's recognized Chicana activists, along with family and friends. It was through this center that I was introduced to the Chicano social and artistic movement. My first performance was at a Chicano rally; after we finished performing, a young man went up on the stage and ingrained in my mind how my f****n' rights were being taken away, and how the system of the f****n' *gabacho*[10] was excluding me as a Chicano.

The first dances I learned were a set from the state of Michoacán; "El jarabe michoacano," "La botella, " and "La costilla."[11] I understood that these dances were from Michoacán because I was told that the peasant-type costume—pants and a shirt made of *manta* (muslin) adorned with strips of materials along the collar, pant bottoms, and wrists—represented the state of Michoacán. The hats that we wore affirmed this, because one of them had stamped inside it *hecho en Michoacán* (made in Michoacán). I would later come to realize that "El jarabe michoacano," "La botella," and "La costilla" were recordings by Mariachi Vargas de Tecalitlán, and the latter two would also be performed as Jalisco dances. To this day I have never heard a recording of these songs played by a *conjunto de arpa grande,*[12] or any other type of traditional musical ensemble of Michoacán.

Performing in San José at St. James, Roosevelt, or Hellyer Parks for rallies, *fiestas patrias* (patriotic holidays), or festivals was common, as was performing alongside groups like Flor del Pueblo, a magnificent musical ensemble that played *huelga* (protest) songs, *corridos* (ballads), or compositions about Che Guevara, César Chávez, Pancho Villa, and Emiliano Zapata.[13] As a child dancer, I shared the stage with other performance groups like the Teatro de la Gente, Teatro Urbano, and Teatro Campesino that were performing *actos* (short skits) and plays about labor, inner-city issues, and Vietnam. One very clear memory of the *muerte* (death) narrator character in a *teatro* performance of Luis Valdez's *Soldado Razo* (buck private) contributed to my understanding of the *teatro* movement. Another vivid memory that stands out was the priest who would show up at the rallies and have a hypnotic effect on the audience when he would recite the *letanía en caló.*[14] I would later learn that the priest was José Antonio Burciaga (*que en paz descanse*)[15]—an inspirational writer, visual artist, and performer who would influence my own desires for higher education.

By the time I was ten, my mother, Theresa Rodríguez, my older sister, Joan, and I would go to San José City College (SJCC) every Saturday morning to attend classes, which were being offered by Susan Cashion and Ramón Morones, the founders of the group Los Lupeños de San José. Joan was performing with the group, so in addition to going to the classes, my mother and I would stay at SJCC and watch the group rehearsal while we waited for my sister. I would also attend her Wednesday evening rehearsals held at the old abandoned Guadalupe Church in east San José. It was an amazing space in which the sound of twenty dancers with wooden heels, *zapateando,*[16] aggressively dancing syncopated rhythms was inspirational to me. The natural reverb of this high-ceilinged wooden building would embrace the sound of the dancers and throw it back at me, instigating a feeling that resonates fondly in my memory today. It was this *sentimiento* (feeling) along with the enthusiasm of all the young Chicanos learning these dances that initiated my desire to become a serious *folklórico.*

The group often practiced the dances called *huapangos* or *sones huastecos* of Tamaulipas. *Sones* like "El querreque," "La rosa," and "El caballito"[17]—played by the three-piece string ensemble, the *trío huasteco,* which utilizes the violin, *jarana huasteca,* and the *huapanguera*[18]— would haunt me until I finally learned the dances by watching. A few years later, I became a student of the music.

After about a year of taking classes at SJCC, five families decided to form a group in which children and adults could perform together (Los Lupeños was primarily an adult group). These families secured rehearsal space in the local schools on the east side[19] and hired some of the members of Lupeños as teachers. The group, of which my mother eventually became the director, was called Los Mestizos. It was a remarkable experience to grow up so closely with these families; many of us children would refer to each other as cousins, and some of our parents actually became *compadres,*[20] affirming our desires to be related.

It was during this time with Los Mestizos that I learned a good portion of the *folklórico* repertoire. I learned *sones* from Veracruz, Jalisco, and San Luis Potosí, and *polcas, chotíz,* and *valses*[21] from Chihuahua, Nuevo León, and Tamaulipas.

People like Tomasita Prado and Barbara Pérez, members of Los Lupeños who taught us, were highly influential and inspiring teachers. Pérez, a musician/dancer, continually supported my development as a musician and dancer, providing opportunities for me to study and perform. Rick Mendoza, the son of Sophie Mendoza, was one of the lead dancers from Lupeños and was learning *huasteca* music at the time; he (along with my mother) was the one who put a *jarana* in my hand and encouraged me to learn music. Pérez and Mendoza were the two that always understood and made me understand that Mexican folk music and dance are not supposed to be separated.

Armando Quintana, another dancer I looked up to, would sometimes pick up my cousin, sister, and me for class in his van, a bright red Chevy with huge UFW eagles on each side. It was Quintana who first explained to me what the eagles symbolized and told me about the farm workers' struggle. There was also Amando Cablas Fink, a Chicano Filipino who was an awesome dancer. He had endless energy and everyone used to love to watch him dance "la culebra," a very physical dance from Jalisco in which the male dancers slam their hats on the floor as if they were killing a snake, *la culebra*. When I was ten years old these three male dancers—Quintana, Mendoza, and Cablas—immediately became my role models. Any chance I got to perform with them was an incredible thrill. In addition to being accomplished *folklórico* dancers and willing to do all the performances at the rallies and protests, they seemed like the coolest guys I knew. While my older brothers and sister were looking up to Santana, the Rolling Stones, Willie Mays, and other pop icons of the time, I was lucky that my idols would become my mentors and friends.

When I was eleven I made it into Los Lupeños, but it was then that my favorite *folklórico* dancers started leaving the group, either going off to university or moving on with their lives. Mendoza attended Santa Clara University, which neighbors San José, so he danced a bit longer in the group, but he ended up leaving and eventually started his own ensemble, Grupo Folklórico Xochipilli de San José.[22]

Around 1975, the Chicana/o movement was in full force. Consumers were encouraged to boycott grapes, Gallo wine, and lettuce; picket lines were forming at grocery stores in cities throughout the state; Chicano studies programs were developing in colleges and universities; and various other political and social developments were emerging as a result of Chicanos organizing.[23] Some members of Los Lupeños were participating in these causes and would ask the group to lend its support through performances. At some point (I don't remember exactly when), the group met to discuss what type of entity Lupeños was to be: a community group or a professional performance ensemble. It was decided that the group was heading more toward being professional; if dancers wanted to perform at the rallies and political events they could do so, but as "members" of Los Lupeños rather than as Los Lupeños de San José. Looking back on it now, it seems as though this was a turning point for the group.

The shift entailed a new approach to performance and practice that would include other dance forms (e.g., modern dance) and more theatrical expressions including acting and singing. This is when the group began its rehearsals for the dance drama *Mextizol*. This decision created tension, because while some participants embraced the new practices, others wanted to simply perform *folklórico*. Another issue was that some liked the idea of becoming a professional ensemble while other people wanted the group to continue as a community-oriented ensemble. I remember feeling that Los Lupeños was diverging from its mission of promoting and preserving Mexican culture; however, I do recognize that I learned much as a performer during this time.

It was during this time that Teatro Campesino actors Noé Montoya and Alan Cruz joined Lupeños to help develop *Mextizol*. Socorro Valdez also came to work with Los Lupeños doing workshops and coaching us in *teatro* techniques. Because Montoya and Cruz were also musicians with Teatro Campesino, through them I was exposed to the music of the Chicano movement. We played *huelga* songs such as "El Picket Sign" and "Huelga en General," the music of Danny Valdez, and a haunting musical version of "El Chuy," based on José Montoya's poem "El Louie," that had been developed by Teatro Campesino. I had already attained experience playing *sones huastecos* and *jarochos*,[24] so there was some mutual exchange of musical knowledge. Montoya and I eventually played much music together as members of the *jarocho/huasteco* ensemble Los Trovadores de la Costa,[25] but we also became the two guys who would play at many of the social events for the group. It was from Montoya that I learned a Chicano musical repertoire.

Despite being a productive time for the group, it was also a confusing time, for it was not clear whether Los Lupeños was becoming a group that was creating art for art's sake or had intentions of speaking directly to local communities by incorporating some of the techniques of *teatro* into its repertoire; I now believe it was both. In conversations with Cashion and Morones, both confirmed that Valdez's Teatro Campesino was a huge influence on their vision for Los Lupeños.[26] However, Los Lupeños never really took on the issues or concerns of the Chicano community in San José or the larger imagined community defined as Chicano.

We were neither professional dancers nor actors; we were highly enthusiastic *folklóricos* who found community in this ensemble. It was from the Mexican American community that the majority of the membership was built, and it was from the Chicana/o social and artistic movement that this group received much momentum and support. However, unlike the *teatros*, Chicano movement musical groups, the collectives of muralists, poets, and even some of the university *folklórico* groups, the members of Los Lupeños had diverse views about politics and cultural identity. Though some group members were student and political activists, there were also many who felt this group provided a space for those who were not participants in the Chicano movement but who wanted to fulfill their desire for something culturally Mexican. In addition, Lupeños was always open to anyone interested in Mexican dance and culture. Through its history, membership included people of Asian American, African American, and Anglo American backgrounds.

I worked with Los Lupeños until 1980, and I developed skills in teaching, choreographing, and directing dance. I moved on to work with Rick Mendoza's group, Grupo Folklórico Xochipilli de San José, which was a great experience where I further developed my skills. Nevertheless, after dancing for ten years I felt dissatisfied, as though I missed out on something or something was not right. Even though I felt this way, I continued to dance while I started shifting my focus more to music. I had already been performing since 1978 with the musical group Los Trovadores de la Costa, playing at restaurants, weddings, and other types of social and political events. Then by 1981 I started performing mariachi music in the San José and Monterey Bay regions. It was through my musical experience that I realized that *folklórico* had no natural contextual setting for its performance. The idea that *folklórico* was always staged was made clear once juxtaposed to the contextual setting of Mexican musical performance. How people participated in our musical performance by requesting songs, singing along, *echando gritos* (stylized shouts), and most importantly spontaneously dancing made clear the vibrancy of this cultural expression. These musical interactions also illuminated how Mexican music becomes recontextualized in the United States.

A desire for *mexicanidad* was shared by the performers and also by those receiving and responding to the expression, in a manner that was never apparent in a *folklórico* performance. It was obvious that collecting, preserving, or promoting *mexicanidad* was not as much a concern as was the desire for direct engagement and reinstatement of culture. I felt as a musician I was providing a tangible grasp of social and cultural gratification to people, which was not as evident performing as a dancer. It is from this position that I am writing this chapter.

Reflection

I share these specific experiences to explain that with all this exposure to *chicanismo* and Chicana/o identity, art, cultural expression, and politics, I still identified much more as Mexican than Chicano for various reasons. First, I was a young boy who simply did not understand the identity politics of the time. Second, because of my entrance into Mexican music and my apprenticeship with two *maestros* from San Luis Potosí—Artemio Posadas and Juan Francisco Díaz—my training was based on performance and practice that was framed in *mexicanidad*. Third, the *folklórico* groups in San José, like most *folklórico* groups, maintained a desire to preserve and promote Mexican culture. These groups did not offer an ideological context for Chicana/os, even though a good portion of the dancers did identify as Chicano and the expression received much momentum from what is recognized as the Chicano artistic movement.

The *folklórico* scene was by no means the only space in which people demonstrated a desire for *mexicanidad*. Chicanos during the 1970s were seeking viable *mexicano* expressions to ground a shared heritage, identity, and national movement. However, for many other artists this desire evolved into a process that moved from imitating a Mexican cultural expression (and sometimes inventing it) to analyzing it, then eventually developing a voice within the expression that spoke to and about their own experience as a member of the Chicano community. As Steven Loza wrote about Los Lobos: "In an important sense, 'tradition' was the ideal that Los Lobos sought to express through their reinterpretation of Mexican music. A larger part of the group's desire to appropriate folkloric *jarocho* genres into their repertory was based on an urge not only to preserve such music, but to promote it as a viable art form in an urban and, in many respects, a culturally hostile environment" (1992, 187–88). As history would illustrate (and as do I below), Los Lobos—along with many other musicians, artists, and poets—experienced a process that led them to develop their own voice to represent their own community in Los Angeles. Instead of preservation and promotion, a method of practice and innovation prevailed and continues to do so. This is not to say that Mexican traditions are learned and then ignored; on the contrary, the more one understands them the better they serve as foundations for the development of emerging forms and practices. It was these emerging forms and practices that constituted a Chicano collective memory contributing to a Chicano history, identity, and culture.

Preservation and Promotion vs. Practice and Creation

The approach of preservation and promotion of *mexicanidad* is currently recognizable not only in the *grupo folklórico* movement but is also apparent in cultural projects such as mariachi programs found in universities, colleges, high schools and middle schools, and community cultural centers throughout the United States. I would argue that the model for preserving and promoting Mexican cultural expression by Chicanos and Mexican Americans stems from a desire to come to terms with the "authentic tradition" that establishes an essence of *mexicanidad*. Meaning there is an engagement with the cultural expression to the convenience of the participant, leaving a question of political intention and accountability to Mexican identity, culture, and community.

Like most *folklórico* dancers, I grew up with an ideology in which terms like "traditional" and "authentic" were accepted largely without challenge. As Robin Kelly states, "terms like 'folk,' 'authentic,' and 'traditional' are socially constructed categories that have something to do with the reproduction of race, class, and gender hierarchies and the policing of the boundaries of modernism" (1992, 1402), but at that time, I didn't understand this crucial point. Like many other young dancers, I did not make the distinction that many of the folkloric dances I was learning and performing were choreographies created for theatrical purposes, rather than maintaining a "traditional" expression or cultural understanding. Indeed the dances I learned were influenced by and had direct connection to some "traditional" Mexican folk dance form, but neither the students nor the teachers seriously explored these connections or the concept of context. Coming to this realization I became disillusioned and angry. I had been wholeheartedly invested and believed that this cultural expression of *folklórico* was an "authentic" performance practice—not one that had been staged, choreographed, and re-interpreted without much regard to context.

I even believed at times that by virtue of my expertise in this "traditional" art form I understood something about Mexican culture that many *mexicanos* themselves did not understand. When I realized my arrogance and ignorance, I felt that *folklórico* dancers could not be trusted and that many of them did not have a clue as to what they were doing. I felt that my identity had been erased from the history of this expression to which I had believed I was contributing.

Another issue inherent in the collection, preservation, and promotion of Mexican *folklórico* dance is the odd "policing" of misunderstood, (re)created traditions or folklorizations by many self-entitled authorities. The practice of *folklórico* within the United States has created a space for cultural transmission that is not practiced in a lived fashion; rather it is rehearsed, choreographed, and performed in the same manner as musical theater. Within this approach to *folklórico,* cultural information that is often thin and lacking nuance is passed on to students without any type of critical analysis. The reality is many students of the practice (not all) are not interested in the historical context or significance of the dances they perform. There are even fewer students interested in researching these cultural symbols.[27]

Realizing that my analysis may sound harsh and unforgiving—I did say I was angry—I want to emphasize that there is much to appreciate in the *folklórico* space and the new U.S. traditions that have been forming in this practice. As Nájera-Ramírez points out, we must view the act of learning and performing Mexican folk dance in the United States in the 1970s as a political act in itself (1989). A political act in the sense that the recovery of a Chicano cultural heritage, history, and identity forces one to search outside the dominant spaces of knowledge, those political and cultural institutes that provide a sense of belonging, entitlement, and authority to the society's majority.

Indeed, as I hope my reflexive narrative makes clear, the *folklórico* group was an incredibly positive space for learning, developing talent and skills, and building community. Some of my fellow practitioners became outstanding performers and flowered into people who became successful in whatever they did in their lives. *Folklórico* gave them opportunities that may not have been available to them had they not danced. The *folklórico* group has also provided a space in which self-esteem is developed. Performing on stage for small and large audiences and having to occasionally do public speaking (introducing regional suites, costumes, and dancers) are not undemanding skills, not to mention learning how to dance, fix, mend, and make costumes, make or paint backdrops, or write up performance programs. I personally learned many technical skills for recording music, creating program soundtracks, and most importantly how to produce a *folklórico* show. But even these positive elements speak to what was lacking: Because of the little time a group spends together (rehearsals of two to three hours, two or three times a week), all the effort is directed toward creating the visual spectacle that is to be performed. There is very little or no time for research, self-reflection, or critical analysis.

I also do not want to give the impression that the *folklórico* scene lacked innovative people and work. Because *folklórico* dance works within the parameters of preservation and promotion, and as a "traditional" dance category,[28] certain types of expectations (e.g. how *folklórico* should look and sound) are placed upon participants. Nevertheless, there were moments in history in which innovation flourished. Susan Cashion and Ramón Morones, directors of Los Lupeños de San José, wrote and produced a two-hour dance drama called *Mextizol.* This work incorporated dance (modern and *folklórico*), theater, music, and poetry to reinterpret the origin story of Aztec deities Omotéotl, Tetzcatlipoca, and Quetzalcoatl, the Spanish invasion of Tenochtitlán, and the caste class condition and oppression of *el indio mexicano.* Framed within the notion of *mexicanidad*—(re)presenting and preserving the history of Mexico—it provided an interestingly nuanced articulation of that history. While it was highly innovative, it could be argued that it was not incorporated within the collective memory of the Chicano community. *Mextizol* was a work that was only performed in theaters. It was not a public piece that could be performed at a park or rally or displayed on a wall, where other Chicano artists were presenting their work.

Following the production of *Mextizol,* Los Lupeños produced other regional suites that incorporated dance and drama, as did other groups throughout the country. In 1978 at the annual ANGF conference held in Topeka, Kansas, a group of young Chicanos from Denver, Colorado, presented a work called "Main Street," an excerpt of a larger piece entitled "Cuatro épocas" (Four Eras). This work, performed by the National Chicano Dance Theater, incorporated *folklórico,* modern, and jazz dance with Chicano music, something that had never been done at this *folklórico* conference. It was the first attempt that I had witnessed to represent a Chicano identity through dance. The group was an umbrella company that included a *folklórico* (the Ballet Folklórico Nezahualcóyotl, at one point affiliated with Denver-based Rodolfo "Corky" Gonzáles and the Crusade for Justice), an ensemble that specifically incorporated African American jazz dance (the Urban Street Dancers), and other Chicano performers such as musicians and *teatristas.* According to Juan Ríos, a former member of this ensemble, Enrique Montoya, who had been a member of the Ballet Folklórico Nezahualcóyotl and had worked in Mexico with the Ballet Folklórico de México de Amalia Hernández, was the creator of this piece.[29] This represents what I am arguing for; unfortunately, this ensemble disbanded by the mid-1980s and it is unclear if their products were documented for public distribution or analysis.

Another moment in which dance provided a medium to represent Chicano experience was Luis Valdez's play *Zoot Suit.* Presented under the rubric of *teatro* (and eventually film), dance was a central focus in the play (specifically a Chicano dance style that *pachucos*[30] created and practiced in the

1940s). The play also created some momentum for dancers like Juan Ríos and Miguel Delgado (who participated in the play and movie) to choreograph dance suites for classes they were teaching and for ensembles with which they were working. But unlike the dance *cuadros* (suites) from Jalisco or Veracruz, jitterbug, swing, and mambo were an ephemeral moment for the very few *folklóricos* that performed these dances—again, too short for public distribution, analysis, and memory.

Chicanidad and *Mexicanidad*

Throughout this article I have brought up the terms "*chicanidad*" and "*mexicanidad*" without any discussion. I consider *mexicanidad* as the manner in which Mexican culture is imagined and sustained continuously through family or sociocultural ties or through Mexican cultural practice and performance that is in dialogue with, or is included in a transnational network that connects to, a context in Mexico. The latter notion is exemplified by the transnational networks of mariachi musicians found in locations such as Los Angeles and San José, California, or Atlanta, Georgia, which maintain strong ties to Mexican locations such as Guadalajara, Jalisco, and Mexico City. Some U.S.-born musicians have become integrated into these networks yet have never worked or lived in the Mexico locations. Nevertheless, through the recontextualization of the practice and the process of transmission—through apprenticeship training with *mexicano* musicians, for example—*mexicanidad* may be the sole foundation in their approach to cultural expression and possibly to their identity formation. In addition to their close interaction with *mexicano* musicians, these U.S.-born musicians are often submerged within the *mexicano* community through their role as mariachi musicians. Not only providing music for religious Masses, weddings, *quinceañeras, serenatas,* and *mañanitas*[31] for a birthday or a saint's day, the U.S. musicians become incorporated and establish an understanding and relationship to the traditions, processes, and practices for these cultural events. As a central participant in such occasions, the U.S. *mariachera/o*[32] contributes and helps define these events that sustain *lo mexicano.*

Aside from the performance settings, participation in social spaces—playing *fútbol* (soccer), attending social events with their *compañeros,* establishing friendships with the *mexicano* musicians—provide other means to sustain *lo mexicano.* It is within this context, which is most often contained within a large *mexicano* community, that the U.S. musicians—specifically those of Mexican descent who have attained their knowledge as mariachi musicians through an apprenticeship process—identify as *mexicano,* embracing and engaging the idea of *mexicanidad.* However, I suggest that Mexicano identity is just one of several identities the U.S. musicians maintain, knowing that they also go through a U.S. educational system, have engaged political and social spaces, and have most likely experienced the popular culture that U.S. society provides.[33] Nevertheless, it is often the case that these musicians will publicly identify as *mexicanos.*

Before addressing the notion of *chicanidad,* it would be helpful to provide some discussion on the formation of Chicano identity in the 1960s and 1970s, which was framed within the concept of political and cultural nationalism. Carlos Muñoz explains how activists/cultural producers such as Luis Valdez and Corky Gonzáles proposed ideology at the first Chicano Youth Conference hosted by Gonzáles's organization Crusade for Justice. In addition to fomenting a political stance of "building nationalism in an era of imperialism,"[34] the conference would make clear that a cultural component to the Chicano movement was just as important. Muñoz states, "From the ranks of this new breed of youth would come the poets, the writers and the artists necessary for the forging of the new Chicano identity. This new identity would base itself on symbols of traditional Mexican culture and would reflect a total rejection of *gabacho* culture—the culture of the white Anglo-Saxon Protestant" (1989, 76). Understanding Muñoz's statement I want to emphasize that the "new identity would base itself on symbols of traditional Mexican culture." However, we have to recognize that expression and culture from other ethnic communities also contribute to Chicano identity and the emerging voices that represent the Chicano experience in the United States. *Chicanidad* is very much tied to the concept of *mexicanidad* in the sense that the latter serves as a foundation to the former. Nevertheless, *chicanidad(es)* is often seen as working "within" *mexicanidad(es),* as Claire Joysmith assesses. She states, in a response to an article by literary critic Norm Klahn,

> [I]n this case [that Chicana writers and poetics want to be read in their difference], the status of the audience as "outsiders" yet within those very *mexicanidades* that Chicana writers/writings lay claim to as constituting a signifier of difference in a U.S. cultural site, exemplified a (dis)location problematizing issues of inclusion/exclusion, among several others. Because the concept of *mexicanidad* has remained monolithic and singular in Mexico as a cultural location until very recently (neozapatista discursivity, for instance, has contributed toward pluralizing it), the participation of and positionality of *chicanidad(es)* within *mexicanidad*(es) is an issue scarcely addressed textually, academically, and theoretically from the specificity of Mexico as a cultural location. (2003, 148)

I agree with Joysmith that if one positions *chicanidad(es)* within *mexicanidades*, that Chicana literature or any Chicana/o expression would be "scarcely addressed . . . from the specificity of Mexico as a cultural location." What it sets up is the relationship of Chicano cultural practitioners to always be expected to look to Mexico as a source of cultural expression, leaving the Mexican cultural producers and practitioners as the unquestionable authorities. Américo Paredes recognized this predicament as the result of both a "diffusionist" and "regionalist" view of Mexican American folklore.[35] He stated that the diffusionist view of Mexican American folklore is seen "as a slight isolated ripple, moving far from its origin in the great waves of Mexican folk culture. . . . The converse of the Hispanophile opinion, it regards Mexican American folklore as in no way different, original, or important, since it is merely a collection of decayed chips scattered from the trunk. We might perhaps find a few variants of texts well known in Mexico, variants which would serve as footnotes to Mexican folklore. That would be about all. Most native Mexican folklorists have viewed Mexican American folklore in this way, as the detritus of Mexican folklore, when they have taken it into account at all" (1993, 5).

If *mexicanos*, folklorists, and academics even recognize *chicanidad*, it is as an extension of *mexicanidad*, rather than as its *own* entity. Instead, if we were to think about expressions, ideologies, and practices regarded as *mexicanidad(es)* as foundational influences on Chicano expression, in the same manner that U.S. popular culture and the expressions of neighboring communities (e.g., African American, Asian American, and so on) influence Chicanos, Mexicanos along with Chicanos will possibly identify the cultural developments that represent and give voice to a Chicano community. Also it is important to understand that just as *mexicanidad* can be maintained, searched for, and desired by non-*mexicanos*, *chicanidad* is enhanced by the participation of many people, Chicanos and non-Chicanos alike. Good examples of expressive culture that illuminate this dynamic and could be framed within *chicanidad* are the products of the musical groups Quetzal and Ozomatli, where the membership is not solely Chicano and the groups as a whole may not identify as a Chicano ensemble; however, songs like "Chicana Skies" (Quetzal 1998), "The Social Relevance of Public Art" (Quetzal 2000), "La Misma Canción" (Ozomatli 1997), and "Guerrillero"[36] (Ozomatli 2002) come out of an experience and memory of living and working collectively within a Chicano community (that is, a U.S. context of ethnic Mexicans).

These musicians, like their predecessors in the Chicano movement, experienced the cultural expressions of Mexico as a process of rediscovery. Rosa-

Linda Fregoso's examination of Chicana/o film culture of this era provides a useful analytical frame based on Stuart Hall's notion of "imagined re-discovery." She states, "The short films of this early period are *actos* of 'imaginative re-discovery'[37] because they work to 're-invent,' 're-cover,' and 're-vision' a 'lost' history of Chicanas and Chicanos" (1993, 1). *Folklóricos* have engaged in the processes of re-covering and re-invention; however, I question if the notion of "re-vision" has been sincerely engaged in this practice.

Llegando a lo Chicano[38]

Like *folklóricos, teatristas* (theater troupes) engaged in different aspects of Mexican culture but, through the notion of "imagined re-discovery," processed them within a Chicano frame, taking ownership by re-envisioning the expression. Examining the work of Luis Valdez we can see that two of the most obvious *mexicano* cultural entities utilized were the music form of the *corrido* and pre-Cortesian mythology. Focusing on the *corrido,* the storytelling musical form, it becomes apparent that it easily lends itself to rediscovery, reinvention, and revision in representing subjugated stories and historical events, specifically by Chicanos. Paredes, who recognized the value of the musical form as an expression of empowerment for Chicanos, states, "For thousands of young Chicanos today, so intent on maintaining their cultural identity and demanding their rights, the Border *corrido* hero will strike a responsive chord when he risks life, liberty and material goods *defendiendo su derecho*"[39] (1976, xviii). Valdez, like Paredes, saw this form not only as an expression of empowerment but also as a strategic tool for attaining attention for the telling of the Chicano story, as well as for developing new innovations in theater.

The full-length medley piece *La Gran Carpa de los Rasquachis*[40] (aired on PBS as "*El Corrido*") is a great example of how Valdez utilized the musical and poetic form of the *corrido.* This collective piece specifically develops a theatrical movement around the character of Jesús Pelado Rasquachi. However, unlike Paredes' "border *corrido* hero," Valdez focuses on the issue of oppressed farm workers and their continuous struggle for survival in the United States.[41] Taking a union stance, Valdez illustrates the traumatic experience of *mexicanos* crossing the border, working in fields, raising a family in a foreign environment, enduring cultural and generational disparity with one's children, falling short economically, asking for government aid, and dying without dignity as possibilities because of a choice not to join the union. Throughout the play, the *corrido* is interjected as a narrative tool to set up each scene.

The centrality of oppression resonates with the Chicano experience, whether in fields, factories, rural areas, cities, homes, or institutions. Jesús Pelado is constantly reminded that he is at the bottom of the social ladder. First there is *el patrón,* then there is *el patroncito,* then you! *El pelado.*[42] The rupture of *actos* between verses of the *corrido* and the inclusion of race and class issues that directly index the Mexican U.S. experience are ways in which Valdez utilizes the Mexican cultural expression to make it his own and to process it as Chicano. *La Gran Carpa de los Rasquachis* is a popular work that has had commercial and critical success as well as scholarly attention, implanting it into a collective memory that influences the development of history, identity, and culture for Chicana/os.

In the same way Valdez has utilized Mexican expressions and has redeveloped them to represent a Chicano experience, musicians like Los Lobos have also learned Mexican folk forms and, after working within a frame of preservation and promotion for many years, developed a voice and a well-recognized body of work that integrates their experiences as U.S. rock, R&B, blues, and Mexican musicians. David Hidalgo shared that it was the song "Be Still," from the album *The Neighborhood,* in which they consciously brought their diverse experiences together in an experimental manner to produce an original hybrid work. The group was concerned with how people would respond to their decision to mix Mexican traditional sounds with other styles; as Hidalgo put it, "I wasn't sure, I felt weird about it, if it's out of line or not, but it might be cool and open up another way of playing, another avenue to combine things."[43] As a result, Los Lobos maintains a vast repertoire of cool "combined things" that speak volumes to the Chicano experience.

Another example is how many Chicano muralists—while developing a Chicano aesthetic in the plastic arts—grounded much of their artistic techniques in layout, color, and mediums on what Mexican artists such as José Clemente Orozco, David Siqueiros, Rufino Tamayo, and Diego Rivera established. More important, Chicanos fervently grasped the ideology that "public art" should always address sociopolitical issues, which these Mexicano artist shared. It is this latter ideology that Chicano activist/artists leave as a legacy explicit in their work, which fortifies the Chicano cultural memory. Thematically, however, the work of muralist collectives such as ASCO, The Street Scapers, and Los Four index a Chicano experience, history, and culture of the United States as opposed to that of Mexico.[44]

Possibilities for Dance (Chicana/o)

It was not until I left the space of the *folklórico* groups that I began to realize different possibilities for working within and reinterpreting traditional music and dance. I would like to present one alternative to the *folklórico* group that I think provides a different type of frame, one that permits Chicana/os to be more creative and innovative within the realms of traditional Mexican dance and music.

Today throughout California there are Chicana/o cultural producers participating in a dialogue with different communities and groups of *jarocho* musicians/dancers from the state of Veracruz. Unlike earlier generations of ethnic Mexicans interested in learning and performing Mexican dance, this current group is focused on the *son* as an expression of music, song, and dance that cannot be separated from each other or from an understanding of the social context, the *fandango,* where these expressions are practiced.[45] Also, by framing this interaction as a *mexicana/o* and Chicana/o dialogue, many of the Chicana/o participants understand that they are not learning *jarocho* music so that they can become torch bearers of the tradition, envisioning the quandary that Kelly (1992) warns us about, but to complement their own cultural understanding and self-expression as dancers, musicians, muralists, actors, or writers. Still, there is an emphasis on developing a strong foundation in the *son,* understanding how the *jarocha/os* visualize their tradition, and being respectful of that vision.

For Chicana/o musicians there is a desire to participate in the *fandango,* taking care in learning the etiquette of performance at this event (which *sones* are danced by partners or which are danced only by women, and so on). There now exist *fandangos* that recreate a cultural setting in which the *son* can be practiced in the United States. This recontextualization of the *fandango* has provided a tool for Chicanos not only to practice the *son* but to develop and affirm community locally, nationally, and transnationally. Unlike *folklórico,* the *fandango* provides a context in which members of the audience are expected to openly participate in the festivity, dance, and music. By blurring the lines of performer and spectator, new conditions are set up so that many more participants are actively involved in constructing the memories of the event, contributing to the process of cultural and identity formation.

In addition to recontextualizing the *fandango,* groups like Quetzal, Ozomatli, Los Otros, Ollín, Candela, and Pochosón have been creative in utilizing the influence of the *son* in writing original music. Martha González of the group Quetzal offers a great example of developing a foundation in Mexican folk dance and music tradition and utilizing it as a basis for her own original compositions. The composition "Planta de los pies," from Quetzal's recording *Worksongs* (2003), provides a model in which the concepts of learning, practicing, and creating (re-cover, re-invent, and re-vision) are employed to develop a new composition within the frame of Chicanidad.[46] González states:

> The *cadencia* of the foot patterns is typical *fandanguero*;[47] specifically they are an original rendition of the *café con pan* . . .
>
> What makes this *zapateado* unusual, however, is that it is in a nontraditional eleven-beat meter. The lyrics reflect my departure from tradition: *Aunque tanto a mí me gusten los colores de su son, siento propia mi cadencia pues el chicano siempre inventa.*[48]

González thus disrupts the "traditional" dance-step groove (which she refers to as *cadencia*, specific to the *son* "La morena") by shifting the meter. She does this by cutting one beat from a four-bar phrase in 3/4 time to re-establish her groove as a single-bar phrase in 11/4 time (understand that one 12/4 bar would be the same as four bars of 3/4), an odd phrasing that may take a while to feel since the groove is *descuadrado* (not squared off). However, González shifts the pattern on beat 9 to deal with the odd feeling of the dance step (see Table 19.1).

More important is González's message to the *jarocho* explaining that we, as Chicanos, need to embrace the way we feel the groove, the rhythm, which is a musical and social statement. The lyrics that precede those quoted above also contain an intriguing interrogation of *chicanidad, Cinco y seis son once, el tiempo de mi compás / Señores, no se asusten, estoy aquí y no allá.*[49] The statement "*estoy aquí y no allá*" is a rupture or distancing from the Chicano notion *no soy de aquí, ni de allá*,[50] which Chicanos have embraced to illustrate their situation as being binationally discriminated: in the United States for

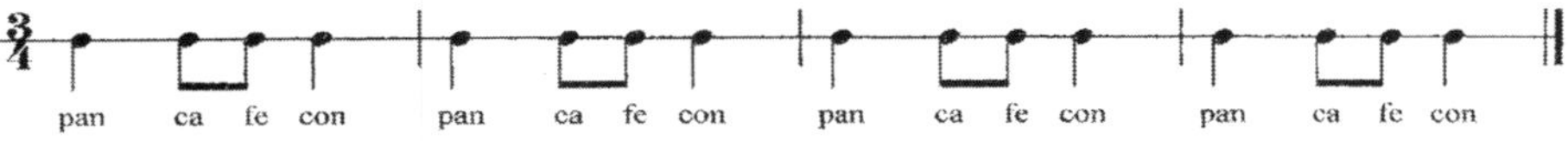

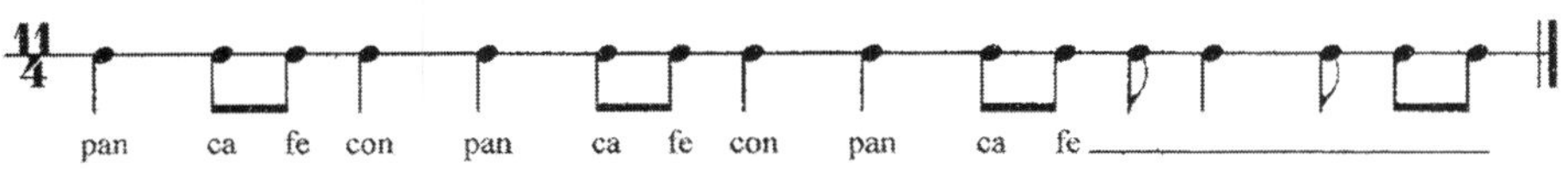

Table 19.1: Martha González's departure from traditional phrasing (see also Table 20.2, p. 371).

being of Mexican descent and in Mexico for being born in the United States. González, embracing a U.S. citizenship, explicates a necessary re-vision of *chicanidad* within the United States, through a mutual dialogue with Mexico, continuing the process as re-imagined discovery keeping our memories in practice; "*pues el chicano siempre inventa.*"[51]

Conclusion

Folklórico has developed into a widely recognized cultural expression in the United States that has created a space for the development of talent, self-esteem, and community building. Unfortunately, it has been largely ignored by academics as a serious topic of research and has been (mis)understood more for its spectacle rather than its positioning in U.S. society. I have argued that the practice of Mexican dance, or *folklórico,* in the United States was developed from the momentum of the Chicano artistic movement and was an important part of this movement. Because it has been framed solely as an expression of *mexicanidad,* however, there does not exist a *direct* contribution to Chicano history, identity, or culture. In addition, because of the desire to preserve *mexicanidad* within the *folklórico,* the form is seen only as an extension of a Mexican expression, blurring the contributions of the U.S. *folklórico* experience. Unlike *folklórico,* other cultural expressions such as Chicano *teatro,* murals, poetry, and music, which emerged from the same era and started with the same desires of engagement with *lo mexicano,* have traced a trajectory in which individuals and collectives, through a process of imagined rediscovery, have recontextualized the Mexican expressions to produce cultural products and events that constitute a Chicano collective memory.

This chapter also presents the reflections of a disillusioned *folklórico* dancer who targets this expression to illustrate how the lack of self-analysis and critique of the method of preservation and promotion has possibly hindered any type of dance developments that may have contributed to constituting Chicano history, culture, and identity. At the same time, this chapter, more importantly, was produced to illuminate some of the history and individuals that have unquestionably given energy to this grand movement and have contributed to the success, failure, and survival of this expression in the San José area, which was undeniably one of the hubs of *folklórico* in the 1970s.

Notes

1. "Each generation has the right to express its interpretation of art and only time and the people will judge its value" (cited in Cashion 1985). I would like to thank the editors for their comments, criticisms, tireless efforts in editing such a project, and

for providing this opportunity to write about something that is dear to my heart. A special thanks to Olga Nájera-Ramírez for her incredible mentoring and to Alicia Nájera for her love and support. I dedicate this work to all the wonderful dancers I have had the opportunity to work with, but most appreciatively to my mother Theresa Rodríguez, who created a space not only for me but for hundreds of children and young adults to experience *folklórico,* this culturally rich U.S. expression.

2. For an in-depth discussion on *folklórico,* see Nájera-Ramírez 1989 and her essay in this volume (chapter 16).

3. Gutiérrez (1995) utilizes the term "ethnic Mexican" to include all people of Mexican descent, regardless of the differing terms they may use to define themselves.

4. National Association of Folklórico Dance Groups.

5. The term ASCO translates as "disgust" or "nausea"; when someone states, "me da asco," it means, "I find it nauseating or disgusting." This visual art collective, by embracing this very common term to represent them, exhibits irony and sarcasm, but more importantly illuminates how Chicanos resignified terms and ideas that became recontextualized spatially and temporally.

6. Eduardo Robledo, telephone communication with author, June 14, 2005.

7. Eduardo Robledo, interview with the author, San José, California, March 5, 1996.

8. Nájera-Ramírez's 1989 essay "Social and Political Dimensions of Folklórico Dance" has been the only serious critical examination of *folklórico* available for many years. In addition to this, the short-lived *ANGF Journal* provides some historical narratives and analyses.

9. As a child unaware of identity politics, I did not understand the maintenance of multiple identities, which I believe many of the *folklóricos* did, specifically those at universities and those who were political activists. What I understood was that claiming to be Mexican during this time was political, yet claiming to be Chicano was radical. I was more concerned with maintaining what I thought was tradition, and I saw Chicanos, at the time, as distorting that tradition.

10. "white, Anglo-Saxon Protestant"

11. *Jarabe* translates to "cough syrup," but refers to the mixture of ingredients that compose the syrup. *Jarabe* is also a musical genre that is characterized by the mixture of melodies and rhythms that compose a musical selection. The songs would translate as the "Michoacan Jarabe," "The Bottle," [and] "The Rib."

12. Literally the "big harp ensemble," but in practice is a four- to five-piece ensemble—two violins, harp, the *guitarra de golpe* (a five-string rhythm guitar also referred to as a *quinta* or *jarana*) or *vihuela* (a small five-string guitar with a convex back)—found in Michoacán and parts of Jalisco. For samples of recordings and a further description of this ensemble, see *Conjunto de Arpa Grande Arpex (2006).*

13. For examples and a discussion on Chicano movement music, see *Rolas de Aztlán: Songs of the Chicano Movement* (2005).

14. "litany in Chicano slang"

15. "may he rest in peace"

16. *Zapateando* comes from *zapatear* (rooted in *zapato,* or shoe) to do footwork in a tap-dance manner, but Mexican *zapateado* is not about tapping your feet as much as it is energetically and precisely utilizing heel, toe, and flat foot stomps, sweeps, brushes, and kicks.

17. The *son* (pl. *sones*) is the regional music form that incorporates song lyrics, music, and dance, typically played on instruments of the specific region. Thus, *sones hustecos* (and also *huapangos*) are from the Huastec region of Mexico. "El querreque" translates to "woodpecker" (the word *querreque* represents the sound that the bird makes when burrowing), "La rosa" "The rose," [and] "El caballito" "The Little Horse." For samples of recordings and further description of this music, see Los Camperos de Valles 2005.

18. The *jarana huasteca* is a small five-string rhythm guitar tuned in thirds. The *huapanguera* is an eight-string, five-course guitar, closer in size to a regular guitar, which fills in the lower harmonic structure of the ensemble. The *huapanguera* is a rhythmic guitar whose player can also *pespuntear,* that is, play melodic lines that outline the chordal patterns.

19. Because of the lack of city funding, Los Mestizos depended on dues and monies from performances to pay their instructors and sustain themselves as a group. In the early 1970s finding a school to offer its cafeteria as rehearsal space was pretty simple. This would change in the late 1970s when school districts' budgets were strained, specifically after California passed Proposition 13.

20. *Compadre* literally translates to "co-parenting." It is a word used for a parent of a child and the godparent of the same child to make reference to each other.

21. "polkas, schottisches, and waltzes"

22. Xochipilli became well-established in the community, along with other groups such as Los Mestizos. Both groups would have their day as being very impressive performance ensembles on the *folklórico* scene in San José.

23. For accounts of the farm workers movement, see Griswold del Castillo and García 1995 and García 1989; for the Chicano power movement and the Chicano student movement see Muñoz 1989.

24. *Sones jarochos* are from the Sotavento region along the Gulf of Mexico in southern Veracruz.

25. "The Troubadors of the Coast"

26. Susan Cashion, personal communications with the author, Stanford, California, April 23, 1996; Los Altos, California, November 11, 1996; Ramón Morones, personal communications with the author, Los Altos, California, November 11, 1996.

27. There are very few skills shared between *folklóricos* on how to do research, document movement or music, or analyze collected materials. One reason is that many of the *folklórico* teachers and directors themselves lack these skills (again, not all).

28. I thank Chicano dancer JohnAvalos (aka Juan Ríos) (telephone communications, June 14, 2005) for reminding me of this point. Juan Ríos changed his name to JohnAvalos in 2007.

29. JohnAvalos, telephone communications with the author, June 14, 2005.

30. *Pachuco* refers to the streetwise Chicanos of the 1940s era, who established, through a resisting character, new styles and aesthetics that pertained to a Chicano experience in the United States. See Burciaga, "Pachucos and the Taxicab Brigade" (1995), for a brief but superb discussion on *pachucos,* zoot suiters, and their predecessors.

31. "coming out celebrations for fifteen-year-old girls, evening serenades, and morning serenades"

32. "female and male mariachi musicians"

33. See Rodríguez 2006.

34. Muñoz (1989, 76) cites Gonzáles's speech presented at the Chicano Youth Conference (printed in Steiner 1970, 385).

35. This specific article presents an analysis of three views of Mexican American folklore. The third not listed above is the Hispanophile, which simply put, recognizes Spain as the main source of Mexican American folklore.

36. "The Same Song" and "Warrior."

37. Fregoso footnotes the citation for the term "imaginative re-discovery" from Stuart Hall (1989, 68–81).

38. Translation of the subhead: "Arriving at what is Chicano"

39. "defending his rights"

40. *The Big Tent [Theater] of the Underdogs.* See Tomás Ybarra-Frausto's "Rasquachismo: A Chicano Sensibility" (1991); also Amalia Mesa-Bains' "'Domesticana': The Sensibility of Chicana Rasquache" (1999) for a further discussion on *rasquachismo.*

41. For a full analysis of this specific work, see Huerta 1982.

42. Paraphrase of a line in La Carpa de los Rasquaches: First there is "the boss," then there is "the little boss," then you! "the pauper." Throughout the play Jesús Pelado is reminded of this hierarchy whether he is crossing the border, working in the fields, in the welfare line, and so on.

43. David Hidalgo, filmed interview with author, San Francisco, California, December, 2000.

44. I want to thank visual artists José Ramírez for sharing with me much of his personal experience and his knowledge of the cultural history of Chicano artists.

45. Generally speaking, earlier generations of dancers were interested in learning solely the dance of Veracruz, as were musicians mostly interested in learning and performing the music. Since the *fandango,* the social event in which the *son* was practiced, had all but disappeared in the 1970s, the *son* dance expression existed mostly in *folklórico* spaces, and musicians were often found in commodified contexts such as restaurants and bars.

46. For more details about the composition, see González's essay in this anthology (chapter 20).

47. "of the *jarocho fandango* context"

48. "We identify with [jarocho] music, the colors of your *son.* We, however, have our own cadence we feel and execute as Chicanos."

49. "Five plus six is eleven, the time meter of my measure / People, don't get scared (offended), I'm over here and not there" (my translation).

50. "I am neither from here nor there."

51. Though González translates this line "we feel and execute as Chicanos," the word *inventa* (invent) is appropriate, for it makes clear that our search and research for history, cultural expression, heritage, and identity is continuous and in motion.

20

Zapateado Afro-Chicana *Fandango* Style

Self-Reflective Moments in Zapateado

MARTHA GONZÁLEZ

Introduction

Both music and dance have been a driving force in my life since my early childhood, beginning with *música mexicana* and *ballet folklórico mexicano.*[1] Free after-school programs and schools of the arts provided most of my dance and musical training as a child. In addition, performing with my family gave me considerable musical practice. As an adult, I discovered my interest in dance and the rhythms of Africa while attending the University of California, Los Angeles (UCLA), where I graduated with a degree in ethnomusicology. Yet it was not until I traveled to Veracruz, Mexico, that I was exposed to the *zapateado fandanguero*[2] and the people who practice it as culture. The culmination of my experiences with dance and musical traditions from around the world has given birth to a dance style that I call Zapateado Afro-Chicana/o Fandanguero.

The *zapateado,*[3] percussive dancing on a wooden platform, is a form of the *fandango,* which is thought to have begun in Spain around the seventeenth century as a dance of courtship.[4] While the *fandango*'s original birthplace is not known, it is believed that its roots are in Africa. Antonio García de León (2003) states that the word "*fandango*" is believed to derive from the Bantu word *fanda,* which means "fiesta."

The *zapateado* is relevant visually as well as sonically, emphasizing the art of improvisation. Syncopated, rhythmic stomping and tapping of the feet are used in *zapateado* as an essential percussive element of the *son,* music traditionally associated with the *zapateado.* The *son* is a combination of Spanish,

African, and indigenous musical traditions, and Veracruz's style of the *son* is known as *son jarocho*[5] or *son veracruzano.*

When I am composing *zapateado* foot patterns, they are based on the traditional musical rhythms from Veracruz. Yet being a Chicana, born and raised in East Los Angeles, is and continues to be the lens through which I humbly offer this highly personal perspective on *zapateado* and its impact on me. In this chapter, I will reflect on dance and musical experiences throughout my life in order to demonstrate the influence they have had in my compositions, and to take the reader through my progression from avid student to novice composer.

My Life before *Zapateado*

MÚSICA EN MI FAMILIA[6]

I was born to immigrant parents from México. My mother was from Tijuana and my father was born and raised in Guadalajara, Jalisco. Ironically, they met in Los Angeles, California, in the United States and married in Guadalajara, Jalisco, in Mexico. They met, like many other couples, in the *bailes* (dances) that the newly arrived immigrants frequented in downtown Los Angeles hotel ballrooms such as the Alexandria.[7] They settled in Los Angeles and immediately started a family. My father was very particular about the influence of American culture. He did not allow English or anything he couldn't understand in his home. He was an aspiring singer and listened to old *corridos*[8] and Mexican crooner hits. At an early age my brother, sisters, and I were exposed to the music of Jorge Negrete, Javier Solís, Lucha Villa, José Alfredo Jiménez, Amalia Mendoza, and Vicente Fernández. My mother, on the other hand, liked Pérez Prado, Estelita Núñez, Chayito Valdez, Chelo Silva, Juan Gabriel, and Roció Durcal. Music was at the center of our cultural experience. My father owned a guitar and a shiny black wall piano, neither of which he knew how to play. Just a few years after they married, my parents had a total of four children in the family. Never able to pursue his dream of establishing a musical career, my father became extremely depressed and turned to the bottle.

Some of my first childhood memories of my father are of him sitting on the floor, intoxicated, gazing at the record player and conducting imaginary musicians and singers. Sometimes my brother, my sisters, and I would be told to sit on the couch and listen. My father would then pretend to sing to a large audience. At times he would make *us* sing to the music. He soon found that Gabriel, my older brother, had natural talent and thus my father spent the next few years vicariously living through Gabriel's musical success.

My uncle, Fernando Hernández, was a small-time Mexican promoter. He saw my brother's potential and ushered him into contests and singing engagements. My brother participated in the *variedades,* or variety shows, that came through California. Such shows would often stop off at the historic Million Dollar Theater in downtown L.A. Gabriel was soon on bills with some of the most respected Mexican artists at the time, the very same artists we had mimicked years earlier.

My sister and I were soon encouraged to join my brother by singing *segunda* (harmony),[9] and our show became known as Gabrielito González, La Actuación Infantil (the Children's Act). Lucha Villa, Mercedes Castro, Aída Cuevas, Vicente Fernández, Federico Villa, and Yolanda del Rió were some of the artists we had the privilege of opening for. I still remember exploring the Million Dollar Theater, running on sticky floors through back stage wings, and dodging rattraps. The smell of stale popcorn and nachos lingered in the air as we listened to the mariachis tune up in the basement. The house mariachi was Mariachi América de Miguel Marquez, and in my brother's best interest my father would bring the mariachis a bottle of *tequila* to keep them happy and have them play well.

Gabrielito González was soon known as "*la sensación infantíl, con el auténtico sentimiento mexicano.*"[10] His birthplace was concealed at first, since he was born in Los Angeles and the record company that signed him felt his birthplace would turn off Mexican patrons who were *ranchera* fans. A lot of his work, and film roles in particular, mostly took place in Mexico, and with

The Million Dollar Theatre marquee. Photograph from the personal collection of Martha González's family.

La Actuación Infantil in the Million Dollar Theatre (*left to right*): Gabriel, Martha, and Claudia Tenorio González. Photograph from the personal collection of Martha González's family.

no child labor protection acts in Mexico and my father's drunken permission, my brother worked like a dog from the time he was nine to eleven years old, frequently missing school, traveling, doing late-night gigs, and filming. My mother was always around, but she was submissive in those days. My father's word was always final. Although she worried tremendously about my brother, she would mostly deal with her daughters, combing our hair, applying makeup, and making our skirts. I am saddened when I think about these times, for although these experiences were rich in music and culture, I knew my family was falling apart. My father's drinking worsened and he became extremely abusive. After many years of a turbulent home life, losing a home and living in and out of our relative's garages and trailers, my mother finally asked my father to leave. After the divorce, my father tried to keep in touch but soon lost his battle with alcoholism and one day disappeared into the streets of East Los Angeles. It was up to my mother to raise four children. Although my father was absent for the rest of my life, I inherited most of my musical interest from him. My father was always the anti-American enforcer in the household. Once he left, my mother began to allow mainstream U.S. culture, its music and ideas, to slowly stream into our home.

As we grew older and had no money for formal music training or education, my mother sought out free extracurricular activities, most of them being art- and music-related. Sports always required some sort of expensive uniform or equipment. If it had anything to do with music, art, dance, or drama, my mother would sign us up. I, along with my brothers and sisters, were a part of many after-school and weekend arts and enrichment programs, some of which offered *ballet folklórico mexicano.*

MUSIC, DANCE, AND THE RETURN OF JOY

Like many children of Mexican immigrant parents, Spanish was my first language. I was in a bilingual kindergarten class, but I was soon thrown into a strictly English classroom. I feel that this early disruptive experience set me up to struggle through the rest of my formal education and contributed to my nervousness as a child.

My first *ballet folklórico* instructor was my fifth grade teacher at Lorena Street School, Ms. Helen Stringos, a Greek American. Ms. Stringos was a talented singer and dancer who taught one of the few classes for gifted students. Although I did not have the grades or the academic skills to be in her class, my brother and I were considered "gifted" because of our performance abilities. Ms. Stringos devoted her life to her students after school and on weekends. She loved the arts, spoke Spanish, and knew *folklórico* well. She taught us many dances from different regions of Mexico, including Jalisco, Chiapas, Nayarit, and, my favorite, Veracruz. My brother, my sister, and I spent these years rehearsing after school, learning a plethora of songs and dances, performing for school assemblies, musical theater shows, and convalescent homes. Ms. Helen Stringos, with all her love, devotion, great talent, and encouragement, redefined my concept of music and performance art.

COMFORT IN SILENCE

During this period I took an interest in pantomime and studied with a mime instructor at the Saturday Conservatory. I vividly recall when he took the class to witness the genius of his French professor, Marcel Marceau. I was mesmerized by the way Marceau was able to transform himself into a complete story and take you with him in silence. I was inspired to be a mime artist, taking as many mime classes as the conservatory offered and putting everything I had into practicing the techniques. Similarly, my main focus at

Bancroft Junior High School Magnet and Los Angeles County High School for the Arts (LACHSA) was theater. Mime and mask, Kabuki,[11] and stage combat were the courses in which I felt the most confident. What appealed to me about pantomime was the silence. I did not want to speak. Many aspects of U.S. culture still felt foreign to me. Through mime I was able to take whatever skills I could from both schools and graduate quietly.

PUBLIC HOUSING AND THE SOUNDS OF L.A.

During the early 1980s and through my older cousins, I was exposed to rap, b-boying, break dancing,[12] and poplocking.[13] These various forms of self-expression were all very popular in the projects. This was also my first encounter with a wide variety of popular mainstream U.S. music, from Led Zeppelin, AC/DC, Earth, Wind and Fire, R&B, the Oldies, and The Huggie Boy Show to hip-hop and rap. This was an exciting time.

My cousins lived with my *tía* Esther in the William Mead Homes projects, otherwise known as Dog Town,[14] just northeast of Downtown L.A. and Olvera Street. Although Dog Town was a notoriously violent neighborhood, we would hang out in the patios and "battle" each other, testing our skills at breaking and poplocking, while listening to whatever radio station was blaring out of someone's apartment.

Much of the music was highly rhythmic in nature with strong beats and grooving bass lines, which was what attracted me to the art of poplocking. The isolation of body parts, the grace of the moves, and the reliance on imagination were all required to battle an opponent. I found it all exhilarating and became quite good at it.

FINDING MY OWN VOICE

I never thought I would revisit the skills of my childhood as an adult, but then I joined the band Quetzal while I was a student in the ethnomusicology department at UCLA. As a teenager, I had had a brief stint with the Hollywood record industry that left me very disillusioned. I refused to dress "sexy," which resulted in my being fired from bands, and when I was not fired I quit for the same reason. The frustration I felt with the entertainment industry took me back to my pain as a young child, and once again, I turned away from pursuing music as an expression.

The first time I heard the band Quetzal was at Troy Café, a coffee shop in L.A.'s Little Tokyo. It was a small space with brick walls, a counter, and a tiny stage. The minute I heard their music I was home. Quetzal melded together lyrics in English and Spanish without sounding contrived. The band also featured a violin, which I found to be extremely unusual and inspiring. Their singer, Lilia Hernández, sang a song called "Agua de la Manguera"[15] beautifully. I related to their distinctly Mexican and U.S. influences, seeing them as a Chicano[16] version of 10,000 Maniacs.[17]

A year later, encouraged by my cousin, I auditioned for the Department of Ethnomusicology at UCLA. My interest in this program was largely due to its focus on world music and classes based on study and performance. In addition, ethnomusicology's emphasis on culture as the medium through which music is expressed and shaped directed me toward my future in the performing arts. Although I did not read Western musical notation, my audition emphasized my knowledge and practice of popular Mexican music.

Once admitted into UCLA's ethnomusicology program, I had the opportunity to absorb the music and dance of Ghana and to study drumming and dances from Cuba. The study of these two particular genres was enlightening, because they both made no distinction between the dance and the music. One is essential to the performance of the other; specific drumbeats signal certain dance movements and vice versa.[18] Additionally, a drummer may have to interpret spontaneous movements of the dancer (Loza 1979, 45).

It was during this time that I joined Quetzal, which gave me a chance to cultivate my talent as a singer, dancer, and percussionist as the band developed as a whole. Moreover, performing with Quetzal greatly complemented my studies. Much of what I learned in the classroom found its way into my performances with Quetzal, incorporating music and influences from the African diaspora or Mexico.

Up to this point, most of what I knew as a singer was through imitation. I had never had formal training to develop my own voice. Suddenly, I was faced with the challenge of finding this hidden voice. I was encouraged by my band to not only sing what I felt but also to write lyrics and melodies. Having been a nervous and traumatized child that found refuge in mime, I was being asked to say something in my own way. After some struggle and reflecting on my studies and my childhood, I soon found that I had many things to say with words, with movement, and with rhythm.

Zapateado Gives Birth

SON JAROCHO AND EL NUEVO MOVIMIENTO JARANERO

In a collaborative project with Chicana cellist and performance artist Maria Elena Gaitan,[19] my band and I discovered that a movement had recently begun to restore *son jarocho* music to its traditional sound. Maria Elena shared with us a tape of Mono Blanco, a band from Veracruz, Mexico, that was at the forefront of this movement. Before this introduction, our only exposure to *son jarocho*[20] had been recordings of the more popularized versions of the *son* made by virtuosos like Lino Chávez.

Son jarocho is festive music, using numerous stringed instruments and incorporating dance and song/poetry, which is characteristic of the villages and small cities of southern Veracruz. This region is *son jarocho*'s birthplace, created out of community celebrations like the *fandango*, where everyone is encouraged to play an instrument, sing, and dance. Yet due to its commercialization, *son jarocho* adopted a faster tempo and altered cadences for the popular market (Salas Peña 2002, 32).

During the 1970s, communities in Veracruz began their efforts to recover their history and culture through workshops and classes. Gilberto Gutiérrez, Juan Pascoe, and Arcadio Hidalgo of the group Mono Blanco were largely responsible for the resurgence of the *son jarocho* (see Pascoe 2003). Mono Blanco, Son de Madera, Chuchumbé, Los Vega, and Los Cojolites represent the few families that have taken their skills to the stage. Such groups are dedicated to bringing *son jarocho fandanguero*, the *son* as it is still practiced in the *ranchos* and *campos*,[21] to the public.

Many of these musical families continue to live, interact, and teach within the communities that afforded them this talent. Although it has been difficult for most groups to record their traditional versions of the *son*, they have been successful with the help of small record companies from Mexico. Quetzal has been fortunate to have the opportunity to study, dialogue, collaborate, and compose with members of this new movement, especially Son de Madera.

LISTENING WITH MY FEET

In 2001, 2002, and 2003, Quetzal Flores (bandleader of Quetzal and my husband) and I made extended trips to Veracruz, where we received invaluable musical direction and hospitality, especially from the members of Son de Madera. We were guided across the state to visit various communities, musicians, and luthiers. Most of what people were eager to show us was the *fandango*.

We quickly realized that there was a common unspoken protocol to this dance form. The *tarima*[22] is the center of the *fandango* and *bailadoras*[23] are respected and praised for their ability to maintain balance, timing, and grace while improvising their movements. *Bailadoras* dance in continuous rotation on the *tarima*, and at the point where they have completed a cycle of *verso* and *estribillo*[24] they are immediately followed by waiting dancers who gently tap them to indicate that their time is up.

Only a pair of women dances the *sones de a montón;*[25] a male and female couple dances the *sones de pareja.* Depending on the *son,* the dance may be regarded as either a competition or a courtship between the two dancers. *Son jarocho* almost always includes various-sized instruments evolved from the early Spanish colonial guitar prototypes, including *jarana* (an eight-stringed rhythm instrument), the *guitarra de son* or *requinto* (a four-, sometimes five-stringed solo instrument), a *leona* ("lion," a four-stringed bass instrument), a *pandero* ("tambourine" with animal skin head), a *quijada* ("jaw of a horse or donkey"), and, of course, the driving pulse of the *son,* the *tarima* (see Sheehy 1979). Only recently have other instruments, such as the *cajón* (a "wooden box" with a sound-hole used for percussion), been re-introduced. I spent most of the initial trip observing the *bailadoras* of all ages, most of whom were dancing *sones de a montón.* The older women in the communities seemed to be highly respected practitioners. After observing my first few *bailadoras,* I had only begun to assimilate the complexity of the *fandango* style of Veracruz *zapateado.* Once I worked up the nerve to get on the *tarima,* I realized it was much harder than it looked. I found that the improvisational aspects of the *zapateado* were most challenging. *Zapateado* uses stomps, strikes, slides, shuffles, and silences (pauses), using the shoe in positions that are fully flat as well as the toe and the heel, to create sounds on the *tarima.* Yet, technically, there is but one main step that the locals call "*café con pan*"[26] because of its rhythm. It was not so much the technical aspects of the dance that were difficult for me to nail,[27] but rather the *cadencia* or cadence ("swing" or "groove") of it. I simply did not understand the feel of the *zapateado* and, as much as I wanted to dance, I sat and listened instead.

Even though there is one basic step pattern in the *sones de a montón,* the *café con pan* is a very different step depending on the *son* and its cadence. Idiosyncratic subtleties in the different *sones fandangueros* are perceptible to members of the community, or to someone who carefully listens and considers the conversations taking place between the music made with the dancers' steps, the musicians' instruments, and the singers' *versos.* The unfamiliar ear might find that the same steps are being used all night long for each *son* that is played. Yet the *cadencia* of each *son* implies a very different *café con pan.* Improvisation is essential to all aspects of this musical-dance form. After observing *zapateado* in its natural environment on and off for about two years, I was finally able to begin to feel comfortable enough to join some of the *señoras*[28] on the *tarima.*

Zapateado Movements and Sounds

A NATURAL EVOLUTION

When I began to incorporate *zapateado* into our music, it came as a natural evolution. As a band, we have followed in the footsteps of Ritchie Valens and Los Lobos, incorporating rock grooves with *son jarocho,*[29] as with our rendition of the traditional Mexican *son* "El cascabel." In Quetzal, I sing and play the *congas,* so I am considered part of the rhythm section (which consists of the drum set, the bass, and other percussion instruments such as the *congas, maracas, chekere,* and *cajón*). During a performance in the late 1990s, I decided to pull out the small *tarima* that I traveled with (and was using as a cable box) and began to improvise *folklórico* dance steps onstage in the middle of "*El Cascabel.*" The tremendous excitement I felt, as well as the response from the audience, led me to incorporate the *tarima* into our songs as a musical instrument, and my footwork began to evolve. By the time my band and I came upon *zapateado,* it felt like the next phase in our growth process as musicians.

Zapateado Afro-Chicana Fandanguero

There is always order within a *son,* as there should be with any song or composition. There are sections within the *son* that require *mudanza*[30] in order to hear the *versador.* After the *estribillo,* there is a break in the singing, and this is where improvisation is expected.

As a practitioner of dance and music, I perceive physical rhythmic dance movements as musical compositions, incorporating *zapateado* into music where I feel it is appropriate sonically. Ultimately, I am a musician and a composer before a dancer. While I am on the *tarima,* I do not prefer one step to another based on its visual aesthetic; rather, I create sounds and silences/rests based on the music. Like any other instrument, I find sections for the *zapateado* and develop them individually as well as within the entirety of the music being composed.

When I compose steps to music, I first consider whether or not the music needs *zapateado.* There must be room for this dialogue. The music must also respect *zapateado* and anything it might want to contribute to the conversation. I consider all the instruments and pay special attention to the percussive instruments in the ensemble. Sometimes the *requinto* or the *jarana* overrule the other instruments. It all depends on who I want to have the conversation with at that particular moment in the composition.

Once the foot patterns have been set, I concern myself with the upper-body movement. Some of the most respected *bailadoras* of the *fandango*, such as Rubí Oseguera Rueda and Martha Vega, have stressed the importance of relaxation.[31] While I do incorporate the traditional stance of *bailadoras* into my compositions, I also include movements from Ghanaian and Afro-Cuban dances with which I am familiar. I do not force any given upper-body movement; if it does not feel right or if it hurts, I do not use it. Yet, given the shared African roots of all the dance forms I rely upon to compose Zapateado Afro-Chicana/o Fandanguero, I am able to create and combine movements without feeling that they are contrived.

I use my overall experience as a musician familiar with the genres of Africa and its diaspora to compose *zapateado* patterns. Intuitively, but not deliberately, I rely on my percussive training with the *congas, batá, chekere* (shaker), and the music and dance of Cuba and Ghana. My musical background has made the transition from an observer of *zapateado* to a practitioner and composer easier. Having studied the rhythmic music of Africa, I immediately sensed the African roots of the *son jarocho.* The 3/4 cadence of the *son jarocho*[32] is a variant of the 6/8 meter, related to practices typical of rhythmic cycles in the African music I have studied.

A feature of my compositions derived from the oral tradition of *zapateado* is that I generally do not notate my steps. In many respects, the feel or *cadencia* of the foot sounds cannot be accurately notated, as is often the case with sound and movement of the African diaspora. Additionally, if a foot pattern is not implicated in the music and is difficult to recall an hour later, then I feel that the pattern's application is not worthy.

COMPOSING

I have always been encouraged by my band mates and feel completely free to experiment in my compositions. I seek to create sections in all my compositions for the various instruments I use—my voice, feet, and hands—always leaving room for improvisation. Maintaining the groove or pulse throughout a song is important to integrating all the instruments within the composition and serves as the foundation for improvisation, both its timing and rhythm.

On our second Quetzal album, *Sing the Real,* the song called "Cenzontle" was composed as our version of a *son jarocho.* It is in 6/8 meter with drums, electric bass, *jarana,* electric guitar, and violin. This song's *zapateado* rhythm is in the feel of the smallest of the Afro-Cuban *batá* drums, the *okonkolo,* at the beginning of the *oro seco.*[33] The *okonkolo* is the timekeeper of the rhythm, and the accents I have created for the *tarima* in "Cenzontle" are emphasized on the second, third, fifth, and sixth beats of the rhythm.

In addition, I have incorporated arm movements from the popular Ghanaian dance *agahu* into the *zapateado.* In *agahu,* the posture is hunched over as if the dancer were picking something up from the floor. When the drum calls, the dancer assumes this position and jerks the forearms forward in conjunction with specific steps. For "Cenzontle," I took the posture from *agahu* and combined this with a *zapateado* foot pattern that I composed similar to what would be seen in the southern region of Veracruz. When I step with one foot in the style of *zapateado,* my arm on the same side of my body jerks forward as in *agahu.*

Another example of one of my compositions, "Planta de los Pies," is on *Worksongs,* our most recent album. The *cadencia* of the foot patterns is typical *fandanguero;* specifically they are an original rendition of the *café con pan* (see Table 20.1).[34]

What makes this *zapateado* unusual, however, is that it is in a nontraditional eleven-beat meter. The lyrics reflect my departure from tradition: "*Aunque tanto a mi me gusten los colores de su son, siento propia mi candencia, pues el chicano siempre inventa.*"[35] In this song, I am addressing my need as a Chicana to express my own voice within the context of my Mexican heritage. The Chicana/o voice in this song is the mixture of the Mexican cadence of *café con pan* altered to fit an 11/4 meter rhythm.

When I composed the dance steps for "Planta de los Pies," I specifically had the traditional *cadencia* of the *son* "La Morena" in mind. The standard footsteps for the *tarima* in a *zapateado* differ for the *versos* and the *estribillo* (see Table 20.2). In "Planta de los Pies" I have added steps specifically for the *coro* (chorus), which is a section not typical of traditional *sones fandangueros,* resulting in three different foot patterns for this song. The foot patterns are actively involved in conversation with the *requinto* during the *estribillo* and with the drums during the *coro,* and the *versos* are accompanied by my version of a *mudanza* (see Table 20.3). My upper-body posture resembles

Table 20.1: Zapateado code for "Planta de los Pies"

	Striking with toe, usually a transitional move with not much accent to it.
	Full flat stomp of the foot.
	Full brush forward.
	Full brush back.

Planta de los Pies
(zapateado)

Table 20.2: The author's composition showing the Mexican cadence of *café con pan* (the zapateado usually in 3/4) altered to fit an 11/4-meter rhythm. The third line in the transcription is a reference to demonstrate the author's departure from the traditional rhythmic pattern. Courtesy of the author.

the *zapateado* for "La Morena," yet my hip and body movements are slightly more pronounced and my rib cage undulates on the down beats.

COLLABORATING WITH CHICANA/OS

Audiences, musicians, and dancers alike have received my compositions with great enthusiasm. *Son jarocho* groups from Veracruz such as Son De Madera,

Planta de los Pies (mudanza)

Table 20.3: The author's composition showing the Mexican cadence of the *mudanza* (the *mudanza* usually in 3/4) altered to fit an 11/4-meter rhythm. The third line in the transcription is a reference to demonstrate the author's departure from the traditional rhythmic pattern. Courtesy of the author.

and Chuchumbé dancer Rubí Oseguera Rueda have been impressed with my rhythmic work and have proposed collaborations on more than one occasion. *Folklórico* groups have also taken interest. One such group is Danza Floricanto/USA, one of the oldest existing professional Mexican *folklórico* dance troupes in Los Angeles. Gema Sandoval is the artistic director and founder of Danza Floricanto/USA. Sandoval works to ensure that this thirty-year-old dance company continues to preserve Mexico's culture by presenting dances that reflect various regions of Mexico as well as the Chicana/o experience. After witnessing one of Quetzal's performances, Sandoval was captivated by the way we had taken *zapateado* and made it our own.[36] Sandoval expressed the urge to collaborate with Quetzal because her exposure to Veracruz's *sones* had only been through the performances of Ballet Folklórico de México de Amalia Hernández, one of the most famous and respected Mexican dance companies. We suggested to Sandoval the she witness the *fandango* as we had in its own context, the *ranchos* of Veracruz, and, with the help of Quetzal Flores, she agreed.

A year later, Quetzal and Danza Floricanto/USA joined forces, composing Fandango sin Fronteras/Fandango Without Borders, which debuted at the John Anson Ford Theatre in Hollywood. The production focused on the discovery of Chicana/o identity. Through music and dance, we demonstrated the common yearning among Chicana/os to tap into our Mexicanidad and the cultural nourishment *fandango* can provide us, culminating with an assertion of a distinctly Chicana/o voice. The musical-dance production featured the music of Quetzal, including "Planta de los Pies," as well as compositions created with Rubí Oseguera Rueda from Chuchumbé and César Castro of Mono Blanco, two of the most respected *fandango* artists and members of the Veracruz community.

The collaboration was difficult for Danza Floricanto/USA: "[T]his process, the change was real painful because we had to learn to think a different way. You didn't know what you were holding on to, the music or the dance. We have always thought of it as two separate elements. [Adjusting] took a while."[37] In the end, our production was a success, and we discussed the possibility of future collaborations that we would tour at other performing arts centers throughout the United States.

DISCUSSION

All of my life experiences have been poured into the lyrics and compositions that I create for Quetzal, including my Zapateado Afro-Chicana/o Fandanguero. I have struggled in my childhood and during my schooling and, as a Chicana, within U.S. society and in my early professional years. More recently, as a member of Quetzal, I have been fortunate to travel to and commiserate with peoples in Mexico (specifically Chiapas and Veracruz), Japan, Canada, and throughout the United States. Twelve years and four albums later, Quetzal continues to be my extended family. The opportunity to be, live, and learn with this band has provided countless life lessons, which I consider to be one of the most powerful aspects of studying and performing art.

Over the years, I have developed a great admiration for *son jarocho,* and I consider myself a student of this music and dance style. Yet I do not strive to be *jarocho;* I do not try to emulate or imitate the *son.* Rather, I study the *son jarocho* and borrow from it, using it as a foundation for creating my own musical expressions. I draw greatly on the strong improvisational emphasis in *son jarocho fandanguero* for my compositions. As far as I know, no other group has developed dance compositions based on the *fandango.* Others replicate the music, lyrics, and the steps of *zapateado* verbatim. Nevertheless, my exposure to *zapateado* is credited to those *son jarocho fandanguero* virtuosos like Son de Madera, Chuchumbé, and Mono Blanco, who have shared the music and dance of Veracruz as it was taught to them in their homeland.

Visits from Veracruz to the United States made by practitioners of *son jarocho fandanguero* have led to a growing interest in this musical art form, particularly in the Southwest, among audiences and dancers alike. Not all seem to be embracing this style of *fandango,* however. Sandoval informs me that a *zapateado fandanguero* workshop held at the 2005 Danzantes Unidos Conference in Los Angeles was met with a lack of interest by members of the *folklórico* community. *Folklórico* dancers in attendance were unwilling to dedicate their weekend to learning this dance style. According to Sandoval, workshop participants did not get the rhythms, and as a result they were bored. She states, "It's not about the steps. It was about the rhythms."[38]

Sandoval points out that the unenthusiastic reception to *zapateado* could have been because the conference took place over a weekend, and it takes much longer to achieve a level of comfort with *zapateado fandanguero.* She feels that a conference may not be the best place to present *zapateado fandanguero* properly, for it needs a communal context. Moreover, Sandoval believes that many *folklórico* practitioners go to these conferences to validate that what they are doing is *folklórico,* which is negated by *zapateado fandanguero* in this environment.[39] Although the improvisational importance placed on *zapateado fandanguero* may conflict with the canonized choreography of both the music and the dance of the *folklórico,* both *folklórico* and *fandango* have their place in history and are of great significance to Chicana/os. Nevertheless, as Sandoval indicates, each may need its own space to evolve.

Despite the unsuccessful exhibition of *zapateado fandanguero* at the Danzantes Unidos Conference, El Nuevo Movimiento Jaranero has taken off, particularly in California. Increasingly, *fandango*s are being established in the United States, and a community is developing that spans the United States and Mexico. Not only have Veracruz's *son jarocho fandanguero* musicians and dancers come to the United States, but those forming in the United States have also gone to Veracruz. There is an understanding on both sides of the importance placed on learning and communing within the larger *fandango* community. I suspect this community will continue to grow, because *zapateado fandanguero* has the ability to connect Chicanas/os to our past and, as I have demonstrated, to absorb experiences, struggles, and elements from the present and from other cultures to create our own unique voice.

Notes

I extend my deepest gratitude and admiration to Russell Rodríguez, Olga Nájera-Ramírez, Brenda M. Romero, and Norma E. Cantú for their belief in me and encouragement to submit this essay; my cheerleader and good friend Sumaiya Olatunde for her editorial assistance and advice; Edson Gianesi for helping me code and transcribe my compositions; Richard Mora for his advice; Gema Sandoval for her constant support of me as a Chicana and a new mother; my first teacher and brother, Gabriel González, as well as my sisters Claudia and Karla; my mother, Martha R. Hernández, for always keeping us positive; Grandma Consuelo and Xochi for their love and support; Son de Madera, Chuchumbé, and the communities of El Hato, Apixita, Chacalapa, Xalapa, and Boca de San Miguel; and last but not least, my life partner, soul mate, and the father of our baby José María Sandino, Quetzal Flores for his love and encouragement.

1. "Mexican music and Mexican folkloric dance." See Nájera-Ramírez's and Rodríguez's essays (chapters 16 and 19) in this volume.

2. "*fandango* footwork." Zapateado Afro-Chicano Fandanguero innovates on this basic format, as described in this chapter.

3. In this chapter, "*zapateado*" refers to *zapateado fandanguero* (as opposed to *folklórico*'s representation of *zapateado*) unless otherwise noted.

4. The *fandango* as dance genre is most notably linked to Spain due to its most widely known form, the *flamenco.* It is found in other regions of the world, however, including Mexico and other parts of Latin America, as well as Africa where it is believed to have originated. Note that the word *fandango* has entered English usage with limited definition, although its courtship aspects are noted in English dictionaries.

5. *Son jarocho* is music from the rural *jarocho/a* peoples in southern Veracruz, Mexico. *Jarocho* is a caste term that was utilized by the church in an attempt to keep track of bloodlines. *Jarocho* refers to the offspring of an indigenous and an African person.

6. In the subhead above: "Music in my family"

7. Downtown Los Angeles, especially on streets such as Broadway, continue to be the hub and safe haven for the newly arrived immigrant. The *callejón* (alley), the cheap bargain shopping, and *taquerias* (taco shops) are all tailored to the Spanish-speaking customer.

8. One of many styles of Mexican rural music forms that are rooted in documenting historical as well as personal accounts.

9. Literally "second," but is often used with regard to all harmonizing voices but the melody, which is the "primera," or first.

10. "the child sensation, with the authentic Mexican sentiment." *Gabrielito González con el auténtico sentimiento mexicano* is the actual title of his debut album on El Rey *discos* (1978).

11. Kabuki is highly stylized traditional Japanese theater.

12. Dance elements of early hip-hop that developed by the disenfranchised poor youth in the Bronx in New York City.

13. Poplocking, believed to have developed on the West Coast of the United States, is a hip-hop dance form that involves joint isolation and locking and releasing, and appears to occur in a jerking motion. Dancers are judged aesthetically on their execution of rhythm and originality.

14. Dog Town is named mainly after the local gang that dominated the William Mead Homes projects on Main Street.

15. "Water from the Hose"

16. Rooted in the politics of the Mexican American experience in the 1960s, Chicana/o is an ideological term used to describe political as well as cultural identity.

17. 10,000 Maniacs is a pop group from the early 1990s that incorporated violins into their music. Natalie Merchant, the lead singer, went on to have a successful solo career.

18. Drums often used in this manner, creating a dialogue with dancers, include the *conga* and the *batá* drums. The *conga* is a Cuban adaptation of a similar tall, single-headed African drum type. There are several types of *conga,* including the small *quinto* solo improvising instrument, the mid-sized *conga,* and the large *tumbadora.* The *batá* is a sacred drum from Nigeria used in worship by the Yoruba and is used in Cuba (where it arrived during slavery) for similar religious purposes as well as in secular music. This drum is double-headed with an hourglass shape where one end is larger than the other. There are three *batá* drums: the *okonkolo* is the smallest, the *itotole* is of medium size, and the *iya* is the largest. Originally, these three drums were cut from a single tree trunk. Traditionally, *batás* are ceremonial drums played in groups of at least three people, each with a different size drum. A *toque* can refer to a drumbeat, a particular drumming session, or a conversation between the dancers. In *batá* drumming, identifiable *toque* patterns are used to summon a specific *orisha* (god), of which there are several. Each *orisha* has different natural elements or human characteristics attributed to it that are expressed through a dancer's movements, which are signaled by the *toques.* Dancers must know the *toques* well and drummers must know the movements well in order to engage in a dialogue that accurately represent the *orisha.* This is true of both religious music and secular music whether the rhythms are standard *toques* or improvisational variations of the *batá* drums.

19. Maria Elena Gaitan is most notably known for her "Chola con Chelo" ("The Chola with Her Cello") piece. For *chola* (feminine form of *cholo*) see also note 8 in Rudy García's essay in this volume (chapter 13).

20. In the subhead above: "The New Movement of Son Jaranero" (*son jaranero* is another term for *son jarocho; jaranero* is also used to refer to the musician who plays this music, from *jarana,* the name for *jarocho* guitars in various sizes and for the fiesta where the music is played). It should be noted that this movement is both a musical-cultural as well as a political movement and is owed in part to the great memory and musical talent of Don Arcadio Hidalgo, an Afro-Mexicano from Nopalapan, who fought alongside Zapata and Pancho Villa in the Mexican Revolution. Having always been a part of the *fandango* tradition, Don Arcadio continued his love affair with the *fandangos* and the *sones* of Mexico after fighting in the Mexican Revolution, going from village to village across his motherland in search of this music and dance form that was banned by the government and the church until after the Revolution. For more information on El Nuevo Movimiento Jaranero, see Pascoe 2003.

21. "ranches" [and] "countryside"

22. The *tarima* is a wooden platform measuring anywhere from 10 x 4 feet to 10 x 12 feet. This instrument/resonator is the heart of the *fandango.*

23. *Bailadoras* dance the *fandango* in couples, as many possible dancing in turn, surrounded by other participants, including musicians, dancers, and singers.

24. *Verso* means verse, and is sung in call and response. *Estribillo* means refrain.

25. Literally *sones* "for many, or group"

26. Literally "*coffee with bread*" but in practice is an onomatopoeic rhythmic phrase to get children and beginners to grasp the mechanics of the steps. Technically, there is but one step pattern to *zapateado:* two flat strokes on one foot, then one flat stomp with the other foot, and then one more flat stroke with the first. This pattern is then continually repeated by alternating the ordering of the feet (for example, right-left-right, then left-right-left, and so on). This rhythmic phrase, "*café con pan,*" changes in feel depending on the *son* accompanying the dance. Other than this term, there is intentionally no terminology to refer to specific steps in *zapateado,* due to the importance placed on improvisation in this dance.

27. I was familiar with the steps of *zapateado* from my early years of learning *folklórico,* which presents choreographed versions of *zapateado* along with other music and dance forms from Mexico.

28. In the community and especially within the context of *fandango, señora* implies a veteran dancer.

29. Ritchie Valens's version of the song "La Bamba" is a well-known example of this fusion.

30. A dance step used to keep time and allow the singer sonic space to sing the *verso* (Gilberto Gutiérrez of the group Mono Blanco, and Rubí Oseguera Rueda, anthropologist and respected *fandango* dancer within the tradition, personal communications with the author, Los Angeles, California, and Veracruz, Mexico, since 2001).

31. Holding the body in a relaxed stance does not mean slouching, nor does it mean being in an erect, overexaggerated ballet posture. One should maintain a comfortable stance with the knees slightly bent and the arms out to the side (for men and women) or slightly picking up one's skirt (for women).

32. The 3/4 and 4/4 meters are used often in *son jarocho,* as in mariachi.

33. There is *oro seco* and *oro cantado. Oro seco* (*toque* with no vocal accompaniment) is the first conversation one learns as a student, along with playing in ceremony to start *misa* (worship). The first conversation in the *oro seco* is a *toque* for *elegua,* the god of the crossroads.

34. This code and transcription was created with the help of Edson Gianesi.

35. "We identify with your music, the colors of your *son.* We, however, have our own cadence we feel and execute as Chicanos."

36. According to Sandoval (2005, personal communication), our style of *zapateado* "stopped being about the way we used to be, and it became [very contemporary] about the way we are today." She felt that our incorporation of *zapateado* into our music as well as our transformation of the dance style gave it a whole new meaning.

37. Gema Sandoval, interview with the author, Los Angeles, California, July 13, 2005.

38. Ibid.

39. Ibid.

Epilogue

We love to dance. Working on *Dancing across Borders: Danzas y Bailes Mexicanos,* we have learned many things. It has not been easy, but it has been worthwhile. When we first sent out the call for papers for this book, we did so with great anticipation, envisioning the exciting journey it indeed turned out to be. Our focus on the varied perspectives of both scholars and practitioners on the dance traditions of Greater Mexico would no doubt bring to light much that had been hidden from all but those closely involved in those traditions. Acutely aware of globalization and the increased trafficking of peoples and their dance expressions within and across national borders, we felt it imperative that *Dancing across Borders* highlight scholarship on the contemporary cross-cultural richness of forms, contexts, and meanings, as well as historical trajectories of dance expressions within the geopolitical entity we refer to as Greater Mexico. As stated by one reviewer, "The geographic spread—across borders and in the borderlands, *lo mexicano y lo chicano*—makes this collection unique and valuable." We received some of the essays in Spanish but were not able to publish them in their original language, only in translation (De la Torre, Zárate, and Sánchez). We plan to publish all the essays in Spanish at a future time so that the conversations that have begun among the contributors can continue among a wider circle of scholars.

Each editor brought particularly valuable expertise to the project, coming as we do from three different disciplines—anthropology/folklore, literature/folklore, and ethnomusicology/composition. We depended on our ample interdisciplinary lenses as we articulated the intellectual framework for the project and prepared the manuscript, reading and rereading our own and the other authors' various revisions. Serendipitously, the essays we accepted fit nicely into four main categories around themes we had first discussed when preparing the call for papers—identity, placiality, traditionality, and authenticity. So we arrived at the sections: Contested Identities, Dimensions of Space and Place, Trajectories of Tradition, and the Politics of Tradition and Innovation. Some essays dealt with more than one of the section themes but ultimately fit better in a particular category. With this in mind, we summarize here the theoretical and conceptual frameworks of each.

In the first section, titled "Contested Identities," we gathered essays that while exploring indigenous, transnational, and gendered identities also manifested a deep exploration of the generational and localized identities of *danzantes,* ritual, and social dance practitioners. It is rare that scholarship demonstrates with such clarity how identities are affirmed or contested in dance traditions. Whether Mexican and mestizo (European and Indigenous mix), Mexican and Indigenous, Chicanas/o (mestizo born or acculturated in the United States), or Indigenous and U.S. citizen, the populations of the geographical area of Greater Mexico have had to negotiate questions of identity for more than five hundred years, and it is no surprise that a discussion of cultural expressions such as dance impelled a discussion of identity. The authors of the essays in this section aptly interrogated how the subject positions of the dancers and the social contexts of the dance traditions shape and reflect identity, both individual and collective.

The essays in the second section, "Dimensions of Space and Place," theorized around the ideas of spatiality and placiality through analyses of performance and ritual and of the spaces and places where they occur. Central to this section was the notion that dance events may imbue the social spaces in which they are enacted with particular meanings. A corollary to these ideas was the interrogation as to what kind of impact the deterritorializing (through migration) of people within the United States and Mexico and to and from Mexico and the United States has on the traditions and on the people, since the transcultural movement of dance traditions results in changes in the dance itself.

In the section we titled "Trajectories of Tradition," we placed essays that dealt with the historical processes that reflect dance as enduring cultural practice. We traced the many paths that social dance and *danza* can take across time and space, then proceeded to individual trajectories along a lifetime devoted to dance. We also explored the manifestation of particular dance genres as sites in which to deploy nationalist and other sociohistorical ideologies as the genres evolve. The essays' central theme shows the multifaceted layers of meaning that are negotiated and produced each time the traditions are enacted.

Finally, in the last section, "The Politics of Tradition and Innovation," we placed essays that engaged in conversations with each other around the polemic surrounding issues of preservation and innovation of traditional dance expressions. If change is inevitable, as many of the essays in the previous sections seem to suggest, then there must be some negotiation of the equally strong forces impelling the preservation of salient traditional dance expressions. As in the discussions of many other Mexican cultural expressions, including material culture items such as *piñatas* or *rebozos* and other textiles, the politics surrounding the tension between change and innovation exists in dance traditions.

Dancing across Borders fulfills a dire need for original scholarship that takes into account not only the transnationality of contemporary dance traditions, but also the intellectual processes that cross disciplines and modalities, and political and philosophical borders, over generations, as they have in Mexico. Such a book matters because it explores issues that will no doubt continue to present themselves in our increasingly globalized social and cultural realities. *Dancing across Borders* is a timely collection because dance is a vibrant and enduring expressive form in Latino communities everywhere. With an increasing mobility of people within and across national borders, regional dances are becoming more widely known beyond their places of origin; localized traditions from Latin America are springing up in new cultural environments. The dance halls in places such as Rupert, Idaho, host social dances where one hears *banda* music; classes on *cumbias, danzón,* tango, and salsa have sprung up around the country; churches throughout the midwestern United States celebrate liturgical festivals with *matachines* dance rituals; in California, Nebraska, Colorado, as in many other northern locations, *danza azteca* or *conchero* dancers join Native North American pow-wow dancers; and Mexican indigenous peoples practice their dance traditions in New York City, Washington, D.C., and Dallas. Moreover, as those who return to Mexico take the social dance traditions back to their communities of origin, and foreigners introduce new dance traditions to those communities, all those involved feel the impact of the transnational aspects that *Dancing across Borders* explores.

Our hope is that through work such as this, we can come to better understand and appreciate the contributions of marginalized groups to the larger cultural fabric of our country, and that we begin to realize how, culturally and intellectually, borders are ever more porous and tenuous—and that there the love of dance continues to feed the spirit.

Selected Bibliography on Folk, Ritual, and Social Dance in Greater Mexico

(This bibliography only contains entries that are not included in the Works Cited.)

Acosta Baez, Francisco. "Danza de los negros de la región Totonaca de Papantla, Veracruz." In *Una caricia a la tierra: danzas y bailes de Veracruz.* México: Gobierno del Estado de Veracruz,Universidad Veracruzana, Instituto de Investigación y Difusión de la Danza Mexicana, A.C, 1991.

Acuña, Rene. *Farsas y representaciones escénicas de los mayas antiguos.* México: Universidad Nacional Autónoma de México, Dirección General de Publicaciones, 1978.

Adams, Doug, and Martha Ann Kirk. *Mexican and Native American Dances in Christian Worship and Education.* Austin: The Sharing Company, 1981.

Aguirre, Coral. *La pasión del diablo: Una visión enamorada.* Nuevo León: Facultad de Filosofía y Letras de la Universidad Autónoma de Nuevo León, 2004.

Aguirre Beltrán, Gonzalo. "Bailes de negros." *Revista de la Universidad de México* 25, no. 2 (1970): 2–5.

Altamirano Zamorano, José de Jesús. *La danza de la conquista de Tetitlán, Nayarit.* Tepic, Nay. Gobierno del Estado de Nayarit, Consejo Estatál para la Cultura y las Artes: Unidad Estatál de Culturas Populares e Indígenas de Nayarit, 2001.

Alvarez, Cecilia. *Atrapar a la danza: Fotografías.* Colima, Col., México: Universidad de Colima, 2001.

Alvarez y Alvarez de la Cadena, Luis. *Leyendas y costumbres, trajes y danzas.* México, D.F.: Editorial Layac, 1945.

Amézquita Borja, Francisco. *Música y danza: Algunos aspectos de la música y danza de la Sierra Norte del estado de Puebla, recopilación del prof. Francisco Amezquita Borja.* Puebla, México, 1943.

Anguiano, Marina, and Guido Munich. *La danza de la Malinche.* México: Dirección General de Culturas Populares, Secretaría de Educación Pública, n.d.

Arispe, Lourdes. "La Sierra de Puebla." *Artes de México* 19 (1972): 155.

Armstrong, Gayle Elizabeth. *Danza Azteca: Contemporary Manifestation of Danza de los Concheros in the United States.* PhD Dissertation, University of California Los Angeles, 1985.

Arriaga, Guillermo, and Leonardo Velásquez. *La danza en México a través del tiempo: [Discurso de ingreso a la Academia de Artes].* México, D.F.: Academia de Artes, 2001.

Aulestia de Alba, Patricia. *Testimonio: 25 años de danza en México: 1934–1959.* México: Instituto Nacional de Belles Artes, Centro de Información y Documentación de la Danza, 1984.

Baja California Sur (Mexico) Dirección General de Acción Social. *Ballet Folklórico Sudcaliforniano: Director Prof. Marco Antonio Ojeda Garcia.* La Paz, B.C.: Dirección General de Acción Social, 1973.

Ballet Folklórico de México. VHS. Mexico: Cinema Mexico, 24 min. 1987.

———. VHS. Los Angeles: Million Dollar Video Corporation, 112 min. 1989.

———. 1962–69. VHS. Photographed by Michael Truppin. New York: Michael Truppin, 9 min., 1995.

Ballet Folklórico del Puerto de Veracruz. VHS. México: Telecast by Estelar Musical, 66 min. 198–[?].

Baud, Pierre-Alain. *Le Mexique face a la transnationalisation des systemes de production culturelle la danse comme enjeu de communication.* Dissertation. Lille: A.N.R.T., Universite de Lille III, 1987.

———. *Una danza tan ansiada: La danza en México como experiencia de comunicación y poder.* México, D.F.: Universidad Autónoma Metropolitana, Unidad Xochimilco, 1992.

Baudez, C. F. "The Maya Snake Dance: Ritual and Cosmology." *Res* 21 (1992): 37–52.

Bautista, Fidencio. *Una danza que nos trajeron los españoles.* México, D.F.: Dirección General de Culturas Populares, Secretaría de Educación Pública, 1982.

Baumann, Roland. "Tlaxcalan Expression of Autonomy and Religious Drama in the Sixteenth Century." *Journal of Latin American Lore* 13 (1987): 139–53.

Beutler, Gisela. "Floripes, la Princesa Pagana en los bailes de moros y cristianos de México: Algunas observaciones sobre las fuentes literarias." *Jahrbuch Geschichte von Staat, Wirtschaft und Gesellschaft Lateinamerikas* 20 (1983): 257–98.

———. *La historia de Fernando y Alamar: Contribución al estudio de las danzas de moros y cristianos en Puebla, Mèxico.* Stuttgart: F. Steiner Verlag Wiesbaden, 1984.

Blanco, Manuel. *Nueva tradición de la danza.* Mexico: Universidad Nacional Autonoma de Mexico, Coordinacion de Difusión Cultural, 1996.

Bonfiglioli, Carlo. *La epopeya de Cuauhtémoc en Tlacoachistlahuaca: Un estudio de contexto, texto y sistema en la antropología de la danza.* México, D.F.: Casa Abierta al Tiempo, Universidad Autónoma Metropolitana, 2004.

Boot, Erik. "A Dance Festival with Litter and Castle and its Possible Classic Maya Antecedents." *Yumtzilob* 10, no. 3 (1998): 233–47.

Bradomín, José María. *Oaxaca en la tradición.* México, 1960.

Brandes, Stanley. "Dance as Metaphor: A Case from Tzintzuntzan, México." *Journal of Latin American Lore* 5, no. 1 (1979): 25–43.

———. *Power and Persuasion.* Philadelphia: University of Pennsylvania Press, 1988.

Bravo, Guillermina. "Cuerpo de gigantes: La danza mexicana y el Palacio de Bellas Artes." *Plural* 19, no. 225 (1990): 62–63.

Brewster, Mela S. *Mexican and New Mexican Folkdances.* Albuquerque: The University of New Mexico Press, 1938.

Bricker, Victoria Reifler. *Humor ritual en la Altiplanicie de Chiapas.* México: Fondo de Cultura Económica, 1986.

Caballero, María Socorro. *Danzas regionales del estado de México.* Secretaría de Educación Pública, 1985.

Caballero Socorro, María del. *Danzas regionales del estado de México.* México, D.F., 1985.

Camacho Diaz Gonzalo. "Danza de sonajitas." In *México Danza* Núm. 1, Año 1, abril–junio. Instituto de Investigación y Difusión de la Danza Mexicana A.C. México. 1994.

———. "A Small Harp Accompanies Dance of the Little Rattlers: The Traditional Indigenous Dance of the Huastec Region of San Luis Potosí." *The Harp Therapy Journal* (Summer 1997).

Camacho, G., and M. E. Jurado. "Cuando la muerte danza: La danza de los huehues en la Huasteca Hidalguense." In *Nuevos aportes al concocimiento de la huasteca,* ed. Jesus Ruvalcaba Mercado, 327–34. México, D.F.: CIESAS, 1998.

Campobello, Nellie. *Ritmos indígenas de México.* México, 1940.

Campos, Ruben M. *El folklore musical de las ciudades: Investigación acerca de la música Mexicana para bailar y cantar, obra integrada con 85 composiciones para piano, cuyas melodias estan intactas.* México: Secretaría de Educacion Pública, 1930.

Canto-Lugo, Ramiro Fernando. "La danza de moros y cristianos en México." PhD Dissertation, University of California at Davis, 1991.

Casar González, Eduardo. "La danza en México: Un apretado nudo de contradicciones." *Plural* 9, no. 108 (1980): 59–60.

Cashion, Susan V. "Dance Ritual and Cultural Values in a Mexican Village: Festival of Santo Santiago." PhD Dissertation, Stanford, 1983.

———. "The Son and Jarabe: Mestizo Dance Form of Jalisco, México." MA Thesis, Stanford, 1967.

Castro, Carlo Antonio. "Los Huehues: Atisbo intercultural de una danza." *La palabra y el hombre* 100 (1996): 51–54.

Castro de la Rosa, María Guadalupe. "Voladores and Hua-huas: Two Ritual Dances of the Region of Papantla." *UCLA Journal of Dance Ethnology* 9 (1985): 46–64.

Ceseña, Maria Teresa. "Negotiating Identity, Politics, and Spirituality: A Comparison of Two Danza Azteca Groups in San Diego, California." MA Thesis, University of California at San Diego, 2004.

Ciechanower, Mauricio. "Gladiola Orozco: La danza en México y otras latitudes." *Plural* 13, no. 153 (1984): 57–63.
Cinco décadas de investigación sobre música y danza indígena. México: Instituto Nacional Indigenista, 2002.
50 encuentros de música y danza indígena. México: FONAPAS, 1981.
Cobos, Ruben. "The New Mexican Game of Valse Chiquiao." *Perspectives in Mexican American Studies* 1 (1988): 61–67.
Cohen, Jeffrey H. "Danza de la Pluma: Symbols of Submission and Separation in a Mexican Fiesta." *Anthropological Quarterly* 66, no. 3 (1993): 149–58.
Collier, Donald. *La danza del sol de los indios de las llanuras.* Pátzcuaro, Michoacán, 1940.
Comstock, Tamara. *New Dimensions in Dance Research: Anthropology and Dance—the American Indian: The Proceedings of the Third Conference on Research in Dance.* March 26th–April 2nd, 1972, the University of Arizona, Tucson, Arizona, and the Yaqui villages of Tucson. Conference. New York: Committee on Research in Dance, 1974.
Correa, Ethel. "Fiestas que fueron: Carnaval, baile de máscaras y máscaradas en la Ciudad de México." *Antropología* 41 (1994): 6–12.
Covarrubia, Luis. *Regional Dances of Mexico.* México, D.F.: E. Fischgrund, 1979.
Croda León, Ruben, and Francisco Acosta Báez. *Entre los hombres y las deidades: las danzas del Totonacapan.* México: CONACULTA, Dirección General de Culturas Populares e Indígenas, 2005.
Cruz Rodríguez, José Antonio. *La misión del espinal.* Mexico, D.F.: Centro de Estudios Antropológicos, Científicos, Artísticos, Tradicionales y Lingüísticos "Ce-Acatl," 2004.
Cuéllar Hernández, Fernando. *La motivación dramática en la escenificación de la danza.* México: Secretaría General Académica, Centro de Actualización y Formación de Profesores, 1980.
Cuerpos de maíz: Danzas agrícolas de la huasteca. México, D.F.: Ediciones del Programa de Desarrollo Cultural de la Huasteca, 2000.
Cupryn, Teresa. "La expresión cósmica de la danza Azteca." *Revista mexicana de ciencias políticas y sociales* 37, no. 147 (1992): 35–52.
Dallal, Alberto. *La danza contra la muerte.* México: Universidad Nacional Autónoma de México, Instituto de Investigaciones Estéticas, 1983.
———. "La danza prehispanica: Abstracción y síntesis de lo ritual." *México en el arte* 1 (1983): 80–83.
———. "Lo nacional como proyecto y realización en la danza mexicana de hoy." *Anales del Instituto de Investigaciones Estéticas* 13, no. 52 (1983): 187–229.
———. "Temas relativos a la danza en la revista romance, 1940–1941." *Anales del Instituto de Investigaciones Estéticas* 14, no. 53 (1983): 163–79.
———. "Guillermina Bravo o la irradiación de la danza." *Mexico en el Arte* 7 (1984–85): 52–57.

———. *Fémina-danza.* México: Universidad Nacional Autónoma de México, Instituto de Investigaciones Estéticas, 1985.

———. *La danza en situación.* Mexico: Ediciones Gernika, 1985.

———. *El "dancing" mexicano.* México, D.F.: Editorial Oasis, 1987.

———. "Procesos espontáneos y proceso inducidos en el arte dancístico." *Revista Universidad de México* 575 (1988): 18–27.

———. *La mujer en la danza.* México, D.F.: Panorama Editorial, 1990.

———. "Guillermo Keys Arenas: Modelo en el desarrollo de la danza de concierto del Siglo XX en México; los Primeros Años." *Anales del Instituto de Investigaciones Estéticas* 20, no. 73 (1998): 161–84.

Dances of the World: Mexico. VHS. Featuring Ballet Folklórico de Colima and Grupo Folklórico del Departmento de Bellas Artes, Guadalajara. [U.S.]: Folk Dance Videos International. Folkmoot USA series, 36 min., 1989.

Danza de las varitas: Tzineja, Huehuetlán, S.L.P. y Zoquitipa, Tamazunchale, S.L.P.: Antecedentes históricos, constantes prehispánicas y estado actual de la danza. San Luis Potosí, México: Gobierno del Estado de San Luis Potosí, 1985.

Danza 'La Virgen y las fieras.' México, D.F.: FONADAN/FONAPAS, 1980.

Danza 'los sembradores.' México, D.F.: FONADAN/FONAPAS, 1980s.

Danzas y bailes de la costa oaxaqueña. Festival Costeño de la Danza. Conference. Oaxaca, Mexico: Instituto Oaxaqueño de las Culturas, 1995.

del Carmen, Patricia. *Crónica historica del huapango huasteco veracruzano.* Xalapa, Ver: Gobierno del Estado de Veracruz, Secretaría de Educación y Cultura, 1991.

Delgado Martínez, César. 1991. *Guillermina Bravo: Historia oral.* México, D.F.: Instituto Nacional de Bellas Artes: Centro Nacional de investigación Documentación e Información de la Danza José Limón, 1994.

———. *Yol-Izma: La danzarina de las leyendas.* México: Escenologia AC, 1997.

de los Reyes, Aurelio. "Tres documentos sobre la fundación de la escuela de danza." *Anales del Instituto de Investigaciones Estéticas* 16, no. 60 (1989): 249–61.

Diaz Roig, Mercedes. "La danza de la conquista." *Nueva revista de filología hispánica* 32, no. 1 (1983): 176–95.

Dickins, Guillermina. *Dances of Mexico.* London: M. Parrish, 1954.

Domínguez-Torres, Jesús. *Historia de la danza, primer curso: Investigación bibliográfica y de campo.* Chihuahua: Escuela Superior de Danza Folklórica Mexicana, Incorporada a la Dirección de Educación Pública del Estado de Chihuahua, 1996.

Duggan, Anne S. "The Folk Dance Library." In *Folk Dances of the United States and Mexico,* ed. Anne Schley Duggan, 159. New York: Barnes, 1948.

Duran, Lin. *La danza mexicana en los sesenta: Antología hemerográfica.* México: INBA, 1990.

El huapango: relato de niños huastecos. Hidalgo, San Luis Potosí: Instituto Nacional Indigenista, 1992.

Encuentros de música y danza indígenas. San Cristóbal de las Casas, Chiapas: Gobierno del Estado de Chiapas, Consejo Estatal para la Cultura y las Artes, Centro Estatal de Lenguas, Arte y Literatura Indígenas, 1997.

Escudero, Alexandrina. *Felipe Segura: Una vida en la danza.* México, D.F.: Instituto Nacional de Bellas Artes: Grupo Editorial Gaceta, 1995.

Fergusson, Erna. *Fiesta in Mexico.* New York: A. A. Knopf, 1934.

———. *The Deer-dance at Taos.* Tucson, Ariz.: Peccary Press, 1983.

Fernández, Justino. *Danzas de los concheros en San Miguel de Allende.* Mexico: FCE, 1941.

Festival artístico. La Paz, Baja California Sur, Mexico: Gobierno del Estado de Baja California Sur, 1987.

Festival costeño de la danza: Danzas y bailes de la costa oaxaqueña. Oaxaca, México: Instituto Oaxaqueño de las Culturas, Consejo Nacionál para la Cultura y las Artes, Dirección General de Culturas Populares, Coordinación de Descentralización del CNCA, 1994.

Figueroa Hernández, Rafaél. *Salsa mexicana: Tranculturación e identidad.* México: ConClave, 1996.

Florencia Pulido, Patricia del Carmen. *Crónica histórica del huapango huasteco veracruzano: Trovas, música, danza y tradiciones.* Xalapa, Ver.: Gobierno del Estado de Veracruz, Secretaría de Educación y Cultura, 1991.

Flores Guerrero, Raúl, and Miguel Covarrubias. *La danza en México.* México, D.F.: Difusión Cultural, Departamento de Danza, Universidad Nacional Autónoma de México, 1980.

Fogelquist, Mark Stephen. *Rhythm and Form in the Contemporary Son Jalisciense.* PhD Dissertation, University of California at Los Angeles, 1975.

Folklórico. VHS. Derry, N.H.: Chip Taylor Communications, 28 min., 1999.

Fondo Nacional para el Desarrollo de la Danza. *La danza del tecuán.* México: FONADAN, 1975.

Forman, Karen, and Amando Cablas. "Mexican Folk Dance Traditions: Jalisco." PhD Dissertation, San Jose State University, 1979.

Forrest, Earle R. *Missions and Pueblos of the Old Southwest; Their Myths, Legends, Fiestas, and Ceremonies, with some Accounts of the Indian Tribes and their Dances; and of the Penitents.* Cleveland, Ohio: The Arthur H. Clark Company, 1929.

Franco Fernández, Roberto. *El folklore de Jalisco: Recopilación e investigación.* Guadalajara, Jal.: Ediciones Kergima, 2002.

Fuentes Mata, Irma. *El diseño curricular en la danza folklórica: Análisis y propuesta.* México, D.F.: Instituto Nacional de Bellas Artes, 1995.

Galovic, Jelena. *Los grupos místico-espirituales de la actualidad.* México: Plaza y Valdés, 2002.

Gagnier Mendoza, Mary Jane. *Oaxaca Celebration: Family, Food, and Fiestas in Teotitlán.* Santa Fe: Museum of New Mexico Press, 2005.

Galarza Cruz, Guillermina. *Evolución del traje regional en Jalisco: Indumentaria de danzas, sones y jarabes de Jalisco.* Guadalajara, Jal.: Gobierno de Jalisco, Secretaría General, Unidad Editorial, 1945.

Galinier, Jacques. *La mitad del mundo: Cuerpo y cosmos en los rituales otomies*. Mexico: UNAM/INI, 1990.

García, Elvira. "La danza como testimonio: Opus 32." *Revista de Bellas Artes* 9, no. 2 (1973): 15–16.

García, Richard A. "Danza de los huesos." *Vuelta* 2, no. 20 (1978): 27.

García Arreola, Román. *La música y el baile de "la chilena" en la costa oaxaqueña*. Oaxaca: Proveedora Escolar, 1990.

García Canclini, Nestor. *Notas sobre las máscaras, danzas y fiestas de Michoacán*. Morelia, Michoacan: Comite Editorial del Gobierno de Michoacan, 1985.

Garrido, Juan S. *Historia de la música popular de México: 1896–1973*. México: Editorial Extemporaneos, 1974.

Gavina, Mario. *La danza folklórica mexicana: Recopilación*. Hermosillo, Son.: Editorial Casa de la Cultura de Sonora, 1988.

Genin, Auguste. *Notes sur les danses, la musique et les chants des mexicains anciens et Modernes: avec 48 figures*. Paris: E. Leroux, 1913.

Gillmor, Frances. *The Dance Dramas of Mexican Villages*. Humanities Bulletin 14, no. 2. Tucson: University of Arizona Press, 1943.

———. *Spanish Texts of Three Dance Dramas from Mexican Villages*. Humanities Bulletin 13, no. 4. Tucson: University of Arizona Press, 1943.

Gomez Severiano, Pablo. *La danza del maíz*. Tancoco, Ver.: Copia Mecanuscrita de Proyecto Cultural Presentado al PACMYC, 1999.

González, Anáhuac. "Los concheros: la (Re)conquista de México." In *Las danzas de conquista*, eds. Jesús Jáuregui and Carlo Bonfiglioli, 207–27. México: Consejo Nacional para la Cultura y las Artes: Fondo de Cultura Económica, 1996.

González, Anita. *Jarocho's Soul: Cultural Identity and Afro-Mexican Dance*. Lanham, Md.: University Press of America, 2004.

González, Aurelio. "La danza y los museos." *Revista de Bellas Artes* 13, no. 2 (1974): 49–51.

Gonzáles, Juan. "El Ballet Folklórico de México." *Artes de México* Número 88/89 (1967).

González Torres, Yolotl. "The 'Concheros,' the Dancers of an Ancient Ritual Dance in Urban Mexico." *Bulletin of the International Committee on Urgent Anthropological and Ethnological Research* 37/8 (1995/96): 69–74.

———. *Danza tu palabra: la danza de los concheros*. México, D.F.: CONACULTA-INAH: Plaza y Valdés Editores, 2005.

Gorbea Soto, Alfonso. "Trabajo comunal y recíproco en la huasteca veracruzana." In *Cuadernos antropológicos* 1, no. 1 (1983): 29–47.

Guemes Jiménez, Román. *Mira, aquí estamos!: Pláticas en torno a la danza los Santiagos de Atzalán, Veracruz*. Xalapa, Ver., Mexico: Universidad Veracruzana, 1996.

Guerra, Elias. *Etnografía del estado de Puebla*. Mexico: Inedito, 1979.

Guerrero, José E. *La chilena: Estudio geomusical*. Mexico, D.F.: FONADAN, 196–?

Guerrero Guerrero, Raul. *Un recorrido por la huasteca hidalguense.* México, D.F.: Instituto Nacional de Antropología e Historia, 1947.

Gutiérrez, Electra. *Danzas y bailes populares.* México: Editorial Hermes, 1976.

Gutiérrez Rodríguez, José Javier. "Soluciones y salidas en la danza de las horas: Primera llamada." *El cotidiano* 15, no. 92 (1988): 84–94.

Guzmán A., José Napoleón. *Uruapan: Paraíso que guarda tesoros enterrados, acordes musicales y danzas de negros.* Morelia, México: Instituto de Investigaciones Históricas, UMSNH; Uruapan, Michoacán, México: Grupo Cultural "Uruapan Visto pos los Uruapenses"; Morelia, Michoacán: Morevallado Editores, 2002.

Harris, Max. "Moctezuma's Daughter: The Role of La Malinche in Mesoamerican Dance." *Journal of American Folklore* 109, no. 432 (1996): 149–77.

———. "The Return of Moctezuma: Oaxaca's Danza de la Pluma and New Mexico's Danza de los Matachines." *The Drama Review* 41, no. 1 (1997): 106–34.

Heller, Lisa L. *Dance Dramas of the Mexican Highlands.* San Francisco: San Francisco Crafts and Folk Arts Museum, 1983.

Heredia Casanova, Marta. *Raíces de nuestro México: Muestra de la indumentaria indígena = A sample of Mexican Indian costumes.* Guadalajara, Mexico: Universidad Autónoma de Guadalajara, 1986.

———. *El legado del maestro Marcelo Torreblanca.* Guadalajara, México: Universidad Autónoma de Guadalajara, 2002.

Hernández, Benjamín. "Mexican Dance in the Los Angeles Public, 1970–1999." MA Thesis, University of California at Los Angeles, 1999.

Hernández, Joanne. *The Art and Tradition of Mexican Indian Dance Masks.* Santa Clara, Calif.: Triton Museum of Art, 1982.

Horcasitas Pimentel, Fernando. "El teatro popular en nahuatl y una danza de Santiago." *Revista de la Universidad de México* 29, no. 5 (1975): 1–9.

———. "La danza de los tecuanes." *Estudios de cultura nahuatl* 14 (1980): 239–86.

———. "Versos de la danza de Santiagos de Taxco, Guerrero." *Anales de antropología* 17, no. 2 (1980): 99–157.

Herrera, Julio. *Cinco décadas de investigación sobre música y danza indígena.* México, D.F.: Instituto Nacional Indigenista, 2002.

Houston, Stephen D. "Quetzal Feather Dance at Bonampak, Chiapas, Mexico." *Sociétè des Amèricanistes* 70 (1984): 127–37.

Huberman, Miriam. "La danza de 1986." *México en el Arte* 13 (1986): 87–90.

———. "Lo mexicano en la danza contemporanea." *México en el Arte* 17 (1987): 28–34.

Huerta, Jorge A. *A Bibliography of Chicano and Mexican Dance, Drama, and Music.* Oxnard, Calif.: Colegio Quetzalcoatl, 1972.

Ibarra, Domingo. *Bailes.* México, D.F., 1858.

Icho, Alain. *La religion de los totonacas de la sierra.* México: Instituto Nacional Indigenista; Secretaria de Educación Pública, 1973.

Illescas Nájera, Idalia. "Sobre la danza de los Santiagos de Huichila." *La palabra y el hombre* 114 (2000): 105–9.

Instituto Nacional de Estadística, Geografía e Informática. *Veracruz: Conteo de poblacion y vivienda.* Resultados definitivos. Tomos II y III, 1996.

Jarabes y fandanguitos: Imagen y música del baile popular. Mexico, D.F.: Museo Nacional de Arte, 1990.

Jara Gámez, Simón, Aurelio Rodríquez Yeyo, and Antonio Zedillo Castillo. *De Cuba con amor . . . el danzón en México.* México: Grupo Azabache: Consejo Nacional para la Cultura y las Artes, 1994.

Jáuregui, Jesus, ed. *Música y danzas del Gran Nayar.* México, D.F.: Centro de Estudios Mexicanos y Centroamericanos: Instituto Nacional Indigenista, 1993.

———. "La serpiente emplumada entre los coras y huicholes." *Arqueología mexicana* 9, no. 53 (2002): 64–69.

Jenkins, Ruth E. *An Historical Study of the Dances of the Mexican Indians in the Latter Pre-Hispanic, Colonial and Modern Periods of Mexico.* New York, 1932.

Jiménez, Guillermo. "The Dance in Mexico." *Pan American Union* 75 (1941): 316–24.

———. *Danzas de México.* México: Ediciones de Arte, 1948.

———. *7 ensayos sobre danza.* México: Universidad Nacional Autónoma de México, 1950.

Jiménez de Báez, Yvette. *Lenguajes de la tradición popular fiesta, canto, música y representación.* México: El Colegio de México, Centro de Estudios Lingüísticos y Literarios, Seminario de Tradiciones Populares, 2002.

Johansson, Patrick. "Cuecuechcuicatl: Canto travieso de los aztecas." *Estudios de cultura nahuatl* 21 (1991): 83–97.

Juarez Cao Romero, Alexis. *La cosmovisión en las danzas tradicionales: Rituales de los nahuas de la Sierra Norte de Puebla: Proceso rituales y sistema festivo en el municipio de Xochitlán.* México: Tesis de licenciatura en Etnohistoria, Escuela Nacional de Antropologia e Historia, 1995.

———. *Entre rituales y teofanías.* Puebla, México: Secretaría de Cultura, 1996.

———. *Catolicismo popular y fiestas: Sistema gestivo y vida religiosa de un pueblo indígena del estado de Puebla.* Mexico: Benermerita Universidad Autonoma de Puebla, 1999.

Juarez Rueda, Perfecto. *Ejtzpidijc tza'ndu'aambi/Los danzantes de Coatlaán: en mixe y español.* Mexico, D.F.: Instituto Linguistico de Verano, 1986.

Kaplan, Bernice A. "Changing Functions of the Huanancha Dance at the Corpus Christi Festival in Paracho, Michoacan, Mexico." *Journal of American Folklore* 64 (1951): 383–92.

Kendrick, Edith Johnston. *Regional Dances of Mexico.* Dallas: B. Upshaw, 1935.

Kenefick, Ruth M. *The Power and Position of the Spanish and Mexican Folk Dance in Southern California.* PhD Dissertation, University of California at Los Angeles, 1936.

Kurath, Gertrude P. "Los Concheros." *Journal of American Folklore* 59, no. 234 (1946): 387–99.

———. "Reconstruction of Precortesian Dances: Distribution of Roles." *El Palacio* 67, no. 6 (1960): 210–13.

Lara Barragan, Antonio. *El danzón es cultura: Colección de ensayos breves sobre el danzón y temas afines.* Guadalajara, Jalisco, México: Ediciones Cuellar, 2000.

Lara González, Everardo. *Matemática y simbolismo en la danza autóctona de México.* México, 1993.

Larson, Helga. "The Mexican Indian Flying Pole Dance." *National Geographic Magazine* 71, no. 3 (March 1937): 387–400.

Lavalle, Josefina. *Danza de las varitas: Tzineja, Huehuetlán, San Luis Potosí: Antecedentes históricos, constantes prehispánicas y estado actual de la danza.* Gobierno del Estado, San Luis Potosí, 1985.

Leal, Luis. "From Ritual to Game: The Flying-pole Dance." *New Scholar* 8 no. 1–2 (1982): 129–42.

Lechuga, Ruth D. "La serpiente en máscaras y danzas contemporaneas." *Artes de México* 56 (2001): 24–33.

Lekis, Lisa. *Folk Dances of Latin America.* New York: The Scarecrow Press, Inc., 1958.

Limón, Jose E. *Dancing with the Devil: Society and Cultural Poetics in Mexican-American South Texas.* Madison: University of Wisconsin Press, 1994.

———. "Texas-Mexican Popular Music and Dancing: Some Notes on History and Symbolic Process." *Latin American Music Review* 4, no. 2 (1983): 229–46.

Llano, Enrique. *Danses indiennes du Mexique.* Bruxelles: M. Hayez, 1939.

Loewe, Ronald. "Yucatan's Dancing Pig's Head (Cuch): Icon, Carnival, and Commodity." *Journal of American Folklore* 116, no. 462 (2003): 420–23.

López Austin, Alfredo. *Cuerpo humano e ideología. Las concepciones de los antiguos nahuas.* México: UNAM, 1984.

"Los Viejitos: The Dance of the Little Old Men." *Folk Dance Scene* 33, no. 7 (1997): 12–17.

Loubat, Joseph Florimond, duc de. "Letra de la 'Danza de Pluma' de Moctezuma y Hernan Cortés con los capitanes y reyes que intervinieron en la conquista de México." Proceedings of the Twelfth International Congress of Americanists held in Paris, 1902, 221–61.

Loza, Steven J. "The Son Jarocho: the History, Style and Repertory of a Changing Mexican Musical Tradition." *Aztlán* 13, no. 1–2 (Spring–Fall, 1982): 327–33.

Lucero-White, Aurora. *Folk-dances of the Spanish-colonials of New Mexico.* Santa Fe, N.M.: Examiner Publishing Co., 1940.

Lupo, Alessandro. "Tatiochihualatzin, valores simbólicos del alcohol en la Sierra Norte de Puebla." In *Estudios de cultura nahuatl.* México: UNAM, 1991.

Macías Moranchel, Rosa María. "La danza de los tlaxinquis y tejamanileros." *Choreography and Dance* 3, no. 4 (1994): 73–79.

Maestas, Enrique G. M. "Grupo Tlaloc and Alternative Forms of Pedagogy." MA Thesis. University of Texas at Austin, 1998.

Mansfield, Portia. *The Conchero Dancers of Mexico.* Ann Arbor, Mich., 1953.

Manzanos, Rosario. "La danza en el México actual." *Cuadernos hispanoamericanos* 549–550 (1996): 225–36.

Martí, Samuel. "Danza precortesiana." *Cuadernos americanos* 18, no. 5 (1959): 129–51.

———. *Canto, danza y música precortesianos.* México: Fondo de Cultura Económica, 1961.

———. *Dances of Anahuac; the Choreography and Music of Precortesian Dances.* New York: Wenner-Gren Foundation for Anthropological Research, 1964.

Martínez, Alma Rosa. "Danzas en la Villa de Guadalupe el 12 de diciembre." *Boletín del Centro de Investigaciones Antropológicas de México* 11 (1961): 13–16.

Martinez Hernandez, Rosendo. *Fiesta en la Huasteca: Una mirada a la huapangueada, los sones, la poesía y las danzas tradicionales de mi tierra.* México: Rosendo Martinez Hernández, 2005.

———. *Xantolo: El día de muertos en la Huasteca veracruzana.* México: Impresora Gráfica del Centro, 2002.

Martínez-Hunter, Sanjuanita. *The Development of Dance in Mexico, 1325–1910.* PhD Dissertation, University of California at Los Angeles, 1984.

Martínez Luna, Esther. "Ciclo Miguel Covarrubias de danza contemporanea." *México en el Arte* 9 (1985): 91.

Martínez Peñaloza, Porfirio. *Sagrado y profano en la danza tradicional de México.* México: M. A. Porrua, 1986.

Martínez Rios, Jorge. "Analisis funcional de la 'Guelaguetza Agricola.'" *Revista Mexicana de Sociología* 26, no. 1 (1964): 79–125.

Mata Torres, Ramón, *Los tastuanes de Nextipac.* Guadalajara, Jalisco, Mexico: Gobierno de Jalisco, Secretaría General, Unidad Editorial, 1987.

———. "Los huicholes." *Casa de la Cultura Jalisciense, Guadalajara, México.* Series title: Ediciones de la Casa de la Cultura Jalisciense, 2002.

Matos Moctezuma, Eduardo. *Estudios de cultura popular.* México, D.F.: Instituto Nacional Indigenista, 1967.

McAfee, Bryon."Danza de la gran conquista." *Tlalocan* III, no. 3 (1952): 246-73.

Memoria: Encuentros de música y danza indígenas. Tuxtla, Gutiérrez, Chiapas: Gobierno del Estado de Chiapas; Consejo Estatal para la Cultura y las Artes de Chiapas; Centro Estatal de Lenguas, Artes y Literatura Indígenas, 1997.

Mendez, Xavier. "Dance Masks of Mexico." *Nuestro* 4, no. 6 (1980): 58.

Mendoza, Vicente. "La danza en la colonia." Mexico: *Artes de Mexico,* no. 3, 1955: 19–30.

———. "La música y la danza." In *Esplendor del México antiguo,* ed. Jorge R. Acosta, 323–54. México: Editorial del Valle de México, 1959.

———. *Panorama de la música tradicional de Mexico.* Mexico: Universidad Nacional Autónoma de México, Instituto de Investigaciones Estéticas, 1984.

Mendoza Cruz, Luciano. *Festival costeño de la danza: Danzas y bailes de la costa oaxaqueña.* Oaxaca: Instituto Oaxaqueño de las Culturas; Consejo Nacional para la Cultura y las Artes; Dirección General de Culturas Populares; Coordinación de Descentralización del CNCA, 1994.

Mérida, Carlos. "Pre-hispanic Dance and Theatre." *Mexican Life* 15, no. 10 (1939): 25–27.

———. *Mexican Costume.* Twenty-five color plates and text by Carlos Mérida, with a note by René d'Harnoncourt. Chicago: The Pocahontas Press, 1941.

———. *Escritos de Carlos Mérida sobre el arte: La danza /* [estudio introductorio y selección de textos, Cristina Mendoza]. México, D.F.: INBA; Centro Nacional de Investigación y Documentación de Artes Plásticas, 1990.

Mesopotamia de Chiapas "Villaflores": Policromia de Chiapas, bailes y danzas. Villaflores, Chiapas: Esc. Prim. Fral. Lic. Adólfo López Mateos, 1988.

Método para aprender por si solo el baile de la polka. México, D.F.: Valdez, 1845.

Molina E., Arturo. *La última danza apache.* Chihuahua, Mex.: Talleres de Magnacolor, 1999.

Mompradé, Electra L., and Tonatiúh Gutiérrez. *Danza y bailes populares.* México: Hermes, 1981.

Montaño Villalobos, Alicia. *Sinaloa: Danza y tradición.* México, D.F.: Subdirección General de Prestaciones Sociales, Jefatura de Servicios de Promoción Cultural, Instituto Mexicano del Seguro Social, 1989.

Montero de Amaya, Gloria. *Perfil de bailes y danzas tradicionales del estado de Campeche.* Campeche, 198–?

Montes de Oca, Jose G. *Danzas indígenas mejicanas.* Tlaxcala, Tlax.: Imprenta del Gobierno del Estado, 1926.

Montoya Briones, José de Jesús. *Jerez y su gente: Región de virgenes, nomadismo y resistencia cultural.* Mexico, D.F.: Plaza y Valdes, Instituto Nacional de Antropología e Historia, 1996.

Moyo, Mauro Rafael, and Adolfo Best-Maugard. *Mexican Regional Folk Dance and Costume.* México: Secretaría de Educación Pública, 1940.

Museo Nacional de Cultura Populares. *Nuestro maíz: Treinta monografías populares.* México: Museo de Culturas Populares, SEP, 1982.

Múzquiz, Rodolfo. *Bailes y danzas tradicionales.* Mexico City: Instituto Mexicano del Seguro Social, 1988.

Nájera-Ramírez, Olga. "Festival Performance as Racial Discourse: Los Tastoanes de Jocotán." *Raíces.* Jalapa, Ver.: Asociación Nacional de Grupos Folklóricos, 1995.

Nava L., E. Fernando. "Danzas con reverencias para una conquista gentil." *Anales de Antropología* 29 (1992): 301–39.

Navarrete, Carlos. "Un escrito sobre danzas zoques de antes de 1940." *Tlalocán* 10 (1985): 449–56.

Núñez Mesta, Martín Antonio. *Bailes del folklore mexicano: Pasos, coreografía y vestuario.* México: Editorial Trillas, 1990.

Obregón Andrade, Luis Felipe. *Mexican Dances.* México: Riveroll's Art Gallery, 1947.

Ocampo, Carlos. *Cuerpos en vilo.* Mexico, D.F.: CONACULTA, 2001.

Ochoa, Alvaro. *Mitote, fandango y mariacheros.* Zamora, Michoacán: El Colegio de Michoacán, 1994.

Ochoa, Lorenzo. *Huaxtecos y totonacos.* México: Consejo Nacional para la Cultura y las Artes, 1989.

Ochoa Campos, Moisés. *La chilena guerrerense.* Chilpancingo de los Bravos, Gro.: Ediciones del Gobierno del Estado, 1987.

Oleszkiewicz, Malgorzata. "'La danza de la pluma' y el sincretismo cultural en México." *Revista de crítica literaria latinoamericana* 23 (1997): 46.

Olgúin, Enriqueta. "Como nacio chicomexochitl." In *Prácticas agrícolas y medicina tradicional,* ed. Jesus Ruvalcaba y Graciela Alcalá, PP. Mexico: CIESAS, 1993.

Olivera Bustamante, Mercedes. *Catálogo nacional de danzas.* México, D.F.: Fondo Nacional para el Desarrollo de la Danza Popular Mexicana, 1974.

Olmos Aguilera, Miguel. *El sabio de la fiesta: Música y mitología en la región Cahitatarahumara.* México: INAH, 1998.

Olvera Estrada, Martha Otilia. *Los tiempos del patrón: Danza de mil soles: los últimos trabajadores de la hacienda en Querétaro.* Querétaro: Talleres Gráficos de Gobierno del Estado de Querétaro, 1661.

Orozco, Gilberto. "Tradiciones y leyendas del Istmo de Tehuantepec." *Revista Musical Mexicana,* 1946.

Orvananos, Genoveva. "La tradición de la danza de los concheros." In *Historia y actualidad de los grupos indígenas de Queretaro,* ed. Carlos Viramontes. Mexico: INAH, 1992.

Oseguera M., Andres. "Mito y danza entre los huaves y los chontales de Oaxaca: La lucha entre el rayo y la serpiente." *Dimensión antropológica* 21 (2001): 85–111.

Oxman, Nelson. "Danza y pintura." *Plural* 9, no. 107 (1980): 83–84.

Parga, Pablo. *Cuerpo vestido de nación: Danza folklórica y nacionalismo mexicano, 1921–1939.* México: CONACULTA/FONCA, 2004.

Peña, Manuel. *The Mexican American Orquesta: Music, Culture, and the Dialectic of Conflict.* Austin: University of Texas Press, 1999.

Peñaloza, Porfirio M. *Sagrado y profano en la danza tradicional de México y otros ensayos afines.* México: M.A. Porrua, 1986.

Petersen, Patricia. *Voladores.* Columbus, Ohio: Peter Bedrick Books, 2002.

Pill, Albert S. *Mexican Regional Dance for the Elementary School.* PhD Dissertation, University of California at Los Angeles, 1963.

Pinkus Rendon, Manuel Jesus. *De la herencia a la enajenación: Danzas y bailes "tradicionales" de Yucatán.* Mexico, D.F.: UNAM, Instituto de Investigaciones Filológicas; Coordinación de Humanidades, Unidad Académica de Ciencias Sociales y Humanidades, 2005.

Pino Memije, Francis. *La danza en Guerrero.* Taxco: Instituto Guerrerense de la Cultura, 1985.

Pomar, María Teresa. *Danza-mascara y rito-ceremonia.* México, D.F.: Fondo Nacional para el Fomento de las Artesanías, 1982.

Poveda, Pablo. "Danza De Concheros en Austin, Texas: Entrevista con Andres Segura Granados." *Latin American Music Review* 2, no. 2 (1981): 280–99.

Priego Martínez, Jorge. *El zapateo tabasqueño.* Villahermosa: Gobierno del Estado de Tabasco, 1989.

Primer encuentro nacional sobre investigación de la danza: 8 y 9 de diciembre de 1984. Mexico, D.F. Conference. México: Instituto Nacional de Bellas Artes, Centro Nacional de Investigación, Documentación e Información de la Danza "Jose Limón," 1984.

Pulido, F. Maria del Carmen. *Crónica histórica del huapango huasteco veracruzano: Trovas, música, danza y tradiciones.* Xalapa, Equiz., Ver.: Gobierno del Estado de Veracruz, Secretaría de Educación y Cultura, 1991.

Quezada, Noemi. "La danza del volador y algunas creencias de Tempoal en el siglo XVIII." *Tlalocan* VII (1977): 357-66.

Ramírez, Maira. *Estudio etnocoreográfico de la danza de conquista de Tlacoachistlahuaca, Guerrero.* México, D.F.: Instituto Nacional de Antropología e Historia, 2003.

Ramírez, Maira, and Itze Valle. "Cortés contra Moctezuma: Cuauhtémoc: el intercambio de mujeres." In *Las danzas de conquista,* eds. Jesús Jáuregui and Carlo Bonfiglioli, 339–98. México: Consejo Nacional para la Cultura y las Artes: Fondo de Cultura Económica, 1996.

Ramírez Canul, Marcos. *Música y músicos tradicionales de Quintana Roo.* Quintana Roo, Mex.: Instituto Quintanarroense de la Cultura: Universidad de Quintana Roo, 2001.

Ramiro, Maritza. *El simbolismo en la danza de 'El volador.'* México: B.A. thesis. Escuela Nacional de Antropología e Historia, 1996.

Ramos Smith, Maya. "Los Noventa." In *La danza en México durante la época colonial.* México, D.F.: Alianza Editorial Mexicana; Consejo Nacional para la Cultura y las Artes, 1990.

Recio Flores, Sergio. *Danza tlaxcalteca de matachines.* Saltillo, Coah., México: Ediciones Recinto de Juarez, 1978.

Reifler, Victoria. *El cristo indígena, el rey nativo.* México: Fondo de Cultura Económica, 1989.

Reyes Sahagún, Carlos. *Danza de quetzales bajo el sol de paris.* Aguascalientes: Instituto Cultural de Aguascalientes, 2001.

Rodríguez Peòa, A. Hilda. "La danza tradicional en México: un análisis bibliográfico." *Sociedad Mexicana de Antropología, Mesa Redonda* 13, no. 3 (1975): 145–60.

Roíz, Carmen Teresa. "La magia del Ballet Folklórico de México." *Vista* 10, no. 1 (1994): 32.

Romero, Brenda M. "Old World Origins of the Matachines Dance of New Mexico." In *Vistas of American Music, Essays and Compositions in Honor of William K. Kearns,* ed. Susan L. Porter and John Graziano, 338–56. Michigan: Harmonie Park Press, 1999.

———. "The Indita Genre of New Mexico: Gender and Cultural Identification." In *Chicana Traditions: Continuity and Change,* ed. Olga Nájera-Ramirez and Norma Cantú, 56–80. Urbana: University of Illinois Press, 2001.

Rostas, Susanna. "The Conchero of Mexico: Changing Images of Indianity." *Cambridge Anthropology* 17, no. 2 (1994): 38–55.

———. "The Production of Gendered Imagery: The Concheros of Mexico." In *Machos, Mistresses, Madonnas: Contesting the Power of Latin American Gender Imagery,* ed. Marit Melhuus and Kristi Anne Stølen, 207–29. New York: Verso, 1996.

———. "'Mexicanidad': The Resurgence Of The Indian Popular Mexican Nationalism." Paper for Latin American Studies Association, Guadalajara, Jalisco, 1997.

———. "From Ritualization to Performativity: The Concheros of Mexico." In *Ritual, Performance, Media,* ed. Felicia Hughes-Freeland, 85–103. New York: Routledge, 1998.

Royce, Anya P. *Mexican Dance Forms: A Bibliography with Annotations.* Palo Alto, Calif.: Institute for the Study of Contemporary Cultures of the Institute of International Relations, Stanford University, 1967.

———. "An Acculturational Study of Some Dances of Oaxaca, Mexico." *Researches in Latin American Society* (1968): 37–79.

———. "Music, Dance, and Fiesta: Definitions of Isthmus Zapotec Community." *Latin American Anthropology Review* 3, no. 2 (1991): 51–60.

Ruiz, E. Cortes. "La guelaguetza en la mayordomia de Cuilapan: Un nivel de la ayuda interpersonal." *Anales: Instituto Nacional de Antropología e Historia México* 7, no. 6 (1976): 71–90.

Ruiz, Luis B. *Breve historia de la danza en México.* México: Libro-Mex, 1956.

Ruvalcaba Mercado, Jesús. *Tecnología agrícola y trabajo familiar: Una etnografía agrícola de la huasteca veracruzana.* México: CIESAS-eds. De la Casa Chata, 1992.

———. "Los huastecos de Veracruz." In *Etnografía de los pueblos indígenas de México, vol. 3. Región oriental,* ed. Marcela Villegas Rodríguez, 105–64. México, D.F.: Instituto Nacional Indigenista, Secretaría de Desarrollo Social, 1995.

Ruyter, Nancy L. "Images of Aztlán and Tenochtitlan in 20th Century Danza Azteca." *Cairon: Revista de Ciencias de la Danza* 3 (1996): 73–81.

———. "La Meri and the World of Dance." *Anales: Instituto de investigaciones estéticas* 77 (2000): 169–88.

Saavedra, Rafael M., and Nabor Hurtado. *Danza de los "tecomates."* México: Secretaría de Educación Pública, Dirección de Misiones Culturales, 1930–39.

———. *"Los inditos": Danza del Señor de Chalma.* México: Secretaría de Educación Pública, Dirección de Misiones Culturales, 1931.

Saldívar, Gabriel. *Historia de la música en México.* México: Biblioteca Enciclopedica del Estado de México, 1981.

Salinero, Fernando G., and Elma Yolanda Gonzáles de Radke, eds. Festival Folklórico Mexicano: ANGF, IV Handbook. Seattle: Shorey's Bookstore, 1977.

Sánchez, Leopoldo. *La danza en México.* Culiacán, Sin.: Colegio de Sinaloa, 2000.

Sánchez García, Rosa Virginia. "La danza del Rey Colorado." *Signos* (1989): 127-36.

Sandoval, Marcela. *Mexican/New Mexican Folk Dance.* Albuquerque: Hispanic Culture Foundation, 1994.

Sandoval Forero, Eduardo A. *La danza de los arrieros: Entre la identitad y la memoria.* México, D.F.: Insumisos Latinoamericanos, 2004.

Sandoval Forero, Eduardo A., and Marcelino Castillo, eds. *Danzas tradicionales: Actualidad u obsolescencia?* México: Autónoma del Estado de Mexico, 1998.

Sanchez-Fernández, Jose Roberto. *Bailes y sones deshonestos en la Nueva España.* Veracruz: Instituto Veracruzano de Cultura, 1998.

Sánchez Flores, Francisco. "Los paixtlis: Version de San Andres Ixtlan, Jalisco." *Fondo Nacional para el Desarrollo de la Danza Mexicana, n.d.*

———. *Danzas fundamentales de Jalisco.* México: Fonodan, 1976.

Sandstrom, Alan. "El nene lloroso y el Espiritu Nahua del Maíz: El cuerpo humano como Simbolismo Clave en la Huasteca Veracruzana." In *Nuevos aportes al conocimiento de la huasteca,* ed. Jesús Ruvalcaba, 59–94. México: Ediciones de la Casa Chata, 1997.

Sareli, Jorge. *El tango en México.* México: Editorial Diana, 1977.

Sarmiento Rubio, Epifanio. *La danza del maíz.* Xalapa, Ver.: Copia mecanuscrita, 2000.

Saucedo Rodríguez, Victor Manuel. "III Congreso de la Asociación Nacional de Grupos de Danza Folclórica Mexicana." Zacatecas, México: Asociación Nacional de Grupos de Danza Folclórica Mexicana, Delegación Zacatecas, 2000.

Scarff, Frances Beatriz González. "A Study of the Matachine Dance in Selected Areas of Mexico and Texas." MA Thesis, University of Texas at Austin, 1962.

Schwendener, Norma. *Legends and Dances of Old Mexico.* New York: Barnes, 1934.

Schwendener, Norma, and Tibbels Averil. *How to Perform the Dances of Old Mexico.* New York: A. S. Barnes and Company, 1998.

Secretaría de Educación Pública. *Monografía y música de danzas y bailes regionales presentados en las jornadas nacionales deportivos y culturales llevadas a cabo en los años 1953–1958.* México: Dirección General de Internados de Enseñanza Primaria y Escuelas Asistenciales. Talleres Gráficos de la Nacion, 1958.

Segovia, Eloisa M., and Cindy Clayman Wesley. *Folklóricos regionales de México.* Colton, Calif.: C and E Prensa, 1975.

Segundo festival costeño de la danza: Danzas y bailes de la costa oaxaqueño. Instituto Oaxaqueño de las Cultura. Gobierno del Estado de Oaxaca, 1995.

Sevilla, Amparo. *De carnaval a Xantolo: contacto con el inframundo.* Ediciones del Programa de Desarrollo Culturual de la Huasteca, CONACULTA, México. 2002.

———. *Cuerpos de maíz: danzas agrícolas de la Huasteca.* Ediciones del Programa de Desarrollo Cultural de la Huasteca, CONACULTA, México. 2000.

———. *Danza, cultura y clases sociales.* México, D.F.: Instituto Nacional de Bellas Artes, 1990.

———. *Danzas y bailes tradicionales del Estado de Tlaxcala.* Tlahuapan, Puebla: Premia, 1985.

———. *Los templos del buen bailar.* México, D.F.: CONACULTA, Culturas Populares e Indigenas, 2003.

Silva Ruelas, Ramón. *Danzantes Unidos Festival '96 Anthology.* Salinas, Calif.: Danzantes Unidos, 1996.

Shelton, Anthony. "Los Tlocololeros: A Structuralist Interpretation of a Mexican Dance Drama." *Antropologia Portuguesa* 16–17 (2000): 43–68.

Sklar, Deidre. "Enacting Religious Belief: A Movement Ethnography of the Annual Fiesta of Tortugas, New Mexico." PhD Dissertation, New York University, 1991.

———. "All the Dances Have a Meaning to That Apparition: Felt Knowledge and the Danzantes of Tortugas, in Las Cruces, New Mexico." *Dance Research Journal* 31, no. 2 (Autumn 1999): 14–33.

Smith, Deborah L. "Mexican Folk Dance in California: A Summary of the Cause and Effects of the Rise in Popularity of Mexican Folk Dancing, 1940–1990." *UCLA Journal of Dance Ethnology* 15 (1991): 68–77.

Smoot, Sharene L. *Frances Toor as an Authority on Mexican Folk Dance.* Greenville, N.C.: East Carolina College, 1963.

Spicer, Edward H. "La danza yaqui del venado en la cultura mexicana." *América indígena* 25, no. 1 (1965): 117–39.

Stark, Alan. "La danza en México durante la época virreinal." *Cairon: Revista de ciencias de la danza* 4 (1998): 9–17.

Straffon Vázquez, Elodia. *Fortalecimiento del nacionalismo en México a través de sus danzas y bailes populares.* México: Academia de la Danza Mexicana, 1978.

Talavera, F. *Cuaderno de la danza de la conquista: Un documento para la historia de México.* Anales: Instituto Nacional de Antropología e Historia, 1976.

Téllez Duarte, Agustín. "Los concheros de Baja California y sus perspectivas de investigación." *Estudios Fronterizos* 5 no. 14 (September–December 1987): 111–16.

Temas para el estudio de la teoría e historia de la danza. Celaya, Gto., Ediciones de la Casa de la Cultura de Celaya "Francisco Eduardo Tresguerras," INBA, SEP, Depto. de Danza, 1978.

Torres, Larry. "Los Matachines Desenmascarados." In *Six Nuevomexicano Folk Dramas for Advent Season.* Albuquerque: University of New Mexico Press, 1999.

Tortajada Quiróz, Margarita. "Danza de mujer: El nacionalismo revolucionario de Nellie Campobello." *El Cotidiano* 13, no. 84 (1997): 87–94.

Tradiciones: Ballet Folklórico. VHS. Escuela Superior de Música y Danza de Monterrey. Mexico: Claroscuro Producciones, 34 min, 1991.

Trajes y danzas de México. Mexico: Porrua: PB Distribuidor, Libros y Servicios, 1984.

Trujillo, Lawrence A. *The Spanish Influence on the Mexican Folkdance of Yucatán, Veracruz, and Jalisco, Mexico.* Denver: Dart Publications, 1974.

Urtubees, Dionisia. "La danza en México." *Revista Nacional de Cultura* (Venezuela) 237 (1978): 44–59.

Valdiosera, Ramón. *Mexican Dances.* México: Editorial Fischgrund, 1900–1949.

———. *Mexican Folklore.* México, D.F.: Editorial Fischgrund, n.d. "Danzantes/Dancers." *Artes de México* 21 (1949): 78–96.

Valle, Liliana, and Bertha Schulte. *Los bailes de salón en el Distrito Federal.* México, D.F.: INBA-Centro Nacional de Investigación, Documentación e Información de la Danza José Limón, 1993.

Vásquez, Raquel. "La organización de la danza: Una experiencia." *Revista de la Universidad de México* 25, no. 8 (1971): 39–40.

Vázquez Hall, Patricia. "El Grupo Frederick: Danza o pantomima?" *México en el Arte* 15, no. 108 (1986–87).

———. "La Danza en el Festival Internacional Cervantino, Ciudad de México." *Plural* 19, no. 219 (1989): 67–78.

———. "Historia de la danza." *Plural* 22, no. 255 (1992): 72–73.

———. "Danza folklórica hoy." *Plural* 22, no. 259 (1993): 72–73.

———. "Danza: De todo en un día." *Plural* (1993).

———. "Waldeen, pensadora y maestra de la danza." *Plural* 22, no. 265 (1993): 85.

Velasco Rivero, Pedro de. *Danzar o morir: Religión y resistencia a la rominación en la cultura tarahumar.* México, D.F.: Centro de Reflexión Teológica, 1987.

Vélez Calvo, Raúl. *El baile y la danza en Guerrero.* Chilpancingo: Instituto Guerrerense de la Cultura, 2003.

Vento, Arnoldo Carlos. "Aztec Conchero Dance Tradition: Historic, Religious and Cultural Significance." *Wicazo SA Review* 10(1): 59–64, 1989.

Villanueva, Alberto. "Parachico, Fiesta de enero en Chiapa de Corzo." *Terra Maya* (January 14, 2001): 4.

Villavicencio Rojas, Josué Mario. *Mojigangas y pachecos: Leyenda, tradición y magia en la mixteca oaxaqueña.* Puebla, Puebla: Benemérita Universidad Autónoma de Puebla, 1998.

Villazana Millan, Pedro. *Danzas y bailes de Morelos.* Cuernavaca, Mor.: Instituto de Cultura de Morelos: Dirección General de Culturas Populares, 2000.

Vivian, Miriam. *La danza de los pájaros.* Hermosillo, Son.: Editorial Unison, 1998.

Waldeen. "El expresionismo y mi participación en la danza moderna mexicana." *Plural* 18, no. 213 (1989): 49–50.

Wilder, Carleton S. *The Yaqui Deer Dance: A Study in Cultural Change.* Washington: United States Government Printing Office, 1963.

Williams, Robert. *Danzas y andanzas.* México: Gobierno del Estado de Veracruz/Instituto Veracruzano de Cultura, 1997.

Wilson, Rebecca Van Sciver. *The Ceremonial of the Conchero Dancers of Mexico.* MA Thesis, University of Oregon, 1970.

Yanaguana Society. *Presentation of the Matachine Dance by Chichimec and other Indians, December thirteenth, nineteen hundred thirty-four.* San Antonio, Tex.: Yanaguana Society, 1934.

Zamarripa Castañeda, Rafael, and Xóchitl Medina Ortiz. *Trajes de danza mexicana.* Colima, Col.: Universidad de Colima, 2001.

Zaleta, Leonardo. *La danza de los voladores: Origen y simbolismo.* Poza Rica de Hidalgo, Ver.: Grupo Editorial León, 1992.

Zárate, Alberto. *Cuando los huaraches se acaban y la tradicion se pierde. El Impacto sociocultural en las expresiones dancísticas de la comunidad de Zihuateutla, Puebla.* México: Tésis de licenciatura en Antropológica Social. Escuela Nacional de Antropología e Historia, 1996.

Zvirie Vazquez, Gema B., and Francisco Acosta Baez. "Problemática de los grupos de danza tradicional en el norte de Veracruz." In *Huasteca II. Prácticas agrícolas y medicina tradicional. Arte y sociedad. Selección de trabajos pertenecientes al V y VI encuentros de investigadores de la Huasteca,* ed. Jesús Ruvalcaba and Graciela Alcalá, 197-203. México: CIESAS, 1993.

Works Cited

Abrahams, Roger. 1983. "Shouting Match at the Border: The Folklore of Display Events." In *"And Other Neighborly Names": Social Process and Cultural Image in Texas Folklore,* ed. Richard Bauman and Roger D. Abrahams, 303–21. Austin: University of Texas Press.

Acevedo Conde, Maria Luisa. 1997. "Historia de la Fiesta de los Lunes del Cerro." In *Historia del arte de Oaxaca: Arte contemporaneo,* ed. Margarita Dalton Palomo, Verónica Loera, and Chávez Castro, 357–78. Oaxaca, México: Instituto Oaxaqueño de las Culturas.

Aceves, Jorge E., Renée de la Torre, and Patricia Safa. 2004. "Fragmentos urbanos de una misma ciudad: Guadalajara." *Revista Espiral: Estudios Sobre Estado y sociedad* 11, no. 31: 277–322.

Adair, Christy. 1992. *Women and Dance: Sylphs and Sirens.* New York: New York University Press.

Adler, Rachel. 2004. *Yucatecans in Dallas, Texas: Breaching the Border, Bridging the Distance.* Boston: Pearson.

Aguirre Beltrán, Gonzalo. 1946. *La población negra de México, 1519–1810: Estudio etnohistórico.* México: Ediciones Fuente Cultural.

———. 1986. *Zongolica: Encuentro de dioses y santos patronos.* Mexico: Fondo de Cultura Económica.

Aguirre Cristiani, Gabriela, and Felipe Segura Escalona. 1994. *Amalia Hernández's Folkloric Ballet of Mexico.* Mexico, D.F.: Fomento Cultural Banamex, A.C.

Ajú, Marta, Jaime González, and Francisco Talavera. 2004. "La noche bárbara: discursos sobre el otro." Unpublished manuscript.

Alarcón, Norma. 1990. "Chicana Feminism: In the Tracks of 'The' Native Woman." *Cultural Studies* 4, no. 3: 147–59.

Almaguer, Tomás. 1994. *Racial Fault Lines: The Historical Origins of White Supremacy in California.* Berkeley: University of California Press.

Althusser, Louis. 1971. *Lenin and Philosophy and Other Essays.* New York: Monthly Review Press.

Alurista. 1995. "El Plan de Aztlán." In *"Takin' it to the Streets": A Sixties Reader,* ed. Alexander Bloom and Wini Breines, 181–83. New York: Oxford University Press.

Amnesty International. 1986. *Mexico: Human Rights in Rural Areas: Exchange of Documents with the Mexican Government on Human Rights Violations in Oaxaca and Chiapas.* London: Amnesty International.

———. 1990. *Mexico: Reports of Human Rights Violations Against Members of the Triqui Indigenous Group of Oaxaca.* London: Amnesty International.

Amorós, Celia. 1985. *Hacia una crítica de la razón patriarcal.* Madrid: Anthropos Editorial del Hombre.

Anderson, Benedict. 1991. *Imagined Communities: Reflections on the Origin and Spread of Nationalism.* London: Verso.

Anzaldúa, Gloria. 1987. *Borderlands/La Frontera: The New Mestiza.* San Francisco: Aunt Lute Books.

Appadurai, Arjun. 1996. "Global Ethnoscapes." In *Modernity at Large. Cultural Dimensions of Globalization,* ed. Arjun Appadurai, 48–65. Minneapolis and London: University of Minnesota Press.

Appelbaum, Nancy P., Anne S. Macpherson, and Karin Alejandra Rosemblatt, ed. 2003. *Race and Nation in Modern Latin America.* Chapel Hill: University of North Carolina Press.

Arellano, A., and Vigil, J., ed. 1980. *Arthur Campa and the Coronado Cuarto Centennial.* Las Vegas, N.M.: Editorial Telaraña.

Arreola, Daniel D. 2002. *Tejano South Texas: A Mexican American Cultural Province.* Austin: University of Texas Press.

———, ed. 2004. *Hispanic Spaces, Latino Places: Community and Cultural Diversity in Contemporary America.* Austin: University of Texas Press.

Arreola, Daniel D., and James R. Curtis. 1993. *The Mexican Border Cities: Landscape Anatomy and Place Personality.* Tucson: University of Arizona Press.

Arreola, Martha Patricia E. 1977. *Los Matachines de las fiestas de San Lorenzo en Bernalillo, Nuevo México.* Tepic, Nayarit: Secretaría de Educación y Cultura, Escuela de la Danza Mexicana.

Artesanías Díaz Zamora. 2001. "Tradicional: Fiesta de Enero en Chiapa de Corzo, Chiapas." Chiapa de Corzo, Chiapas.

Atencio, Tomas. 1985. "Social Change and Community Conflict in Old Albuquerque, New Mexico." PhD Dissertation, University of New Mexico.

Aulestia, Patricia. 1995. *La danza premoderna en México (1917–1939).* Caracas, Venezuela: UNESCO.

Ávila Palafox, Ricardo, and Tomás Calvo Buezas. 1993. *Identidades, nacionalismos, y regiones.* Guadalajara, Jalisco: Universidad de Guadalajara.

Báez-Jorge, Félix. 1988. *Los oficios de las diosas: dialéctica de la religiosidad popular en los grupos indios de México.* Xalapa, México: Universidad Veracruzana.

Ballet Folklórico de México. 1961–1983. Programs and press releases. New York Public Library, Performing Arts Division, Dance Collection.

———. 1968? *Ballet Folklórico de México.* México, D.F.: Instituto Nacional de Bellas Artes de Mexico.

Barbieri, Teresita de. 1986. *Movimientos feministas.* México: UNAM.

Barendrect, John. 1996–2002. "Dance Terms." http://www.centralhome.com/ballroomcountry/dance_terms.htm.

Barrios, Walda, and Leticia Pons. 1995. *Sexualidad y religión en los Altos de Chiapas.* Tuxtla Gutiérrez, México: Universidad Autónoma de Chiapas.

Barro Rojo. 1992. *Barro Rojo 1992; 10 años en la danza mexicana.* México: Centro Cultural Universitario (November).

Barth, Frederik, ed. 1976. *Los grupos étnicos y sus fronteras.* México: Fondo de Cultura Económica.

Basch, Linda, Nina Glick Schiller, and Christine Blanc-Szanton, ed. 1992. "Towards a Transnational Perspective on Migration: Race, Class, Ethnicity, Nationalism Reconsidered." *Annals of the New York Academy of Social Sciences* 65: 1–24.

Bateson, Gregory. 1977. *Vers une ecologie de l'esprit.* Paris: Éditions du Seuil.

Bauman, Richard. 1986. "Performance and Honor in 13th-Century Iceland." *Journal of American Folklore* 99, no. 392: 131–50.

Bohannan, Paul, and Mark Glazer. 1973. *High Points in Anthropology.* New York: Knopf.

Bonfiglioli, Carlo. 1991. ¿Quiénes son los matachines? *México Indígéna* no. 18, March: 33–39.

———. 1995. *Fariseos y matachines en la Sierra Tarahumara.* Mexico, D.F.: Instituto Nacional Indigenista.

———. 1996a. "Fariseos y matachines: El conflicto y la armonia cosmicos." In *Las danzas de conquista, I. México contemporáneo,* ed. Jesús Jáuregui and Carlo Bonfiglioli, 255–84. México, D.F.: Consejo Nacional para la Cultura y las Artes, Fondo de Cultura Economica.

———. 1996b. "Chichimecas contra franceses: De los 'Salvajes' y los Conquistadores." In *Las danzas de conquista, I. México contemporáneo,* ed. Jesús Jáuregui and Carlo Bonfiglioli, 91–115. México, D.F.: Consejo Nacional para la Cultura y las Artes, Fondo de Cultura Economica, 1996.

Bonfil Sanchez, Paloma, and Raul Marco del Point Lalli. 1999. *Las mujeres indígenas al final del milenio.* Mexico: Secretaría de Gobernación, Comision Nacional de la Mujer-FUNAP.

Booth, George C. 1969. *Mexico's School Made Society.* New York: Greenwood Press Publishers.

Bourdieu, Pierre. 2003. *La dominación masculina.* Translated by Joaquin Jorda. Barcelona: Anagrama, Tercera Edición.

Brettell, Caroline. 2003. *Anthropology and Migration. Essays in Transnationalism, Ethnicity, and Identity.* Walnut Creek, Lanham, New York, and Oxford: Altamira.

Brisset, Demetrio. 1996. "Cortés derrotado: la vision indígena de la conquista." In *Las danzas de conquista, I. México contemporáneo,* ed. Jesús Jáuregui and Carlo Bonfiglioli, 69–90. México, D.F.: Consejo Nacional para la Cultura y las Artes.

Brown, Barry. 2001. "Geographies of technology: Some comments on place, space and technology." http://www.fxpal.com/ConferencesWorkshops/ECSCW2001/brown.doc.

Broyles-González, Yolanda. 1994. *El Teatro Campesino: Theater in the Chicano Movement.* Austin: University of Texas Press.

Bruno Ruiz, Luis. 1956. *Breve historia de la danza en México.* México: Libro-Mex.

Burciaga, José Antonio. 1995. "Pachuchos and the Taxicab Brigade." In *Spilling the Beans: Lotería Chicana,* 59–71. Santa Barbara, Calif.: Joshua Odell Editions.

Butler, Judith. 1990a. "Performative Acts and Gender Constitution: An Essay in Phenomenology and Feminist Theory." In *Performing Feminisms: Feminist Critical Theory and Theatre,* ed. Sue-Ellen Case, 270–82. Baltimore: Johns Hopkins University Press.

———. 1990b. *Gender Trouble: Feminism and the Subversion of Identity.* New York: Routledge.

Buxó, María Jesús. 1991. *Antropología de la mujer: Cognición, lengua e ideología cultural.* Barcelona: Anthropos.

Campa, Arthur. 1979. *Hispanic Culture in the Southwest.* Norman: University of Oklahoma Press.

Campbell, Patrick, ed. 1996. *Analysing Performance: A Critical Reader.* Manchester and New York: Manchester University Press.

Canales, I. Alejandro. 2003. "Mexican Labour Migration to the United States in the Age of Globalisation." *Ethnic and Migration Studies* 29, no. 4: 741–61.

Cancian, Francesca. 1964. "Interaction Patterns in Zinacateco Families." *American Sociological Review* 29: 540–50.

Candelaria, Michael. 2002. "Images in *Penitente* Ritual and *Santo* Art: A Philosophical Inquiry Into the Problem of Meaning." In *Nuevomexicano Cultural Legacy: Forms, Agencies, and Discourse,* ed. Francisco A. Lomelí, Víctor A. Sorell, and Genaro M. Padilla, 270–82. Albuquerque: University of New Mexico Press.

Cantú, Norma E. 1974. "Barrio Names in Laredo." Unpublished paper.

———. 1982. "*The Offering and the Offerers: A Generic Illocation of a Laredo Pastorela in the Tradition of Shepherds' Plays.*" PhD Dissertation, University of Nebraska.

———. 1989. "The Barrios of Laredo" and "Los Matachines de la Santa Cruz." *Sí Laredo,* Fall/Winter.

———. 1991. "Las radiodifusoras en Laredo y Nuevo Laredo: Apuntes basados en la aportación de Luciano Duarte y Ramoncita Esparza." South Central Organization of Latin American Studies, Monterrey, Nuevo León. Unpublished paper.

———. 1992a. *Los Matachines de la Santa Cruz: un acto de resistencia cultural, mito y leyenda.* Tijuana, B.C.: Colegio de la Frontera Norte.

———. 1992b. "Costume as Cultural Resistance and Affirmation: The Case of a South Texas Community." In *Hecho en Texas: Texas-Mexican Folk Arts and Crafts,* ed. Joe S. Graham, 117–30. Denton: University of North Texas Press.

———. 1995a. "Los Matachines de la Santa Cruz de la Ladrillera: Notes Toward a Socio Literary Analysis." In *Feasts and Celebrations in North American Ethnic Communities,* ed. Ramón Gutierrez and Genevieve Fabre, 57–67. Albuquerque: University of New Mexico Press.

———. 1995b. "The Streets of Laredo: Myth and Reality of a Legendary Site." Presented at the Conference on Barrios and Other Ethnic Neighborhoods in the U.S. Université Paris VII. Unpublished paper.

———. 1996. *Los Matachines.* VHS. San Antonio: KLRN: Alamo Public Telecommunications Council (produced by Marlene Richardson for the PBS station in San Antonio).

———. 2003. "Pastoras and Malinches: Women in Traditional Folk Drama." In *Recovering the U.S Literary Heritage Project,* ed. Ramon Gutierrez and Genaro Padilla, 172–83. University of Houston, Arte Público Press.

———. 2005. "Processions and Parades." *Encyclopedia of Latinos and Latinas in the United States,* Volume 3, ed. Suzanne Oboler and Deena J. González, 452–54. New York: Oxford University Press.

———. Forthcoming. *Soldiers of the Cross: Los Matachines de la Santa Cruz.* Texas A&M University Press.

Casey, Edward S. 1996. "How to Get From Space to Place in a Fairly Short Stretch of Time: Phenomenological Prolegomena." In *Senses of Place,* ed. Steven Feld and Keith H. Basso, 13–52. Santa Fe: School of American Research Press.

Cashion, Susan V. 1985. "1983 ANGF Conference." *Asociación Nacional de Grupos Folkoricos Journal* 7 (Summer): 12.

Cazés Menache, Daniel. 2001. "El tiempo en masculino." Paper presented at the VII Congreso Español de Sociología del Tiempo, Salamanca, September 20–22.

Ceballos, Manuel Ramírez. 1991. "La onda de la frontera: las radiodifusoras en Laredo y Nuevo Laredo." Unpublished paper presented at the Universidad Valle del Bravo, Semana de la Comunicación, Nuevo Laredo, Tamaulipas.

Chamorro E., and J. Arturo. 2000. *Mariachi antiguo, jarabe y son: Símbolos compartidos y tradición musical en las identidades jaliscienses.* Zapopan, Jalisco: El Colegio de Jalisco.

Champe, Flavia Waters. 1983. *The Matachines Dance of the Upper Rio Grande: History, Music, and Choreography.* Lincoln: University of Nebraska Press.

Chasteen, John Charles. 2004. *National Rhythms, African Roots: The Deep History of Latin American Popular Dance.* Albuquerque: University of New Mexico Press.

Chávez Hayhoe, Salvador. 1944–48. *Historia sociológica de México.* México, D.F.: Editorial Salvador Chávez Hayhoe.

Chavira Cárdenas, J. C. 1999. *Vida en Cristiano* 137 (October 19): 2–6.

Chen, Nancy. 2003. *Breathing Spaces: Qigong, Psychiatry, and Healing in China.* New York: Columbia University Press.

Christian, William A. Jr. 1981. *Local Religion in Sixteenth-Century Spain.* Princeton, N.J.: Princeton University Press.

Cifuentes-González, Rita Del Carmen. 1964. "*La Fiesta de Enero y la danza de parachicos.*" MA Thesis. Mexico, D.F.

Clifford, James. 1997. *Routes: Travel and Translation in the Late Twentieth Century.* Cambridge, Mass., and London: Harvard University Press.

Colaizzi, Giulia, ed. 1990. *Feminismo y teoría del discurso.* Madrid: Cátedra.

Coleman, Lucinda. 1995. "Worship God in Dance." *Renewal Journal* 6, no. 2: 35–44. http://www.pastornet.net.au/renewal/journal6/coleman.html.

Collier, George, with Elizabeth Lowery Quarantiello. 1999 [1994]. *Basta: Land and the Zapatista Rebellion in Chiapas.* Oakland, Calif.: Institute for Food and Development Policy.

Collier, Jane. 1968. "Courtship and Marriage in Zinacatan, Chiapas, Mexico." *Middle American Research Institute* 25: 149–201.

———. 1973. *Law and Social Change in Zinacatan.* Stanford, Calif.: Stanford University Press.

Conjunto de Arpa Grande Arpex. 2006. *¡Tierra Caliente! Music from the Hotlands of Michoacán.* Produced by Daniel Sheehy. Washington D.C.: Smithsonian Folkways Recordings, SFW40536.

Consejo Estatal para la Cultura y las Artes de Chiapas. 2001. *Fiesta grande de Chiapa de Corzo.* Tuxtla Gutiérrez, Chiapas: Consejo Estatal para la Cultura y las Artes de Chiapas.

Corzo, Alejandro C. 1999. *Chiapas: voces desde la danza.* Tuxtla Gutiérrez, Chiapas: Consejo Estatal para la Cultura y las Artes de Chiapas.

Cowan, Jane. 1990. *Dance and the Body Politic in Northern Greece.* Princeton, N.J.: Princeton University Press.

Crawford, Polly Pearl. 1925. "The Beginnings of Spanish Settlements in the Lower Rio Grande Valley." MA Thesis, University of Texas.

Crease, Robert P. 2002. "The Pleasure of Popular Dance." *Journal of the Philosophy of Sport* 29, no. 2: 106–21.

Cruz-Manjarrez, Adriana. 2001. "Performance, Ethnicity and Migration: Dance and Music in the Continuation of Ethnic Identity among Immigrant Zapotecs from the Oaxacan Highlands Village of Villa Hidalgo Yalálag to Los Angeles." MA Thesis, University of California at Los Angeles.

Da Camara, Kathleen. 1949. *Laredo on the Rio Grande.* San Antonio, Tex.: Naylor Co. Press.

Dallal, Alberto. 1995. *La danza en México.* Primera parte: "Panorama critico." 2nd ed. México: UNAM.

———. 1997a. "Elementos míticos e históricos de la Danza de la Pluma." In *Historia del arte de Oaxaca: Arte contemporaneo,* ed. Margarita Dalton Palomo, Verónica Loera, and Chávez Castro, 339–55. Oaxaca, México: Instituto Oaxaqueño de las Culturas.

———. 1997b. *La danza en México en el siglo XX*. México: CNCA.

———. 1998. "Procesos espontáneos y procesos inducidos en el arte dancístico." *Revista Universidad de México* 575: 18–27.

Dalton Palomo, Margarita, and Verónica Loera y Chávez C., eds. 1997. *Historia del arte de Oaxaca. Volumen III: Arte contemporáneo*. Oaxaca, México: Instituto Oaxaqueño de las Culturas.

Daniel, Yvonne. 1995. *Rumba*. Bloomington: Indiana Press.

De la Fuente, Julio. 1949. *Yalálag. Una villa zapoteca serrana*. Serie Científica. México: Museo Nacional de Antropología.

———. 1994. "La cultura zapoteca." In *Los zapotecos de la Sierra Norte de Oaxaca. Antología Etnográfica*, ed. Manuel Ríos, 99–128. México: Centro de Investigaciones y Estudios Superiores en Antropología Social and Instituto Oaxaqueño de las Culturas.

De la Peña, Francisco. 2003. "Milenarismo, nativismo y neotradicionalismo en el México actual." *Ciencias Sociales y Religión* 3, no. 3: 95–114.

De la Peña, Guillermo. 2001. "Fiestas de tastoanes." *Revista Artes de México. Zapopan* 60: 54–64.

De la Torre, Renée. 1998. "Guadalajara vista desde la Calzada: Fronteras culturales e imaginarios urbanos." *Revista Alteridades* 8, no. 15: 45–55.

———. 2001. "La eclesialidad representada en la romería de la Virgen de Zapopan." *Revista Ciencias Religiosas* 2, no. 4: 39–46.

———. 2002. "La Romería de la Virgen." *Revista Artes de México. Zapopan* 60: 30–36.

———. 2005. "Danzar, una manera de practicar la religion." *Revista Estudios Jaliscienses* 60: 6–18.

de las Casas, Bartolomé. 1875–76. *Historia de las Indias*. Madrid, Imprenta de M. Ginesta.

de Velasco Rivero, Pedro. 1983. *Danzar o morir*. Mexico, D.F.: Centro de Reflexión Teológica, A.D.

Delgado, Celeste Fraser, and José Esteban Muñoz, eds. 1997. *Everynight Life: Culture and Dance in Latin/o America*. Durham, N.C.: Duke University Press.

Delgado Martínez, César. 1991a. "Mexican Dance Panorama: A Country of Dancers." *Ballet International* 14 (November): 32.

———. 1991b. *Laberinto de voces que danzan*. México: INBA/CENIDI-DANZA.

———. 1995. "Tierno abril nocturno: entre Kundera, Foucault y Genet." *Blanco Movil* 67: 7–9.

———. 1999. "Santos, sombras y otras lunas." *Zona de Danza* 1/6 (May–June): 9.

———. 2000. *Waldeen: La coronela de la danza mexicana*. México: Escenología.

Delpar, Helen. 2000. "Mexican Culture, 1920–1945." In *The Oxford History of Mexico*, ed. Sherman Meyer and William Beezley, 532–72. New York: Oxford University Press.

Dempster, Elizabeth. 1998. "Women Writing the Body: Let's Watch a Little How She

Dances." In *The Routledge Dance Studies Reader*, ed. Alexandra Carter, 223–29. London and New York: Routledge.

Desmond, Jane C., ed. 1997. *Meaning in Motion: New Cultural Studies of Dance.* Durham, N.C., and London: Duke University Press.

DeWalt, Billie R. 1975. "Changes in the Cargo System of Mesoamerica." *Anthropological Quarterly* 48: 87–105.

Díaz, Bernal. 1963. *The Conquest of New Spain.* New York: Penguin.

———. 2004. *The Discovery and Conquest of Mexico, 1517–1521.* Cambridge, Mass: Da Capo Press.

Dibble, Sandra. 2003. "In Tijuana, Danzón Classes Bring Together People of All Ages and Walks of Life." *The San Diego Union Tribune,* Oct. 26: B.1.

Dils, Ann, and Ann Cooper Albright, eds. 2001. *Moving History/Dancing Cultures: A Dance History Reader.* Middletown, Conn.: Wesleyan University Press.

Doi, Mary Masayo. 2001. *Gesture, Gender, Nation: Dance and Social Change in Uzbekistan.* Westport, Conn.: Greenwood Publishing Group.

Doremus, Anne. 2001. "Indigenism, Mestizaje, and National Identity in Mexico During the 1940s and the 1950s." *Mexican Studies/Estudios Mexicanos* 17, no. 1: 375–402.

Dorson, Richard M. 1976. *Folklore and Fakelore: Essays Toward a Discipline of Folk Studies.* Cambridge, Mass.: Harvard University Press.

Douglas, Mary. 1996. *Pureza y peligro: Un análisis de los conceptos de contaminación y tabú.* España: Siglo XXI.

Dozier, Edward P. 1980 (1970). *The Pueblo Indians of North America.* New York: Holt, Rinehart, and Winston.

Dundes, Alan. 1965. *The Study of Folklore.* Englewood Cliffs, N.J.: Prentice-Hall.

Eber, Christine. 1995. *Women and Alcohol in a Highland Maya Township.* Austin: University of Texas Press.

Eber, Christine, and Christine Kovic. 2003. *Women of Chiapas: Making History in Times of Struggle and Hope.* New York and London: Routledge.

Eliade, Mircea. 1981. *Lo sagrado y lo profano.* Barcelona: Guadarrama & Omega.

Estabrook, Emma Franklin. 1931. *Givers of Life: the American Indians as Contributors to Civilization.* Albuquerque: University of New Mexico Press.

Farnell, Brenda. 1995. *Human Action Signs in Cultural Context: The Visible and the Invisible in Movement and Dance.* Metuchen, N.J.: Scarecrow Press.

Feld, Steven, and Keith Basso. 1996. *Senses of Place.* Santa Fe, N.M.: School of American Research Press.

Flores y Escalantes, Jesús. 1993. *Salón México.* México: Asociación Mexicana de Estudios Fonográficos, A. C.

———. 1994. *Imágenes del danzón.* México: Dirección General de Culturas Populares.

Flores, Richard R. 1995. *Los Pastores: History and Performance in the Mexican Shepherd's Play of South Texas.* Washington: Smithsonian Institution Press.

Foster, Susan, ed. 1995. *Choreographing History.* Bloomington: University of Indiana Press.

Foucault, Michel. 1977. *Discipline and Punish: the Birth of the Prison.* Translated from French by Alan Sheridan. New York: Pantheon Books.

Fraleigh, Sondra, and Penelope Hanstein, ed. 1995. *Researching Dance: Evolving Modes of Inquiry.* Pittsburgh, Pa.: University of Pittsburgh Press.

Fregoso, Rosa-Linda. 1993. *The Bronze Screen: Chicana and Chicano Film Culture.* Minneapolis: University of Minnesota Press.

Freyermuth Enciso, Graciela, and Gabriel Torres. 2001. *Historias, comité pro una maternidad voluntaria y riegos en Chiapas.* Chiapas, Mexico: ACASAC.

Friedlander, Judith. 1981. "The Secularization of the Cargo System: An Example from Postrevolutionary Central Mexico." *Latin American Research Review* 16, no. 2: 132–43.

Friedler, Sharon E., and Susan B. Glazer, eds. 1997. *Dancing Female: Lives and Issues of Women in Contemporary Dance.* Amsterdam: Harwood Academic Publishers.

Gandert, Miguel. 2002 "Retratos de Mestizaje, A Photographic Survey of Indo-Hispanic Traditions of the Rio Grande Corridor." In *Nuevo México Profundo: Rituals of an Indo-Hispano Homeland,* ed. Francisco A. Lomelí, Víctor A. Sorell, and Genaro M. Padilla, 73–90. Santa Fe: Museum of New Mexico Press; Albuquerque: National Hispanic Cultural Center of New Mexico.

Garcia, Elaine. 2000. "Las matachines de Alcalde." http//www.webspawner.com/users/elainegarcia/Copyright 2000 Elaine Garcia/elaineroyal.

García Canclini, Néstor. 1993. *Transforming Modernity: Popular Culture in Mexico.* Translated by Lidia Lozano. Austin: University of Texas Press.

———. 1995. *Hybrid Cultures.* Minneapolis: University of Minnesota Press.

———. 2001. *Culturas híbridas: Estrategias para entrar y salir de la modernidad,* rev. ed. Buenos Aires: Editorial Paidós.

García de León, Antonio. 2003. "Foreword." In *Algo sobre los bailes de tarima en el son jarocho,* ed. Claudia Cao Romero, Mexico: Consejo Nacional para la Cultura y las Artes, FONCA; Sotavento.

Garcia, Alma M., ed. 1997. *Chicana Feminist Thought: The Basic Historical Writings.* New York: Routledge.

García, Mario T. 1989. "Arthur L. Campa and the Cultural Question." In *Mexican American: Leadership, Ideology, & Identity 1930–1960,* 273–90. New Haven, Conn., and London: Yale University Press.

García, Peter. 2001. "La Onda Nuevo Mexicana: Multi-Sited Ethnography, Ritual Contexts, and Popular Traditional Musics in New Mexico." PhD Dissertation, University of Texas at Austin.

———. 2004. "Baile." In *Encyclopedia of Latino Popular Culture,* ed. Cordelia Candelaria, Arturo J. Aldama, and Peter J. García, 51–52. Westport, Conn.: Greenwood Press, 2004.

Gerholm, T. 1993. "On Ritual: A Postmodernist View." *Ethnos* 3, no. 4: 190–203.

Geurts, Kathryn Linn. 2002, *Culture and the Senses: Bodily Ways of Knowing in an African Community.* Berkeley: University of California Press.

Gil Martinez, Juan. 2002. "Baja California." *Congreso XX Syllabus for the 2002 Conference,* ed. Rey Cuesta, 39–44. Riverside, California: Asociación Nacional de Grupos Folklóricos.

Gilbert, Helen. 1995. "Dance, Movement, and Resistance Politics." In *The Post-Colonial Studies Reader,* ed. Bill Ashcroft, Gareth Griffiths, and Helen Tiffin, 341–45. New York: Routledge.

Giménez, Gilberto. 1978. *La cultura popular y religión en el Anáhuac.* México: Centro de Estudios Ecuménicos.

Glick Schiller, Nina, Linda Basch, and Christine Blanc-Szanton. 1995. "From Immigrant to Transimmigrant: Theorizing Transnational Migration." *Anthropological Quarterly* 68, no. 1: 48–63.

Godelier, Maurice. 1986. *La producción de grandes hombres: Poder y dominación masculina entre los baruya de Nueva Guinea.* Madrid: Akal.

Goertzen, Chris. 2001. "Crafts, Tourism, and Traditional Life in Chiapas, Mexico: A Tale Told by a Pillowcase." In *Selling the Indian: Commercialism and the Appropriation of American Indian Cultures,* ed. Diana Royer and Carter Meyer, 236–69. Tucson: University of Arizona Press.

Goffman, Erving. 1987. *Façons de parler.* Paris: Les Éditions de Minuit.

———. 1993. *La presentación de la persona en la vida cotidiana.* Buenos Aires: Amorrortu Editores.

González Escoto, Armando. 1998. *Historia breve de la iglesia de Guadalajara.* Guadalajara, UNIVA/Arzobispado de Guadalajara.

González Torres, Anáhuac. 1996. "Los concheros: la (re)conquista de México." In *Las danzas de conquista I. México contemporáneo,* ed. Jesus Jáuregui and Carlo Bonfiglioli, 207–27. México: Conaculta/ Fondo de Cultura Economica.

González, María Angela. 1978. "La danza de concheros: una tradición sagrada." *México Indígena,* México, D.F., Año IV: 59–62.

González Torres, Yólotl. 2000. "El movimiento de la mexicanidad." *Religiones y sociedad* 8: 9–36.

———. 2005. *Danza tu palabra: La danza de los concheros.* Mexico, D.F. Plaza Y Valdes, S.A. de C.V.

Goodman, Lizbeth. 1996. "Feminisms and theatres: canon fodder and cultural change." In *Analysing Performance: A Critical Reader,* ed. Patrick Campell, 19–42. Manchester and New York: Manchester University Press.

Goodman, Lizbeth, with Jane de Gay. 1988. *The Routledge Reader in Gender and Performance.* London and New York: Routledge.

Gossen, Gary. 1974. *Chamulas in the World of the Sun: Time and Space in a Maya Oral Tradition.* Cambridge, Mass.: Harvard University Press.

Graburn, Nelson H. H. 1989. "Tourism: The Sacred Journey." In *Hosts and Guests,* ed. Valene Smith, 21–36. Oxford: Blackwell.

Gramsci, Antonio. 1981. *Antología*. Selected and translated by Manuel Sacristán. México, Siglo XXI, Editores.

Green, Lucy. 2001. *Música, género y educación*. Translated by Pablo Manzano. Madrid: Ediciones Morata, Coleccion Pedagogia, Manuales.

Greenberg, James B. 1981. *Santiago's Sword: Chatino Peasant Religion and Economics*. Berkeley: University of California Press.

Greenfield, Patricia. 1972. "Cross-Cultural Studies of Mother-Infant Interaction: Toward A Structural-Functional Approach." *Human Development* 15: 131–38.

Griswold del Castillo, Richard. 1996. *Aztlán Reocupada: A Political and Cultural History Since 1945*. México: Universidad Nacional Autónoma de México.

Griswold del Castillo, Richard, and Richard A. Garcia. 1995. *César Chávez: A Triumph of Spirit*. Norman: University of Oklahoma Press.

Gross, Joan, David McMurray, and Ted Swedenburg. 1996. "Arab Noise and Ramadan Nights: Rai, Rap, and Franco-Maghrebi Identities." In *Displacement, Diaspora, and Geographies of Identity*, ed. Smadar Lavie and Ted Swedenburg, 120–55. Durham, N.C.: Duke University Press.

Gupta, Akhil. 1992. "The Song of Non-Aligned World: Transnational Identities and the Reinscription of the Space in Late Capitalism." *Cultural Anthropology* 7, no. 1: 63–79.

Guss, David M. 2000. *The Festive State: Race, Ethnicity, and the Nationalism as Cultural Performance*. Berkeley: University of California Press.

Gutiérrez, David. 1995. *Walls and Mirrors: Mexican Americans, Mexican Immigrants, and the Politics of Ethnicity*. Berkeley: University of California Press.

Gutmann, Matthew. 2000. *Ser hombre de verdad en la ciudad de México: Ni macho ni mandilón. México,* COLMEX-Centro de Estudios Sociológicos-Programa Interdisciplinarios de Estudios de la Mujer/Centro de Estudios Demográficos y de Desarrollo Urbano-Programa Salud Reproductiva y Sociedad.

Hall, Stuart. 1989. "Cultural Identity and Cinematic Representation." *Framework* 36: 68–81.

———. 1996a. "What Is This 'Black' in Black Popular Culture?" In *Stuart Hall: Critical Dialogues in Cultural Studies*, ed. David Morley and Chen Kuan-Hsing, 465–75. London: Routledge.

———. 1996b. "New Ethnicities." In *Stuart Hall: Critical Dialogues in Cultural Studies*, ed. David Morley and Chen Kuan-Hsing, 441–49. London: Routledge.

———. 1998. "Introduction: Who Needs Identity?" In *Questions of Cultural Identity*, ed. Stuart Hall and Paul du Gay, 1–17. London: SAGE.

Hamilton, Nora, and Norma Stoltz Chinchilla. 2001. *Seeking Community in a Global City: Guatemalans and Salvadorans in Los Angeles*. Philadelphia: Temple University Press.

Handbook of Texas Online. *"Hernandez v. State of Texas."* http://www.tsha.utexas.edu/handbook/online/articles/HH/jrh1.html.

Handler, Richard, and Jocelyn Linnekin. 1984. "Tradition, Genuine or Spurious." *Journal of American Folklore* 97: 273–90.

Harris, Max. 2000. *Aztecs, Moors, and Christians: Festivals of Reconquest in Mexico and Spain.* Austin: University of Texas Press.

Harvey, David. 2000. *Spaces of Hope.* Los Angeles: University of California Press.

Haviland, John B. 1993. "Anchoring, Iconicity, and Orientation in Guugu Yimithirr Pointing Gestures." *Journal of Linguistic Anthropology* 3, no. 1: 3–45.

———. 2000. "Pointing, Gesture Spaces, and Mental Maps." In *Language and Gesture: Window into Thought and Action,* ed. David McNeill, 13–46. Cambridge: Cambridge University Press.

Hebdige, Dick. 1972. *Subculture: The Meaning of Style.* London: Routledge.

Henderson, Richard. 1991. "Liner notes." *Grandson of Frat Rock! Vol. 3. Even More of the Greatest Rock 'n' Roll Party Tunes of All Time.* Santa Monica, Calif.: Rhino Records.

Henry, Rosita, Fiona Magowan, and David Murray. 2000. "Introduction." *Australian Journal of Anthropology* Special Dance Issue, 11, no. 3: 253–60.

Heredia Casanova, Marta. 1999. *El jarabe: Baile tradicional de México.* Jalisco, México: Secretaría de Cultura, Gobierno del Estado de Jalisco.

Hernández-Ávila, Inés. 2005. "La Mesa del Santo Nino de Atocha and the Conchero Tradition of Mexico-Tenochtitlán: Religious Healing in Urban Mexico and the United States." In *Religion and Healing in America,* ed. Linda L. Barnes and Susan S. Sered, 359–74. New York: Oxford University Press.

Hernández Castillo, Rosalva Aida. 2001. *Histories and Stories from Chiapas; Border Identities in Southern Mexico.* Austin: University of Texas Press.

Hershfield, Joanne. 1999. "Race and Ethnicity in the Classical Cinema." In *Mexico's Cinema: A Century of Film and Filmmakers,* ed. Joanne Hershfield and David R. Maciel, 81–100. Wilmington, Del.: Scholarly Resources.

Hershfield, Joanne, and David R. Maciel, eds. 1999. *Mexico's Cinema: A Century of Film and Filmmakers.* Wilmington, Del.: Scholarly Resources.

Hervieu-Léger. 1996. "Por una sociología de las nuevas formas de religiosidad: algunas cuestiones teóricas previas." In *Identidades religiosas y sociales en México,* ed. Giménez, Gilberto, 23–46. México: IFAL/UNAM.

———. 1993. *Cultural Capital: Mountain Zapotec Migrant Associations in Mexico City.* Tucson: University of Arizona Press.

Hobsbawn, Eric. 1983. "Introduction: Inventing Traditions." In *The Invention of Tradition,* ed. Eric Hobsbawn and Terrance Turner, 1–14. New York: Cambridge University Press.

Hobsbawm, Eric, and Terence Ranger. 1983. *The Invention of Tradition.* Cambridge: Cambridge University Press.

Huerta, Elisa. Forthcoming. "Buscando la Armonia: Discursive Embodiments of Indigeneity in la Danza Azteca." PhD Dissertation, University of California, Santa Cruz.

Huerta, Jorge. 1982. *Chicano Theater: Themes and Forms.* Ypsilanti, Mich.: Bilingual Press.

Hulshof, Marije. 1991. "Zapotec Moves: Networks and Remittances of U.S.-Bound Migrants from Oaxaca, Mexico." *Nederlandse Geografische Studies* 128: 1–110.

Hurtado, Milena M., and Carlos Mata Induráin. 2002. "Algo más sobre comedia burlesca y Carnaval: a propósito de El Mariscal de Virón, de Juan de Maldonado." *eHumanista* 2: 161–75.

Huxley, Aldous. 1925. *Along the Road.* London: Chatto and Windus.

Ibarra, Ricardo. 2001. *Gaceta Universitaria.* November 12.

Ickx, Wonne. 2002. "Los fraccionamientos cerrados en la zona metropolitana de Guadalajara" and "Nuevas formas y viejos valores: urbanizaciones cerradas de lujo en Guadalajara." In *Latinoamérica: países abiertos, ciudades cerradas,* ed. Luis Felipe Cabrales, 117–44. Guadalajara: UdeG/UNESCO.

Illescas, Francisco. 1995. Press conference, October 2, Mexico City. Unpublished transcription by Angelica del Angel Magro.

Instituto Nacional de Estadistica Geografía e Informática. 1991. *Estado de Oaxaca México: Guía turística.* Aguascalientes: Instituto Nacional de Estadistica Geografía e Informática.

———. 2000a. *Estados Unidos Mexicanos. Xii censo general de población y vivienda, 2000. Resultados Preliminares.* Mexico: INEGI.

———. 2000b. *Estadística sociodemográficas: Dínamicas de la población,* http://www.inegi.gob.mx/est/contenidos/espanol/tematicos/mediano/mun.asp?t=mpob93&c=3839&e=07.

———. 2000c. *XII Censo general de población y vivienda, 2000. Puebla, resultados definitivos. Datos por localidad. Integración Territorial.* México, INEGI. http://www.inegi.gob.mx/difusion/espanol/poblacion/definitivos/pue/sintesis/presentacion.pdf.

Jacorzynski, Witold. 2004. *El crepúsculo de los ídolos en la antropología social: más allá de Malinowski y los posmodernistas.* México: Centro de Investigaciónes Estudios Superiores en Antropología Social (CIESAS)-Porrúa.

Jáuregui, Jesús. 1990. *El mariachi: símbolo musical de México.* Mexico: Banpaís.

Jáuregui, Jesús, and Carlo Bonfiglioli, eds. 1996a. *Las danzas de conquista, I. México contemporáneo.* México, D.F.: Consejo Nacional para la Cultura y las Artes, Fondo de Cultura Economica.

———. 1996b. "Introduccion: El complejo dancístico—teatral de la conquista." In *Las danzas de conquista,* ed. Jesus Jauregui and Carlo Bonfiglioli, 7–30. Mexico, D.F.: Consejo Nacional para la Cultura y las Artes; Fondo de Cultura Economica.

———. 1996c. "Cortés contra Moctezuma. Cuauhtémoc: el intercambio de mujeres." In *Las danzas de conquista,* ed. Jesus Jáuregui and Carlo Bonfiglioli, 33–68. México: Consejo Nacional para la Cultura y las Artes: Fondo de Cultura Económica.

Jimenez, Guillermo. 1932. "La danza en Mexico." *Maestro Rural* 1, no. 3: 23.

Johnston, Edith Louise. 1937. *The Use of Mexican Folk Dance in School Activities.* MA Thesis, University of Texas at Austin.

Joysmith, Claire. 2003. "Response: (Re)Mapping *Mexicanidades:* (Re)Locating Chicana Writings and Translation Politics." In *A Critical Reader: Chicana Feminisms*, ed. G. Arrendondo, A. Hurtado, N. Klahn, O. Nájera-Ramírez, and P. Zavella, 148–54. Durham, N.C.: Duke University Press.

———. 1992. "Theoretical and Methodological Considerations for Anthropological Studies of Dance and Human Movement Systems." *Ethnographica: The Dance in Greece* 8: 151–57.

Kealiinohomoku, Joanna. 1979. "Theory and Methods for Anthropological Studies of Dance." Ph.D. Dissertation, Indiana University.

Kearney, Michael. 1991. "Borders and Boundaries of State and Self at the End of Empire." *Journal of Historical Sociology* 4, no. 1: 52–74.

Kelly, Robin D. 1992. AHR Forum Notes on Deconstructing "The Folk." *American Historical Review* (December): 1400–1408.

Kirshenblatt-Gimblett, Barbara. 1998a. "Objects of Ethnography." In *Destination Culture: Tourism, Museums, and Heritage*, ed. Barbara Kirshenblatt-Gimblett, 17–78. Berkeley: University of California Press.

———. 1998b. *Destination Culture: Tourism, Museums, and Heritage.* Berkeley: University of California Press.

Klaver, Jeanine. 1997. "From the Land of the Sun to the City of Angels. The Migration Process of Zapotec Indians from Oaxaca, Mexico to Los Angeles, California." *Netherlands Geographical Studies* 228: 231. Utrecht, Amsterdam: Department of Human Geography, UVA.

Knight, Alan. 1990. "Racism, Revolution, and *Indigenismo:* Mexico, 1910–1940." In *The Idea of Race in Latin America, 1970–1940*, ed. Richard Graham, 71–114. Austin: University of Texas Press.

Krauze, Enrique. 1997. *Mexico, Biography of Power: A History of Modern Mexico, 1810–1996.* Translated by Hank Heifetz. New York: Harper Collins Publishers.

Krippendorf, Jost. 1987. *The Holiday Makers: Understanding the Impact of Leisure and Travel.* Translated by Vera Andrassy. London: Heinemann.

Kurath, Gertrude P. 1967. "La danza de los matachines entre los indios y los mestizos." *Revista Mexicana de Estudios Antropológicos* 21: 261–85.

Kurath, Gertrude Prokosch, and Samuel Martí. 1964. *Dances of Anáhuac: The Choreography and Music of Precortesian Dances.* New York: Foundation for Anthropological Research, Inc.

Kurath, Gertrude P., and Antonio Garcia. 1970. "Matachines: A Midwinter Drama from Iberia." In *Music and Dance of the Tewa Pueblos*, 257–58. Santa Fe: Museum of New Mexico.

Lagarde, Marcela. 1993. *Los cautiverios de las mujeres: Madresposas, monjas, putas, presas y locas.* México: Universidad Nacional Autónoma de Mexico.

Lakoff, George, and Johnson, Mark. 1980. *Metáforas de la vida cotidiana.* Madrid: Cátedra Teorema.

Lamadrid, Enrique R. 2003. *Hermanitos Comanchitos, Indo-Hispano Rituals of Captivity and Redemption.* Albuquerque: University of New Mexico Press.

Lameiras, José. 1999. *El Tuxpan de Jalisco. Una identidad danzante.* Zamora: El Colegio de Michoacán.

Lau Jaiven, Ana. 1987. *La nueva ola del feminismo en Mexico: Conciencia y acción de lucha de las mujeres.* México: Grupo Editorial Planeta.

Laughlin, Robert M. 1963. *Through the Looking Glass: Reflections on Zinacantan Courtship and Marriage.* PhD Dissertation, Harvard University.

Lavalle, Josefina. 1987. "Waldeen." *Cuadernos del CID-DANZA,* núm. 17. México: Instituto Nacional de Bellas Artes.

———. 1988. *El Jarabe el jarabe ranchero or jarabe de Jalisco.* Mexico, D.F.: Instituto Nacional de Bellas Artes.

Lavie, Smadar, and Ted Swedenburg. 1996. "Introduction." In *Displacement, Diaspora, and Geographies of Identity,* ed. Smadar Lavie and Ted Swedenburg, 1–26. Durham, N.C., and London: Duke University Press.

Lea, Aurora Lucero-White. 1963–64. "More About the Matachines." *New Mexico Folklore Record* 20: 7–10.

Leach, Edmund. 1979. "Two Essays Concerning the Symbolic Representations of Time." In *Reader in Comparative Religion. An Anthropological Approach,* ed. William A. Lessa and Evon Z. Vogt, 108–15. New York: Harper & Row Publishers.

León-Portilla, Miguel. 1963. *Aztec Thought and Culture: A Study of the Ancient Nahuatl Mind.* Norman: University of Oklahoma Press.

Levelt, Willem J. M. 1996. "Perspective-Taking and Ellipsis in Spatial Descriptions." In *Language and Gesture,* ed. Paul Bloom, 77–107. Cambridge, Mass.: MIT Press.

Levinson, Stephen C. 1996. "Language and Space." *Annual Review of Anthropology* 25: 353–82.

———. 1997. "Language and Cognition: The Cognitive Consequences of Spatial Description in Guugu Yimithirr." *Journal of Linguistic Anthropology* 7, no. 1: 98–131.

———. 1998. "Studying Spatial Conceptualization across Cultures: Anthropology and Cognitive Science." *Ethos* 26, no. 1: 7–24.

Levitt, Peggy. 2001. *Transnational Villagers.* Berkeley: University of California Press.

Limón, José. 1981. "Expressive Dimensions of Heterogeneity and Change: The Folk Performance of 'Chicano' and the Cultural Limits of Political Ideology." In *"And Other Neighborly Names": Social Process and Cultural Image in Texas Folklore,* ed. Roger D. Abrahams and Richard Bauman, 197–225. Austin: University of Texas Press.

Linn, Priscilla Rachun. 1976. "The Religious Office Holders of Chamula: A Study of Gods, Rituals and Sacrifice." PhD Dissertation, Oxford University.

Livingston, Jessica. 2004. "Murder in Juarez: Gender, Sexual Violence, and the Global Assembly Line." *Frontiers — A Journal of Women's Studies* 25, no. 1: 59–76.

Loeffler, Jack. 1999. *La Música de los Viejitos: Hispano Folk Music of the Río Grande del Norte.* With Katherine Loeffler and Enrique R. Lamadrid. Albuquerque: University of New Mexico Press.

Los Camperos de Valles. 2005. *El ave de mi soñar: Mexican Sones Huastecos featuring Los Camperos de Valles.* Produced by Artemio Posadas. Washington D.C.: Smithsonian Folkways Recordings, SFW40512.

Los Lobos. 1990. *In the Neighborhood.* Producers Larry Hirsch and Los Lobos. Slash/ Warner Bros. 9 26131–2.

Low, Setha M., and Denise Lawrence-Zuaniga. 2003. *The Anthropology of Space and Place: Locating Culture.* Malden, Mass.: Blackwell Publishing, 2003.

Loza, Steven J. 1979. "Origins, form, and development of the Son Jarocho: Veracruz, Mexico." *Aztlán* 13, no. 1: 257–74.

———. 1992. "From Veracruz to Los Angeles: The Reinterpretation of the 'Son Jarocho.'" *Latin American Music Review* 13, no. 2: 179–94.

Lozano, Tomás. 2007. *Cantemos al alba.* Translated into English by Rima Montoya. Albuquerque: University of New Mexico Press.

Lynton, Anadel. 1988. "Anna Sokolow." *Cuadernos del CENIDI-DANZA,* no. 20. Mexico: Instituto Nacional de Bellas Artes.

MacAloon, John. 1984. "Olympic Games and the Theory of Spectacle in Modern Societies." In *Rite, Drama, Festival, Spectacle: Rehearsals Toward Theory of Cultural Performance,* ed. John MacAloon, 241–81. Philadelphia: Institute for the Study of Human Issues.

MacCannell, Dean. 1975. *The Tourist: A New Theory of the Leisure Class.* New York: Schocken Books.

Macías, Anna. 1982. *Against All Odds: The Feminist Movement in Mexico to 1940.* Westport, Conn.: Greenwood Press.

Maestas, Enrique G. M. 1997a. "Danza Azteca en Aztlán." BA Thesis, University of Colorado at Denver.

———. 1997b. "Danza Azteca: The Rebirth of a Cultural Renaissance." *RazaTeca Magazine,* no. 5 (January/February).

———. 1999. "Danza Azteca: Xicana/o Life-Cycle Ritual and Autonomous Culture." In *Mapping strategies: NACCS and the challenge of multiple (re)oppressions: Selected proceedings of the XXIII Annual Conference of the National Association for Chicana and Chicano Studies,* ed. María Antonia Beltrán-Vocal, Manuel de Jesús Hernández-Gutiérrez, and Silvia Fuentes, 60–90. Phoenix, Arizona: Editorial Orbiz Press.

Malone, Jacqui. 1996. *Steppin' on the Blues: The Visible Rhythms of African American Dance.* Urbana: University of Illinois Press.

Manuel, Peter. 1989. "Andalusian, Gypsy and Class Identity in the Contemporary Flamenco Context." *Ethnomusicology* 33, no. 1: 47–65.

Martin, John. 1939. *Introduction to Dance.* Brooklyn, N.Y.: Dance Horizons.

Martínez, Oscar J. 1996. "Introduction." In *U.S.-Mexico Borderlands. Historical and Contemporary Perspectives,* ed. Oscar J. Martínez, xii–xix. J. Wilmington, Del.: Scholarly Resources Inc.

Martínez Casas, Regina. 2001. "Una cara indígena de Guadalajara: La resignificación de la cultura otomí en la ciudad." Ph.D dissertation. México: UAM-Iztapalapa.

Mata Garcia, María Eugenia. 1996. "Economic Crisis and Rural Violence in Oaxaca Mexico." Presentation at the Washington Office on Latin America in Washington, D.C., September 26. http://uscis.gov/graphics/services/asylum/ric/documentation/Oaxaca.htm.

Mazón, Mauricio. 1994. *Zoot Suit Riots.* Austin: University of Texas Press.

McKean, Philip F. 1989. "Towards a Theoretical Analysis of Tourism: Involution in Bali." In *Hosts and Guests,* ed. Valene Smith, 124–44. Oxford: Blackwell.

McKinnon, James, ed. 1991 [1990]. *Antiquity and the Middle Ages.* Englewood Cliffs, N.J.: Prentice-Hall.

McRobbie, Angela. 1991. *Feminism and Youth Culture: From "Jackie" to "Just Seventeen."* Boston: Unwin Hyman.

Medrano de Luna, Gabriel. 2001. *Danza de indios de mesillas.* Zamora: El Colegio de Michoacán.

Meier, Richard P., ed. 2002. *Modality and Structure in Signed and Spoken Languages.* West Nyack, N.Y.: Cambridge University Press.

Melhuus, Marit, and Kristi Anne Stølen, eds. 1996. *Machos, Mistresses, Madonnas: Contesting the Power of Latin American Gender Imagery.* London and New York: Verso.

Menchaca, Martha. 2001. *Recovering History, Constructing Race: The Indian, Black, and White Roots of Mexican Americans.* Austin: University of Texas Press.

Mendoza, Vicente T., 1956. *Panorama de la música tradicional de México.* México: Imprenta Universitaria.

Mendoza, Zoila S. 2000. *Shaping Society through Dance: Mestizo Ritual Performance in the Peruvian Andes.* Chicago: University of Chicago Press.

Middleton, Richard. 1989. *Studying Popular Music.* Milton Keynes: Open University Press.

Modiano, Nancy. 1973. *Indian Education in the Chiapas Highlands.* New York: Holt, Rinehart and Winston.

Montejano, David. 1987. *Anglos and Mexicans in the Making of Texas.* Austin: University of Texas Press.

Mooney, Gertrude X. 1957. *Mexican Folk Dances for American Schools.* Coral Gables, Fla.: University of Miami Press.

Moraga, Cherríe. 1993. *The Last Generation: Prose and Poetry.* Boston: South End Press.

———. 2000 [1983]. *Loving in the War Years: Lo que nunca pasó por sus labios.* Second ed. South End Press Classics.

Moreno Navarro, Isidoro. 1985. *Cofradías y hermandades andaluzas: Estructura, simbolismo e identidad.* Sevilla: Biblioteca de la cultura Andaluza.

Mummert, Gail, and Luis Alfonso Ramírez Carrillo, eds. 1998. *Rehaciendo las diferencias.* México: El Colegio de Michoacán y Mérida; Universidad Autónoma de Yucatán.

Muñoz, Carlos, Jr. 1989. *Youth, Identity, and Power: The Chicano Movement.* New York: Verso.

Muñoz, Jose Esteban. 1999. *Disidentifications: Queers of Color and the Performance of Politics.* Minneapolis: University of Minnesota Press.

Murguía Rábago, Mariana. 1975. "*Las danzas coloniales en Puebla.*" M.A. thesis. México, ENAH - UNAM.

Nader, Laura. 1969. "The Zapotec of Oaxaca." *Handbook of Middle American Indians* 7: 329–59. Austin: University Press of Texas.

Nahachewsy, Andry. 1995. "Participatory and Presentational Dance as Ethnochoreological Categories." *Dance Research Journal* 27, no. 1 (Spring): 73–80.

Nájera-Ramírez, Olga. 1989. "Social and Political Dimensions of *Folklórico* Dance: The Binational Dialectic of Residual and Emergent Culture." *Western Folklore* 48 (January): 15–32.

———. 1997a. *La Fiesta de Los Tastoanes: Critical Encounters in Mexican Festival Performance.* Albuquerque: University of New Mexico Press.

———. 1997b. "Of Fieldwork, Folklore, and Festival: Personal Encounters." *Journal of American Folklore* 112, no. 444: 183–99.

———. 2001. "Haciendo Patria: La Charreada and the Formation of a Transnational Identity." In *Transnational Latina/o Communities: Politics, Processes, and Cultures,* ed. Carlos Velez-Ibanez and Anna Sampaio, 167–80. Rowman & Littlefield Press.

———. 2002. "Reclaiming Aztlán, Resisting Borders: Danza Azteca." Paper delivered at Annual Meeting of American Anthropological Association, New Orleans, La., November 20.

Nash, June. 1964. "The Structuring of Social Relations in Ametenango." *Estudios de Cultura Maya* 4: 335–59.

———. 1970. *In the Eye of the Ancestors: Belief and Behavior in a Maya Community.* New Haven, Conn.: Yale University Press.

———. 1977. "Gendered Deities and the Survival of Culture." *Journal of the History of Religion* 36, no. 4: 333–56.

———. 2001. *Mayan Visions: The Quest for Autonomy in an Age of Globalization.* New York: Routledge.

Nash, June, and Helen Icken Safa. 1980. *Sex and Class in Latin America: Women's Perspectives on Politics, Economics, and the Family in the Third World.* Brooklyn, N.Y.: J. F. Bergin Publishers.

Nash, June, and Maria Patricia Fernandez-Kelly. 1983. *Women, Men and the International Division of Labor.* Albany: State University of New York Press.

Novaro, María. 1991. *Danzón.* VHS, Mexico City: George Sánchez, Producer.

Ocampo, Carlos. 1993. "Danza: Mujeres de barro." *Siempre!* (June 11): 5.

Ochoa, Alvaro. 2005. *Mitote, fandango y mariacheros.* Zamora, México: Colegio de Michoacán; Colegio de Jalisco.

Olivera Bustamante, Mercedes. 1974. *Las danzas y fiestas de Chiapas.* México: Fondo Nacional para el Desarrollo de la Danza Popular Mexicana.

Omi, Michael, and Howard Winant. 1994. *Racial Formation in the United States from the 1960s to the 1990s*, 2nd ed. New York: Routledge.

Ozomatli. 1997. "La Misma Canción." *Ozomatli*. Produced by T-Ray and Ozomatli, Alamo Sounds, AMSD 80020.

———. 2001. "Guerrillero." *Embrace the Chaos*. Produced by Bob Power, Alamo Sounds and Interscope Records 0694931162.

Palley, Julian. 1998. "Somos el borrador de un texto." *Revista Universidad de México* 575: 12.

Paredes, Américo. 1970. "Introduction." In *Folktales of Mexico*, ed. Américo Paredes, ivii–lxxxiii. Chicago: University of Chicago Press.

———. 1976. *A Texas-Mexican Cancionero: Folksongs of the Lower Border*. Urbana: University of Illinois Press.

———. 1983. "The Corrido: Yesterday and Today." In *Ecology and Development of the Border Region: Second Symposium Mexican and United States Universities in Border*, ed. Stanley Ross, 293–97. Mexico: Asociación Nacional de Universidades e Institutos de Enseñanza Superior.

———. 1993a. "The Folklore of Groups of Mexican Origin in the United States." In *Folklore and Culture on the Texas-Mexican Border*, ed. Richard Bauman, 3–18. Austin: University of Texas, Center for Mexican American Studies. Originally published as "El Folklore de los grupos de origen mexicano en Los Estados Unidos." *Folklore Americano* 14 (1966): 146–63.

———. 1993b. "The Mexican *Corrido:* Its Rise and Fall." In *Folklore and Culture on the Texas-Mexican Border*, ed. Richard Bauman, 129–41. Austin: University of Texas Press. Originally published in *Madstones and Twisters*, ed. Mody C. Boatright, Wilson M. Hudson, and Allen Maxwell. *Publications of the Texas Folklore Society* 28(1958): 91–105.

———. 1993c. *Folklore and Culture on the Texas-Mexican Border*. Austin: University of Texas Press.

Pascoe, Juan. 2003. *La mona*. Universidad Veracruzana.

Paz, Octavio. 1987. *El laberinto de la soledad*. México: Fondo de Cultura Económica.

Pedelty, Mark. 2004. *Musical Ritual in Mexico City*. Austin: University of Texas Press.

Peña, Alfonso. 1972. "Los Matachines de Laredo." Unpublished essay.

Peña, Manuel. 1980. "Ritual Structure in a Chicano Dance." *Latin American Music Review* 1: 47–73.

———. 1982a. "The Emergence of the Conjunto Music, 1935–1955." In "*And Other Neighborly Names*": *Social Process and Cultural Image in Texas Folklore*, ed. Richard Bauman and Roger Abrahams, 280–99. Austin: University of Texas Press.

———. 1982b. "Folksong and Social Change: Two Corridos as Interpretive Sources." *Aztlán* 13, nos. 1 and 2: 13–42.

———. 1985a. *The Texas-Mexican Conjunto: History of a Working Class Music*. Austin: University of Texas Press.

———. 1985b. "From Ranchero to Jaitón: Ethnicity and Class in Texas-Mexican Music. (Two Styles in the Form of a Pair)." *Ethnomusicology* 29, no. 1: 29–55.
Pérez, Emma. 1991. *The Decolonial Imaginary: Writing Chicanas into History.* Bloomington: Indiana University Press.
Peterson, Anya. 1968. "An Acculturation Study of Some Dances of Oaxaca, Mexico." In *Researchers in Latin American Society,* ed. Anya Peterson and Ronald Royce, 37–79. Stanford, Calif.: Institute for the Study of Contemporary Culture.
Peterson, Anya, and Ronald Royce, eds. 1968. *Researchers in Latin American Society.* Stanford, Calif.: Institute for the Study of Contemporary Culture.
Pina, Michael. 1989. "The Archaic, Historical and Mythicized Dimensions of Aztlán." In *Aztlán: Essays on the Chicano Homeland,* ed. Rudolfo Anaya and Francisco Lomelí, 14–48. Albuquerque, N.M.: Academia/El Norte Publications.
Pineda del Valle, César. 1999. *Las Fiestas de Enero en Chiapa de Corzo, Chiapas.* Tuxtla Gutiérrez, Chiapas: Ediciones y Sistemas Especiales, S.A. De C.V.
Piñón, Diego. "Statement of Purpose." http://www.diegopinon.com/personal%20statement.html.
Pizano, Margarita. 2001. *El triunfo de la masculinidad.* Chile: Surada Ediciones. Also at http://www.mpisano.cl/index.htm. July 2, 2004.
Place of the Plumed Serpent. 196–? [Production information not given.] VHS. 52 min.
Polkinhorn, Harry, Gabriel Trujillo Muños, and Rogelio Reyes, eds. 1994. *Bodies Beyond Borders: Dance on the U.S.-Mexico Border.* Calexico, Calif.: Binational Press; Mexicali, Baja California: Editorial Binacional.
Portal, Ma. Ana. 1990. "La identidad como objeto de estudio de la antropología." En *Alteridades: "Identidad," Identidad.* México, UAM—I, Año I, no. 2: 3–5.
Preston, Julia. 1997. "Arts Abroad; Transforming Mayan Mysteries Into Fancy Footwork." *New York Times,* September 18: E2.
Price, Sally H. 1966. "I was Pashu and my husband was Telesh." *Radcliffe Quarterly* 50: 4–8.
Pugh, Grace Thompson. 1944. *Mexican Folk Dances.* New York: Curriculum Service Bureau for International Studies, Inc.
Quetzal. 1998a. *Quetzal.* Son del Barrio Music, SDB998–01.
———. 1998b. "Chicana Skies." *Quetzal.* Produced by Quetzal and John Avila. Son del Barrio Records, SDB998-01.
———. 2002a. "The Social Relevance of Public Art." *Sing the Real.* Produced by Greg Landau. Vanguard Records, 79712–2.
———. 2002b. *Sing the Real.* Produced by Greg Landau. Vanguard Records, 79712-2.
———. 2003a. "Planta de Los Pies." *Worksongs.* Produced by Steve Berlin. Vanguard Records, 79738-2.
———. 2003b. *Worksongs.* Produced by Steve Berlin. Vanguard Records, 79738-2.
Ramírez Sáiz, Juan Manuel. 1998. *¿Cómo gobiernan Guadalajara? Demandas ciuda-*

danas y respuestas de los ayuntamientos. México: Editorial Porrúa-IIS/UNAM-Universidad de Guadalajara.

Reed, Susan. 1998. "The Politics and Poetics of Dance." *Annual Review of Anthropology* 27: 503–32.

Rémy, Siméon. 1999. *Diccionario de la lengua náhuatl o mexicana.* Mexico: Siglo XXI.

Reyes, David, and Tom Waldman. 1998. *Land of a Thousand Dances: Chicano Rock 'n' Roll from Southern California.* Albuquerque: University of New Mexico Press.

Reyes-Arias, Alejandro. 2005. "Pensar México." *Berkeley Review of Latin American Studies* (Spring): 9–13.

———. 1994. *La conquista espiritual de México. Ensayo sobre el apostolado y los métodos misioneros de las órdenes mendicantes en la Nueva España de 1523–1524 a 1572.* México: Fondo de Cultura Económica.

Robb, John Donald. 1961. "The Matachines Dance — A Ritual Dance Drama." *Western Folklore* 20 (April): 87.

———. 1980. *Hispanic Folk Music of New Mexico and the Southwestern United States.* Norman: University of Oklahoma Press.

Rodrigo Alvarez, Luis. 1995. *Historia general de estado de Oaxaca.* Oaxaca: Carteles Editores.

Rodríguez, Hilda. 1988. "La danza popular." In *La antropología en México: Panorama histórico,* ed. Carlos Mora, 333–84. México: Instituto Nacional de Antropología e Historia.

Rodríguez, Jeanette. 1994. *Our Lady of Guadalupe: Faith and Empowerment Among Mexican American Women.* Austin: University of Texas Press.

Rodriguez, Gabriela. 1996. "Jalisco Contemporaneo." *Congreso XXIII Syllabus for the 1996 Conference.* Corpus Christi, Texas: Asociación Nacional de Grupos Folklórico.

Rodriguez, Roberto. 1997. *The X in La Raza II.* Albuquerque: Roberto Rodriguez.

Rodríguez, Russell. 2006. "Cultural Production, Legitimation, and the Politics of Aesthetics: Mariachi Transmission, Practice, and Performance in the United States." PhD Dissertation, University of California at Santa Cruz.

Rodríguez, Sylvia. 1991. "The Taos Pueblo Matachines: Ritual Symbolism and Interethnic Relations." *American Ethnologist* 18, no. 2: 234–56.

———. 1996. *The Matachines Dance: Ritual Symbolism and Interethnic Relations in the Rio Grande Valley.* Albuquerque: University of New Mexico Press.

———. 1997. "The Taos Fiesta: Invented Tradition and the Infrapolitics of Symbolic Reclamation." *Journal of the Southwest* 39, no. 1: 34–57.

Rodríguez Aceves, J. Jesús. 1988. *Danzas de moros y cristianos.* Guadalajara: Unidad Editorial del Gobierno de Jalisco.

Rojas, Rosa. 1994. Edicion 1. *Chiapas, ¿y las mujeres qué?* Ediciones la Correa Feminista.

———1995. Edicion 2. *Chiapas ¿y las mujeres que?* Ediciones La Correa Feminista.

Rolas de Aztlán: Songs of the Chicano Movement. 2005. Produced by Estevan Azcona and Russell Rodríguez. Smithsonian Folkways Recordings SF40516.

Romero, Brenda. 1993. *The Matachines Music and Dance in San Juan Pueblo and Alcalde, New Mexico: Context and Meanings.* PhD Dissertation, University of California at Los Angeles.

———. 1997. "Cultural Interaction in New Mexico as Illustrated in the Matachines Dance." In *Musics of Multicultural America,* ed. Kip Lornell and Anne Rasmussen, 155–85. New York: Schirmer.

———. 2003. "The New Mexico, Texas, and Mexico Borderlands and the Concept of Indio in the Matachines Dance." In *Musical Cultures of Latin America: Global Effects, Past and Present,* ed. Steven Loza, 81–87. Los Angeles: The Regents of the University of California.

———. 2007. "La Danza Matachines as New Mexican Heritage." In *Expressing New Mexico: Nuevomexicano Creativity, Ritual, and Memory,* edited by Phillip B. Gonzalez. Tucson: University of Arizona Press.

———. Forthcoming. "La Danza Matachines as New Mexican Heritage." In *Expressing Culture/Expressing Place: Nuevomexicano(a) Creativity, Everyday Ritual, and Collective Remembrance,* ed. Phillip B. Gonzalez. Tucson: University of Arizona Press.

Rönstrom, Owe. 1999. "It Takes Two-or More to Tango: Researching Traditional Music/Dance Interrelations." In *Dance in the Field: Theory, Methods and Issues in Dance Ethnography,* ed. Theresa Buckland, 134–44. New York: St. Martin's Press.

Rosaldo, Renato. 1993. *Culture and Truth: The Remaking of Social Analysis.* Boston: Beacon Press.

Rosenbaum, Brenda. 1993. *With Our Heads Bowed: The Dynamics of Gender in a Maya Community.* Albany: Institute for Mesoamerican Studies, State University of New York.

Rouse, Peter. 1991. "Mexican Migration and the Social Space of Postmodernism." *Diaspora* 1, no. 1: 8–23.

Rovira, Guiomar. 1996. *Mujeres de maiz. La voz de las indigenas de Chiapas y la rebelion zapatista.* Barcellona: Ed. Virus.

Royball, Jimmy Newmoon. 2004. "*Danza*" "*Baile Folklórico.*" In *Encyclopedia of Latino Popular Culture,* ed. Cordelia Candelaria, Arturo J. Aldama, and Peter J. Garcia, 218–20. Westport, Conn.: Greenwood Press.

Rus, Jan. 1994. "The 'Comunidad Revolucionaria Institucional': The Subversion of Native Government in Highland Chiapas, 1936–1968." In *Everyday Forms of State Formation: Revolution and the Negotiation of Rule in Modern Mexico,* ed. Gilbert M. Joseph and Daniel Nugent. 265–300. Durham, N.C.: Duke University Press.

Rus, Jan, and Roberto Wasserstrom. 1980. "Civil-Religious Hierarchies in Central Chiapas: A Critical Perspectives." *American Ethnologist* 7, no. 3: 466–78.

Ruyter, Nancy Lee Chalfa. 1979. *Reformers and Visionaries; The Americanization of the Art of Dance.* New York: Dance Horizons.

Sáenz, Moises. 1927. Nuestras Escuelas Rurales. *Mexican Folkways* 3, no. 1: 44–52.
Sahagún, Bernardillo. 1829. *Historia de la conquista de México.* Mexico: Imprenta de Galván.
Salas Peña, Fernando. 2002. "El fandango y los ballets folclóricos." *Son Del Sur* 9: 32–37.
Saldívar, Gabriel. 1937. *El jarabe: Baile popular mexicano.* México: Talleres Gráficos de la Nación.
Salinas, Martín. 1990. *Indians of the Rio Grande: Their Role in the History of Southern Texas and Northeastern Mexico.* Austin: University of Texas Press.
Sánchez, George. 1936. *Mexico: A Revolution by Education.* New York: The Viking Press.
Sánchez, José. 2000. "Radiografía de un santiaguero." *Diario de campo.* Octubre 5, Coshuaca, Hidalgo.
———. 2004a. "No nos vamos a ir como venimos." PhD Dissertation, CIESAS, México.
———. 2004b. *Diario de campo.* October 4, Coshuaca, Hidalgo.
Sánchez Flores, Francisco. 1982. *Danzas Fundamentales de Jalisco.* Mexico: FONADAN.
Saunders, Lawrence I. 1976. *The Son Huasteco: A Historical, Social, and Analytical Study of a Mexican Regional Folk Genre.* MA Thesis, University of California at Los Angeles.
Schechner, Richard. 1985. *Between Theater and Anthropology.* Philadelphia: University of Pennsylvania Press.
———. 1994. "Ritual and Performance." In *Companion Encyclopedia of Anthropology,* ed. Tim Ingold, 613–47. London: Routledge.
Schwendener, Norma. 1933. *How to Perform the Dances of Old Mexico: A Manual of their Origins, Legends, Costumes, Steps, Patterns, and Music.* Detroit: Blaine Ethridge Books.
Sedillo Brewster, Mela. 1938. *Mexican and New Mexican Folkdances.* Albuquerque: The University of New Mexico Press.
Seidler, Victor J. 2000. *La sinrazón masculina: Masculinidad y teoría social.* Mexico: UNAM, Programa Universitario de Estudios de Género.
Segal, Lewis. 1989. "Inner City Cultural Center Hosts Barro Rojo." *Los Angeles Times,* July 10.
Senelick, Laurence. 2000. *The Changing Room: Sex, Drag and Theatre.* London: Routledge.
Serret, Estela. 2001. *El género y lo simbólico. La constitución imaginaria de la identidad femenina.* México: Universidad Autónoma Metropolitana Azcapotzalco.
Shay, Anthony. 1999. "Parallel Traditions: State Folk Dance Ensembles and Folk Dance in 'The Field.'" *Dance Research Journal* 31, no. 1: 29–56.
———. 2002. *Choreographic Politics: State Folk Dance Companies, Representation, and Power.* Middletown, Conn.: Wesleyan University Press.

Sheehy, Daniel Edward. 1979. "The Son Jarocho: The History, Style, and Repertoire of a Changing Mexican Musical Tradition." PhD Dissertation, University of California, Los Angeles.

———. 2005. "Music of the African Diaspora in the Americas." *Encyclopedia of Diasporas: Immigrant and Refugee Cultures Around the World,* ed. Melvin Ember, Carol R. Ember, and Ian Skoggard. New York: Kluwer Academic/Plenum.

———. 2006. *Mariachi Music in America: Experiencing Music, Expressing Culture.* New York: Oxford University Press.

Sheriff, Robin E. 2001. *Dreaming Equality: Color, Race, and Racism in Urban Brazil.* New Brunswick, N.J.: Rutgers University Press.

Shipley, Charles. 1987. "The Matachines Dance of New Mexico." Channel 13, Albuquerque.

Silva Meinel, Javier (editor and photography), and Antonio Muñoz Monge (text). 1998. *Peru, tiempos de fiesta, calendario.* Lima, Peru: Unión de Cervecerías Peruanas Backus y Johnston S.A.A.

Singer, Milton. 1972. *When a Great Tradition Modernizes: An Anthropological Approach to Indian Civilization.* New York: Praeger.

Siskel, Suzanne E. 1974. *With the Spirit of a Jaguar: A Study of Shamanism in Ichinton, Chamula.* BA Honors Thesis, Anthropology Department, Harvard University.

Sklar, Deirdre. 2001. *Dancing with the Vírgen. Body and Faith in the Fiesta of Tortugas, New Mexico.* California: University of California Press.

Smith, Linda Tuhiwai. 1999. *Decolonizing Methodologies: Research and Indigenous Peoples.* London; New York: Zed Books; Dunedin: University of Otago Press; New York: distributed in the USA exclusively by St. Martin's Press.

Smith, Robert. 1998. "Transnational Public Spheres and Changing Practices of Citizenship, Membership and Nation: Comparative Insights from the Mexican and Italian Cases." ICCCR Conference on Transnationalism.

Smith, Waldermen. 1977. *The Fiesta System and Economic Change.* New York: Columbia University Press.

Snyder, Allegra. 1972. "The Dance Symbol." *CORD Research Annual* 6: 213–24.

Solomon, Loes Madalynne. 1941. "Some Mexican Folk Dances as Found in Los Angeles, California." PhD Dissertation, University of California at Los Angeles.

Sommer, Doris. 1991. *Foundational Fictions: The National Romances of Latin America.* Berkeley: University of California Press.

Son de Madera. 1997. *Son de Madera.* Produced by Ramón Gutiérrez Hernandez. Urtext, UL 3003.

———. 2004. *Las Orquestas del Día.* Produced by Robert Carranza, Quetzal Flores, Martha Gonzalez, and Dante Pascuzzo. Independent release.

Stanford, Thomas. 1984. *El son mexicano.* México: Fondo de Cultura Económica, 1984.

Stanton, Andra Fischgrund. 1999. *Zapotec Weavers of Teotitlán.* Santa Fe: Museum of New Mexico Press.

Steiner, Stan. 1970. *La Raza: The Mexican American.* New York: Harper.
Sten, María. 1990. *Ponte a bailar, tú que reinas.* México: Editorial Joaquín Mortiz.
Stephenson, Claude D. 2001. "A Comparative Analysis of Matachines Music and Its History and Dispersion in the American Southwest." PhD Dissertation, University of New Mexico.
Stoller, Paul. 1997. *Sensuous Scholarship.* Philadelphia: University of Pennsylvania Press.
Stone, Martha. 1975. *At the Sign of Midnight: The Concheros Dance Cult of México.* Tucson: The University of Arizona Press.
Tamayo, Jaime, and Alejandra Vizcarra. 2000. *Jalisco.* México: Biblioteca de las Entidades Federativas: UNAM.
Terry-Azios, Diana A. 1999. "Color & Heritage: Ballet Folklorico de Mexico Production." *Hispanic* 12, no. 9 (September): 52.
Tibol, Raquel. 1982. *Pasos en la danza mexicana.* Mexico: UNAM.
Tijerina, Andrés. 1977. *Tejanos and Texas: The Native Mexicans of Texas, 1820–1850.* College Station: Texas A&M Press.
———. 1994. *Tejanos and Texans under the Mexican Flag: 1821–1836.* College Station: Texas A&M Press.
Titon, Jeff Todd. 1999. "'The Real Thing': Tourism, Authenticity, and Pilgrimage among the Old Regular Baptists at the 1997 Smithsonian Folklife Festival." *World of Music* 41, no. 3: 115–39.
Tobar, Héctor. 2005. *Translation Nation: Defining a New American Identity in the Spanish Speaking United States.* New York: Riverhead Books.
Toor, Frances. 1947. *A Treasury of Mexican Folkways.* New York: Crown Publishers.
Tortajada Quiroz, Margarita. 1995. *Danza y poder.* Mexico, D.F.: Instituto Nacional de Bellas Artes. Centro Nacional de Investigación, Documentación, e Información de la Danza José Limón.
———, ed. 1998. *Mujeres de danza combativa.* México: CENIDI-DANZA/CONACULTA.
———. 2000. *La danza escénica de la revolución mexicana, nacionalista y vigorosa.* Mexico, D.F.: Instituto Nacional de Estudios Históricos de la Revolución Mexicana.
———. 2001. *Frutos de mujer: Las mujeres en la danza escénica.* México: CONACULTA y CENIDI-DANZA.
Treviño, Adrian and Barbara Gilles. 1994. "A History of the Matachines Dance." *New Mexico Historical Review* 69, no. 2: 105–26.
———. 1997. *The Dance of Montezuma: Some Remarks on the Origins and History of the Matachines in Northern New Mexico.* Unpublished manuscript.
Tuñón, Esperanza. 1997. *Mujeres en escena: De la tramoya al protagonismo. El quehacer político del movimiento amplio de mujeres en México (1982–1994).* México: UNAM; El Colegio de la Frontera Sur.
Turino, Thomas. 2003. "Nationalism and Latin American Music: Selected Case

Studies and Theoretical Considerations." *Latin American Music Review* 24, no. 2: 169–209.
———. 1995. *The Ritual Process: Structure and Anti-Structure.* New York: Aldine de Gruyter.
Valcárcel, Amelia. 2002. "Ética para un mundo global. Una apuesta por el humanismo frente al fanatismo." Madrid, Colección Temas de Hoy.
Valdez, Luis. 1982. Screenplay and producer. *Zoot Suit.* Based on the original (1981) play by Luis Valdez. Music by Daniel Valdez. Motion Picture (103 minutes). California: Universal Studios.
———. 1992. *Zoot Suit and Other Plays.* Houston, Tex.: Arte Publico Press.
Valencia, Marylou. 1994. "Danza Azteca." In *From Bodies Beyond Borders: Dance on the U.S.-Mexico Border/ Cuerpos más allá de las fronteras: la danza en la frontera Mexico-E.U.A,* ed. Harry Polkinhorn, Gabriel Trujillo Muñoz, and Rogelio Reyes, 128–78. Calexico, Calif.: Binational Press; Mexicali, Baja Calif.: Editorial Binacional.
Van Den Berghe, Pierre L. 1994. *The Quest for the Other: Ethnic Tourism in San Cristóbal, Mexico.* Seattle: University of Washington Press.
Vázquez, Aguado, and María Ana Portal. 1991. "Ideología, identidad y cultura." *Boletín de Antropología Americana* 23 (July): 67–82.
———. 1997. *El retorno de lo sagrado.* México Grijalbo/Círculo cuadrado.
Vertovec, Steven. 2001. "Transnationalism and Identity." *Ethnic and Migration Studies* 27, no. 4: 573–82.
Vila, Pablo. 1991. "Tango to Folk: Hegemony Construction and Popular Identities in Argentina." *Studies in Latin American Popular Culture* 10: 107–40.
———. 2000. *Crossing Borders, Reinforcing Borders: Social Categories, Metaphors, and Narrative Identities on the U.S.-Mexico Frontier.* Austin: University of Texas Press.
Vogt, Evon Z. 1969. *Zinacantan: A Maya Community in the Highlands of Chiapas.* Cambridge, Mass.: Harvard University Press, 1969.
———. 1994. *Fieldwork among the Maya: Reflections on the Harvard Chiapas Project.* Albuquerque: University of New Mexico Press.
Wade, Peter. 2003. "Race and Nation in Latin America: An Anthropological View." In *Race and Nation in Modern Latin America,* ed. Nancy P. Appelbaum, Anne S. Macpherson, and Karin Alejandra Rosemblatt, 263–82. Chapel Hill: University of North Carolina Press.
Wali, Alaka. 1974. *Dependence and Dominance: The Status of Women in Zinacantán.* BA Honor Essay presented to the Anthropology Department, Radcliffe College.
Warman, Arturo. 1972. *La danza de moros y cristianos.* México: INAH, Coleccion Divulgacion.
Warren, Larry. 1991. *Anna Sokolow: The Rebellious Spirit.* Princeton, N.J.: Princeton Book Company.

Wasserstrom, R. 1983. *Class and Society in Central Chiapas.* Berkeley: University of California Press.
Waters, Mary C. 1990. *Ethnic Options. Choosing Identities in America.* Berkeley, Los Angeles, and Oxford: University of California Press.
Whipperman, Bruce. 2000. *Oaxaca Handbook: Mountain Craft Regions, Archaeological Sites, and Coastal Resorts.* Emeryville, Calif.: Avalon Travel Publishing.
Williams, Drid. 1995. "Space, Intersubjectivity, and the Conceptual Imperative: Three Ethnographic Cases." In *Human Action Signs in Cultural Context: The Visible and the Invisible in Movement and Dance,* ed. Brenda Farnell, 44–81. Metuchen, N.J.: Scarecrow Press.
Williams, Raymond. 1977. *Marxism and Literature.* New York: Oxford University Press.
Wimer, Sara. 1995. "Ballet *Folklórico* Today: Tejano Culture Inspires San Antonio's Rio Bravo Dance Company." *Hispanic Magazine* (August): 54–56.
Yoder, Don. 1974. "Toward a Definition of Folk Religion." *Western Folklore* 33, no. 1 (January): 2–15.
Zárate Rosales, Alberto. 2003. "Las danzas tradicionales en el estado de Puebla en el nuevo milenio." In *Etnografía del estado de Puebla, Puebla,* ed. Elio Masferrer, 78–85. Secretaría de Cultura del Estado de Puebla. 3 Tomos (Tomo "Puebla Norte").
Zavella, Patricia. 1997. "Feminist Insider Dilemmas: Constructing Ethnic Identity with 'Chicana' Informants." In *Situated Lives: Gender and Culture in Everyday Life,* ed. Louise Lamphere, Helena Ragoné, and Patricia Zavella, 42–61. New York: Routledge.
Zedillo Castillo, Antonio. 1996. "The Danzón in Mexico." *México en el tiempo* 13 (June–July). México, D.F.: Editorial Jilguero. http://www.mexicodesconocido.com/english/cultura_y_sociedad/fiestas_y_tradiciones/detalle.cfm?idpag=642&idsub=61&idsec=15.
Žižek, Slavoj. 1989. *The Sublime Object of Ideology.* London: Verso.
Zuñiga Benavides, Norma, in collaboration with Blanca Zuñiga Azíos. 1995. *Holidays and Heartstrings: Recuerdos de la Casa de Miel.* Laredo, Texas: Border Studies.

Contributors

NORMA E. CANTÚ is a professor of English at the University of Texas, San Antonio. In addition to her scholarly work, she has published poetry, short fiction, essays, and a novel, *Canícula: Snapshots of a Girlhood en la frontera* (1995), which received the Premio Aztlán. She is completing *Soldiers of the Cross: Los Matachines de la Santa Cruz,* forthcoming from the Texas A&M University Press, where she is editor of the Rio Grande/Rio Bravo: Borderlands Culture and Traditions series. She is also writing a second novel, *Champú, or Hair Matters.*

SUSAN CASHION, a senior lecturer emerita in the Dance Division at Stanford University, received her doctorate from Stanford University. Her scholarship centers on the *danzas* and *bailes* of Mexico. In her role as artist/choreographer, she was a cofounder of Los Lupeños de San José Mexican Dance Company, and the director of the Ballet Folklórico de Stanford for twenty years.

MARÍA TERESA CESEÑA is a doctoral candidate in ethnic studies at the University of California, San Diego. Her current research compares historical and contemporary representations of Mexican and American Indians under projects of respective nation building, examining how indigenous identity is constructed and represented on both sides of the border.

XÓCHITL C. CHÁVEZ is currently a doctoral candidate in cultural anthropology at the University of California, Santa Cruz. Her area of study includes folklore, festival and ritual, dance, identity formation, gender, Greater Mexico, and Latin America. She has coauthored articles on community relations and education, as well as Latino political and artistic identities.

ADRIANA CRUZ-MANJARREZ, professor of Cultural Studies at Universidad de Colima, México, received her doctorate from the University of California Los Angeles. Her interdisciplinary work specializes in the study of indigenous Mexican migration into the United States, transnationalism, identity, gender, and social and cultural change in expressive culture. She is the author of "The Social Construction of the Yalálag Zapotec Transnational Community, Networks, and Membership Practices" in *Migración internacional: Efectos de la globalización y las políticas migratorias* (México: Universidad del Estado de México), "Performing Zapotec Religiosity in the International Context of Migration" in *Dance and Society: Dancer as a Cultural Performer,* and "Rethinking Theory in Practice: Moving from the Past to the Present."

RENÉE DE LA TORRE CASTELLANOS is a professor of anthropology at CIESAS Occidente in Guadalajara, Jalisco, Mexico. She received her doctorate in social sciences, specializing in social anthropology through CIESAS at the University of Guadalajara, in 1998. She has specialized in the study of religion and new urban identities. She is the author of *Los hijos de la luz,* which received the Premio Casa Chata 1993 and Premio CONEIC 1993, and *La ecclesia nostra,* which received the Premio Casa Chata 1998. She has also published close to a hundred scholarly articles.

PETER J. GARCÍA is an assistant professor of ethnomusicology and folklore in the Department of Chicana/o Studies at California State University, Northridge. He was senior subject editor for the *Encyclopedia of Latino Popular Culture* and has published several articles and book reviews. His book *Decolonizing Enchantment: Lyricism, Ritual, and Echoes of Nuevo Mexicano Popular Music* is forthcoming with University of New Mexico Press. He is also a 2007 Fulbright Grantee to Mexico, where he investigated the Fiestas de San Francisco in Magdalena, Sonora, and is also visiting assistant professor in the Department of Chicana/o Studies at the University of California, Santa Barbara.

RUDY F. GARCÍA began his dance training while a student at Stanford University. He has danced with many Bay Area Mexican dance groups, has served as artistic director of Los Lupeños and Alegría de San José, and has performed with Il Quartiere Italiano and the Jubilee American Dance Theater. His "Folklorico Handbook" is used in *folklórico* curricula in colleges throughout California and Arizona.

CHRIS GOERTZEN is an associate professor of music at the University of Southern Mississippi and writes about United States, Latin American, and European vernacular music. He received his doctorate from the University of Illinois and was a student of Bruno Nettl.

MARTHA GONZÁLEZ is currently a graduate student in women's studies at the University of Washington, Seattle. She holds a bachelor's degree in ethnomusicology from the University of California at Los Angeles and is singer, songwriter, and percussionist for Los Angeles–based Quetzal. She has recorded and performed with various bands and believes in using art as a tool for the redefinition and reconstruction of society. She is a 2007 recipient of the Fulbright–Garcia Robles Grant, which allowed her to study and collaborate with women dancers and musicians from Veracruz, Mexico, who practice the *son jarocho.*

ELISA DIANA HUERTA received a bachelor's degree in cultural anthropology, ethnic studies, and Plan II Honors Program from the University of Texas at Austin and is currently a doctoral candidate in the anthropology department at the University of California, Santa Cruz. She was awarded the University of California President's Postdoctoral Fellowship for 2007.

SYDNEY HUTCHINSON is a doctoral candidate in ethnomusicology at New York University, where her research focuses on issues of migration, gender, transnationalism, and cultural policy in Dominican *merengue típico.* She is the author of articles on *merengue,* salsa dancing, and public folklore, as well as *From Quebradita to Duranguense: Dance in Mexican American Youth Culture.*

MARIE "KETA" MIRANDA is an associate professor in the Mexican American Studies Program at the University of Texas, San Antonio. Her publications include ethnography of representational politics for young women in gangs and examination of the East L.A. music scene, focusing on teenage girls. Her current project examines the mod subculture among Los Angeles Mexican American youth in the 1960s.

OLGA NÁJERA-RAMÍREZ, professor of anthropology at the University of California, Santa Cruz, received her doctorate from the University of Texas in Austin. As an anthropologist specializing in folklore, she has concentrated on documenting and critically examining expressive culture among Mexicans in both Mexico and the United States. Author of *La Fiesta de los Tastoanes: Critical Perspectives in a Mexican Festival Performance*, she also produced the award-winning video *La Charreada: Rodeo a la Mexicana*. Her most recent books include *Chicana Traditions: Continuity and Change,* coedited with Norma E. Cantú, and *Chicana Feminisms: A Critical Reader,* coedited with Gabriela Arredondo, Aida Hurtado, Norma Klahn, and Pat Zavella.

SHAKINA NAYFACK received his doctorate in dance history and theory at the University of California, Riverside, where he also earned a masters in fine arts in experimental choreography. He holds a bachelor's degree in community studies and a graduate certificate in theater arts from the University of California, Santa Cruz. As a performance artist, theater director, and educator, Nayfack's work explores the social and political efficacy of postmodern ritual in process and performance.

RUSSELL RODRÍGUEZ received his doctorate in anthropology at the University of California, Santa Cruz. He has worked closely with the Smithsonian Center for Folklife and Cultural Heritage and is coproducer of the Smithsonian Folkways Recordings CD compilation *Rolas de Aztlán: Songs of the Chicano Movement*. He was awarded the University of California President's Postdoctoral Fellowship for 2007 and 2008.

BRENDA M. ROMERO holds a doctorate in ethnomusicology from the University of California at Los Angeles and is an associate professor/coordinator of ethnomusicology at the University of Colorado in Boulder. She has worked extensively on the *matachines* music and dance and other music genres that reflect both Spanish and Indian origins in New Mexico, and she has played the violin for the Pueblo of Jemez Matachina for nine years. She did extensive fieldwork on the genre throughout Mexico and began to investigate the *matachines* in South America in 2007.

NANCY LEE CHALFA RUYTER has a doctorate in history from Claremont Graduate School and extensive practical experience in dance and choreography. She is a professor of dance at the University of California, Irvine. She currently teaches dance history, graduate seminars, and Spanish dance. She has written extensively on the Delsarte system and on dance and theater in Latin America, Spain, the Balkans, and Italy. She has also taught modern technique, choreography, and Balkan dance, as well as Spanish dance at many institutions including Tufts University, UCLA, UC Riverside, and Pomona College.

JOSÉ SÁNCHEZ JIMÉNEZ teaches social anthropology and experimental ethnography at the Universidad de Guanajuato, México. He received his doctorate in 2004 from the Centro de Investigaciones y Estudios Superiores en Antropología Social (CIESAS, México). His main research interests involve the overlapping fields of language, culture, and cognition. He is editor of *El día que disfrutemos en la diversidad: Concreciones e indeterminaciones de la interculturalidad* (Universidad de Guanajuato, 2008). He has also written several articles on interpretative anthropology and cultural semiotics. He is responsible for supervising anthropology students engaged in fieldwork at the Universidad de Guanajuato.

ALBERTO ZÁRATE ROSALES is a research professor at the Academia de Arte y Patrimonio Cultural of the Universidad Autónoma de la Ciudad de México and is a doctoral student of anthropology at the Universidad Autónoma de México. He was a member of the editorial board of the *Revista Diálogo Antropológico* (UNAM) and serves as Consejo Asesor Externo of the journal *Herencia* at the University of Costa Rica. He specializes in gender studies in popular culture and has coordinated various national and international conferences.

Index

The University of Illinois Press
is a founding member of the
Association of American University Presses.

University of Illinois Press
1325 South Oak Street
Champaign, IL 61820-6903
www.press.uillinois.edu